CORNERSTONE
B I B L I C A L
COMMENTARY

CORNERSTONE
BIBLICAL
COMMENTARY

Romans
Roger Mohrlang

Galatians
Gerald L. Borchert

GENERAL EDITOR
Philip W. Comfort

with the entire text of the
NEW LIVING TRANSLATION

TYNDALE HOUSE PUBLISHERS, INC. CAROL STREAM, ILLINOIS

Cornerstone Biblical Commentary, Volume 14

Visit Tyndale's exciting Web site at www.tyndale.com

Library of Congress Cataloging-in-Publication Data

Cornerstone biblical commentary.
    p. cm.
    Includes bibliographical references and index.
    ISBN-13: 978-0-8423-8342-4 (hc : alk. paper)
    ISBN-10: 0-8423-8342-5 (hc : alk. paper)
    1. Biblical—Commentaries. I.

Printed in Malaysia

12	11	10	09	08	07	
7	6	5	4	3	2	1

CONTENTS

CONTRIBUTORS TO VOLUME 14

Romans: Roger Mohrlang
BS, Carnegie Institute of Technology/Carnegie Mellon University;
MA, Fuller Theological Seminary;
DPhil, University of Oxford;
Professor of Biblical Studies, Whitworth College.

Galatians: Gerald L. Borchert
BA, LLB, University of Alberta Law School;
MDiv, Eastern Baptist Theological Seminary;
ThM, PhD, Princeton Theological Seminary and Princeton University;
Retired Professor of New Testament and Director of Doctoral Studies,
Northern Baptist Theological Seminary.

GENERAL EDITOR'S PREFACE

The *Cornerstone Biblical Commentary* is based on the second edition of the New Living Translation (2004). Nearly 100 scholars from various church backgrounds and from several countries (United States, Canada, England, and Australia) participated in the creation of the NLT. Many of these same scholars are contributors to this commentary series. All the commentators, whether participants in the NLT or not, believe that the Bible is God's inspired word and have a desire to make God's word clear and accessible to his people.

This Bible commentary is the natural extension of our vision for the New Living Translation, which we believe is both exegetically accurate and idiomatically powerful. The NLT attempts to communicate God's inspired word in a lucid English translation of the original languages so that English readers can understand and appreciate the thought of the original writers. In the same way, the *Cornerstone Biblical Commentary* aims at helping teachers, pastors, students, and lay people understand every thought contained in the Bible. As such, the commentary focuses first on the words of Scripture, then on the theological truths of Scripture—inasmuch as the words express the truths.

The commentary itself has been structured in such a way as to help readers get at the meaning of Scripture, passage by passage, through the entire Bible. Each Bible book is prefaced by a substantial book introduction that gives general historical background important for understanding. Then the reader is taken through the Bible text, passage by passage, starting with the New Living Translation text printed in full. This is followed by a section called "Notes," wherein the commentator helps the reader understand the Hebrew or Greek behind the English of the NLT, interacts with other scholars on important interpretive issues, and points the reader to significant textual and contextual matters. The "Notes" are followed by the "Commentary," wherein each scholar presents a lucid interpretation of the passage, giving special attention to context and major theological themes.

The commentators represent a wide spectrum of theological positions within the evangelical community. We believe this is good because it reflects the rich variety in Christ's church. All the commentators uphold the authority of God's word and believe it is essential to heed the old adage: "Wholly apply yourself to the Scriptures and apply them wholly to you." May this commentary help you know the truths of Scripture, and may this knowledge help you "grow in your knowledge of God and Jesus our Lord" (2 Pet 1:2, NLT).

PHILIP W. COMFORT
GENERAL EDITOR

ABBREVIATIONS

GENERAL ABBREVIATIONS

b.	Babylonian Gemara	Heb.	Hebrew	NT	New Testament
bar.	baraita	ibid.	*ibidem,* in the same place	OL	Old Latin
c.	*circa,* around, approximately	i.e.	*id est,* the same	OS	Old Syriac
cf.	*confer,* compare	in loc.	*in loco,* in the place cited	OT	Old Testament
ch, chs	chapter, chapters	lit.	literally	p., pp.	page, pages
contra	in contrast to	LXX	Septuagint	pl.	plural
DSS	Dead Sea Scrolls	𝔐	Majority Text	Q	Quelle ("Sayings" as Gospel source)
ed.	edition, editor	*m.*	Mishnah	rev.	revision
e.g.	*exempli gratia,* for example	masc.	masculine	sg.	singular
et al.	*et alli,* and others	mg	margin	*t.*	Tosefta
fem.	feminine	ms	manuscript	TR	Textus Receptus
ff	following (verses, pages)	mss	manuscripts	v., vv.	verse, verses
fl.	flourished	MT	Masoretic Text	vid.	*videur,* it seems
Gr.	Greek	n.d.	no date	viz.	*videlicet,* namely
		neut.	neuter	vol.	volume
		no.	number	*y.*	Jerusalem Gemara

ABBREVIATIONS FOR BIBLE TRANSLATIONS

ASV	American Standard Version	NCV	New Century Version	NKJV	New King James Version
CEV	Contemporary English Version	NEB	New English Bible	NRSV	New Revised Standard Version
ESV	English Standard Version	NIV	New International Version	NLT	New Living Translation
GW	God's Word	NIrV	New International Reader's Version	REB	Revised English Bible
HCSB	Holman Christian Standard Bible	NJB	New Jerusalem Bible	RSV	Revised Standard Version
JB	Jerusalem Bible	NJPS	The New Jewish Publication Society Translation (*Tanakh*)	TEV	Today's English Version
KJV	King James Version			TLB	The Living Bible
NAB	New American Bible				
NASB	New American Standard Bible				

ABBREVIATIONS FOR DICTIONARIES, LEXICONS, COLLECTIONS OF TEXTS, ORIGINAL LANGUAGE EDITIONS

ABD *Anchor Bible Dictionary* (6 vols., Freedman) [1992]

ANEP *The Ancient Near East in Pictures* (Pritchard) [1965]

ANET *Ancient Near Eastern Texts Relating to the Old Testament* (Pritchard) [1969]

BAGD *Greek-English Lexicon of the New Testament and Other Early Christian Literature,* 2nd ed. (Bauer, Arndt, Gingrich, Danker) [1979]

BDAG *Greek-English Lexicon of the New Testament and Other Early Christian Literature,* 3rd ed. (Bauer, Danker, Arndt, Gingrich) [2000]

BDB *A Hebrew and English Lexicon of the Old Testament* (Brown, Driver, Briggs) [1907]

BDF *A Greek Grammar of the New Testament and Other Early Christian Literature* (Blass, Debrunner, Funk) [1961]

BHS *Biblia Hebraica Stuttgartensia* (Elliger and Rudolph) [1983]

CAD *Assyrian Dictionary of the Oriental Institute of the University of Chicago* [1956]

COS *The Context of Scripture* (3 vols., Hallo and Younger) [1997–2002]

DBI *Dictionary of Biblical Imagery* (Ryken, Wilhoit, Longman) [1998]

DBT *Dictionary of Biblical Theology* (2nd ed., Leon-Dufour) [1972]

DCH *Dictionary of Classical Hebrew* (5 vols., D. Clines) [2000]

DJD *Discoveries in the Judean Desert* [1955–]

DJG *Dictionary of Jesus and the Gospels* (Green, McKnight, Marshall) [1992]

DOTP *Dictionary of the Old Testament: Pentateuch.* (T. Alexander, D.W. Baker) [2003]

DPL *Dictionary of Paul and His Letters* (Hawthorne, Martin, Reid) [1993]

EDNT *Exegetical Dictionary of the New Testament* (3 vols., H. Balz, G. Schneider. ET) [1990–1993]

HALOT *The Hebrew and Aramaic Lexicon of the Old Testament* (L. Koehler, W. Baumgartner, J. Stamm; trans. M. Richardson) [1994–1999]

IBD *Illustrated Bible Dictionary* (3 vols., Douglas, Wiseman) [1980]

IDB *The Interpreter's Dictionary of the Bible* (4 vols., Buttrick) [1962]

ISBE *International Standard Bible Encyclopedia* (4 vols., Bromiley) [1979–1988]

KBL *Lexicon in Veteris Testamenti libros* (Koehler, Baumgartner) [1958]

LCL Loeb Classical Library

L&N *Greek-English Lexicon of the New Testament: Based on Semantic Domains* (Louw and Nida) [1989]

LSJ *A Greek-English Lexicon* (9th ed., Liddell, Scott, Jones) [1996]

MM *The Vocabulary of the Greek New Testament* (Moulton and Milligan) [1930; 1997]

NA^{26} *Novum Testamentum Graece* (26th ed., Nestle-Aland) [1979]

NA^{27} *Novum Testamentum Graece* (27th ed., Nestle-Aland) [1993]

NBD *New Bible Dictionary* (2nd ed., Douglas, Hillyer) [1982]

NIDB *New International Dictionary of the Bible* (Douglas, Tenney) [1987]

NIDBA *New International Dictionary of Biblical Archaeology* (Blaiklock and Harrison) [1983]

NIDNTT *New International Dictionary of New Testament Theology* (4 vols., C. Brown) [1975–1985]

NIDOTTE *New International Dictionary of Old Testament Theology and Exegesis* (5 vols., W. A. VanGemeren) [1997]

PGM *Papyri graecae magicae: Die griechischen Zauberpapyri.* (Preisendanz) [1928]

PG *Patrologia Graecae* (J. P. Migne) [1857–1886]

TBD *Tyndale Bible Dictionary* (Elwell, Comfort) [2001]

TDNT *Theological Dictionary of the New Testament* (10 vols., Kittel, Friedrich; trans. Bromiley) [1964–1976]

TDOT *Theological Dictionary of the Old Testament* (8 vols., Botterweck, Ringgren; trans. Willis, Bromiley, Green) [1974–]

TLNT *Theological Lexicon of the New Testament* (3 vols., C. Spicq) [1994]

TLOT *Theological Lexicon of the Old Testament* (3 vols., E. Jenni) [1997]

TWOT *Theological Wordbook of the Old Testament* (2 vols., Harris, Archer) [1980]

UBS^3 *United Bible Societies' Greek New Testament* (3rd ed., Metzger et al.) [1975]

UBS^4 *United Bible Societies' Greek New Testament* (4th corrected ed., Metzger et al.) [1993]

WH *The New Testament in the Original Greek* (Westcott and Hort) [1882]

ABBREVIATIONS FOR BOOKS OF THE BIBLE

Old Testament

Gen	Genesis	1 Sam	1 Samuel	Esth	Esther
Exod	Exodus	2 Sam	2 Samuel	Ps, Pss	Psalm, Psalms
Lev	Leviticus	1 Kgs	1 Kings	Prov	Proverbs
Num	Numbers	2 Kgs	2 Kings	Eccl	Ecclesiastes
Deut	Deuteronomy	1 Chr	1 Chronicles	Song	Song of Songs
Josh	Joshua	2 Chr	2 Chronicles	Isa	Isaiah
Judg	Judges	Ezra	Ezra	Jer	Jeremiah
Ruth	Ruth	Neh	Nehemiah	Lam	Lamentations

Ezek	Ezekiel	Obad	Obadiah	Zeph	Zephaniah
Dan	Daniel	Jonah	Jonah	Hag	Haggai
Hos	Hosea	Mic	Micah	Zech	Zechariah
Joel	Joel	Nah	Nahum	Mal	Malachi
Amos	Amos	Hab	Habakkuk		

New Testament

Matt	Matthew	Eph	Ephesians	Heb	Hebrews
Mark	Mark	Phil	Philippians	Jas	James
Luke	Luke	Col	Colossians	1 Pet	1 Peter
John	John	1 Thess	1 Thessalonians	2 Pet	2 Peter
Acts	Acts	2 Thess	2 Thessalonians	1 John	1 John
Rom	Romans	1 Tim	1 Timothy	2 John	2 John
1 Cor	1 Corinthians	2 Tim	2 Timothy	3 John	3 John
2 Cor	2 Corinthians	Titus	Titus	Jude	Jude
Gal	Galatians	Phlm	Philemon	Rev	Revelation

Deuterocanonical

Bar	Baruch	1–2 Esdr	1–2 Esdras	Pr Man	Prayer of Manasseh
Add Dan	Additions to Daniel	Add Esth	Additions to Esther	Ps 151	Psalm 151
Pr Azar	Prayer of Azariah	Ep Jer	Epistle of Jeremiah	Sir	Sirach
Bel	Bel and the Dragon	Jdt	Judith	Tob	Tobit
Sg Three	Song of the Three Children	1–2 Macc	1–2 Maccabees	Wis	Wisdom of Solomon
		3–4 Macc	3–4 Maccabees		
Sus	Susanna				

MANUSCRIPTS AND LITERATURE FROM QUMRAN

Initial numerals followed by "Q" indicate particular caves at Qumran. For example, the notation 4Q267 indicates text 267 from cave 4 at Qumran. Further, 1QS 4:9-10 indicates column 4, lines 9-10 of the *Rule of the Community*; and 4Q166 1 ii 2 indicates fragment 1, column ii, line 2 of text 166 from cave 4. More examples of common abbreviations are listed below.

CD	Cairo Geniza copy of the *Damascus Document*	1QIsa[b]	Isaiah copy [b]	4QLam[a]	Lamentations
		1QM	*War Scroll*	11QPs[a]	Psalms
		1QpHab	*Pesher Habakkuk*	11QTemple[a,b]	*Temple Scroll*
1QH	*Thanksgiving Hymns*	1QS	*Rule of the Community*	11QtgJob	*Targum of Job*
1QIsa[a]	Isaiah copy [a]				

IMPORTANT NEW TESTAMENT MANUSCRIPTS

(all dates given are AD; ordinal numbers refer to centuries)

Significant Papyri (𝔓 = Papyrus)

𝔓1 Matt 1; early 3rd
𝔓4+𝔓64+𝔓67 Matt 3, 5, 26; Luke 1-6; late 2nd
𝔓5 John 1, 16, 20; early 3rd
𝔓13 Heb 2-5, 10-12; early 3rd
𝔓15+𝔓16 (probably part of same codex) 1 Cor 7-8, Phil 3-4; late 3rd

𝔓20 James 2-3; 3rd
𝔓22 John 15-16; mid 3rd
𝔓23 James 1; c. 200
𝔓27 Rom 8-9; 3rd
𝔓30 1 Thess 4-5; 2 Thess 1; early 3rd
𝔓32 Titus 1-2; late 2nd
𝔓37 Matt 26; late 3rd

𝔓39 John 8; first half of 3rd
𝔓40 Rom 1-4, 6, 9; 3rd
𝔓45 Gospels and Acts; early 3rd
𝔓46 Paul's Major Epistles (less Pastorals); late 2nd
𝔓47 Rev 9-17; 3rd

𝔓49+𝔓65 Eph 4-5; 1 Thess
  1-2; 3rd
𝔓52 John 18; c. 125
𝔓53 Matt 26, Acts 9-10;
  middle 3rd
𝔓66 John; late 2nd
𝔓70 Matt 2-3, 11-12, 24; 3rd
𝔓72 1-2 Peter, Jude; c. 300

𝔓74 Acts, General Epistles; 7th
𝔓75 Luke and John; c. 200
𝔓77+𝔓103 (probably part of
  same codex) Matt 13-14, 23;
  late 2nd
𝔓87 Phlm; late 2nd
𝔓90 John 18-19; late 2nd
𝔓91 Acts 2-3; 3rd

𝔓92 Eph 1, 2 Thess 1; c. 300
𝔓98 Rev 1:13-20; late 2nd
𝔓100 James 3-5; c. 300
𝔓101 Matt 3-4; 3rd
𝔓104 Matt 21; 2nd
𝔓106 John 1; 3rd
𝔓115 Rev 2-3, 5-6, 8-15; 3rd

Significant Uncials

א (Sinaiticus) most of NT; 4th
A (Alexandrinus) most of NT;
  5th
B (Vaticanus) most of NT; 4th
C (Ephraemi Rescriptus) most
  of NT with many lacunae;
  5th
D (Bezae) Gospels, Acts; 5th
D (Claromontanus), Paul's
  Epistles; 6th (different MS
  than Bezae)
E (Laudianus 35) Acts; 6th
F (Augensis) Paul's Epistles; 9th
G (Boernerianus) Paul's
  Epistles; 9th

H (Coislinianus) Paul's
  Epistles; 6th
I (Freerianus or Washington)
  Paul's Epistles; 5th
L (Regius) Gospels; 8th
Q (Guelferbytanus B) Luke,
  John; 5th
P (Porphyrianus) Acts—
  Revelation; 9th
T (Borgianus) Luke, John; 5th
W (Washingtonianus or the
  Freer Gospels) Gospels; 5th
Z (Dublinensis) Matthew; 6th
037 (Δ; Sangallensis) Gospels;
  9th

038 (Θ; Koridethi) Gospels;
  9th
040 (Ξ; Zacynthius) Luke; 6th
043 (Φ; Beratinus) Matt,
  Mark; 6th
044 (Ψ; Athous Laurae)
  Gospels, Acts, Paul's
  Epistles; 9th
048 Acts, Paul's Epistles,
  General Epistles; 5th
0171 Matt 10, Luke 22;
  c. 300
0189 Acts 5; c. 200

Significant Minuscules

1 Gospels, Acts, Paul's Epistles;
  12th
33 All NT except Rev; 9th
81 Acts, Paul's Epistles,
  General Epistles; 1044
565 Gospels; 9th
700 Gospels; 11th

1424 (or Family 1424—a
  group of 29 manuscripts
  sharing nearly the same
  text) most of NT; 9th-10th
1739 Acts, Paul's Epistles; 10th
2053 Rev; 13th
2344 Rev; 11th

f^1 (a family of manuscripts
  including 1, 118, 131, 209)
  Gospels; 12th-14th
f^{13} (a family of manuscripts
  including 13, 69, 124, 174,
  230, 346, 543, 788, 826,
  828, 983, 1689, 1709—
  known as the Ferrar group)
  Gospels; 11th-15th

Significant Ancient Versions

SYRIAC (SYR)
syr^c (Syriac Curetonian)
  Gospels; 5th
syr^s (Syriac Sinaiticus)
  Gospels; 4th
syr^h (Syriac Harklensis) Entire
  NT; 616

OLD LATIN (IT)
it^a (Vercellenis) Gospels; 4th
it^b (Veronensis) Gospels; 5th
it^d (Cantabrigiensis—the Latin
  text of Bezae) Gospels, Acts,
  3 John; 5th
it^e (Palantinus) Gospels; 5th
it^k (Bobiensis) Matthew, Mark;
  c. 400

COPTIC (COP)
cop^{bo} (Boharic—north Egypt)
cop^{fay} (Fayyumic—central Egypt)
cop^{sa} (Sahidic—southern Egypt)

OTHER VERSIONS
arm (Armenian)
eth (Ethiopic)
geo (Georgian)

TRANSLITERATION AND NUMBERING SYSTEM

Note: For words and roots from non-biblical languages (e.g., Arabic, Ugaritic), only approximate transliterations are given.

HEBREW/ARAMAIC

Consonants

א	aleph	= '	מ, ם	mem	= m
בּ, ב	beth	= b	נ, ן	nun	= n
גּ, ג	gimel	= g	ס	samekh	= s
דּ, ד	daleth	= d	ע	ayin	= '
ה	he	= h	פּ, פ, ף	pe	= p
ו	waw	= w	צ, ץ	tsadhe	= ts
ז	zayin	= z	ק	qoph	= q
ח	heth	= kh	ר	resh	= r
ט	teth	= t	שׁ	shin	= sh
י	yodh	= y	שׂ	sin	= s
כּ, כ, ך	kaph	= k	תּ, ת	taw	= t, th (spirant)
ל	lamedh	= l			

Vowels

ַ	patakh	= a	ָ	qamets khatuf	= o
חַ	furtive patakh	= a	ֹ	holem	= o
ָ	qamets	= a	וֹ	full holem	= o
הָ	final qamets he	= ah	ֻ	short qibbuts	= u
ֶ	segol	= e	ֻ	long qibbuts	= u
ֵ	tsere	= e	וּ	shureq	= u
ֵי	tsere yod	= e	ֲ	khatef patakh	= a
ִ	short hireq	= i	ֳ	khatef qamets	= o
ִ	long hireq	= i	ְ	vocalic shewa	= e
ִי	hireq yod	= i	ַי	patakh yodh	= a

Greek

α	alpha	= a	ε	epsilon	= e
β	beta	= b	ζ	zeta	= z
γ	gamma	= g, n (before γ, κ, ξ, χ)	η	eta	= ē
			θ	theta	= th
δ	delta	= d	ι	iota	= i

κ	kappa	= k		τ	tau	= t
λ	lamda	= l		υ	upsilon	= u
μ	mu	= m		φ	phi	= ph
ν	nu	= n		χ	chi	= ch
ξ	ksi	= x		ψ	psi	= ps
ο	omicron	= o		ω	omega	= ō
π	pi	= p		ʽ	rough	= h (with
ρ	rho	= r (ῥ = rh)			breathing	vowel or
σ, ς	sigma	= s			mark	diphthong)

THE TYNDALE-STRONG'S NUMBERING SYSTEM

The Cornerstone Biblical Commentary series uses a word-study numbering system to give both newer and more advanced Bible students alike quicker, more convenient access to helpful original-language tools (e.g., concordances, lexicons, and theological dictionaries). Those who are unfamiliar with the ancient Hebrew, Aramaic, and Greek alphabets can quickly find information on a given word by looking up the appropriate index number. Advanced students will find the system helpful because it allows them to quickly find the lexical form of obscure conjugations and inflections.

There are two main numbering systems used for biblical words today. The one familiar to most people is the Strong's numbering system (made popular by the *Strong's Exhaustive Concordance to the Bible*). Although the original Strong's system is still quite useful, the most up-to-date research has shed new light on the biblical languages and allows for more precision than is found in the original Strong's system. The Cornerstone Biblical Commentary series, therefore, features a newly revised version of the Strong's system, the Tyndale-Strong's numbering system. The Tyndale-Strong's system brings together the familiarity of the Strong's system and the best of modern scholarship. In most cases, the original Strong's numbers are preserved. In places where new research dictates, new or related numbers have been added.[1]

The second major numbering system today is the Goodrick-Kohlenberger system used in a number of study tools published by Zondervan. In order to give students broad access to a number of helpful tools, the Commentary provides index numbers for the Zondervan system as well.

The different index systems are designated as follows:

TG Tyndale-Strong's Greek number　　　　ZH Zondervan Hebrew number
ZG Zondervan Greek number　　　　　　　TA Tyndale-Strong's Aramaic number
TH Tyndale-Strong's Hebrew number　　　ZA Zondervan Aramaic number

So in the example, "love" *agapē* [TG26, ZG27], the first number is the one to use with Greek tools keyed to the Tyndale-Strong's system, and the second applies to tools that use the Zondervan system.

---

1. Generally, one may simply use the original four-digit Strong's number to identify words in tools using Strong's system. If a Tyndale-Strong's number is followed by a capital letter (e.g., TG1692A), it generally indicates an added subdivision of meaning for the given term. Whenever a Tyndale-Strong's number has a number following a decimal point (e.g., TG2013.1), it reflects an instance where new research has yielded a separate, new classification of use for a biblical word. Forthcoming tools from Tyndale House Publishers will include these entries, which were not part of the original Strong's system.

Romans

ROGER MOHRLANG

INTRODUCTION TO
Romans

PAUL'S LETTER TO THE ROMANS is one of the most significant writings ever to come from the hand of a Christian. Theologically, it is certainly the most important of all of Paul's letters, and many would say it is the single most important document in the entire New Testament—indeed, "arguably the single most important work of Christian theology ever written" (Dunn 1993:838). It is the most fully developed theological statement we have from the earliest Christians. Of all the New Testament writings, it is Romans that gives us the most comprehensive exposition and analysis of the Christian gospel, the Good News of salvation in Jesus Christ.

Because of this, Romans has been extremely influential in the history of the Christian church and, indeed, in the history of the western world. It was instrumental in the formulation of the early Christian creeds, and it shaped the lives and thinking of such key figures as Augustine (reflected in his understanding of human sinfulness and of grace), Luther (justification by faith), Calvin (God's sovereignty and predestination), Wesley (the transforming work of the Holy Spirit), and Barth (God's sovereign revelation of grace). It played a key role in the rise of the Protestant Reformation and, more than any other single work, has shaped the theology of the modern-day evangelical movement (reflected, for example, in the preaching of Billy Graham and in Campus Crusade for Christ's "Four Spiritual Laws"). Luther thought the book to be so important that "every Christian should know it word for word, by heart, [and] occupy himself with it every day, as the daily bread of the soul. It can never be read or pondered too much," he wrote, "and the more it is dealt with the more precious it becomes, and the better it tastes" (Luther 1954:xi).

Without question, of all the letters of Paul, Romans is the weightiest and most significant theologically and comes closest to being a carefully constructed theological exposition. Here, in well-organized form, Paul gives us all the central elements of his understanding of the Christian faith: God's saving work in Christ, the doctrine of justification by faith, the claims of Christ as Lord, the life-transforming work of the Holy Spirit, the confident expectation of sharing in God's glory, and much more. Here we have the quintessence of Paul's theological thought. A good grasp of Romans is crucial, then, if we are to understand Paul.

But understanding Romans is no easy task; it is difficult to know how to put all the pieces together. (The title of John A. T. Robinson's book, *Wrestling with Romans*, is apropos.) Of all Paul's writings, this one, more than any other, has challenged—

and continues to challenge—the intellectual powers of interpreters. The seeming inconsistencies and enigmatic logic give rise to many questions and make Romans the most perplexing of Paul's letters. There may well be more written about Romans than about any other book of the New Testament. (For an extensive list of commentaries up to 1973, see Cranfield 1980:xiii-xviii.) But the book of Romans is well worth the struggle.

Here, then, is the greatest of all Paul's letters, a letter that many Christians believe is the single most important writing in the entire New Testament—indeed, perhaps the most significant Christian document in the whole of human history. Here God in his mercy has given us a window into the single most important thing in life, our salvation, with all of its life-changing ramifications. A good grasp of Romans is essential not only for our understanding of Paul but for our understanding of the early Christians' perception of Jesus and his significance, and of the message that lies at the very heart of the New Testament.

AUTHOR

There is no question that Paul is the author of the Letter to the Romans. Though doubts are frequently raised about the authenticity of several of the other writings bearing Paul's name (esp. 1 and 2 Timothy and Titus—but also Ephesians, Colossians, and 2 Thessalonians), there is almost universal acknowledgment among scholars that Paul is the author of Romans.[1] The letter is included in every early list of Paul's letters, and its language, style, and theology are all characteristically Pauline.

Though Paul is the author, it is clear that he was not the actual writer per se, inasmuch as Tertius is named as the writer of the epistle (16:22). In keeping with common practice in the Roman world, Paul used the services of Tertius as a secretary (or amanuensis) to write the letter for him. How much of this letter, then, actually came from Paul? Did Paul dictate the letter word by word? Or did Tertius take down Paul's thoughts in a form of shorthand and then later write them out in his own words? Or did Paul simply give Tertius a sketch of what he wanted to say, allowing him a free hand in composing a letter that expressed those ideas? In other words, how much freedom did the secretary have in the actual writing?[2]

It is impossible to know exactly what Paul communicated to Tertius. But given (1) the importance of the subject matter—the eternal Good News, (2) the careful and extensive way the complex case is argued, (3) the seriousness with which Paul took his apostolic calling and his readers' response to it, and (4) his concern that he not be misinterpreted, it seems likely that Paul would have had a strong interest in making sure that the final wording expressed his thoughts accurately. So, however he used his secretary, we may be reasonably confident that the letter as it stands is an accurate expression of Paul's thought and that he would have been careful to ensure that. With respect to Paul's direct involvement in the whole writing process, Cranfield observes, "In view of the inherent improbability that someone capable of the highly original, closely articulated and also extremely difficult thought which has gone into the Epistle to the Romans would ever have voluntarily entrusted the expression of it to another person, we conclude that Tertius either wrote the epistle in longhand directly from Paul's dictation or else took it down first in shorthand, and that we may be confident that we have in the text which Tertius wrote the thought of Paul for all intents and purposes expressed as Paul himself expressed it" (1980:2-5).

There is some question as to whether Paul wrote the final invocation of grace (16:20, 24), the final doxology (16:25-27), and the final long list of greetings (16:3-23); see "Canonicity and Textual History" below.

DATE AND OCCASION OF WRITING

The Letter to the Romans was written near the end of Paul's third major mission trip (described in Acts 18:23–20:38), when he was about to set off for Jerusalem with money he had been collecting for the poverty-stricken Christians in Judea (15:25-26). (It is possible that he thought this gift would help to allay Jewish suspicions about him and his work among Gentiles and serve to bring the two branches of the church closer together [Käsemann 1980:403ff; Dunn 1988a:xlii]). The letter seems to have been written during the three months Paul spent in southern Greece (the Roman province of Achaia) before leaving for Jerusalem (Acts 20:2-3). Most probably it was written from Corinth, the capital and home of the key church of the province. Hints of this are found in the references to Phoebe of Cenchrea, Corinth's eastern port (16:1), and to Gaius and Erastus, who may have lived in Corinth (16:23; cf. Acts 19:22; 1 Cor 1:14; 2 Tim 4:20). Thus, the letter was most probably written during the winter or early spring of AD 55–56 or 56–57 (Cranfield 1980:12-16; Dunn 1988a:xliii-xliv).

After a decade of productive evangelism and church planting in the Aegean area (in the major towns of the Roman provinces of Galatia, Asia, Macedonia, and Achaia especially), Paul felt his missionary work in the northeastern end of the Mediterranean was over, at least for a time. Following his trip to Jerusalem he intended to head west—all the way to Spain, the oldest Roman province in the West, which, at that time, was beginning to produce some of the great men of the Roman Empire (Seneca, Trajan, and Hadrian all had Spanish ancestry). On the way, he hoped to stop for a time in Rome—a visit he had long anticipated—to see the Christians and do evangelistic work there before being assisted by them on his way to the western end of the Mediterranean (1:13-15; 15:23-29). This letter, sent on ahead, served to notify the Christians in Rome of his plans.

Why did Paul choose this particular occasion to spell out in such detail his understanding of the Good News and its relevance to both Jews and Gentiles? Were there tensions in the church between the two groups, or conflicting understandings of salvation or the role of the Jewish law? Or was Paul attempting to head off such problems before they erupted? (By this time he was certainly aware of the strength of Jewish-Christian sentiment against his seemingly law-free gospel, but how much this sentiment had surfaced in the church in Rome is not clear.) Was there confusion over the role of Jews and Gentiles in God's overall plan? Was there opposition to Paul himself? In other words, was Paul addressing specific problems in the Roman church, or was he simply hoping to lay a solid theological foundation for an important young and growing church whose establishment and development he had not personally overseen?

The answers are not entirely clear, and scholarly opinions vary widely. In reality, Paul may well have been concerned with a number of issues such as tensions or disagreements in the church, potential or real opposition to himself and his message, the need to lay a foundation for his evangelistic work, and the role of Rome in his future missionary work in the western Mediterranean (Cranfield 1981:814-823; Fitzmyer 1993:68-80; Dunn 1988a:lv-lviii; cf. Moo 1996:20-21).[3] Nonetheless, his primary concern was clearly to expound in some depth, against the background of the Jewish law, the Good News itself—and to show its broader implications for *both* Jews and Gentiles. (Note his repeated emphasis that the Good News is for *everyone* who believes: 1:16; 3:29-30; 4:9-17; 9:24-26; 10:11-13; 11:11-32; 15:7-12.) This is what dominates his thought in Romans. The other issues—for example, the matter of the relationship between the two groups, which some take to be the central concern of the letter (so Kaylor 1988:18ff)—are clearly secondary. Such issues may well have helped to shape what Paul wrote and emphasized (cf. chs 9–11, 14–15), but they are not the primary issues he deals with in this letter. Although it is popular today to emphasize the importance of understanding the letter in light of the specific problems facing the church or the author (cf. Dunn 1988a:lvii; Wedderburn 1988:140-142; Moo 1996:16-22), a careful reading of the letter makes it clear that the dominant focus is not on the problems of the church or the author per se but on the all-absorbing content of the Good News itself (so Cranfield 1981:818-819; Moo 1996:21-22; cf. Mounce 1981:8: "Romans is a magnificent presentation of the gospel"). The local problems may lie in the background, but it is the Good News that dominates the foreground. It is the inner logic of his argument itself, not the sociological setting of the letter, which provides the primary key to understanding Romans.

In any case, for those who didn't know the man well, this letter, written at the end of a major period in Paul's missionary career, served the very practical function of providing a useful introduction to Paul and the Good News he preached prior to his anticipated visit to Rome. At the same time, it laid a solid theological foundation for what was to become a key church in the Empire, a church that Paul hoped would actively support his missionary work in the West.

When Paul finally arrived in Rome three years later, it was not at all as he had planned. According to Luke's account in Acts, his trip to Jerusalem resulted in such a violent uproar in the Jewish community that he was arrested and then imprisoned for two years in Caesarea. Subsequently, when at his request he was sent under guard to Rome to have his case tried by an imperial court,[4] he spent two more years under house arrest in the capital city while awaiting trial. During this time he was allowed to evangelize and minister freely to all who visited him (Acts 28:16-31). After that, details are less certain. A letter written about AD 96 by Clement, an elder in the church in Rome, suggests that Paul got his wish to preach the Good News in the western end of the Mediterranean. (Clement speaks of Paul reaching "the furthest limits of the West," commonly understood as a reference to Spain; 1 Clement 5; cf. Radice 1968:25). This indicates that the case against him in the Roman courts came to nothing. A few years later (AD 64–65, in the reign of Nero), according to early tradition, Paul was rearrested, sentenced to death in Rome as a leader of the Christians, and beheaded outside the city. (For a full account of the various early traditions about the end of Paul's life, see Bruce 1977:441-455; cf. Hennecke 1965:2.73.) Shortly before his death, in full anticipation of the glorious future awaiting him, he wrote,

> As for me, my life has already been poured out as an offering to God. The time of my death is near. I have fought the good fight, I have finished the race, and I have remained faithful. And now the prize awaits me—the crown of righteousness, which the Lord, the righteous Judge, will give me on the day of his return. (2 Tim 4:6-8)

AUDIENCE

No one knows precisely when the church in Rome first came into being or what its exact makeup was. Ever since 62 BC, when Pompey returned from Judea with many captives, there had been a large community of Jews in Rome. By the time of Paul, it may have numbered 40,000–50,000 and many synagogues had sprung up. (The Jewish catacombs list 10–13 synagogues that may have been in existence in Paul's time; Dunn 1988a:xlvi.) Most likely the Good News was first spread in these synagogues—by ordinary Jewish Christians returning from Jerusalem rather than by evangelists who had targeted the city. There is no evidence for the tradition that Peter was the founder and first bishop of the church in Rome, though it is clear that he later preached in Rome and that he was eventually executed for his witness there (Eusebius 1965:88, 104-105). That there was a Christian community in Rome for at least seven years before Paul wrote this letter seems certain from Suetonius's reference to Claudius's mass expulsion of Jews from Rome in AD 49 because of riots caused (in the synagogues presumably) by a certain Chrestus—a name commonly taken as a reference to Christ (cf. Dunn 1988a:xlv-liv).

Judging by the number of Jews Paul mentions in the last chapter of Romans (which I assume to be part of the original writing) and by the priority he gives to addressing issues relevant to Jews, it appears that the decree was later relaxed and that many Jews had returned to Rome and were then part of the church. It is also clear that a number of Gentiles were in the church (cf. 1:5-6, 13; 11:13-32; 15:7-12, 15-16). Most of them were probably originally connected with the synagogues, given Paul's frequent reference to the Scriptures. But whether the church was dominantly Jewish or Gentile at the time of Paul's writing is difficult to tell (Cranfield 1980:21). In the fourth century, Ambrosiaster says the Romans "had embraced the faith of Christ, albeit according to the Jewish rite" (cited by Bruce 1985:15-16). The names listed in chapter 16 reflect a mix of Jewish, Greek, and Roman backgrounds

(Sanday and Headlam 1902:xxxiv). The fact that there was often tension between Jews and Gentiles probably accounts for some of Paul's emphases in the letter (e.g., 1:16; 2:9ff; 14:1–15:13).

The social status of the Christians is likewise not easy to ascertain and appears to have been mixed. A number appear to have been slaves or "freedmen"—at least 14 of the 24 greeted by name in chapter 16 have commonly used slave names; several of them (perhaps as many as 8 of the 14) may have been well-to-do (Dunn 1988a:lii). Given the size of the capital city and the references in chapter 16 to various groups in the church, it is probable that the Christians in Rome were divided into a number of small house groups, partly on the basis of these ethnic and social distinctions—even though Paul writes a single letter to "all of you in Rome who are loved by God" (1:7).

Although Paul had never visited Rome, he seems to have known a number of the Christians there personally, judging from the number of people to whom he sends his greetings in the final chapter. We may safely assume, then, that many of them already knew what he stood for and had at least a rough idea of the Good News he preached. Paul was not writing to a totally foreign audience.

CANONICITY AND TEXTUAL HISTORY

Because it was acknowledged as authentically Pauline, the Letter to the Romans has from the earliest days been accepted as canonical Scripture. All the early lists of New Testament Scripture include it. The exact form of the end of the letter, however, varies in the manuscript traditions as follows (Metzger 1971:533-536):

1. The doxology (16:25-27) occurs in various places: at the end of chapter 14, at the end of chapter 15, at the end of chapter 16, and in some manuscripts it is repeated at the end of both chapter 14 and chapter 16. In a few manuscripts, it is omitted entirely.
2. The invocation of "grace" (16:20) occurs in various places: after 16:19, after 16:23, after both 16:19 and 16:23, and after 16:27 in a few authorities.
3. The bulk of chapters 15 and 16 (15:1–16:23/24) is missing in a few manuscripts of the Latin Vulgate, and some of the early fathers are strangely silent on these two chapters.

Several different explanations of these variations have been proposed. Some scholars think that Paul originally wrote 1:1–14:23 as a general letter to be circulated and that 15:1–16:27 was added to a copy specifically addressed to the church in Rome. Others think that chapter 16 (with its commendation of Phoebe and its long list of personal greetings) was never a part of Paul's original letter to the church at Rome but was added later when a copy of the letter was sent to the church in Ephesus, which Paul knew much more intimately. (For a critical evaluation of this hypothesis, see Dodd 1932:12-17.) Still others think that Paul wrote the whole of 16:1-23 but that the doxology represents a later addition to the end of all the varying early forms of Romans (at least one of which was truncated at chapter 14 by Marcion, according to Origen; Metzger 1971:533; Kümmel 1975:315). (For detailed discussion of the arguments for and against the alternative explanations, see Cranfield 1980:5-11; also cf. Comfort 2007:[Rom 14:23; 15:33].)

However, it is equally possible that Paul wrote the whole of 1:1–16:27, including the fitting doxology (Nygren 1949:457; Guthrie 1970:407-408; Harrison 1976:171; cf. Cranfield 1980:11), and that parts of the last two chapters (being somewhat lengthy and more personal) were simply omitted by some early copyists because they were perceived as less important or less significant theologically or were omitted by Paul himself in an abridged version he edited for wider circulation (Guthrie 1970:408 [citing Lightfoot]; cf. Robinson 1979:5). The resulting abbreviated copies would still have been understood as communicating the essence of this long theological letter. This is the position I have adopted.

LITERARY STYLE AND STRUCTURE

The language and style of Romans is characteristic of a good, competent speaker of Koine Greek. Though not intended as a piece of literary art per se, the Letter to the Romans occasionally expresses both literary refinement and knowledge of Greek philosophy. Passages such as 8:31-39 show genuine elegance. Much of the vocabulary reflects the influence of the Septuagint (the Gr. translation of the OT that was used in Hellenistic synagogues); this is seen in such words as "righteous" (*dikaios* [TG1342, ZG1465]), "righteousness" (*dikaiosunē* [TG1343, ZG1466]), "justify" (*dikaioō* [TG1344, ZG1467]), "covenant" (*diathēkē* [TG1242, ZG1347]), "law" (*nomos* [TG3551, ZG3795]), "glory" (*doxa* [TG1391, ZG1518]), "Lord" (*kurios* [TG2962, ZG3261]), and "elect" (*eklogē* [TG1589, ZG1724]). Paul's thought is shaped by the traditional Jewish concepts of the Old Testament, in which he was steeped from childhood, having been brought up in the Pharisaic tradition (Acts 22:3; 23:6; 26:5; cf. Phil 3:5).

Paul's style of writing varies naturally with the subject. Frequently, he shows a preference for the rhetorical style of Hellenistic diatribe (Watson 1993:213-214) in posing the questions or arrogant objections of a would-be opponent and then answering them himself (2:1-5, 17-29; 3:1-9, 27ff; 9:19-21; 11:17-24). In some cases, the objections take the form of false conclusions or misinterpretations drawn from his argument, which Paul rejects—often with the phrase "Of course not!"—and then goes on to correct (3:1-9, 31; 6:1-3, 15-16; 7:7, 13; 9:14, 19-20; 11:1, 11). New steps in his argument are often introduced by "Well then" or "What shall we say" (3:5, 9; 4:1; 6:1, 15; 7:7; 8:31; 9:14, 30). In these passages we catch glimpses of a larger dialogue going on within Judaism.

Recently a few scholars (esp. Räisänen 1983:264ff; cf. Sanders 1983:144-148) have alleged that Paul's writing in Romans is contradictory and incoherent, especially with regard to the Jewish law—which they take as a sign of Paul's own confusion over the issue. Much of this seeming confusion, however, may be accounted for by Paul's desire to both affirm the law while qualifying the traditional understanding of it and to distinguish varying functions of the law, according to the context. (See "The Law of Moses" below.)

On the whole, the Letter to the Romans is a fine early-Christian example of a well-organized, comprehensive, sustained theological argument, with the relationship between sentences often carefully marked by connecting words. The way Paul develops this argument may be seen in the brief overview below.

1:1-17 Introduction. Introducing himself as a missionary apostle, chosen by God to proclaim the Good News of salvation in Christ (1:1-15), Paul gets right to the heart of his message: God saves those who put their trust in Christ. Only by trusting in Christ can a person be made right with God. Whether one is a Jew or Gentile, one must have faith in Christ to be considered righteous (1:16-17).

1:18–3:20 The Universal Need of Salvation. Why is this so? In short, there is a universal need for salvation because no one can be made right with God on his or her own. There is no person, Jew or Gentile, who has lived up to God's moral standards—and God holds people accountable for what they can know of him and his demands.

Even Gentiles are responsible for what they can learn about God from the world of nature and are, thus, obligated to him. But instead of giving God the worship and gratitude due him, Gentiles have chosen rather to worship idols and engage in moral perversity. The terrible consequences may be seen in the depraved way of life God has allowed them to experience. Intuitively aware of their moral responsibilities and of God's judgment upon them, they nonetheless live as though they were oblivious to both (1:18-32).

Jews (even pious ones) are little better. Although they have the written law of God and pride themselves in their adherence to it, they fall as far short of keeping it as the Gentiles do. And God will judge them, not on the basis of their knowledge of the law, but on the basis of their obedience to it. Though superior to Gentiles in their own eyes, they are equally guilty in God's eyes (2:1-29).

What is the tragic conclusion of it all? The whole world, Jews and Gentiles alike—every single person who has ever lived—has failed to measure up to God's holy standards. As Scripture itself shows, there is no one who can be considered truly righteous from God's point of view: "For everyone has sinned; we all fall short of God's glorious standard" (3:23). The whole world, then, stands guilty under the holy scrutiny of God, deserving of his retribution; no one is exempt. Everyone stands desperately in need of God's mercy and forgiving grace (3:1-20).

3:21–5:21 God's Gift of Salvation. The amazing, good news is that God, in his mercy, has provided salvation for a doomed world! By giving up his own Son to die as a sacrifice for sin, God in his grace has made it possible for us to be forgiven and made right with himself—something we could never achieve on our own. This gracious gift is freely given to all who put their trust in Christ; it is not dependent on a person's observance of the law of Moses (3:21-31).

Scripture confirms the point by what it says about Abraham, the founder of the Jewish nation: "Abraham believed God, and God counted him as righteous because of his faith" (4:3). It was because of his faith that Abraham received God's blessing, not because of his observance of God's law. Here the principle of justification by faith is drawn from the law of Moses itself, in opposition to those who would argue that the principle represents a denial of the law (4:1-25).

Paul then expounds in greater detail the amazing nature of God's grace in Christ and its related benefits—peace with God, joy, character transformation, the experience of God's love, the power of his Spirit, and the assurance of ultimate glory. He then contrasts the deadly effects of Adam's sin with the life-giving results of Christ's obedience, showing how the latter overcomes the former in every way (5:1-21).

6:1–7:25 Objections to the Good News. A troublesome objection is now posed: If salvation is simply a matter of grace and not dependent on obedience to the law of Moses, what is to keep a person from sinning (6:1; cf. 6:15)? Do away with the law and what is left as the basis of morality and ethics? The real basis of Christian morality, Paul replies, is not the Jewish law but one's relationship to Christ. When we are joined to Christ in baptism, we enter into Christ's experience of dying and rising again: we "die" to our former way of life, and we "rise" to live a new life as a new person. We are to behave, then, as people who are dead to the power of sin but alive to God. There is to be no yielding to sin in the life of one who has died with Christ (6:1-14).

Further, as Christians we now have a new master, and we live in obedience to him and his desires. If we continue in a life of sin, it shows that our master is not the Lord but sin—and the end of that way of life is eternal doom. How one lives, then, reveals the real driving force—the real "master"—of a person's life (6:15-23).

Here Paul lays a basis for Christian morality and ethics in one's relationship to Christ, quite apart from obedience to the law of Moses. As one who has died with Christ, the Christian is no longer bound by the demands of the law and the power of sin. Joined to the resurrected Lord, the Christian is now empowered by the Spirit to live the kind of life God desires (6:14; 7:1-6).

But does this mean that the law of Moses is bad? No, not at all, Paul responds; the law comes from God and serves God's purposes. But its most important function is not what people think. The real purpose of the law is not to legislate goodness or to be a means of salvation but to show people their sin—to make them aware of their failings and their guilt before God, of their need of divine mercy. Confronting people with the strong demands of God, the law offers no answer to the problem of sin; it simply condemns it. The law of Moses in itself, then, provides no salvation; its role is to make people aware of their need of salvation. But its moral demands remain a valid expression of the will of God in any case (7:7-13).

The problem is not that the demands of the law are too strong, but that human nature is too weak; the real problem is the power of sin. No matter how well intentioned a person may be, no one has what it takes to live out the demands of the law fully. Morally schizophrenic, human beings by nature are dominated by the terrible power of sin. The picture Paul paints in 7:14-25 is one of utter frustration and despair: no matter how much we may desire to obey the law of God, in our own power we are simply unable to do so. Herein lies the dilemma of the pious Jew—and herein lies the problem for all who would make obedience to the law a requirement for salvation.

8:1-39 The Power and Glory of the New Life. Where then do we find power over sin? We find it in our new life in Christ, which brings the power of the Holy Spirit into our life—a power that breaks the enslaving chains of sin and makes real goodness actually possible. We who have experienced the power of the Spirit should no longer be frustrated by our inability to do what is right, for the power of the life-giving Spirit frees us from the power of sin that results in death. A new potential for goodness has come into our life, the power of the "age to come," enabling us to live in a way that we never could under the law. This, too, is part of the Good News of salvation (8:1-4).

But—and here Paul carefully qualifies his statement—such a life is only possible for those who intentionally turn from sin and allow the Spirit to rule their lives. Though this life-transforming power is given to all believers, its actual effect in a person's life depends on the extent to which a person yields to its influence. And if a person does not yield to its control, questions will inevitably be raised about the authenticity of that person's relationship to God, for it is those who are *led* by the Spirit of God who are the true children of God. Those who continue to yield to sin, allowing the old, sinful nature to drive their life, will ultimately die. Thus, there must be a correlation between what we claim to believe and how we actually live if our faith is to be considered real. We cannot validly claim to be righteous in God's sight if there is no concern to live out that righteousness in our daily life (8:5-14).

The Spirit is more than simply a life-transforming power. The Spirit's presence assures us that we are true children of God and recipients of all the benefits of Christ. The Spirit also gives us a foretaste of the glory that awaits us beyond this life—and the entire universe looks forward longingly to the day when that glory will be fully revealed. In the meantime, as we live out our calling to suffer with Christ, the Spirit prays for us in our difficulties. The role of the Spirit is to aid us in every way and to transform us into the likeness of Christ himself according to God's purposes for us. This assurance is why we can be absolutely confident that God will cause everything to work for our ultimate good if we love him. So the Spirit of God plays a wide-ranging and crucial role in the living out of the Christian life (8:15-30).

The salvation that God provides in Jesus Christ, then, is a comprehensive one. It meets our deepest needs in several ways: it makes us right with God, it gives us power over sin, and it provides an effective intercessor for us. It affects our life for good in a thoroughgoing way and works to transform us into the likeness of the Son of God himself.

Having dealt at length with the subject of salvation, and having reflected on the glory that awaits believers beyond this life, Paul draws chapters 1–8 to a close by contemplating the wonder of God's love revealed in it all. In light of all that God has done for us in Jesus Christ, he concludes, surely there is nothing—absolutely nothing—that can ever separate us from his eternal love. Even though we must take the judgment of God seriously, if we rest in Christ we need have no fear or trepidation; we are completely safe in his care (8:31-39).

9:1–11:36 The Jews and the Good News. At this point Paul digresses to address an agonizing question arising from the Good News he preaches: What about the salvation of Jews? They have always been considered God's people; why have they not responded to Christ? How are we to account for their failure to receive God's salvation? (9:1-5)

Has God failed to bless his chosen people as he promised? No, Paul responds, we have to remember that not all who call themselves Jews are true Jews—i.e., real people of God. The real children of Abraham have always been those specially chosen by God, by his sovereign grace. He decides who will be his people (9:6-13).

But doesn't this mean that God is unfair? No, Paul counters, God has the sovereign right to choose whomever he wishes (an implicit acknowledgment that some are not chosen), and we must respect his authority to do so. It is God alone who decides who will be the recipients of his mercy (9:14-18).

This being the case, how can God hold people accountable if they don't respond? Aren't they simply doing what he has already decided they will do? Paul's response is simple and direct: "Who are you, a mere human being, to argue with God?" (9:20) Mere mortals cannot challenge the wishes of their Creator any more than clay jars can challenge the intent of the potter who makes them. If God chooses to pour out his judgment on some (including Jews, 9:27) and his mercy on others (including Gentiles, 9:25) just as Scripture predicts, that is his prerogative. God is sovereign (9:19-29).

Paul also explains that the Jews bear responsibility for their own plight: they have been so preoccupied with the law of Moses, so desperately determined to get right with God by keeping the law, that they have failed to recognize God's way of making them right with himself through Christ. They have refused to receive God's free gift of salvation by faith, and the responsibility for the consequences lies squarely on their own shoulders (9:30–10:4).

The law of Moses itself speaks of the essentially easy nature of getting right with God by faith. As the Good News affirms, all that is required is a simple confession that Jesus is Lord and a simple belief in his resurrection. All people have to do is call "on the name of the LORD" (10:13), and they will be saved—whether they are Jews or Gentiles. The Jews heard this message, but they refused to respond, so they have no excuse. Their whole history has been one of resistance and disobedience to God (10:5-21).

Yet there is hope, for not all Jews have rejected Jesus. By God's kindness, there are a small number of them who, like Paul, have come to believe in Christ; they are the chosen few. So even though the majority of Jews have not found the salvation they so earnestly seek in the law, a few have through Christ—those chosen by the sheer mercy of God. The rest, at least for the present, have been made unresponsive (11:1-10).

The situation is not as tragic as it seems, however. For as a result of their failure to respond, a most ironic thing has happened—salvation has been extended to

Gentiles! And here we see God's hidden purposes in this seeming tragedy: the turning-away of the Jewish people has resulted in God's amazing acceptance of Gentiles. However, Gentile believers must never take their newly privileged status for granted or presume on God's grace. If they do not continue in their faith and obedience, God can remove them just as he did the Jews (11:11-24).

In the end, God will bring the Jews back to himself. When all the chosen Gentiles are "in," the Jews will once again be restored—"all Israel will be saved" (11:26). Without spelling out the details, Paul affirms his confidence in the future return and salvation of his own people because God will be faithful to keep his ancient promises to them. "For God's gifts and his call can never be withdrawn" (11:29). So ultimately, for both Jews and Gentiles, everything depends on the sheer mercy of God (11:25-32).

Paul concludes this parenthetical section with a fine note of praise to God, whose ways are beyond human understanding, and to whom his people are indebted for everything. The whole of life is to be understood as a gift (11:33-36).

12:1–15:13 Living the Good News. Having written at length about the Good News, Paul now turns his attention to the practical matters of Christian living. How are we to respond to God's great mercy in saving us? By giving the whole of our life back to him—a kind of "living sacrifice," fully dedicated to a way of life that pleases him in all things. This means living in a way that is significantly different from the way the world around us lives, which requires a change in our whole way of thinking, brought about by the transforming power of the Holy Spirit (12:1-2).

In the remainder of chapter 12, Paul gives some very specific suggestions about the kinds of attitudes and behavior that should characterize Christians as they relate both to other Christians and to non-Christians. The life of the Christian should at all times reflect humility, patience, kindness, gentleness, devotion, enthusiasm, and (above all) love. This chapter gives us a beautiful summary of the Christian life as it ought to be lived (12:3-21).

Beginning in chapter 13, Paul provides practical guidelines for a few specific issues. The first concerns the attitude of Christians to secular authorities. On this question, Paul's advice is simple and straightforward: As a general rule, Christians are to respect those who have authority over them and to be compliant subjects. Whether they know it or not, those in administrative positions in the government indirectly serve God, and as Christians we must acknowledge that; our duty is to be respectful citizens (13:1-7).

Christians must always remember the supreme importance of love. Love both sums up and fulfills the ethical demands of the law of Moses, for the person who truly loves will never intentionally hurt another person. Love is the primary ethical expression of new life in Christ (13:8-10). At all times, Christians are to live in an exemplary, Christlike way, remembering that the Lord is returning soon (13:11-14).

In chapter 14, Paul deals with two relatively minor issues on which there were different opinions in the church: the question of whether Christians ought to be vegetarians, and the question of whether they ought to observe special holy days. On issues like these, of relatively little theological or moral significance, Christians should do whatever their conscience permits them to do and allow those with different opinions (whether more traditional or more free) to do the same, without ridiculing or condemning them. The important thing is to be considerate of others and to avoid doing anything that would lead another person into sin—even if that means giving up doing something we ourselves feel quite free to do. Christian freedom must always be subordinated to the more important consideration of what is most helpful for others because Christian love is sacrificial love (14:1-23).

This principle means that in a mixed community like the church in Rome, comprising both Jews and Gentiles, there must be a concerted effort to respect the different opinions of one another and to live together harmoniously in love. Christians are to build one another up, not tear one another down (15:1-13).

15:14–16:27 Conclusion. In the last chapter and a half, Paul deals with more personal issues. After reminding his readers of the authority God has given him to proclaim the Good News to Gentiles (15:14-22), he writes of his plans to visit Rome in the near future, on his way west to Spain. First, however, he must deliver a gift of money he's been collecting for the needy Christians in Jerusalem—a risky trip for which he seeks their prayers (15:23-33). Finally, he asks that his personal greetings be relayed to a number of Christian individuals he knows in Rome, and he passes along greetings from the Christians around him (16:1-23). The letter closes fittingly on a note of praise, with a doxology (16:25-27).

MAJOR THEMES AND THEOLOGICAL CONCERNS

Human Sinfulness. Romans, more than any other writing in the New Testament, highlights the full extent of human sinfulness. Here, as throughout the Bible, sin is the single greatest problem with which human beings have to deal, the problem behind all other problems. Though Paul nowhere defines sin, it is clear that he thinks of it as an offense not primarily against other people but against God himself. And God holds people accountable for their sins.

Though sin entered the world through Adam (5:12-21), every individual is responsible for his or her own sin, for "everyone has sinned" (3:23). And sin is all-pervasive—so much so that Paul can say, from God's point of view, "No one is righteous. . . . No one does good, not a single one" (3:10, 12). The entire human race is infected with sin in a thoroughgoing way; everything people do is radically tainted with sin.

As a result, all people—Jews and Gentiles alike—deserve to die, for "the wages of sin is death" (6:23; cf. 5:12; 7:5, 9-11). Everyone stands guilty under the judgment of God (3:19; Eph 2:1-3). Gentiles are responsible for what they can know of God in nature (1:18-32); Jews, for the word of God in the Scriptures (2:17-29). And no one, Gentile or Jew, has ever fully lived up to what he or she knows to be right and good in God's sight. "We all fall short of God's glorious standard" (3:23). So the whole world stands condemned before God, the ultimate Judge, in desperate need of his forgiving grace.

For Paul, sin is not simply a matter of violating the commandments of God's law; it runs much deeper than that. To know the reality of the living God, who has given us every good thing we have, and yet fail to honor and thank him for his kindness—*that* is sin. To treat the Everlasting One to whom we owe everything as if he weren't important, to ignore him and his word—*that* is sin. To fail to acknowledge the Almighty for who he is, to desire the created things more than the Creator himself—*that* is sin (1:19-25). For a person like Paul, whose life has been immersed in Scripture, sin would be anything that falls short of the two all-encompassing biblical commandments—the commandment to love God with all our heart, soul, and strength (Deut 6:5), and the commandment to love our neighbors as much as we love ourselves (Lev 19:18). So sin is defined as much by what people fail to do as by what they do.

The function of the law of Moses, with its clearly defined statements of what is right and wrong, is not simply to prevent sin but, more importantly, to make people aware of their sin (3:19-20). Indeed, Paul would not have recognized certain patterns in his own life as sinful without the law (7:7). In a perverse way, the power of evil even uses the explicit prohibitions of the law to arouse sin (7:8-13).

Paul conceptualizes sin as a force or "power" (like a demon) at work in the world and within individuals (5:21; 6:6ff, 11-20). As a result of sin's dominating power, unregenerate people live as sin's "slaves" (6:6, 14-20). Because of the weakness of human nature in combating sin, it is impossible for people to live a life that is truly good on their own, even if they desire to do so (7:14-25). Their desire to do what is right will inevitably be frustrated as they are driven by powers greater than they are (Eph 2:1-3). This is the maddening plight in which all human beings find themselves. The greatest need that people have is to be delivered from the power and consequences of sin.

The answer to sin lies in the atoning death and resurrection of Jesus Christ, through which God both forgives sins and provides the life-transforming power of his Spirit to overcome sin. As a result, Christians are freed from the power of sin and enabled to live a life of true goodness (7:4-6; 8:1-14). Though they still feel the temptation of sin (Gal 5:17), now they are the Lord's slaves, and they must no longer continue in a life of sin (6:1-23). (For a fuller discussion of sin, see Morris 1993b:877-881.)

God's Holiness and Judgment. Behind this understanding of the all-pervasive nature of sin stands the sober awareness of the holiness and purity of God, informed by the Old Testament Scriptures. The "high and lofty one who lives in eternity" (Isa 57:15), the Holy One who made us and holds us accountable, demands purity: "You must . . . be holy, because I am holy" (Lev 11:44; 19:2). Because he cannot tolerate sin, God pronounces a fearful judgment on all that is not holy. As a result, the relationship between God and humans has been utterly severed; that is why everyone stands guilty before his holy judgment (3:19).

The awareness of the absolute holiness of God goes hand in hand with Paul's emphasis on the coming day of judgment, the terrible day when God's righteous anger will be poured out on all unforgiven sin. On that day, every person will stand individually before God and receive eternal blessing or damnation, depending on his or her attitude and response to Christ. (The key issue is whether a person trusts in Christ.) The day of ultimate accountability is always just beyond the horizon for Paul; it looms large in all his considerations and shapes his thinking about everything else. It is the one great future event for which all people must prepare with deep reverence and fear. The solemn reality of it is one of the factors motivating Paul's evangelism (2 Cor 5:11) and his frequent calls for holy living (13:11-14; note the references to "fear" in 2 Cor 7:1; Phil 2:12; and the desire to be found "blameless" in Phil 1:10; 1 Thess 3:13; 5:23). The final judgment will reveal whether each person has an authentic relationship to Christ or not.

Although committed Christians stand forgiven before God and assured of eternal life because of their trust in Christ, they too will be held personally accountable for how they have lived (14:10, 12; cf. 2 Cor 5:10, "We must all stand before Christ to be judged"). However, in the case of true believers, what is at stake is not their eternal salvation but certain unspecified rewards that God will give to those who have served him faithfully (1 Cor 3:12-15). See "Salvation by Faith and Judgment by Works" below. (For a fuller discussion of judgment, see Travis 1993:516-517; Mohrlang 1984:57-67.)

Salvation by Grace and Justification by Faith. The heart of the Good News is that God, in his mercy, has provided salvation for a doomed world, through the atoning sacrifice of Jesus Christ—his death on the cross for our sins, in fulfillment of the prophecy of Isaiah 53 (3:21-26). It is in Romans that Paul spells out the details of this most fully.

Salvation becomes a personal experience when each person puts his or her trust individually in Christ to save them, relying on God's grace rather than on their own efforts to obey his demands. This is how we are made right with God (1:16-17; 3:25-26, 28, 30; 4:3-8; 5:1; 10:9-11). Saving faith results in righteousness (the righteousness of Christ) being freely credited to us by God because of Christ's sacrifice for our sins. This is what Paul calls the "righteousness of God" (God's way of making us right with himself) and what theologians call "justification by faith." When we put our trust in Christ, God mercifully considers us righteous in his sight, quite apart from our efforts to achieve righteousness by keeping the law of Moses (3:21–4:25; 9:30–10:13). In contrast to the common Jewish way of thinking, Paul emphasizes repeatedly that salvation (righteousness) is a free gift of God for those who put their trust in Christ; in no way is it dependent on keeping the demands of the law of Moses (cf. 2 Cor 5:21; Phil 3:8-9).

Salvation is a comprehensive concept for Paul, with multiple dimensions—all of them dealing with the problem of sin, and all of them viewed as gifts of grace. It provides, above all, the forgiveness of our sins (in Paul's terms, "righteousness") and reconciliation with God. This results in deliverance from the coming wrath of God and the assurance of eternal life (3:21-26; 5:1-5), but, more than that, it also provides power for the living of life here and now, the life-transforming power of the Holy Spirit—which is nothing less than the life of the resurrected Christ himself within us (Gal 2:20; Col 1:27). As a result, believers are given new desires and a new potential—the potential to begin to live the kind of truly good life that God desires (7:4-6; 8:1-14; 12:2), just as God promised in the Old Testament (Jer 31:31-34; Ezek 11:19-20; 36:25-27).

Salvation also means being adopted into the family of God, which brings with it the promise of all the blessings that God has for his children (8:15-17). It also brings us into the community of God's people, the church, which itself is a means of ministering the saving grace of God to his people (12:6-8; 1 Cor 12:4-31; 14:1-33; Eph 4:11-16). The church, the "body of Christ," is the context within which we are called to live out this new life.

Salvation is spoken of in past, present, and future terms. We _have been_ saved—by Christ's death on the cross and our faith in him. We _are being_ saved—by the transforming work of the Holy Spirit, changing us day by day increasingly into the likeness of Christ. We _will be_ saved—from God's wrath on the day of final judgment, when those who belong to Christ will experience salvation in all its fullness. Though we are already saved and experience something of God's glory here and now, the full experience of salvation always awaits the future. This dual outlook is what gives rise to the already/not-yet tension found in Paul's letters.

Thus, salvation, in Paul's letters, is not simply a matter of being forgiven or rescued from God's wrath. It is a much more comprehensive, multifaceted concept, with past, present, and future dimensions, all dealing with the fundamental problem of sin. The goal of salvation is to free us in every way from sin and its consequences—to make us God's pure people, reflecting the likeness of Christ and the glory of God himself, both in this life and in the life to come (8:29-30; 2 Cor 3:18). (For a fuller discussion of salvation, see Morris 1993a:858-862.)

The Holy Spirit. In fulfillment of the Old Testament promises (Ezek 11:19-20; 36:25-27; Joel 2:28ff; cf. Jer 31:31-34), God has now sent his Spirit into the hearts of his people. This Spirit, the Holy Spirit—Paul also speaks of him as the Spirit of Christ, representing the living Christ himself (8:9-11)—is given to those who believe (8:1ff; Gal 3:1-2). Without the Holy Spirit, one has no relationship to Christ (8:9).

Just as Paul's view of salvation is a comprehensive one, so is his understanding of the role of the Spirit in the life of the believer. It is the Spirit who opens our heart, evokes saving faith, and makes our experience of God real. The Spirit gives us power over sin and liberates us to live the life that God desires; by means of the Spirit we are gradually transformed into the likeness of Christ. The Spirit also aids us in our weakness, praying for us and reassuring us that we are indeed the children of God. And it is the Spirit who, by filling our heart with the love of God, gives us strong and joyful confidence in the life to come (7:4-6; 8:1-17, 26-30; 12:2; 15:13). Indeed, the Spirit is our pledge and guarantee that we shall one day fully experience all the eschatological blessings that God has for his children (5:5; 8:23; cf. 2 Cor 1:22; 5:5; Eph 1:14).

It is the life-transforming work of the Spirit in the believer, giving power over sin, which Paul especially emphasizes in the salvation-centered Letter to the Romans. People, on their own, dominated by their sinful nature, are incapable of living the kind of life God desires. Driven as they are by the power of sin, their attempts to live a life of goodness are constantly frustrated (7:14-25). The answer, Paul claims, lies not in a more determined attempt to obey the law of Moses but in the infusion of a new power that is greater than the power of sin—the power of the Holy Spirit, given to all who put their trust in Christ. The Spirit brings the life and power of God himself into our life and with it the potential for a transformed way of living (8:1-14).

But the transformation of a Christian's life is not an automatic thing to be taken for granted. All life long we live in a state of tension, pulled in two different directions by the power of sin and the power of the Spirit—the result of living in two different ages (this age and the age to come) simultaneously (Gal 5:17). But no longer is defeat inevitable, for "the power of the life-giving Spirit has freed you from the power of sin that leads to death" (8:2). Much, however, depends on which power we allow to dominate our life (8:5-14; Gal 5:16-23). Only by letting the Holy Spirit fill and control our life (Eph 5:18) can we begin to live out the kind of good and godly life that God desires of us.

In Paul's letters, this emphasis on the power of God's Spirit to transform a believer's life is only part of a more comprehensive understanding of the Spirit's role as the driving force behind all effective Christian life and ministry, both in the individual and in the church (15:18-19; cf. 1 Cor 2:1-16; 14:1-33). Because the Spirit represents the life and presence of God himself (the living Christ) in the believer, the whole of the Christian life is to be lived "in the Spirit"—i.e., directed and empowered by the Spirit. In this way, we can begin to experience the life of the Kingdom of God here and now. (For a fuller discussion of the Holy Spirit, see Fee 1994; Mohrlang 1984:115-123; Paige 1993:404-413.)

Love. The primary ethical characteristic of life in the Spirit is love. For Paul, love is the most important of all the Christian graces and the very heart of Christian ethics. Motivated by the supreme expression of God's own love in the sacrificial death of Christ (5:5, 8; Eph 2:4ff; cf. 2 Thess 2:16-17), love springs from a transformed life filled with the Spirit of God—for it is the Spirit's work to produce in us the qualities of Christ (12:2; Gal 5:22-23).

Having a good grasp of God's saving love in Christ is crucial for believers because it is the foundation for all true Christian theology and ethics and it is important for a believer's sense of security ("Nothing can ever separate us from God's love," 8:38). One of Paul's deepest desires for his converts is that they come to a full awareness of this love (Eph 3:18-19). Indeed, the overwhelming sense of Christ's love was one of the chief forces driving Paul's own Christian life and ministry (2 Cor 5:14-15). In turn, believers are called to a life of loving others.

The priority that Paul gives to love may be seen in chapters 12–16. When he gives specific instructions on practical Christian living, he begins with an appeal for love (12:9-10), and the emphasis on love runs throughout the final chapters (cf. esp. 13:8-10; 14:15). Though the primary focus is on showing love to fellow Christians (12:16; 14:19; 15:2, 5ff), believers are to express kindness to non-Christians also (12:14-21; cf. Gal 6:10). God's people are to "live in harmony with each other" and to "live in peace with everyone" (12:16, 18). A Christian's whole life is to be an expression of sacrificial love, as Christ's was.

This emphasis on love in Paul's writings is a reflection of the priority given to love throughout the New Testament. Jesus speaks of the two love commandments as the most important of all the commandments of God, the foundation and essence of all that is written in the law and the prophets (Matt 22:34-40). For Paul, love is the greatest of all the Christian virtues, the single most important ethical trait to seek in life. Of greater value than the more popularly desired charismatic gifts such as tongues, prophecy, knowledge, and faith (1 Cor 8:1; 12:31–13:3, 8, 13), love is the moral quality with which believers are to clothe themselves above all else (Col 3:12, 14). Significantly, love occurs first in Paul's list of the "fruit" of the Spirit (Gal 5:22-23). Regarded as both summing up and fulfilling the ethical demands of the law of Moses (13:8-10; Gal 5:14, 22-23), love is the one unending debt that Christians owe to others. The love commandment is the new "law of Christ" (Gal 6:2), and love plays a key role in Christians being found "pure and blameless" when Christ returns (Phil 1:9-10; 1 Thess 3:12-13). Paul often mentions "faith" and "love" together (Eph 1:15; 3:17; 1 Thess 3:6; 2 Thess 1:3)—with "hope" sometimes added (1 Cor 13:13; Col 1:3-5; 1 Thess 1:3; 5:8)—as the key elements of the Christian life. Together, "faith" and "love" sum up Paul's deepest theological and ethical desires for his converts. His view of the Christian life is perhaps best summed up in the words "faith expressing itself in love" (Gal 5:6). (For a fuller discussion of love, see Mohrlang 1984:101-106; 1993:575-578.)

The Law of Moses. For those influenced by traditional Jewish teaching especially, Paul emphasizes that salvation is not dependent on keeping the demands of the law of Moses. In particular, this means that one's standing with God is not dependent on "the big three"—the laws pertaining to circumcision, Sabbath-keeping, and eating kosher foods—the practices that served to identify Jews living in the Roman world distinctively. By severing the link to these, Paul frees the Good News for a much wider acceptance by Gentiles. But for Paul, this is not simply a matter of severing ethnic links; there is a crucial theological principle at stake. Salvation must always be understood as a sheer gift of God's grace, not something that one achieves by performance (i.e., by keeping the demands of the law; 3:21–4:25; 9:30–10:13).

The statements Paul makes about the law appear somewhat contradictory. On the one hand, he states that Christ is the "end" of the law (10:4, NRSV); yet he insists that the Good News does not do away with the law but rather "upholds" it (3:31,

NRSV). He speaks of the "curse" of the law (Gal 3:10, 13), yet he still sees the law's commandments as "holy and right and good" (7:12). How are we to reconcile such seemingly divergent statements?

Scholars continue to come to different conclusions on this question. Some see Paul as simply confused and his statements on the law (sometimes positive, sometimes negative) as inconsistent and incoherent. Others attempt to trace a chronological development in his thinking that would account for the confusing data. Some interpret the data in light of the dual nature of his audience (Jew and Gentile). In reality, the positive and negative statements address quite different points and focus on different functions of the law. On the one hand, Christ signifies the "end" of the law when the law is viewed as (1) a means of gaining salvation, (2) a comprehensive body of legislation governing the details of daily life and behavior, and (3) a power that gives sin its authority. In these respects, the law has no jurisdiction over the Christian. On the other hand, as a God-given moral guide, the law remains a valid expression of the will of God. Like Jesus before him, Paul makes an implicit distinction between its moral and ritual aspects. In this sense, its commandments are still "holy and right and good"—though the focus has now shifted away from the multitude of individual commandments to the all-encompassing love commandment that sums up and fulfills the law (13:8-10). The ethical standards of the law are maintained, but the Christian life is understood to be governed not by a massive body of legal precepts but by a single basic principle (the principle of love) operating on a much deeper level and motivated by the renewing power of the Holy Spirit.

With regard to salvation, the deeper function of the law is a negative one. Its ultimate purpose is to make people aware of their failings—their inability to keep the demands of the law, no matter how good their intentions (3:20; 5:20; 7:7-13; Gal 3:19). Thus, its real purpose is to make people aware of their desperate need for forgiveness and the saving grace of Christ apart from their observance of the law. For Paul, then, the law serves in a distinctly secondary way and must never be viewed as a means of gaining salvation in itself. Those who rely on their observance of the law for their salvation are under a curse: "Cursed is everyone who does not observe and obey all the commands that are written in God's Book of the Law" (Gal 3:10, citing Deut 27:26). It is only by faith in Christ that one can be rescued from the curse of the law because Christ assumed the curse for us: "Cursed is everyone who is hung on a tree" (Gal 3:13). Those who place their trust in him, then, receive his gift of righteousness and eternal life.

It goes without saying that many of Paul's Jewish Christian contemporaries considered Paul's view of the law too lax and felt that all Christians (whether Jewish or Gentile) must take the law more seriously than Paul taught if they wanted an authentic relationship with God. For these Jewish Christians, of course, the law was not simply the law of Moses; it was the law of God, in its entirety. It was these two different positions taken on the law that most sharply divided the early Christian community. In the end, as Christianity became increasingly centered in the non-Jewish world, it was Paul's position that came to be accepted as normative. (For a fuller discussion of the law, see Mohrlang 1984:26-42; cf. Thielman 1993:529-542, who includes a historical summary of scholarly interpretation of Paul's understanding of the law.)

Jews and Gentiles. For Paul, God's grace is always for "everyone who believes—the Jew first and also the Gentile" (1:16; cf. 2:9ff)—a point he emphasizes in Romans. As the premier Jewish missionary to Gentiles, Paul argues that, when it comes to relating to God, the same principles have always applied to both groups. Though Jews have a certain formal advantage in being considered the chosen people of God historically, the true people of God have always been those who put their trust in him, whether Jewish or Gentile. Both groups stand equally in need of God's forgiving grace, equally guilty before God (1:18–3:20). And in Jesus Christ, God's grace is extended equally to both, quite apart from their observance of the law of Moses (3:21–4:25). Obedience to God was never intended to be defined by mere outward observance of the Torah but by a reverent response from the heart (2:1-29). In the same way, salvation was never intended to be understood as a reward for legal observance but as a gift of grace given to those with true faith— whatever their ethnic background.

In chapters 9–11, Paul wrestles with the agonizing question of why so many Jews have failed to respond to Christ. One of the things we have to remember, he concludes, is that through this seeming tragedy, God's mercy has now been graciously extended to the Gentiles. But when the full number of Gentiles has come to Christ, the door will once again be opened to the Jews, and "all Israel will be saved" (11:26). In the meantime, Gentiles face the same threat of judgment as Jews if they fail to take Christ seriously.

Because God has now accepted believers from both groups into the family of Christ, converted Jews and Gentiles are to be warmly welcoming and accepting of one another in the church, even though they may see some things quite differently (15:7-12; cf. 14:1–15:6). Here the Good News has clear implications for how Jews and Gentiles are to relate to one another in the body of Christ. (For a fuller discussion of Gentiles, see de Lacey 1993:335-339.)

Predestination and Human Responsibility. In chapters 9–11, where Paul presents his struggle with the question of the Jews' relationship to God in light of their failure to respond to Christ, Paul's belief in divine election and predestination is clearly affirmed (9:6-29; 11:1-10). Historically, though God had selected the Jewish people as a whole to be his own, it was always only the "chosen few" from among them—the minority specifically designated by God—who proved to be the true Israel, just as it is now (9:6-13; 11:1-10). And to those who would challenge the fairness of this, Paul argues that ultimate destinies are always decided by God's sovereign choice alone, not by human desires or efforts. Everything depends not on what we want or do but on God's sheer mercy alone: "God chooses to show mercy to some, and he chooses to harden the hearts of others so they refuse to listen" (9:18). As people created by God, we cannot fault him for what he chooses to do or not do, for he has the right to do whatever he wishes (9:14-24). God himself defines what is "fair." From his Jewish background, then, Paul has no hesitations in speaking of God's true people as the "elect" or the "chosen" (8:33; 11:5, 7; Eph 1:4; Col 3:12; 1 Thess 1:4; 2 Thess 2:13; 2 Tim 2:10; Titus 1:1), those who from the beginning of time have been specially "called" to be his people (1:6-7; 8:28, 30; 1 Cor 1:2, 24). It is solely by God's mercy that anyone finds himself to be among the people of God; believers are infinitely indebted to God for choosing them.

God's sovereign choice of people is not an arbitrary end in itself but part of a much larger plan for the universe. His ultimate goal is to perfect for himself a group of people who, by the Spirit of his Son living in them, will grow to become like his Son and one day share the full glory of his Son (8:28-30; Col 1:27). In the end, God's desire is to unite the entire universe, including both Jews and Gentiles, under the authority of his Son, to the endless praise of his own glory and grace (Eph 1:9-12; 3:3-6). Election and predestination must always be understood in the larger context of God's ultimate plan and purposes.

At the same time, paradoxically, Paul also speaks of God's desire for "everyone" to be saved (1 Tim 2:4; cf. 2 Pet 3:9), and Paul very explicitly warns people about the clear responsibility they bear for the choices they make and the eternal consequences of failing to continue in the saving faith (9:31-32; 10:3, 21; 11:11-14, 20-22). Side by side, then, lie statements that affirm both the sovereign choice of God and people's responsibility—both divine causation and human accountability. Both, paradoxically, are somehow true—which implies that we cannot adequately account for the mysterious complexities of life without taking account of both. The affirmation of God's sovereign choice in salvation does not eliminate the need for us to take seriously our responsibility to God. Here we come to the limitations of rational systematic theology; Paul gives us instead a "theology of paradox."

The crucial question is, "When does he emphasize one as opposed to the other?" In general, Paul emphasizes God's sovereign choosing when he addresses believers. It is a doctrine for the saved, to remind them of their indebtedness. Human responsibility, on the other hand, is emphasized when he speaks of unbelievers or the disobedient. Those who refuse to respond to the Good News have no one to blame but themselves. Generally speaking, then, while salvation is always the gift of God's sovereign grace, God's judgment is the consequence of human refusal to believe and obey. (For a fuller discussion of election and predestination, see Elwell 1993:225-229; for discussion of the relation between God's sovereignty and human responsibility, see Carson 1994.)

Theology and Ethics. Several of Paul's writings (notably Romans, Galatians, Ephesians, and Colossians) divide into two parts: first, a statement of what God has graciously done for us in Christ, or an issue pertaining to the Good News (e.g., Rom 1–8); and second, an appeal for a truly Christian lifestyle (e.g., Rom 12:1–15:13). The order is significant: first the Good News, then Christian living—first theology, then ethics. Here the Christian life is understood as a response to the

Good News of God's grace. The experience of God's mercy obligates us to live in a way that pleases him—but it is the obligation of grace, not of law. So Christian living, for Paul, is never understood as autonomous; instead, it is a response of gratitude to God for his saving grace, a way of saying thank you for the Good News. As those who live and die solely by the grace of God, we owe him everything, and our gratefulness is to be expressed in everything we say and do.

This idea is reflected in the emphasis Paul places on joy and thanksgiving as key elements of the Christian life. Just as "joy" (*chara* [TG5479, ZG5915]), "thanksgiving" (*eucharistia* [TG2169, ZG2374]), and "grace" (*charis* [TG5485, ZG5921]) are related linguistically in Greek, so they are related theologically in Paul's letters. Joy and thanksgiving derive from the experience of grace and represent the appropriate response to it. Those who know they are saved by the grace of God will reflect it in the joyful, thankful lives they live.

The relation in Paul's thinking between the Good News and Christian living is clearly seen at the very beginning of chapter 12: "And so, dear brothers and sisters, I plead with you to give your bodies to God because of all he has done for you. Let them be a living and holy sacrifice—the kind he will find acceptable. This is truly the way to worship him" (or, "This is the only appropriate response you can make"). The greatness of God's mercy in the Good News (spelled out in chs 1–8 especially, but also highlighted in chs 9–11) calls for the dedication of our whole life to God as an expression of gratitude (chs 12–15). The Christian life is not a half-hearted show of dreary obligation but a full-blown expression of heartfelt love and dedication to the one who died for us. It is a "living sacrifice" that demands not simply the patching up of a few bad habits but the transformation of our whole way of living and thinking (12:1ff). Anything less is unworthy of the immeasurable grace God has shown us in Jesus Christ. (For a fuller discussion of Pauline ethics, see Mohrlang 1984; Mott 1993.)

Salvation by Faith and Judgment by Works. Because of the close relationship in Paul's thinking between theology and ethics—belief and behavior—his writings reflect his simultaneous belief in the seemingly contradictory principles of justification by faith and judgment by works. When he focuses on salvation, the emphasis always falls on God's grace and the need to trust in Christ because there is nothing we can do to earn salvation. We are saved by faith alone, not by our works (Eph 2:8-9). Salvation must always be understood as a sheer gift of God's grace for those who believe.

However, when he addresses problems of morality, the accent falls on the traditional Jewish doctrine of judgment by works (cf. Yinger 1999). Thus, he warns that those whose lives are dominated by obvious vices will not inherit the Kingdom of God (1 Cor 6:9-10; Gal 5:19-21; Eph 5:5-6; Col 3:5-6). Strong threats of eschatological judgment like this reflect his conviction that certain kinds of behavior are simply incompatible with new life in Christ and therefore, generally speaking, mark one who is outside the sphere of God's saving grace.

How is this to be reconciled with his belief in justification by faith apart from works? For Paul (as for all the biblical writers), theology and ethics cannot be divorced. How we live shows whether our faith is real or not; it confirms or denies our claim to be "in Christ." True saving faith is always life-changing faith, for *imputed* righteousness cannot be separated from *realized* righteousness; the lack of the latter brings into question one's claim to the former. So although moral living in itself does not earn salvation, the lack of moral living may demonstrate a person's exclusion from it. Believers are under a certain continual obligation, therefore, to show by their obedience that they really are among those whom God has called and chosen by his grace (cf. 2 Pet 1:10) and that they therefore remain safely within the circle of his kindness.

As a result, Paul simultaneously affirms what seem to be two contradictory principles: justification by faith and judgment by works. Though our works may condemn us, it is always our faith—and faith alone—that saves us, by God's grace. It is a subtle but important distinction: our works can never save us, but true saving faith will always be evidenced by how we live. Or, as it is commonly put, "We are saved by faith and faith alone, but saving faith is never alone." This seeming paradox shows the strong connection in Paul's thinking between faith in Christ and moral behavior. In the end, Christian faith cannot be divorced from an obedient lifestyle. The God who saves us is the God who calls us to holy living (2 Tim 1:9). (For a fuller discussion of justification by faith and judgment by works, see Mohrlang 1984:60-64.)

The Radical Claims of Christ as Lord. The Christian life is motivated also by the awareness that Christ is Lord—not simply in an abstract sense, but also in a personal sense: if he is Lord, he must be Lord of *my* life. If he is our Lord (master), then we are his slaves. And as slaves, we recognize that our life is forfeited; we belong no longer to ourselves but to him who has claimed us for himself. So we must no longer live simply for ourselves but for the Lord. "We don't live for ourselves or die for ourselves. If we live, it's to honor the Lord. And if we die, it's to honor the Lord. So whether we live or die, we belong to the Lord" (14:7-8). "He died for everyone so that those who receive his new life will no longer live for themselves. Instead, they will live for Christ" (2 Cor 5:15). So there is no room for halfhearted commitment. From the moment of our conversion, our whole life is to be thoroughly devoted to Christ as Lord and lived for the glory of God (1 Cor 10:31). True Christian faith means that, as those "under new management," we die to ourselves—to sin and to our own desires (6:1-23; cf. Gal 6:14)—in order to live for Christ. A commitment to Christ as Lord lays claim to every part of a believer's life.

How seriously we take the lordship of Christ may be viewed as a measure of the reality of our faith. True believers will demonstrate their faith by attempting to live in a way that is pleasing to him at all times. Those who allow sin to continue to dominate their lives reveal their lack of true devotion to Christ, and this inevitably raises questions about the reality of their claims to believe in him. To accept Christ as Savior is to accept Christ as Lord, and if that is to mean anything, it must mean everything.

OUTLINE

I. The Good News of Salvation (1:1–8:39)
   A. Introduction (1:1-17)
      1. Greetings (1:1-7)
      2. Paul's desire to visit Rome (1:8-15)
      3. The Good News that saves (1:16-17)
   B. The Universal Need of Salvation (1:18–3:20)
      1. The world has become corrupt (1:18-32)
      2. God will judge all sinners (2:1-16)
      3. Jews are sinners, too (2:17–3:8)
      4. All people are sinners (3:9-20)
   C. God's Gift of Salvation (3:21–5:21)
      1. God's way of saving us (3:21-31)
      2. Abraham as an example of saving faith (4:1-25)
      3. The results of saving faith (5:1-11)
      4. Adam and Christ contrasted (5:12-21)
   D. Objections to the Good News (6:1–7:25)
      1. Why not continue in sin? (6:1-23)
         a. We have "died" to sin (6:1-14)
         b. We have become slaves of righteousness (6:15-23)
      2. What about the law? (7:1-25)
         a. We are no longer bound by the law (7:1-6)
         b. God's law reveals our sin (7:7-13)
         c. The power of sin in our lives (7:14-25)
   E. The Power and Glory of the New Life (8:1-39)
      1. Living by the power of God's Spirit (8:1-17)
      2. The glorious future (8:18-30)
      3. God's never-ending love (8:31-39)
II. God's Plan for the Jews and Gentiles (9:1–11:36)
   A. God Chooses Whomever He Wishes (9:1-29)
   B. Jews Have Refused God's Salvation (9:30–10:4)
   C. Whoever Believes Will Be Saved (10:5-13)
   D. Jews Have No Excuse for Refusing the Message (10:14-21)
   E. A Few Jews Have Been Saved (11:1-10)
   F. Salvation Has Now Come to Gentiles (11:11-24)
   G. All Israel Will Be Saved One Day (11:25-32)
   H. The Mysterious Ways of God (11:33-36)
III. Living the Good News (12:1–15:13)
   A. A Fully Dedicated Life (12:1-21)
   B. Respect for Authority (13:1-7)
   C. The Importance of Love (13:8-10)

ENDNOTES

1. For a more skeptical view of the Pauline authorship of certain passages, see O'Neill 1975:11-22.
2. Conceding even a minimum of secretarial initiative and responsibility in drafting the letters—and the use of different secretaries—is one way of accounting for the differences in style and vocabulary that we find in Paul's various letters (cf. Kelly 1963:27).
3. For further discussion of Paul's purposes in writing, see Minear 1971; Wedderburn 1988; Donfried 1991.
4. For Paul and the Roman legal system, see Sherwin-White 1963:57-70, 108-119.

COMMENTARY ON

Romans

◆ **I. The Good News of Salvation (1:1–8:39)**
  A. Introduction (1:1–17)
   1. Greetings (1:1–7)

This letter is from Paul, a slave of Christ Jesus, chosen by God to be an apostle and sent out to preach his Good News. ²God promised this Good News long ago through his prophets in the holy Scriptures. ³The Good News is about his Son. In his earthly life he was born into King David's family line, ⁴and he was shown to be* the Son of God when he was raised from the dead by the power of the Holy Spirit.* He is Jesus Christ our Lord. ⁵Through Christ, God has given us the privilege* and authority as apostles to tell Gentiles everywhere what God has done for them, so that they will believe and obey him, bringing glory to his name.

⁶And you are included among those Gentiles who have been called to belong to Jesus Christ. ⁷I am writing to all of you in Rome who are loved by God and are called to be his own holy people.

May God our Father and the Lord Jesus Christ give you grace and peace.

1:4a Or *and was designated.*   1:4b Or *by the Spirit of holiness;* or *in the new realm of the Spirit.*
1:5 Or *the grace.*

NOTES

1:1 *This letter is from Paul.* Paul always refers to himself as *Paulos* [ᵀᴳ3972, ᶻᴳ4263], the Gr. form of his Roman name *Paulus.* Saul was his Jewish name, used only in Acts (cf. Acts 13:9).

a slave of Christ Jesus. This implies that Paul was wholly claimed by Christ and utterly devoted to his service, as one who belonged entirely to him. The phrase may have positive connotations: in the OT, "slave of the Lord" (or its equivalent) was a title of honor for people who served God, such as Abraham, Moses (e.g., Deut 34:5), Joshua (e.g., Josh 24:29), David, the prophets, and the psalmists (Cranfield 1980:50); similarly, in some languages of the Middle East, the title "slave of the king" was used of important officials (L&N 1.741). For background on slavery in the Greco-Roman world, see Rupprecht 1993:881. Instead of "Christ Jesus," some Gr. mss (𝔓26 ℵ A) have "Jesus Christ."

chosen. Lit., "called" (*klētos* [ᵀᴳ2822, ᶻᴳ3105]). Not in the weaker sense of "invited" ("Many are called, but few are chosen," Matt 22:14), but in the stronger sense of being especially designated or appointed, either by God or by Jesus himself. The calling came at the time of Paul's conversion (Acts 26:12-18; Gal 1:1). Cf. 1:6-7; 8:28-30; 9:12, 24; 11:29; 2 Thess 2:14; comments on 8:28-30.

apostle. One especially commissioned by the Lord to proclaim his word. Though it often refers specifically to the Twelve (esp. in Luke–Acts), the word may also refer more widely to others (cf. 1 Cor 15:5, 7, 9).

sent out to preach his Good News. Lit., "set apart for the Good News of God"—i.e., set apart for the service or proclamation of the good news of salvation through Jesus Christ, which Paul spells out in chs 1-8.

1:2 *through his prophets.* This may refer generally to the inspired men of the OT (including Moses and David, who were called prophets, Acts 2:29-31; 3:21-24), not simply those associated with the section we know as "the prophets."

1:3 *In his earthly life.* Or, "From a human point of view"; or, "On the human level"; or, "As a human." Lit., "According to the flesh" (*kata sarka* [TG2596/4561, ZG2848/4922]). The phrase stands in contrast to the parallel phrase "according to the spirit of holiness" (*kata pneuma hagiōsunēs* [TG4151/42, ZG4460/43]) in 1:4 (cf. note). Verses 3-4 may come from an early confession of faith (Cranfield 1980:57-58; Moo 1996:45-46).

he was born into King David's family line. Lit., "who came from the seed of David." The fact that Paul uses the verb "came" (*genomenou* [TG1096, ZG1181]) instead of the more common "was born" (*gennēthentos* [TG1080, ZG1164]) may imply that he was familiar with the tradition of Jesus' unusual birth (Moo 1996:46). There was a widespread expectation among Jews that the Messiah would come from the family line of David (Isa 11:1-11; Jer 23:5-6; 33:14-16; Ezek 34:23-24; 37:24-25). Jesus' Davidic descent rests on Joseph's acceptance and legitimization of Jesus as his son, even though Joseph was not his natural father (Cranfield 1980:58-59).

1:4 *and he was shown to be the Son of God.* Or, "and he was designated the Son of God"; cf. *orizō* [TG3724, ZG3988].

by the power of the Holy Spirit. Or, "from the viewpoint of the Holy Spirit"; or, "from the viewpoint of his divine holiness." Lit., "with power according to the spirit of holiness." The phrase "with power" (*en dunamei* [TG1411, ZG1539]) may be understood as modifying either "shown" or "Son of God." The phrase "according to the spirit of holiness" (*kata pneuma hagiōsunēs* [TG42, ZG43]) is a reference either to the Holy Spirit (Bruce 1985:69; Dunn 1988a:14-15) or to Christ's own inner spirit (Mounce 1995:62). Note the contrast in 1:3-4: "on the human level, . . . but on the level of the spirit—the Holy Spirit" (REB); "as to his humanity, . . . as to his divine holiness" (TEV). Stott (1994:50-51) understands it rather as a contrast between Jesus' pre-Resurrection and post-Resurrection ministries, "the first frail and the second powerful through the outpoured Spirit." For a discussion of the complexities of this verse, see Cranfield 1980:61-64. The NLT rendering is accurate.

1:5 *God has given us.* The word "us" refers either to Paul and the other apostles or to Paul himself (as in REB, TEV, CEV).

the privilege and authority as apostles. Or, (preferably) "the grace [divine gift] of apostleship." Lit., "grace and apostleship" (cf. 15:15-16)—not two separate things; the divine gift of being an apostle (Moo 1996:51).

Gentiles. A Jewish term for people who are not Jews. Though *ethnesin* [TG1484, ZG1620] may be translated "the nations" or "the pagans," the word is better translated "Gentiles" in most of its occurrences in Romans. This verse and those immediately following may imply that the letter is addressed primarily to Gentiles (cf. 11:13-14; 15:15-16) or that the church in Rome is predominantly Gentile. See, however, "Audience" in the Introduction.

so that they will believe and obey him. Lit., "for the obedience of faith" (*eis hupakoēn pisteōs* [TG4102, ZG4411]), a phrase that could mean either "obedience that results from faith" (cf. "obedience inspired by faith"; Williams 1952:328) or, more probably (in the context of chs 1-8), "obedience that consists of faith" (Cranfield 1980:66 n.3; cf. 10:16; 11:30-31; 15:18; 16:19—all of which speak of people's response to the Good News as an expression of their obedience to God; cf. 16:26; Schlatter 1995:11). The NLT leaves the relationship between the two terms ambiguous (so also REB, TEV).

bringing glory to his name. Lit., "for the sake of his name," i.e., for the sake of glorifying either Christ or God.

1:6 *called to belong to Jesus Christ.* Or, "called by Jesus Christ" (*klētoi Iēsou Christou*). The word "called" (*klētoi* [TG2822A, ZG3105]) implies "chosen, selected"; cf. note on 1:1; cf. 8:28, 30; 9:12, 24; 11:29.

1:7 *I am writing to all of you in Rome who are loved by God.* The words "in Rome" are omitted in a few ancient authorities (G 1739^mg Origen). Instead, these manuscripts read, "to all those in the love of God." G also omits "in Rome" in 1:15. This raises questions about the destination of the original letter and its later recensions (see "Canonicity and Textual History" in the Introduction).

called to be his own holy people. Lit., "called to be saints," i.e., chosen to be God's holy people—those set apart for him. For the meaning of "called," see note on 1:1.

May God our Father and the Lord Jesus Christ give you grace and peace. A common invocation often found at the beginning of Paul's letters, which may represent a combining and Christianizing of the traditional Greek greeting (*chairein* [TG5463, ZG5897G]) with the traditional Jewish greeting (*shalom* [TH7965, ZH8934], "peace"). "Grace" (*charis* [TG5485, ZG5921]), the keynote of the Good News, refers to God's blessing, love, and kindness, always undeserved. "Peace" (*eirēnē* [TG1515, ZG1645]), when used generally as here, probably refers to a state of well being and contentedness embracing the whole of one's life, deriving from the Good News (see comments on 15:13). In some of Paul's invocations, the word "mercy" (*eleos* [TG1656, ZG1799]) is added (1 Tim 1:2; 2 Tim 1:2; cf. Gal 6:16), just as the combination "mercy and peace" is found in some earlier Jewish invocations (Dunn 1988a:20; Käsemann 1980:16).

COMMENTARY

The beginning section of Romans (1:1-17) serves as a general introduction and is best divided into three paragraphs. In these paragraphs, Paul introduces himself and greets the church (1:1-7), speaks of his desire to come see them in the near future (1:8-15), and states the main theme of the letter (1:16-17).

Paul introduces himself as a missionary apostle called by God to proclaim the Good News of Jesus Christ, the resurrected Son of God and Lord of the universe, so that people all over the world will come to believe and obey him. Paul then invoked God's blessing and peace upon those in Rome who belong to Jesus. This unusually long beginning paragraph (1:1-7), a single complex sentence in Greek, represents a Christian expansion of the typical way of beginning ancient Greek letters. Most letters from this period begin by simply listing the names of the sender and recipient and giving a brief greeting: "Person A to Person B, greetings" (Bruce 1985:67).

Paul's Missionary Calling. The beginning of the letter focuses immediately on the main point—the Good News of Jesus Christ, the most important message in the world. What Paul said about himself is entirely subservient to this: He was a missionary apostle specifically chosen by God to preach the Good News, one who was wholly claimed by Christ to serve his cause (1:1, 5; 15:15-16). He knew that Christ had been revealed to him in order that he might make him known to the world (Gal 1:16). In a most unusual way, recounted three times in Acts, he seems to have sensed his missionary calling from the earliest days of his conversion (Acts 9:3-6, 15-16; 22:14-15; 26:16-18). So he wrote as one who was passionately convinced that he had been given a crucial role to play in the most important work in the world, the proclamation of the Good News of salvation.

He clearly understood that it was God himself who had commissioned him for this work (1:1). Writing to the Galatians, he speaks of having been appointed directly by Jesus Christ himself and by God the Father (Gal 1:1; cf. the words of the risen Lord, "Saul is my chosen instrument to take my message to the Gentiles," Acts 9:15). Indeed, he was convinced that God ordained him for this work long before he was ever born (Gal 1:15). F. F. Bruce (1985:67) concludes, "All the rich and diversified gifts of Paul's heritage (Jewish, Greek, and Roman), together with his upbringing, were fore-ordained by God with a view to his apostolic service."

Though we can see a number of ways in which Paul's heritage and upbringing served him well in his missionary work, it is not clear how much Paul thought of these as "fore-ordained by God with a view to his apostolic service"—or, for that matter, how much he thinks of any Christian's background as fore-ordained by God with a view to his or her special calling in the service of Christ. True, Paul acknowledges that God "chose us in advance, and he makes everything work out according to his plan" (Eph 1:11). But generally speaking, his foreordination language is limited to the idea of God choosing his people for salvation (8:29; 11:2, 5; Eph 1:4-5, 11; 2:4-6, 8-10; Col 3:12; 1 Thess 1:4; 5:9; 2 Thess 2:13). His understanding of an individual's ministry seems to be shaped more by the notion of charismatic giftedness than by considerations of natural heritage (12:6-8; 1 Cor 12:4-11, 28; Eph 4:11). Nonetheless, because here and there in the Old Testament clear traces of God's providential hand can be seen in the background of the people he chooses to use (as in the cases of Joseph, Moses, Samuel, Ezra, Esther, and Daniel, for instance), it is not unreasonable to assume that such notions may be in Paul's thought, as well. Nor is it unreasonable for us to look for traces of God's providential goodness in our own individual backgrounds, preparing us for our own specific callings in the service of Christ.

As a "slave" of Christ (1:1), he knows that his life is no longer his own—no longer to be lived for himself but for his master (Phil 1:21). He has been "bought . . . with a high price" (1 Cor 6:20), and every part of his life now belongs to Christ and must be devoted to his work in the world. Nothing else is ultimately important. As a slave of Christ, Paul viewed himself as a slave of Christ's people also (2 Cor 4:5). Furthermore, in his missionary evangelism, he regarded himself as a slave of all those to whom he preached (1 Cor 9:19-22)—in the sense that his whole life was devoted to the spiritual welfare of others.

And so it is for every Christian, in Paul's thinking: as redeemed people, our self-identity is defined by our conversion to Christ. Loyalty to Christ transcends the importance of everything else in our lives. Like Paul, all of us who confess Christ as Lord are to consider ourselves "slaves" of Christ; we too are claimed by Christ—"bought with a high price"—to serve his cause. Though not all of us are called to a life of pioneer evangelism as Paul was, all of us are called to be witnesses for Christ in everything we say and do and to be devoted ministers of God's grace to the body of Christ. Like Paul, every serious follower of Christ must say, "For to me, living means living for Christ" (Phil 1:21). Because Christ died for us, we recognize that we, too, are called to live no longer for ourselves but for him (2 Cor 5:14-15). And if we take seriously our "slavery" to Christ—if we really mean what we say when we confess Christ as our Lord—then every part of our life must be devoted to his service because we belong to him. The whole of our life must be considered his, not ours. Slaves do not have the privilege of living for themselves like everyone else.

Here Paul's words reflect a strong and radical understanding of Christian discipleship that challenges the softer, more comfortable view of the Christian life so common in the modern world. Paul knows that we only "find" our life by "losing" it, that dying is the necessary prelude to living. As slaves of Christ, we must constantly die to ourselves in order to live for the one who has claimed us, body and soul. This kind of commitment will never be easy to live out, but it is the life to which all true disciples know themselves to be called.

Christ as the Fulfillment of the Scriptures. In the second verse of this introduction, we discover that the amazing Good News that Paul was called to preach was predicted—indeed, promised—in the Hebrew Scriptures themselves (1:2). This was a key element in the early Christian apologetic. This messianic way of reading the Old Testament is reflected throughout Paul's writings (1:17; 3:21; 4:3-25; 10:5-20; 15:8-12, 21). As he testifies to King Agrippa, "I teach nothing except what the prophets and Moses said would happen—that the Messiah would suffer and be the first to rise from the dead, and in this way announce God's light to Jews and Gentiles alike" (Acts 26:22-23). Though it is primarily the servant texts of Isaiah that Paul seems to have been thinking of here (Isa 42:6; 49:1, 5-6; 52:13–53:12), he clearly understood the Old Testament as a whole to point to Christ and the Good News, and read it in that light—as did the entire early Christian community. After all, didn't Jesus himself say, "The Scriptures point to me!" (John 5:39)? Luke especially, one of Paul's converts and long-term missionary associates, highlighted Jesus' endorsement of this perspective:

> Then Jesus took them through the writings of Moses and all the prophets, explaining from all the Scriptures the things concerning himself. . . . Then he said, ". . . everything written about me in the law of Moses and the prophets and in the Psalms must be fulfilled. . . . Yes, it was written long ago that the Messiah would suffer and die and rise from the dead on the third day." (Luke 24:27, 44, 46)

From a Christian point of view, then, the Old Testament must always be read, interpreted (judiciously), and taught in light of its fulfillment in Christ and the New Testament. Christians do not read the Old Testament in isolation or merely as the Hebrew Scriptures but as part of a larger canonical whole.

In the New Testament, the coming of Jesus Christ as the Messiah is viewed as the fulfillment of all the deepest hopes and dreams of the Jewish people and the ultimate fulfillment of God's promises under the old covenant (cf. esp. Heb 8:1–10:18). Paul went even further when he spoke of Jesus as the fulfillment of the deepest hopes and dreams of human beings universally: he is the ultimate reality, to which all other religious aspirations and teachings point, and of which they were but "shadows" (Col 2:17).

Jesus Christ is from the family line of David—a "Son of David" (a requirement for the Messiah, from a Jewish point of view)—yet at the same time he is the Son of God, sharing the nature of God himself, as the miracle of the Resurrection attests (1:3-4). This dual emphasis on Jesus as both human and divine anticipates the creeds of the early church, in which the early Christians struggled to put into words their understanding of who Jesus is and how he relates to God. Among the New Testament writers, it is the writer of Hebrews who places the greatest emphasis on the humanness of Jesus (considered essential for his work of atonement and intercession; Heb 2:10, 14-18; 5:8). And it is John, Paul, and the writer of Revelation who place the greatest emphasis on his deity (John 1:1-4, 18; 20:28; Col 1:15-19; 2:9; Rev 5:6-14). (There are three places where Paul seems to speak of Jesus as "God": 9:5; 2 Thess 1:12; Titus 2:13; cf. Rom 1:7.) Though the early Christians thought it was essential to have a genuine appreciation of both the human and divine aspects of Jesus (he is always to be understood as simultaneously "fully human and fully divine"), the overall emphasis in this passage is on his divine power and authority as the Son of God, shown above all in the Resurrection.

The Resurrection was a historical event; it shows that God was clearly at work in Jesus' life (1:4) and confirms that Jesus Christ is truly the Son of God—the Lord and ultimate Judge of every human being. The historical fact of the Resurrection, then, played a central role in the proclamation of the Good News by the early Christians (Acts 2:31-33; 3:15; 5:30-32; 10:40-41; 13:30-31; 17:3, 31-32; 23:6; 24:21; 25:19; 26:6-8, 22-23; 1 Cor 15:1-8). It must also be a central element in the proclamation of the historic faith today, when skepticism abounds. Unlike other religions, the Christian faith is founded on a crucial historical event, the death and resurrection of Jesus Christ, and all else flows from that.

The historicity of the Resurrection also plays a vital role in our understanding of the Good News, focused as it is on the promise of life beyond death. The resurrection of Christ assures us not only that there is life beyond death but also that we who belong to him will one day fully share in that resurrection life (1 Cor 15:20). To deny the historicity of the Resurrection, then, is to deny the heart of the Good News itself, leaving us with no sure hope of anything beyond this life (1 Cor 15:12-19).

The Resurrection plays another role in Paul's thinking: it opens the door for believers to begin to experience the age to come. As a result of the Resurrection, believers can experience, here and now, something of the life and power of the Kingdom of God—"resurrection life"—by the power of the Holy Spirit (6:4-11; 7:4-6; 8:2-4, 9-14). This is nothing less than the power of the resurrected Christ himself at work in his people (Gal 2:20; Col 1:27). One of Paul's deepest desires is to experience the full extent of this power in his own life—to "know Christ and experience the mighty power that raised him from the dead" (Phil 3:10). In the same way, he prays that the Ephesians will come to know the incredible greatness of this power at work in their own lives—"the same mighty power that raised Christ from the dead" (Eph 1:19-20). So the resurrection of Christ not only confirms the truth of Jesus, the Good News, and the Christian hope, it also makes it possible for us to experience the living Christ and his power in our lives today.

Paul's way of thinking about the Christian life was radically shaped by his awareness that the Spirit of the resurrected Christ lives in those who belong to him. It is the Spirit of the living Christ within—not simply our own efforts—that produces in us Christlike qualities and character (Gal 5:22-23). Further, because our body is a sanctuary, we must do nothing that would offend the living presence of Christ within (1 Cor 6:18-19; Eph 4:30; 1 Thess 4:8). The awareness of Christ's presence in believers also influences Paul's way of thinking about Christian ministry, for here, too, the real power and effectiveness lie with Christ (the Spirit of Christ) and not with us (1 Cor 2:4-5, 13; 2 Cor 4:7, 10-11; 12:8-10). So in both Christian living and Christian ministry, the real power lies with the living Christ within; believers are simply channels through which the power of the resurrected Christ flows. The awareness of Christ's presence working in and through us assures us that we will one day share in his full glory (Col 1:27).

Believing and Obeying. Paul then tells his readers that he was given his apostleship in order to proclaim the Good News so that people would "believe and obey" (1:5; 16:26). Though the exact relationship between believing and obeying is ambiguous in the text, Paul probably means "obey by believing" in this context (cf. note on 1:5). Elsewhere he makes it clear that it is our faith in Christ, not our works, that saves us (1:16-17; 3:22-26; 4:3-8; 5:1; 9:30-32; 10:9-10; Gal 2:16; 3:2, 6, 11, 26). Salvation is always to be understood as a gift of God's grace that we receive solely by faith, not as a reward for our efforts (Eph 2:8-9). At the same time, however, true faith will always be expressed in obedience, for true faith can never be divorced from a serious attempt to live it out. That is why Paul speaks of "faith expressing itself in love" (Gal 5:6). So, although we are saved by faith, we are paradoxically judged by works. This is a point made throughout the New Testament—by Jesus (Matt 7:21-27; John 5:29), Paul (2 Cor 5:10), John (1 John 1:5-6; 2:4-6; 3:4-10), and especially James (Jas 2:14-26). Though our works can never save us, the lack of them can damn us—by putting the lie to our claim to believe—if we are not serious about living out our faith. So although we are saved by faith alone, true saving faith is never alone. Authentic faith is always life-changing faith that is reflected in our works, i.e., in how we live (Eph 2:10). That is the point emphasized in the seemingly contradictory passage, James 2:14-26, which ends with the statement "Faith is dead without good works"—a statement with which Paul would agree. (For the relation between faith and works, see the comments on 4:1-8; 6:15-23; 8:5-14; see also "Salvation by Faith and Judgment by Works" in the Introduction.)

The Roman Christians were among those who had obeyed the Good News. As such, they were those whom God himself had "called" (or chosen) to belong to Jesus Christ. They are called to be "saints," God's own holy people, those whom God has specially chosen and set apart for himself. They are the ones specially loved by God (1:6-7). So even saving faith must be understood ultimately as a gift of God, the result of God's sovereign work in the hearts of those he has mercifully selected to become part of his family. Behind all true faith in the living Christ, then, lies the gracious work of God, calling people to himself and making such faith possible (Eph 2:8-10; cf. Matt 11:25-27; John 6:44; 15:16). That is why, in both the Old Testament and the New Testament, God's people are spoken of as the "elect," those who by God's mercy are chosen and predestined to belong to him. (For election and predestination, see the comments on 9:6-29; see also "Predestination and Human Responsibility" in the Introduction.)

With a privileged calling come great responsibility and a sense of infinite indebtedness. Those who by the grace of God are rescued from his anger and judgment and chosen to be his people should dedicate their lives to him and live the rest of their days in joyful, grateful devotion to his service (12:1-2). As his people, they are to be holy, just as he is holy (Lev 11:44-45; 19:2; 1 Pet 1:15-16). Everything Paul writes about the Christian life presupposes a sense of total indebtedness to God, who in sheer mercy grants believers their salvation.

◆   ## 2. Paul's desire to visit Rome (1:8-15)

⁸Let me say first that I thank my God through Jesus Christ for all of you, because your faith in him is being talked about all over the world. ⁹God knows how often I pray for you. Day and night I bring you and your needs in prayer to God, whom I serve with all my heart* by spreading the Good News about his Son.

¹⁰One of the things I always pray for is the opportunity, God willing, to come at last to see you. ¹¹For I long to visit you so I can bring you some spiritual gift that will help you grow strong in the Lord. ¹²When we get together, I want to encourage you in your faith, but I also want to be encouraged by yours.

¹³I want you to know, dear brothers and sisters,* that I planned many times to visit you, but I was prevented until now. I want to work among you and see spiritual fruit, just as I have seen among other Gentiles. ¹⁴For I have a great sense of obligation to people in both the civilized world and the rest of the world,* to the educated and uneducated alike. ¹⁵So I am eager to come to you in Rome, too, to preach the Good News.

1:9 Or *in my spirit.*   1:13 Greek *brothers.*   1:14 Greek *to Greeks and barbarians.*

NOTES

1:8 *your faith in him.* Though the words "in him" are omitted in the Gr. text, when Paul speaks of "faith" (*pistis* [TG4102, ZG4411]), he usually means faith in Jesus Christ. Saving faith is not an intellectual affirmation of the truth of Christ; rather, it is personal trust in Christ as Savior. See note on 3:22.

all over the world. This does not imply that their faith was extraordinary but rather that news of it had spread far and wide (Cranfield 1980:75), particularly in the places where Christianity had already been established.

1:9 *Day and night.* Lit., "without ceasing."

with all my heart. Lit., "in [or with] my spirit"—i.e., with my whole being. For other interpretations, see Cranfield 1980:76-77.

1:11 *some spiritual gift.* Here *charisma pneumatikon* [TG5486, ZG5922] is best understood generally, as a blessing bestowed by God through Paul's ministry (so Cranfield 1980:79) —not as one of the specific gifts referred to in 12:6-8 and 1 Cor 12:8-10, 28, or as the apostolic understanding of the gospel (contra Schreiner 1998:54).

1:12 *When we get together, I want to encourage you in your faith, but I also want to be encouraged by yours.* Lit., "that is, that we might be mutually encouraged by each other's faith, yours and mine."

1:13 *I want you to know.* Lit., "I do not want you to be ignorant," a favorite phrase of Paul (11:25; 1 Cor 10:1; 12:1; 2 Cor 1:8; 1 Thess 4:13). A few mss (D G) read, "I do not suppose you to be ignorant," but the support for this reading is less reliable.

dear brothers and sisters. Gr. *adelphoi* [TG80, ZG81] (brothers).

I was prevented. Whether it was God, Satan, or other people or events that had prevented the visit is not clear. In 15:22, Paul attributes the long delay to the pressures of his evangelistic work in the northeastern Mediterranean area.

see spiritual fruit. The results of his evangelistic work; cf. 1:14-15.

among other Gentiles. Or, "in the other nations."

1:14 *I have a great sense of obligation.* Because of the great grace and wide-ranging missionary charge God had given him, Paul felt the obligation of proclaiming the Good News to all people everywhere.

to people in both the civilized world and the rest of the world. Lit., "both to Greeks (*hellēsin* [TG1672, ZG1818]) and to barbarians (*barbarois* [TG915A, ZG975])," i.e., both to the cultured and to the uncultured. To the Greeks, all who rejected Greek culture were barbarians. Here "Greeks" is not so much an ethnic designation as a term applying to all who identified themselves with Greek culture, as most Romans would; but in Paul's usage generally, the word is synonymous with "Gentiles."

1:15 *in Rome.* Omitted in a few ancient authorities (G it\^g Origen\^lat), as it is in 1:7. The textual evidence for its inclusion is much stronger. The omission may well be the result of the letter being edited for wider distribution at a later time.

COMMENTARY

Paul begins this section by expressing his thanks to God for the Romans' faith and by telling them how much he prays for them and longs to come see them—something he has been wanting to do for a long time. He hoped that his coming would serve to strengthen them spiritually and that both they and he would be encouraged by each other's faith. Because his divine calling as an evangelist obligated him to all people, he looked forward to the day when he would have the chance to proclaim the Good News in Rome.

Seeking to encourage them, Paul told the Christians in Rome how grateful he was for them because their faith in Christ had become so widely known (1:8). Apparently they were quite open in confessing their faith and made no attempt to hide it. For Paul, Christian faith was never simply a private matter but something to be confessed openly and proclaimed publicly for all the world to hear. Later in his life, face to face with death (presumably in Rome), Paul encouraged Timothy to carry on the same bold proclamation of the Good News that has characterized his own life, without the slightest sense of embarrassment—even if that entailed suffering for his witness (2 Tim 1:7-8; 2:1-3; 3:12; 4:1-5). Some things are simply so important that the world *must* hear them, whatever the cost.

The Romans' faith in Christ evoked Paul's thanksgiving. A number of Paul's letters begin with his expression of gratitude for the "faith and love" of his readers—i.e., for their faith in Jesus Christ and their love for one another in the church (Eph 1:15; Col 1:4; 1 Thess 1:3; cf. 1 Thess 3:6; 5:8; 2 Thess 1:3). Taken together, these two terms represent his deepest desires for his converts: saving faith, which establishes their relationship to God, and heartfelt love, which "binds us all together in perfect harmony" (Col 3:14). In Paul's theology and ethics, faith and love represent the crucial twin responses of the Christian believer to the Good News. The two are joined by Paul in what is perhaps the best single-sentence summary of his view of the Christian life—"faith expressing itself in love" (Gal 5:6)—just as they ought to be joined in every Christian's life. If either is missing, one's experience of the Christian faith is deficient. The fact that Paul's beginning affirmation in this letter focuses only on the faith of the Roman Christians may imply a certain lack in their expression of love (cf. 14:1–15:7), but we cannot be sure; his dominant concern in this theologically focused letter is with matters of faith. (For more on love, see comments on 12:9-21; 13:8-10.)

Paul desired to make a visit to the Romans because he wanted to communicate a spiritual blessing to them, so that they might be strengthened in their faith (1:9-11). Paul's dominant concern for Christians was always a spiritual one, as may be seen in his prayers recorded in the Prison Letters (Eph 1:15ff; 3:14ff; Phil 1:9ff; Col 1:9ff). The focus of these prayers was not on the physical needs of his readers but on their need for a deeper experience of God and the resurrected Christ, his power and his Spirit—and the outworking of that in their love for one another. For Paul, the most important things center on one's relation to God and Christ; all else is secondary—if not unimportant. As Christians, our concern for one another must go beyond our physical and social needs (as important as they are) to the health and vitality of our spiritual life—our walk with God and our experience of Christ.

Paul said he prayed "day and night" (lit., "without ceasing") for the Christians in Rome (1:9). These words reveal not only his sense of utter dependence on God and his belief in the real power of prayer to change things but also his understanding of prayer as a way of life. For Paul, every part of a Christian's life is to be immersed in prayer; everything is to be done prayerfully. The whole of life is to be filled with prayer—prayer is to become the proverbial air that we breathe. So, as Christians, we are not to worry about anything but to pray about everything (Phil 4:6-7). We are to pray at all times because this is God's will for us (1 Thess 5:17-18)—it is the life to which he calls us, the life that pleases him. God even gives us his own Spirit to pray for us (8:26-27). So for us as Christians, prayer is to become a way of life because it expresses our dependence on him for everything. This amazing God, who calls us to be his own special people in the world and the undeserving recipients of his grace and love, wants us to pray constantly, in and for all things, so he can give us the help we need to live for him.

Paul qualified his desire to come see them with the simple phrase "God willing" (1:10), a phrase the early Christians commonly voiced when talking about their plans or hopes for the future. With this simple phrase they expressed their awareness of being dependent upon God for all things, and their submission to his sovereign will. Indeed, to fail to acknowledge such dependence and submission was interpreted as an expression of self-sufficiency and arrogance. ("What you ought to say is, 'If the Lord wants us to, we will live and do this or that.' Otherwise you are boasting about your own plans, and all such boasting is evil," Jas 4:15-16.) In all our planning for the future, we must never forget that we are dependent upon God for everything and that we are to be subject to his will in all things. Whatever we do, all life long, it must always be "God willing."

To avoid any one-sided impressions he may have communicated in expressing his desire to come minister to them, he emphasized that the fellowship they would experience together would be mutually edifying: their faith would encourage him, just as his faith would strengthen them (1:12). This is Christian fellowship at its best—Christians strengthening one another in their faith; anything less will seem superficial and unsatisfying to those who long for real communion on the deepest level. If our fellowship with one another is to be genuine Christian fellowship, it must be characterized not merely by social niceties and chit-chat but by mutual sharing of our experience of the Lord.

Paul had long wanted to visit the Roman Christians but had been prevented from coming to see them earlier (1:13). Exactly what prevented any previous visit is not stated—though later on he says it was the pressure of his evangelistic work in the East that had kept him from coming (15:22). It is this same evangelistic calling— this passion to win converts for Christ—that fueled his desire to go to Rome. Evangelism was in his blood—it was the passion of his life. As F. F. Bruce (1985:71-72) said, "He is never off duty but must constantly be at it, discharging a little more of that obligation which he owes to the whole human family—an obligation which he will never fully discharge so long as he lives." Paul's "mission field" was broad; he felt obligated to preach the Good News to all cultures and all levels of society— to everyone from simple peasants to sophisticated urbanites (1:14,16). Because all people stand guilty before God, Paul felt called to evangelize everyone. Even though his primary calling was to the Gentile world, he did not limit himself to reaching Gentiles (1 Cor 9:19-22). This says a great deal about the burden he felt for all who do not know God.

In the same way, as Christ's people we are called to bear witness to all the people in our world, even though our primary ministry may be to a more limited group. Not all of us, of course, are called to be evangelists as Paul was, but we are all called to bear witness to Christ in everything we say and do. And because evangelism lies at the very heart of the Great Commission that Jesus entrusted to his church (Matt 28:18-20; Mark 16:15-16; Luke 24:47), we must all do everything we can to pray for and support the work of evangelism all over the world.

◆   ## 3. The Good News that saves (1:16-17)

16For I am not ashamed of this Good News about Christ. It is the power of God at work, saving everyone who believes—the Jew first and also the Gentile.* 17This Good News tells us how God makes us right in his sight. This is accomplished from start to finish by faith. As the Scriptures say, "It is through faith that a righteous person has life."*

1:16 Greek *also the Greek.*   1:17 Or *"The righteous will live by faith."* Hab 2:4.

NOTES

1:16 *I am not ashamed of this Good News about Christ.* Sometimes interpreted as an understatement (litotes) and translated accordingly: "I have complete confidence in the gospel" (TEV); "I am proud of the good news!" (CEV). But it may be preferable to understand it literally, with regard to Paul's fearless proclamation in the face of opposition (Cranfield 1980:86-87; cf. NIV, RSV, et al.). The words "about Christ" are added in the NLT for clarity.

It is the power of God at work. God works powerfully through the simple preaching of the Good News to bring about the salvation of those whom he calls. See 1 Cor 1:17-25; 2:1-5.

saving everyone who believes. God saves everyone who trusts in Christ from the effects, power, and eternal consequences of sin. Throughout the Bible, the greatest problem confronting people is the problem of sin, and their greatest need is to be saved from it (cf. Gen 3, 6; Ps 51).

the Jew first and also the Gentile. As his chosen people, Jews have a prior claim to the Good News (cf. chs 9–11); but the message is fundamentally universal—it is also for Gentiles. The word "first" is omitted in a few ancient witnesses (B G cop^sa Marcion), though this may be due to the influence of Marcion's anti-Jewish emphasis (Metzger 1971:506). God's judgment, like God's salvation, is also spoken of as "for the Jew first and also for the Gentile" (2:9-10).

1:17 *tells us how God makes us right in his sight.* Lit., "in it the righteousness of God is revealed." The phrase "righteousness of God" (*dikaiosunē theou* [TG1343, ZG1466]) occasionally refers to the character of God and has sometimes been interpreted that way here (cf. N. T. Wright 2002:30, 32, who interprets the phrase as "the faithful covenant justice of God"), but in this verse, as in 3:21, it refers rather to the righteousness that God graciously attributes (or credits) to those who put their trust in Christ—God declares them righteous—and is synonymous with the "righteousness of faith." Paul contrasts it with the righteousness Jews traditionally tried to achieve by keeping the law of Moses (10:3). It may also be translated, "how God puts people right with himself" (TEV). For a full discussion of Paul's understanding of the important phrase "righteousness of God" and its role as theme of Rom 1–8, see Cranfield 1980:91-99; Moo 1996:79-90; Schreiner 1998:63-71.

This is accomplished from start to finish by faith. Lit., "from faith to faith" (*ek pisteōs eis pistin* [TG4102, ZG4411]), a difficult phrase that may be translated in various ways (Cranfield 1980:99-100; Moo 1996:76). It is probably best taken as an emphatic expression: "entirely a matter of faith"; "through faith from beginning to end" (TEV; cf. NIV; Murray 1965:363-374). For the meaning of "faith," see notes on 1:8; 3:22.

It is through faith that a righteous person has life. Or, "The one who is righteous by faith will live" (*ho de dikaios ek pisteōs zēsetai* [TG1342, ZG1465])—a text from Hab 2:4, cited by Paul to validate his emphasis on justification by faith—i.e., his teaching that a believer is declared righteous by God because of his faith in Christ. The text is also found in Gal 3:11 and Heb 10:38. The original wording of Hab 2:4 in Heb. ("The righteous one will live because of his faithfulness") and Gr. ("The righteous one will live because of my faithful-ness" or ". . . because of his faith in me," *ek pisteōs mou*) makes it clear that Paul is interpret-ing this text in light of the Good News of Christ and in line with Gen 15:6, which he cites in 4:3—"Abraham believed God, and God counted him as righteous."

COMMENTARY

Getting to the heart of the matter, Paul stated the main theme of the letter—the Good News of salvation in Christ. This message has the power to save all who believe, no matter what their ethnic background. The Good News reveals how people can be made right with God—by putting their trust in Christ. As the Old Testament Scripture says, it is faith that makes people right with God and gives them life (Hab 2:4).

Paul knew that many people would find this message laughable. How could a convicted criminal make people right with God? He also knew that many would be offended by its exclusivity—its claim that salvation is to be found in Christ alone (1:16; 3:22, 25; 10:9; cf. John 14:6; Acts 4:12; 1 John 5:11-12). Yet because this is the God-given message of eternal life, Paul proclaimed it without the slightest sense of embarrassment: "I am not ashamed of this Good News about Christ" (1:16). Even face to face with death, he remained undaunted. Shortly before dying he wrote to Timothy, "Never be ashamed to tell others about our Lord. . . . be ready to suffer with me for the sake of the Good News" (2 Tim 1:8). The one who died for us asks us to be willing to live—and die—unashamedly for him (2 Cor 5:14-15). And he warns us, "If anyone is ashamed of me and my message . . . , the Son of Man will be ashamed of that person when he returns" (Mark 8:38).

Paul knew that his success as a missionary was not due to his own abilities or powers of persuasion but, rather, to the power of the message he preached, a mes-sage that can convict and convert human hearts. "It is the power of God at work, sav-ing everyone who believes" (1:16). Paul's reliance was not on himself but on the power of God to work in a saving manner in the lives of those who hear the Good News. When criticized by the Corinthian Christians because his speaking ability was not as impressive as that of others, he argued that the important thing was not his rhetorical skills but God's work in and through him (1 Cor 1:17-25; 2:1-5, 13; cf. 2 Cor 4:7; 12:8-10). As servants of God, Christians are nothing more than channels; the real life-changing work is always done by the one with the real power, God himself (1 Cor 3:5-7).

Paul emphasized that the Good News is for everyone who believes, "the Jew first and also the Gentile" (1:16; cf. 2:9-10). In God's scheme of things, the Jews, those traditionally considered his people, had a prior claim to the Good News; this Paul readily acknowledged (cf. chs 9–11). At the same time, in light of his own special calling to the Gentile world, he wanted to stress the universal nature of the Good News—it is also for Gentiles.

The pattern of "the Jew first and also the Gentile" may be seen in Paul's own evan-gelism: he typically began work in a new area by preaching in the synagogues but then turned to the Gentiles when Jews reacted negatively (Acts 13:46; 18:6; 19:9).

However, the order that pertains to the preaching of the Good News and the receiving of God's eternal blessing also holds true for its rejection: God's judgment is likewise "for the Jew first and also for the Gentile" (2:9). With privilege comes responsibility.

The precise nature of the tensions that give rise to Paul's emphasis here on "the Jew first and also the Gentile" are not spelled out. (Whether the words are directed to anti-Jewish or anti-Gentile sentiments is not clear.) But the larger point is unambiguous: the Good News that has its origin and roots in Judaism is intended for Jews and non-Jews equally. As a result, the Jew-Gentile distinction—and any other ethnic distinction—loses its force in the body of Christ. Christians are to treat one another equally as brothers and sisters, regardless of their ethnic background. ("There is no longer Jew or Gentile. . . . For you are all one in Christ Jesus," Gal 3:28; cf. Eph 2:11-22.) As Christians, it is our relationship to Christ that defines our fundamental identity, not our ethnicity or cultural background; the family to which we now belong is the universal family of Christ. (See "Jews and Gentiles" in the Introduction.)

The Good News that Paul preached was very straightforward: God, in his mercy, saves those who put their trust in Christ as Savior (1:17). Because of their simple faith, God regards believers as righteous in his sight, quite apart from their observance of the Mosaic law. This is God's definition of righteousness—what Paul calls "the righteousness of God," God's way of making people right with himself. It is a truth affirmed in the Old Testament Scripture itself, as Paul points out in a text from the prophets: "It is through faith that a righteous person has life" (cf. Hab 2:4, which may be rendered, "The person who is put right with God through faith shall live"; cf. Gal 3:11). It was this emphasis on salvation by faith alone that Paul's Jewish-Christian contemporaries found so hard to accept because it seemed to deny the validity and role of the law of Moses. Of all the New Testament writers, Paul is the one who articulates this principle most forcefully, usually in the context of arguing against certain Jewish Christians who were trying to convince his young converts of the necessity of obeying the Jewish law (cf. 3:21–4:25).

The emphasis on "justification by faith alone" is one of the most important tenets of the Good News, and it is essential that Christians understand it clearly and grasp it firmly. Our only hope of salvation lies in throwing ourselves wholly onto Christ our Savior, trusting him to do for us what we cannot do for ourselves. We must never rely on what we have done; it will always be inadequate to satisfy the holy demands of God. To the very day we die, our reliance must be wholly on what Christ has done for us in his sacrificial death for our sins; that alone is able to save us. Our own righteousness will always be insufficient; his righteousness—the righteousness God credits to us when we put our trust in Christ—is the only thing that can save us. God accepts us as righteous because of him. It is this that sets the Christian faith fundamentally apart from all other religions, which typically stress what people must do to *earn* salvation. (See "Salvation by Grace and Justification by Faith" in the Introduction.)

It was Paul's words in 1:17 that proved to be so life-changing for Martin Luther in 1513 and that eventually sparked the Protestant Reformation. Burdened by his desire to experience God's forgiving grace, Luther struggled to understand the phrase "the righteousness of God." In his own words,

> I had greatly longed to understand Paul's letter to the Romans, and nothing stood in the way but that one expression, "the righteousness of God", because I took it to mean that righteousness whereby God is righteous and acts righteously in punishing the unrighteous. . . . Night and day I pondered until . . . I grasped the truth that the righteousness of God is that righteousness whereby, through grace and sheer mercy, he justifies us by faith. Thereupon I felt myself to be reborn and to have gone through open doors into paradise. The whole of scripture took on a new meaning, and whereas before "the righteousness of God" had filled me with hate, now it became to me inexpressibly sweet in greater love. This passage of Paul became to me a gateway into heaven. (Luther 1960:34.336-337)

Through Luther, these words of Paul brought about a revolution in the church that has changed the entire course of history in the western world and transformed the nature of the Christian community around the world.

◆   ## B. The Universal Need of Salvation (1:18–3:20)
1. The world has become corrupt (1:18-32)

[18]But God shows his anger from heaven against all sinful, wicked people who suppress the truth by their wickedness.* [19]They know the truth about God because he has made it obvious to them. [20]For ever since the world was created, people have seen the earth and sky. Through everything God made, they can clearly see his invisible qualities—his eternal power and divine nature. So they have no excuse for not knowing God.

[21]Yes, they knew God, but they wouldn't worship him as God or even give him thanks. And they began to think up foolish ideas of what God was like. As a result, their minds became dark and confused. [22]Claiming to be wise, they instead became utter fools. [23]And instead of worshiping the glorious, ever-living God, they worshiped idols made to look like mere people and birds and animals and reptiles.

[24]So God abandoned them to do whatever shameful things their hearts desired. As a result, they did vile and degrading things with each other's bodies. [25]They traded the truth about God for a lie. So they worshiped and served the things God created instead of the Creator himself, who is worthy of eternal praise! Amen.

[26]That is why God abandoned them to their shameful desires. Even the women turned against the natural way to have sex and instead indulged in sex with each other. [27]And the men, instead of having normal sexual relations with women, burned with lust for each other. Men did shameful things with other men, and as a result of this sin, they suffered within themselves the penalty they deserved.

[28]Since they thought it foolish to acknowledge God, he abandoned them to their foolish thinking and let them do things that should never be done. [29]Their lives became full of every kind of wickedness, sin, greed, hate, envy, murder, quarreling, deception, malicious behavior, and gossip. [30]They are backstabbers, haters of God, insolent, proud, and boastful. They

invent new ways of sinning, and they disobey their parents. ³¹They refuse to understand, break their promises, are heartless, and have no mercy. ³²They know God's justice requires that those who do these things deserve to die, yet they do them anyway. Worse yet, they encourage others to do them, too.

1:18 Or *who, by their wickedness, prevent the truth from being known.*

NOTES

1:18 *God shows his anger from heaven.* Lit., "the wrath of God is revealed from heaven." The wrath of God is the anger of God expressed in judgment, either present or future; Paul speaks of both aspects in this passage.

sinful, wicked. Both terms are broad and comprehensive and probably not intended to be sharply distinguished. Some understand the terms to denote two distinct categories of sinfulness, with "sinful" (*asebeian* [TG763, ZG813], "ungodly") denoting sins against God and "wicked" (*adikian* [TG93, ZG94], "unrighteous") denoting sins against others, thus summing up the two tables of the Ten Commandments. However, it is probably more accurate to see the first as expressing ungodly behavior generally and the second as focusing on violations of God's just decrees. Together they are intended to characterize sinful attitudes and behavior in their totality (Cranfield 1980:111-112; Günther 1976:94).

people who suppress the truth. Or, "people who prevent the truth from being known." They suppress the truth about God, whom they oppose (cf. 1:19-20).

1:19 *he has made it obvious to them.* Here the focus is on what God has revealed about himself in nature; cf. 1:20.

1:20 *divine nature.* God's nature and characteristics (*theiotēs* [TG2305, ZG2522]). Though this is the only occurrence of this term in the NT, a similar term occurs in Col 2:9: "For in Christ lives all the fullness of God (*theotēs* [TG2320, ZG2540]) in a human body."

1:21 *they knew God.* They knew *about* God, but they had no sense of their need to acknowledge his authority over them.

their minds became dark and confused. Lit., "their undiscerning heart was darkened." They were unable to think correctly, either about God or about moral issues.

1:22 *they instead became utter fools.* The reference is to moral obtuseness in God's sight rather than intellectual deficiency (cf. Ps 14:1; Prov 1:7).

1:23 *instead of worshiping the glorious, ever-living God, they worshiped idols.* Lit., "they exchanged the glory of the immortal God for images."

1:24 *God abandoned them.* Lit., "God gave them up" (*paredōken* [TG3860, ZG4140]); also in 1:26, 28. God abandoned them to their desires and let them go their own way, resulting in the misuse of their bodies.

1:25 *They traded the truth about God for a lie.* A similar concept is expressed in 2 Thess 2:10-12.

they worshiped and served the things God created. A reference to the worship of idols depicting created things; cf. 1:23. Such practices were expressly forbidden by God's special revelation in Exod 20:4-5, and here it is implicit that they are also contrary to his general revelation.

1:27 *Men did shameful things with other men.* A reference to homosexual practices. Pederasty was widely accepted in ancient Greek and Roman society and was viewed by some as superior to heterosexual love (Cranfield 1980:127; Dunn 1988a:65; Edwards 1992:55-56; Fitzmyer 1993:286-287). Such practices were considered perversions and abominations by orthodox Jews, and this view is reflected throughout the Bible (Lev 18:22; 20:13; 1 Cor 6:9;

1 Tim 1:10; cf. D. F. Wright 1993). For a critique of modern reinterpretations of the biblical view of homosexual practices, see Dunn 1988a:64-66; Fitzmyer 1993:285-288; Moo 1996:113-117.

they suffered within themselves the penalty they deserved. A reference either to some unspecified form of God's judgment or to the sexually perverse lifestyle itself as a form of punishment for abandoning God. The latter was the interpretation of at least some church fathers (e.g., Chrysostom, Calvin; cf. Cranfield 1980:126-127).

1:28 *Since they thought it foolish to acknowledge God, he abandoned them to their foolish thinking.* There is word play here that is difficult to translate in English. Since they did not "approve" (*edokimasan* [TG1381, ZG1507]) of acknowledging God in their lives, God in turn abandoned them to their "depraved way of thinking" (*adokimon noun* [TG96/3563, ZG99/3808]), of which he does not "approve." Such people have no moral or spiritual sensitivity, and their lives are full of sin.

1:29-31 *full of every kind of wickedness, sin.* The terms used in 1:29-31, which include several groups of synonyms, are not intended to be precisely distinguished from one another in every case but to give the cumulative effect of a lifestyle that is utterly antithetical to God and his ways. The first four terms occur in varying order in the ancient authorities, and "immorality" is added in the TR. Similar lists of sins, together with the explicit warning of God's judgment, may be found in 1 Cor 6:9-10; Gal 5:19-21; Eph 5:5-6; Col 3:5-6.

1:30 *haters of God.* Or, "hateful of God"; or "enemies of God"; this term is found nowhere else in the NT.

insolent. Disrespectful, insulting; elsewhere in the NT, the term is found only in 1 Tim 1:13.

1:32 *those who do these things deserve to die.* The death referred to here is not simply physical death but ultimate death as the penalty for sin on the day of judgment, the final expression of the wrath of God. "Death" has the same meaning in 6:16, 21, 23; 7:5; 8:6.

COMMENTARY

In this section Paul carefully lays the foundation for his case by showing the universal nature of sin and God's judgment upon it. All human beings—Jews as well as Gentiles—have turned from God and failed to live up to his holy standards. As a result, all people are guilty sinners in God's sight and deserve his judgment. The entire world stands in need of his salvation.

God's Holy Anger and Judgment. Paul begins his argument by stating a fundamental biblical conviction: God's anger and judgment are upon those who live in sin. Human beings, created by God, are morally accountable for their behavior because God has shown them something of himself, and they know intuitively something of his demands upon them. The amazing nature of the cosmos—all that can be seen in the earth and the sky, the whole world of nature—speaks volumes about the one who made it and reveals his divine power. Yet people as a whole have turned away from the God who created them. The people of the Gentile world pay little attention to God; they don't bother to worship or thank him. Instead, they worship their own distorted conceptions of God and go their own perverse ways—all of which reflects the extent to which their thinking has become clouded and confused. They desire the things God has made more than they desire God himself; indeed, they treat created things as if they were God. So God has abandoned them, and the result is seen in the obscene and degraded lifestyle of the Gentile world, epitomized especially by their depraved homosexual practices. As a result of their wrong ideas about God, their lives have come to be filled with sin and detestable practices. But one day they will suffer the consequences; they will feel the full brunt of the anger and judgment of God against them because retribution is a must in a moral universe.

Paul's beginning statement in this section reflects one of the most basic tenets of orthodox Jewish and Christian theology—namely, God's anger is directed against human sin (1:18). Behind this statement lie two fundamental convictions: (1) God is utterly holy and hates sin, and (2) God holds people accountable and punishes them for their sins. This high view of God's holiness, emphasized throughout the Old Testament, stands in sharp contrast to the "softer" view of God held by many people today. The modern-day understanding of the Christian God as all-tolerant and all-accepting could not be further removed from that of the early Christians, who lived before God "with deep reverence and fear" (Phil 2:12). The Old Testament prophets speak strongly of God's "fury," "anger," "vengeance," "rage," and "wrath"—all directed against human sin. Jesus himself spoke of the need to fear God, "who can destroy both soul and body in hell" (Matt 10:28). So it is not surprising that Paul also spoke freely about the wrath of God—he refers to it in eight of the sixteen chapters of Romans.

The New Testament writers speak as much about God's judgment as they do about God's love (cf. Matt 7:13-14, 22-23; 10:28; 23:33; 2 Thess 1:8; Heb 10:26-31; 2 Pet 3:7, 10; Jude 1:7; Rev 20:11-15). Without a clear understanding of the utter holiness of God, which gives rise to these severe warnings of judgment on human sin, we shall understand neither Jesus nor the Good News—nor the New Testament perspective on life as a whole. The full significance of God's love can only be appreciated when it is seen against the backdrop of God's holy anger; only then can we appreciate the grace of God for what it really is. For Christians, the modern secular understanding of God must be enlarged, deepened, and purified by the biblical view of God (see "God's Holiness and Judgment" in the Introduction).

God's Revelation of Himself in Nature. Another important truth Paul puts forward in this section is that this all-holy God has revealed something of himself in the amazing cosmos he has created. Therefore, people are responsible for what they can instinctively learn about him through it (1:19-20). More specifically, the cosmos shows us there is indeed a God and reveals his immense power and divine nature. Every created thing bears his signature. As the psalmist writes,

> O LORD, our Lord, your majestic name fills the earth! . . . When I look at the night sky and see the work of your fingers—the moon and the stars you set in place—what are mere mortals that you should think about them, human beings that you should care for them? (Ps 8:1-4)

Many modern people are out of touch with the magnificence of creation and the majesty of the Creator—perhaps in part because so much of modern life is lived indoors, in a man-made world full of man-made complexities and distractions. In our scientific world, many people no longer have eyes to see God's hand in the glorious majesty of the created world—the snowcapped mountains, the shimmering lakes, the beautifully forested hills and grassy valleys, the endless miles of golden grain. Even less do they have eyes to see God's hand in the profound magnificence of the ultimate revelation—the eternal Word, Jesus Christ. For if something of God's nature (*theiotēs*) is shown in the world of creation, his full deity (*theotēs*) is seen only in Jesus Christ himself—"For in Christ lives all the fullness of God in a human body" (Col 2:9; cf. Bruce 1985:80; see note on 1:20). Many people are taken up with the fascination of worldly things and unable to see beyond them. And behind this inability to "see" lies the insidious influence of the evil one, according to Paul. "Satan, who is the god of this world, has blinded the minds of those who don't believe. They are unable to see the glorious light of the Good News. They don't understand this message about the glory of Christ, who is the exact likeness of God" (2 Cor 4:4).

The love of nature itself is as close as many people get to the recognition of anything transcendent in the world of creation. But this in itself may reflect the longing of the modern heart for the lost experience of that transcendence. Tragically, even though the reality of God is clearly recognizable in the amazing world of nature, the Gentile world as a whole shows relatively little concern for God. They refuse to acknowledge God for who he really is, and they express no gratitude to him (1:21), even though they stand infinitely indebted to him for everything. And for this refusal to acknowledge him and give him thanks, God will pour out his holy anger and judgment upon them. The sovereign and holy God, who has created all things, holds human beings accountable for what he has revealed of himself to them. This is why Paul speaks of the mass of humanity as dead, doomed forever, because of their many sins (Eph 2:1-3).

To those who protest that the universe does not convincingly evidence the creative work of God and who insist that the origin of the universe is wholly explainable scientifically to people with scientific minds, Paul would respond that such a response in itself reflects the extent to which human minds and hearts have become "dark and confused" (1:21), clouded to the reality of God. In actuality, the whole world reflects the hand of the living God—the presence of design clearly suggests the hand of a Designer. (The fact that this is acknowledged by virtually all traditional tribal societies suggests that atheism is not a natural state.) From God's point of view, then, there is no excuse whatsoever for failing to recognize his hand in it all and for failing to acknowledge him (1:20).

Paul's Radical View of Sin. In this section, Paul also presents a very radical view of sin. Notice that sin is not simply a matter of breaking the divine commandments or violating the decrees of God. Sin runs much deeper than that—it concerns even the attitudes of the heart and how people think about God. To know the reality of the living God, who has given us every good thing we have, and yet fail to honor and thank him for his kindness—that is sin. To enjoy God's good gifts with little sense of gratitude or indebtedness—that is sin. To treat God as if he weren't all that important or relevant, to ignore him, to live life independently of him—that is sin. To fail to acknowledge God for who he is, to desire the created things more than the Creator himself—that is sin (1:19-25). For Paul, immersed from childhood in

Scripture, sin is anything that falls short of the two great biblical commandments—the commandment to love God with all our heart, all our soul, and all our strength (Deut 6:5), and the commandment to love our neighbor as much as we love ourselves (Lev 19:18; cf. Mark 12:30-31). Sin is anything that falls short of acknowledging our full dependence on God for everything.

From this point of view, sin is defined as much by what we fail to do as by what we do. Here Paul reflects a profound understanding of the magnitude of human failing before God. Sin, then, is not simply a surface-level phenomenon, a matter of violating the laws of God but something defined on a much deeper level by the essential attitude and orientation of a person's heart. This is similar to Jesus' view of sin—that it is not the external things that defile a person but what comes from a person's heart (Mark 7:18-23; cf. Prov 4:23). Paul's conception of sin is much bigger and more radical than most people's conception of sin because his conception of God is much bigger and more radical than most people's conception of God. This is why the entire world stands guilty under the judgment of God (see "Human Sinfulness" in the Introduction.)

Idolatry: Distorted Conceptions of God. The behavior of the Gentile world reveals how far away from God people's thoughts really are. Arrogant and foolish, they devote themselves to their own distorted conceptions of God—silly images of humans and animals (1:21-23). The seriousness with which God takes idolatry is seen in the priority given to its prohibition at the very beginning of the Ten Commandments (Exod 20:3-5) and in the harsh judgment pronounced on it by many of the prophets (cf. esp. Isa 44:9-20; cf. Isa 57:3-13; Jer 10:1-16; Ezek 8:1-18; 14:1-11; 20:27-39; 23:1-49; Hos 4:11–5:15). As absurd as the practice of idolatry may sound to our ears, it is not far removed from the popular modern acceptance of a wide diversity of views about the nature of God. For whenever people feel they have the right to conceive of ultimate reality as they wish, they have lost sight of the truth of the living God. The acceptance of a distorted conception of God is in itself a form of idolatry. Our understanding of God must always be shaped by God's own revelation of himself, not by our wishful thinking about him. We must resist the temptation to make God fit our sense of what he ought to be like.

Behind distorted conceptions of God lies the dark countenance of human pride. "Claiming to be wise," people devise and propagate their own imaginings of divinity as if they were ultimate reality (1:22). The multiplied, diverse expressions of religion in the world today may in themselves be a reflection, paradoxically, both of the longing of human beings for the experience of the divine and of their refusal to submit to it. There is a dark and arrogant side to the human heart that refuses to submit to the claims of the living God as Lord over all. The irony is that the result of people's desire to be seen as wise—their idolatry—reveals them to be "utter fools" (1:22). The contrast between human and divine conceptions of wisdom, or between human pride and divine wisdom, runs throughout the Bible (Gen 3:1-7; Prov 1:7; 3:5-7; 1 Cor 1:18–2:16; Jas 3:13-18). A person with true wisdom (divine wisdom), on the other hand, is always characterized by genuine humility—humility that recognizes its utter dependence on God and submits to him. And it is the truly humble person with whom God—"the high and lofty one who lives in eternity, the Holy One"—has promised to live (Isa 57:15).

The concept of idolatry is extended in Paul's letters to include anything that wrongfully consumes a person's life—for example, greed ("A greedy person is an idolater, worshiping the things of this world," Eph 5:5; Col 3:5) and sensual desires ("Their god is their appetite, they brag about shameful things, and they think only about this life here on earth," Phil 3:19). Figuratively speaking, then, idolatry may be understood as a matter of giving one's allegiance to anything other than God himself. In most cases, that allegiance is ultimately to oneself—it is making an idol of oneself and one's own desires. So when the writer of 1 John warns God's people to guard themselves from idols, it is accurate to translate this, "Keep away from anything that might take God's place in your hearts" (1 John 5:21). If we are to love the Lord our God with all our heart, all our soul, and all our strength—and he asks for nothing less—we must be careful not to let anything else take God's place as the chief love of our life. God's love is a jealous love, and like a jealous lover he wants nothing less than the full love of our hearts—single-minded devotion to himself.

Immoral Sexual Practices. Idolatry is not the only problem with the sinful world. Filled with darkness and driven by immoral desires, the people of the world engage in behavior that could only be described as filthy and shameful, vile and embarrassing. Instead of enjoying normal sexual relations, as God intended, these people (both men and women) engage in depraved homosexual practices (1:24-27). Here Paul explicitly condemns homosexual behavior as a perversion of the life intended by God for men and women; God originally created them "male and female" for each other (Gen 1:27-28; 2:18-24). Other passages that condemn the practice of homosexuality include Lev 18:22; 20:13; 1 Cor 6:9-10; 1 Tim 1:10-11; these texts reflect the perspective of early Judaism as a whole. On this issue, the teaching of Scripture in both the Old Testament and the New Testament is uniform.

The widespread acceptance of the homosexual lifestyle in the modern world reflects a contemporary tendency to assess morality by societal norms rather than by the revealed truth of Scripture. Behind this contemporary tendency lies not only a lost sense of the authority of Scripture but also a distorted view of God—as well as a failure to grasp the holiness of God. As Creator and ultimate Judge, God alone has the right to define moral truth (i.e., what is to be considered right and good). Those who engage in sexual practices contrary to the will of God suffer the consequences, and their perverse lifestyle itself is a reflection of that (1:27).

A World Filled with Sin. Because of their immoral lifestyle and perverse way of thinking, God abandoned the people of the Gentile world to the things their darkened hearts desired (1:24, 26, 28). As a result, they became utterly depraved. Their lives were dominated by selfishness, hate, evil, and pride (Paul's list is much longer—1:29-31). They had no more concern for others than they did for God.

Their whole way of life was the antithesis of the two great love commandments. As a result, they were bringing upon themselves the punishment they deserved. Sin hardens people, leads them into more sin, and ultimately brings the judgment of God upon them.

In spite of recent rejections or modifications of the idea, the sins that Paul lists here (esp. in 1:29-31) confirm the traditional understanding that he was thinking primarily of the Gentile world in this description (Moo 1996:96-97). These are the sins that typified Greek culture in the thinking of pious Jews. Not all Gentiles, of course, would have fit the more extreme statements made about them in this section. Some, like the Stoic moralist Seneca, genuinely sought to promote virtuous living and humane values. But all, Paul would argue, in their clouded, self-centered way of thinking, have failed in their obligation to make God the center and focus of their lives. (Even the great Seneca had his failings—such as his connivance at Nero's murder of Agrippina, Nero's mother; cf. Bruce 1985:82-83.) And in their failure to make God the center of their lives and loves, they reveal the deepest roots of sin in their lives—indeed, the deepest roots of sin in the hearts of all people. It is not simply what people do against God that condemns them; it is what they fail to do that marks them as guilty—for it is what we do not do that most deeply reflects our failure to love God with all our heart. So people are responsible for their sins of *omission*, as well as their sins of *commission*. The general confession in the Anglican Book of Common Prayer expresses the dual emphasis well: "We have left undone those things which we ought to have done, and we have done those things which we ought not to have done."

In this passage, Paul asserts that the weight of responsibility for human sin falls squarely on the shoulders of sinners themselves. Driven by their own evil desires, humans have turned their back on God and thus invoked God's judgment on themselves. In other passages, however, Paul reveals his belief in a more sinister force at work behind all this: "Satan, who is the god of this world, has blinded the minds of those who don't believe" (2 Cor 4:4). Enslaving humanity, Satan is "the spirit at work in the hearts of those who refuse to obey God" (Eph 2:2), and people are "held captive by him to do whatever he wants" (2 Tim 2:26). Throughout the New Testament, Satan is understood as the great enemy of human souls. Paradoxically, however, the work of Satan in people's lives does not excuse them from their responsibility to obey God. So here, where the focus is on the universal guilt of humanity, the whole emphasis falls on the responsibility of people for their own behavior, rather than on the work of the evil one.

Either way, the utter seriousness of sin is highlighted in the final verse. A life of sin merits not merely severe discipline but the ultimate death penalty—the final expression of the anger and retribution of God on the day of judgment (1:32). As the writer of Hebrews warns, "It is a terrible thing to fall into the hands of the living God" (Heb 10:31). It is the fearful nature of the coming day of judgment, when every human being will stand before God and be held accountable, that makes the Good News of God's saving grace so urgent and important.

◆ 2. God will judge all sinners (2:1-16)

You may think you can condemn such people, but you are just as bad, and you have no excuse! When you say they are wicked and should be punished, you are condemning yourself, for you who judge others do these very same things. ²And we know that God, in his justice, will punish anyone who does such things. ³Since you judge others for doing these things, why do you think you can avoid God's judgment when you do the same things? ⁴Don't you see how wonderfully kind, tolerant, and patient God is with you? Does this mean nothing to you? Can't you see that his kindness is intended to turn you from your sin?

⁵But because you are stubborn and refuse to turn from your sin, you are storing up terrible punishment for yourself. For a day of anger is coming, when God's righteous judgment will be revealed. ⁶He will judge everyone according to what they have done. ⁷He will give eternal life to those who keep on doing good, seeking after the glory and honor and immortality that God offers. ⁸But he will pour out his anger and wrath on those who live for themselves, who refuse to obey the truth and instead live lives of wickedness. ⁹There will be trouble and calamity for everyone who keeps on doing what is evil—for the Jew first and also for the Gentile.* ¹⁰But there will be glory and honor and peace from God for all who do good—for the Jew first and also for the Gentile. ¹¹For God does not show favoritism.

¹²When the Gentiles sin, they will be destroyed, even though they never had God's written law. And the Jews, who do have God's law, will be judged by that law when they fail to obey it. ¹³For merely listening to the law doesn't make us right with God. It is obeying the law that makes us right in his sight. ¹⁴Even Gentiles, who do not have God's written law, show that they know his law when they instinctively obey it, even without having heard it. ¹⁵They demonstrate that God's law is written in their hearts, for their own conscience and thoughts either accuse them or tell them they are doing right. ¹⁶And this is the message I proclaim—that the day is coming when God, through Christ Jesus, will judge everyone's secret life.

2:9 Greek *also for the Greek;* also in 2:10.

NOTES

2:1 *You may think you can condemn such people.* It is not clear whom Paul is addressing in this section (lit., "O man, everyone who judges"; cf. 2:3). Though 1:18-32 speaks primarily of Gentiles and 2:17ff is clearly addressed to Jews, opinion differs as to whether 2:1-16 is best interpreted as directed to Jews specifically (so Nygren, Murray, Cranfield, Dunn, Moo) or to self-righteous people generally (so Calvin, Barrett). The passage is probably best interpreted as addressed to Jews, who would be quick to condemn the idolatry and immorality of the pagan world. One strong reason for this understanding is Paul's emphasis in 2:9 that God's judgment is "for the Jew first and also for the Gentile." Cranfield (1980:137ff) presents numerous additional reasons. As such, 2:17ff would then be understood as a continuation of Paul's criticism of Jewish self-righteousness.

you who judge others. Not in the sense of evaluating objectively, but in the sense of condemning; this is the meaning of the word "judge" (*krinō* [TG2919, ZG3212]) throughout this section.

2:2 *And we know.* A reference to Paul and his readers. There is no need to interpret this as a statement of the Romans, as in the NRSV: "You say, 'We know . . .'"

2:4 *Don't you see how wonderfully kind, tolerant, and patient God is with you?* Reflection on God's judgment on the Gentiles should lead the Jews to a greater sense both of their own sin and of God's mercy on *them,* for they deserve his judgment, too.

Can't you see that his kindness is intended to turn you from your sin? The awareness of his mercy ought to evoke a deep spirit of repentance. "Repentance" (*metanoia* [TG3341, ZG3567], "change of thinking") implies a change in one's whole way of thinking and living, marked by a turning away from sin and a turning to God.

2:5 *you are storing up terrible punishment for yourself.* Lit., "you are storing up wrath for yourself on the day of wrath." On the day of judgment, God's wrath will fall on all who are unrepentant, whether they are Gentile or Jewish.

2:6 *He will judge everyone according to what they have done.* Lit., "who will render to each one according to his works." The difficult passage that follows (2:6-10), in which Paul seems to contradict himself by speaking of salvation by works rather than by faith, is to be understood in light of the point he is making in the larger context (1:18–3:20)—namely, that *all* have sinned and stand under the judgment of God. This means that *no one* merits salvation by his works. Cf. note on 2:7 and the discussion in Moo 1996:139-142.

2:7 *He will give eternal life to those who keep on doing good.* Cf. 2:10: "There will be glory and honor and peace from God for all who do good." In light of the main point being made in the larger context (cf. note on 2:6), these statements are to be understood as a theoretical possibility only. In reality there is no one who fully does "good." As Paul later says, "No one is righteous—not even one. . . . No one does good, not a single one" (3:10, 12). Some interpreters, however, assume that in 2:7, 10 Paul is referring to the sanctified state of those who have come to believe in Christ and who now really do "keep on doing good, seeking after the glory and honor and immortality that God offers" (2:7). Such interpreters understand these words to refer to works of faith—i.e., the lifestyle that grows out of a relationship with God established by faith (Newman and Nida 1973:35).

glory. In this context, it means eternal blessedness. The term "glory" (*doxa* [TG1391, ZG1518]), a difficult term to translate, may have a broad range of meaning ("brilliance," "splendor," "honor," "greatness," "majesty," "grandeur," "praise," "power"), depending on the context.

2:8 *who refuse to obey the truth.* This refers to those who refuse to live the kind of life God demands of them. In this context, "truth" is not abstract but moral.

2:9 *for the Jew first and also for the Gentile.* Cf. 1:16. For the rationale of judgment on "the Jew first," see Amos 3:2; Luke 12:48. This emphasis probably implies that it is primarily Jews who are being addressed in 2:1-16. God's judgment falls upon the sins of Jews, just as it does upon the sins of Gentiles.

2:10 *glory.* Cf. note on 2:7.

peace. Gr., *eirēnē* [TG1515, ZG1645]. In this context the word refers to overall wholeness or well-being (like the Heb. *shalom* [TH7965, ZH8934]), embracing the whole of one's life. Cf. note on 1:7.

2:11 *For God does not show favoritism.* God judges both Jews and Gentiles by the same moral standard and holds them equally accountable. For similar statements, see Gal 2:6; Eph 6:9; Col 3:25; cf. Acts 10:34.

2:12 *When the Gentiles sin, they will be destroyed, even though they never had God's written law.* Lit., "all who have sinned apart from the law (*anomōs* [TG460, ZG492]) will also perish apart from the law" (*anomōs*); a reference to Gentiles, who did not live according to the law of Moses.

And the Jews, who do have God's law, will be judged by that law when they fail to obey it. Lit., "all who have sinned under the law (*en nomō* [TG3551, ZG3795]) will be judged by the law" (*dia nomou*); a reference to Jews, whose lives are traditionally governed by the law of Moses. In Paul's letters, "the law" commonly refers to the law of Moses, the large body of Jewish legislation found in the first five books of the Bible (the Pentateuch), though some-

times the meaning of the term is extended to include the even larger body of oral interpretation (the "traditions," now codified in the Mishnah) that was popularly understood to
define its application to specific situations. The phrase "the law" (*nomos*) is thus often
used in a broad, general sense, referring to the religious legislation that governs the life
of practicing Jews.

2:13 *For merely listening to the law doesn't make us right with God.* The distinction
between listening to and doing the law is described in Matt 7:21-27; Jas 1:22-25.

It is obeying the law that makes us right in his sight. Here Paul states the traditional
Jewish understanding of how one achieves righteousness before God; it is drawn from
texts like Lev 18:5: "If you obey my decrees and my regulations, you will find life through
them." Note, however, Paul's later qualification: "The law's way of making a person right
with God requires obedience to all of its commands" (10:5; cf. Gal 3:10, 12). This is why he
concludes that, by the absolute standards of the law, "no one is righteous—not even one"
(3:10). The "righteousness of God" comes only through Jesus Christ (1:17; 3:21-26).

2:15 *They demonstrate that God's law is written in their hearts.* They have a God-given
intuitive sense of the distinction between right and wrong. This awareness is not to be confused with Jeremiah's prophecy about the new covenant: "I will put my instructions deep
within them, and I will write them on their hearts" (Jer 31:33)—a prophecy that finds its
fulfillment in the regenerating work of the Holy Spirit in Christian believers.

*for their own conscience and thoughts either accuse them or tell them they are doing
right.* This verse reveals the close connection in Paul's thinking between the "conscience"
(*suneidēsis* [TG4893, ZG5287]) and the "heart" (*kardia* [TG2588, ZG2840]). Opinion differs as to
whether this work of the conscience is to be understood as taking place in the present or
on the day of judgment. The second interpretation is favored by the close link to the following verse; see 2:16. Though not included in the Gr. text, "them" is the most probable
object of "accuse" and "tell."

2:16 *And this is the message I proclaim—that the day is coming when God . . . will
judge everyone's secret life.* Lit., "on the day when God judges the secrets of people
according to my Good News." Most translations, including the NLT, link this statement
about the day of judgment to the earlier statements about judgment in 2:12-13, rather
than to the immediately preceding comment about the conscience of Gentiles in 2:15,
because the accusing or vindicating action of the conscience is assumed to take place in
the present, not on the day of judgment. For a closer link between 2:15 and 2:16, in which
the work of the conscience itself is understood to take place on the day of judgment, see
Cranfield 1980:161-162.

COMMENTARY

Having described the extent to which the Gentile world has turned from God, Paul
now speaks of the judgment of God upon those who do such things—and upon
those who self-righteously condemn such behavior in others but fail to recognize it
in themselves. On the day of judgment, God will judge *all* people on the basis of
how they live, regardless of their ethnic backgrounds; Jews and Gentiles will be
treated equally. Eternal life will be given to those who live a truly good life, but
God's wrath will fall on those who live a self-centered, sinful life. (As Paul continues
his argument in this section, it becomes clear that, due to the universal problem of
sin, the former is only a hypothetical outcome—no one actually lives a truly good
life.) Gentiles will be judged on the basis of what their conscience tells them is right
or wrong, while Jews will be judged on the basis of the law of God that has been

revealed to them. Both groups are responsible for what they've been given. And the judgment, when it comes, will not concern mere superficialities; it will probe even the depths of a person's secret life—the thoughts and attitudes of the heart. Divine judgment will fall on all who sin, Jews and Gentiles alike.

Before we explore this section in detail, it is important to note that Paul often wrote as if he was addressing someone who was raising questions or objections, which he then answered or corrected (a style known as "diatribe"; see "Literary Style and Structure" in the Introduction). Several passages in chapters 1–11 reflect this style of teaching, beginning with this section in chapter 2. The question is, "Who was Paul addressing in this section?" Though 1:18-32 clearly speaks of Gentiles and 2:17ff is clearly addressed to Jews, opinions differ as to whether this section in between (2:1-16) is best interpreted as addressed to Jews specifically or to self-righteous people generally, both Jews and Gentiles (cf. note on 2:1). On balance, it is probably best to assume that Paul was here addressing Jews, who would be quick to condemn the pagan practices described in the preceding section.

We Are All Sinners. The vivid description of the lifestyle of pagans in the preceding section (1:18-32) would have been abhorrent to pious Jews, who thought of themselves as taking God and his demands seriously. But Paul sought to awaken in self-righteous Jews a sense of their own sin (2:1-5). Although not all sin is as explicit or blatant as that described in the preceding section, those who recognize and condemn such behavior as sin must acknowledge, if they look deeply enough into their own hearts, that their lives reflect self-centered, evil tendencies, too. Sin, if understood in its most profound sense as being anything that violates the utter holiness of God—anything that falls short of the two great love commandments that sum up the law of God—lies deep within the heart of every person. "The human heart is the most deceitful of all things, and desperately wicked. Who really knows how bad it is?" (Jer 17:9).

God's judgment does not fall simply on those whose vile acts clearly identify them as "sinners" in the eyes of the righteous; God's judgment falls upon everyone who sins—all of us. Indeed, our readiness to condemn the sin we see in the lives of others may simply reflect our insensitivity to the sin that is covertly present in our own life—an insensitivity that will result in an accumulated sense of guilt on that day when God will judge *us*. And behind such insensitivity lies an inadequate grasp both of the full depths of human sin and of the utter holiness of God himself—an inflated view of human nature and a deficient view of God, precisely the kind of perspective the Old Testament prophets inveigh against. This inflated view of human nature and deficient view of God is widespread in the modern world and underlies much of the theological skepticism that is so prevalent today. We must recognize that the biblical view of human nature and God is fundamentally different from that of the society in which we live. Like ancient Israel, we must guard ourselves from the influence of the pagan culture that surrounds us and be very wary of its fundamental assumptions. We must constantly remind ourselves of the unqualified holiness of God and all its implications.

The tendency to excuse, in ourselves, sins that we are quick to condemn in others is a common human failing but one that must be rooted out in Christians. Jesus himself spoke of the need to remove the log in our own eye before getting upset about the speck in another's (Matt 7:1-5), and both Paul and James teach us to judge ourselves rather than others (14:3-4, 10-13; Jas 4:11-12). God alone knows the hearts of people, and we can leave the judgment of their failings in his hands; our job is to live the life he demands of *us*. One of the marks of authentic spirituality is a heightened sensitivity to sin in one's own life (cf. Jas 4:7-10; 1 John 1:8-10).

Rather than focusing on the failings of others, then, we are called to address the failings in our own lives. This, in turn, will heighten our sensitivity to God's great mercy and kindness to *us*—his patience with *our* sins as he waits for us to turn from them (2:4). This perspective will have the effect of making us more patient with the sins and failings of others. Even on a purely human level, remembering just how much others have to put up with our failings can have the salutary effect of helping us to put up with theirs (see "Human Sinfulness" in the Introduction).

God Will Judge Us All. In the end, God will judge us all; his standards apply universally to all people ("the Jew first and also . . . the Gentile," 2:9, 10). To those who measure up to his demands for selfless goodness, "those who keep on doing good," he will give eternal life and peace. But for those whose lives are self-centered and wicked, those "who refuse to obey the truth"—"everyone who keeps on doing what is evil"—there will be nothing but wrath and suffering (2:6-9). The standard is constant: God judges all people according to their lifestyle ("according to what they have done"), in light of his holy expectations (2:6-11).

How does this enigmatic passage, which seems to teach salvation by works, square with Paul's constant emphasis on salvation by faith apart from works? Some assume that when Paul speaks of "those who keep on doing good," he is referring to believers—those who have the Spirit of God and a new desire to live out the will of God—and that when he speaks of "everyone who keeps on doing what is evil," he is referring to unbelievers. With this view, the principle of salvation by faith is preserved. More likely, however, Paul is giving us here a general principle that was widely accepted in Judaism: God judges all people equally, on the basis of how they live (Job 34:11; Ps 62:12; Prov 24:12; Jer 17:10; 32:19)—which then has to be interpreted in light of the primary point he's making in the larger context (1:18–3:20), namely, that no one, in reality, consistently does what is "good"; all people fall short and therefore stand guilty under God's judgment.

So, in spite of the theoretical truth that God saves those who truly do good, in practice, no one can ever be saved that way because no one is wholly committed to doing good, as measured by God's standards. For example, even the pious Gentile Cornelius, whom Peter speaks of as being among "those who fear him and do what is right"—even he had to be saved by the message of salvation like everyone else (Acts 10:34-35). That is why salvation must always be understood as a gift of God's forgiving grace. We are constitutionally unable to achieve salvation by living up to the demands of God fully; we can never come to the point of deserving salvation.

But don't Jews come closer to living out the ideals of God than Gentiles? Isn't the lifestyle of the pagan world inherently more sinful than the lifestyle of God's chosen people, who have and revere the law of God? Aren't Gentiles fundamentally more guilty because of their "lawless" way of life? Paul responded to this anticipated objection by insisting that the measure of one's goodness is defined not by one's possession of the law but by one's actual obedience to its demands (2:12-15). Theoretically, he argued, it is possible even for Gentiles, without formally having the law, to live out the demands of God because they have something of God's expectations "written in their hearts." They have an intuitive sense of the distinction between right and wrong; in other words, they have a conscience. When they violate their conscience, they know they are doing wrong, and by that knowledge they will be judged on the day when the secret thoughts of every human heart will be revealed. Jews, on the other hand, who have been given the sacred law of God, are responsible to live out what they can know of that law and will be held absolutely accountable for it. All people, then, Jews and Gentiles alike, are judged on the basis of their actual obedience to what has been revealed to them, not on the basis of their mere formal adherence to it (2:12-15). God judges the actual acts of people— and the hidden thoughts of their hearts—not just their words of intent. Here Jews and Gentiles stand on the same ground before God, as sinners in need of God's mercy and forgiveness because the day is coming when God will judge everyone's secret life (2:16). If we look deep within our hearts, we all know how far our secret life is from pleasing God. When God, through Jeremiah, warned of the desperate wickedness of the human heart and asked, "Who really knows how bad it is?" he went on to say, "I the LORD, search all hearts and examine secret motives" (Jer 17:9-10). If God judges us on the basis of our secret thoughts and motives, we all stand in need of his mercy and forgiving grace; none of us is free of guilt. (See "Jews and Gentiles" and "Salvation by Faith and Judgment by Works" in the Introduction.)

◆   ## 3. Jews are sinners, too (2:17–3:8)

[17]You who call yourselves Jews are relying on God's law, and you boast about your special relationship with him. [18]You know what he wants; you know what is right because you have been taught his law. [19]You are convinced that you are a guide for the blind and a light for people who are lost in darkness. [20]You think you can instruct the ignorant and teach children the ways of God. For you are certain that God's law gives you complete knowledge and truth.

[21]Well then, if you teach others, why don't you teach yourself? You tell others not to steal, but do you steal? [22]You say it is wrong to commit adultery, but do you commit adultery? You condemn idolatry, but do you use items stolen from pagan temples?* [23]You are so proud of knowing the law, but you dishonor God by breaking it. [24]No wonder the Scriptures say, "The Gentiles blaspheme the name of God because of you."*

[25]The Jewish ceremony of circumcision has value only if you obey God's law. But if you don't obey God's law, you are no better off than an uncircumcised Gentile. [26]And if the Gentiles obey God's law, won't God declare them to be his own people? [27]In fact, uncircumcised Gentiles

who keep God's law will condemn you Jews who are circumcised and possess God's law but don't obey it.

²⁸For you are not a true Jew just because you were born of Jewish parents or because you have gone through the ceremony of circumcision. ²⁹No, a true Jew is one whose heart is right with God. And true circumcision is not merely obeying the letter of the law; rather, it is a change of heart produced by God's Spirit. And a person with a changed heart seeks praise* from God, not from people.

CHAPTER 3

Then what's the advantage of being a Jew? Is there any value in the ceremony of circumcision? ²Yes, there are great benefits! First of all, the Jews were entrusted with the whole revelation of God.*

³True, some of them were unfaithful; but just because they were unfaithful, does that mean God will be unfaithful? ⁴Of course not! Even if everyone else is a liar, God is true. As the Scriptures say about him,

"You will be proved right in what
    you say,
  and you will win your case in
    court."*

⁵"But," some might say, "our sinfulness serves a good purpose, for it helps people see how righteous God is. Isn't it unfair, then, for him to punish us?" (This is merely a human point of view.) ⁶Of course not! If God were not entirely fair, how would he be qualified to judge the world? ⁷"But," someone might still argue, "how can God condemn me as a sinner if my dishonesty highlights his truthfulness and brings him more glory?" ⁸And some people even slander us by claiming that we say, "The more we sin, the better it is!" Those who say such things deserve to be condemned.

2:22 Greek *do you steal from temples?*   2:24 Isa 52:5 (Greek version).   2:29 Or *receives praise.*   3:2 Greek *the oracles of God.*   3:4 Ps 51:4 (Greek version).

NOTES

2:17 *you boast about your special relationship with him.* Or, "you take pride in your God" (REB). Lit., "you boast in God." In 2:17-20, Paul lists a number of special privileges and roles Jews prided themselves in as a result of their being the covenant people of God.

2:18 *You know what he wants.* Lit., "you know the will"—i.e., the will of God, the ultimate will.

you know what is right. Or, "you discern what is best"; or, "you know what really matters" (REB); or, "you . . . are able to discern what is important" (NAB).

2:19 *the blind.* In context, those who are spiritually blind.

people who are lost in darkness. The word "lost" is added in the NLT for clarity.

2:20 *the ignorant.* Those who are morally and spiritually ignorant, not educationally deficient.

children. Those who in their faith are young, immature, or uninstructed; not literal children.

2:21-22 *do you steal? . . . do you commit adultery?* Having listed the special privileges and role of the Jews, Paul now exposes their hypocrisy with several rhetorical questions. They may be understood literally or in the more radical sense of Matt 5:21-48, assuming the demand for absolute purity of both thoughts and actions. For Paul, as for Jesus, sin is not a matter of simply breaking the letter of the law but of breaking the intention of the law—even in one's heart and thoughts.

2:22 *do you use items stolen from pagan temples?* Lit., "do you do temple-robbing?" (The word "pagan" is added in the NLT for clarity.) This may be understood literally, as a reference to taking things from pagan shrines (or using things taken by others from them), or figuratively, as a reference either to inadequate giving to the Jewish Temple (cf. Mal 3:8: "You have cheated me!") or to treating holy things in an unholy way generally ("Do you desecrate holy things yourself?" NJB; Cranfield 1980:169-170; Moo 1996:163-165). Temple robbery was regarded as a serious offense in the Roman world (cf. Acts 19:37, where Paul is publicly defended as having stolen nothing from the temple of Artemis). Though Jews were quick to condemn idolatry, some apparently felt free to make use of things taken from pagan temples for their own advantage.

2:23 *you dishonor God by breaking it.* Alternatively, a question parallel to the preceding four questions: "Do you dishonor God by breaking it?" (cf. NRSV, TEV).

2:24 *The Gentiles blaspheme the name of God because of you.* This is a quotation from Isa 52:5, LXX. To "blaspheme" is to denounce or speak irreverently of God or the things of God. The despising of God's name by the pagans in Isa 52:5 is due to the tragic plight of the Jews in exile, leaving the impression that their God has either no power or no care; but here, the despising of God's name is due to the moral faults of the Jews, not their misfortune.

2:25 *circumcision.* Circumcision was traditionally understood in the Jewish community as the identification mark of a male devoted to God and committed to living according to God's will, a member of the people of God—i.e., a true Jew (cf. Gal 5:3). Failure to live according to the will of God, then, in effect denied one's circumcision—one's claim to be part of God's people. Hence Judah, several centuries earlier, was likened by Jeremiah to the neighboring countries that traditionally practiced circumcision but were in reality "uncircumcised": "The people of Israel also have uncircumcised hearts" (Jer 9:25-26; cf. Deut 10:16).

has value. Or, "means something."

you are no better off than an uncircumcised Gentile. Lit., "your circumcision has become uncircumcision."

2:26 *won't God declare them to be his own people?* Lit., "won't his uncircumcision be counted as circumcision?"

2:28 *you are not a true Jew just because you were born of Jewish parents or because you have gone through the ceremony of circumcision.* Lit., "being a Jew is not an outward thing (*en tō phanerō* [ᵀᴳ5318A, ᶻᴳ5745]), nor is circumcision an outward thing in the flesh." A relationship with God is defined not by external things but by the heart.

2:29 *a true Jew is one whose heart is right with God.* Lit., "being a Jew is an inward [or hidden] thing" (*en tō kruptō* [ᵀᴳ2927A, ᶻᴳ3220]); cf. 9:6-9. The word "Jew" (Heb. *Yehudi* [ᵀᴴ3064, ᶻᴴ3374]), derived from the name of the ancient ancestor Judah (*Yehudah* [ᵀᴴ3063, ᶻᴴ3373]), is linked to the word "praise" (*yadah* [ᵀᴴ3034A, ᶻᴴ3344]); cf. the exclamation of Judah's mother at his birth, "Now I will praise the LORD!" (Gen 29:35), and the deathbed blessing of his father, "Judah, your brothers will praise you" (Gen 49:8). Readers with a Jewish background may have sensed wordplay here. Paul was emphasizing that the real Jew is the one who is genuinely concerned with God's praise, not just going through the motions (Cranfield 1980:175-176; Bruce 1985:89-90).

true circumcision is not merely obeying the letter of the law. Lit., "circumcision is not a literal thing" (*ou grammati* [ᵀᴳ1121, ᶻᴳ1207]).

it is a change of heart produced by God's Spirit. Or, "it is a matter of the heart, a spiritual thing" (*kardias en pneumati* [ᵀᴳ2588/4151, ᶻᴳ2840/4460]).

And a person with a changed heart seeks praise from God, not from people. Or, ". . . his commendation comes from God, not from people" (cf. REB). Lit., "whose praise is not from people but from God."

3:2 *the whole revelation of God.* Lit., "the words (*ta logia* [TG3051, ZG3359]) of God," a general reference that probably includes the OT as a whole, not just the revelation of the law on Mount Sinai.

3:3 *some of them were unfaithful; but just because they were unfaithful.* Or, "some of them did not believe; but just because they were unbelieving." The terms *ēpistēsan* [TG569, ZG601] and *apistia* [TG570, ZG602] can be translated either "were unfaithful" and "unfaithfulness" (so Dunn, Schreiner, Moo) or "were unbelieving" and "unbelief" (so Murray, Cranfield). The other occurrences of the terms in the NT favor the latter, but the immediate context, which speaks of the contrasting "faithfulness" of God, favors the former. Because the terms embrace both ideas, early readers may not have made the distinction; "unfaithfulness" and "unbelief" are closely related.

3:4, 6 *Of course not!* This emphatic negation (*mē genoito* [TG3361/1096, ZG3590/1181]) occurs ten times in Romans (3:4, 6, 31; 6:2, 15; 7:7, 13; 9:14; 11:1, 11) but nowhere else in Paul's writings.

As the Scriptures say about him. Lit., "as it is written." The words "about him" are added in the NLT for clarity.

You will be proved right in what you say, and you will win your case in court. This is a quotation from Ps 51:4, LXX, showing God's verdict always to be right.

3:5 *our sinfulness serves a good purpose, for it helps people see how righteous God is.* Or it could be phrased as a question: "If our doing wrong only serves to highlight God's doing right, then isn't it unfair of God to judge us?" This is a preposterous question, refuted by Paul to show that God's judgment on human sin is merited. The phrase "how righteous God is" (lit., "God's righteousness" [so NIV, NAB], *theou dikaiosunēn* [TG1343, ZG1466]) is translated in a variety of ways: "God's doing right" (TEV); "how right God is" (CEV); "God's justice" (REB, cf. NRSV); "God's saving justice" (NJB); "his integrity" (JB).

This is merely a human point of view. Or, "I am using a human argument" (NIV). Lit., "I speak in a human way" (*kata anthrōpon* [TG444, ZG476]); cf. 6:19; Gal 3:15.

3:6 *judge the world.* This is a reference to the final day of judgment.

3:8 *And some people even slander us by claiming that we say, "The more we sin, the better it is!"* Lit., "Let's do evil (*ta kaka* [TG2556B, ZG2805]) so that good (*ta agatha* [TG18C, ZG19]) may come of it." Paul's comment about slander should be understood as a parenthetical statement: "If that is true, then you might as well say 'The more we sin, the better it is!' (Some people slander us by saying that's actually what we teach. Such people deserve to be condemned.)" Such slander may be a response to Paul's emphasis on salvation by grace apart from the law and to the way he speaks of grace as transcending all human sin (5:20). For Paul's response to the charge that the Good News of grace undermines the foundation of morality and ethics, see 6:1-23. For a discussion of the grammatical complexities of this verse, see Cranfield 1980:185-187.

Those who say such things deserve to be condemned. The reference is to the divine condemnation of those who slander Paul and the church (3:8), not those speaking in 3:5, 7.

COMMENTARY

After describing the depraved lifestyle of the Gentile world (1:18-32) and then emphasizing that the judgment of God falls equally upon all who sin, Jews as well as Gentiles (2:1-16), Paul now specifically addresses those who are Jewish, reminding them of their own sins. Though intensely proud of their religious heritage and their devotion to the law of Moses, in reality they have fallen far short of faithfully keeping that law. And Jews who fail to keep the law are no better in God's sight than uncircumcised Gentiles; indeed, Gentiles who faithfully obey the law are better off than Jews who don't! So a real relationship with God is defined not by mere ethnicity (being Jewish) or by external criteria (being circumcised) or by mere formal adherence to the law of Moses but by something deeper—genuine devotion of the heart, a circumcised heart. This can only come about by the transforming work of the Spirit of God, when one comes to personal faith in Christ.

Addressing those who are Jewish, Paul now seeks to make the children of Abraham aware of their own sin, to help them see that Jews stand as guilty before God as pagan Gentiles. To those who prided themselves in their Jewishness and their devotion to the law of God, who thought of themselves as the chosen people of God and the "people of the Book," superior to all others because of their privileged calling and religious insight (2:17-20), Paul raised the uncomfortable question of their actual obedience to the revealed truth of God. Hadn't they, too, committed acts of thievery, adultery, and temple-robbing (2:21-22)? After all, the Jews had a long history of dishonoring God by breaking his law. No wonder Gentiles ridiculed the name of God (2:23-24)!

Most pious Jews would have been shocked by Paul's suggestion that they, too, were guilty of such blatant sins as thievery, adultery, and temple-robbing—as most people who consider themselves good, moral people would be, if accused of such things. But sin runs deeper than the letter of the law; it is all-pervasive and is reflected not only in actions but also in the thoughts and intents of the heart. So thievery occurs whenever we selfishly take for ourselves something that belongs to someone else, no matter how small it may be (cf. Paul's reflection on the prohibition of coveting in 7:7-8). Adultery is expressed even in the way we look at people, or the way we think about people, if it reflects an underlying spirit of lust or faithlessness to our spouse (Matt 5:28). Traces of even the most blatant sins, then, can be found even in the people who seem to be most moral. We are all radically infected with sin.

The failure to live out the ideals one professes—especially when a person is unaware of this failing or blatant in disregarding it—lies close to the essence of hypocrisy, and such hypocrisy is condemned throughout the New Testament. Jesus, for example, excoriates the Pharisees for their hypocrisy: "They don't practice what they teach. . . . [Their] hearts are filled with hypocrisy" (Matt 23:3, 28; cf. 23:1-33); "These people honor me with their lips, but their hearts are far from me. Their worship is a farce" (Mark 7:6-7). Both Jesus and James warn God's people against hypocrisy (Matt 6:1-18; Jas 2:14-26), and Jesus emphasizes that only those who actually live out their faith will be in the Kingdom of Heaven (Matt 7:21). James reminds us that a hypocritical faith—a faith that is not lived out—won't save anyone (Jas 2:14). So one of the marks of God's true people is—and always has been—their serious attempt to live out what they claim to believe. As Christians, we need to be ever vigilant lest there be aspects of our lives that blatantly contradict what we say we believe. Christian living should be a fully integrated expression of our confession of faith.

In this light, Paul asks, "Who, then, is the real Jew?" His answer is that a real Jew is not one just born of Jewish parents or one that is circumcised. The outward mark of circumcision by itself means nothing, Paul argues, if a person is not actually committed to obeying the demands of God. It is the ones who actually do what God commands who are regarded as the people of God, even if they are not circumcised (2:25-27). The real mark of one's "Jewishness," then, is internal rather than external. The real Jew is defined inwardly, and real circumcision is a matter of the heart—something spiritual, not literal (2:28-29; cf. 4:9-12). Those with "circumcised hearts" (converted hearts) are less concerned with the commendation of others than they are with the commendation of God himself. Failure to take seriously the demands of God, which one professes to follow, merits nothing but the judgment of God, regardless of whether a person is circumcised or not. (For more on circumcision, see notes and comments on 4:9-12.)

With deep insight, Paul makes it clear in this passage that a relationship with God can never be defined by external or merely formal criteria. On this basis, Christian baptism, often taken as a parallel to Jewish circumcision in marking a person's relationship to God, is no more effective than circumcision in establishing such a relationship if it is not accompanied by a commitment that goes deeper than the baptism itself. It is not the physical act of baptism per se that defines our relationship to God but what the baptism signifies on a deeper level about our belonging to Christ and our commitment to Christ. Throughout the Bible, a relationship with God is never defined by mere externalities; God always looks at the heart and judges by the heart. "People judge by outward appearance, but the LORD looks at the heart" (1 Sam 16:7). That is why Jesus, in contrast to the legalistic Pharisees, consistently emphasized that the important thing is not religious rituals in themselves but what comes from the heart (Mark 7:18-23). Both Jesus and Paul emphasize that everything significant springs from the heart—the heart must be converted and changed.

Of all the New Testament writers, it is Paul who explored most deeply the question of *how* the heart is to be changed. The real secret to an obedient life, Paul writes, lies not in a more emphatic determination to observe the law of God but in the life-transforming power of the Holy Spirit, who alone has the power to convert and change the human heart (2:29). Only in this way can Christians begin to obey God and live out the kind of life that God desires of them. Although he hints at the importance of the transforming work of the Spirit, Paul says nothing more about it here, leaving his discussion of the Spirit's role for a later stage in his argument (7:4-6; 8:1-14).

What, then, is the advantage of being circumcised—or for that matter, of being a Jew at all (3:1)? Here Paul poses a question that he knows will be in the minds of Jewish readers objecting to his argument. Behind the question lies a deeper and more troubling concern: Don't Paul's teachings deny the basic principles of the law of Moses? Don't Paul's ideas fundamentally contradict the teaching of the Hebrew Scriptures?

For 2000 years, Christian scholars have wrestled with the difficult question of how to reconcile Paul's teaching with the Old Testament, or whether there are fundamental contradictions between the two. The question of how Paul's teaching relates to the Hebrew Scriptures—especially the law of Moses—is part of the larger question of how the New Testament as a whole relates to the Old Testament that precedes it. This is a crucial question because our understanding of the relationship between the two, to a large degree, determines our understanding of the Christian life. We shall return to this question later, when we consider 3:31 and 4:3. (See "The Law of Moses" in the Introduction.)

Paul responded to the anticipated concern of his readers (3:1) by affirming one of the most basic convictions of the Old Testament: God has indeed singled out the Jewish people for himself and entrusted them with his revealed word (3:2). And God remains faithful to his chosen people, even if some of them have not remained faithful to him (3:3-4). So whatever new thing has come about in Jesus, it does not negate the validity of what God has done in the past or his faithfulness to the people he originally chose to be his own. Indeed (as Paul says later), God will honor the promises he made long ago to the ancestors by one day restoring all of Judaism to himself—"All Israel will be saved" (11:26). God's faithfulness remains, as do his promises; he can be fully trusted to keep his word.

Paul then addressed another question posed by some: Is it really fair of God to judge people so harshly for their sins, especially his own people? If even their failings serve, by way of contrast, to validate his righteous judgment or to show the rightness of all he does, then on what basis can he punish them? If even their disobedience serves his more ultimate purposes and brings him glory, how can God properly call them "sinners" (3:5-7)? The ridiculous nature of this argument is seen in the extreme to which some had accused Paul of taking it: "The more we sin, the better it is!" (3:8). His point is clear: The fact that human sin may result in glory being given to God in no way excuses the sin. Because of his righteousness, God must punish sin, whoever's sin it is—even if, in some strange way, such sin serves his ultimate purposes. Sin is sin, and in his holiness God has decreed judgment on all sin. So, yes, God will indeed judge the failings of the Jewish people, just as he judges the failings of all people.

In the modern world, skepticism about the notion of God's judgment is widespread. Belief in the traditional understanding of the judgment of God seems largely to have died out in many parts of the Christian community. "Hell has been in steady decline as a doctrine since the seventeenth century. By 1985 Martin Marty, the church historian, could quip that 'hell disappeared but nobody noticed'" (Hunsinger 1998:409). Such skepticism mirrors the relativistic perspectives of the modern culture that have shaped our thinking and reflects a lost sense of the radical holiness of God. This is a common way of thinking today, but it is strikingly at odds with the perspective of the biblical writers, who take the holiness of God and the thoroughgoing nature of human sin much more seriously.

◆   ## 4. All people are sinners (3:9-20)

⁹Well then, should we conclude that we Jews are better than others? No, not at all, for we have already shown that all people, whether Jews or Gentiles,* are under the power of sin. ¹⁰As the Scriptures say,

"No one is righteous—
   not even one.
¹¹ No one is truly wise;
   no one is seeking God.
¹² All have turned away;
   all have become useless.
No one does good,
   not a single one."*
¹³ "Their talk is foul, like the stench
   from an open grave.
Their tongues are filled with
   lies."

"Snake venom drips from their lips."*
¹⁴ "Their mouths are full of cursing
    and bitterness."*
¹⁵ "They rush to commit murder.
¹⁶ Destruction and misery always
    follow them.
¹⁷ They don't know where to find
    peace."*
¹⁸ "They have no fear of God at all."*

¹⁹Obviously, the law applies to those to whom it was given, for its purpose is to keep people from having excuses, and to show that the entire world is guilty before God. ²⁰For no one can ever be made right with God by doing what the law commands. The law simply shows us how sinful we are.

3:9 Greek *or Greeks*.   3:10-12 Pss 14:1-3; 53:1-3 (Greek version).   3:13 Pss 5:9 (Greek version); 140:3.
3:14 Ps 10:7 (Greek version).   3:15-17 Isa 59:7-8.   3:18 Ps 36:1.

NOTES

3:9 *should we conclude that we Jews are better than others?* The single Gr. word underlying the last six words of this question (*proechometha* [TG4284A, ZG4604]) may be interpreted in three different ways: (1) Are we Jews any better off (than Gentiles)? (2) Are we Jews any worse off (than Gentiles)? (3) What excuse can we Jews give? The first interpretation fits the context best. For a full discussion of the textual problems and alternative interpretations, see Cranfield 1980:187-191.

No, not at all. The alternative translation, "Not altogether," is less likely. This strong negative response to the question seems, on the face of it, to contradict Paul's earlier positive response to the question, "What's the advantage of being a Jew?" (3:1). There, however, he was speaking of the privileges of being the chosen people; here he is speaking of their moral standing before God. Regardless of their privileges, Jews are as guilty as Gentiles before the judgment of God.

under the power of sin. Sin is a power that dominates people's lives and enslaves them.

3:10-18 *As the Scriptures say.* Here Paul strings together a series of texts taken from the LXX to prove his point that all people stand condemned before God because of their sin. In their original OT setting, many of these texts refer specifically to the unrighteous, in contrast to the righteous. But when unrighteousness is understood in its absolute sense —i.e., when human behavior is measured against the righteousness of God—the distinction becomes irrelevant and the texts apply to all people. No one is truly righteous in God's sight.

3:10-12 *No one is righteous.* These verses come from Ps 14:1-3, LXX (cf. parallel, Ps 53:1-3). Significantly, Paul altered the first line to include the word "righteous" (*dikaios* [TG1342, ZG1465]), implying that no one is right with God. That is the point emphasized throughout 3:10-18.

No one is truly wise. This means that no one is wise in a moral or spiritual sense, in the understanding of God and his ways—not in an intellectual sense. In OT wisdom literature, wisdom and folly are defined by whether or not one's life is lived in accord with the ways of God.

All have turned away. That is, they have turned away from God and his ways.

all have become useless. Or, "all have become worthless."

No one does good. Or, "No one shows *kindness*" (*chrēstotēta* [TG5544, ZG5983]) (cf. NRSV, REB).

3:13 *Their talk is foul, like the stench from an open grave.* Lit., "Their throat is an opened grave," meaning either that the words people speak are foul (like the stench of a corpse) or that they are deadly in their effect (they "kill" people). This is a quotation from Ps 5:9, LXX.

Snake venom drips from their lips. Their words are poisonous and deadly, a quote taken from Ps 140:3.

3:14 *Their mouths are full of cursing and bitterness.* The word "cursing" (*aras* [TG685, ZG725]) here refers to the act of invoking God's judgment on others with evil intent. This is a quotation from Ps 10:7, LXX.

3:15-17 *They rush to commit murder.* Lit., "their feet are quick to pour out blood"—i.e., they are quick to hurt and kill. This is a quotation from Isa 59:7-8 and Prov 1:16.

Destruction and misery always follow them. Lit., "ruin and misery are in their paths." Wherever they go, they destroy people and cause grief.

They don't know where to find peace. Lit., "the way of peace (*hodon eirēnēs* [TG3598/1515, ZG3847/1645]) they have not known." This may be interpreted three different ways: (1) they do nothing to bring about peace between people; (2) they have no experience of peace with God; or, (3) they have no peace in their lives. The first fits the context best: their hurtful speech and murderous ways leave behind misery.

3:18 *They have no fear of God at all.* This is a quotation from Ps 36:1.

3:19 *the law applies to those to whom it was given.* This refers to the Jews; they are the ones guilty of the sins described in the preceding verses. "The law" here refers to the Hebrew Scriptures in general, since none of the texts quoted comes from the law in its narrower sense (i.e., the law of Moses, the Pentateuch).

its purpose is to keep people from having excuses. Lit., "so that every mouth may be silenced."

and to show that the entire world is guilty before God. The Scriptures make it clear that all people, Jews as well as Gentiles, stand guilty before God because of their sins, deserving of his holy wrath.

3:20 *For no one can ever be made right with God by doing what the law commands.* Lit., ". . . by the works of the law." This is a free quotation and expansion of Ps 143:2 (cf. Gal 2:16; 3:11).

The law simply shows us how sinful we are. Lit., "for through the law [comes] the knowledge of sin." The real purpose of the law is not to save us but to show us our need of salvation by making us aware of our sins and of our failure to measure up to God's demands. This deeper purpose of the law is further expounded in 5:20; 7:7-11; Gal 3:19, 22-24.

COMMENTARY

In this section, Paul sums up the point he had been making in 1:18–3:8. In spite of certain traditional advantages favoring Jews, there is no one—Jew or Gentile—who fully lives up to the holy standards of God. No one can claim to be truly good or righteous in God's sight. The Scriptures themselves say as much—and here Paul strings together a number of texts from the Old Testament to make the point that the whole world has turned from God's ways to a life of sin. And since the words of Scripture are addressed primarily to Jews, these texts apply as much to Jews as to Gentiles. The conclusion, then, is that all people are sinners in the eyes of God; everyone stands guilty before the divine Judge. The entire world lies under the judgment of God, in need of his mercy, and there is nothing people can do to save themselves, for salvation does not come by observing the law of Moses.

In their natural state, people live "under the power of sin," driven by the impetus of sin (3:9)—the terrible, self-serving bent toward evil that is so all-pervasive in human nature. Like the law itself, sin is here viewed as a perverse force dictating the direction of people's lives, effectively enslaving people (cf. 6:6, 20; 7:14-25). For Paul, as for the New Testament writers generally, humans by nature are not autonomous beings freely choosing their own lifestyles but people subject to sinister spiritual forces linked to the ultimate power of evil in the universe. In Ephesians 2:2, Paul describes the situation: "You used to live in sin, just like the rest of the world, obeying the devil—the commander of the powers in the unseen world. He is the spirit at work in the hearts of those who refuse to obey God."

For Paul and the writers of the New Testament, the greatest problem any individual faces—the problem behind all other problems—is the problem of sin. The answer to it lies not in determined moral reformation but in God's gracious gift of forgiveness and the transforming power of the Holy Spirit, received when a person converts to Christ. The world of the New Testament is essentially a spiritual world, and the early Christians took spiritual forces seriously. They recognized that there was more to life than meets the eye, and they were convinced that one could not deal adequately with human problems without taking account of spiritual factors and the enslaving power of sin. The reality of sin as a powerful driving force in the world is one of the most basic elements shaping the Christian view of the world and of human nature. It helps us to understand the widespread phenomenon of evil, both in human history and in people's lives individually.

To drive his point home, Paul cited a string of Old Testament texts that, when taken together, make the point that all human beings have turned away from God to go their own evil way (3:10-18). This rebellion is reflected in both their words and their actions. As a result, there is *no one*—Jew or Gentile—who can be considered truly good or righteous from God's point of view. *No one* has a heart fully devoted to God or lives consistently in the fear of God. *No one* is genuinely kind and caring toward others—both the words and the deeds of people are often destructive. *No one* consistently lives a life of pure goodness, perfectly obedient to God's desires. And the terrible conclusion of it all is that the entire world—every single person—stands guilty before God, deserving of divine retribution (3:19).

For Jews, in particular, this means that one cannot think of becoming righteous in God's eyes by obeying God's law. Why? Humans are constitutionally unable to fully live out the demands of the law. The law functions, then, not as a means of achieving righteousness but as a means of showing us how far we fall short (3:20). Here Paul's words reflect his understanding of the deeper purpose of the law, the real purpose of the law from God's point of view: it makes us aware of our sin. But in itself, the law provides no answer to the problem of sin (i.e., its power over a person's life). (For the role of the law, see comments on 5:20; 7:7-13; cf. 4:15; Gal 3:19, 23ff; see also "The Law of Moses" in the Introduction.)

Though many of the Scriptures cited by Paul were lifted out of their original context and used to make a much broader point than they were originally intended to make, the point being made accurately reflects Paul's understanding of the insidious nature of sin. Driven by perverse, self-serving desires, with minds darkened by the evil one, people by themselves simply cannot obey God or live out their love for God to the extent he deserves. "For everyone has sinned; we all fall short of God's glorious standard" (3:23). There is something uncontrollable, something fundamentally evil and destructive within, that drives people to disobey God and hurt others. People by themselves simply do not have what it takes to give God the honor he deserves.

The fact that human nature is so often viewed today as good (or at least as "not so bad") reflects the superficial nature of the modern understanding of sin and the extent to which people have lost a profound sense of the holiness of God. It also reflects the extent to which individualism and relativism have come to dominate our thinking in a pluralistic world. In the modern world, people are hesitant to call anything or anyone really "bad" because there is little sense of any universal absolute. Badness, like goodness, is simply relative—it all depends on your point of reference. In the modern world, often it is the acceptance of human thinking in all its diversity, the toleration of widely differing points of view, which constitutes the only absolute. It is considered simply inappropriate to judge the opinions of others as wrong. So the demand for tolerance and acceptance of a wide range of human thinking and behavior often becomes the measure of all else.

For Paul, the awareness of the universal nature of sin is of fundamental importance; it is the beginning point for any understanding and appreciation of salvation. But if that is true, how do we communicate the message of salvation to people today who have lost any sense of sin? How do we proclaim the Good News to a society that has little sense of its need of a Savior? What does "salvation from sin" mean to people who have little sense of their moral failing? If we are to be true to the biblical gospel, we *must*—at some point, in some way—speak of the reality of sin and of our need, above all, to be forgiven. This may mean that we have to engage in some form of preevangelism first, to heighten people's awareness of their sin in light of the holy nature of God. For some people today, however, the normal sequence of conversion may be reversed: a deeper sense of sin may come about only after a person has embraced Jesus on other grounds (e.g., a conviction of the truth of the claims made by or about him, or a sense of needing him for the healing of personal brokenness, or a belief in his ultimate meaningfulness, or a need to "find closure with the universe"). There is, however, no true understanding of the biblical Good

News if there is no awareness of sin. Fortunately, he who is "the way, the truth, and the life" is not limited in his ability to illuminate the darkness of the human heart and draw people to himself.

Behind Paul's argument lie certain traditional Jewish assumptions about the nature of God that are not widely held in the modern world—assumptions about his holiness and moral demands, his judgment and punishment of sin. Many people in the twenty-first century have a much more benevolent view of God and find it hard to believe that God would condemn anyone; but the New Testament writers speak as much of God's holiness and judgment as they do of his love and grace, and everything they write reflects the dominance of the final day of judgment (Rev 20:11-15) in their thinking. God is the one who, on the final day, will judge all people according to the good or evil they have done (2 Cor 5:10). So people must live with "deep reverence and fear" (Phil 2:12) before him—for "our God is a devouring fire" (Heb 12:29; cf. Luke 12:5). The New Testament reflects a more radical conception of God than that of many modern Christians.

Paul's letter to the Romans seems to reflect the conviction that one cannot come to an adequate appreciation of the grace of God without first feeling the full weight of the judgment of God. This classic ordering of the gospel message, with the statement of sin and judgment preceding the message of grace—while not consistently characteristic of Paul's own preaching of the Good News (cf. Acts 13–28)—has proved to be a highly effective approach to evangelism at many points in the history of the church's witness. The popular "Four Spiritual Laws" approach to evangelism today, which begins with a statement of human sinfulness, is one example of this. (See "Human Sinfulness" and "God's Holiness and Judgment" in the Introduction.)

◆   C. God's Gift of Salvation (3:21–5:21)
      1. God's way of saving us (3:21-31)

21But now God has shown us a way to be made right with him without keeping the requirements of the law, as was promised in the writings of Moses* and the prophets long ago. 22We are made right with God by placing our faith in Jesus Christ. And this is true for everyone who believes, no matter who we are.

23For everyone has sinned; we all fall short of God's glorious standard. 24Yet God, with undeserved kindness, declares that we are righteous. He did this through Christ Jesus when he freed us from the penalty for our sins. 25For God presented Jesus as the sacrifice for sin. People are made right with God when they believe that Jesus sacrificed his life, shedding his blood. This sacrifice shows that God was being fair when he held back and did not punish those who sinned in times past, 26for he was looking ahead and including them in what he would do in this present time. God did this to demonstrate his righteousness, for he himself is fair and just, and he declares sinners to be right in his sight when they believe in Jesus.

27Can we boast, then, that we have done anything to be accepted by God? No, because our acquittal is not based on obeying the law. It is based on faith. 28So we are made right with God through faith and not by obeying the law.

²⁹After all, is God the God of the Jews only? Isn't he also the God of the Gentiles? Of course he is. ³⁰There is only one God, and he makes people right with himself only by faith, whether they are Jews or Gentiles.* ³¹Well then, if we emphasize faith, does this mean that we can forget about the law? Of course not! In fact, only when we have faith do we truly fulfill the law.

3:21 Greek *in the law.* 3:30 Greek *whether they are circumcised or uncircumcised.*

NOTES

3:21 *God has shown us a way to be made right with him.* Lit., "the righteousness of God has been revealed." Here, as in 1:17 (cf. note), "the righteousness of God" (*dikaiosunē theou* [TG1343, ZG1466]) refers not to the character of God (cf. N. T. Wright 2002:30, 32, who interprets it as the faithful covenant justice of God) but to God's act of declaring people righteous because of their faith, the "righteousness of faith." It may be translated "God's way of putting people right with himself" (TEV). For a full discussion of Paul's understanding of the important phrase "righteousness of God," see Cranfield 1980:91-99; Moo 1996:79-90; Schreiner 1998:63-71.

without keeping the requirements of the law. Lit., "apart from law" (*chōris nomou* [TG5565/ 3551, ZG6006/3795]). Salvation is dependent neither on the law of Moses nor on any sort of legal system.

the writings of Moses and the prophets. A common designation for the OT as a whole. Cf. Matt 5:17; 7:12; 22:40; Luke 16:29; Acts 24:14; 28:23.

3:22 *by placing our faith in Jesus Christ.* Lit., "through faith in Jesus Christ" (*dia pisteōs Iēsou Christou*). The faith that saves is not "faith" in a vague, general sense but faith specifically in Jesus Christ. Saving faith is not an intellectual affirmation of the truth of Christ (or of a set of theological convictions) as much as a personal trust in Christ as Savior. To translate the phrase as "the faith [or faithfulness] of Jesus Christ"—as if it were Jesus' faith (or faithfulness), not ours, that saves us (so Howard 1992:758-760; NRSV mg)—would be to miss the point of the simple contrast Paul draws between believing and doing (4:4-8) and the parallel he draws with God's declaration of Abraham as righteous because of his faith. For a full discussion of the crucial phrase "faith in Jesus Christ," see Schreiner 1998:181-186; cf. Fitzmyer 1993:345-346; Moo 1996:224-226. For other references to faith *in* God or Christ, see 3:25; Mark 11:22; Acts 3:16; Gal 2:16, 20; 3:22; Eph 3:12.

no matter who we are. Whether we are Jews or Gentiles.

3:23 *we all fall short of God's glorious standard.* Lit., "all fall short of the glory of God" (*tēs doxēs* [TG1391, ZG1518] *tou theou*). We all fail to measure up to the full goodness of God's own character, which is God's holy standard for all people.

3:24 *with undeserved kindness.* Lit., "as a gift, by his grace." Righteousness (salvation) must always be understood as a sheer gift from God, never as something we achieve by our own efforts.

God . . . declares that we are righteous. Lit., "being justified" (*dikaioumenoi* [TG1344, ZG1467]), an important Pauline term meaning "regarded as righteous" or "made righteous" in God's eyes—"made right" with God. It is another way of talking about being forgiven. Cf. 1:17; 3:21.

He did this through Christ Jesus when he freed us from the penalty for our sins. Lit., "through the redemption that is in Christ Jesus." As a result of the sacrificial death of Christ, we are set free both from our slavery to sin and from the threat of God's eternal judgment on us. "Redemption" is the word used for buying a slave in order to set the slave free (cf. Moo 1996:229-230; Schreiner 1998:189-191). Elsewhere Paul spoke of redemption from the enslaving power of the law (Gal 3:13; 4:4-5).

3:25 *as the sacrifice for sin.* Lit., "[as] a sacrifice of atonement" (*hilastērion* [TG2435, ZG2663]); cf. NIV. This term has been understood either in the sense of "propitiation" (a sacrifice to satisfy the righteous anger of God; KJV, NASB) or "expiation" (a sacrifice to cover the sins of people; NAB; cf. "means of expiating sin," REB). In either case, the sacrifice is intended to avert the anger and judgment of God (cf. 1:18: "God shows his anger from heaven"). The term may be translated more broadly as "the means by which people's sins are forgiven" (TEV). For a full discussion of *hilastērion*, see Cranfield 1980:214-218; Bruce 1985:99-101; Moo 1996:231-237; Schreiner 1998:191-194.

Jesus sacrificed his life, shedding his blood. Behind this image lies the OT emphasis on the atoning blood of sacrifices ("I have given you the blood on the altar to purify you, making you right with the LORD. It is the blood, given in exchange for a life, that makes purification possible," Lev 17:11). The NT consistently speaks of Jesus as the ultimate atoning sacrifice ("We have been made right in God's sight by the blood of Christ," 5:9; "Look! The Lamb of God who takes away the sin of the world!" John 1:29; cf. Heb 9:11–10:18; esp. 10:1-7.)

shows that God was being fair when he held back and did not punish those who sinned in times past. Lit., "to show his righteousness because of the passing-over of the previously committed sins." For God simply to leave sins unpunished indefinitely would be a denial of his righteousness; he cannot condone evil. The sacrificial death of Christ is thus an expression of his holy sense of justice. God has patiently refrained from fully punishing people's sins in the past (cf. Acts 17:30: "God overlooked people's ignorance") because of his plan from the beginning to deal with sin once and for all in the death of his Son, the quintessential expression of grace. Here the phrase "to show his righteousness" is not to be interpreted "to show God's way of putting people right with himself" (as in 1:17; 3:21) but rather "to demonstrate his justice" (cf. 3:26).

3:26 *to demonstrate his righteousness, for he himself is fair and just, and he declares sinners to be right in his sight when they believe in Jesus.* Lit., "to show his righteousness in the present time, that he might be righteous and make righteous the one who has faith in Jesus." The sacrificial death of Christ shows both the *righteousness* of God in punishing sin and the *rightness* of God in forgiving sinners who put their reliance in Jesus (cf. Schreiner 1998:198: "in the death of Jesus the saving and judging righteousness of God meet"). God's forgiving grace does not compromise his holy justice. For the meaning of "faith in Jesus," see note on 3:22.

3:27 *our acquittal is not based on obeying the law. It is based on faith.* Lit., "By what law? Of works? No, but through the law of faith." The two contrasting "laws" represent two contrasting ways of thinking about how one becomes right with God (cf. 4:4-8).

3:28 *we are made right with God through faith.* Luther's translation of the Bible into German was criticized for adding the word "alone" to the end of this statement, but his rendering accurately conveys the meaning of the text in its context.

3:29 *is God the God of the Jews only?* If salvation were given on the basis of obeying the law, it would be limited to the people of the law; but God is concerned for the salvation of all people.

3:30 *There is only one God.* The implication is that he is the God of the whole world, concerned for Jews and Gentiles alike.

whether they are Jews or Gentiles. Lit., "circumcised and uncircumcised."

3:31 *does this mean that we can forget about the law?* Lit., "do we nullify (*katargoumen* [TG2673, ZG2934]) the law?"

Of course not! This emphatic negation (*mē genoito* [TG3361/1096, ZG3590/1181]) occurs ten times in Romans (3:4, 6, 31; 6:2, 15; 7:7, 13; 9:14; 11:1, 11) but nowhere else in Paul's writings.

In fact, only when we have faith do we truly fulfill the law. Lit., "rather, we affirm (endorse, validate, confirm, substantiate) the law." Though the message of the Good News seems to deny the law (because it teaches salvation by faith apart from the law), in reality it affirms the law in at least three ways: (1) it accepts the holy standards of the law as a measure of human behavior, (2) it acknowledges the deeper purpose of the law—to show people their sin and their need of salvation (cf. 4:15; 5:20; 7:7-11; Gal 3:19, 22-24), and (3) it affirms the teaching of the law itself—that righteousness is conferred on the basis of faith (4:3; Gal 3:6). It is the latter point that is primarily in focus here, as the following context (4:1-3) makes clear.

COMMENTARY

This section of Romans is the heart of the Good News. With the entire world guilty under the judgment of God, God in his mercy has provided a way for us to be saved. By sending his own Son to die as a sacrifice for sin, God has made it possible for us to be forgiven—if we simply put our trust in Christ to save us. This simple act of faith makes us right with God without sacrificing his holy standards, for Christ has borne the punishment for our sins.

So when it comes to salvation, there are no grounds for pride. Salvation cannot be earned by doing good things or keeping the law of Moses. It is a free gift, received by simple faith when we throw ourselves upon Christ, trusting him to save us. Here Jews and Gentiles stand on equal ground before God. But, someone will object, doesn't this emphasis on faith deny the fundamental teaching of the law of Moses? No, not at all, Paul emphasizes, it affirms it—because this is the same principle (salvation by faith) that the law itself teaches.

The Gift of Salvation. Romans 3:21-26, the most theologically concentrated passage in Romans, contains the core of Paul's message, the Good News he preached everywhere. God, in his mercy, has done something for us that we could not do for ourselves—he has provided a means by which we can be saved. By sending his own Son as a sacrifice for sin, God has made it possible for us to be made right with him. This gracious gift of salvation is in no way dependent on our keeping the law of Moses; it is a free gift to all who put their trust in Christ, relying on him to save them (3:21-26). It is the same principle expressed in the law of Moses and the prophets—that we are made right with God by our faith. Even though its origins lie in traditional Judaism, the salvation that God has given the world in Christ is for Jews and Gentiles equally, on the very same basis—personal faith in Christ.

Because we are all sinners in the sight of God, all of us "fall short of the glory of God" (3:23, NRSV)—we all fail to measure up to the full goodness of God's own character. As humans, we were originally made to reflect the glory of God ("Then God said, 'Let us make human beings in our image, to be like us,'" Gen 1:26), but the tragedy of sin has resulted in the diminishing of that glory. The experience of salvation is intended to restore something of the glory of God to our lives so that we "can see and reflect the glory of the Lord" (2 Cor 3:18)—and one day come to share his glory fully, in all its splendor (5:2). Day by day, through all the experiences of life, God is working to make us more and more like his Son

(8:29), who is the full reflection of his glory (John 1:14), so that we, too, can increasingly reflect his glory. For Christians, life is to be an ever-increasing experience and expression of the glory of God in Jesus Christ. (For further discussion of glory, see comments on 8:18-30.)

The gracious gift of Christ takes away our sins in two different senses: (1) It removes the intolerable burden of sin's guilt from our conscience. (2) It removes our sin as an object of judgment in God's sight. As a result, God can truly say, "I will never again remember their sins" (Heb 8:12; 10:17; cf. Jer 31:34). The book of Hebrews especially emphasizes the once-for-all nature of this perfect sacrifice: "With his own blood . . . he entered the Most Holy Place once for all time and secured our redemption forever" (Heb 9:12); "Once for all time, he has appeared at the end of the age to remove sin by his own death as a sacrifice" (Heb 9:26); "Our High Priest offered himself to God as a single sacrifice for sins, good for all time" (Heb 10:12); "For by that one offering he forever made perfect those who are being made holy" (Heb 10:14); "And when sins have been forgiven, there is no need to offer any more sacrifices" (Heb 10:18). As a result, we can now come to God with a completely free conscience, "sprinkled with Christ's blood" (Heb 10:19-22). Here we have a vast, limitless view of God's forgiving grace, immense and free. Because of that grace, we can live today knowing that we are fully forgiven; God himself, in his kindness, declares that we are righteous—not guilty (3:24). In 8:1-14 we will see yet another way this gift of salvation "takes away" our sins—by giving us the strength to overcome the dominating power of sin in our lives.

Behind this emphasis on Jesus as a sacrifice for sin lies the earlier Jewish practice of offering animal sacrifices for atonement in accordance with the Mosaic law (Lev 1–7, 16), as well as the strange but key passage in Isaiah 52:13–53:12 about the Suffering Servant who sacrifices his life so that others might be forgiven and live:

> He was pierced for our rebellion, crushed for our sins. He was beaten so we could be whole. He was whipped so we could be healed. . . . The LORD laid on him the sins of us all. . . . My righteous servant will make it possible for many to be counted righteous, for he will bear all their sins. (Isa 53:5-11)

Jesus himself understood this to be his calling, for he said, "The Son of Man came . . . to give his life as a ransom for many" (Mark 10:45) and "This is my blood, . . . poured out as a sacrifice to forgive the sins of many" (Matt 26:28). The early Christian community after him was convinced that Jesus was indeed the Suffering Servant of Isaiah, the ultimate sacrifice for sins. (This can be observed in John 1:29; cf. 1 Cor 11:24-26; 15:3; Eph 1:7; Col 1:14; Titus 2:14; Heb 1:3; 10:12-14; 13:20-21; 1 Pet 1:18-19; 3:18; 1 John 2:2; Rev 5:9, 12.) Indeed, it was in his sacrificial death that the early Christians found the greatest significance of Jesus' life.

Christ as Our Righteousness. Christ's death on the cross provided the means by which we can be saved and the means by which God can make us righteous. Paul spoke of salvation as a gift of "righteousness," the perfect righteousness of Jesus Christ that God graciously gives the believer so that the believer is made acceptable in his sight (3:21-26). So righteousness is "credited" to those who put their trust in

Christ—an experience referred to as "justification," or "being put right with God." In the words of the Westminster Shorter Catechism (answer to question 33), "Justification is an act of God's free grace, wherein he pardoneth all our sins, and accepteth us as righteous in his sight, only for the righteousness of Christ imputed to us, and received by faith alone."

This is the "righteousness of God" of which Paul so often spoke. It is the righteousness that God graciously confers and counts as valid. This stood in contrast to the more traditional concept of righteousness popular in Judaism, measured by one's observance of the law of Moses. This concept is what Paul introduced earlier as the main point of the Good News (1:17). The Good News of Jesus Christ shifts the focus from our righteousness to the gift of God's righteousness—the righteousness he mercifully confers upon us because of Christ's sacrifice for our sins.

At the same time, the sacrificial death of Christ expresses the "righteousness of God" in another sense—his holy sense of justice—because forgiveness is bestowed only on the basis of Christ's sacrifice for sin. Although God was very patient with his people's sins in the past (3:25; cf. Acts 17:30), his righteous character demanded that there be some form of judgment exacted for such sins (sin must be atoned for), and Christ bore that terrible judgment for us. The patience God has shown sinners in the past is understandable only in light of the justice now expressed in the death of Christ, who is "the sacrifice that atones for our sins—and not only our sins but the sins of all the world" (1 John 2:2). This passage hints at the potential efficacy of the sacrifice of Christ even for earlier generations, "those who sinned in times past" (3:25); here the death of Christ is viewed as atoning for the sins of the past as well as the sins of the future. However, the underlying assumption would seem to be that for the people of the past to be forgiven, they too must have placed their trust in God's grace; for salvation is only for those who place their trust in God and live by faith.

The death of Christ, then, shows both the *righteousness* of God in punishing sin, and the *rightness* of God in forgiving sinners who put their trust in the sacrifice of his Son (3:25-26). God can rightly show grace to those who put their trust in his sacrifice, for the price of sin has now been paid. In Jesus Christ, then, God reveals both his holy justice and his forgiving grace—neither is compromised. There is an interesting parallel to this dual understanding of righteousness in *The Rule of the Community* (1QS 10:11; 11:11-15) of the Dead Sea Scrolls:

> I will declare His judgment concerning my sins. . . . I will say to God, "My Righteousness" and "Author of my Goodness". . . . As for me, if I stumble, the mercies of God shall be my eternal salvation. If I stagger because of the sin of flesh, my justification shall be by the righteousness of God. . . . He will draw me near by His grace, and by His mercy will He bring my justification. . . . Through His righteousness He will cleanse me . . . that I may confess to God His righteousness. (Vermes 1975:90-94)

Further, we should note the linking of the two in the prophets' description of God as "a righteous God and Savior" (Isa 45:21; cf. "righteous and saving," Zech 9:9 LXX). "For Christ occupies a unique position as God's representative with man and man's representative with God. As the representative man he absorbs the judgment incurred by human sin; as the representative of God he bestows God's pardoning grace on men and women" (Bruce 1985:103). So the Atonement both reflects the righteousness of God himself (his holy justice) and results in the free gift of the righteousness of God (his forgiving grace) for the person who trusts in it (3:25ff). Just as salvation is a matter of "faith from beginning to end" (1:17, TEV), so it is a matter of the "righteousness of God" from beginning to end.

Most pious Jews earnestly hoped that by their sincere attempts to observe the law of God they would in the end be judged as righteous on the last day, when everyone stands before God. The Good News of Christ reverses the order: believers are pronounced righteous at the beginning of their course, not at the end—as the result not of their works but of God's free gift! There was always a degree of uncertainty and anxiety associated with the attempt to achieve righteousness by the observance of the law: how could a person ever be sure that he or she had done enough to satisfy God? Even if one did his best (and no one consistently does that), how could he be certain that his behavior measured up to the minimum requirement of God's holy standards? One could hope, but one could never be sure (Bruce 1985:97-98). By contrast, the Good News of Christ promises us that we are fully forgiven quite apart from our attempts to measure up—entirely because of the death of Christ, the "perfect sacrifice for our sins" (Heb 9:14). The word of God assures us, "I will never again remember their sins and lawless deeds" (Heb 10:17). This is the message that proved so freeing to John Bunyan:

> As I was walking up and down in the house, as a man in a most woeful state, that word of God took hold of my heart, *Ye are justified freely by his grace, through the redemption that is in Christ Jesus,* Rom. 3.24. But oh what a turn it made upon me! Now was I as one awakened out of some troublesome sleep and dream, and listening to this heavenly sentence, I was as if I had heard it thus expounded to me; Sinner, thou thinkest that because of thy sins and infirmities I cannot save thy Soul; but behold my Son is by me, and upon him I look, and not on thee, and will deal with thee according as I am pleased with him: at this I was greatly lightened in my mind, and made to understand that God could justify a sinner at any time; it was but looking upon Christ, and imputing of his benefits to us, and the work was forthwith done. (Bunyan 1962:80)

Salvation, then, is the result of two acts: (1) God's gracious giving of Christ to die for our sins, by which it becomes possible for God to forgive and accept us; and (2) our coming to trust in that sacrifice, by which the gift of salvation becomes personally effective in our own lives. "For God presented Jesus as the sacrifice for sin. People are made right with God when they believe that Jesus sacrificed his life, shedding his blood" (3:25). This is the heart of the Good News, and it is of crucial importance to understand and grasp it well.

For John Wesley, hearing this message expounded from Luther's commentary on Romans in the small society in Aldersgate Street on May 24, 1738, was a life-changing experience:

About a quarter before nine, while he was describing the change which God works in the heart through faith in Christ, I felt my heart strangely warmed. I felt I did trust in Christ, Christ alone, for salvation: and an assurance was given me, that he had taken away my sins, even mine, and saved me from the law of sin and death. (Wesley 1879:1.97)

The assurance of salvation that Wesley received that evening, trusting in Christ, made him a different man, and marked the beginning of the evangelical revival of the eighteenth century. And Paul would remind us that this same assurance can be experienced by everyone who truly trusts in Christ as Savior. Because of his death for our sins, we can indeed be assured of *our* salvation; we can know that *our* sins are forgiven—if we put our trust in him (cf. commentary on 4:4-8).

In this section, then, Paul uses the language of the law-court ("God . . . declares that we are righteous," 3:24), the slave market ("through Christ Jesus . . . he freed us," 3:24), and the altar ("God presented Jesus as the sacrifice for sin," 3:25) to communicate the full significance of Christ's death. Salvation brings us justification, redemption, and atonement—pardon, liberation, and forgiveness (Bruce 1985: 101-102), and it is all a free gift, by God's sheer grace. We can never earn it; we can only receive it with gratitude and wonder, simply taking God at his word and putting our trust in him.

Because salvation is a free gift and not something we can ever earn, there are two inferences that may be drawn. First, there is absolutely no room for human pride (3:27; 4:2)—the only boasting is in what the Lord has done (1 Cor 1:31). We receive salvation not because of what we have done but because of what Christ did for us, and our trust must be in that alone. Salvation is always *sola gratia, sola fide, soli Deo gloria* (by grace alone, through faith alone, to God alone be the glory). There is no room here for the person who says, "I do the best I can, I try to live a decent life—what more can God expect of me?" Such self-reliance reflects both an inadequate view of sin and a failure in understanding the Good News of grace (cf. comments on 4:1-8). Second, there is no preferential consideration given to those who keep the law; Gentiles are accepted on the same basis as Jews (3:28-30). Paul's emphasis on this point would seem to be directed to Jewish Christians who may be critical of Gentile believers.

But What about the Law of Moses? All of this, however, was sure to raise troubling questions in the minds of those from Jewish backgrounds. What about the law of Moses? Doesn't this understanding of the Good News undermine the God-given role of the law? Not at all, Paul asserted—it confirms and endorses it (3:31). But how can this be true, when Paul speaks so negatively of the law so often? There are three ways in which the Good News of salvation in Christ may be said to affirm the role of the law of Moses:

1. It validates the absolute demands of the moral law; in other words, it takes the righteous demands of God seriously and acknowledges that judgment must be meted out for failure to obey them.

2. It recognizes the deeper purpose (the true purpose) of the law in God's scheme
   of things—namely, the law's function in making people aware of their moral
   failures so that they might be wakened to their need of God's forgiving grace.
3. It confirms and fulfills the teaching of the law itself—that God considers people righteous on the basis of their faith (Gen 15:6; cf. Hab 2:4). It is this point
   that seems to be in focus here, judging from what follows (4:1-25).

Far from denying the validity of the law of Moses, the emphasis of the Good News
on justification by faith is entirely in line with the demanding character, the deeper
purpose, and the very teaching of the law itself.

Having said this, however, we must acknowledge that Paul's writing clearly
reflects a denial of certain aspects of the law as it was popularly understood in the
Jewish community. These are instructive to note, both for our understanding of
Paul and for our consideration of the role of Old Testament law in Christian theology today. Like Jesus, Paul made an implicit distinction between the moral and
ritual (ceremonial) aspects of the law. The moral laws remain a valid expression of
the will of God, but the ritual laws (the regulations pertaining to circumcision, the
Sabbath, and food rules especially) are considered no longer relevant—at least for
Gentile Christians. But even the moral laws are relegated to the background of
Paul's thinking, where they provide a backdrop, against which the sheer forgiving
grace of the Good News stands out in magnificent contrast.

If we follow Paul's lead as we read the Old Testament law today, we will not read it
as a legal manual (a book of specific instructions authoritatively legislating the details of our life) but rather as Scripture that shows us the nature of God and his *moral*
desires for his people and that points us to the Good News of Jesus Christ as its ultimate fulfillment. As Christians, we read and interpret the Old Testament law in light
of Christ and the Good News—in light of its fulfillment in the New Testament. The
Old Testament law provides background for understanding Christian theology, but
it is the New Testament that gives us the shape of Christian theology and the primary principles for living the Christian life.

In the end, we can say that Paul's focus was no longer on the law at all as a way of
life, a regimen to be followed; his focus had shifted to Christ and the Good News
and the way this new life is lived out by the power of the Spirit. For Paul, life in
Christ—life "in the Spirit"—had replaced life "under the law." Commitment to
Christ and the power of the Spirit replaced the law as the driving force of life (7:4-6;
8:1-14).

◆   2. Abraham as an example of saving faith (4:1-25)

Abraham was, humanly speaking, the
founder of our Jewish nation. What did
he discover about being made right with
God? ²If his good deeds had made him
acceptable to God, he would have had

something to boast about. But that was
not God's way. ³For the Scriptures tell us,
"Abraham believed God, and God counted
him as righteous because of his faith."*
⁴When people work, their wages are not

a gift, but something they have earned. ⁵But people are counted as righteous, not because of their work, but because of their faith in God who forgives sinners. ⁶David also spoke of this when he described the happiness of those who are declared righteous without working for it:

⁷"Oh, what joy for those
whose disobedience is forgiven,
whose sins are put out of sight.
⁸Yes, what joy for those
whose record the LORD has cleared
of sin."*

⁹Now, is this blessing only for the Jews, or is it also for uncircumcised Gentiles?* Well, we have been saying that Abraham was counted as righteous by God because of his faith. ¹⁰But how did this happen? Was he counted as righteous only after he was circumcised, or was it before he was circumcised? Clearly, God accepted Abraham before he was circumcised!

¹¹Circumcision was a sign that Abraham already had faith and that God had already accepted him and declared him to be righteous—even before he was circumcised. So Abraham is the spiritual father of those who have faith but have not been circumcised. They are counted as righteous because of their faith. ¹²And Abraham is also the spiritual father of those who have been circumcised, but only if they have the same kind of faith Abraham had before he was circumcised.

¹³Clearly, God's promise to give the whole earth to Abraham and his descendants was based not on his obedience to God's law, but on a right relationship with God that comes by faith. ¹⁴If God's promise is only for those who obey the law,

then faith is not necessary and the promise is pointless. ¹⁵For the law always brings punishment on those who try to obey it. (The only way to avoid breaking the law is to have no law to break!)

¹⁶So the promise is received by faith. It is given as a free gift. And we are all certain to receive it, whether or not we live according to the law of Moses, if we have faith like Abraham's. For Abraham is the father of all who believe. ¹⁷That is what the Scriptures mean when God told him, "I have made you the father of many nations."* This happened because Abraham believed in the God who brings the dead back to life and who creates new things out of nothing.

¹⁸Even when there was no reason for hope, Abraham kept hoping—believing that he would become the father of many nations. For God had said to him, "That's how many descendants you will have!"* ¹⁹And Abraham's faith did not weaken, even though, at about 100 years of age, he figured his body was as good as dead—and so was Sarah's womb.

²⁰Abraham never wavered in believing God's promise. In fact, his faith grew stronger, and in this he brought glory to God. ²¹He was fully convinced that God is able to do whatever he promises. ²²And because of Abraham's faith, God counted him as righteous. ²³And when God counted him as righteous, it wasn't just for Abraham's benefit. It was recorded ²⁴for our benefit, too, assuring us that God will also count us as righteous if we believe in him, the one who raised Jesus our Lord from the dead. ²⁵He was handed over to die because of our sins, and he was raised to life to make us right with God.

4:3 Gen 15:6. 4:7-8 Ps 32:1-2 (Greek version). 4:9 Greek *is this blessing only for the circumcised, or is it also for the uncircumcised?* 4:17 Gen 17:5. 4:18 Gen 15:5.

NOTES

4:1 *humanly speaking.* Lit., "according to the flesh" (*kata sarka* [ᵀᴳ2596/4561, ᶻᴳ2848/4922]). God was the true founder of the nation (Gen 12:1-3).

the founder of our Jewish nation. Lit., "our forefather" (*propatora* [ᵀᴳ3962A, ᶻᴳ4635]). This is the reading of ℵ* A B C* syr cop. Other Gr. mss (ℵ¹ C³ D F G 33 1739 𝔐) read *patera*

[TG3962, ZG4252] (father). Paul later speaks of Abraham as the spiritual ancestor of all believers in Christ, both Jew and Gentile. He is "the father of all who believe," just as God had promised that he would be "the father of many nations" (4:16-17; see also 4:11-12; Gen 17:4-6).

What did he discover about being made right with God? The words "about being made right with God" are an expansion, reflecting the focus of the passage.

4:2 *If his good deeds had made him acceptable to God.* Lit., "If he was made righteous because of works."

But that was not God's way. Lit., "but not before God." Abraham had no grounds for boasting before God because his righteousness was not an achievement of his own but a gift of God based solely on his faith.

4:3 *Abraham believed God, and God counted him as righteous because of his faith.* This is a quotation from Gen 15:6 (also cited in Gal 3:6). Abraham put his trust in God, relied on God—this is the common meaning of "believed" (*episteusen* [TG4100, ZG4409]) in Paul's usage. What follows in this chapter is Paul's expanded exposition of this decisive OT text.

God counted him as righteous because of his faith. Lit., "and it was counted to him as righteousness." In lieu of a fully righteous life, God counted (or reckoned) Abraham's faith as righteousness (cf. Moo 1996:262: "the 'reckoning' of Abraham's faith as righteousness means 'to account to him a righteousness that does not inherently belong to him.'"). The same verb, "count," occurs in 4:8 (cf. note).

4:4 *When people work, their wages are not a gift, but something they have earned.* In 4:4-5 Paul draws a contrast between two different ways of thinking about how to be made right with God. If salvation is understood as "wages for work," one may seek to achieve it by obeying the law of Moses; if it is understood as a sheer gift of mercy, we must simply trust God for it. Paul's point is that salvation is given only to those who rely upon God's mercy for it.

4:5 *because of their faith in God who forgives sinners.* Lit., "to the one who believes in the one who makes the ungodly righteous." Many Jews were bound to be offended by Paul speaking of the ungodly being declared righteous because in traditional Jewish thinking, God's blessings were for the genuinely righteous, not the ungodly.

4:7 *Oh, what joy for those whose disobedience is forgiven, whose sins are put out of sight.* In 4:7-8, a quotation from Ps 32[31]:1-2, LXX, Paul shows that being justified or declared righteous (4:6, 9) is simply another way of talking about being forgiven. There is no significant difference between "disobedience" and "sins"; the three parallel relative clauses are essentially synonymous and simply reinforce each other.

4:8 *whose record the LORD has cleared of sin.* Lit., "against whom the LORD will not count (*logisētai* [TG3049A, ZG3357]) sin." The same verb, "count" (credit, reckon), occurs in both of the texts cited in 4:3 and 4:8 (Gen 15:6 and Ps 32:2). The occurrence of the same word in two texts was taken by Jewish exegetes of Paul's time as a rationale for interpreting one in light of the other, which Paul does here (Bruce 1985:107). In this case, the ideas in the two verses are similar: justification is virtually synonymous with forgiveness. Having one's faith counted as righteousness means not having one's sins counted against oneself.

4:10 *Clearly, God accepted Abraham before he was circumcised!* Abraham was declared righteous in Gen 15:6; the account of his circumcision occurs later, in Gen 17:23-27.

4:11 *Circumcision was a sign that Abraham already had faith and that God had already accepted him and declared him to be righteous—even before he was circumcised.* Here Paul interprets the significance of Abraham's circumcision (Gen 17:9-14, 23-27) in light of the earlier declaration of his righteousness (Gen 15:6). Circumcision was the outward and visible "sign" (*sēmeion* [TG4592, ZG4956]) and "attestation" (*sphragida* [TG4973, ZG5381]) of the righteousness already granted him by God because of his faith.

So Abraham is the spiritual father of those who have faith but have not been circumcised. The NLT adds the word "spiritual" for clarity. Paul saw a divine purpose in the ordering of circumcision in Abraham's life: so that Abraham could be a key person in God's program for both Jews and Gentiles—all those who live trusting in God's promises. Some mss (ℵ² C D F G 𝔐) add "also" after "father," but superior documentation (ℵ* A B 1739) affirms its exclusion in the original.

4:12 *if they have the same kind of faith Abraham had.* Lit., "if they follow in the footsteps of Abraham's faith." The reference is to Jewish Christians, Jews who have faith in Jesus.

4:13 *God's promise to give the whole earth to Abraham and his descendants.* Though nowhere found in the OT itself, the idea of Abraham and his descendants inheriting the whole earth was a commonly accepted Jewish interpretation of the promises God made to Abraham in Genesis (cf. Gen 12:2-3, 7; 13:14-17; 15:5, 7, 18-21; 17:4-6, 8; 18:18; 22:17-18)—the promises that he would be the father of many nations, that he would inherit the land, and that all nations would be blessed through him.

was based not on his obedience to God's law. Lit., "[it was] not through law." In the context of Rom 1–8, this must be interpreted as a reference to the law of Moses, not to the general principle of law (as in Sanday and Headlam, Murray). The law was not formally given to the Israelites until the time of Moses, more than 400 years later (Exod 20:1ff).

but on a right relationship with God that comes by faith. Lit., "but through the righteousness of faith" (*dia dikaiosunēs pisteōs* [TG1341/4102, ZG1466/4411])—that is, because Abraham trusted God and was therefore declared righteous (Gen 15:6).

4:14 *God's promise.* The promise referred to in 4:13.

faith is not necessary and the promise is pointless. Lit., "faith is invalidated (*kekenōtai* [TG2758, ZG3033]) and the promise is nullified (*katērgētai* [TG2673A, ZG2934])." If God's blessings are given on the basis of obedience to the law, then trusting him counts for nothing and God's promise of undeserved grace is rendered invalid.

4:15 *For the law always brings punishment on those who try to obey it.* Lit., "for the law works wrath." Attempts to follow the law inevitably lead to failure. Far from bringing a person to God (the common understanding of the law's function), such attempts instead bring about the awareness of transgression and guilt before the judgment of God—a point Paul expands on elsewhere (3:20; 5:20; 7:7-13; Gal 3:19). "Its actual effect . . . is to bring God's wrath upon them by turning their sin into conscious transgression and so rendering it more exceeding sinful" (Cranfield 1980:241).

The only way to avoid breaking the law is to have no law to break! Lit., "where there is no law, neither is there violation." One cannot technically speak of "violations" if there is no law to violate. Not only this sentence (as in the NLT) but the entire verse may be taken as a parenthesis (Fitzmyer 1993:385).

4:16 *So the promise is received by faith. It is given as a free gift.* Lit., "Because of this, [it is] by faith (*ek pisteōs* [TG4102, ZG4411]) in order that [it might be] by grace (*kata charin* [TG5485, ZG5921])." The unspecified subject could be the promise of 4:13 or the promise of salvation more generally.

if we have faith like Abraham's. If we trust in God like Abraham did.

Abraham is the father of all who believe. This is a restatement of 4:11-12.

4:17 *I have made you the father of many nations.* A parenthetical quotation from Gen 17:5, LXX, where these words represent the meaning of the name Abraham. "In Genesis these [many nations] are his descendants through Isaac (the Israelites and Edomites), together with the twelve tribes of the Ishmaelites (Gen 25:12-18) and his descendants by

Keturah (Gen 25:2-4). For Paul they are the multiplicity of Jewish and Gentile believers" (Bruce 1985:112). The quotation confirms the immediately preceding statement in 4:16.

This happened because Abraham believed in the God. Lit., "in the presence of the God in whom he believed." This is an awkward phrase in the Gr., probably intended to connect with 4:16b (cf. NASB, where 4:17a is a parenthetical statement), pointing out that Abraham is the father of us all *in God's sight*. Alternatively, if the phrase is intended to connect with 4:16a, it would speak of the promise being confirmed *in God's sight* to all Abraham's descendants (cf. ESV).

who brings the dead back to life. Abraham's body and Sarah's womb are both spoken of as "dead" in 4:19.

and who creates new things out of nothing. This serves as an introduction for the verses that follow, which speak about Abraham's trusting response in his old age to God's promise that he would be given a son and, through that son, countless descendants.

4:18 *Even when there was no reason for hope.* Other renderings include "against all hope" (NIV); "hoping against hope" (NRSV, NAB); "when hope seemed hopeless" (REB); "and when it all seemed hopeless" (CEV).

That's how many descendents you will have! This is a quotation from Gen 15:5, part of God's promise to Abraham.

4:19 *And Abraham's faith did not weaken.* Cf. 4:20: "Abraham never wavered in believing God's promise." What is reflected in Paul's characterization here is the idealized Abraham of later Jewish tradition, the model of faith and obedience—not the more fallible Abraham of Gen 17:17.

even though . . . he figured his body was as good as dead—and so was Sarah's womb. This is the reading of the best mss (א A B C 1739). Inferior mss (D F G 𝔐) read, "He did not figure his body as good as dead." This alteration is a scribal attempt to show that Abraham believed that his body could produce seed for conception. The point of the text is that Abraham knew that his body was incapable to do so and thus had to trust God for a miracle. Both Abraham and Sarah were well beyond childbearing years when God promised them a son, and Sarah had long been considered barren. When their son Isaac was born, Abraham was 100 years old and Sarah 90 (Gen 17:17).

4:20 *Abraham never wavered in believing God's promise.* Cf. note on 4:19; cf. Gen 17:17.

his faith grew stronger. Or, "his faith filled him with power"; or, "he was empowered by faith" (NAB).

in this he brought glory to God—that is, by trusting him to do the impossible.

4:22 *God counted him as righteous.* Lit., "it was credited to him for righteousness" (*elogisthē autō eis dikaiosunēn* [TG3049/1343, ZG3357/1466]).

4:25 *He was handed over to die because of our sins.* The NLT adds the words "to die" for clarity. "Because of" here is the Gr. *dia* [TG1223, ZG1328] (cf. the next clause).

and he was raised to life to make us right with God. Lit., "and he was raised for our justification" (*dia tēn dikaiōsin* [TG1347, ZG1470] *hēmōn*). Here *dia* is prospective ("for the sake of"), not retrospective ("because of") as in the first clause. These two clauses are possibly taken from an early traditional theological formulation, clearly shaped by Isa 52:13–53:12 (note the parallels with Isa 53:5, 8, 10-12 especially). No sharp distinction is to be made between the functions of the death and resurrection of Christ; elsewhere it is the sacrificial death of Christ that is said to make us right with God (3:24-26; 5:9). The two are part of a single saving event; together they bring us forgiveness and right standing with God.

COMMENTARY

Having stated the heart of the Good News—that we are saved by faith in Christ alone, not by obedience to the law of Moses—Paul now sets out to show that the principle of salvation by faith lies at the heart of the law itself. Drawing on a key text from the law of Moses (Gen 15:6), Paul points out that even venerable father Abraham was considered righteous because of his faith, not because of any works he did. The principle is further corroborated by the greatest of all the Israelite kings, David himself, who speaks of the joy of undeserving sinners who, only because of God's mercy, are declared righteous by God and forgiven (Ps 32:1-2). In Abraham's case, the fact that he was pronounced righteous long before he was circumcised shows that circumcision is not a factor in salvation. This fact means salvation is open to everyone who believes—Gentiles as well as Jews. Thus, to insist that salvation is only for those who obey the law of Moses is to deny the fundamental truth that we are saved by faith and not by our observance of the law. In traditional Jewish thinking, Abraham's life stood as a rich testimony to his faith: he trusted God's promises with unwavering confidence, even when their fulfillment seemed impossible, and that's why God declared him righteous. But this gracious declaration wasn't just for Abraham's sake; it is also for us, to show us that we, too, can be declared righteous if we believe in the one who miraculously raised our Lord Jesus from the dead. It is by our faith that we are made right with God.

Even Abraham Was Saved by Faith. At the very end of the preceding chapter, Paul posed the question of whether the Good News—with its emphasis on salvation by faith alone, quite apart from obedience to the law of Moses—doesn't in reality deny the basic tenets of the law (3:31). Having refuted this charge, Paul supports his refutation by appealing to a crucial text from the law itself: "Abraham believed God, and God counted him as righteous because of his faith" (4:3; cf. Gen 15:6), a text he also cites in his letter to the Galatians (Gal 3:6). Here, from the Mosaic law itself, Paul validates the doctrine of justification by faith. Even the great father Abraham was saved by his faith, not by his "works" (as good as they were—for God himself said of Abraham, "[He] obeyed all my requirements, commands, decrees, and instructions," Gen 26:5).

With great insight, Paul puts his finger on a commonly overlooked theme that runs throughout the Hebrew Scriptures—namely, that God accepts those who put their trust in him and blesses people according to their faith in him. To trust in God is to know and rely on his character—his heart of forgiving love. God delights in those who trust in his grace and the kindness of his heart. To fail to trust in God, however, is to refuse to accept him for who he claims to be. Our relationship to God, then, is defined essentially by our trust in him, based on our understanding of his character—not by our observance of his law. God wants us to come to know and trust his mercy. (Compare Jesus' response to the disciples' question about what kind of "work" God wanted them to do: "This is the only work God wants from you: Believe in the one he has sent," John 6:29.) "Faith," said Luther (1954:xv), "is a living, daring confidence in God's grace"—and for believers that must be a daily experience. Our faith in God's grace must be kept vital and fresh; it must always be real, not merely formal. In the rest of the chapter, Paul gives a full exposition of the principle of justification by faith based on the text that speaks of Abraham believing God (4:3; cf. Gen 15:6).

The Contrast between Faith and Works. In order to appreciate Paul's perspective on justification, we need to understand that there are two fundamentally different ways to think of approaching God and that God recognizes only one as valid. We can either come to him as people striving to be "good," relying on what we have done to earn his favor, or we can come to him as sinners, simply trusting in his forgiving grace. Throughout Romans 4, a sharp contrast is drawn between the two. The traditional Jewish understanding of righteousness, based on observance of the law and the concept of "wages for work," is the antithesis of God's way of faith (4:4-5). It reflects an inadequate view both of human sin and of the holiness of God. By contrast, the understanding of righteousness proclaimed in the Good News, based on simple trust in Christ, depends wholly on God's mercy and the gift of his grace. The only way we can be made right with God is to throw ourselves—just as we are, with all of our sins—on the unfailing mercy and love of God and to accept with gratitude and trust the forgiveness he promises us in Christ. Salvation lies not in a desperate, hopeless attempt to win God's approval by observing his law but in the humble, penitent acceptance of the love and grace that he offers in the gift of his Son. Given the holiness of God and the imperfections of human beings, we simply cannot rely on the idea of merit to be put right with God. The point is well expressed in the words of the hymn "Rock of Ages, Cleft for Me":

> Not the labors of my hands,
> Can fulfill Thy law's demands;
> Could my zeal no respite know,
> Could my tears forever flow,
> All for sin could not atone;
> Thou must save, and Thou alone.
>
> Nothing in my hand I bring,
> Simply to Thy cross I cling;
> Naked, come to Thee for dress,
> Helpless, look to Thee for grace;
> Foul, I to the fountain fly;
> Wash me, Savior, or I die.

In contrast to the popular way of thinking, then, it is not the person who strives to be good who ends up being considered good by God. Rather, it is the person who acknowledges that he or she is not good and simply comes to God to receive freely the gift of righteousness (forgiveness) that defines a person as "good." Saving righteousness must always be viewed as a sheer, undeserved gift of God.

Paul's reference to God as one who "justifies the ungodly" (4:5, NRSV) would have been both shocking and offensive to many Jews, who would have understood it as contradicting several specific texts in the law of Moses. For example, in Exodus God says, "I never declare a guilty person to be innocent" (Exod 23:7)—which might well be translated, "I will not justify the ungodly." Here, in the Greek version, the very terms the law uses to express what God *refuses* to do (justify the ungodly) are the exact terms Paul uses to express what God *promises* to do! No wonder, then, that Paul finds it necessary to defend the personal integrity of God for forgiving those who are guilty: "God was being fair when he held back and did not punish those who sinned. . . . He himself is fair and just, and he declares sinners to be right in his sight when they believe in Jesus" (3:25-26; cf. Luke 18:9-14; Bruce 1985:106-107). The shocking nature of the reference to God as one who "justifies the ungodly" should be understood in light of just how serious a matter ungodliness is in the law of Moses (cf. Gen 6:5-8; Exod 23:7; Deut 9:4-5). The key to the dilemma, of course, lies in Paul's statement, "Christ died for the ungodly" (5:6, NRSV). It's because of the sacrificial death of Christ that sinners can be forgiven and the ungodly clothed with the righteousness of Christ himself.

If we are saved by faith alone, then what is the role of works in a Christian's life? It all depends on what one means by "works." If by "works" we mean the legalistic observance of certain rituals in the Mosaic law, the answer is "none" because these have absolutely no bearing on one's relationship to God. But if by "works" we mean good deeds and a life of integrity, goodness, and love, these—though they do not save us— are the natural outcome and intended result of a person's faith. ("For by grace you have been saved through faith, and this is not your own doing; it is the gift of God— not the result of works," Paul emphasizes—but then immediately adds, "We are . . . created in Christ Jesus for good works, which God prepared beforehand to be our way of life," Eph 2:8-10 NRSV.) Part of God's purpose in saving us is to produce a people for himself who are utterly devoted to living a good life (Titus 2:14). A true Christian lifestyle is also what validates a person's claim to saving faith, the evidence that one's faith is real. If someone claims to be a Christian but doesn't show it by how he or she lives, questions are inevitably raised about the reality of the person's faith. True faith is always life-transforming faith, resulting in a life of good deeds.

The Assurance of God's Forgiveness. The point Paul was making—that we are saved by faith, not by works—is further validated by Psalm 32:1-2, 5. In this psalm, great King David himself speaks of the joy of undeserving sinners whom God, in his mercy, declares righteous (4:4-8). Here again the Old Testament Scripture shows that a relationship with God is defined by God's grace, not by the work people do. The psalm from which the text is quoted leaves the impression that a person's acquittal is the result solely of his acknowledging his guilt and throwing himself on the mercy of God, trusting his forgiving grace alone. Paul's appeal to this text on forgiveness shows that, in his thinking, justification is virtually synonymous with forgiveness. Justification and forgiveness are two different ways of talking about the same experience.

When Paul spoke of the unmitigated joy of those who are forgiven, he was reflecting his conviction that forgiveness is something believers can be sure of, not something they vaguely hope for with uncertainty. Throughout the New Testament, a restored relationship with God (whether described in terms of "forgiveness," "justification," or "reconciliation") is spoken of as something Christians can be sure of, for it is as sure as the promises of God. The early Christians *knew* they were forgiven people and proclaimed it joyfully (cf. Heb 10:22; 1 John 1:9). Assurance of God's forgiving grace is one of the great gifts of the Good News for believers. The writer of 1 John emphasizes, "I have written this to you who believe in the name of the Son of God, so that you may know you have eternal life" (1 John 5:13). Thus, the book of Hebrews, with its emphasis on the once-for-all nature of the sacrifice of Christ, a sacrifice that has "forever made perfect" those who belong to him (Heb 10:14), encourages Christians to come "boldly" into the presence of God (Heb 4:16; 10:19), "with sincere hearts fully trusting him . . . without wavering" (Heb 10:22-23). In the same way, Paul speaks of believers' salvation as something that has already been accomplished, something believers may boldly claim as their own—not because of anything they merit in themselves, but because of the sure efficacy of Christ's death on the cross. True saving faith in Christ brings with it, then, the confident assurance of one's salvation; the lack of assurance may raise questions about the reality of one's faith.

The saving grace of God should never become mundane to us; it must always be understood as *amazing* grace—absolutely undeserved, a sheer gift of God's mercy. Grace ceases to be understood for what it is when it is no longer amazing—if it is simply taken for granted or viewed as just another Christian doctrine. We must never lose the wonder of it all or the sense of joy it is intended to evoke. In the words of Paul's quotation from Psalm 32:1-2, LXX, "Oh, what joy for those whose disobedience is forgiven, whose sins are put out of sight. Yes, what joy for those whose record the LORD has cleared of sin" (4:7-8)—and both statements properly ought to end with an exclamation point!

In this chapter, then, Paul draws on texts from both the law (4:3; cf. Gen 15:6) and the writings (4:7-8; Ps 32:1-2), just as earlier he drew on a text from the prophets (1:17; cf. Hab 2:4), to show that all three parts of the Hebrew Bible—the law, the prophets, and the writings—validate the principle of salvation by faith. So the Good News of Christ does not contradict the Old Testament Scriptures in its understanding of how one relates to God; both teach that it is by faith that we are saved.

Salvation Does Not Require Circumcision. In promoting the principle of justification by faith, Paul needed to make it clear that salvation is not dependent on circumcision. He knew that others could argue that the practice of circumcision was instituted by God, that the law of Moses defines it as the mark of one who belongs to God and has been accepted by God (Gen 17:9-14). (Traditionally, Gentiles were allowed into the community of God's people only if they agreed to be circumcised and baptized as converts and to submit to the ceremonial obligations of the law of Moses; Schreiner 1986:1009-1010.) To these traditional Jewish objections, Paul responded by pointing out that even in the case of father Abraham, circumcision was not the defining factor. For God's acceptance of Abraham took place before—

at least fourteen years before—not after, his circumcision (cf. Gen 15:6 with Gen 17:9-12, 23-27). So God's acceptance of a person is not dependent on circumcision but on a person's faith alone (4:9-12). A relationship with God is defined not by circumcision but by one's faith. Circumcision is simply a formal sign of the relationship to God that one already has by faith. "Real" circumcision, Paul emphasizes, is not literal circumcision but circumcision of the heart (2:29)—the mark of the transforming work of the Holy Spirit that accompanies genuine faith. A relationship with God is never established by external things but by real trust in God and the converting work of God's Spirit in a person's heart. (This has important implications for those who would draw a parallel between Jewish circumcision and Christian baptism. The physical act of baptism is no more effective than the physical mark of circumcision in establishing a relationship with God if it is not accompanied by a life-changing faith on a deeper level; cf. comments on 2:28-29.) Thus, Abraham is not the father of the Jews exclusively but the father of all who truly trust in God, whether they be Jews or Gentiles, circumcised or uncircumcised.

Salvation Does Not Require Obedience to the Law. But what of the promise God made to Abraham—the promise that the whole world would belong to him? This was a traditional Jewish interpretation of the promises God made to Abraham in Genesis (Gen 12:2-3, 7; 13:14-17; 15:5, 7, 18-21; 17:4-8; 18:18; 22:17-18)—the promises that he would be the father of many nations, that he would inherit the land, and that all nations would be blessed through him. Was this not dependent on Abraham's keeping the law? No, Paul argues, it could not have been dependent on his keeping the law or else the biblical principle of justification by faith would be meaningless and the promise of God's undeserved grace pointless; grace, by definition, could not be dependent on works (4:13-15). As Paul argues in his letter to the Galatians, the law came about long after the promise was made—430 years after, according to Galatians 3:17—and could in no way limit or invalidate the earlier promise. So God's promises and grace are not just for those who keep the law but for all who have true faith—Gentiles as well as Jews. God's promise is a sheer gift of grace. (See Gal 3:15-18 for a similar argument about the priority of God's promise over the law.)[1]

In any case, Paul argues, the law of God is not something that brings God's blessing on those who obey it. Instead, it brings God's punishment on those who disobey it (4:15), as all people inevitably do. Contrary to popular understanding, the function of God's law is not so much to instruct people in the way of righteousness as to convict people of their unrighteousness—to show them their failings, to make them aware of how far they fall short of God's demands—and so reveal to them how much they need God's forgiving grace (3:20). That's why people cannot rely on their observance of the law to gain God's approval. The first step in coming to God is to realize how far away we are from him—to become aware of the magnitude and dreadfulness of our sin, of the fearful reality of God's judgment on us, of our desperate need of God's saving grace. In this, the law of God serves a very useful role in reminding us of the high standards of the Holy One and of how far we fall short of his expectations. That's why the message of salvation by simple faith in God's grace is such good news.

Salvation, then, cannot be understood as dependent on a person's obedience to the law of Moses, but only as dependent on a person's faith—just as Abraham received the promise of God solely on the basis of his faith (4:16-22). And what is true faith? Faith is the ability to trust God to do the seemingly impossible—just as Abraham, almost 100 years old, with an 87-year-old wife who was unable to bear children, was able to trust God to give him a son, as God had promised. As Hebrews 11:1 says, "Faith is the confidence that what we hope for will actually happen; it gives us assurance about things we cannot see." Although he was as good as dead, Abraham's eyes were fixed on the power of God, not on the impotence of his own body or the sterility of his aged wife. He reckoned that the certainty of God's promise counted for more than any human improbability. He had confidence in God in spite of the circumstances (4:19-21). He believed in "the God who brings the dead [in this case, Abraham's body and Sarah's womb] back to life and who creates new things [a son, and all the descendants to follow] out of nothing" (4:17). In the same way, Christians put their faith in the God of the seemingly impossible, the God who raised the Lord Jesus from death (4:24). Such bold faith brings glory to God and results in God declaring those who trust him to be righteous.

Belief in the seemingly impossible event of the Resurrection is spoken of in Paul's letters as the expression of true faith (10:9; cf. 1 Thess 4:14). In this passage, Paul speaks of the Resurrection in particular as that which effects our justification: the Crucifixion effects our atonement; the Resurrection, our justification (4:25). Elsewhere, Paul speaks of the Crucifixion as that which effects our justification and the Resurrection as that which guarantees our full salvation because of Jesus' life and work for us now (5:9-11). The fluidity of the concepts shows that the Crucifixion and Resurrection merge together in Paul's thought as the great saving event and that everything else flows from that. Belief in the Crucifixion and the Resurrection—and in what they represent theologically—lies at the very heart of Christian faith.

Is Paul's Message Different from that of Jesus? In conclusion, I should note that various scholars have raised the question of whether Paul, in emphasizing the principle of salvation by faith in Christ apart from human efforts, is teaching something fundamentally different from what Jesus taught. Is Paul's Good News really the same as the Good News of Jesus? The differences are more apparent than real. The Pauline theme of God's forgiving grace for unworthy sinners is a dominant one in the Gospels, too. In Luke's Gospel, there are two passages especially that speak of God's delight in forgiving the unworthy. In the story of the Lost Son (Luke 15:11-32), God's mercy is portrayed in the warm and welcoming response of the forgiving father to the undeserving son. In the story of the Pharisee and the Tax Collector (Luke 18:9-14), God's approval is given not to the proud Pharisee parading his good deeds but to the undeserving tax collector, whose only words are "O God, be merciful to me, for I am a sinner" (Luke 18:13). Jesus' comment, "I tell you, this sinner, not the Pharisee, returned home justified before God," shows the importance in his thinking of a simple reliance on God's forgiving grace (Luke 18:14). Jesus' concern for sinners is also reflected in the way his enemies spoke of him as "a friend of tax collectors and other sinners" (Matt 11:19). When criticized for keeping such company, he responded, "I have come to call not those who think they are righteous, but those who know they are sinners" (Matt 9:13). Indeed, Jesus said, "There is more joy in heaven over one lost sinner who repents and returns to God than over ninety-nine others who are righteous and haven't strayed away" (Luke 15:7). At the heart of Jesus' ministry lay the message of God's forgiveness for sinners who turn to him; and it is this message of repentance and forgiveness that his disciples were to proclaim to the world: "There is forgiveness of sins for all who repent" (Luke 24:47). Notice the close parallels: the Gospels speak of the need for repentance—a turnaround of one's life, a reorientation toward God—in order to receive forgiveness; Paul speaks of the need for faith—a personal trust in Christ—in order to be made right with God. A moment's reflection will reveal how close the ideas are—repentance and faith, forgiveness and justification. Though the language is different, the underlying convictions are similar. The teachings of both Jesus and Paul reflect the assumption that human righteousness per se is an inadequate basis for a relationship with the Holy One. Both share the conviction that when it comes to being accepted by God, we are always dependent on God's forgiving grace alone. On this most basic point, the perspectives of Jesus and Paul are in fundamental agreement, not in conflict.

Further, careful comparison of the Gospels and Paul's letters shows that Jesus placed as much emphasis on faith as Paul did. On numerous occasions in the synoptic Gospels, Jesus especially commends people whose faith in him is strong: "I haven't seen faith like this in all Israel!" (Matt 8:10). "Your faith has made you well" (Matt 9:22). "Because of your faith, it will happen" (Matt 9:29). "Your faith is great. Your request is granted" (Matt 15:28). On other occasions, he clearly rebuked the disciples because of their lack of faith: "Why are you afraid? You have so little faith!" (Matt 8:26). "You have so little faith. . . . Why did you doubt me?" (Matt 14:31). "You don't have enough faith" (Matt 17:20). The Gospel of John is even stronger in its emphasis on the importance of personal faith—the word "believe" occurs almost 100 times—though the focus is somewhat different from that of the synoptic Gospels. Here again, we see that the perspectives of Jesus and Paul are not in fundamental conflict.[2]

ENDNOTES

1. Perhaps it is worth noting that the land promised to Abraham and his descendants in the Old Testament included everything between the border of Egypt and the Euphrates River (Gen 15:18). In the New Testament, however, where the ultimate fulfillment of the Old Testament promises is often understood in a spiritual and not a literal way, and this world is no longer considered the believers' home, there is no emphasis on the promise of literal land for ethnic Israel. The focus has shifted instead to the promise of a heavenly home for God's "new Israel," the people of Christ. Hence, the book of Hebrews speaks of God's people seeking no literal Canaan but "a better

place, a heavenly homeland" (Heb 11:16); "For this world is not our permanent home; we are looking forward to a home yet to come" (Heb 13:14; cf. the eschatological nature of Jesus' promises in the Beatitudes, Matt 5:3-10). In the New Testament, the focus has shifted away from the promise of literal land for ethnic Israel, to the promise of salvation for all God's children, whatever their ethnicity (see comments on 11:25-32).

2. For further comparison of the teaching of Paul and Jesus, see Wenham 1995.

3. The results of saving faith (5:1-11)

Therefore, since we have been made right in God's sight by faith, we have peace with God because of what Jesus Christ our Lord has done for us. ²Because of our faith, Christ has brought us into this place of undeserved privilege where we now stand, and we confidently and joyfully look forward to sharing God's glory.

³We can rejoice, too, when we run into problems and trials, for we know that they help us develop endurance. ⁴And endurance develops strength of character, and character strengthens our confident hope of salvation. ⁵And this hope will not lead to disappointment. For we know how dearly God loves us, because he has given us the Holy Spirit to fill our hearts with his love. ⁶When we were utterly helpless, Christ came at just the right time and died for us sinners. ⁷Now, most people would not be willing to die for an upright person, though someone might perhaps be willing to die for a person who is especially good. ⁸But God showed his great love for us by sending Christ to die for us while we were still sinners. ⁹And since we have been made right in God's sight by the blood of Christ, he will certainly save us from God's condemnation. ¹⁰For since our friendship with God was restored by the death of his Son while we were still his enemies, we will certainly be saved through the life of his Son. ¹¹So now we can rejoice in our wonderful new relationship with God because our Lord Jesus Christ has made us friends of God.

NOTES

5:1 *we have peace with God.* Human beings, by nature enemies of God standing under the judgment of God because of their sin (1:18–3:20; Eph 2:1-3, 12), become God's friends when they put their trust in Christ. The ancient mss are divided as to whether the verb is an indicative, *echomen* [TG2192, ZG2400] ("we have [peace]"; א¹ B² F G P Ψ), or a subjunctive, *echōmen* ("let us have [peace]"; א* A B* C D K L). Most interpreters favor the former.

5:2 *Because of our faith.* Lit., "by faith." Though this phrase is not included in a few important mss (B D F G 0220), it probably reflects the original text. Later copyists may have judged the phrase as unnecessary because 5:1 has already made it clear that justification is by faith.

Christ has brought us into this place of undeserved privilege where we now stand. Lit., "through whom [i.e., Christ] we have gained access to this grace in which we stand." This is a reference to the experience of God's gracious forgiveness and salvation for those who trust in Christ.

and we confidently and joyfully look forward to sharing God's glory. Lit., "and we boast in the hope of the glory of God." Here, *kauchōmetha* [TG2744, ZG3016] (boast) could also be translated "let us boast." In either case, it is better to understand "boast" as "rejoice" (cf. 5:3). Paul is not speaking of gloating but rather of joyful exaltation. The biblical term "hope" (*elpis* [TG1680, ZG1828]) expresses not the uncertainty of a wish but strong confidence and expectation; it is usually eschatological in its orientation—it anticipates the coming of Christ and the life beyond (see commentary below). "God's glory" in this context is best taken as a reference to the eternal blessedness of being with God forever, experiencing his life and goodness in all its fullness. It refers to "that illumination of man's whole being by the radiance of the divine glory which is man's true destiny but which was lost through sin, as it will be restored (not just as it was, but immeasurably enriched through God's own personal participation in man's humanity in Jesus Christ—cf. 8:17), when man's redemption is finally consummated at the parousia of Jesus Christ" (Cranfield 1980:260).

5:3 *We can rejoice, too, when we run into problems and trials.* Lit., "and not only, but we also boast (*kauchōmetha*, [TG2744, ZG3016], which, as in 5:2, could also be translated "let us boast") in troubles."

for we know that they help us develop endurance. For the importance of patient endurance and perseverance (*hupomonē* [TG5281, ZG5705G]), see 2:7; 8:25; 15:4-5.

5:4 *strength of character.* Or, "proven character" (*dokimēn* [TG1382, ZG1509]; NAB), "tested character" (NJB), "approval" (REB). Cf. Jas 1:2-4: "When troubles come your way, consider it an opportunity for great joy. For you know that when your faith is tested, your endurance has a chance to grow. So let it grow, for when your endurance is fully developed, you will be perfect and complete, needing nothing."

and character strengthens our confident hope of salvation. Lit., "and [tested] character (*dokimē* [TG1382, ZG1509]) [produces] hope" (*elpis* [TG1680, ZG1828]; cf. note on 5:2). To have our faith tested and proved in the fire of difficulties strengthens our anticipation of what lies beyond this life.

5:5 *And this hope will not lead to disappointment.* Lit., "and hope does not disappoint" (*kataischunei* [TG2617, ZG2875]). The same verb occurs as "will not be disgraced" (*kataischunthēsetai*) in 9:33 and 10:11. We can be sure that our confidence in what lies beyond this life will not be disappointed because we know the reality of God's love for us experientially.

For we know how dearly God loves us, because he has given us the Holy Spirit to fill our hearts with his love. Lit., "because the love of God has been poured out in our hearts through the Holy Spirit given to us." "The love of God" (*hē agapē tou theou* [TG26, ZG27]), a phrase that may refer either to our love for God or God's love for us, here refers to the Spirit-given certainty of God's love for us, expressed in Christ's dying for us while we were still sinners. This love assures us that our hope is well founded (5:8).

5:6 *When we were utterly helpless.* Lit., "[being] weak" (*asthenōn* [TG772, ZG822])—i.e., unable to help ourselves.

just the right time. God's appointed time (*kata kairon* [TG2540, ZG2789]). Cf. Gal 4:4; Mark 1:15.

died for us sinners. Lit., "died for the ungodly." Cf. note on 5:8.

5:7 *an upright person . . . a person who is especially good.* Lit., "a righteous one" (*dikaiou* [TG1342A, ZG1465]) . . . "a good one" (*tou agathou* [TG18A, ZG19]). Grammatically, these terms may be either masculine or neuter. Some, like the NLT, interpret these terms as largely synonymous references to good persons, with the second clarifying the first. Others see a distinction in meaning intended, with the second contrasting with the first—though the distinction is understood in different ways: (1) "a just cause" versus "the public good" (understanding both terms as neuter—a less likely interpretation); (2) "a righteous person" (masculine) versus "a good thing" (neuter); (3) a "righteous person" versus "his benefactor" (understanding both terms as masculine). None of these contrasts fits the context as well as the NLT translation. In any case, the overall point is clear: it is rare for anyone to be willing to sacrifice his life for someone else, even for someone who is worthy—though, Paul adds, a few people might go so far as to do so (cf. 1 John 4:9-10).

5:8 But God showed his great love for us by sending Christ to die for us while we were still sinners. This is why the "ungodly"—if they put their trust in Christ's sacrifice—can now be considered righteous (see note on 4:5).

5:9 by the blood of Christ. By the sacrificial death of Christ (cf. 3:25). In the NT, "blood" usually refers to the death of a sacrifice for sins.

he will certainly save us from God's condemnation. Lit., "we shall be saved through him from the wrath" (cf. 1:18; 12:19). In 1 Thess 1:10 Paul speaks of Jesus as "the one who has rescued us from the terrors of the coming judgment [wrath]." Those who have been made right with God through their trust in Christ can rest assured that they will be safe on the day of wrath.

5:10 our friendship with God was restored. Lit., "we were reconciled (*katēllagēmen* [TG2644, ZG2904]) to God."

we will certainly be saved through the life of his Son. Here the focus is again on the Resurrection as part of the great saving event. If, through the death of Christ, God was merciful to us when we were his enemies, how much more, through the resurrected life of Christ, will he care for us—now that we are his friends?

COMMENTARY

In this section, Paul reflects on the various benefits we receive as a result of our salvation in Christ. Salvation brings us, above all, peace with God, and with it come the full experience of his blessing and grace, as well as the joyful anticipation of one day sharing fully in his glory. In the meantime, we have the joy of knowing that all things—even the difficult experiences of life—work for our good. Difficult times develop endurance and strength of character, making us people whose eyes are fixed confidently and expectantly on that future day when the full experience of salvation will be ours. Our confidence in the future is based on the certainty of God's love for us; his love fills our hearts as a result of the Spirit's work within us.

The supreme manifestation of God's love is the Cross itself. God loved us so much that he sent his own Son to die for us when we were still ungodly to make us right with himself. If he did that when we were still his enemies, how much more will he do for us now that we are his friends! We can rejoice because of all that God has done for us in Jesus Christ.

Peace with God. The first benefit of salvation is that we have peace with God (5:1). Alienated from God because of our sin, we all stand under his holy judgment. By nature God's "enemies" (5:10), "separated from him by [our] evil thoughts and actions" (Col 1:21), we were all "dead because of [our] disobedience and [our] many sins. . . . subject to God's anger, just like everyone else" (Eph 2:1-3). It is only Christ's sacrifice for sin that makes reconciliation with God possible, and it is our faith in that sacrifice that makes it effective for us individually. As one who has been given the task of reconciling people to God, Paul appealed to his readers, "We entreat you on behalf of Christ, be reconciled to God" (2 Cor 5:20, NRSV). The ministry of the Good News is a ministry of reconciliation.

However, it is important to note that when Paul speaks of reconciliation, he is speaking primarily about being reconciled to God. Today, when Christians speak of reconciliation, the focus is often on the social dimension of reconciliation—ethnic or racial reconciliation, or the reconciliation of family members to one another, for example. Though there are clear social implications in the emphasis on reconciliation in the Good News (14:1–15:13; Eph 2:11–3:6), the greatest need is always for reconciliation with God, and this is the primary focus of Paul's Good News of reconciliation.

Peace with God can easily be taken for granted by those who come to know personally the forgiving grace of God; we quickly grow accustomed to our privileged status as God's friends. For that reason we must constantly remind ourselves of God's anger and judgment upon all that is unholy and never forget that we, like everyone else, were once "subject to God's anger," "without God and without hope" (Eph 2:3, 12), doomed forever because of our sins. Only then will we treasure peace with God for the precious gift it is.

God's Blessing and Grace. The second benefit of salvation is the full experience of God's blessing and grace (5:2). As his forgiven people, we have the indescribable privilege of living day by day in fellowship with God himself as the blessed recipients of his forgiving grace and love. Freed from slavery to sin and the law, we can now delight in the undeserved experience of God's grace. Of all the New Testament writers, it is Paul who waxes most eloquent on the grace of God—who makes the grace of God "sing," just as Luther did centuries later. We live and die, Paul emphasizes, only by the mercy and kindness of God. Everything good that we have and are, both in this life and in the life beyond, is a gift of God's grace. As a result, the Christian life is to be understood not as a heavy, burdensome obligation but as a joyful, free response to God's grace and goodness to us. The Christian ethic, properly conceived, is an "ethic of gratitude"—a way of saying thank you to God for his astounding grace. It is this strong emphasis on grace that makes Paul's depiction of the Christian life so joyful and attractive, especially in the Prison Letters.

As with the peace we have with God, the grace of God must never be taken for granted. We must never forget that God's kindness is wholly undeserved—that we merit nothing but punishment for our sins. When we appreciate grace for what it really is, it will always be understood as genuinely amazing grace—undeserved kindness. Grace is no longer grace if we cease to think of it as amazing. If we are fully to appreciate God's grace for what it is, then, we must never forget the terrible nature of our sin in God's sight and God's holy judgment on it. Grace is perceived as grace only by those who take God's judgment seriously. This is why Paul devoted so much attention to emphasizing the judgment of God on human sin in chapters 1–3; he knew that it is crucial for us to feel the full weight of divine judgment if we are to feel the full greatness of divine grace. In Romans, God's holiness and judgment serve as the backdrop against which the Good News of God's grace is magnificently highlighted.

The Hope of Future Glory. The third benefit of salvation is that we are given the confident and joyful anticipation of one day sharing the full glory of God himself (5:2). "Christ lives in you. This gives you assurance of sharing his glory" (Col 1:27; for "glory," see comments on 3:23; 5:2; 8:18ff). This confident anticipation is what Paul usually means when he uses the word "hope." The Christian's hope is not some ill-defined, vague desire for everything to turn out well; instead, it is a strong confidence, solidly grounded in the promises of Christ and the Scriptures, that everything *shall* turn out well. Further, "hope" for Paul is almost always eschatological hope, expressing not one's desires for this life but the vision of sharing God's glory beyond this life. This strong anticipation of the life beyond is a central element in Paul's theology and ethics. For Paul, faith in Christ always has an eager expectancy about it, a focus on the horizon—an awareness that the "real" life lies in the unseen world beyond, soon to come. As a result, the proper focus of the Christian is not on the visible things of this world, which will soon disappear, but on the invisible things of eternity—the world of God and the glory of the life beyond (2 Cor 4:18). This orientation to the future world is reflected both in the focus of Paul's preaching (salvation in light of the coming day of judgment) and in his sense of priorities for Christian life and ministry.

For many Christians today in the Western world, the comfortable affluence of modern society has resulted in a much greater focus on life in this world—and, with it, a loss of the early Christian emphasis on the joyful anticipation of the life beyond. Just as the modern world has lost a sense of the holiness and judgment of God, it has also lost sight of what lies beyond this life. As a result, for many Christians today, the Christian life has a different shape and feel than it did for Paul; the forward-looking focus and the emphasis on eternal life are less dominant or missing. These elements are also less central in much contemporary preaching of the Good News. The great danger is that, with the change of focus, the heart of the Christian message itself will be subtly changed or differently understood. At the heart of the Good News preached by Paul lies the Christian hope, the promise of eternal life—"eternal comfort and a wonderful hope" (2 Thess 2:16), "salvation and eternal glory" (2 Tim 2:10). The Good News, as Paul proclaimed it, is the truth that gives us "confidence that [we] have eternal life" (Titus 1:2). If we lose our focus on the great Christian hope, we lose something at the very heart of the early Christians' understanding of the Good News. And, as Paul reminds us, "If our hope in Christ is only for this life, we are more to be pitied than anyone in the world" (1 Cor 15:19).

Strength of Character through Suffering. Another outcome of salvation is that it brings with it the assurance that everything we face in this life—even the most difficult experience—works for our ultimate good. The love of God is sufficiently great to take everything that comes our way and use it for God's good purposes in our lives (8:28). Therefore, when problems or difficulties arise, we can rejoice and take heart in knowing that difficulties develop resilience in us—an ability to endure the tough times. (Another problem of an affluent culture is that it inclines us to a soft and comfortable life, leaving us weak and ill-equipped for the demands of trying times.) This resiliency, in turn, develops strength of character and makes us the kind of people God wants us to be (5:3-4; cf. Jas 1:3-4: "When your faith is tested, your endurance has a chance to grow. So let it grow, for when your endurance is fully developed, you will be perfect and complete, needing nothing"). Christians, then, have nothing to fear when difficult times strike. Indeed, as James teaches, we are to find joy in facing difficulties (Jas 1:2). Paul's view of God's love is such that nothing lies beyond its power; God's love is able to take everything that comes our way and turn it into good. Here is a radically different view of life and a thoroughly positive approach to life's problems (cf. comments on 8:31-39).

Suffering, on the whole, was viewed much more positively in the New Testament than it is in the modern Western world. Persecution and suffering were common experiences for the early Christians, and new converts were warned about them in advance (Acts 14:22). Suffering was accepted as a given part of being a Christian. (Cf. Jesus' words, "Since they persecuted me, naturally they will persecute you" John 15:20.) Christians knew that they "must suffer many hardships to enter the Kingdom of God" (Acts 14:22); after all, Jesus himself had told his disciples that they must be prepared to die for him (Mark 8:34-38). Suffering was more than simply inevitable, though; it was understood as something used by God to make his people "worthy of his Kingdom" (2 Thess 1:5). So it is not surprising that suffering for Christ was actually considered a privilege (Acts 5:41; Phil 1:29). This theology of suffering has been rediscovered in the twentieth century by the persecuted church in many parts of the world, where it has suffered—and continues to suffer—under the rule of Communism, Islam, Hinduism, and Buddhism.

The development of endurance and the steadfastness of character deriving from it serve, in turn, to sharpen our focus on the Christian hope—the joyful anticipation of the full experience of salvation in the life to come (5:4). With suffering as the norm for so many of the early Christians, it is not surprising that their focus shifted to the joyful hope of the life beyond. (The same thing happened among Christian slaves in nineteenth-century America and has happened more recently among persecuted Christians in many parts of the world.) This confident expectation of future glory is fueled by the strong conviction of God's love for us—love poured into our hearts by the gift of the Holy Spirit (5:5), by which God gives us a touch of the glory that lies beyond this life. (For the Spirit's role in our lives as believers, see the comments on 7:4-6, 14-25; 8:1-17, 26-30; 12:2; 13:8-10; 15:13; see also "The Holy Spirit" in the Introduction.) So in the midst of our suffering, we who belong to Christ can rest assured that God's blessing is on us, no matter what comes our way, and that the full experience of God's glory will one day be ours—such is the greatness of God's love for his children.

Because we have received such an abundance of grace and experience it continually in our lives, we can be joyful. We are to find joy in the anticipation of the coming glory (5:2), joy in the problems we face here and now (5:3), and joy especially in knowing God himself, the giver of all good gifts (5:11; or, as the psalmist says, "the source of all my joy," Ps 43:4). For Paul, joy—like thanksgiving—is one of the chief characteristics of the Christian life, even in times of suffering. Addressing two suffering churches, Paul wrote: "Always be joyful. . . . Be thankful in all circumstances" (1 Thess 5:16-18); "Always be full of joy in the Lord. . . . and thank him for all he has done" (Phil 4:4-6). In Greek, the words for "joy" (*chara* [TG5479, ZG5915]) and "thanksgiving" (*eucharistia* [TG2169, ZG2374]) are related etymologically to the word for "grace" (*charis* [TG5485, ZG5921]). The three are also related in Paul's theology—joy and thanksgiving are the result of God's grace and represent heartfelt responses to that grace. Because we live by the grace of God in Jesus Christ, it is only appropriate that our lives, in response, be filled with joy and thanksgiving for that grace—even in the midst of our suffering.

The Greatness of God's Love. Reflect, then, on the greatness of this grace—this divine love shown to us in Jesus Christ. Impelled by a love that far transcends the limits of normal human love, Christ came to die for us—not because we were good or righteous, but when we were still ungodly, deserving nothing but the anger and judgment of God. If God loved us enough to do that when we were still sinners, how much more will he do for us, now that we are saints? If, when we were still enemies, God made us his friends through his Son's death, how much more, now that we are his friends, will he save us from eternal judgment by his Son's resurrected life (5:6-11; cf. 8:32)? We are God's friends, and he is our benefactor; even more, we are his children, and he is our Father (8:15-17). Is there anything too great for his concern and care? What incredible joy should be ours over this amazing grace, brought to us by the reconciling death of our Lord Jesus Christ!

The salvation that God gives us in Christ brings us a veritable world of good things. In addition to assuring us that we shall be saved on the day of judgment, it makes God himself our friend, giving us peace with him and the priceless privilege of experiencing his blessings and grace. It also gives us the wonderful anticipation of sharing all his goodness in the life beyond. And in the meantime, it assures us that whatever comes our way, no matter how difficult it is, it will all be used by God for our ultimate good—to shape our character according to his will. By the gift of his Spirit in our hearts, we sense something of just how much God loves us in everything. "The guilty past has been cancelled, the glory of the future is assured, and here and now the presence and power of the Spirit of God secure to believers all the grace they need to endure trials, to resist evil, and to live as befits those whom God has declared righteous" (Bruce 1985:115). Such is the astounding grace that God has given us in his Son! In return, as his blessed people, our lives should be filled with joy and thanksgiving for all his goodness to us.

◆   4. Adam and Christ contrasted (5:12-21)

¹²When Adam sinned, sin entered the world. Adam's sin brought death, so death spread to everyone, for everyone sinned. ¹³Yes, people sinned even before the law was given. But it was not counted as sin because there was not yet any law to break. ¹⁴Still, everyone died—from the time of Adam to the time of Moses—even those

who did not disobey an explicit commandment of God, as Adam did. Now Adam is a
symbol, a representation of Christ, who was
yet to come. [15]But there is a great difference between Adam's sin and God's
gracious gift. For the sin of this one man,
Adam, brought death to many. But even
greater is God's wonderful grace and his
gift of forgiveness to many through this
other man, Jesus Christ. [16]And the result of
God's gracious gift is very different from
the result of that one man's sin. For Adam's
sin led to condemnation, but God's free gift
leads to our being made right with God,
even though we are guilty of many sins
[17]For the sin of this one man, Adam, caused
death to rule over many. But even greater is
God's wonderful grace and his gift of righteousness, for all who receive it will live
in triumph over sin and death through this
one man, Jesus Christ.

[18]Yes, Adam's one sin brings condemnation for everyone, but Christ's one act of
righteousness brings a right relationship
with God and new life for everyone.
[19]Because one person disobeyed God,
many became sinners. But because one
other person obeyed God, many will be
made righteous.

[20]God's law was given so that all people
could see how sinful they were. But as
people sinned more and more, God's wonderful grace became more abundant. [21]So
just as sin ruled over all people and
brought them to death, now God's wonderful grace rules instead, giving us right
standing with God and resulting in eternal life through Jesus Christ our Lord.

NOTES

5:12 *sin entered the world.* Here "world" means humankind or human life.

Adam's sin brought death. Lit., "and through sin death [entered the world]."

for everyone sinned. This may be taken to mean that all sinned in their own personal lives
(Cranfield 1980:274-279) or, representatively, in Adam's primal sin ("Adam is mankind,"
Bruce 1985:122-123). For a full discussion of the complexities of this verse and the alternative interpretations, see Cranfield 1980:271-281; Moo 1996:316-329; Schreiner
1998:271-279.

5:13 *people sinned even before the law was given.* The law was not given until the time
of Moses (Exod 20:1ff), but sin was a reality in people's experience before then. Romans
5:13-14 is a digression to deal with the question of how one can speak of sin prior to the
giving of the law that defined sin.

But it was not counted as sin because there was not yet any law to break. Or, "Where
there is no law, no account is kept of sins" (TEV). Lit., "But sin is not counted when there
is no law." Technically, one cannot speak of "transgressions" if there is no formal law to
define transgressions.

5:14 *Still, everyone died—from the time of Adam to the time of Moses.* The fatal effects of
sin were still experienced, even before the law defined sin formally. Genesis 5 drives this
point home with its repetition of the phrase "and then he died."

even those who did not disobey an explicit commandment of God, as Adam did. Lit.,
"even . . . those whose sin was not like Adam's transgression" (cf. Gen 2:16–3:24).

Now Adam is a symbol, a representation of Christ, who was yet to come. Lit., ". . . a proto-
type (*tupos* [TG5179, ZG5596]) [i.e., example] of the coming one." Though there are parallels
between Adam and Christ, the following verses highlight the contrasts between the two.

5:15 *Adam's sin.* Lit., "the trespass."

God's gracious gift. Lit., "the gift of grace."

brought death to many. . . . forgiveness to many (*hoi polloi . . . tous pollous* [TG4183, ZG4498]).
Here "many" is practically equivalent to "all"; cf. 5:12, 18-19.

5:16 *God's free gift leads to our being made right with God.* Lit., "the gift of grace [leads] to justification [acquittal]" (*to charisma . . . eis dikaiōma* [TG5486/1345, ZG5922/1468]); this implies forgiveness.

5:17 *will live in triumph over sin and death.* Lit., "will reign in life" (*en zōē basileusousin* [TG2222/936, ZG2437/996]). This phrase may be interpreted with regard either to this life or to the coming one; NLT includes both (cf. 8:2).

5:18 *Christ's one act of righteousness.* The word *dikaiōmatos* [TG1345, ZG1468] here refers not to justification (as in 5:16; so Morris) nor to Christ's righteous life as a whole (so Leenhardt, Murray, Cranfield, Schreiner), but rather to his crowning act of dying for our sins (so Käsemann, Bruce, Dunn, Mounce, Stuhlmacher). Notice the term is contrasted in this verse with the one sin of Adam and defined as his great act of obedience (cf. Phil 2:5-11) in 5:19.

brings a right relationship with God and new life for everyone. Lit., "[brings] justification of life (or, "justification that is life"; *dikaiōsin zōēs* [TG1347/2222, ZG1470/2437]) for all people." Though the gift of justification and new life is potentially for everyone, it is effective only for those who put their trust in Christ (3:21-26; Gal 2:16).

5:19 *many became sinners. . . . many will be made righteous.* For the meaning of "many," see notes on 5:15, 18.

5:20 *God's law was given so that all people could see how sinful they were.* Lit., ". . . so that the trespass might increase," or, ". . . so that it might increase the trespass" (*hina pleonasē to paraptōma* [TG412/900, ZG4429/4183]). "Trespass" may be taken as either the subject or object (though the parallel with 5:20b suggests it is to be taken as the subject), and *hina* [TG2443, ZG2671] may be interpreted as indicating either purpose (REB, NAB, NJB, NIV) or, less likely, result (NRSV). This clause may be understood in three different ways: (1) The law brings a heightened awareness of sin (NLT). (2) The law increases the "sinfulness" of sin (continuing violation of the explicit will of God now becomes conscious, willful disobedience). (3) The law results in a quantitative increase in sin itself (a perverse tendency in humans inclines them to do what they know is wrong). All three are true and could be part of Paul's thinking (3:20; 4:15; 5:20; 7:7-13; Gal 3:19). The negative effects of the law, in any case, serve God's more ultimate purposes of salvation by increasing people's awareness of their need of forgiveness and deliverance.

But as people sinned more and more, God's wonderful grace became more abundant. Or, "where sin increased, God's grace increased much more" (TEV); or, "where sin was powerful, God's kindness was even more powerful" (CEV). Lit., "But where sin increased, grace abounded." His grace is greater than all our sin.

5:21 *now God's wonderful grace rules instead, giving us right standing with God.* Lit., "[so] grace might rule through righteousness."

COMMENTARY

In this section, Paul draws a comparison between Christ and Adam, showing that the positive effects of Christ's saving work overcome all the negative effects of Adam's tragic fall. Though the comparison between the "first Adam" and the "last Adam" seems strange to us, the parallels between the two were apparently a matter of discussion in the Jewish-Christian world of Paul's day (cf. 1 Cor 15:21-22, 45-49). Both figures represent defining moments in human history: Adam, the origin of human sin, with all its ruinous consequences; Christ, the origin of God's forgiving grace, with all its accompanying blessings. The point of the comparison is clear: The new situation now made possible by Christ completely transcends the old, brought about by Adam. Christ, "the other man," has the power to undo all the catastrophic effects of Adam's fall. Just as the sin of Adam affected the whole of humanity for evil, so the sacrifice of Christ has the potential to affect the whole of humanity for good.

Building on the traditional understanding of the Creation story, in which sin—and consequently death—entered the world through the tragic failure of Adam, Paul relates how sin and death then spread to all human beings (5:12-14). In Paul's comparison, Adam is more than a historical personality; he represents what his name means in Hebrew: "humanity." His sin represents the sin of the whole of humanity, which has now become alienated from God. The story of Adam, then, is the story of every person—the story of each one of us. "For everyone has sinned; we all fall short of God's glorious standard" (3:23; cf. 2 Esdr 7:118: "O Adam, what have you done? For though it was you who sinned, the fall was not yours alone, but ours also who are your descendants," NRSV). Like Adam, we too have disobeyed the command of God, and we, too, suffer the consequences. Just as "in Adam" all sin, so "in Adam" all die. This is our natural state as human beings descended from Adam.

In traditional Jewish thinking, people are not simply individuals; they are always part of a larger community, and the whole community may be represented by or considered as being "in" a single individual or earlier ancestor with whom they are linked. For example, the Jews are spoken of in the Bible as "Israel" or "Judah"; the people of God are represented in Daniel by the "son of man" (Dan 7:13); the Levitical priests are understood as being "in" their ancestor Abraham when Abraham paid his tithe to Melchizedek (Heb 7:9-10). Similarly, Paul speaks of the natural state of all human beings as being "in Adam"—infected by the sin of Adam. In the same way, all who have been redeemed by receiving the forgiving grace of Christ are spoken of as being "in Christ." "As all die in Adam, so all will be made alive in Christ" (1 Cor 15:22, NRSV). Linked by sin to Adam, we stand under the judgment of God; but linked by faith to Christ, we stand as forgiven people, recipients of God's forgiving grace. Our destiny is determined, if you will, by the community of which we are most essentially a part—"in Adam" or "in Christ." In the quaint words of an earlier Oxford scholar, "In God's sight, there are two men—Adam and Jesus Christ—and these two men have all other men hanging at their girdle strings."[1]

The contrast between the two men is striking: Adam's sin brings us death and condemnation by God; Christ's righteousness brings us life and a warm welcome by God. Adam's wrongdoing puts us under the judgment of God; Christ's sacrifice brings us into the grace of God. Adam's disobedience dooms us; Christ's obedience saves us. And the good news is that the freeing power of the latter is greater than the enslaving power of the former (5:15-21). "For all who receive it [God's grace and his gift of righteousness] will live in triumph over sin and death" (5:17; cf. 8:2-4). "When death reigns, human beings are its helpless victims; when Christ reigns, they share his risen life and royal glory" (Bruce 1985:125). "That one single misdeed should be answered by judgment, this is perfectly understandable: that the accumulated sins and guilt of all the ages should be answered by God's free gift, this is the miracle of miracles, utterly beyond human comprehension" (Cranfield 1980:286).

We must be careful, however, not to read too much into Paul's words about the grace of God in Christ bringing a right relationship with God and a new life for "everyone" (5:18). There is no basis for universal salvation here; Paul is clearly an exclusivist, not a universalist. Everything he says in the larger context makes it clear that salvation is given not to everyone but only to those who put their trust in Christ. The grace of God is indeed an undeniably wonderful thing—greater than all our sin—but it is only so for those who accept it for the gift it is. It has the potential to make everyone right with God, but in reality it does so only for those who have faith in Christ (1:17; 3:25-26; 5:1; Gal 2:16). The heart of the Good News proclaimed by Paul is that, by God's grace, people can now freely be made right with God—if they put their faith in Christ.

Now, let's turn our attention to another matter: original sin. Parts of Paul's argument seem to reflect the assumption of original sin—the assumption that there is something inherently evil in the heart of every person born into the world as a result of being a descendant of Adam (5:15-19). As the psalmist says, "I was born a sinner—yes, from the moment my mother conceived me" (Ps 51:5). However, it is important to note that neither Paul nor the psalmist is making a statement about the genetic origins of sin; instead, they are speaking of the universality of sin and the ingrained, all-pervasive nature of sin. The overall focus of the New Testament writers is not so much on "original sin" as on actual sin; not so much on the origin of sin as on the reality of sin as it is expressed here and now in the lives of people.[2] Whenever and however sin arises, Paul emphasized that it is a universal experience with tragic consequences—death and the judgment of God for all who sin.

Paul knew that some of his readers were sure to be troubled by this brief analysis of the history of sin and God's dealing with it because it omits all reference to the law, which Jewish people commonly assumed God had instituted to deal with sin. Early in this section, Paul acknowledged that, technically, sin cannot be classified as legal culpability before the era of the law, for the law is what legally defines sin. Nonetheless, the reality and the consequences of sin as an expression of disobedience were felt from the very beginning, long before the time of Moses and the law (5:13-14). Sin was a problem long before the law was ever given—and sin remained a problem after the law was given.

The important point implied by Paul is that the law is not really the answer to the problem of sin at all. The law was only instituted to help people see their sin more clearly—until Christ could come to deal with sin effectively. So the law was only a stopgap measure "until the coming of the child who was promised . . . until the way of faith was revealed" (Gal 3:19, 23). Now Christ spells the end (termination) of the law as a way of life so that righteousness may be credited to everyone who believes (10:4).

The ultimate purpose of the law—its deeper function—is not simply to control wrongdoing by restricting people's behavior but (ironically) to increase their sense of wrongdoing—to give sin its bite, to heighten people's sense of sin, to make them feel their wrongdoing. The real purpose of the law is to make people aware of how far they fall short of actually keeping God's law (5:20; cf. Gal 3:19: "Why, then, was the law given? It was given alongside the promise to show people their sins,"). Here, with great insight, Paul goes well beyond the Judaism of his day in his understanding of the negative function of the law of Moses and of "law" as a way of life in general. Paul was keenly aware that no system of law could ever be an adequate basis for the motivation of true love or of the kind of life and attitudes that truly please God. Real goodness cannot be legislated; it has to come from a completely different source of motivation, the awareness of being deeply loved by God. A life of heartfelt goodness is a response not to the demands of law but to God's wholly undeserved grace.

The astonishing message of the Good News is that, however great our sin and its grip upon us, the amazing grace of God in Jesus Christ is greater still (5:20-21)! Indeed, the more profound our understanding of sin and its consequences, the greater our appreciation of God's grace—of all he has done for us, undeserving as we are. It is our awareness of the full depths of our sin that makes us realize we can never merit his love; all we can do is accept it as a gift. The heightened awareness of our sin makes us realize the full extent of our dependence on God's forgiving grace and thus pushes us to a life of simple trust in Christ as Savior. So in the end, in the service of the Good News, the law of Moses performs a most useful function—but not the one most people think. Only in Jesus Christ can the bonds of sin and death be broken (8:1-4). As Paul proclaimed to the people in Antioch of Pisidia, "Through this man Jesus there is forgiveness for your sins. Everyone who believes in him is declared right with God— something the law of Moses could never do" (Acts 13:38-39).

ENDNOTES

1. These are the words of Thomas Goodwin, seventeenth-century president of Magdalen College, Oxford—cited in Bruce 1985:120.
2. The question of infant baptism and its relation to "original sin" is a question that arose only later, in the second century, as the church began to consider the relationship between God and children born into Christian families. In the early days of the Christian movement, the dominant concern was with adult converts who were clearly aware of their sin.

◆   D. Objections to the Good News (6:1–7:25)
        1. Why not continue in sin? (6:1–23)
           a. We have "died" to sin (6:1–14)

Well then, should we keep on sinning so that God can show us more and more of his wonderful grace? ²Of course not! Since we have died to sin, how can we continue to live in it? ³Or have you forgotten that when we were joined with Christ Jesus in baptism, we joined him in his death? ⁴For we died and were buried with Christ by baptism. And just as Christ was raised from the dead by the glorious power of the Father, now we also may live new lives.

⁵Since we have been united with him in his death, we will also be raised to life as he was. ⁶We know that our old sinful selves were crucified with Christ so that sin might lose its power in our lives. We are no longer slaves to sin. ⁷For when we died with Christ we were set free from the power of sin. ⁸And since we died with Christ, we know we will also live with him. ⁹We are sure of this because Christ was raised from the dead, and he will never die again. Death no longer has any power over him. ¹⁰When he died, he died once to break the power of sin. But now that he lives, he lives for the glory of God. ¹¹So you also should consider yourselves to be dead to the power of sin and alive to God through Christ Jesus.

¹²Do not let sin control the way you live;* do not give in to sinful desires. ¹³Do not let any part of your body become an instrument of evil to serve sin. Instead, give yourselves completely to God, for you were dead, but now you have new life. So use your whole body as an instrument to do what is right for the glory of God. ¹⁴Sin is no longer your master, for you no longer live under the requirements of the law. Instead, you live under the freedom of God's grace.

6:12 Or *Do not let sin reign in your body, which is subject to death.*

NOTES

6:1 *should we keep on sinning so that God can show us more and more of his wonderful grace?* This is a false conclusion that might be drawn from 5:20b ("As people sinned more and more, God's wonderful grace became more abundant").

6:2 *Of course not!* This emphatic negation (*mē genoito* [TG3361/1096, ZG3590/1181]) occurs ten times in Romans (3:4, 6, 31; 6:2, 15; 7:7, 13; 9:14; 11:1, 11) but nowhere else in Paul's writings.

6:3 *Or have you forgotten.* Lit., "Or do you not know."

we were joined with Christ Jesus in baptism. Lit., "we were baptized into Christ Jesus." In the NT, baptism is the immediate public expression of one's conversion to Christ and is spoken of as the point at which one becomes united to Christ.

we joined him in his death. Lit., "we were baptized into his death." This may be understood either from God's point of view (we are now considered recipients of all the benefits of Christ's death) or from the individual's point of view (we now consider ourselves "dead" to the life of sin we once lived—the point of the immediate passage). The two are closely related, and Paul moves easily from one to the other in this passage. Cranfield (1980:299-300) distinguishes four interrelated senses in which Christians die to sin and are raised with Christ: the juridical (i.e., judicial—as it appears in the sight of God the Judge), baptismal, moral, and eschatological senses.

6:4 *For we died and were buried with Christ by baptism.* Lit., "Therefore we were buried together with him through baptism into his death."

by the glorious power of the Father. Lit., "through the glory (*doxa* [TG1391, ZG1518]) of the Father." The life-transforming power we have now received is "the same mighty power that raised Christ from the dead" (Eph 1:19-20; cf. Col 2:12).

now we also may live new lives. Lit., "so that (*hina* [TG2443, ZG2671]) we may also walk in newness of life"; this is the purpose of our dying with Christ in baptism. The Greek verb "walk" (*peripateō* [TG4043, ZG4344]) is used similarly in 8:4; 13:13; 14:15.

6:5 *we will also be raised to life as he was.* The words "raised to life" may be understood either in a future sense (eschatologically) or a present sense (figuratively). Because the overall emphasis of the passage is on the present experience of resurrection life, the present sense is more likely.

6:6 *our old sinful selves.* Lit., "our old person," a phrase also used in Eph 4:22; Col 3:9.

so that sin might lose its power in our lives. Lit., "so that the body of sin might be destroyed." Most interpreters understand "the body of sin" (*to sōma tēs hamartias* [TG4983/266, ZG5393G/281]) to mean the sinful nature as a whole (cf. "the power of the sinful self," TEV), not the sinful desires of the physical body. But the way that Paul speaks of "the law of sin that dwells in my members" (*en tois melesin* [TG3196, ZG3517] *mou*) and "this body of death" (*tou sōmatos tou thanatou* [TG2288, ZG2505]; 7:23-24, NRSV; cf. 8:3) suggests that the phrase could equally well be interpreted as the sinful drives of the physical body. Note the way he speaks of putting to death "the deeds of the body" (8:13, NRSV), of killing our "members upon the earth" (a literal rendering of Col 3:5), of not letting sin rule "in your mortal body," and of not giving in to "its passions" (a literal rendering of 6:12). Paul is clear on this point: the power of sin at work in the body has now been overcome (cf. 8:10). However, the extent to which this will be experienced in believers' lives depends on their submission to the influence of the Spirit (8:5-14 and notes on 7:23-24; 8:13).

6:7 *set free from the power of sin.* Lit., "made righteous from sin." This is best interpreted in the context as "set free from the power of sin" (NLT; Schreiner 1998:319), not "justified" from sin (as in Cranfield 1980:311, n. 1; Bruce 1985:131).

6:8 *we will also live with him.* As in 6:5b, this is best understood in the context as a reference to the present experience of resurrection life, not to future eschatological existence. But it is true for both, and the two are closely related.

6:9 *Death no longer has any power over him.* Lit., "Death no longer rules over (*kurieuei* [TG2961, ZG3259]) him."

6:10 *he died once to break the power of sin.* Lit., "he died once to sin." The book of Hebrews especially emphasizes the once-for-all nature of Jesus' sacrifice (Heb 7:27; 9:12; 10:10).

he lives for the glory of God. Lit., "he lives to God."

6:11 *consider yourselves to be dead to the power of sin.* Lit., "dead to sin." This is the first of a sequence of four present-tense imperatives in 6:11-13, urging believers to live out their new resurrection life.

and alive to God through Christ Jesus. Lit., "but living to God in Christ Jesus." Some Gr. mss (𝕏 C 𝔐) expand the divine title to "Christ Jesus our Lord."

6:12 *Do not let sin control the way you live.* Lit., "Therefore sin must not rule in your mortal body." See note on 6:6.

sinful desires. Lit., "its desires" (*epithumiais autou* [TG1939, ZG2123]), referring to the desires of "your mortal body." This reading is supported by 𝔓94 𝕏 A B C* 81 1739. Other Gr. mss (𝔓46 D F G) read "it" (*autē*, the fem. sg. pronoun), referring to "sin."

6:13 *Do not let any part of your body become an instrument of evil to serve sin.* Lit., "do not present your members (*ta melē* [TG3196, ZG3517]) as instruments of wickedness (*hopla adikias* [TG3696/93, ZG3960/94]) to sin"; cf. 13:14.

for you were dead, but now you have new life. Lit., "as those who are alive from the dead" (*ek nekrōn zōntas* [TG3498A/2198, ZG3738/2409]).

So use your whole body as an instrument to do what is right for the glory of God. Lit., "present . . . your members (*ta melē* [TG3196, ZG3517]) as instruments of righteousness (*hopla dikaiosunēs* [TG3696/1343, ZG3960/1466]) to God."

6:14 *Sin is no longer your master.* Lit., "For sin will not rule over (*kurieusei* [TG2961, ZG3259]) you." This declaration does not mean that the believer no longer feels the temptation of sin but that the believer is no longer hopelessly enslaved to sin (as in 7:14-25). Cf. 8:1-4 and Gal 5:17.

for you no longer live under the requirements of the law. Instead, you live under the free-dom of God's grace. Lit., "for you are not under law but under grace." The law, like sin, is a power dominating the lives of those under its authority; but believers are no longer subject to the all-enslaving power of either. "The law demanded obedience, but grace supplies the will and the power to obey; hence grace breaks the mastery of sin as law could not" (Bruce 1985:132).

COMMENTARY

In this section, Paul addresses some anticipated objections to his emphasis on God's grace apart from the law of Moses: If you do away with the law of Moses, what's to keep believers from sinning? If God's forgiving grace multiplies in propor-tion to our sin (as Paul seems to imply in 5:20), why not sin even more? Paul responded by explaining the radical change that comes into a believer's life at con-version (ch 6) and by challenging his opponents' view of the law as a sufficient foundation for moral living (ch 7).

Why Not Keep on Sinning? These objections to Paul's emphasis on grace alone are not simply theoretical. Unfortunately, throughout church history there have been individuals who have found justification for sin in the doctrine of God's grace. A notable example is the infamous Russian monk Gregory Rasputin (1871–1916), who preached that salvation comes through repeated experiences of sin and repen-tance. He maintained that, since those who sin more require more forgiveness, believers who continue to sin with abandon enjoy, every time they repent, more of God's forgiving grace than ordinary sinners (Bruce 1985:127). Even in New Testa-ment times there were those who attempted to justify sin on the basis of a distorted understanding of God's grace. The small letter of Jude, for example, is a response to problems caused by certain people in the church who were saying that God's for-giveness allows Christians to live an immoral life (Jude 1:4).

From Paul's letters we also find evidence of Christians whose lives seemed to reflect this self-indulgent way of thinking—judging, for example, from the lax atti-tudes to sex expressed by some of the Christians in Corinth (1 Cor 5:1-2; 6:12-20) and from Paul's strong warnings of God's judgment on certain activities (1 Cor 6:9-10; Gal 5:19-21; Eph 5:5-6; Col 3:5-6). It was bad enough for his opponents to charge him with preaching a gospel that encouraged immoral living (3:8) but even worse when his own converts began to live in a way that seemed to substanti-ate such claims. No wonder some Christians felt it was essential for believers to be under the regime of the Mosaic law. It is a problem that Paul frequently had to address—the temptation to take sin lightly, to presume on God's grace and forgiveness, to abuse the doctrine of grace.

This remains a problem today, for there are still many Christians (in name) who live as if morality and ethics were a matter of indifference—people for whom the Good News of God's grace has become a subtle pretext for indulging in sin. Such a crass attitude toward sin reflects a lost sense of the holiness and judgment of God and a desire for "cheap grace"—not the costly grace of the gospel. Where such distorted conceptions of God's grace exist, there is no true understanding of the God of grace.

Therefore, to the question "should we keep on sinning?" Paul's stinging response was, "Of course not!" (6:2, 15). This response shows how utterly opposed he was to a carefree attitude about sin. True Christians, he reminded us, are those who have turned their back on sin. Together with Christ, we have died to sin, so we cannot take it lightly. And if we do take it lightly, it raises questions about how seriously we take our commitment to Christ. The writer of 1 John goes so far as to say that those who continue to live in sin have never really known or understood God—they belong to the devil. The true children of God show the authenticity of their faith by their abstention from sin, in compliance with God's desires (1 John 3:6-10). It is true that we are saved by grace alone; but if we know the true meaning of grace, we will never presume upon it.

We Have "Died" and "Risen Again" with Christ. When we embrace Jesus Christ and are baptized, something changes in our lives: we become joined to Christ—or as Paul writes elsewhere, we become "clothed" with Christ (Gal 3:27, NRSV). We come to live in him, and he comes to live in us (cf. the words of Jesus, "You are in me, and I am in you," John 14:20). This means that, in some inscrutable way, believers become united with his death and resurrection. To be baptized into Christ, then, is to die and rise again with Christ: we die to sin and rise to live as a new person (6:3-11; cf. Col 2:12). There is symbolism expressed in the act of immersion: going down into the water signifies our burial, and rising out of the water signifies our resurrection to new life. Christian baptism, then, signifies both the death of our old life in sin and the experience of new life in Christ that replaces it. For this reason, Paul speaks of our former sinful self as "crucified with Christ" (6:6; Gal 2:20; cf. Gal 6:14), which means the power of sin has effectively been broken in our lives ("When we died with Christ we were set free from the power of sin," 6:7). A new life has been given to us— the resurrection life of Christ—and with it a new power for living so that now we may live new lives (6:4-14). When we become Christians, then, a fundamental change takes place in our identity and motivation. As 2 Corinthians 5:17 puts it, "The old life is gone; a new life has begun!" As Christians, we see all of life through new eyes and live life with a new power and potential. In embracing Jesus Christ we become different people. Our old sinful self has been crucified with Christ, and sin no longer has the same power over us that it once had. Risen with Christ, we have been given a new life and power that enables us to overcome the power of sin. So the Good News of God's grace does not lead to a life of self-indulgence and sin.

Though Paul's focus is not on the rite of baptism itself but on what it signifies, he assumes that all those who call themselves Christians have been baptized. In New Testament times, Christian baptism—usually in the form of immersion— seems to have been understood as the public expression of one's confession of Christ and was not considered optional. (For a description of baptismal practices in the early church, see *Didache* 7 in Radice 1968:230-231.) It was commonly administered to adult converts (including, at least sometimes, their families; Acts 16:14-15, 31-33) at the time of their conversion (see Acts 2:38, 41; 8:12, 36; 9:18; 10:47-48; 16:14-15, 31-33; 18:8; 19:5) and required no additional time for Christian instruction. As a result, in the New Testament baptism is often spoken of in the context of conversion; it served as the public declaration of a person's conversion. The physical act of baptism itself seems not to have been considered salvific, but the conversion to Christ that it expressed was. There may be a hint of this in Paul's words to the Corinthians, "Christ didn't send me to baptize, but to preach the Good News" (1 Cor 1:17). This distinction may also be seen in the numerous accounts of conversions in Acts where there is no reference to baptism. The imagery of burial and resurrection that Paul sees in baptism suggests how closely linked conversion is, in his thinking, to the idea of submission to Christ as Lord. To be a confessing Christian is to die to a self-centered way of life and to embrace a new, Christ-centered life—a life that acknowledges Christ as Lord in everything.

We Must Say No to Sin. Christian conversion is ultimately the result of God's gracious initiative and work in joining a person to Christ and bringing about a new life, but Paul also makes it clear that Christians must choose to live out this new life. (Note the four present-tense imperatives in 6:11-13.) We must actively commit ourselves to the new life we are called to live upon coming to Christ. Although we have already "died" and "risen again" with Christ as a result of being joined to him, we must now commit ourselves to living out this death and resurrection (6:11-14).

This commitment means, first of all, saying no to all temptation and sin. "Do not let sin control the way you live," Paul writes; "do not give in to sinful desires. Do not let any part of your body become an instrument of evil to serve sin" (6:12-13). As Christians, we are to consider ourselves "dead to the power of sin" (6:11). The power to live this out lies in the transforming work of the Holy Spirit, who not only opposes the desires of the sinful nature but effectively frees us from the power of sin over us (7:4-6; 8:1-14; cf. Gal 5:16-18).

Paul spoke very specifically of the need for self-denial. What is called for is nothing less than the crucifixion of our sinful desires. ("Those who belong to Christ Jesus have nailed the passions and desires of their sinful nature to his cross and crucified them there," Gal 5:24.) But self-denial has never been popular, and in the modern world especially, with its emphasis on self-gratification, it is very much out of vogue—even in the Christian community, where it is sometimes deprecated as an expression of "works theology." Earlier generations of Christians were much more conscious of the New Testament emphasis on self-denial and the central role it plays in Jesus' teachings, and many of the Christian classics reflect this. A good example is Thomas à Kempis's *Of the Imitation of Christ*, which places self-denial and obedient commitment to the will of God at the very heart of the Christian life, as it was in Christ's own life:

> Thou canst not possess perfect liberty unless thou wholly renounce thyself. . . . Forsake all and thou shalt find all. . . . Forsake thyself, and thou shalt find Me. . . . Forsake thyself, resign thyself, and thou shalt enjoy much inward peace. . . . Let this be thy whole endeavor . . . that thou mayest be stript of all selfishness, and with entire simplicity follow Jesus only; mayest die to thyself, and live eternally to Me. . . . Truly the life of a good Christian is a Cross, yet it is also a guide to Paradise. (1903:131, 139, 177)

In the Gospels, Jesus clearly speaks of self-denial as a central part of Christian disci-pleship: "If any want to become my followers, let them deny themselves and take up their cross and follow me" (Mark 8:34, NRSV). Committing ourselves to dying with Christ—dying to the life of sin—demands self-denial at its very core; and such a way of life is never easy.

We Must Say Yes to the New Life. Living out the life of Christ calls for much more than self-denial. It involves resurrection as well as crucifixion; it means actively pursu-ing the new life as well as dying to the old (6:5-11). Christ did not simply die; he rose to a new life, victorious over sin and death. In the same way, we do not simply "die" to sin; we "rise again" to live by the power of the Resurrection, which transcends the power of sin and death. Now, like Christ, we are to live for the glory of God—a life that pleases God in every way, free from the enslaving power of sin—because we are no longer dominated by the tyrannical rule of the law (6:13-14). When giving instruc-tions on Christian living in the Prison Letters, Paul follows up injunctions to "put off" the old sinful way of life with encouragement to "put on" the new (Eph 4:17–5:20; Col 3:5-17). Christian living, then, calls for the active pursuit of Christian virtues as well as for self-denial; it means saying "yes" to goodness as well as "no" to sin.

Though the ultimate experience of resurrection life awaits the future, in this pas-sage of Romans Paul calls Christians to the fullest possible experience of it here and now by the power of the Spirit. (This is sometimes called "inaugurated eschatol-ogy"—eschatological existence that begins to be experienced in the life of the be-liever here and now.) Though some of the references to resurrection in this passage could be interpreted in a future, literal sense, the context is primarily concerned with the living out of the resurrection life in the present. We must remember that for Paul, the power of the Spirit is nothing less than the power of the resurrected Christ within us: "My old self has been crucified with Christ. It is no longer I who live, but Christ lives in me" (Gal 2:20). It is this life of the resurrected Christ within that assures us of future glory (Col 1:27). Herein lies the key to understanding much of what Paul writes so glowingly about the Christian life: the dynamic that drives us as believers is nothing less than the life of the resurrected Lord himself at work within us.

A Strange Paradox: Both God's Work and Our Work. In the end, Christian conver-sion brings together the divine and the human—God's work and our work. It involves both God's sovereign grace at work in our lives and our response to it. By God's grace we have become joined to Christ and his life and have thereby received a new power for living; in response, we turn our backs on sin and commit ourselves to living the holy life he desires of us. It involves both a divinely ordained change in us and a personal commitment on our part to living that change out.

In this we come face to face with what theologians call "the indicative-imperative" paradox. Side by side in Paul's letters we find (1) statements speaking of things already accomplished for believers as a result of the Cross—changes already effected by Christ (the "indicatives"); and (2) commands for believers to do these things, to live them out (the "imperatives"). We have died with Christ (6:2-8)—but we are also to consider ourselves dead (6:11) and put to death the evil desires within us (Col 3:5). We have been set free from the power of sin (6:7, 14, 18, 22)—but we must also no longer let sin control the way we live (6:12). For Paul, the truth of the indicatives (what God has already done for us) in no way eliminates the need for the imperatives (what we, in turn, must do). Divine sovereignty in no way excludes human responsibility. Both, paradoxically, are true, and we must take both seriously. Whereas the indicatives express the new situation in which we find ourselves in Christ (the life of the Spirit, the power of the new age), the imperatives reflect the fact that we still have to deal with the realities of the old (the sinful self, or what Paul calls the "flesh"). The powers of the old age are conquered, but not destroyed—and certainly not rendered totally ineffective. Although as believers we are transferred from the dominion of sin to the realm of grace (6:14), the human "flesh" remains an active force, constantly pulling us in the opposite direction. Our experience of the Spirit, then, in no way guarantees a sin-free existence—and it is precisely this that renders the imperatives not only valid in Paul's thinking but indeed necessary. As throughout the Bible, divine and human perspectives lie side-by-side in a paradoxical relationship. Both are true and valid, and both must be taken seriously.

◆   ## b. We have become slaves of righteousness (6:15-23)

¹⁵Well then, since God's grace has set us free from the law, does that mean we can go on sinning? Of course not! ¹⁶Don't you realize that you become the slave of whatever you choose to obey? You can be a slave to sin, which leads to death, or you can choose to obey God, which leads to righteous living. ¹⁷Thank God! Once you were slaves of sin, but now you wholeheartedly obey this teaching we have given you. ¹⁸Now you are free from your slavery to sin, and you have become slaves to righteous living.

¹⁹Because of the weakness of your human nature, I am using the illustration of slavery to help you understand all this. Previously, you let yourselves be slaves to impurity and lawlessness, which led ever deeper into sin. Now you must give yourselves to be slaves to righteous living so that you will become holy.

²⁰When you were slaves to sin, you were free from the obligation to do right. ²¹And what was the result? You are now ashamed of the things you used to do, things that end in eternal doom. ²²But now you are free from the power of sin and have become slaves of God. Now you do those things that lead to holiness and result in eternal life. ²³For the wages of sin is death, but the free gift of God is eternal life through Christ Jesus our Lord.

NOTES

6:15 *Of course not!* This emphatic negation (*mē genoito* [TG3361/1096, ZG3590/1181]) occurs ten times in Romans (3:4, 6, 31; 6:2, 15; 7:7, 13; 9:14; 11:1, 11) but nowhere else in Paul's writings.

6:16 *You can be a slave to sin, which leads to death.* Here "death" refers to ultimate death in the final judgment. "Death" has the same meaning in 1:32; 6:21, 23; 7:5; 8:6.

choose to obey God, which leads to righteous living. "To righteous living" is lit., "to righteousness" (*eis dikaiosunē* [TG1343, ZG1466]). "Righteousness" here could be interpreted either as "righteous living" (as in 6:18-19; so Mounce, Moo) or as "a right standing with God" (i.e., final justification), which provides a clearer contrast with "death" (so Cranfield, Bruce). A right standing with God, given freely on the basis of faith in Christ, requires obedience as a response, if faith is to be considered authentic. In the context of ch 6, obedience refers to moral living; it is not to be equated with the act of believing (as in 1:5; 16:26).

6:17 *this teaching we have given you.* An awkward passive construction (*hon paredothēte tupon didachēs* [TG1322, ZG1439]), here translated more freely as an active. It is a reference to the way of life demanded by the Good News. There is no need to understand it as a set body of teaching representing a summary of Christian ethics based on the teaching of Christ (as in Bruce 1985:134; Mounce 1995:156-157).

6:18 *Now you are free from your slavery to sin.* Lit., "and having been freed from sin"— that is (in this context), freed from the enslaving power of sin, not from sin's condemnation.

6:19 *Because of the weakness of your human nature, I am using the illustration of slavery to help you understand all this.* Lit., "I speak in a human way (*anthrōpinon* [TG442, ZG474]) because of the weakness of your flesh (*sarx* [TG4561, ZG4922])"—that is, because of the proneness to self-deception and to forgetting the obligations imposed by grace. As inadequate as it is, Paul used the human illustration of slavery to help them understand both their previous bondage and their present obligation.

you let yourselves be slaves to impurity and lawlessness. "Impurity" and "lawlessness" (wickedness) were terms commonly used by Jews to describe Gentile sins (Newman and Nida 1973:123).

which led ever deeper into sin. Or, "for wicked purposes" (*eis tēn anomian* [TG458, ZG490]) —an emphatic amplification ("to greater and greater iniquity," NRSV).

slaves to righteous living so that you will become holy. Lit., "slaves to righteousness (*tē dikaiosunē* [TG1343, ZG1466]) for sanctification" (*eis hagiasmon* [TG38, ZG40]). Here, sanctification is not a single experience or a state but a process—the continuing process of being transformed by the Spirit into the kind of person God desires, more and more like his Son (8:29), a reflection of the glory of the Lord himself (2 Cor 3:18). Cf. commentary on 8:29.

6:20 *you were free from the obligation to do right.* Lit., "you were free [with regard] to righteousness" (*dikaiosunē* [TG1343, ZG1466]). Their lives were formerly dominated by sin and not righteousness. However, the clause could be interpreted in other ways: "you were free from the control of righteousness" (REB, NIV); "you felt no obligation to uprightness" (NJB). Here the focus is on ethical righteousness, not imputed righteousness.

6:21 *And what was the result?* Lit., "what fruit did you have?" A better translation than the traditional renderings, "And what was the gain/benefit/advantage?" (cf. NIV, NRSV, REB, NASB)

things that end in eternal doom. Lit., "the end of those things is death"—that is, ultimate death in the final judgment. "Death" has the same meaning in 1:32; 6:16, 23; 7:5; 8:6.

6:22 *things that lead to holiness.* Lit., "fruit for sanctification" (*eis hagiasmon* [TG38, ZG40]). See note on 6:19.

eternal life. Though linked to the coming age, eternal life is given to the believer at the moment of believing, so it is experienced already in the present. It is the eternal life of the resurrected Christ himself, now resident in the believer through the Holy Spirit. The present experience of eternal life is emphasized especially in the Johannine writings (John 3:36; 5:24; 6:47, 54; 11:25-26; 1 John 5:11-13).

6:23 *death.* Ultimate death in the final judgment. "Death" has the same meaning in 1:32; 6:16, 21; 7:5; 8:6.

COMMENTARY

In this section, Paul addresses another anticipated objection, closely related to the first: If Christians are now freed from the jurisdiction of the law and governed solely by the principle of grace, what's to keep them from continuing in sin? Doesn't such a denial of the God-given role of the Mosaic law undermine the foundation of all morality and ethics? Not at all, Paul responds, because true Christians submit themselves to God and are committed to obeying his desires. If a person chooses to continue in sin, it shows that sin—not the will of God—is the real "master" of that person's life. Real Christians are committed to living a morally good life because they have made God's desires their "master." How a person lives, then, shows who or what that person's master is, for that to which we submit becomes our "lord." One cannot claim to be a follower of God and continue to live in sin; the two are mutually exclusive—to continue to live in sin results in eternal death. But to submit to the lordship of God and his desires (the mark of genuine faith) results in holy living and eternal life. There must be a correlation, then, between what we confess and how we live, if our faith is to be considered authentic. So even though Christians are not governed by the legislation of the Mosaic law, they are committed to a life of righteousness and obedience because of their submission to the Lord.

Those who think that a Christian can keep on sinning and still be given God's grace have little understanding of the true meaning of God's grace. True Christians cannot continue in a life of sin because they have submitted themselves to God as Lord and therefore live in obedience to his holy desires. Just as Christ was driven by a single-minded desire to obey the Father's will in all things ("I want your will to be done, not mine," Luke 22:42), so those who are truly committed to Christ are driven by the desire to please God in all things. As a result, those who are real Christians have become slaves of obedience (6:16), "slaves to righteous living" (6:18), "slaves of God" (6:22); for to submit to someone as Lord means becoming that person's slave, with the whole of one's life subordinated to that person's desires. Such a life of devoted obedience to God results in holy living and eternal life (6:16, 22-23), for it represents the outworking of an authentic faith in Christ. If one chooses instead to live in sin, it shows that sin, not God, is still the ruling force—the "master"—of that person's life. Such a person has chosen, in effect, to remain a slave of sin, and that choice will ultimately prove to be fatal. That kind of life ends in death (6:16), in "eternal doom" (6:21). So one cannot claim to be a true Christian, submitted to God as Lord, and at the same time continue in a life of sin; the two are mutually incompatible. As Jesus says, "A tree is identified by its fruit" (Matt 12:33).

In this passage, there are only two choices, two different ways of living: one is a slave either of God or of sin. There is no such thing as an autonomous person, free of any master. The person who imagines himself to be free because he acknowledges no god but himself is deluded; for such a self-serving perspective is nothing less than idolatry, the very essence of slavery to sin (1:21-25). One can either remain a slave of sin or choose to serve God as a joyful slave of righteous living. To remain a slave of sin is to be driven by the desires of the old sinful self; to be a slave of righteous living is to be driven by the liberating power of the Holy Spirit. The end of the former is eternal doom; the end of the latter is eternal life and a share in the glory of God. "For the wages of sin is death, but the free gift of God is eternal life through Christ Jesus our Lord" (6:23).

Someone might ask whether this emphasis on obedience and righteous living contradicts the heart of the Good News, the message of grace—the truth that we are saved by faith alone. It does not; for Paul, submission to the Lord is the necessary correlate of true faith in Christ because the Christ in whom we believe is Lord as well as Savior. "If you confess with your mouth that Jesus is Lord and believe in your heart that God raised him from the dead, you will be saved" (10:9). (It should be noted that when Paul speaks of submitting to the Lord, sometimes he speaks of God and sometimes of Christ—which shows how closely related the two are in his thinking.) Confessing Christ (or God) as Lord is not a matter of simply acknowledging an abstract truth; it must be a statement of what is personally true—an acknowledgment that he is *my* Lord. So submission to the Lord is not an optional extra for the Christian who claims to be saved by faith; it is part of the essence of being a true Christian. This is very much in line with the teaching of the Sermon on the Mount, which stresses that not everyone who claims to be a believer will find a home in the Kingdom of God but only those who take seriously their calling to obey (Matt 7:21-23).

It is possible for us to so overemphasize God's grace and the principle of salvation by faith alone that we lose sight of the demands of God's lordship over us. In the New Testament, however, grace and demand always go hand in hand; if we accept God's forgiving grace, we must accept his demands as well. To accept Christ as Savior means we must also submit to him as Lord. God's grace, though free, is never cheap.

Some might ask, then, if submission to Christ (or God) as Lord is an essential element of Christian salvation, doesn't that mean, in reality, that we're saved in part by our "works"—by how we live, by what we do—and not simply by our faith alone? Only to the extent that our works are understood as vindicating or validating our claim to saving faith. As James emphasizes, "Faith is dead without good works" (Jas 2:26); a faith that is not lived out is not true saving faith at all. That kind of "faith" will save no one.

In discussing the relation between faith and works, it is important to distinguish exactly what is meant by the term works. When Paul speaks of salvation by faith "apart from works," he usually means that salvation is not conditional on the "works of the law"—that is, the careful observance of the law of Moses (which for most Jews focused on the regulations pertaining to circumcision, food, and the Sabbath). Paul does however teach that true, saving faith must always be expressed in the transformed quality of one's life—that is, in how one lives. True faith is always life-changing faith. So, faith and works (in a moral sense) are always married: though it is always our faith (our trust in Christ as Savior) that saves us, the reality of our faith is attested by our works—that is, by how we live. Hence one finds a paradoxical tension in Paul's writings between the principles of salvation by faith and judgment by works (cf. Yinger 1999). That is why Paul can say such things as the following: "Don't you realize that those who do wrong will not inherit the Kingdom of God?" (1 Cor 6:9); "Anyone living that sort of life will not inherit the Kingdom of God" (Gal 5:21); "The anger of God will fall on all who disobey him" (Eph 5:6; cf. Col 3:5). If our lifestyle does not reflect our faith, there is no reason to suppose that we have any real experience of true saving faith, or God's saving grace, at all. That is why Paul can speak of obedience as resulting in righteousness and eternal life (6:16, 22)—obedience is the mark of true faith. (See comments on 1:5.)

True faith in Christ, then, takes seriously the call to obedience and holy living (sanctification). Holiness, in a Pauline sense, is not to be understood in a legalistic way, as the result of following a strict moral code, but as a life of utter goodness and wholehearted dedication to God, one manifestly set apart for him. Those who choose to become "slaves to righteous living" recognize that they are called to become holy and therefore, "do those things that lead to holiness" (6:19, 22). God, by his nature, is utterly holy; it is not surprising, then, that he asks his people to pursue a life of holiness also (Lev 11:44-45; 19:2; 1 Pet 1:15-16). Paul often speaks of Christians as those who are called to a life of holiness (1:7; 1 Cor 1:2; Eph 1:4; 2 Tim 1:9; cf. Col 1:22). In the Prison Letters, Paul says Christ's purpose in dying for the church was "to make her holy and clean," so that he might "present her to himself as a glorious church without a spot or wrinkle or any other blemish" (Eph 5:25-27). In the Pastoral Letters, he writes, "He gave his life to free us from every kind of sin, to cleanse us, and to make us his very own people, totally committed to doing good deeds" (Titus 2:14). The ultimate goal of salvation, God's highest desire for his people, is that they become holy like his Son (8:29). So they are to grow "in every way more and more like Christ" (Eph 4:15). Therefore, Paul encourages his young converts to live a transformed life: "Put on your new nature, created to be like God—truly righteous and holy" (Eph 4:24). As God's holy ones, submitted to him as Lord and chosen to become like Christ, then, Christians are called to live holy lives, fully dedicated to him and his purposes in the world. This will inevitably set them apart as different from the people around them—not because they legalistically follow a different moral code but because they live in this world as people dedicated to God, as truly good people who acknowledge God in all they do.

The language of slavery that Paul uses to illustrate submission shows well the sense of total obligation felt by one who recognizes God as Lord—just as it shows the inescapable bondage of nonbelievers to sin. "It is doubtful whether there is any other [figure] which can so clearly express the total belongingness, the total obligation, the total commitment and the total accountability, which characterize the life under grace" (Cranfield 1980:326). The analogy of slavery, however, fails to do justice to Paul's understanding of submission to the Lord as a response of warmhearted gratitude for God's mercy and grace; hence, he acknowledges the inadequate nature of the analogy (6:19). The language of slavery is not intended to negate the importance of human choice (6:16): "Don't you realize that you become the slave of whatever you choose to obey? You can be a slave to sin . . . or you can choose to obey God." For the Christian, then, slavery—either to the terrible bondage of sin or the joyful bondage of the Lord—is a choice we make. Because Christ gave up everything for us, we gladly give up our lives to serve him as slaves, with joy and gratitude (12:1-2; 14:7-9; 2 Cor 5:14-15). The result is liberating—a life of holiness freely lived for him as our Lord. Ironically, in giving up ourselves to become a slave of the one who created us and loved us, even to the point of giving up his own Son for us, we have the sense of being freed to become who we are really meant to be. We only "find" our life by "losing" it; as Jesus says, "If you try to hang on to your life, you will lose it. But if you give up your life for my sake and for the sake of the Good News, you will save it" (Mark 8:35). Real life, then—the liberated life, the life of freedom—is found, paradoxically, in devoted slavery—to the Lord. For, as Paul says to the Corinthians, in Christ, "slaves" are really free, and the "free" are really slaves (1 Cor 7:22). In Jesus Christ, slavery and freedom are defined no longer by external circumstances but inwardly, by the orientation of one's heart. The result is a radically different way of thinking about slavery and freedom.

In this chapter, then, Paul is responding to potential objections to his emphasis on salvation as a free gift of God's grace apart from obedience to the law of Moses, and the rejection of the law as a foundation for morality and ethics that this seems to imply. Here Paul lays a foundation for Christian morality and ethics that is based not on obedience to the law but on one's relationship to Christ and commitment to God. Christians are no longer governed by the demands of the Mosaic law but by the power of a new life and commitment that transcends both the demands of the law and the power of sin (6:14, 18, 22). As a result, they are to turn their back on sin, considering themselves "dead" to sin and "alive" to Christ. Free of the law, they are to live the whole of their life in submission and obedience to the Lord and to the life of holiness he desires.

With a nice touch of theological sophistication, Paul finishes the chapter by reminding us that, though our sin merits the sentence of death, eternal life must always be understood as a sheer gift of God's grace (6:23). So we must never rely on the quality of our moral life itself to save us—that will always be insufficient; but genuine, saving faith in Christ will change the quality of our moral life.

◆　　2. What about the law? (7:1-25)
　　　a. We are no longer bound by the law (7:1-6)

Now, dear brothers and sisters*—you who are familiar with the law—don't you know that the law applies only while a person is living? ²For example, when a woman marries, the law binds her to her husband as long as he is alive. But if he dies, the laws of marriage no longer apply to her. ³So while her husband is alive, she would be committing adultery if she married another man. But if her husband dies, she is free from that law and does not commit adultery when she remarries.

⁴So, my dear brothers and sisters, this is the point: You died to the power of the law when you died with Christ. And now you are united with the one who was raised from the dead. As a result, we can produce a harvest of good deeds for God.

⁵When we were controlled by our old nature,* sinful desires were at work within us, and the law aroused these evil desires that produced a harvest of sinful deeds, resulting in death. ⁶But now we have been released from the law, for we died to it and are no longer captive to its power. Now we can serve God, not in the old way of obeying the letter of the law, but in the new way of living in the Spirit.

7:1 Greek *brothers;* also in 7:4.   7:5 Greek *When we were in the flesh.*

NOTES

7:1 dear brothers and sisters. Gr., *adelphoi* [TG80, ZG81].

you who are familiar with the law. Because the word "the" is omitted in the Gr., this ambiguous phrase could refer to the nature of law in general, or the Roman law, or the Jewish law (the law of Moses). The last is the most likely in this context.

the law applies. Lit., "the law governs" (*kurieuei* [TG2961, ZG3259]).

7:2 For example. Not in the Gr. text, but implied.

7:3 she would be committing adultery. Or, "she incurs the stigma of adultery" (Phillips translation). Lit., "she will be called (*chrēmatisei* [TG5537, ZG5976]; i.e., be publicly known as) an adulteress." Cf. Mark 10:12.

7:4 brothers and sisters. Cf. note on 7:1.

You died to the power of the law. Lit., "you died to the law." Believers are no longer subject to the law's enslaving power.

when you died with Christ. Lit., "through the body of Christ." When one is joined to Christ in baptism, one comes to share in his death and in the freedom derived from it. Here the "body of Christ" is not a reference to the Eucharist or the church (Fitzmyer 1993:458) but to Christ's atoning sacrifice on the cross.

And now you are united with the one who was raised from the dead. Lit., "so that you might belong to another, to the one who was raised from the dead." Unlike the marriage relationship, one's relationship to Christ will not be broken by death.

As a result, we can produce a harvest of good deeds for God. Lit., "in order that (*hina* [TG2443, ZG2671]) we might bear fruit for God"; cf. 7:5. A life of true goodness is possible for those who are joined to Christ because the life of Christ (the Spirit of Christ) is now active within them (Gal 2:20; 5:22-23).

7:5 When we were controlled by our old nature. Lit., "For when we were in the flesh" (*en tē sarki* [TG4561, ZG4922])—that is, in our preconversion state, dominated by the power of sin.

sinful desires were at work within us, and the law aroused these evil desires. Lit., "the sinful desires [that come] through the law were working in our members." For a description of the way the law stimulates covetousness, see 7:7-13.

that produced a harvest of sinful deeds, resulting in death. Lit., "to bear fruit for death"— that is, ultimate death in the final judgment. "Death" has the same meaning in 1:32; 6:16, 21, 23; 8:6. Cf. the contrasting phrase "bear fruit for God" in 7:4 (NRSV; cf. NLT's "produce a harvest of good deeds for God").

7:6 *we have been released from the law.* Some inferior Gr. mss (D F G) read, "we have been freed from the law of death," as in 8:2. The reference is to the law of Moses.

for we died to it and are no longer captive to its power. Lit., "having died [to that] by which we were held down"—that is, the law.

not in the old way of obeying the letter of the law. Lit., "not by the oldness of the letter" (*palaiotēti grammatos* [TG3821/1121, ZG4095G/1207]), or "not by an antiquated code." Paul understood the life of an observant Jew—as traditionally conceived—to be a life of literal observance of an external code.

but in the new way of living in the Spirit. Lit., "in newness of spirit" (*en kainotēti pneumatos* [TG2538/4151, ZG2786/4460]). Cf. 2 Cor 3:6, where Paul speaks of a "new covenant . . . not of written laws, but of the Spirit. The old written covenant ends in death; but under the new covenant, the Spirit gives life." "Now the Spirit supplies from within that regulative principle which once the law, and that imperfectly, supplied from without" (Bruce 1985:139). In the background lies the OT promise of a new covenant and a transformed, obedient heart, empowered by the Spirit of God (Jer 31:31-34; Ezek 11:19-20; 36:25-27). The contrast between "letter" and "Spirit" found in Romans and 2 Corinthians is paralleled by a contrast between "flesh" and "Spirit" in Romans and Galatians (Bruce 1985:46, n.1). Here we see the link between law ("letter") and sin ("flesh") in Paul's thinking.

COMMENTARY

The statement made by Paul in 6:14 ("Sin is no longer your master, for you no longer live under the requirements of the law") might well have left some of his readers confused and even offended. How could Paul speak so disparagingly of the law? After all, it wasn't just the "law of Moses" or the "Jewish law"—it was the law of God, sacred Scripture, the authoritative word of God. Hadn't it been given as a revelation from God himself, to reveal his ways to his people, so they would live the kind of life he wanted them to live? How then could Paul speak of it in such a derogatory way, as something that stimulates the power of sin in a person's life?

Many pious Jews, especially those from a Pharisaic background, took the demands of the law seriously and earnestly attempted to order the whole of their life according to its regulations and the orthodox interpretation of those regulations. Psalm 119 is a fine expression of early Jewish devotion to the law:

> How I delight in your commands! How I love them! . . . Your decrees have been the theme of my songs wherever I have lived. . . . Oh, how I love your instructions! I think about them all day long. . . . How sweet your words taste to me; they are sweeter than honey. . . . Your word is a lamp to guide my feet and a light for my path. . . . Your laws are my treasure; they are my heart's delight. I am determined to keep your decrees. . . . Truly, I love your commands more than gold, even the finest gold. . . . I pant with expectation, longing for your commands. (Ps 119:47, 54, 97, 103, 105, 111-112, 127, 131)

Paul himself speaks of his zealous preconversion devotion to the law as irreproachable by normal Jewish standards: "As for righteousness, I obeyed the law without fault" (Phil 3:6). Devout Jews like Paul traditionally relied on their strict observance of the law to gain God's approval and blessing.

More ordinary Jews, however—typical Jews in the towns and rural areas, many of whom were minimally literate at best—often found the law of Moses over-whelming. Who could ever observe it all? (Peter speaks of the law as "a yoke that neither we nor our ancestors were able to bear," Acts 15:10.) Indeed, who could even remember it all? It wasn't simply the 613 regulations of the law of Moses itself; it was all the multiplied minutiae of its oral interpretation, called "the tradition of the elders"—thousands upon thousands of meticulous legal opinions accumu-lated and handed down over the generations, spelling out in great detail exactly how the law was to be understood in specific cases. These legal opinions were even-tually organized and written down in the Mishnah and later greatly expanded in the Jewish Talmud. There were hundreds of specific rulings, for example, regarding the Sabbath law alone—specific activities that were permitted or prohibited on the Sabbath. There was no way that ordinary Jews could acquire a comprehensive grasp of the details of the law as they would have been discussed among the rabbis, let alone live them all out. No wonder, then, that most ordinary Jews were viewed as "sinners" (nonobservant Jews) by the religious elite who attempted to observe the law scrupulously. Though most ordinary Jews spoke of the law of Moses with re-spect and reverence, many simply found it a burden.

Paul, for his part, had come to a whole new understanding of the law as a result of his conversion to Christ. Paul had discovered in Christ a new life and power—a new sense of God's forgiving grace, of joy and peace—that he had never known before. And in Christ he had discovered a new "righteousness"—"not . . . a righteousness of my own that comes from the law, but one that comes through faith in Christ, the righteousness from God based on faith" (Phil 3:9, NRSV), a righteousness available to Jews and Gentiles alike. As a result of his conversion and his understanding of salvation in Christ, Paul had been led into deeper reflection on the law and its rela-tion to the Christian Good News. In the process, he had come to a deeper awareness of the limitations of the law and the difficulties it poses for those who seek to take it seriously. He had become aware of the subtle but clear connection between the law and sinning—the surprising way that the demands of the law actually serve to stim-ulate and reinforce sin and heighten people's awareness of their sin. He was pain-fully aware that, in his own life, it was his devotion to the law that brought about the worst of his sins, his persecution of the church (Gal 1:13-14; Phil 3:6; cf. 1 Tim 1:13, 15-16). So his own experience validated what he had learned through his conver-sion and what the Good News revealed to him—that freedom from sin is linked to freedom from the law.

Thus, in this chapter, he gives us his Christian understanding of the Mosaic law and its inadequacies and the role it plays on a deeper level in the service of Christ and the Good News. Just as in chapter 6 he illustrated the Christian's freedom from sin by drawing a parallel to slaves and masters, here Paul illustrates the Christian's freedom from the tyrannical rule of the Mosaic law by drawing a parallel to the tra-ditional laws of marriage, which lose their binding power when one of the spouses dies (7:1-3). For example, as long as a woman's husband is alive, she is bound by the aw to remain faithful to her husband; but if the husband dies, she is free to remarry. In the same way, because we died with Christ on the cross, our relation to the law of Moses is now "dead," and we have become remarried—to the resurrected Christ himself (7:4). Though the analogy may not be exact, the point is clear: Just as death breaks the binding relation between husband and wife, so death—our death, effected by Christ's death on the cross—breaks our relation to the binding authority of the law. As a result, it is no longer the Mosaic law that governs our lives, but the living Christ to whom we have now become bound. Whereas the law could only arouse and reinforce the sinful desires of the old life, producing sinful acts resulting in the sentence of death (7:5), Christ now makes it possible to live a new life with new desires, making us productive in the service of God (7:4; cf. Gal 2:19-20). In the old life, we were enslaved by the law of Moses; in the new life, we are empowered by the Spirit of the resurrected Christ (7:6). The Christian life, then, is not a life driven by the accumulated legislation of Mosaic law ("the letter of the law") but by the life and power of the Spirit of God himself—"for the letter kills, but the Spirit gives life" (2 Cor 3:6, NRSV). So the Christian life has a completely different "feel" to it, compared with life "under the law"; now it is possible to be joyfully obedient, knowing that our lives can be productive in God's service. This passage has implications for the interpretation of the problematic passage that follows in 7:14-25. For here, as in 8:1-17, it is clear that the Christian is no longer under the enslaving power of sin and the law ("When you are directed by the Spirit, you are not under obligation to the law of Moses," Gal 5:18, 23)—and that is precisely the point that Paul is making in this context.

In the background lies the promise of the "new covenant" that God made long ago through the prophet Jeremiah—a promise that includes these words: "I will put my instructions deep within them, and I will write them on their hearts" (Jer 31:33). Similarly, through Jeremiah's younger contemporary Ezekiel, God said, "I will give you a new heart, and I will put a new spirit in you. I will take out your stony, stubborn heart and give you a tender, responsive heart. And I will put my Spirit in you so that you will follow my decrees and be careful to obey my regulations" (Ezek 36:26-27; cf. Ezek 11:19-20).

From time to time in Jewish piety there had arisen the awareness that a fully obedient life required something more than determined observance of the letter of the law. There was the realization that if true goodness and piety were to be experienced, God himself had to transform the heart of his people and give them new desires—desires to obey his wishes. Consider, for example, the repentant psalmist's prayer: "Create in me a clean heart, O God. Renew a loyal spirit within me" (Ps 51:10). In the understanding of orthodox Judaism, this renewal was clearly linked to the work of God's Spirit and to the expectation of the eschatological "pouring out" of his Spirit spoken of by the prophet Joel (Joel 2:28-29). The pure desires required of true goodness could only arise from a pure and obedient heart—one transformed by the work of God's Spirit.

Paul's understanding and experience of the Christian life as a life filled with the Spirit of God (Eph 5:18) is very much in line with this tradition. He knows that the only hope for a truly good life lies not in determined attempts to follow the law more exactly but in opening one's heart and life to the full power of God's Spirit and in letting one's life be fully controlled by his Spirit. "The Holy Spirit produces this kind of fruit in our lives: love, joy, peace, patience, kindness, goodness, faithfulness, gentleness, and self-control. There is no law against these things!" (Gal 5:22-23; cf. Rom 8:2-4). The Spirit is nothing less than the life of the resurrected Christ himself at work in the hearts of his redeemed people (Gal 2:20; Col 1:27). So for Paul, Christian living at its best represents the ultimate fulfillment of Jeremiah's new covenant. The whole of the Christian life is to be understood as life "in the Spirit."

Practically speaking, the evangelical tradition has always emphasized the close link between a Spirit-controlled life and the practice of reading Scripture. The reading of Scripture is a means to living life "in the Spirit." Although Paul was not speaking strictly of Scripture when he spoke of the word of God as "the sword of the Spirit" (it is rather the sword the Spirit provides or uses in spiritual war; Eph 6:17), in a broader sense sacred Scripture—the "word of God"—does function as an instrument the Spirit uses to conform our life to the will of God.

So Scripture and the Spirit of God function together as sanctifying agents in the believer's life. It is the reading of Scripture that lifts our sights beyond the mundane and brings us into the dimension of the Spirit. It is the reading of Scripture that sensitizes us to the life of the Spirit and strengthens our desires for a deeper, fuller experience of that life. So the word of God and the Spirit of God work hand-in-hand to sanctify our lives, and serious Christians will open their hearts to both. Immersing ourselves in the prayerful reading of Scripture is a very practical means to a life filled with the Spirit.

However, the picture of the Christian life that Paul draws in this passage cautions us against all conceptions of it as a life scrupulously lived according to a certain set of rules or demands. There is a freedom and spontaneity about the Christian life that keeps it from fitting into any legalistic framework. Of course, there are moral absolutes (defined by Scripture) that the Christian must take seriously; but the Christian life can never be understood simply as a matter of the scrupulous observance of rules or the detailed fulfillment of one's duty, like a heavy and burdensome responsibility. Paul's view of Christian living is a more buoyant and cheerful thing—a free, joyous, and grateful response to the marvelous grace of God, motivated by the Spirit of God that fills, empowers, and directs one's life according to the will of God.

◆   ### b. God's law reveals our sin (7:7-13)

7Well then, am I suggesting that the law of God is sinful? Of course not! In fact, it was the law that showed me my sin. I would never have known that coveting is wrong if the law had not said, "You must not covet."* 8But sin used this command to arouse all kinds of covetous desires within me! If there were no law, sin would not have that power. ⁹At one time I lived without understanding the law. But when I learned the command not to covet, for instance, the power of sin came to life, ¹⁰and I died. So I discovered that the law's commands, which were supposed to bring life, brought spiritual death instead. ¹¹Sin took advantage of those commands and deceived me; it used the commands to kill me. ¹²But still, the law itself is holy, and its commands are holy and right and good.

¹³But how can that be? Did the law, which is good, cause my death? Of course not! Sin used what was good to bring about my condemnation to death. So we can see how terrible sin really is. It uses God's good commands for its own evil purposes.

7:7 Exod 20:17; Deut 5:21.

N O T E S

7:7 *Of course not!* This emphatic negation (*mē genoito* [ᵀᴳ3361/1096, ᶻᴳ3590/1181]) occurs ten times in Romans (3:4, 6, 31; 6:2, 15; 7:7, 13; 9:14; 11:1, 11) but nowhere else in Paul's writings.

it was the law that showed me my sin. Lit., "I would not have known sin except through the law."

I would never have known that coveting is wrong. Or, "I would not have known what it is to covet" (NRSV). Lit., "I would not have known covetousness"—that is, the experience of coveting as sin. In this section (7:7-13), "I" would seem to be a reference primarily to Paul himself, but with clear implications for all who see themselves as under the law. Cf. note on 7:14.

You must not covet. The last of the Ten Commandments (Exod 20:17; Deut 5:21).

7:8 *sin used this command to arouse all kinds of covetous desires.* Here sin is personified as a power active in a person's life (cf. 7:11). There is a strange propensity in human beings to desire things they know to be forbidden. Cf. Col 3:5, which speaks of covetousness as a form of idolatry.

If there were no law, sin would not have that power. Lit., "apart from the law sin is dead"—that is, inactive, powerless, or at least relatively so (cf. 1 Cor 15:56: "The law gives sin its power"). In another sense, it is the awareness of breaking the law that makes sin a conscious reality to us.

7:9 *At one time I lived without understanding the law.* Or, "There was a time when, in the absence of law, I was fully alive" (REB)—that is, blissfully unconvicted. Lit., "I was once alive apart from the law" (cf. NIV). Though this may refer to an earlier time in Paul's own life when he was less convicted by the rigorous demands of the law, it also applies more broadly to Israel as a whole before the giving of the law (Moo 1996:437). Some see in it a reference to the experience of Adam—and therefore of every person, as a result of their link to him.

7:9-10 *But when I learned the command not to covet, for instance, the power of sin came to life, and I died.* Lit., "but when the commandment came, sin came alive, and I died." Though this may refer to a specific point in Paul's own life, it also applies more generally to all who seek to take the law seriously and to the historical result of the giving of the law (represented by the tenth commandment). In the background of Paul's thinking may lie God's command to Adam and Eve (Gen 2:16-17), whose sin of disobedience arose from covetousness. The law activates sin in two senses: (1) It stimulates sin as a power in our life, arousing in us a desire to do what we know is wrong. (2) It convicts us when we do sin because we know the commands we have broken.

7:10 *the law's commands, which were supposed to bring life.* Cf. Lev 18:5: "If you obey my decrees and my regulations, you will find life through them" (cf. Rom 10:5).

brought spiritual death instead. The word "spiritual" is added by the NLT for clarity.

7:11 *Sin took advantage of those commands and deceived me; it used the commands to kill me.* See notes on 7:8, 9, 10, and the parallels to the serpent's deception of Eve in Gen 3 (Cranfield 1980:352-353).

7:12 *But still, the law itself is holy.* In spite of its negative function, the law remains in essence a "holy" (*hagios* [TG40, ZG41]) gift of God.

right. Or, "just" (*dikaia* [TG1342, ZG1465]).

7:13 *Of course not!* See note on 7:7.

So we can see how terrible sin really is. Or, "thereby sin exposed its true character . . . sin became more sinful than ever" (REB)—that is, by its use of God's good commands for its own evil purposes. Lit., "in order that it might be revealed as sin, and . . . become sinful beyond measure."

C O M M E N T A R Y

Does this mean that the law of Moses is something bad? If the Mosaic law actually serves to stimulate sin, is the law inherently evil? No, not at all, Paul replies, the law is a holy gift from God and it has a God-given purpose—but its deepest purpose is not what people commonly think. In its hundreds of detailed regulations, the law is intended to reveal to us not the way of salvation but our sin. Its most important function is to show us how desperately we need God's forgiving grace. Confronting people with the strong demands of God, the law of Moses provides no moral answer to the problem of sin (i.e., its power over people)—it simply condemns it. (Here the focus is on the law's negative moral function, not its teaching about justification by faith, as in 4:3.) The problem, however, is not the law itself; the problem is the terrible power of sin within us, to which we are all enslaved.

Though the law of Moses is in no way to be viewed as something sinful, it does serve the purpose of making us painfully conscious of our sin. By way of example, Paul speaks of the devastating effect on his own life of the last of the Ten Commandments, "You must not covet" (7:7-11; Exod 20:17; Deut 5:21). (It is significant that, of all the Ten Commandments, Paul highlights the one that focuses on inner attitudes—in this case, attitudes of greed—and not simply on overt acts.) If it weren't for the law of Moses that spells out this commandment, he would never have recognized the full depths of this selfish and illicit tendency in his own life. But once recognized, the desire to covet was further aroused and reinforced by the constant reminder of the law not to do it. In other words, the law had the perverse effect of stimulating the very sin it banned. As long as Paul remained oblivious to the command, his sense of sin and guilt lay dormant; but once he became aware of the law's demands, sinful desires—and with them, guilt—sprang to life, and he knew himself to be a condemned man. So the very law that he had assumed to be the way to life, in reality, proved to be the sentence of death. Such is the perverse effect of decrees that prohibit immoral actions—or rather, such is the strange response of immoral human nature to them. (Compare the effect of a "No

Smoking" sign on habitual smokers who may have forgotten, until they see it, how much they want to smoke; Bruce 1985: 140.) This propensity is precisely why legislation can never produce truly virtuous living. Human nature being what it is, no legal code has the power to produce a truly virtuous life. Real goodness, then, cannot be legislated; it has to arise from a deeper motivation within.

Does this mean that the law of Moses itself is fundamentally a bad thing? No, says Paul, the law itself is not bad. It may be frustrating, it may be maddeningly exasperating, but it remains a holy gift of God, intended for our good. ("The law itself is holy, and its commands are holy and right and good," 7:12; cf. 9:4.) But the way the law does its God-given work is to make us feel the full weight of our sin—to make us feel our need of forgiveness. So its most important function, in the service of the Good News and our salvation, is a negative one.

Does this mean that the law itself, a sacred revelation from the Holy One, is the cause of our ultimate doom? No, Paul says, it is sin that dooms us, not the law (7:13). Here we observe the diabolical nature of sin: sin takes the holy law of God and destroys us with it. It uses the divine law for its own evil purposes, to arouse forbidden desires within us. The problem, then, lies not in the good law of God but in the sinful nature of human beings. The problem is not that the demands of the law are too great or the standards of the law too high but that human nature is too weak. The power of sin in a person's life is too great, too all-pervasive, too perverse. No matter how well intentioned a person may be, no one has what it takes to live out the demands of the law fully; this is the ultimate predicament confronting those who view the law as a way of salvation. And this is the point Paul drives home in the section that follows.

◆   ## c. The power of sin in our lives (7:14-25)

14So the trouble is not with the law, for it is spiritual and good. The trouble is with me, for I am all too human, a slave to sin. 15I don't really understand myself, for I want to do what is right, but I don't do it. Instead, I do what I hate. 16But if I know that what I am doing is wrong, this shows that I agree that the law is good. 17So I am not the one doing wrong; it is sin living in me that does it.

18And I know that nothing good lives in me, that is, in my sinful nature.* I want to do what is right, but I can't. 19I want to do what is good, but I don't. I don't want to do what is wrong, but I do it anyway. 20But if I do what I don't want to do, I am not really the one doing wrong; it is sin living in me that does it.

21I have discovered this principle of life— that when I want to do what is right, I inevitably do what is wrong. 22I love God's law with all my heart. 23But there is another power* within me that is at war with my mind. This power makes me a slave to the sin that is still within me. 24Oh, what a miserable person I am! Who will free me from this life that is dominated by sin and death? 25Thank God! The answer is in Jesus Christ our Lord. So you see how it is: In my mind I really want to obey God's law, but because of my sinful nature I am a slave to sin.

7:18 Greek my flesh; also in 7:25.   7:23 Greek law; also in 7:23b.

NOTES

7:14 *the trouble is not with the law, for it is spiritual and good. The trouble is with me.*
Lit., "the law is spiritual (*pneumatikos* [TG4152, ZG4461]), but I am fleshly" (*sarkinos* [TG4560, ZG4921])—that is, "The law comes from God and is an expression of the will of God, but I am driven by sinful desires." Apart from the Spirit of God, sinful humans on their own cannot fulfill the demands of the law. In this section (7:14-25), the first person singular pronoun "I" is used for the first time in the present. It is best understood, however, as a reference not simply to Paul himself but to Paul as a representative of people generally, especially those who seek to obey the law ("I, as a typical follower of the Torah") apart from the power of the Spirit. Cf. note on 7:7 and see comments below. For a full discussion of the alternative interpretations of "I," see Cranfield 1980:342-347; Moo 1996:443-451; Schreiner 1998:379-392.

for I am all too human, a slave to sin. Lit., "sold [as a slave] under sin." Apart from the regenerating work of the Spirit, humans stand helplessly enslaved to the power of sin.

7:15 *I don't really understand myself.* In their natural state, humans cannot fully understand their inability to overcome the power of sin.

I want to do what is right, but I don't do it. Instead, I do what I hate. In their natural state, driven by the perverse power of sin, people do things their minds disapprove of because the power of sin is greater than the power of rational motives. Cf. the classical parallels from Horace ("I pursue the things that have done me harm; I shun the things I believe will do me good") and Ovid ("I see and approve the better course, but I follow the worse one") cited in Bruce 1985:145.

7:17 *So I am not the one doing wrong; it is sin living in me that does it.* Here Paul distinguishes between "himself" and the power of sin at work within him (cf. 7:20).

7:18 *in my sinful nature.* Lit., "in my flesh" (*en tē sarki mou* [TG4561, ZG4922])—that is, apart from the experience of the Holy Spirit.

7:20 *I am not really the one doing wrong; it is sin living in me that does it.* A repetition of 7:17.

7:21 *this principle of life.* Or, "this rule." Lit., "the law" (*ton nomon* [TG3551, ZG3795]).

I inevitably do what is wrong. Lit., "evil lies ready."

7:22 *with all my heart.* Lit., "according to the inner man" (*ton esō anthrōpon* [TG2080/444, ZG2276/476])—that is, "with my deepest desires" (cf. 2 Cor 4:16; Eph 3:16). In our natural state, it is possible to have right desires (cf. Ps 119:97, 111, 127) yet have no power to live them out.

7:23 *there is another power.* Lit., "I see a different law"—that is, the law of sin, different from the law of God (7:22), of which the mind approves (7:23).

within me. Lit., "in my members" (*en tois melesin mou* [TG3196, ZG3517]). Here Paul seems to distinguish between the desires of the mind and the actions of the body. Sin expresses itself in or through the "body" (*sōma* [TG4983, ZG5393]; see notes on 6:6; 7:24; 8:13), in opposition to the desires of the mind.

7:24 *Oh, what a miserable person I am!* Though some understand this as the sentiment of a frustrated Christian, it is better understood as the cry of a frustrated lover of the Mosaic law (of which Paul makes himself an example). The point of the larger context (7:4-6; 8:1-14) is that by the Holy Spirit Christians are given power to overcome sin.

Who will free me from this life that is dominated by sin and death? Lit., "Who will rescue me from this body of death?" Because the human body serves the cause of sin (sin works in and through our "members," 7:23), the body must die (8:10). (For the link between sin and the body, see notes on 6:6; 8:13; cf. Black 1973:104, 110.) Some wrongly assume that these words reflect Paul's eschatological desire to be free of bodily existence. In longing to be free from the weak-willed body (cf. Mark 14:38), Paul is really expressing his desire to be free here and now from the controlling power of sin that uses the weakness of the body for its own evil purposes.

7:25 Thank God! The answer is in Jesus Christ our Lord. This interjection anticipates ch 8, which speaks of the power of the life-giving Spirit to deliver believers from the power of sin and death, though it occurs before the final summary comment of 7:25b. Lit., "Thanks be to God through our Lord Jesus Christ." This is the reading of ℵ¹ B 33. Other mss (ℵ* A 1739 𝔐) read, "I thank God."

So you see how it is. These words introduce a final summary of 7:14-25. There is no need to think that this sentence was misplaced; 7:25a is an interjection anticipating ch 8.

In my mind. In the mind of the devout Jew seeking to follow the law of Moses, of which Paul makes himself an example—not the Spirit-renewed mind of 12:2.

because of my sinful nature. Lit., "in the flesh."

C O M M E N T A R Y

In this section, which overflows with frustration and despair, Paul probes the full depths of the weakness of human nature—the inability of people to do the good they want to do. Using himself as an example, Paul says in essence, "The problem is not the law of Moses, the problem is my own human weakness. It's not that the demands of the law are too high; I simply don't have within myself the power to live them out. Deep within me I really want to obey the demands of God, but I find I am simply unable to do so. I know what is right, but I don't do it; and I know what is wrong, but I can't keep from doing it. There is this terrible propensity within me to always do the wrong thing, which keeps me from living the kind of obedient life I long to live. I find myself imprisoned, enslaved to this dark and perverse power within that forces me to sin, and I find absolutely no power in myself to deal with it. What a wretched existence! Where do I turn for help?"

This is not just Paul's problem; it is the dilemma facing every pious Jew who wants to take the law seriously, and that's why obedience to the law cannot be considered a requirement for salvation. (This section functions as part of Paul's larger argument against those who are objecting that people must observe the Mosaic law in order to be saved.) People may know the law inside and out, Paul contends—and even have the most sincere desire to obey it—but in themselves they have no power to live it out fully. Given the perversity of human nature, full obedience to the holy standards of the law lies well beyond the capabilities of any human being. So keeping the law cannot be viewed as essential for salvation.

Before we go further with our interpretation of this passage, it is essential to identify who this person is—this "I" that is speaking. On the surface, it sounds like Paul is talking about himself—and because of his use of the present tense, about his current life as a Christian ("I, Paul, as a Christian"). Hence, many readers take this passage to be a reflection of his own frustration in trying to live out the Christian life—and an indication, therefore, of the difficulties that we as Christians inevitably face in trying to live out our Christian life today. As a result, many Christians have resigned themselves to a pessimistic view of the Christian life, to the lifelong frustration of being unable to do what they know they should do or to live the way they know they should live. The assumption is that the depressing experience Paul describes in Romans 7 is to be understood as normative for the Christian life (so Augustine, Luther, Calvin, Hodge, Nygren, Knox and Cragg, Cranfield, Dunn, Morris, Edwards).

However, such an interpretation sharply conflicts with the much more positive view of the Christian life that Paul gives us elsewhere. Even here, the point he is making in the larger context is that now, in Jesus Christ, the believer is no longer helpless under the enslaving power of sin and the law but is liberated from its rule by the new life of the Spirit. In chapter 6, challenging the claim that the Good News of grace leaves Christians free to sin, he wrote, "Sin is no longer your master, for you no longer live under the requirements of the law. Instead, you live under the freedom of God's grace. . . . Now you are free from your slavery to sin. . . . Now you are free from the power of sin and have become slaves of God" (6:14, 18, 22). Similarly, at the beginning of chapter 7, he emphasized that because Christians are free from the enslaving power of the law and joined to Christ, they can now produce "a harvest of good deeds for God" (7:4); and immediately following the present section, in chapter 8, Paul makes the same point again: "The power of the life-giving Spirit has freed you from the power of sin that leads to death. . . . God declared an end to sin's control over us" (8:2ff; cf. Gal 5:18). So the whole point of the larger context (7:4-6; 8:1-17) is that God has now given believers power over sin, and as a result, sin can no longer dominate their lives the way it once did. Part of the Good News of Christ is that now we are freed from the enslaving power of sin and the law so that by the power of the Spirit of God we can actually begin to live the kind of life God wants us to live! Salvation, then, gives us not only the forgiveness of our sins but also a new power over sin—because Jesus Christ came to "take away our sins" (1 John 3:5; cf. Matt 1:21).

It is this sharp contrast with statements in the immediate context, both preceding and following this section, that most clearly suggests 7:14-25 is describing the conflict not of the regenerated Christian with the Holy Spirit but of the person living helplessly under the power of sin and the law *apart from* the power of the Spirit. (Notice also that there is no reference to the Spirit in this passage and that the conflict described is between sin and the mind, not between sin and the Spirit.) Romans 7:14-25 is a continuation, then, of the discussion in 7:7-13 about the function of the law of Moses, showing the way sin is aroused by the law. Apart from a shift in tense, necessitated by the use of the present tense in 7:14a and continued naturally from that point on, there is no sharp break with the immediately preceding context, which explicitly describes the situation of a person under the law. Though Paul uses his own life as an example, the "I" is intended to be representative of all who try to live by the law, in order to show the impossibility of doing so. Paul is writing here not primarily of his own experience but of the plight of people more generally. The point he is making is that in and of ourselves we simply do not have what it takes to live out the life demanded by the law of Moses (so Origen and most of the early Greek fathers, Denney, Leenhardt, Achtemeier, Stuhlmacher).

In view of the seemingly strong arguments that can be mustered for each of the two main interpretations of 7:14-25—as either a postconversion or preconversion experience—it is not surprising that several commentators argue for a compromise position (so Scott, Brunner, Mitton, Best, Fung, Thomas, Schreiner). Some interpret the passage as the cry of a person under conviction of sin but not yet regenerate. Others interpret it as the experience of an immature Christian trying to fight sin by using his willpower. Still others see it as the experience of the sin-prone part of every person, whether Christian or not. (The arguments for the various interpretations are spelled out clearly in Moo 1996:441-451.)

Those who interpret this passage as referring to the conflict Paul was experiencing as a Christian sometimes draw parallels to Galatians 5:17, which speaks of the continuing tension between the "flesh" (the sinful drives) and the Spirit in the believer's life: "These two forces are constantly fighting each other." But there are clear differences between the two passages. In Romans 7:14-25, the conflict is not between the flesh and the Spirit but between the flesh and the mind. In 7:14-25, it is not simply the *possibility of sinning* that is being described (as in Gal 5:17) but the *impossibility of not sinning*—the situation of a person who has no experience of the Spirit. The picture of one who is "a slave to sin," unable to do what is good because he is held captive by the power of sin (7:14, 23), is simply not in keeping with Paul's view of the Christian life generally, empowered as it is by the Spirit of God.

We conclude, then, that to interpret 7:14-25 as Paul's understanding of what is normative for the Christian life, and therefore as the norm for Christians today ("I want to do what is right, but I simply can't"), does a disservice both to Paul and to the New Testament view of the Christian life generally. Overall, Paul's letters reflect a much higher view of the potential and power characteristic of the Christian life, resulting from the gift of the Spirit that is now given to God's people. Though he nowhere speaks of a state of perfection or sinlessness to be attained in this life (cf. Phil 3:12-14), Paul certainly suggests that we can now actually begin to experience something of the kind of life that God desires because of the salvation from sin that is ours in Jesus Christ. This, too, is part of the Good News.

The point Paul was making is summed up at the very end of the passage: "In my mind I [as a typical devout Jew] really want to obey God's law, but because of my sinful nature I am a slave to sin" (7:25b). That is, on our own—by our own power— we simply do not have what it takes to live out the law of God; but there is hope for something much better, and it is anticipated in Paul's exclamation in 7:25a: "Thank God! The answer is in Jesus Christ our Lord." This "answer" is spelled out in the immediately following passage (8:1-14), which heralds the power of the Spirit that has now come into the Christian's life. This is what is missing in the despairing experience of those who would live by the law.

In summary, then, anticipating criticism of his "low" view of the Mosaic law in God's scheme of things, Paul shows there is a foundation for Christian morality that is not based on the law (ch 6), and then points out the inadequacy of the law itself as a basis for moral living (ch 7). The deeper function of the law, he insists, is not to serve as a basis for salvation or Christian living but to make us aware of our need of God's forgiving grace and to point us to the Savior who provides a more adequate basis for Christian living, by the power of his life-transforming Spirit (ch 8).

◆   E. The Power and Glory of the New Life (8:1-39)
     1. Living by the power of God's Spirit (8:1-17)

So now there is no condemnation for those who belong to Christ Jesus. ²And because you belong to him, the power* of the life-giving Spirit has freed you* from the power of sin that leads to death. ³The law of Moses was unable to save us because of the weakness of our sinful nature.* So God did what the law could not do. He sent his own Son in a body like the bodies we sinners have. And in that body God declared an end to sin's control over us by giving his Son as a sacrifice for our sins. ⁴He did this so that the just requirement of the law would be fully satisfied for us, who no longer follow our sinful nature but instead follow the Spirit.

⁵Those who are dominated by the sinful nature think about sinful things, but those who are controlled by the Holy Spirit think about things that please the Spirit. ⁶So letting your sinful nature control your mind leads to death. But letting the Spirit control your mind leads to life and peace. ⁷For the sinful nature is always hostile to God. It never did obey God's laws, and it never will. ⁸That's why those who are still under the control of their sinful nature can never please God.

⁹But you are not controlled by your sinful nature. You are controlled by the Spirit if you have the Spirit of God living in you.

(And remember that those who do not have the Spirit of Christ living in them do not belong to him at all.) ¹⁰And Christ lives within you, so even though your body will die because of sin, the Spirit gives you life* because you have been made right with God. ¹¹The Spirit of God, who raised Jesus from the dead, lives in you. And just as God raised Christ Jesus from the dead, he will give life to your mortal bodies by this same Spirit living within you.

¹²Therefore, dear brothers and sisters,* you have no obligation to do what your sinful nature urges you to do. ¹³For if you live by its dictates, you will die. But if through the power of the Spirit you put to death the deeds of your sinful nature,* you will live. ¹⁴For all who are led by the Spirit of God are children* of God. ¹⁵So you have not received a spirit that makes you fearful slaves. Instead, you received God's Spirit when he adopted you as his own children.* Now we call him, "Abba, Father."* ¹⁶For his Spirit joins with our spirit to affirm that we are God's children. ¹⁷And since we are his children, we are his heirs. In fact, together with Christ we are heirs of God's glory. But if we are to share his glory, we must also share his suffering.

8:2a Greek *the law;* also in 8:2b.   8:2b Some manuscripts read *me.*   8:3 Greek *our flesh;* similarly in 8:4, 5, 6, 7, 8, 9, 12.   8:10 Or *your spirit is alive.*   8:12 Greek *brothers;* also in 8:29.   8:13 Greek *deeds of the body.* 8:14 Greek *sons;* also in 8:19.   8:15a Greek *you received a spirit of sonship.*   8:15b *Abba* is an Aramaic term for "father."

NOTES

8:1 *those who belong to Christ Jesus.* Lit., "those in Christ Jesus." Some Gr. manuscripts (A D¹) add "who do not walk according to the flesh," and other mss (א² D² 𝔐) add to this "but according to the Spirit," the reading reflected in the KJV. This longer reading almost certainly represents a later scribal qualification of the original text, emphasizing the point Paul is making in 8:1-14.

8:2 *And because you belong to him, the power of the life-giving Spirit has freed you.* Lit., "For the law of the Spirit of life in Christ Jesus has freed you." In this context, "law" is to be understood as "power"; "the law of the Spirit" contrasts with "the law of sin," already introduced in 7:23. For the different possible grammatical relationships between "law," "Spirit," "life," and "Christ Jesus," see Cranfield 1980:373-376. Instead of the final "you," evidenced by the best documentation (א B F G 1739*), some Gr. mss have "me" (A D 𝔐 1739ᶜ).

from the power of sin that leads to death. Lit., "from the law of sin and of death." The Spirit both liberates believers from the power of sin and gives them eternal life. Alternatively, "the law of sin and of death" may be understood as a reference to the law of Moses (Dunn 1988a:418-419; Schreiner 1998:400), but the parallel phrase "the law of the Spirit of life in Christ Jesus" (8:2, NASB) suggests that it is better understood as "the power of sin that leads to death."

8:3 *The law of Moses was unable to save us.* Lit., "For what the law was unable to do" —that is, in this context, to break the power of sin.

because of the weakness of our sinful nature. Lit., "because it was weak through the flesh." In this verse the weakness of the "flesh" is linked to the weakness of the body; see notes on 7:23, 24.

God did what the law could not do. Not in the Gr. text, but implied.

He sent his own Son in a body like the bodies we sinners have. Lit., "God sent his own Son in the likeness of sinful flesh" (*en homoiōmati* [TG3667, ZG3930] *sarkos hamartias*). In order to save us, it was necessary for Christ to become like us (see esp. Heb 2:17-18; 4:15-16) yet remain sinless. Paul's belief in the sinlessness of Christ is affirmed in 2 Cor 5:21 (cf. Heb 4:15; 1 Pet 2:22; 1 John 3:5). For different interpretations of "in the likeness of sinful flesh," see Cranfield 1980:379-382.

God declared an end to sin's control over us. Lit., "God . . . condemned sin in the flesh," thereby overcoming its power in the life of believers.

as a sacrifice for our sins. Lit., "for sin" (*peri hamartias* [TG266, ZG281])—that is, as a sin offering (as the phrase is commonly used in the LXX). The NLT adds "sacrifice" to convey this concept. Some interpret the phrase more generally—"with reference to sin."

8:4 *He did this so that the just requirement of the law would be fully satisfied for us.* Lit., "in order that the righteous demand (*to dikaiōma* [TG1345, ZG1468]) of the law might be fulfilled in us." The idea is either that the law would be satisfied for us or lived out in/by us— the second meaning fits the context better. As a result of Christ's sacrifice, we are enabled to live the kind of righteous life the law demands, by the power of the Spirit (cf. REB). "The just requirement of the law" does not refer to the demand for an atoning sacrifice but to the demand for moral living—now made effectively possible by the Holy Spirit (cf. Schreiner 1998:404-406).

who no longer follow our sinful nature but instead follow the Spirit. Lit., "who walk not according to the flesh but according to the Spirit." Only by the power of the Spirit can we live out the law's demands for a life of righteousness.

8:5 *sinful things.* Lit., "the things of the flesh" (*ta tēs sarkos* [TG4561, ZG4922]).

things that please the Spirit. Lit., "the things of the Spirit" (*ta tou pneumatos* [TG4151, ZG4460]).

8:6 *So letting your sinful nature control your mind leads to death.* Lit., "For the way of thinking (*phronēma* [TG5427, ZG5859]) of the flesh is death"—that is, ultimate death in the final judgment. "Death" has the same meaning in 1:32; 6:16, 21, 23; 7:5.

But letting the Spirit control your mind leads to life and peace. Lit., "but the way of thinking (*phronēma*) of the Spirit is life and peace" (*zōē kai eirēnē* [TG2222/1515, ZG2437/1645]). The word "life" refers to eternal life. For the meaning of "peace," see note on 1:7.

8:7 *It never did obey God's laws, and it never will.* Lit., "it [the flesh] does not submit to the law of God, for it cannot." The law of God is spiritual (7:14), and the "flesh" is always at war with the Spirit (Gal 5:17).

8:9 *those who do not have the Spirit of Christ living in them do not belong to him at all.* It is the presence of the Spirit in a believer's life that defines an authentic relationship with Christ (cf. 1 John 3:24; 4:13).

8:10 *And Christ lives within you, so even though your body will die because of sin.* Lit., "And if Christ is in you, the body is dead because of sin." For the connection between the body and sin, see notes on 6:6; 7:23, 24; 8:13.

the Spirit gives you life. Or, "your spirit will live." Lit., "the spirit is life" (*to pneuma zōē* [TG4151/2222, ZG4460/2437]). This may be understood as a reference to either the Holy Spirit or the human spirit, and to either the future resurrection or present experience. In both cases, the one implies the other—the two are closely linked. The following verse clearly refers to the Holy Spirit but could be understood as referring to either future resurrection or (more likely) present experience.

because you have been made right with God. Lit., "because of righteousness" (*dia dikaiosunēn* [TG1343, ZG1466])—that is, the righteousness of God (justification) received by faith in Christ (1:17; 3:21-26).

8:11 *Christ Jesus.* According to the mss ℵ* A C 1739 D*. Other Gr. mss have "the Christ" (ℵ² 𝔐) or "Christ" (B D² F G).

he will give life to your mortal bodies. Though this may be understood with regard to future resurrection, it is better interpreted in this context as a reference to the renewal of one's life in the present. "He is not speaking of the last resurrection . . . but of the continual operation of the Spirit, by which He gradually mortifies the remains of the flesh and renews in us the heavenly life" (Calvin 1960:166). For the opposite opinion, see Cranfield 1980:391; Moo 1996:492-493.

by this same Spirit. Or, "by his Spirit" (*dia autou pneumatos* [TG4151, ZG4460]). Instead of "by" (*dia* [TG1223, ZG1328] with the genitive), found in ℵ A C, some mss (B D F G 33 1739 𝔐) have "because of" (*dia* with the accusative).

8:12 *dear brothers and sisters.* Lit., "brothers" (*adelphoi* [TG80, ZG81]).

you have no obligation. Lit., "we are not debtors."

8:13 *you will die.* See note on 8:6.

if . . . you put to death the deeds of your sinful nature. Lit., "if . . . you put to death the deeds of the body" (*tas praxeis tou sōmatos* [TG4234/4983, ZG4552/5393]; cf. Col 3:5). Here Paul seems to link sinful tendencies to the passions of the body; see notes on 6:6; 7:23, 24; cf. 8:10. Generally, however, Paul identifies sinful tendencies with the "flesh" (*sarx* [TG4561, ZG4922]; i.e., sinful nature), not the "body" (*sōma*); cf. "sinful actions" (TEV).

8:14 *all who are led by the Spirit of God are children of God.* Here true believers are identified by the spiritual quality of their lives ("all who are led by the Spirit"), not simply by their claims of having the Spirit. The focus in this context is on the ethical power of the Spirit, not charismatic enthusiasm (as claimed by Dunn and Käsemann).

8:15 *So you have not received a spirit that makes you fearful slaves.* Lit., "For you did not receive a spirit of slavery [leading you back] again into fear." Cf. the contrast between slavery to the law and freedom in the Spirit in Gal 4:1-7, 21-31.

Instead, you received God's Spirit when he adopted you as his own children. Lit., "but you received a spirit of sonship" (*pneuma huiothesias* [TG4151/5206, ZG4460/5625]). The idea of adoption seems to be implied.

Abba, Father. A phrase also found in Mark 14:36 and Gal 4:6. "Abba" was an intimate Aramaic term for "Daddy," the familiar term used by Jewish children to address their fathers. By Jesus' time the term had come to be used more broadly, though it was not a term commonly used of God. The common use of "Abba, Father" in the Greek-speaking churches may derive from Jesus' use of the term "Abba" when praying. See discussion of the term in Fee 1994:410-412.

8:16 *joins with our spirit to affirm.* Lit., "bears witness to our spirit." This is the NT basis of the doctrine of the "inner witness of the Holy Spirit" (cf. 1 John 5:7-8).

God's children. There is no significant difference between "sons of God" (*huioi theou* [TG5207, ZG5626]; 8:14) and "children of God" (*tekna theou* [TG5043, ZG5451]; 8:16) in Paul's usage. In the writings of John, however, believers are not called "sons of God" but "children of God," and the phrase "Son of God" is reserved for Christ.

8:17 *In fact, together with Christ we are heirs of God's glory.* Lit., "fellow-heirs with Christ." For the meaning of "glory," see note on 5:2.

C O M M E N T A R Y

In chapter 8, Paul focuses on another aspect of the amazing salvation he has been describing since 3:21—the gift of the Spirit, which gives believers power over sin (8:1-14), confirms their status as sons of God (8:15-17), and assures them of ultimate glory (8:18-30). He brings the chapter to a close with a ringing declaration of the assurance of God's eternal love for all who belong to his Son (8:31-39), a fitting conclusion to chapters 1-8.

The Spirit Gives Us Power over Sin. In sharp contrast to the despair that marks the end of chapter 7, Paul begins chapter 8 with the strong affirmation, "Now there is no condemnation for those who belong to Christ Jesus" (8:1). And why is there no condemnation? Because God declares us "not guilty" when we receive his Son and put our trust in him to save us, because Christ bore the condemnation we deserved—or such, at least, would be the theological response we would expect from Paul (1:16; 3:21-26; 5:1). But here, in a different context making a different point, he words it differently: Those who belong to Jesus Christ face no condemnation because the power of his life-giving Spirit has freed them from the dreaded power of sin and death to which they were enslaved (8:2; cf. 6:14, 18, 22). They no longer need to live in despair, under a cloud of failure and guilt. This emphasis on the Spirit as the ultimate liberating agent has already been expressed in 7:4-6, where the focus was on freedom from the law. Here, after the digression of 7:7-25, Paul returns to the same emphasis, but with the focus on freedom from sin and death. Freedom from sin and death (8:2) is clearly linked in Paul's thinking to freedom from the law (6:14; 7:4-6), which evokes sin and gives the death sentence (7:7-11). In either case, true freedom is found only in the life-giving Spirit, for "wherever the Spirit of the Lord is, there is freedom" (2 Cor 3:17).

In 7:14-25, Paul argues that the law of Moses has no power to overcome a person's moral weakness, or to produce the life of integrity and goodness demanded by God. The real power, Paul claims, lies not in the law but in the new life in Christ—in the transforming power of his Spirit, the power that breaks the chains of sin and makes true goodness possible at last. In the past, the desire of serious Jews to live out the law of Moses was constantly frustrated by the sheer weakness of human resolve—the power of sin within. But Christ's death on the cross has overcome that weakness and "declared an end to sin's control over us" (8:3), thereby opening up the possibility of a genuinely transformed life. Christ has pronounced the sentence of death on sin and by his own presence within us gives us the power we need to live a transformed life.

When Paul speaks of God sending his Son as a sacrifice, to do "what the law could not do" (8:3), he is not speaking simply of God's desire to forgive us but rather of his desire to free us from sin's grip, to enable us to overcome the actual power of sin in our lives. Part of the purpose of Christ's coming is to enable us to meet "the just requirement of the law" so that we can actually begin to live the kind of righteous life he's always wanted us to live (8:4), and it is his Spirit that gives us the power to do so. In this context, "the just requirement of the law" is probably not to be understood as the requirement of a sacrifice for forgiveness but the require-ment of righteous living. Christ died so that the righteous demands of the law might be lived out in our lives. This, too, is part of God's saving work, the transforming work of salvation, exactly as is prophesied by Jeremiah and Ezekiel: "This is the new covenant I will make with the people of Israel on that day. . . . I will put my instruc-tions deep within them, and I will write them on their hearts" (Jer 31:33); "I will give you a new heart, and I will put a new spirit in you. I will take out your stony, stubborn heart and give you a tender, responsive heart. And I will put my Spirit in you so that you will follow my decrees and be careful to obey my regulations" (Ezek 36:26-27).

The liberating and transforming work of the Spirit was a strong emphasis in the ministry of the Wesley brothers (John and Charles) in the evangelical movement of eighteenth-century Britain and Ireland. Just as Luther rediscovered Paul's doctrine of justification by faith, so the Wesleys are often held to have rediscovered Paul's emphasis on the sanctifying work of the Holy Spirit (though, in reality, it was medi-ated to them through the work of the European Moravians). The legacy of the Wesleyan "rediscovery" of the sanctifying power of the Spirit may be seen in the twentieth-century Holiness and Pentecostal movements; the influence of the latter especially has been felt around the world. Both these movements trace their roots, at least in part, to Paul's emphasis on the life-changing work of the Holy Spirit in the hearts of believers.

The Choice Is Ours: Which Power Will Rule Us? Salvation, then, is not simply a matter of being forgiven. The Good News of Christ gives us power over sin, as well as the forgiveness of sin. However, a transformed life is only possible if we inten-tionally turn from our old ways and allow the Spirit to govern our lives. The righ-teous demands of the law can only be lived out by us "who no longer follow our sinful nature but instead follow the Spirit" (8:4). This idea is linked in Paul's under-standing to living no longer "under the requirements of the law" (in bondage) but "under the freedom of God's grace" (in freedom; 6:14). Ironically, the ability to live out the demands of the law comes only when we are freed from the rule of the law. The life-transforming power of the coming Kingdom is accessible to all believers, but its actual effect in an individual's life depends on the extent to which that individual is open and submissive to its influence. The power of the Spirit is not a relentless moral force asserting its way in our lives, irrespective of our wills; its potential to change our lives depends on just how fully we yield to its influence.

So the choice is always there: will we allow our life to be "dominated by the sinful nature" or "controlled by the Holy Spirit" (8:5)? As Paul makes clear in Galatians, all life long we will feel the tension between these two forces, pulling us in opposite directions (Gal 5:17). If we allow sin to rule us, sinful thoughts will inevitably fill our minds—and that kind of life can never please God. Only if we let the Spirit of God control our thinking can we experience real life and peace from God (8:5-8). The good news for believers is that their lives will no longer be inevitably dominated by the power of sin (as was true in 7:14-25) because the power of the Spirit is greater than the power of sin. Nonetheless, Paul still writes as if the choice is ours as to which force will have control over our lives and thinking.

If a person is resistant to the influence of the Spirit, the question is inevitably raised as to whether that person has any real experience of God, for it is those who are led by the Spirit of God who are the true children of God (8:14). Those who are controlled by their sinful nature remain hostile to God (8:7), and if they continue in that way of life, the result is "death" in the final judgment (8:6, 13; cf. Gal 5:19-21). Here again, Paul emphasizes that there must be a correlation between what we say we believe and how we actually live if our faith is to be considered authentic saving faith. One cannot validly claim to be right with God if there is no concern to live out that holy status in one's daily life; such a person shows no sign of the regenerating work of God's Spirit. How we live shows whether our faith is real or not.

The Key Is the Spirit of Christ in Us. This is why the New Testament writers speak of the experience of the Holy Spirit as an essential part of Christian salvation. Without the Spirit of Christ there is no comprehension of the Good News, no spiritual sensitivity (1 Cor 2:14), and no power to live the kind of life that God wants. Indeed, without the Spirit of Christ there is no personal relationship to Christ: "Those who do not have the Spirit of Christ, living in them do not belong to him at all" (8:9). In this statement we hear an echo of the words of Jesus in the Gospel of John: "No one can enter the Kingdom of God without being born of water and the Spirit" (John 3:5); "For God is Spirit, so those who worship him must worship in spirit and in truth" (John 4:24). The writer of 1 John adds, "We know he lives in us because the Spirit he gave us lives in us. . . . God has given us his Spirit as proof that we live in him and he in us" (1 John 3:24; 4:13). Without the regenerating work of the Holy Spirit, there is no living experience of God. This is why the reception of the Spirit should not be viewed as a secondary or later stage of Christian conversion (cf. Gal 3:2). As Acts 2:38 makes clear, it is part of the essence of the salvation experience.

Though the body is doomed to die because of its susceptibility to sin, those who have the Spirit of God have received a powerful new life—eternal life. God, having made them right with himself, has now come to live within them (cf. John 14:23). And those who demonstrate the presence of his Spirit in their lives—those whose lives authenticate their claim to spiritual life—can be sure that just as Christ was raised from the dead by the power of the Spirit, so they too will experience "resurrection power" in their mortal bodies, both now and in the age to come (8:11). In this context the reference to receiving life in one's mortal body pertains not so much to a future resurrection as to the renewal and transformation of one's lifestyle here and now, by the life-changing power of the Spirit.

Because this Spirit is the Spirit of Christ (Paul uses the terms "Spirit of God" and "Spirit of Christ" interchangeably), this means that nothing less than the life of the resurrected Christ himself is at work in the believer (8:10). "This is the secret," Paul writes to the Colossians, "Christ lives in you" (Col 1:27). To the Galatians he writes, "It is no longer I who live, but Christ lives in me" (Gal 2:20; cf. 1 Cor 15:10 and the words of Jesus in John 14:20, "You are in me, and I am in you"). So it is the power of the risen Christ himself, working in us, that frees us from "the power of sin that leads to death" (8:2). The synoptic Gospels speak of the promise of Christ to be *with* his people (Matt 18:20; 28:20; cf. Matt 1:23), but it is the Gospel of John and Paul's letters that emphasize his living presence *in* his people. This reality radically affects Paul's view of Christian living and Christian ministry: no longer is it Paul himself who is the primary agent at work but the resurrected Lord Jesus at work in and through him.

In 8:12-14, Paul pauses to sum up his point thus far and presses it home to emphasize its importance. Every single day we are confronted with a choice: Will we yield to the desires of our sinful nature and ultimately die in the final judgment? Or will we, by the power of the life-transforming Spirit, put to death our sinful actions and ultimately live (8:13; cf. 6:11-13; Gal 5:24; Col 3:5)? The choice we make reflects whether or not our faith is real—for it is those who yield to the control of the Spirit who are the true children of God (8:14). Our relationship to God is always reflected in how we live.

In this chapter, where Paul deals *theologically* with the issues of sin and the Spirit, the choice seems to be clear-cut: a person's life is dominated either by the old sinful desires or by the new life of the Spirit. Paul gives us two sharply delineated and mutually exclusive options—the flesh or the Spirit—linked to two different ultimate destinies. Elsewhere, however, when he has to deal *practically* with people in the church whose lives are compromised, the issues and categories become less clear-cut. Thus, even within the Christian community, he distinguishes between those who are spiritual and those who are not (cf. Gal 6:1, NRSV) and frankly even speaks of some Christians as "people of the flesh. . . . behaving according to human inclinations" (1 Cor 3:1-3, NRSV)—and this in spite of the "holy" status he attributes to them elsewhere (1 Cor 1:2; 6:11). So it is possible in Paul's thinking for a person to have an authentic relationship to God (be a genuine Christian) and still be spiritually immature—characterized by something less than full dedication, living too much like the people of the world. This treatment reflects Paul's awareness that in reality, for many people, sanctification is a slow and gradual process—though his own radical conversion and thoroughgoing theology of the Spirit may have made it difficult for him to understand or be patient with the slower transformation of others. In any case, it is clear that Paul was never very comfortable with a compromised commitment to Christ or a Christian life reflecting sinful desires. His strong warnings of God's judgment serve to remind us that we can never presume on God's grace or take God's demands for holy living lightly (1 Cor 6:9-10; Gal 5:19-21; Eph 5:5-6; Col 3:5-6) because a sinful lifestyle is, generally speaking, the mark of an unbeliever, not a believer. As the writer of 1 John says, "Anyone who keeps on sinning does not know him or understand who he is. . . . When people keep on sinning, it shows that they belong to the devil" (1 John 3:6, 8).

The Spirit Confirms that We Are God's Children. At the end of this section, Paul speaks of other aspects of the Spirit's work. The Spirit does more than simply give us new power for living. Deep within, moving us to address God as "Abba, Father" (just as Jesus addressed him, Mark 14:36), the Spirit of God assures us that we are indeed children of God, part of God's own dearly loved family—and that we can therefore boldly lay claim to children's privileges (8:15-17). As Luther wrote so nicely,

> [The word "Father"] is but a little word, and yet notwithstanding it comprehendeth all things. . . . Although I be oppressed with anguish and terror on every side, and seem to be forsaken and utterly cast away from thy presence, yet am I thy child, and thou art my Father for Christ's sake: I am beloved because of the Beloved. Wherefore this little word, Father, conceived effectually in the heart, passeth all the eloquence of Demosthenes, Cicero, and of the most eloquent rhetoricians that ever were in the world. (Luther's *Commentary on Galatians,* on "Abba! Father!" [Gal 4:6], cited in Bruce 1985:157-158)

So we needn't cower in fear and timidity like slaves. Christ has liberated us from the clutches of evil and death—he has made us God's children! (Wesley later described his Aldersgate conversion as his exchanging "the faith of a servant" for "the faith of a son.") Just as Christ can lay claim to the Father's blessings because he is God's Son, so we can lay claim to the Father's blessings because we are God's children. As Jesus himself says, if ordinary human parents have a heart to give good things to their children, how much more does the heavenly Father delight in giving good things to his children (Matt 7:11)? The fact that Paul speaks of us as "adopted" children in no way restricts the blessings, as F. F. Bruce (1985:157) explains:

> In the Roman world of the first century AD an adopted son was a son deliberately chosen by his adoptive father to perpetuate his name and inherit his estate; he was no whit inferior in status to a son born in the ordinary course of nature, and might well enjoy the father's affection more fully and reproduce the father's character more worthily.

Thus, as his children, together with Christ and because of Christ, we are the designated heirs of all his gifts—we are the heirs of God (8:17; cf. Gal 4:7)! So the presence of God's Spirit in our lives is nothing less than a foretaste of the ultimate glory, a touch of all that we shall experience of God's power and goodness beyond this life. Indeed, Paul was so sure of it that he spoke of the Spirit as a "guarantee" of all that God has for us in the future (2 Cor 5:5; Eph 1:14; cf. 2 Cor 1:22).

However, the full experience of that future glory is only for those who recognize Christ's claim upon their lives and who demonstrate that by their willingness to share in his sufferings in this life (8:17). It is encouraging to know that it is these very sufferings that God uses to develop our character and make us worthy of his glory (see comments on 5:3-5; cf. 2 Thess 1:11). The difficulties that wear down our bodies are the very things that renew our spirits and conform us to the likeness of Christ (2 Cor 4:16-17; cf. Col 3:10). "Through suffering, our bodies continue to share in the death of Jesus so that the life of Jesus may also be seen in our bodies" (2 Cor 4:10; cf. 2 Cor 3:18).

This section (8:1-17), then, reminds us that, for the Spirit's work to be effective, we must turn away from sin and open ourselves to his full influence. The only way to experience real goodness is to allow the Spirit to become the driving force of our lives. Those who allow sin to rule their lives will ultimately die, but those who cooperate with the life-transforming influence of his Spirit find life and peace. Those who have no experience of the Spirit have no relationship to Christ, but those who have the Spirit—the life of the resurrected Christ within them—are "clothed" with the righteousness of Christ and experience his resurrection power in their bodies, both now and in the life to come. The presence of his Spirit within also confirms that we are the children of God and that, together with Christ, we shall therefore inherit the full glory of God.

◆   ## 2. The glorious future (8:18-30)

18Yet what we suffer now is nothing compared to the glory he will reveal to us later. 19For all creation is waiting eagerly for that future day when God will reveal who his children really are. 20Against its will, all creation was subjected to God's curse. But with eager hope, 21the creation looks forward to the day when it will join God's children in glorious freedom from death and decay. 22For we know that all creation has been groaning as in the pains of childbirth right up to the present time. 23And we believers also groan, even though we have the Holy Spirit within us as a foretaste of future glory, for we long for our bodies to be released from sin and suffering. We, too, wait with eager hope for the day when God will give us our full rights as his adopted children,* including the new bodies he has promised us. 24We were given this hope when we were saved. (If we already have something, we don't need to hope* for it. 25But if we look forward to something we don't yet have, we must wait patiently and confidently.)

26And the Holy Spirit helps us in our weakness. For example, we don't know what God wants us to pray for. But the Holy Spirit prays for us with groanings that cannot be expressed in words. 27And the Father who knows all hearts knows what the Spirit is saying, for the Spirit pleads for us believers* in harmony with God's own will. 28And we know that God causes everything to work together* for the good of those who love God and are called according to his purpose for them. ²⁹For God knew his people in advance, and he chose them to become like his Son, so that his Son would be the firstborn among many brothers and sisters. ³⁰And having chosen them, he called them to come to him. And having called them, he gave them right standing with himself. And having given them right standing, he gave them his glory.

8:23 Greek *wait anxiously for sonship.*   **8:24** Some manuscripts read *wait.*   **8:27** Greek *for God's holy people.*
8:28 Some manuscripts read *And we know that everything works together.*

NOTES

8:18 *the glory he will reveal to us.* Lit., "the glory to be revealed into (*eis* [TG1519, ZG1650]) us." The last phrase is translated in different ways: "to us" (NRSV, TEV, CEV), "for us" (NJB, NAB, REB), "in us" (KJV, NIV). The last is the best choice; God's glory will transform us. For the meaning of "glory," see note on 5:2.

8:19 *all creation.* The whole of the created world (apart from human beings), both animate and inanimate (Cranfield 1980:411), both "sub-human and supra-human" (Edwards 1992:212). Cf. J.B. Phillips's picturesque translation of this verse: "The whole creation is on tiptoe to see the wonderful sight of the sons of God coming into their own."

that future day when God will reveal who his children really are. Lit., "the revelation of the sons of God." "Believers are already sons of God in this life, but their sonship is veiled and their incognito is impenetrable except to faith" (Cranfield 1980:412-413).

8:20 *subjected to God's curse.* Or, "made subject to frustration." Lit., "subjected to futility" (*mataiotēti* [TG3153, ZG3470]). A reference probably to Gen 3:17-19, which speaks of God placing a curse on the ground as a result of human sin. See Cranfield 1980:413-414 for a full discussion of various interpretations of the term (mutability, mortality, vain men, idolatry, celestial powers, futility, absurdity, frustration).

But with eager hope. Lit., "in hope," a phrase that goes better with what follows than with what precedes.

8:21 *will join God's children in glorious freedom from death and decay.* Lit., "will be freed from the slavery of decay into the freedom of the glory of the children of God." Just as death and decay are linked to slavery, so glory is linked to freedom. Cf. Jas 1:18, which speaks of believers as "a kind of first fruits of his creatures" (NRSV). Cf. 8:23.

8:22 *groaning as in the pains of childbirth.* That is, in the hope of new life for all creation. In this passage, just as the creation groans with longing (8:22), so believers groan (8:23), and even the Holy Spirit groans (8:26).

8:23 *And we believers also groan.* Cf. 2 Cor 5:2: "In this tent we groan, longing to be clothed with our heavenly dwelling" (NRSV). See note on 8:22.

even though we have the Holy Spirit within us as a foretaste of future glory. Lit., "having the firstfruits of the Spirit." "Firstfruits" (*aparchēn* [TG536, ZG569]) is a technical term derived from the Jewish sacrificial system, designating the first crops of the harvest, which were to be offered to God in acknowledgment of his provision, thus invoking his blessing on the whole crop. (See 11:16 for another use of the term.) Here the term refers to something given by God to his people in pledge of a fuller gift yet to come. Cf. 2 Cor 1:22; 5:5; Eph 1:14, where the Holy Spirit is spoken of as the "pledge" or "guarantee" (*arrabōn* [TG728, ZG775]) of what is to come, a "first installment" or "deposit" guaranteeing the promise.

for we long for our bodies to be released from sin and suffering. Lit., "[awaiting] the redemption of our body"—that is, full freedom from sin and suffering, to be experienced on the "day of redemption" (Eph 4:30).

We, too, wait with eager hope for the day when God will give us our full rights as his adopted children. Lit., "awaiting sonship" ["adoption," NRSV]. Though already children of God, Christians look forward to the full manifestation of that relationship in the future with all of its blessings. Some Gr. mss (𝔓46^vid D F G) omit "sonship" (*huiothesian* [TG5206, ZG5625]), perhaps because of the contradiction it seems to pose with 8:15, which speaks of sonship as a present experience.

including the new bodies he has promised us. This reference to the future resurrection is not in the Gr. text. The NLT supplies this as one aspect of the "full rights" referred to, to correspond to the release of our bodies from the sin and suffering referred to earlier in this verse. See 1 Cor 15:35-57 for a fuller discussion of future resurrection bodies.

8:24 *We were given this hope when we were saved.* Lit., "For we were saved by hope" (*tē elpidi* [TG1680, ZG1828])—that is, by our strong and confident trust in the future that God has for us. For the meaning of "hope," see comments on 5:2-5.

If we already have something, we don't need to hope for it. Lit., "But hope being seen is not hope; for who hopes for that which he sees?" Instead of "hopes" (*elpizei* [TG1679, ZG1827]; 𝔓46 ℵ² B C D), some Gr. mss (ℵ* A 1739^mg) have "waits" (*hupomenei* [TG5278, ZG5702]).

8:26 *we don't know what God wants us to pray for.* Or, "we don't know how we should pray."

But the Holy Spirit prays for us. The words "for us" are not included in ℵ* A B D F G.

with groanings that cannot be expressed in words. The word *stenagmos* [TG4726, ZG5099] may be interpreted either as "groaning" or "sighing": "through our inarticulate groans" (REB); "with inexpressible groanings" (NAB); "with sighs too deep for words" (NRSV). The word connotes the deepest longings that well up in the human spirit, for which no words are adequate. The phrase is probably not a reference to glossolalia or a prayer language. See note on 8:22.

8:27 *the Father who knows all hearts.* Lit., "the one who searches the hearts."

knows what the Spirit is saying. Lit., "knows^vid the thinking (*phronēma* [TG5427, ZG5859]) of the Spirit."

in harmony with God's own will. Lit., "according to God."

8:28 *God causes everything to work together for the good.* This follows the mss 𝔓46 A B. Other mss (ℵ C D F G 1739) read, "everything works together for the good" (so NRSV, NAB).

of those who love God. The promise is not for everyone but specifically for believers, those who are truly devoted to God.

called. Not in the weaker sense of "invited" ("Many are called, but few are chosen," Matt 22:14) but in the stronger sense of an "effectual call," resulting in saving faith and conversion (1:1, 6-7; 8:30; 9:12, 24; 11:29; 2 Thess 2:14). See note on 1:1.

8:29 *For God knew his people in advance, and he chose them.* Lit., "And those whom he foreknew (*proegnō* [TG4267, ZG4589]) he also predestined" (*proōrisen* [TG4309, ZG4633]). The word "foreknew" implies God's sovereign choosing (as in Calvinism) and does not simply mean that God knew ahead of time how people would respond (as in Arminianism). "God's foreknowledge here connotes that electing grace which is frequently implied by the verb 'to know' in the Old Testament. When God takes knowledge of people in this special way, he sets his choice on them. Note the usage in Amos 3:2, 'You only have I known of all the families of the earth'; and the Qumran *Rule of the Community*: 'From the God of Knowledge comes all that is and shall be. Before ever they existed He established their whole design, and when, as ordained for them, they come into being, it is in accord with His glorious design that they fulfil their work'" (Vermes 1975:75).

brothers and sisters. Lit., "brothers."

8:30 *he called them to come to him.* Lit., "he called (*ekalesen* [TG2564, ZG2813]) them." This is an "effectual call," resulting in saving faith and conversion. See notes on 1:1; 8:28.

he gave them his glory. If the focus here is on heavenly glory, or eternal blessedness (5:2; 8:18), this may be a carryover from Paul's Hebrew background—an example of the "prophetic past," whereby a future event is viewed with such certainty that it is spoken of as having already happened. Or, it may refer to the glory they already have been given as believers, a foretaste of the ultimate glory that lies in the future (8:23; 2 Cor 3:18; cf. John 17:22: "I have given them the glory you gave me").

COMMENTARY

Looking beyond the experience of suffering he refers to in 8:17, in this section (8:18-30) Paul speaks of the full experience of God's glory that awaits believers beyond this life, the ultimate goal of becoming like Christ, and the Spirit's role in bringing that about. This section serves as the conclusion of his discussion of the role of the Spirit in God's saving work in 8:1-30.

Suffering Now—but Glory Then!

Writing not long after one of the most intense periods of suffering he ever experienced—his difficult time in Ephesus (for his comments about this, see 2 Cor 1:8-9; cf. 2 Cor 4:8-12, 16-18; 6:4-10; 11:23-28)—Paul knew firsthand that suffering is part of the Christian's life and calling. Persecution and suffering seem to have been widespread in the early church, judging from Peter's words about "Christian brothers and sisters all over the world . . . going through the same kind of suffering" (1 Pet 5:9). This is exactly what Jesus told his disciples to expect: "You will be handed over to the courts and will be flogged with whips in the synagogues. . . . All nations will hate you because you are my followers" (Matt 10:17, 22); "You will be expelled from the synagogues, and . . . those who kill you will think they are doing a holy service for God" (John 16:2). Paul typically taught his converts that they "must suffer many hardships to enter the Kingdom of God" (Acts 14:22). After many years of suffering, shortly before he died, Paul wrote to Timothy that "everyone who wants to live a godly life in Christ Jesus will suffer persecution" (2 Tim 3:12). As the book of Acts vividly portrays, this is what Paul himself repeatedly experienced in his missionary work for Christ.

Paul's eyes, however, were fixed not on his suffering but on the unspeakable glory of the life beyond (8:18). As he wrote to the church at Corinth shortly before this, "Our present troubles are small and won't last very long. Yet they produce for us a glory that vastly outweighs them and will last forever! So we don't look at the troubles we can see now; rather, we fix our gaze on things that cannot be seen. For the things we see now will soon be gone, but the things we cannot see will last forever" (2 Cor 4:17-18).

His perspective models that of Jesus, who encouraged his disciples to rejoice over their persecution: "Be happy about it! Be very glad! For a great reward awaits you in heaven" (Matt 5:12). Here Paul, like Jesus, speaks of the future glory not simply as the antithesis of present suffering but (in part at least) as a reward for it, as something brought about by suffering for Christ. So in the strange providence of God, while suffering serves both to develop our character in this life and to strengthen our anticipation of what lies beyond this life (5:3-5), it also results in an even greater experience of glory in the life beyond. Our focus, then, is to be not on the passing trials of the present but on the eternal glories of the future—the magnificent things that lie beyond this life.

Of course, Christians already reflect something of the divine glory—the distinctive quality of God, the magnificence of his grace—here and now, as a result of their experience of "the glory of God that is seen in the face of Jesus Christ" (2 Cor 4:6; cf. Jesus' words, "I have given them the glory you gave me," John 17:22). In a corporate sense, this reflection of divine glory is also suggested by Paul's description of the church as "a holy temple for the Lord," a "dwelling where God lives by his Spirit" (Eph 2:21-22)—just as the union of Jews and Gentiles in the church is intended to be a reflection of God's "wisdom in its rich variety to all the unseen rulers and authorities in the heavenly places" (Eph 3:10). So the church, as the body of Christ, reflects God's glory just as individual believers do. Further, in Paul's thinking, the ministry of the Good News itself, the ministry of the new covenant, also expresses the glory of God—vastly more than the old covenant, under the system of law, ever could (2 Cor 3:7-11). As Christian believers and ministers of the grace of God, then, we already reflect, both individually and as the body of Christ, something of the glory of the Lord—something of the distinctive wonderfulness of God and the greatness of his grace. And as his Spirit works in us to transform us increasingly into the likeness of Christ, we come to reflect his glory more and more (2 Cor 3:18), and that's what God desires for us. At all times and in all situations, our lives, our relationships, and our ministries are to reflect the greatness of the Lord and the magnificence of his grace. But we must remember that the glory we reflect in this life will always be diminished by our imperfections. As for now, we are only a pale reflection of the divine glory that we will one day experience in its full splendor when Christ returns. (For more on "glory," see commentary on 3:23 and note on 5:2.) And when that day comes, how indescribably magnificent it will be! If, with all of our human failings, God pours out so much grace and glory upon us in this fallen world, what will it be like in the pristine world that lies beyond this vale of tears? The indescribable glory of it will make the sufferings we experience now pale as nothing in comparison (8:18).

It was this focus on the glorious life beyond, the great Christian hope (5:2-5), that enabled the early Christians to endure the suffering and persecution they bore for Christ's sake (cf. 1 Pet 1:13)—just as Christ endured the cross "because of the joy awaiting him" (Heb 12:2). At least partly because of persecution, the eschatological promise was dominant in the thinking of the early believers; their eyes were fixed on the incredible glory that lay waiting for them in the future, beyond their suffering. They knew that they could never consider this passing world their home; their real home lay in the unseen world beyond. So Peter reminds his persecuted readers that they are only "temporary residents and foreigners" in this world (1 Pet 2:11), and the writer of Hebrews—also addressing persecuted believers—says much the same: "This world is not our permanent home; we are looking forward to a home yet to come" (Heb 13:14). In contrast to those whose minds are set on earthly things, Paul speaks of Christians as "citizens of heaven, where the Lord Jesus Christ lives"—and goes on to add, "And we are eagerly waiting for him to return as our Savior" (Phil 3:20). So biblical Christians over the years have lived their lives in the strong and confident anticipation of Christ's return, and they have understood their temporal lives as simply a journey to their ultimate home in heaven (see, e.g., Bunyan's *Pilgrim's Progress*).

In the modern world, however, many Christians have lost sight of heaven. We find ourselves so comfortably settled into this affluent world that it seems very much as if it *is* our home. The idea of heaven does not excite us as it did earlier generations of Christians, and we tend to think little of the life beyond. The focus of modern Christians is often on life here and now, and this is reflected in the orientation of contemporary understandings of ministry and missions to the needs of this life. Much of the otherworldly focus of the early church has been lost; indeed, it is often ridiculed as "pie in the sky by and by." But we must remember that the Kingdom of Jesus is "not of this world" (John 18:36), and as Jesus reminds his followers, the loss of an otherworldly focus is a potentially costly one: "Those who love their life in this world will lose it. Those who care nothing for their life in this world will keep it for eternity" (John 12:25). The early Christians were much more aware of the ultimate issues, the eternal concerns—the final judgment, heaven and hell—and much more focused on the eternal destiny of the human soul. So they constantly reminded themselves not to become too attached to the things of this life, not to love the evil "things it offers you," for "this world is fading away, along with everything that people crave. But anyone who does what pleases God will live forever" (1 John 2:15-17). If we lose sight of the life beyond, we run the risk of losing something of the very essence of the Christian message as the early Christians understood it. The Christian hope, Paul reminds the Corinthians, is distinctly not "only for this life" (1 Cor 15:19).

Even nature itself—indeed the whole of creation, which has also experienced the tragic effects of sin (Gen 3:14-19)—eagerly awaits the amazing day when God's children will be revealed in all their true glory, reflecting the full love and perfection of their heavenly Father. For on that day, the entire created universe will share in that magnificent transformation; it, too, will be recreated (8:19-21). The prophets had visions of this future day of universal peace, when the disorder of nature will be restored to its pristine harmony:

> In that day the wolf and the lamb will live together; the leopard will lie down with the baby goat. The calf and the yearling will be safe with the lion, and a little child will lead them all. The cow will graze near the bear. The cub and the calf will lie down together. The lion will eat hay like a cow. The baby will play safely near the hole of a cobra. Yes, a little child will put its hand in a nest of deadly snakes without harm. Nothing will hurt or destroy in all my holy mountain, for as the waters fill the sea, so the earth will be filled with people who know the LORD. (Isa 11:6-9; cf. Isa 65:25; Ezek 47:7-12; 2 Pet 3:13; Rev 21:4; 22:1-5)

Just as the natural world has shared in the terrible consequences of human sin, so it will share in the full glory of human redemption. Drawing a parallel between the death and decay evident in nature and the suffering that Christians experience in this life, Paul observed that both nature and Christians look forward with longing to the day when they will be free of their problems—that day when they will be fully transformed and will experience the full glory of God. So Paul's view of the glory beyond is all-inclusive in its scope: it applies to the whole of the created order, presently under the curse of God.

There is no mention here of the cataclysmic final annihilation of the created world, prior to the revealing of a "new heaven and a new earth," as commonly described in Jewish apocalyptic literature (cf. 2 Pet 3:7, 10-13). Here in Romans the focus is rather on the transformation of the created world. But both of these forms of the apocalyptic tradition build on the anticipation of the "new heavens and new earth" found in the prophets (Isa 65:17; 66:22; cf. 2 Pet 3:13; Rev 21:1). This anticipation is part of the apocalyptic worldview that underlies the entire New Testament—a worldview that presupposes that world history is not directionless or endlessly cyclical but moving toward an eventual climax in which the ultimate purposes of God for his people are brought to completion. There is an ultimate goal, and in all the seeming happenstances of history, God is quietly at work bringing that to pass; his purposes will finally triumph.

The Spirit Is a Foretaste of Glory. Christians have been given a foretaste of the glory that lies beyond in their experience of the indwelling Spirit. Earlier in this chapter, Paul wrote of the Spirit's role in overcoming sin (8:2-14) and in confirming our identity as the children of God (8:15-17). Now he speaks of the Spirit as the guarantee and pledge of the glory that lies beyond—a touch of heaven, if you like, to whet our appetites for the full experience of that glory (8:23; 2 Cor 1:22; 5:5; Eph 1:14).

However, there is no experience of perfection in this life. Perfection always lies in the future; it awaits that final day, both for the created order and for the children of God. In our lives in this world, we never fully escape our limitations. Even with the marvelous gift of his Spirit—with all his transforming power, a hint of the full power of the coming Kingdom—the experience of perfection eludes us as long as we live in these mortal bodies. We agonize over our imperfections and long to be free of them. We "long for our bodies to be released from sin and suffering" (8:23). But as long as we have our mortal bodies, we must learn to live with pain and suffering—and with imperfection; for this is part of what it means to be human. Paul himself, energetically pursuing the life to which God had called him, openly confessed that he had not attained perfection: "I don't mean to say that I have already achieved these things or that I have already reached perfection." But he kept working toward "that perfection for which Christ Jesus first possessed me"—all his energies were focused on that goal (Phil 3:12-13; cf. 2 Cor 5:9). Our energies, too, are to be fully focused on living in a way that pleases God, by the power of his Spirit (Eph 5:18). But we must be patient: full transformation always awaits the future.

One day, however, we will be fully and gloriously changed—and when that day comes, we will receive mysterious new bodies, "the new bodies he has promised us" (8:23). The classic Christian doctrine of the afterlife includes some form of bodily existence, for it is a doctrine of resurrection. Just as Christ was given a resurrection body, so we will be given resurrection bodies. These bodies will be radically different from our present mortal bodies; they will be glorious, immortal, spiritual bodies like Christ's resurrection body (see Paul's extended discussion of resurrection bodies in 1 Cor 15:35-57).

Until believers are raised with new bodies on the final day, however, Paul simply speaks of Christians who have died as being "with Christ" (Phil 1:23). This phrase clearly implies something more than soul sleep until the time of the resurrection—for Paul said he would prefer to die and go to be with Christ immediately. (The idea of soul sleep arises from a misinterpretation of the New Testament idiom "fallen asleep," which is a euphemism for dying; cf. 1 Thess 4:13-15.) Until the day of resurrection, then, the spirit of a Christian who has died continues to live on in the presence of Christ himself—but in what form, we simply do not know. It is enough to know that eternal life, which begins the moment we receive Christ into our lives (John 5:24; 11:25-26; 1 John 5:11-13), does not cease. The one who speaks of himself as "the resurrection and the life" declares to us, "Those who believe in me, even though they die, will live, and everyone who lives and believes in me will never die" (John 11:25-26, NRSV).[1]

This strong and confident anticipation of future glory, the Christian hope in what lies beyond this life, is one of the most distinctive marks of the faith that saves us. We have seen how often Paul speaks of hope (along with faith and love) as one of the most important characteristics of the Christian way of life. This eschatological hope is always in something unseen, something invisible to the naked eye—and that, according to the writer of Hebrews, is the essence of Christian faith (Heb 11:1). As Paul says elsewhere, "We live by believing and not by seeing" (2 Cor 5:7). It is precisely to this life of faith in the unseen future that God calls us (8:24-25). It is the same kind of faith Abraham modeled in the face of seeming impossibilities (4:17); and it is this strong confidence, this sure eschatological hope, that enabled Paul himself to endure all the sufferings he experienced (2 Cor 4:17-18). As those called to live in hope, we, too, must learn to live patiently with the problems we encounter in this life. The secret is to keep our eyes firmly fixed on the future glory, as Christ's eyes were (Heb 12:2), and to remain strong in our faith in God's promise. Our hope is strengthened by the presence of Christ himself within us; "this," Paul says, is what gives us "assurance of sharing his glory" (Col 1:27).

The Ultimate Goal: To Become Like Christ. Between now and that coming day of glory, we have much for which to praise God—especially the help of his Spirit. With all our imperfections, weaknesses, and limitations in this life, the Spirit is always present to help us. He is our *paraklētos* [TH3875, ZH4156] (cf. John 14:16, 26; 15:26; 16:7), our "Counselor" (NIV), "Advocate" (NLT, NRSV, REB, NAB), "Helper" (TEV), and "Comforter" (KJV)—the word could also be translated "Encourager" or "Defender." When we don't even know what God would have us pray for, the divine

Spirit prays for us (8:26). In the deepest longings of the heart, longings that can't begin to be expressed in human words, God's own Spirit is at work, praying for us. Even though we're unable to verbalize our deepest desires, God knows them—for God knows the human heart and the yearnings of his Spirit (8:26-27), and those yearnings are always for our ultimate good. God, who in his grace has given us his Spirit and cares for us as his children, listens and responds to the longings of the Spirit he has placed within us.

But the Spirit does more than simply pray for us. The role of the Spirit in our lives, ultimately, is to transform us into the likeness of Christ himself (8:29). That is why we can be absolutely confident that "God causes everything to work together for the good of those who love God" (8:28)—one of the most encouraging promises in the entire New Testament. By means of his Spirit, God himself is at work in our lives, using everything that happens to accomplish his purposes for us, turning everything into our good. (Note, however, that this promise is specifically for believers, for "those who love God and are called according to his purpose"—not for everyone. There is no glib assurance here that things in life generally turn out well for everyone.) Paul had experienced this in his own life; even in prison he could write, "Everything that has happened to me here has helped to spread the Good News" (Phil 1:12). He knew that the difficulties he had faced were, in the end, working for his good (see 5:3-5). So he spoke of learning to "take pleasure in [his] weaknesses, and in the insults, hardships, persecutions, and troubles" because they were all "for Christ" (2 Cor 12:10)—and he had learned that Christ could work most powerfully, even through his weaknesses.

Through all the difficulties of life, then, God is at work shaping us into the likeness of his Son, who is the likeness of himself—"the visible image of the invisible God" (Col 1:15; cf. 2 Cor 4:4). This shaping process will continue right up to that day when, at last, we will be perfectly conformed to his image (Phil 1:6). This is the ultimate goal to which God has called us, the end he had in mind from the very beginning when he chose us, which is in line with his original intent in creating humans ("Let us make human beings in our image, to be like us," Gen 1:26). His desire is to produce a family, a group of perfected brothers and sisters—all of them reflecting the likeness of the oldest son, who is the likeness of the Father himself—by the transforming work of his Spirit in their hearts. This is the end toward which his Spirit is at work in our lives.

The reason Christians can be assured of God's loving work in all aspects of their lives is that they know themselves to be those who are specially "called" by God—called to belong to Jesus Christ (1:6), called to be God's very own beloved people (1:7), called to have God's holy purposes fulfilled in their lives (8:28). In every way, their salvation is "not by works but by his call" (9:12, NRSV). They have the infinite privilege of being, by the sovereign choice of God Almighty, among the chosen ones, those who are called by God himself to experience his saving grace. The "calling" that Paul speaks of here is not that of a general invitation (as in "Many are called, but few are chosen," Matt 22:14); it is a matter of being especially selected—

an "effectual calling" (as theologians speak of it), resulting in saving faith and conversion. It is a calling which, in the words of the Westminster Shorter Catechism, is "the work of God's Spirit, whereby, convincing us of our sin and misery, enlightening our minds in the knowledge of Christ, and renewing our wills, he doth persuade and enable us to embrace Jesus Christ, freely offered to us in the gospel."[2] We who know ourselves to be the blessed recipients of God's sovereign grace and call can rest assured that his redeeming love is sufficient to embrace every aspect of our life and turn it all into our eventual good. He uses everything we experience to conform us to the likeness of Jesus Christ because that is his ultimate goal for us.

Christians are also called to pursue this goal actively for themselves—the goal of becoming "mature in the Lord, measuring up to the full and complete standard of Christ. . . . growing in every way more and more like Christ. . . . following the example of Christ" (Eph 4:13, 15; 5:2). Thus, Paul calls the Christians in Philippi to adopt the humble attitude of Christ, giving up their own desires and expressing the sacrificial love of Christ in all their relations with one another (Phil 2:4-8). Intentionally seeking to become more like Christ was a goal Paul took seriously in his own life; as he wrote the Corinthians, "You should imitate me, just as I imitate Christ" (1 Cor 11:1). As followers of Christ, we must always take seriously the call to become more like Christ and the priority that God assigns to Christlikeness; when we pursue that end, our desires merge with his.

But in the end, we have to acknowledge that even our right intentions come from the Lord—everything is a gift of God. So while Paul encouraged the Philippian Christians to work hard to live out their salvation, he acknowledged on a deeper level that God himself must be actively working in them, giving them both "the desire and the power to do what pleases him" (Phil 2:13). Therefore, it is not surprising that Paul speaks of all the different facets of salvation, the whole progression, as God's work (8:29-30)—God bringing to fruition his ultimate desires for his people. God is the one who chooses who will be his people; he is the one who calls us to himself; he is the one who makes us right with himself because of our faith in Christ; and he is the one who gives us his glory. It is all God's work, a matter of sovereign grace, from beginning to end. The fact that the progression moves directly from justification to glory with no mention of sanctification is probably due to the fact that sanctification itself is interpreted as an expression of the glory we have been given—an ever-increasing experience of the holiness that will one day culminate in our complete conformity to the likeness of Christ. Sanctification is progressive conformity to the likeness of Christ here and now (see 2 Cor 3:18; Col 3:10); ultimate glory is perfect conformity to the likeness of Christ there and then. Sanctification is the present experience of glory; ultimate glory is sanctification consummated (Bruce 1985:168). Both are the work of God. Paul was convinced that God, who started his good work in the believers, would continue that work until its completion at the return of Christ Jesus (Phil 1:6).

In closing this section, Paul refocuses our eyes on God himself in all his sovereignty and reminds us that, because God is God, we can rest assured that what he decides to do will be done. The one who chose us from the beginning, called us to himself, and set us right in his sight will surely fulfill his promise to bring us one day into the full splendor of his glory, the climax of his divine purpose for us (8:30). "When Christ, who is your life, is revealed to the whole world, you will share in all his glory" (Col 3:4). In the meantime, we can rest at peace, knowing that just as the initiative rests with him, so the responsibility for carrying through his plans for us rests finally with him. He can be trusted to fulfill his word. We are simply the blessed recipients of his kindness and grace.

Summary of the Spirit's Role. By way of summary, it can be said that the Spirit of God plays a wide-ranging and crucial role in the living out of the Christian life. The Spirit overcomes the enslaving power of sin and sets us free; he confirms to us that we are indeed the children of God; he is our assurance that we will one day experience the glory of God fully. In the meantime, he prays for our deepest needs, ensures that everything we encounter works for our ultimate good, working through it all to shape us into the likeness of our older Brother, Jesus.

Of all the New Testament writers, it is Paul who has the fullest and most comprehensive understanding of the Spirit's work in the life of the believer. Every aspect of salvation and Christian living is the result of the Holy Spirit working in and through us individually. Christian ministry also—in all of its varied forms—is a matter of the Spirit working in and through us, both individually and communally (see 1 Cor 12:4-31; 14:1-33). In his emphasis on the active role played by the Spirit in Christian life and ministry, Paul is very much a charismatic in his thinking (see esp. 1 Cor 2:10-16; 12:1-13; 14:1-5, 26-31).[3] In Paul's understanding, Christians are simply channels through which the Spirit works to accomplish God's purposes in his people (see 1 Cor 2:1-5; cf. 3:5-9; 2 Cor 3:5-6; 4:7; 12:8-10; 13:3). For Paul, then, the whole of the Christian life—and Christian ministry as well—is life "in the Spirit."

ENDNOTES
1. Some scholars think that Paul's understanding of eschatology changed as time passed and it became apparent to him that the return of Christ was not imminent. Some suggest that Paul eventually came to see death as the point at which believers receive their new bodies; they say this on the basis of what he writes about the exchange of our "earthly tent" for a "building from God" or "heavenly dwelling" when we die, in 2 Cor 5:1-4 (NRSV). However, the exact meaning of the latter two phrases (translated "eternal body" and "heavenly body" in NLT) is debated.
2. Westminster Shorter Catechism, answer to question 31.
3. Luke's account of Paul's ministry in Acts confirms this impression (Acts 13:2-4, 9-11; 14:8-10; 16:6-10, 16-18; 19:6, 11; 20:22-23; 23:11; 27:21-26; 28:3-9).

◆   3. God's never-ending love (8:31-39)

³¹What shall we say about such wonderful things as these? If God is for us, who can ever be against us? ³²Since he did not spare even his own Son but gave him up for us all, won't he also give us everything else? ³³Who dares accuse us whom God

has chosen for his own? No one—for God himself has given us right standing with himself. ³⁴Who then will condemn us? No one—for Christ Jesus died for us and was raised to life for us, and he is sitting in the place of honor at God's right hand, pleading for us.

³⁵Can anything ever separate us from Christ's love? Does it mean he no longer loves us if we have trouble or calamity, or are persecuted, or hungry, or destitute, or in danger, or threatened with death? ³⁶(As the Scriptures say, "For your sake we are killed every day; we are being slaughtered like sheep."*) ³⁷No, despite all these things, overwhelming victory is ours through Christ, who loved us.

³⁸And I am convinced that nothing can ever separate us from God's love. Neither death nor life, neither angels nor demons,* neither our fears for today nor our worries about tomorrow—not even the powers of hell can separate us from God's love. ³⁹No power in the sky above or in the earth below—indeed, nothing in all creation will ever be able to separate us from the love of God that is revealed in Christ Jesus our Lord.

8:36 Ps 44:22. 8:38 Greek _nor rulers._

NOTES

8:32 _he did not spare even his own Son._ God's words to Abraham may be in the background of Paul's thinking: "You have not withheld from me even your son, your only son" (Gen 22:12).

won't he also give us everything else? Cf. Matt 6:33: "All these things will be given to you as well" (NRSV).

8:34 _Christ Jesus._ This is the reading of ℵ A C F G L. Other Gr. mss (B D 0289 1739 𝔐) read "Christ."

raised to life. Lit., "raised." This is the reading of 𝔓27ᵛⁱᵈ 𝔓46 ℵ² B D F G 𝔐. Other Gr. mss (ℵ* A C Ψ 33) add "from the dead."

he is sitting in the place of honor at God's right hand. Lit., "at the right side of God," an idiom expressing the authority of one who is second in command. Cf. the messianic text Ps 110:1: "The LORD said to my Lord, 'Sit in the place of honor at my right hand.'"

pleading for us. Cf. Isa 53:12: "He bore the sins of many and interceded for rebels." For other references to Jesus as intercessor, see Heb 7:25; 1 John 2:1.

8:35 _Christ's love._ This is the reading of C D F G 33 1739. Other mss (ℵ copˢᵃ) have "God's love"; codex B reads, "God's love in Christ Jesus"; these readings may have been influenced by the wording of 8:38-39. In Paul's understanding, there is a very close link between Christ's love and God's love.

Does it mean he no longer loves us if . . . ? This is a rhetorical question.

8:36 _For your sake we are killed every day; we are being slaughtered like sheep._ This quotation is from Ps 44:22. The phrase "every day" is lit. "all day long."

8:37 _despite all these things._ Lit., "in all these things."

overwhelming victory is ours. Lit., "we triumph overwhelmingly," or "we are super-conquerors" (_hupernikōmen_ [ᵀᴳ5245, ᶻᴳ5664]).

Christ, who loved us. Lit., "the one who loved us."

8:38 _neither our fears for today nor our worries about tomorrow._ Lit., "nor present things nor future things," possibly a reference to the two ages of Jewish apocalyptic thinking (this present age and the coming one).

not even the powers of hell. Lit., "nor powers" (_dunameis_ [ᵀᴳ1411, ᶻᴳ1539]), a reference to spiritual forces—"evil rulers and authorities of the unseen world" (Eph 6:12). Some mss

(L 𝔐), followed by the KJV, place this term before the two preceding ones ("nor powers, nor things present, nor things to come"); some mss (C 81) add the phrase "nor authorities" (*exousiai* [ᵀᴳ1849, ᶻᴳ2026]).

8:39 *No power in the sky above or in the earth below.* Lit., "nor height nor depth." Possibly a reference to spiritual forces in the sky and beneath the earth, as interpreted in the early church (cf. REB), or a reference to geographical extremes (cf. Ps 139:8: "If I go up to heaven, you are there; if I go down to the grave, you are there"). A possible idiomatic equivalent is "neither heaven nor hell."

COMMENTARY

After his detailed discussion of salvation in chapters 1–8, Paul now draws this section to a close by reflecting on the wonder of God's love revealed in it all. He concludes that, in view of all that God has done for us as believers—sacrificing his own Son, forgiving our sins and making us right with himself, bringing us into his own family, giving us the gift of his Spirit, promising us eternal glory—we need have no fear or trepidation. In Jesus Christ we are safe and secure in God's care, and nothing in the whole world can change that (1 Cor 1:8; Phil 1:6; cf. John 10:28-29).

If there is anything the Good News of Christ reveals, it is that God is fundamentally for us—he is on our side. From beginning to end, salvation is a matter of God's gracious initiative, an expression of his sovereign love for us, his chosen ones. And if the God of the whole universe has declared himself for us, who can ever stand against us (8:31)? His power transcends everything—who can stand against him?

The full extent of God's love is shown in the sacrificial gift of his own dear Son, sent to die for us when we were still sinners, enemies of God. Who can grasp the full measure of that kind of love? And if God has loved us that much, won't he also give us everything else we will ever need (8:32)? He's committed himself to us—he's made us his own children, the "apple of his eye"; how can we ever doubt his care for us?

Piling rhetorical question upon rhetorical question, Paul drives his point home—perhaps especially for those burdened with an overactive sense of guilt (8:33-34). Drawing a parallel to a court case, he asks, "Who dares accuse us whom God has chosen for his own?" After all, it is God himself, the Judge, who has declared us not guilty and made us his friends! What person could think he has the right to condemn us? (Cf. Isa 50:8-9: "He who gives me justice is near. Who will dare to bring charges against me now? Where are my accusers? Let them appear! See, the sovereign LORD is on my side! Who will declare me guilty?" Cf. Rom 3:4.) If God takes the side of the defendant, the prosecution's case is lost, no matter what the evidence. And it is Jesus Christ, the very Son of the Judge himself, who died for all our wrongs so we might be forgiven. Further, it is Christ himself who now intercedes for us before God his Father—he's our defense lawyer! How could anyone condemn us before *him*? Just as the Spirit intercedes for us from within, so Christ intercedes for us in the presence of God himself; by his grace God has arranged for double intercession for his people. As God's people, then, we can rejoice and rest assured that we are indeed acquitted—not because of our own virtue but because of the eternally effective virtue of Christ, who died for us. The intended effect of all this on a believer's troubled conscience is well portrayed by John Bunyan in *Grace Abounding* (1962:72):

> But one day, as I was passing in the field, and that too with some dashes on my conscience, fearing lest yet all was not right, suddenly this sentence fell upon my soul, *Thy righteousness is in heaven*; and methought withal, I saw with the eyes of my soul, Jesus Christ at Gods right hand, there, I say, as my righteousness; so that wherever I was, or whatever I was a doing, God could not say of me, *He wants my righteousness*, for that was just before him. I also saw moreover, that it was not my good frame of heart that made my righteousness better, nor yet my bad frame that made my righteousness worse: for my righteousness was Jesus Christ himself, *the same yesterday, and today, and forever*, Heb 13.8.

There is nothing, absolutely nothing, which can ever negate Christ's unfailing love for us. No matter what comes our way—problems of all kinds, pain and suffering, persecution, crises of life that leave us anxious and unsure that our future needs will be met, situations that threaten our well-being or even our life itself—nothing can touch the most important thing, our relationship with Jesus Christ and his love for us. Even though life may be difficult (and as Scripture reminds us, God's people have never had an easy time of it in this life), we can rest assured that we are absolutely secure in the caring hand of Christ our Savior (8:35-36). Indeed, it's not just a question of our *surviving* the difficulties that come our way; through the sure love of Christ, we can be confident of our *transcending* them—and transcending them gloriously, magnificently (8:37)! That is how great Christ's love for us is. The passage is reminiscent of God's magnificent words to anxious Israel, spoken through Isaiah:

> Do not be afraid, for I have ransomed you. I have called you by name; you are mine. When you go through deep waters, I will be with you. When you go through rivers of difficulty, you will not drown. When you walk through the fire of oppression, you will not be burned up; the flames will not consume you. For I am the LORD, your God, the Holy One of Israel, your Savior. . . . You are precious to me. You are honored, and I love you. Do not be afraid, for I am with you. . . . You have been chosen to know me. (Isa 43:1-5, 10)

It should be noted that this absolute love of God toward his children does not mean that Christians can take their relationship with God lightly or frivolously. There is still the need for perseverance, and (paradoxically) the danger of losing the gifts and blessing of God seems to be a real one in Paul's thinking for those who abandon Christ. Thus, side by side with his emphasis on the keeping power of God's love, we find strong warnings of the eternal consequences of abandoning one's faith in Christ (11:20-22; Col 1:23; cf. Heb 3:14; 6:4-8; 10:35-39) and of continuing to live a life of sin (8:5-8, 12ff; 1 Cor 9:24-27; cf. Heb 10:26-31; 12:16ff; 1 John 3:4-8). In either case, the result is the loss of salvation in the final judgment of God. But those who remain firmly committed to Christ, resolutely trusting in him, may rest assured that God will indeed keep them safe in his love, no matter what comes their way, and for that he deserves our endless thanks and praise, as well as the dedication of our whole life to his service.

The conclusion? Surely there is absolutely nothing in all creation that can separate the committed believer from God's love in Jesus Christ (8:38-39). Whether we live or die, we are safe. We have nothing to fear from either the angelic or the demonic realm—or from any kind of spiritual evil, no matter how hellish. Our anxieties and fears of the moment, our worries about the future—these things have no power to sever our relationship with Christ. There is nothing, absolutely nothing in the whole universe—from one end to the other, from the heights of heaven to the depths of hell—that has the power to overcome God's love for us in Jesus Christ. For "your real life is hidden with Christ in God" (Col 3:3). It is this resounding affirmation of God's love for us that makes chapter 8 "perhaps the greatest chapter in the New Testament" (Robinson 1979:ix).

◆ II. God's Plan for the Jews and Gentiles (9:1–11:36)
   A. God Chooses Whomever He Wishes (9:1-29)

With Christ as my witness, I speak with utter truthfulness. My conscience and the Holy Spirit confirm it. ²My heart is filled with bitter sorrow and unending grief ³for my people, my Jewish brothers and sisters.* I would be willing to be forever cursed—cut off from Christ!—if that would save them. ⁴They are the people of Israel, chosen to be God's adopted children.* God revealed his glory to them. He made covenants with them and gave them his law. He gave them the privilege of worshiping him and receiving his wonderful promises. ⁵Abraham, Isaac, and Jacob are their ancestors, and Christ himself was an Israelite as far as his human nature is concerned. And he is God, the one who rules over everything and is worthy of eternal praise! Amen.*

⁶Well then, has God failed to fulfill his promise to Israel? No, for not all who are born into the nation of Israel are truly members of God's people! ⁷Being descendants of Abraham doesn't make them truly Abraham's children. For the Scriptures say, "Isaac is the son through whom your descendants will be counted,"* though Abraham had other children, too. ⁸This means that Abraham's physical descendants are not necessarily children of God. Only the children of the promise are considered to be Abraham's children. ⁹For God had promised, "I will return about this time next year, and Sarah will have a son."*

¹⁰This son was our ancestor Isaac. When he married Rebekah, she gave birth to twins.* ¹¹But before they were born, before they had done anything good or bad, she received a message from God. (This message shows that God chooses people according to his own purposes; ¹²he calls people, but not according to their good or bad works.) She was told, "Your older son will serve your younger son."* ¹³In the words of the Scriptures, "I loved Jacob, but I rejected Esau."*

¹⁴Are we saying, then, that God was unfair? Of course not! ¹⁵For God said to Moses,

"I will show mercy to anyone I choose,
   and I will show compassion to
   anyone I choose."*

¹⁶So it is God who decides to show mercy. We can neither choose it nor work for it.

¹⁷For the Scriptures say that God told Pharaoh, "I have appointed you for the very purpose of displaying my power in

you and to spread my fame throughout the earth."* ¹⁸So you see, God chooses to show mercy to some, and he chooses to harden the hearts of others so they refuse to listen.

¹⁹Well then, you might say, "Why does God blame people for not responding? Haven't they simply done what he makes them do?"

²⁰No, don't say that. Who are you, a mere human being, to argue with God? Should the thing that was created say to the one who created it, "Why have you made me like this?" ²¹When a potter makes jars out of clay, doesn't he have a right to use the same lump of clay to make one jar for decoration and another to throw garbage into? ²²In the same way, even though God has the right to show his anger and his power, he is very patient with those on whom his anger falls, who are destined for destruction. ²³He does this to make the riches of his glory shine even brighter on those to whom he shows mercy, who were prepared in advance for glory. ²⁴And we are among those whom he selected, both from the Jews and from the Gentiles.

²⁵Concerning the Gentiles, God says in the prophecy of Hosea,

"Those who were not my people,
  I will now call my people.
And I will love those
  whom I did not love before."*

²⁶And,

"Then, at the place where they were
  told,
  'You are not my people,'
there they will be called
  'children of the living God.'"*

²⁷And concerning Israel, Isaiah the prophet cried out,

"Though the people of Israel are as
  numerous as the sand of the
  seashore,
only a remnant will be saved.
²⁸For the LORD will carry out his
  sentence upon the earth
  quickly and with finality."*

²⁹And Isaiah said the same thing in another place:

"If the LORD of Heaven's Armies
  had not spared a few of our
  children,
we would have been wiped out like
  Sodom,
destroyed like Gomorrah."*

9:3 Greek my brothers. 9:4 Greek chosen for sonship. 9:5 Or May God, the one who rules over everything, be praised forever. Amen. 9:7 Gen 21:12. 9:9 Gen 18:10, 14. 9:10 Greek she conceived children through this one man. 9:12 Gen 25:23. 9:13 Mal 1:2-3. 9:15 Exod 33:19. 9:17 Exod 9:16 (Greek version). 9:25 Hos 2:23. 9:26 Greek sons of the living God. Hos 1:10. 9:27-28 Isa 10:22-23 (Greek version). 9:29 Isa 1:9.

NOTES

9:1 *My conscience and the Holy Spirit confirm it.* A further example of the inner witness of the Holy Spirit (cf. 8:15-16); "My conscience, enlightened by the Holy Spirit, assures me" (REB). For the meaning of "conscience," see note on 2:15.

9:3 *my people, my Jewish brothers and sisters.* Lit., "my brothers, my kinsmen according to the flesh."

forever cursed. Or, "eternally damned" (*anathema* [TG331, ZG353]).

if that would save them. Added for clarity.

9:4 *chosen to be God's adopted children.* Lit., "of whom is the sonship" (*huiothesia* [TG5206, ZG5625]). The people of Israel were called collectively the "son" of God (Exod 4:22; Hos 11:1) or the "sons" of God (Hos 1:10, NASB).

God revealed his glory to them. A reference to the brilliant shekinah glory of his holy presence, revealed in the Tabernacle (Exod 40:34-35) and the Temple (1 Kgs 8:10-11).

covenants. This is the reading of ℵ C Ψ 0285 33 𝔐 it syr cop^bo. Other mss (𝔓46 B D F G it^b cop^sa) read, "the covenant"—i.e., the covenant made at Mt. Sinai, when God gave the law to Moses. If the pl. is original (as in Eph 2:12), it would refer to the covenants made with Abraham (Gen 15:18-21; 17:4-21), with Israel in the days of Moses and Joshua (Exod 24:3-8; 34:10ff; Deut 29:1; Josh 8:30-35; 24:25), and with David (2 Sam 23:5; Ps 89:28; Bruce 1985:175).

his law. The law of Moses (Exod 20:1ff).

He gave them the privilege of worshiping him. Lit., "of whom is the worship" (*hē latreia* [TG2999, ZG3301]; "service, divine service"). A reference to the divine regulations pertaining to worship in the Tabernacle and the Temple, especially those found in the book of Leviticus.

his wonderful promises. These would include especially the Messianic promises (cf. Acts 13:23, 32-34).

9:5 *Abraham, Isaac, and Jacob are their ancestors.* Lit., "of whom are the fathers," a reference to the venerable patriarchs listed.

Christ himself. Or, "the Messiah himself" (*ho Christos* [TG5547, ZG5986]).

as far as his human nature is concerned. Lit., "according to the flesh" (*kata sarka* [TG2596/4561, ZG2848/4922]).

And he is God, the one who rules over everything and is worthy of eternal praise! Lit., "the one being over all things God blessed forever." This ambiguous Gr. structure may be rendered in three other ways: (1) "May God, who rules over all things, be praised forever." (2) "Christ rules over everything, blessed by God forever." (3) "Christ rules over everything; may God be praised forever." For a detailed analysis of the alternatives and an argument for the NLT interpretation, which asserts that Christ is God, see Cranfield (1981:464-470). This is one of three scriptures where Paul possibly calls Christ "God" (see 2 Thess 1:12; Titus 2:13). That Paul thought of Christ in divine terms may be argued from (1) his reference to Christ as "Lord," the same term used of God in the LXX (10:13-14); (2) the link between Christ and God in his invocations (1:7); (3) his calling upon Christ in prayer (10:13ff); (4) his parallel references to Christ and God (8:35, 39; "the judgment seat of God" in 14:10 becomes "the judgment seat of Christ" in 2 Cor 5:10 (NRSV); cf. his application of Isa 45:23 to Jesus in Phil 2:10-11); and (5) his descriptions of Christ as being "in the form of God" (Phil 2:6, NRSV), the one in whom "lives all the fullness of God in a human body" (Col 2:9), the one through whom and for whom all things were created (Col 1:16; cf. 1 Cor 8:6; Cranfield 1981:468; Bruce 1985:176). Taking into account the need for something to balance the immediately preceding reference to his "human nature," we may conclude with F. F. Bruce that, "Here the Messiah is said, with regard to his human descent, to have come of a long line of Israelite ancestors; but as regards his eternal being, he is 'God over all, blessed for ever'" (1985:176). Murray Harris's detailed study of whether or not Paul was calling Christ "God" concludes, "Given the high Christology of the Pauline letters, according to which Jesus shares the divine name and nature, . . . it should generate no surprise if on occasion Paul should refer to Jesus by the generic title *theos* [TG2316, ZG2536]" (1992:171).

Amen. A concluding affirmation often appended to expressions of praise (1:25; 11:36; 16:27; Gal 1:5; Eph 3:21; Phil 4:20; 1 Tim 1:17; 6:16; 2 Tim 4:18).

9:6 *has God failed to fulfill his promise to Israel? No.* Or, "Does this mean God's promises to them have come to nothing, that God's purposes for them have been thwarted? No, not at all." Lit., "It is not as if the word of God has failed." The "word of God" refers to the promises alluded to in 9:4.

truly members of God's people! Those who have a real relationship with God. Note Paul's definition of a true Jew in 2:29, "A true Jew is one whose heart is right with God."

9:7 *Isaac is the son through whom your descendants will be counted.* This is a quotation from Gen 21:12. God told Abraham not to resist his wife Sarah's demand that the slave woman Hagar and her son Ishmael be put out of the home because Abraham's descendants would be counted through his son Isaac, not Ishmael (who was also his son).

though Abraham had other children, too. The NLT adds this for clarity.

9:8 *the children of the promise.* Those who, like Isaac, trace their origin to the promise of God—i.e., the sovereign choice of God. (Cf. Gal 4:28: "And you, dear brothers and sisters, are children of the promise, just like Isaac.") In Galatians Paul seems to think of Christians as "children of the promise" in two other senses also: (1) Having been baptized into Christ, believers are now the recipients of the promise God made to Abraham and "his child" (namely, Christ; Gal 3:16). (2) Simply relying on God to fulfill his promises, like Abraham did, believers now become the beneficiaries of those promises (cf. Gal 3:26-29). These ideas seem linked in Paul's thinking; Christians are those who live by the promises of God—in more than one way.

9:9 *I will return about this time next year, and Sarah will have a son.* This is a quotation from Gen 18:10, 14. God predicted the birth of Isaac, the promised son, by the same time the following year.

9:10 *This son was our ancestor Isaac. When he married Rebekah, she gave birth to twins.* God's sovereign choice was manifested in Rebekah's children, just as it was in Isaac their father.

9:11 *This message shows that God chooses people according to his own purposes.* Lit., "in order that the will of God, according to his choice, might be determinative."

9:12 *Your older son will serve your younger son.* A quotation from Gen 25:23. Lit., "The greater will serve the lesser"—in sharp contrast to the traditional pattern of Heb. society, which favored the firstborn. The prophecy relates not simply to Esau and Jacob but also to their descendants—to the future submission of the Edomites to Israel and Judah (cf. 2 Sam 8:13-14; 1 Kgs 22:47; 2 Kgs 14:7).

9:13 *I loved Jacob, but I rejected Esau.* A quotation from Mal 1:2-3, which refers not to the individuals Jacob and Esau but to their descendants, the people of Judah and the Edomites. The word "rejected" is lit. "hated" (*emisēsa* [TG3404, ZG3631]), though this is often interpreted to mean the Lord chose Jacob over against Esau.

9:14 *Of course not!* This emphatic negation (*mē genoito* [TG3361/1096, ZG3590/1181]) occurs ten times in Romans (3:4, 6, 31; 6:2, 15; 7:7, 13; 9:14; 11:1, 11) but nowhere else in Paul's writings.

9:15 *I will show mercy to anyone I choose, and I will show compassion to anyone I choose.* This is a quotation from Exod 33:19, where God responded to Moses's request to see his glory.

9:16 *We can neither choose it nor work for it.* "It does not depend on human will or effort" (REB).

9:17 *I have appointed you for the very purpose of displaying my power in you.* This is taken from Exod 9:16, LXX, showing God's desire to pour out his judgment on Pharaoh and his people. Paul's rewording of the LXX text highlights God's initiative ("I have appointed you").

and to spread my fame throughout the earth. So that the entire world would acknowledge and respect God for who he is. For the response of the nations to the events of the Exodus, see Exod 15:14ff; Josh 2:10-11; 9:9ff; 1 Sam 4:8-9.

9:18 *God chooses to show mercy to some.* Lit., "God has mercy on the one he wants to" (cf. 9:15).

and he chooses to harden the hearts of others so they refuse to listen. Lit., "he hardens (*sklērunei* [TG4645, ZG5020]) the one he wants to," just as he hardened Pharaoh's heart (Exod 4:21; 7:3; 9:12; 10:1, 20, 27; 11:10; 14:4, 17; cf. Rom 11:7-10, 25). When Paul speaks of God's sovereign choice, his focus is usually on God's gracious role in saving people—i.e., it is with regard to the "elect," those chosen for salvation. But here we have his strongest statement on God's role in excluding people from salvation. Though not his usual focus, it is Paul's logical conclusion that only some are chosen for salvation; however, it seems to stand in tension with Paul's assertion that God "wants everyone to be saved" (1 Tim 2:4). Attempts to reconcile the two fail to take adequate account of Paul's ability to live with paradox.

9:19 *Haven't they simply done what he makes them do?* Lit., "Who can resist his will?"

9:21 *When a potter makes jars out of clay, doesn't he have a right.* See the parallel potter passages in Isa 29:16; 45:9; Jer 18:6; Wis 15:7; Sir 33:10-13—all of which speak of the potter's right to do whatever he wishes with the clay. In the same way, God has the right to do whatever he wishes with those he creates.

one jar for decoration and another to throw garbage into. Lit., "one vessel for honor and another for dishonor." Cf. "one object for special use and another for ordinary use" (NRSV).

9:22 *In the same way, even though God has the right to show his anger and his power, he is very patient with those on whom his anger falls, who are destined for destruction.* Lit., "[What] if God, desiring to show [his] wrath and to make known his power, has endured with much patience the objects of wrath that are made for destruction." The interpretation of this difficult passage (perhaps the most difficult in the entire letter) depends in part on whether the reader interprets "desiring" to mean "although he desires" (Dunn 1988b:566-568) or "because he desires" (Cranfield 1981:493-497; Moo 1996:604-606). In the first case, his "enduring" seems to run *counter to* his desire to manifest his wrath and power. In the second case, his enduring is *the result of* his desire to manifest his wrath and power. Though the first would seem to be preferable, translations and commentaries are split in their interpretations of this passage. The introductory "[What] if" suggests this is to be interpreted as a possibility rather than as a fact.

9:23 *He does this to make the riches of his glory shine even brighter.* Lit., "and in order to make known the riches of his glory." A few Gr. mss (B 1739mg) omit the difficult "and," for this clause is a continuation of the question begun in 9:22. The introductory "[What] if" suggests that this, like the first part of the question (9:22), is to be interpreted as a possibility rather than as a fact.

those to whom he shows mercy. Lit., "objects of mercy."

who were prepared in advance for glory. Those pre-chosen to receive his eternal blessings.

9:24 *selected.* Lit., "called" (*ekalesen* [TG2564, ZG2813])—that is, "chosen." See note on 1:1; cf. 1:6-7; 8:28, 30; 9:12; 11:29.

9:25 *Concerning the Gentiles.* The NLT has added this for clarity.

Those who were not my people, I will now call my people. And I will love those whom I did not love before. A free rendering of Hos 2:23: "I will show love to those I called 'Not loved.' And to those I called 'Not my people,' I will say, 'Now you are my people.'" In the original context of Hosea, the words are about Israel, who abandoned God; but as Paul used them, they applied to the Gentiles, traditionally outside of God's loving embrace. Among the early Christians, this seems to have been a common interpretation of the Hosea passage (cf. 1 Pet 2:10). See note on 9:26.

9:26 *Then, at the place where they were told, 'You are not my people,' there they will be called 'children of the living God.'* This a quotation from Hos 1:10, which in its original context refers to Israel. See note on 9:25.

9:27-28 This is a quotation from Isa 10:22-23, LXX.

9:27 *only a remnant will be saved.* Though the original text in Isaiah refers to the small number of Jews in exile in Assyria who will return to the Lord, Paul's use of it applies to the small number of Jews who have turned to the Lord in his day (cf. 11:5).

9:28 *the LORD will carry out his sentence upon the earth quickly and with finality.* This is the most likely translation of the Greek text (a rather free rendering of Isa 10:22-23 LXX), though it is difficult to be certain of the exact meaning. Lit., "for the LORD will do his word on the earth, completing and cutting short." Some mss (ℵ² D F G 𝔐) filled out the quotation from Isaiah by adding the words "in righteousness, because the sentence has been shortened" (cf. the KJV). All modern translations assume the "word" refers to God's judgment rather than to God's salvation.

9:29 *If the LORD of Heaven's Armies had not spared a few of our children.* A verbatim quotation from Isa 1:9 LXX. Lit., "If the Lord of Sabaoth (*sabaōth* [TG4519, ZG4877]) had not left a seed [survivors, descendants] for us." Paul simply transliterated the Heb. word "Sabaoth" (meaning "armies") rather than translate it into Gr.

COMMENTARY

Though some see chapters 9–11 as an integral part of Paul's letter, dealing with God's eternal plan for Israel especially (so Nygren, Cranfield, Dunn, Morris, Moo, Schreiner, Stuhlmacher), and some even view the section as the center or climax of the letter (so Baur, Munck, Fitzmyer, Beker, N. T. Wright), Romans 9–11 is best taken as a digression or excursus (so Augustine, Sanday and Headlam, Dodd, Denney)—albeit an important one, closely related to Paul's emphasis on God's concern for both Jews and Gentiles (1:16-17; cf. Edwards). This digression is inserted between Paul's explanation of the Good News (chs 1–8) and his instructions on Christian living (chs 12–15a). If this somewhat self-contained section is omitted, Paul's thought flows naturally from the end of chapter 8 to the beginning of chapter 12—from his concluding reflection on the greatness of God's love in Jesus Christ (8:31-39) to the beginning of his discussion of how Christians are to live in light of that (12:1ff).

Beginning in chapter 9, Paul deals with what, for him, were agonizing questions (though not the central concerns of his letter): Why have more Jews not responded to the Good News of Christ? Has God turned his back on his chosen people? At stake here is not only the eternal destiny of Paul's own people but also the credibility of God—and the Good News itself. ("If the Good News were really true and Jesus were really the long-awaited Messiah," some might well have argued, "would the Jews not have been the first to recognize it?") These questions may also have been actively discussed among the Jews and Gentiles in the church in Rome. Thus, Paul discusses the purposes of God vis-à-vis Jews and Gentiles throughout history. These reflections are probably the result of years of thinking and praying about these troublesome questions.

At the beginning of chapter 9, Paul reminds us that Jews, as the favored people of

God, have a long history of special blessings. So why have they turned away from the salvation God has now revealed in Jesus Christ? First, we have to remember that not all Jews are true Jews—that is, real, spiritual descendants of Abraham (2:28-29; cf. 4:11-12). The real people of God, the truly faithful, have always been a minority specially chosen by God (as Isaac and Jacob were), quite apart from anything they have done to earn it (9:6-13). But isn't this unfair of God—to choose some and not others? No, not at all, Paul argues; God has the right to choose whomever he wishes, and the choice is completely up to him, not us (9:14-16). The question of who receives his eternal blessings is a matter decided not by human desires or efforts but by God alone—it is a matter of God's sheer mercy. But how, then, can God hold people accountable for their responses if their responses are predetermined by him? To this question no answer is given—only the warning not to criticize the Almighty (9:20). It is God's prerogative to choose whomever he wishes—and if that means rejecting some and choosing others, so be it. To reinforce the point, Paul quotes several Scripture texts that speak of God's judgment on Jews and his mercy on Gentiles. In this chapter we have the strongest statement of God's sovereignty in the entire New Testament.

Paul's Agony over the Plight of His Own People. Paul's agony over the plight of the Jewish people (9:2-3) reflects his clear conviction that, apart from Christ, they stand under the judgment of God as condemned sinners like everyone else. Paul was clearly not a universalist: everything he wrote reflects his conviction that the whole world stands under the judgment of God because of its sin—Jews and Gentiles alike (1:18–3:20)—and that salvation is exclusively for those who put their trust in Christ to save them. By nature all people are sinful and therefore "subject to God's anger" (Eph 2:1-3). In Paul's understanding, evangelism is as necessary for Jews as for everybody else.

His excruciating sense of pain over the lost state of his own people ("My heart is filled with bitter sorrow and unending grief. . . . I would be willing to be forever cursed—cut off from Christ!—if that would save them," 9:2-3) is a rebuke to our callous indifference to the spiritual plight of the people around us. Do we agonize over a world that is lost—or do we no longer really believe it is lost? Behind much of our apathy would seem to lie a modern-day hesitance to believe in eternal judgment, shaped by the relativistic ethos of our times. The serious conviction that God's judgment is real is one of the factors that gave the apostle's evangelism such passion and urgency. If we, like Paul, were seriously to believe that the world stands condemned under the anger and judgment of God, perhaps we would begin to take evangelism as seriously as he did.

As a Jew, Paul knew the privileged position historically held by the Jewish people (9:4-5). From the earliest days, they had been God's chosen people, his "adopted children." They were blessed with all that God had given them—his glory and goodness, his eternal covenants and promises, his divine law, the privilege of knowing and worshiping the true and living God. All the great people of God of earlier days were Jews. And the Messiah, humanly speaking, was also a Jew—though in actuality he was nothing less than God himself, the one who is over all things, deserving of our praise forever (9:5). This recital of traditional Jewish privileges only serves to increase the painfulness of the question Paul raises: how can it be that God's own chosen people have now failed to respond to the one who has given them one gracious blessing after another?

God Chooses Some and Not Others. Does their failure to respond mean that God's plan has gone wrong—that God's intentions for his people have been thwarted, that his promises to them have come to nothing? Has God failed his own people? Not at all, Paul says; we have to remember that they were never all God's people in the first place (9:6), any more than all of Abraham's offspring were considered Abraham's true children. When God said to Abraham, "Isaac is the son through whom your descendants will be counted" (Gen 21:12), he made it clear that not all the children of Abraham would be considered God's adopted children (cf. 9:4), but only Isaac, the child God himself had promised and given Abraham in his old age, would bear the special blessing; Isaac was the chosen one (9:7; cf. Gen 17:18-21). In the same way, not everyone who is physically descended from Abraham, or who calls himself or herself a Jew, is a true child of God but only those so designated by God; they are the true "children of the promise" (9:8), the chosen ones. Here Paul expands on his earlier assertion that a true Jew is defined not by his ethnicity or circumcision but by his heart ("A true Jew is one whose heart is right with God. And true circumcision is not merely obeying the letter of the law; rather, it is a change of heart produced by God's Spirit," 2:28-29). A true Jew is one in whose heart God's Spirit, by his sovereign grace, has worked to evoke faith in Christ. So the fact that the majority of Jews have not responded to Christ doesn't at all mean that God has failed his people. His *chosen* people from among Abraham's physical descendants, a small minority, have responded to him.

The pattern of God choosing who will be his people may also be seen in the story of Isaac's sons Jacob and Esau. Of the two sons, it was Jacob who was chosen by God to inherit the promises. God picked him out before he was even born, before he or his twin brother Esau had done anything good or bad (9:10-12). In this case, the traditional pattern of Hebrew society was broken by God himself: the older son was to serve the younger one. This shows that the final choice is always God's and not ours. So it is only those chosen by God himself who can truly be called "God's children"—an implicit acknowledgment that some are not chosen (11:7-10). As the Scripture itself says, "I loved Jacob, but I rejected Esau" (9:13). The sovereign choice of God is what ultimately counts (see comments on 1:6-7).

Is God's Choosing Unfair? However, if God chooses some and not others, isn't that unfair (9:14)? Paul knew that some would pose this question—especially in light of the Old Testament texts that emphasize the fundamental fairness of God (e.g., "God is an honest judge," Ps 7:11; "Everything he does is just and fair," Deut 32:4). Doesn't this choosing of some and not others smack of favoritism rather than fairness? Paul replies that we must remember that God has the right to do whatever he wants;

we cannot judge him simply on the basis of what seems fair or unfair to us. We do not sit in judgment on him; he sits in judgment on us. He is not accountable to us; we are accountable to him. After all, God himself has said, "I will show mercy to anyone I choose, and I will show compassion to anyone I choose" (9:15; Exod 33:19). So the choice is his—and has always been his.

This means that God has the right to condemn as well as to save. As he said (through Moses) to the stubborn Pharaoh, "I have appointed you for the very purpose of displaying my power in you and to spread my fame throughout the earth" (9:17; cf. Exod 9:16). These fearful words remind us that, in the end, everything depends not on what humans want or strive for but simply on what God desires; everything depends on the mercy of God (9:16). "So you see," Paul concludes, "God chooses to show mercy to some"—that's his prerogative; "and he chooses to harden the hearts of others so they refuse to listen" (9:18)—that's his prerogative, too. And so it seems, at least for now, that he has put Jews "into a deep sleep. . . . He has shut their eyes so they do not see, and closed their ears so they do not hear" (11:8). In those awful words we sense something of the enormity of God's sovereignty and learn to live in reverence of it. God has the sovereign right to do whatever he wishes and to choose whomever he desires, and we cannot condemn him for doing so. The fact that he does not reveal his reason for choosing some and not others does not mean we can criticize him for his choices; he does not answer to us. Further, we must always remind ourselves that, in light of the immensity of human sin before the holiness of God, it is by his mercy that he chooses to save anyone. None of us is deserving of his grace; as sinners, we have all forfeited everything—and that puts a whole different perspective on the question. So the real question is not "How could God ever condemn anyone?" but "How could God ever save anyone?"

We must be careful not to misinterpret the apostle on this point. When Paul uses predestination language or talks about God's selection, his focus is generally on the predestination of the saved, not on the predestination of the damned. He speaks of it much more in a positive sense than in a negative sense. Predestination, for Paul, is intended to evoke gratitude in the hearts of God's people—to make us eternally grateful for God's grace, to remind us how infinitely indebted we are to God for choosing *us*. On the other hand, when he speaks of the condemnation of unbelievers, his focus is generally on their own refusal to respond or believe, not on God's role in determining their response. Paul did not place the blame simply on God for the damnation of those who refuse to believe. Logically speaking, of course, to affirm that some are chosen for salvation implies that others are not. "But here," writes A. M. Hunter (1966:74-75), "Paul is splendidly illogical. . . . He says in effect: 'If you perish, it is your own fault. If you have saving faith, then know that it is a gift of God's grace.'" However, rather than saying Paul is "splendidly illogical," perhaps it is more accurate to say that here Paul had learned to live with paradox, the paradox of taking seriously both God's sovereign choice in salvation and the responsibility of individuals to respond to his message. Generally speaking, then, when Paul addresses believers, he freely speaks of God's sovereign grace, which has placed them among the elect; but when he addresses unbelievers, his emphasis falls on their own failing and sin. Predestination, for Paul, is to be preached not to unbelievers but to believers; it is a doctrine not for sinners but for saints. It is to be understood not as a decree of damnation on those predetermined for hell but as an expression of God's grace on those destined for heaven (see, however, comments on 11:7-10). The truth of predestination means that at every point in life, believers must fall on their knees and confess that it is only by God's grace that they are saved.

How Then Can God Hold Anyone Accountable? Paul anticipates a further question in response to God's sovereignty: If God is the one who decides who is and is not saved, how can he hold people accountable for their responses to him? If God himself chooses who is "in" and who is "out," how can he hold people responsible for their refusal to come "in"? Aren't they simply doing what he has already decided they will do (9:19)? To this question, which naturally follows, Paul has no reply—other than to say, Who are you, a mere mortal, to criticize God? How can you challenge the wishes of the one who created you? Does a potter not have the right to shape the clay as he wishes—to make part of it into something beautiful and precious and another part into something to be used for menial purposes if he so desires? What right do the things that are made have to question their maker's intent? Paul warns us here that we must be very careful not to challenge God, for God has the right to do whatever he wishes, and we must respect his authority to do so. However, what Paul cautions against is not the humble questioning of a bewildered, genuine follower of the Lord but the critical and defiant challenge of a skeptic or unbeliever. Indeed, there is a world of difference between an honest question asked of God in humility and an arrogant challenge uttered in ridicule and disbelief. Scripture attests that God graciously abides the genuine questions of his confused and hurting children, but he has little patience with the defiant challenges of stubborn and unbelieving hearts.

This strong view of God's sovereignty, before which all people must bow, is shaped by the Hebrew Scriptures in which Paul's thought was steeped. The Old Testament writers respected the sovereign rights of God as the ultimate King; they readily accepted that he has the right to do whatever he wishes. The words of Isaiah reflect the respect for God's sovereign "otherness" that is found throughout the Old Testament: " 'My thoughts are nothing like your thoughts,' says the LORD. 'And my ways are far beyond anything you could imagine. For just as the heavens are higher than the earth, so my ways are higher than your ways and my thoughts higher than your thoughts' " (Isa 55:8-9). Because of their respect for the otherness of God, the Old Testament writers were much more reluctant to sit in judgment upon God or to challenge God than are many people today. Even Job, who suffered so much and whose example is so often invoked by those seeking to justify the venting of anger to God, was forced to acknowledge that he was wrong to challenge God:

> I am nothing—how could I ever find the answers? I will cover my mouth
> with my hand. I have said too much already. . . . I know that you can do
> anything, and no one can stop you. You asked, "Who is this that questions

my wisdom with such ignorance?" It is I—and I was talking about things I knew nothing about, things far too wonderful for me. . . . I take back everything I said, and I sit in dust and ashes to show my repentance. (Job 40:4-5; 42:2-3, 6)

In the same way, said Martin Luther with regard to God's sovereignty, "All objections to predestination proceed from the [foolish] wisdom of the flesh. . . . [which] exalts itself above God and judges His will" (1954:114). Though such a strong view of the sovereignty of God is unpopular today, both the Old Testament and the New Testament emphasize that those who are created by God are called to bow to the will of God, not to sit in judgment upon it. Because of the utter transcendence of God, we must accept the mysteries of life and learn to live with them. So with regard to the question of why not all of the Jews are saved (and the larger question of why not all people are saved), we must allow full room for God's sovereignty—the right of God to choose whomever he wishes and to do whatever he sees fit.

God Has the Right to Condemn as well as Save. Viewed from the perspective of transcendence, far from being unfair to people, God has shown remarkable patience in tolerating people—especially those whose behavior merits the utmost punishment and who therefore deserve to be called the objects of wrath. But even if his purpose is to pour out his anger and power on the objects of his wrath—in order to highlight, by contrast, the immensity of his grace poured out on the objects of his mercy, those Jews and Gentiles chosen from the beginning of time to receive his mercy—who can contest it? (cf. 9:22-24, NRSV). Surely God has the right to condemn as well as to save. God is God, and whatever he does is his prerogative. We who are created by God have no right to criticize the Creator for his seeming inconsistency or unfairness. We must remember that, in the end, God will surely do what is just; "Should not the Judge of all the earth do what is right?" (Gen 18:25).

Notice here that Paul does not flatly declare that God's purpose is to pour out his anger and power on the objects of wrath. Instead, he poses the possibility more tentatively and shifts the emphasis: *What if* his purpose is to pour out his anger and power on the objects of wrath (though he has borne very patiently with them)—*in order to* highlight the immensity of his grace shown to us, the chosen objects of his mercy? Who can condemn him for it? Rather than focusing baldly on God's wrath on those "made for destruction," he preferred to highlight God's long-standing patience with sinners (even though they deserve his wrath) and his more ultimate purpose of showing grace to the objects of his mercy. At the same time, it must be kept in mind that Paul presented this idea in a tentative way (What if . . . ?). Paul did not say outright that this is God's purpose but simply posed it as a possibility to make the point that this is certainly God's prerogative if he so chooses. Once again, we see that when Paul speaks of predestination, of God's sovereign choosing in the matter of salvation, his overall emphasis falls not on the predestination of the damned but on the predestination of the saved—those specially chosen to be the recipients of his grace.

The Chosen Include Gentiles as well as Jews. The chosen now include both Jews and Gentiles (9:24), though there are relatively few Jews who have responded. But that is exactly what the prophet Isaiah predicted: "Only a remnant will be saved" (9:27; Isa 10:22 LXX). Indeed, Isaiah said that it is only by God's mercy that any Jews are saved at all (9:29; Isa 1:9). The implication is that the nation as a whole deserves nothing but the judgment of God. That which from a human point of view seems unjust, from God's perspective is sheer mercy.

The undeserved mercy of God on Gentiles is also predicted in Scripture, even as the prophets anticipated the future inclusion of Gentiles from all over the world among God's people. Isaiah 40–66 especially reflects this more inclusive vision, as we will see later (see commentary on 11:11-24), but other prophets reflect it also (Mic 4:1-4; Zech 9:10). Hosea spoke openly of God's beckoning love for those who have not known it before (9:25-26)—though in the texts Paul quoted (Hos 1:10; 2:23), Paul was referencing Gentiles while Hosea was speaking of wayward Israel. In any case, both texts quoted by Paul are intended to emphasize the sovereign choice of God in including Gentiles among his people.

In conclusion, it should be said that this entire section (9:6-29) focuses on the sovereign choice of God in designating who his people will be. The choice is not dependent on human desires or efforts but solely on the grace of God, and because God is God, his choice cannot be criticized as unfair—he has the right to do whatever he wishes. With regard to the Jews as a whole, then, Paul implies that the door to his saving grace simply has not been opened to them at this time. Citing Scripture, he concludes, "God has put them into a deep sleep. . . . He has shut their eyes so they do not see, and closed their ears so they do not hear" (11:8; cf. Deut 29:4; Isa 29:10). But there are other considerations also, and it is to these that Paul now directs his attention.

◆ **B. Jews Have Refused God's Salvation (9:30–10:4)**

30What does all this mean? Even though the Gentiles were not trying to follow God's standards, they were made right with God. And it was by faith that this took place. 31But the people of Israel, who tried so hard to get right with God by keeping the law, never succeeded. 32Why not? Because they were trying to get right with God by keeping the law* instead of by trusting in him. They stumbled over the great rock in their path. 33God warned them of this in the Scriptures when he said,

"I am placing a stone in Jerusalem*
  that makes people stumble,
a rock that makes them fall.

But anyone who trusts in him
  will never be disgraced."*

CHAPTER 10
Dear brothers and sisters,* the longing of my heart and my prayer to God is for the people of Israel to be saved. 2I know what enthusiasm they have for God, but it is misdirected zeal. 3For they don't understand God's way of making people right with himself. Refusing to accept God's way, they cling to their own way of getting right with God by trying to keep the law. 4For Christ has already accomplished the purpose for which the law was given.* As a result, all who believe in him are made right with God.

9:32 Greek by works. 9:33a Greek in Zion. 9:33b Isa 8:14; 28:16 (Greek version). 10:1 Greek Brothers. 10:4 Or For Christ is the end of the law.

NOTES

9:30 *Even though the Gentiles were not trying to follow God's standards.* Lit., "Gentiles, the ones not seeking righteousness."

9:31 *But the people of Israel, who tried so hard to get right with God by keeping the law, never succeeded.* Lit., "But Israel, pursuing a law of righteousness (*nomon dikaiosunēs* [TG3551/1343, ZG3795/1466]), did not attain it." The unusual phrase "law of righteousness" has been interpreted in different ways: "principle of righteousness," "law that testifies to righteousness," "law that promises righteousness," "law as a way of achieving righteousness"— the latter roughly equivalent to the more common Pauline phrase, "righteousness of the law" (cf. "the righteousness that is based on the law," NRSV). Human beings, on their own, can neither fulfill the righteous demands of the law (cf. 7:14-25) nor achieve righteousness before God by their attempts to obey the law (cf. 9:32).

9:32 *by keeping the law.* Lit., "by works" (*ex ergōn* [TG2041, ZG2240]). Some Gr. mss (ℵ² D 33 𝔐) read "by works of law." For "works of the law," see note on 3:20.

They stumbled over the great rock in their path. Cf. 1 Pet 2:8, which speaks of Christ as "the stone that makes people stumble, the rock that makes them fall."

9:33 *God warned them of this in the Scriptures when he said.* Lit., "As it is written."

I am placing a stone in Jerusalem that makes people stumble, a rock that makes them fall. But anyone who trusts in him will never be disgraced. A combined quotation from two Isaiah "stone" texts (Isa 8:14; 28:16 LXX) that were commonly used in early Christian apologetics. Cf. 1 Pet 2:6, 8, where they are combined with a third "stone" text from Ps 118:22; and Luke 20:17-18, where there may be an allusion to yet another "stone" text from Dan 2:34-35. The original Isaiah texts, addressing the threat of the Assyrian invasion sweeping over the land like a flood (8th century BC), speak of God as the great rock of refuge for those who put their trust in him but a stumbling stone for those who put their trust elsewhere.

in Jerusalem. Lit., "in Zion," a traditional Jewish way of speaking of Jerusalem.

trusts in him. Or, "trusts in it [the rock]." The words "in him" (or "in it") are not found in the MT of Isa 28:16 but are added in the LXX.

will never be disgraced. Or, "will never be put to shame"; cf. 10:11. In the MT, Isa 28:16 reads, "One who trusts will not panic" (NRSV). Believers can rest secure in the knowledge that God will keep safe those who trust in him and that God's purposes will be fulfilled in their own time.

10:1 *brothers and sisters.* Gr., *adelphoi* [TG80, ZG81] (brothers).

10:2 *it is misdirected zeal.* Lit., "zeal . . . not according to knowledge."

10:3 *they don't understand God's way of making people right with himself.* Lit., "being ignorant of the righteousness of God" (*tēn tou theou dikaiosunēn* [TG1343, ZG1466]).

they cling to their own way of getting right with God. Or, "they want to become righteous on their own." Lit., "seeking to establish their own [righteousness]." Cf. Phil 3:9, where Paul contrasts God's righteousness and his own righteousness.

by trying to keep the law. The NLT adds this for clarity.

10:4 *Christ has already accomplished the purpose for which the law was given.* Lit., "Christ is the end (*telos* [TG5056, ZG5465]) of the law." This Gr. clause may be understood in three different ways: (1) Christ is the fulfillment of the law (cf. Matt 5:17: "I did not come to abolish the law of Moses. . . . No, I came to accomplish their purpose"). (2) Christ is the goal of the law (Cranfield 1981:516-520). (3) Christ is the termination of the law (Dunn 1988b:596-598; Käsemann 1980:282-283). Some combine the possible senses (e.g., "He puts an end to the law, not by destroying all that the law stood for but by realizing it," [Barrett 1957:197-198]). Though all three senses are present in Paul's thinking, the third interpretation fits the context best. The point is that Christ (not the law) is now the means of obtaining a right standing with God.

COMMENTARY

When it comes to the question of why the Jews are not saved, just as we have to take account of the sovereign right of God to choose his people, so we have to take account of the Jews' own responsibility for their standing before God. They have been so insistent on establishing their own righteousness before God that they have failed to recognize the righteousness that God freely offers them in his Son. Instead of accepting it as a free gift by faith, they have been determined to achieve it by their own works—that is, by their dutiful observance of the law of Moses. In so doing, they have failed to submit themselves to God's way of making people right with himself (9:30-32). In the strange providence of God, Gentiles—who traditionally have had no interest in God's ways—have now found God's favor because of their faith in Christ, while Jews—who have always been zealous for God's ways—have failed to find favor because of their determination to gain it by obeying the law of Moses. They failed to see that Christ, not the law, is the way to be accepted by God. From this perspective, it is not God who is to be blamed for their tragic situation but the Jews themselves; the responsibility lies squarely on their own shoulders.

For them, Jesus Christ—or more accurately, the Good News of his free grace—has proven to be the great stumbling block (9:32-33). They could not accept the idea that people can be saved by simply accepting God's grace as a free gift from Christ. The natural instinct of human beings to think they must do something to earn salvation is deeply rooted; many people naturally shy away from the notion of salvation as a free gift. This is just as the Scripture predicts (Isa 8:14; 28:16 LXX): Jesus was both a stone that brought about the downfall of those who stumble over him and a rock of refuge for those who put their trust in him.

At the beginning of chapter 10, Paul reiterates the longing of his heart for the salvation of his own people and then adds, significantly, that he prays for that (10:1). Here again we see the way that divine and human perspectives sit side by side, paradoxically, in Paul's thinking. On the one hand, God is the one who, in his sovereignty, chooses who will belong to him—it has nothing to do with human choice or striving (9:16). On the other hand, Paul prays for the salvation of the Jews because he cannot do otherwise. If we truly care for others, we are compelled to pray for them, especially when their salvation is at stake. After all, does not the whole of Scripture say that God cares for his people and listens to their prayers? (Remember God's willingness to accommodate to Abraham's request for mercy for the people of Sodom in Gen 18:23-32.) If it were a simple case of logic, one might assume that there is no need to pray or that nothing is to be gained by praying, since it all depends on God's choice and not on our desires; but in the paradoxical world of God, it is never a simple case of logic. Consequently, even with Scripture's strong emphasis on the sovereign choice of God, we find ourselves compelled to pray for those who do not know his saving grace, just as Paul prays for them—we cannot do otherwise. And our prayers are directed to the One who cares for the lost more than we ever can—the one whose heart for the lost compelled him to send his own Son into the world, "so that everyone who believes in him will not perish but have eternal life. God sent his Son into the world not to judge the world, but to save the world through him" (John 3:16-17).

So in this strange and complex world that God has made, we must take account of both divine and human factors. God's sovereignty and human responsibility are both true; neither invalidates the other, neither renders the other unimportant. What this means is that, although we cannot reconcile the two logically, we cannot do away with either and still maintain an adequate view of life. The whole of life, with all its complexities, cannot be reduced simply to a Calvinistic emphasis on the sovereignty of God or a Wesleyan emphasis on human choice and responsibility; both are important and necessary. This paradoxical way of thinking, with its seeming inconsistency between the affirmation of God's sovereignty and the acknowledgment of human responsibility, is characteristic of Paul's thinking and may be observed throughout his letters. Indeed, it is one of the keys to understanding his thinking and writing. The old saying "Pray as if everything depends on God; work as if everything depends on you" accurately reflects the way Paul thought and lived. What Paul gives us, then, is not a thoroughgoing systematic theology but a theology of paradox. He teaches us that the phenomenon of paradox lies at the very heart of life and that the acceptance of a paradoxical way of thinking is part of learning to live with the mysteries of God. The acceptance of paradox provides the most adequate explanation of some of life's complexities.

In this section (chs 9–11), Paul's paradoxical recognition of both divine and human factors is clearly observed in his simultaneous acknowledgment of God's role in choosing his people and the Jews' own responsibility for their failure to accept God's salvation. Though the Jews were zealous for God, their zeal was unenlightened: They did not understand or submit to God's way of thinking about righteousness. Instead, they insisted on going their own way, thinking they could achieve righteousness by fulfilling the demands of the law of Moses (10:2-3).

What they failed to realize, however, is that the coming of Christ signifies the "end" (*telos* [TG5056, ZG5465]) of the law of Moses (10:4, NRSV)—that is, the termination of the law (cf. 6:14; 7:4-6; Gal 2:16-21). Though Christ is the "end" of the law in other senses also (he is both its goal and its ultimate fulfillment, as in 3:31; 8:3-4; Gal 3:19, 23-24; cf. Matt 5:17), Paul emphasizes the termination of the law in three ways: (1) as a way of life—that is, as a set of comprehensive legislation governing the details of daily life; (2) as a negative force (like sin) driving people's lives and dooming them to failure; and (3) as a way of trying to achieve righteousness with God. It is in this third sense especially that Paul speaks of Christ as the "end" of the law of Moses in this context; righteousness is achieved not by trying to obey the law but by trusting in Christ as Savior.

◆ **C. Whoever Believes Will Be Saved (10:5-13)**

⁵For Moses writes that the law's way of making a person right with God requires obedience to all of its commands.* ⁶But faith's way of getting right with God says, "Don't say in your heart, 'Who will go up to heaven' (to bring Christ down to earth). ⁷And don't say, 'Who will go down to the place of the dead' (to bring Christ back to life again)." ⁸In fact, it says,

"The message is very close at hand;
    it is on your lips and in your heart."*

And that message is the very message about faith that we preach: ⁹If you con-fess with your mouth that Jesus is Lord and believe in your heart that God raised him from the dead, you will be saved. ¹⁰For it is by believing in your heart that you are made right with God, and it is by confessing with your mouth that you are saved. ¹¹As the Scriptures tell us, "Anyone who trusts in him will never be disgraced."* ¹²Jew and Gentile* are the same in this respect. They have the same Lord, who gives generously to all who call on him. ¹³For "Everyone who calls on the name of the LORD will be saved."*

10:5 See Lev 18:5. 10:6-8 Deut 30:12-14. 10:11 Isa 28:16 (Greek version). 10:12 Greek *and Greek.* 10:13 Joel 2:32.

NOTES

10:5 *the law's way of making a person right with God requires obedience to all of its commands.* Lit., "[concerning] the righteousness of the law, the person who does them will live by them." The last clause is a quotation from Lev 18:5. Paul intends it as an expression of the hopelessness of seeking righteousness by following the law (as in Gal 3:12, where he uses the same text to contrast the way of law with the way of faith) and not as an expression of the achievement of Christ in fulfilling the law (as in Barth 1933:376-377; Cranfield 1981:521-522). The assertion of the hopelessness of seeking righteousness by careful observance of the law is not contradicted by Paul's statement in Phil 3:6 that, with regard to righteousness under the law, he was "without fault"—for there he means "without fault" as judged by the traditional standards of Judaism, not by God.

10:6 *Don't say in your heart, 'Who will go up to heaven.'* Romans 10:6-8 includes quotations from Deut 30:12-14, which, in their original context, concern the law, not Christ. What Paul gives us is a Christian reinterpretation of this passage, applied to Christ, with Christian explanations inserted (in parentheses) for each line he quotes. This is influenced, perhaps, by the way the Deuteronomy passage is interpreted in terms of wisdom in Bar 3:29-30 because for Paul, Christ is wisdom (1 Cor 1:30; Bruce 1985:191-192). As a result, Paul takes a passage that was originally intended to show the easiness of following the law and reinterprets it to show the easiness of following Christ in contrast to the impossibility of following the law! The validity of such a reinterpretation may seem questionable to modern thinkers, but it simply reflects contemporary Jewish practices of interpreting Scripture (see Shulam 1997:347-350) and Paul's Christological way of reading the OT.

to bring Christ down to earth. Paul's Christian interpretation of the OT quotation.

10:7 *And don't say, 'Who will go down to the place of the dead'.* Lit., "Who will go down to the abyss (*abusson* [ᵀᴳ12, ᶻᴳ12])?"

to bring Christ back to life again. Paul's Christian interpretation of the OT quotation.

10:8 *In fact, it says.* Lit., "But what does it say?"

The message is very close at hand; it is on your lips and in your heart. In contrast to the rigorous demands of the law, all that faith requires is a simple response of confessing and believing.

10:9 *If you confess with your mouth that Jesus is Lord.* Cf. 1 Cor 12:3; Phil 2:11. The phrase "Jesus is Lord" seems to have been the earliest form of a Christian statement of faith, perhaps voiced at a convert's baptism.

believe in your heart that God raised him from the dead. Belief in the resurrection of Christ was considered a central part of Christian faith among the early Christians. Cf. 1 Cor 15:17: "If Christ has not been raised, then your faith is useless and you are still guilty of your sins."

10:10 *it is by believing in your heart that you are made right with God, and it is by confessing with your mouth that you are saved.* The actions of believing and confessing are closely linked and ought not to be sharply distinguished—just as being "made right with God" is not to be distinguished from being "saved." These are two ways of describing the same event—Christian conversion.

10:11 *Anyone who trusts in him will never be disgraced.* Or, "will never be put to shame." A quotation from Isa 28:16 LXX, already cited in 9:33.

10:12 *Jew and Gentile are the same in this respect.* Lit., "There is no difference between Jew and Greek (*Hellēnos* [TG1672, ZG1818])." The phrase "There is no difference" had a negative connotation in 3:22, declaring that all have sinned; it has a positive connotation here, declaring that all can be saved.

10:13 *Everyone who calls on the name of the LORD will be saved.* This is a quotation from Joel 2:32, also cited by Peter on the Day of Pentecost in Acts 2:21.

COMMENTARY

In this section, Paul sharpens the contrast between the law of Moses and the Good News. The two represent quite different ways of thinking about how people can be made right with God, quite different understandings of righteousness. The traditional Jewish way of thinking understands righteousness as a matter of obedience to the law of Moses. As the law itself says, "The person who does these things will live by them" (10:5, NRSV; cf. Lev 18:5)—that is, they will gain life as a result of their observance of the law. But there is no allowance for mistakes; the promise of life is only for those who observe the law completely (Gal 3:10, 12). This is what Paul means by "the righteousness of the law" or "the righteousness that comes from the law." It is a righteousness that, in reality, is unattainable because the standard is impossibly demanding; everyone fails at some point or other.

Most people in the world today, when they think of finding favor with God, probably think of it in a somewhat similar way, as something to be earned. They expect to be approved by God on the basis of how they live, or because of the things they do, on the assumption that the good things they do will outweigh the bad. The problem with this whole way of thinking is that it reflects a deficient view both of human sinfulness and of God's holiness. It fails to take account of the radical nature of sin in God's sight and our absolute need of God's forgiving grace. The way we live, the things we do, will never be sufficient to make ourselves acceptable to God; those are the things that have placed us under the judgment of God. (That is the point of 1:18–3:20.)

The only way to come to God and be accepted by him is to come simply trusting in his forgiving grace. All we can do is come with our sin and throw ourselves on his mercy, trusting in Christ alone to save us. Citing a text from the law of Moses that shows the essentially simple nature of responding to God's word ("The message is very close at hand; it is on your lips and in your heart," Deut 30:14), Paul emphasizes that there is nothing difficult we need to do to obtain salvation. We don't need to scale the ladder to heaven or descend into hell to get Christ. All we need to do is embrace the Savior and put our trust in him to save us, and that is within easy reach of everyone—it is a simple matter of trusting Christ and confessing our faith in him (10:6-8). So there is nothing difficult or complicated about acquiring salvation—God has made it easy; we simply receive it as a gift. "God saved you by his grace when you believed. And you can't take credit for this; it is a gift from God. Salvation is not a reward for the good things we have done" (Eph 2:8-9). The result is what Paul speaks of as "the righteousness of faith" or "the righteousness that comes from faith"—the righteousness that God himself credits to us because of our trust in Christ's death for our sins. It is nothing less than the righteousness of Christ himself, and it is the only righteousness that can save us.

Paul concludes with the well-known text, "If you confess with your mouth that Jesus is Lord and believe in your heart that God raised him from the dead, you will be saved" (10:9ff)—a text that reflects the way the simple confession "Jesus is Lord" functioned as the earliest Christian creed. Public confession is here viewed as the expression of true faith. (Christian faith was never intended to be a private, hidden thing but something to be confessed openly to the world.) Though there are clear implications for how the believer is to live (to confess Jesus as Lord means he must be Lord of the confessor's life), the overall focus of this passage is not on living out the Good News but on simply believing it and putting our trust in it. Scripture itself teaches us that "Anyone who trusts in him will never be disgraced" (10:11; cf. Isa 28:16). God will be absolutely faithful to his promise to accept us in Christ.

Because this way of coming to God is not dependent on obeying the law of Moses, it is open to everyone—Jews and Gentiles alike. Christ came to be Lord of all, and his grace is poured out abundantly upon all who call upon him. As Scripture reassures us, "Everyone who calls on the name of the LORD will be saved" (10:13; Joel 2:32).

◆ D. Jews Have No Excuse for Refusing the Message (10:14-21)

¹⁴But how can they call on him to save them unless they believe in him? And how can they believe in him if they have never heard about him? And how can they hear about him unless someone tells them? ¹⁵And how will anyone go and tell them without being sent? That is why the Scriptures say, "How beautiful are the feet of messengers who bring good news!"*

¹⁶But not everyone welcomes the Good News, for Isaiah the prophet said, "LORD, who has believed our message?"* ¹⁷So faith comes from hearing, that is, hearing the Good News about Christ. ¹⁸But I ask, have the people of Israel actually heard the message? Yes, they have:

"The message has gone throughout the earth,
and the words to all the world."*

¹⁹But I ask, did the people of Israel really understand? Yes, they did, for even in the time of Moses, God said,

"I will rouse your jealousy through people who are not even a nation.
I will provoke your anger through the foolish Gentiles."*

²⁰And later Isaiah spoke boldly for God, saying,

"I was found by people who were not looking for me.
I showed myself to those who were not asking for me."*

²¹But regarding Israel, God said,

"All day long I opened my arms to them,
but they were disobedient and rebellious."*

10:15 Isa 52:7. 10:16 Isa 53:1. 10:18 Ps 19:4. 10:19 Deut 32:21. 10:20 Isa 65:1 (Greek version).
10:21 Isa 65:2 (Greek version).

NOTES

10:15 *How beautiful are the feet of messengers who bring good news!* Or, "How wonderful is the coming of those who bring good news!" This free rendering of Isa 52:7 is found in 𝔓46 ℵ* A B C 81 1739. It is also possible that the Gr. word *hōraioi* [TG5611, ZG6053] should be translated "timely" rather than "beautiful" (so Käsemann, Dunn), giving the text a more eschatological interpretation. Some Gr. mss (ℵ² D F G 𝔐), followed by the KJV, fill out the last phrase: "the good news of peace." Paul makes use of several passages from Isa 40–66 (a part of Scripture anticipating God's deliverance of the Jews from Babylonia) in a way that shows he reads and interprets texts in this section from a Christian point of view, as texts referring to the Good News of salvation in Christ.

10:16 *welcomes.* Lit., "obeys" (*hupēkousan* [TG5219, ZG5634]).

Isaiah the prophet. Lit., "Isaiah."

LORD, *who has believed our message?* This is a quotation from Isa 53:1, with the word "LORD" added from the LXX. In its original context, it refers to the Jews' incredulous response to the Suffering Servant's exaltation; here it refers to the Jews' failure to believe the Good News about Jesus, who represents the fulfillment of Isaiah's prophecy. Cf. John 12:38, where the quotation refers to their failure to believe in Jesus and his miracles.

10:17 *the Good News about Christ.* Lit., "the word (*rhēma* [TG4487, ZG4839]) of Christ." This reading is strongly supported by 𝔓46ᵛⁱᵈ ℵ* B C D* 81 1739 cop and Old Latin. Other mss (ℵ¹ A D¹ 𝔐 syr), followed by the KJV, read "the word of God." The same word (*rhēma*) is used in 10:8 for "message."

10:18 *have the people of Israel actually heard the message?* Lit., "have they not heard?" (*mē ouk ēkousan* [TG191, ZG201]); this implicitly expects the answer, "Yes, they have heard."

Yes, they have. The NLT adds this for clarity.

The message has gone throughout the earth, and the words to all the world. This is a quotation from Ps 19:4, which in its original setting refers to the revelation of God's glory in creation; here it is applied to the Good News, which has been proclaimed in Jewish communities everywhere. (Some—e.g., Calvin, Schreiner—interpret it as a reference to the Gentile mission.) The quotation is not to be taken as strictly literal (cf. the literal reading "all over the world" in Col 1:6, 23). "It is unnecessary to suppose that Paul regarded Psalm 19:4 as a regular *prediction* of the worldwide dissemination of the gospel; the dissemination of the gospel, it is implied, is becoming as worldwide as the light of the heavenly bodies" (Bruce 1985:197).

10:19 *did the people of Israel really understand?* Lit., "did Israel not know?" (*mē Israēl ouk egnō* [TG1097, ZG1182]); this implicitly expects the answer, "Yes, they knew."

Yes, they did. The NLT adds this for clarity.

I will rouse your jealousy through people who are not even a nation. I will provoke your anger through the foolish Gentiles. Lit., "I will make you jealous by a non-nation, I will make you angry by a nation without understanding"—that is, by people who have no knowledge of God (cf. 11:11). This is a quotation from the Song of Moses (Deut 32:21), which is a pronouncement of God's judgment on Israel for its history of disobedience. (For other Pauline references to the Song of Moses, see 11:11; 12:19; 15:10; 1 Cor 10:20; Phil 2:15; cf. Heb 1:6; 10:30.) Cf. Bruce 1985:197-198: "Because they had provoked God to jealousy by their worship of a 'no-god' (Heb., *lo'-'el* [TH3808/410A, ZH4202/446]), he would provoke *them* to jealousy by means of a 'no-people' (Heb., *lo'-'am* [TH3808/5971A, ZH4202/6639])"—that is, by those not included in God's covenant purposes. Those familiar with the Heb. Bible (as Paul was) may have recognized the close relation between Moses's "no-people" (Heb. *lo'-'am*) and Hosea's "not my people" (Heb. *lo'-'ammi* [TH3818, ZH4204]; 9:25ff; Hos 1:10). Cf. the Jews' understanding of themselves as those who could "instruct the ignorant" (2:20).

10:20 *And later Isaiah spoke boldly for God.* Lit., "And Isaiah shows great daring and says." Isaiah is even more daring than Moses in speaking of the blessing of God upon those who have shown no interest in God.

I was found by people who were not looking for me. I showed myself to those who were not asking for me. A quotation from Isa 65:1, LXX, which in its original context refers to Israel. Paul here finds the words equally valid for Gentiles. In its original context, Isa 65:1-2 refers to rebellious Israel; in quoting it here, Paul takes v. 1 to refer to Gentiles and v. 2 to refer to Israel.

10:21 *All day long I opened my arms to them, but they were disobedient and rebellious.* This is a quotation from Isa 65:2, LXX.

COMMENTARY

The preceding section ended with the strong biblical affirmation, "Everyone who calls on the name of the LORD will be saved" (10:13)—and for Paul, of course, the Lord is Jesus Christ. This, however, only leads to other perplexing questions, and here Paul poses four of them (10:14-15), each one leading logically to the next:

> How can people call on the name of the Lord if they don't believe in him?
> How can people believe in him if they don't hear the message?
> How can people hear the message if someone doesn't tell them?
> How can anyone tell them if no one is called and commissioned to do so?

This leads Paul to ask whether it might be that the people of Israel have never really heard or understood the Good News (10:18-19) and therefore have never really had a chance to believe and be saved. No, Paul says, the reality is that many have simply chosen not to believe. Even Isaiah, in his time, was dismayed at how few people seemed to have ears to hear God's message (10:16; Isa 53:1). It is true that faith comes from hearing the message, and the message is heard when people preach about Christ (10:17). However, people *have* heard the message. Just as the Psalms speak of the way the skies proclaim the glory of God throughout the world, so we may speak, in a sense, of the worldwide proclamation of the Good News, the missionary witness of Christian evangelists everywhere—"to all the world" (10:18; cf. 1:19-20; Ps 19:4). This statement, of course, is not intended to be taken literally; what Paul means to say is that, like the skies' witness to God's glory, the Good News is spreading all around the world. By now the Good News has been heard throughout the northeastern Mediterranean area—that is the focus of Paul's thought here. The problem is not that people have not heard; the problem is that their disobedient and rebellious hearts have kept them from believing.

But who are the people that Paul is talking about in 10:14-18—these people who seem, at least in the eyes of some, to have had no chance to hear the Good News? Is he speaking of human beings generally (both Jews and Gentiles) or of Jews specifically? Either interpretation is possible; the passage itself is ambiguous. In either case, it is clear that, beginning in 10:19, Paul focuses explicitly on the Jewish people and the question of why *they* have not believed—and that is the primary question underlying the whole of chapters 9–11. Since the larger context is concerned with the lack of response of Jews specifically, that is almost certainly the focus of Paul's thinking here, too.

It is not a question of Jews not knowing the Good News; they have heard it, they understand it, they know it. It is a question of why they have not believed it. Paul reminds us that Israel has a long history of unbelief, dating right back to her earliest days as a nation. Even Moses himself was frustrated with the people's disobedience and ingratitude. Paul cites the Song of Moses (Deut 32) to show that even back then God said he would use Gentiles to shame the Jews for their failure to respond and to make them "jealous" when they see all his blessings poured out on Gentiles who do respond (10:19; 11:11; Deut 32:21). Paul also quoted the words of Isaiah to make his point that the Gentiles had found God while the Jews continued in disobedience. The Gentiles were "people who were not looking for me," "those who were not asking for me" (10:20). Jews, on the other hand, had had God's welcoming arms extended to them "all day long," but they had repeatedly turned away from him (10:21; Isa 65:1-2). So the Scriptures themselves—both the law of Moses and the prophets—bear witness to their rebellious, disobedient spirit.

The overall point Paul was making, then, is clear: The Jews had heard the Good News, they could have believed in Jesus—but they chose not to. So the responsibility lies squarely on their own shoulders; they are without excuse. Notice that Paul shifted the focus away from the theoretical questions about people not knowing the Good News to the practical responsibility that people have to respond to what they do know—that is, to what God has clearly shown them. In the same way, when we find ourselves preoccupied with theoretical questions about those who have never heard, we would do well to remind ourselves of the responsibility that lies upon people to respond to what they *have* heard—and the responsibility that lies upon *us* to respond to what we have heard.

Difficult questions remain, however: If the message of eternal salvation requires a response of faith to become personally effective, what about those who have never heard, or have never heard adequately? What about those who live in remote places where the message has never reached? What about those who die prematurely, before they get a chance to hear and understand? What about those who, because they are disadvantaged in one way or another, are unable to comprehend the significance of the message? These and related questions trouble many Christians today. Unfortunately, there is no comprehensive treatment of such questions in the New Testament. Here we must learn to live with unanswered questions.

The New Testament is clear that it is only through Jesus Christ that one can come to God. What is not so clear, however, is how that is to be interpreted. All kinds of questions arise: What constitutes an authentic conversion to Christ? Are there different ways of coming to God "through Jesus Christ"? What defines saving "faith in Christ"? For example, what about people who, keenly aware of their sin, throw themselves upon God's mercy and in a gospel-like way come to rely on his forgiving grace, even though they may never have heard the Good News explicitly? Do Paul's words in 10:18, quoting Psalm 19:4 ("The message has gone throughout the earth, and the words to all the world"), offer any hope of a larger understanding of God's evangelistic work in the world, of God speaking his word in a more widespread way? Who can tell just how much of the Good News God has revealed in the hearts of "unreached" people all over the world? (Stories abound about people who seem to have been given premonitions of gospel truth before missionaries ever arrived in their area.)

These questions, as agonizing and urgent as they are (because they deal with people's eternal salvation), must finally be left in the hands of God. The One who gave up his own Son for us all surely cares even more than we do about the salvation of people all over the world. Our job is to live with the light we have, to be concerned with the truth we know. As Moses said near the end of his life, "The LORD our God has secrets known to no one. We are not accountable for them, but we and our children are accountable forever for all that he has revealed to us, so that we may obey all the terms of these instructions" (Deut 29:29). And the charge God has left with us is the great commission—the responsibility to devote ourselves wholeheartedly to spreading Christ's message of salvation all over the world. We must be faithful, but the eternal destiny of the world's people ultimately lies in God's hands—it is a burden too great for us to bear. And it is ultimately God's job to move effectively in the hearts of people to bring them to himself.

◆   ### E. A Few Jews Have Been Saved (11:1-10)

I ask, then, has God rejected his own people, the nation of Israel? Of course not! I myself am an Israelite, a descendant of Abraham and a member of the tribe of Benjamin.

²No, God has not rejected his own people, whom he chose from the very beginning. Do you realize what the Scriptures say about this? Elijah the prophet complained to God about the people of Israel and said, ³"LORD, they have killed your prophets and torn down your altars. I am the only one left, and now they are trying to kill me, too."*

⁴And do you remember God's reply? He said, "No, I have 7,000 others who have never bowed down to Baal!"*

⁵It is the same today, for a few of the

people of Israel* have remained faithful because of God's grace—his undeserved kindness in choosing them. ⁶And since it is through God's kindness, then it is not by their good works. For in that case, God's grace would not be what it really is—free and undeserved.

⁷So this is the situation: Most of the people of Israel have not found the favor of God they are looking for so earnestly. A few have—the ones God has chosen—but the hearts of the rest were hardened. ⁸As the Scriptures say,

"God has put them into a deep sleep.
To this day he has shut their eyes so
    they do not see,

and closed their ears so they do not hear."*

⁹Likewise, David said,

"Let their bountiful table become
    a snare,
a trap that makes them think all
    is well.
Let their blessings cause them to
    stumble,
and let them get what they
    deserve.
¹⁰Let their eyes go blind so they cannot
    see,
and let their backs be bent
    forever."*

11:3 1 Kgs 19:10, 14.   11:4 1 Kgs 19:18.   11:5 Greek *for a remnant.*   11:8 Isa 29:10; Deut 29:4.   11:9-10 Ps 69:22-23 (Greek version).

N O T E S

11:1 *his own people.* This reading has the support of ℵ B C 33 1739. Some Gr. mss (𝔓46 F G) have "his inheritance."

the nation of Israel. This is not in the Gr. text but implied.

Of course not! This emphatic negation (*mē genoito* [TG3361/1096, ZG3590/1181]) occurs ten times in Romans (3:4, 6, 31; 6:2, 15; 7:7, 13; 9:14; 11:1, 11) but nowhere else in Paul's writings.

a member of the tribe of Benjamin. Paul's Jewish name, Saul, may reflect this (cf. Phil 3:5); King Saul was the most famous of all the Benjamites in the OT.

11:2 *whom he chose from the very beginning.* Lit., "whom he foreknew" (*proegnō* [TG4267, ZG4589])—that is, pre-chose. See note on 8:29.

11:3 This verse is a quotation from 1 Kgs 19:10, 14.

11:4 *I have 7,000 others who have never bowed down to Baal!* This is a quotation from 1 Kgs 19:18, which refers to the faithful minority who will escape the swords of Hazael, Jehu, and Elisha as those three execute God's wrath (see 1 Kgs 19:17).

11:5 *a few of the people of Israel have remained faithful because of God's grace—his undeserved kindness in choosing them.* Lit., "a remnant has come about according to the free choice of grace"—that is, because of God's grace in choosing them. The Bible often portrays God's people as a faithful minority, or "remnant."

11:6 *in that case, God's grace would not be what it really is—free and undeserved.* Lit., "otherwise grace is no longer grace." Some Gr. mss (ℵ² B Ψ 33ᵛⁱᵈ 𝔐), followed by the KJV, add, "But if it is by works, then it is no longer grace; otherwise work is no longer work."

11:7 *the hearts of the rest were hardened.* Lit., "the rest were hardened" (*epōrōthēsan* [TG4456, ZG4800]). Cf. 9:17-18, 21-22; 11:25. This represents the judgment of God for their spiritual insensitivity. Translations that attempt to soften the language ("The rest grew deaf to God's call," TEV; "The rest of them were stubborn," CEV) fail to express the element of God's judgment inherent in the people's response.

11:8 This verse is a conflated quotation from Isa 29:10 and Deut 29:4. Cf. Isa 6:10: "Harden the hearts of these people. Plug their ears and shut their eyes," a passage cited by Jesus (Matt 13:14-15; Mark 4:12; Luke 8:10; John 12:40). Cf. also Acts 28:26-27.

11:9-10 These verses are a periphrastic quotation of Ps 69[68]:22-23, LXX. This psalm was widely interpreted in the early Christian community as an expression of the suffering of Christ. The point of the quotation is in 11:10a: "Let their eyes go blind so they cannot see," reinforcing the text quoted in 11:8.

11:9 *a snare, a trap that makes them think all is well. Let their blessings cause them to stumble, and let them get what they deserve.* Lit., "a snare, a trap, a stumbling block, and retribution." Various explanations have been offered of precisely how the table becomes a snare and a trap, a stumbling block, and retribution (see Cranfield 1981:551-552), but Paul is probably less interested in the details than in the general point the psalmist is making—that God himself has blinded the eyes of his unfaithful people, just as Isaiah predicted (11:8).

11:10 *let their backs be bent forever.* The exact significance of the original imagery is uncertain. "The thought could be of . . . being bowed down under oppressive slavery, being bent under a heavy burden, cowering with fear, being bowed down by grief, being too weak to stand upright, or stooping to grope on the ground because one's sight is bad or one is blind" (Cranfield 1981:552). Cf. "Bend their backs beneath a burden that will never be lifted" (CEV); "make them bend under their troubles at all times" (TEV). As mentioned in the previous note, Paul's primary interest is not in the details of the imagery of this quotation but in its agreement with the verses from Isaiah quoted in 11:8.

COMMENTARY

Does the failure of the Jews to respond to Christ mean that God has rejected his people entirely, written them off *in toto*? No, Paul replied, God has not rejected his people as a whole because there are clearly some Jews who *have* come to believe in Christ—Paul himself is a living example. But these are a chosen few, those whom God, in his mercy, claimed for himself from the very beginning of time (11:1-2, 5, 7; cf. Eph 1:4, 11). As it was in the days of Elijah, so it is now: only a small minority can be called the true people of God, because it is only a small minority that God, in his kindness, has chosen to belong to himself (11:2-4). Here Paul returns to his earlier emphasis on God's sovereignty in choosing who will be his people (see 9:6-29).

The Bible often portrays God's people, those who truly belong to him, as a small minority of the population, a "faithful remnant." In passages throughout the Old Testament, the overall impression we get is that only a small minority of the people who considered themselves God's people remained wholeheartedly faithful to the Lord. The notion of the faithful remnant may be seen in the accounts of Joshua and Caleb, whose trust in God allowed them to enter Canaan when the rest of their generation were excluded (Num 14:30, 36-38); in Elijah's sense that he was the only faithful servant of the Lord left, in the terrible days of King Ahab (1 Kgs 19:10, 14; cf. 1 Kgs 19:18); in the courageous acts of the two great reformers, Hezekiah and Josiah, when pagan practices were widespread in the land (2 Kgs 18:1-8; 23:1-25); in God's promises of mercy and deliverance for the small remnant that would survive his judgment on Judah (Isa 10:20-22; Jer 23:3; 31:7; 50:20; Mic 2:12; 4:7; 5:7-8; Zeph 2:7); in the return of a small minority after the Exile, with God's promise of blessing on them (Ezra 9:8-15; Zech 8:6, 11); and in the apocalyptic stories of

Daniel and this three friends in the threatening environment of a foreign country (Dan 1-6). In the New Testament, the idea of the faithful few is expressed in Jesus' words, "Many are called, but few are chosen" (Matt 22:14); "The highway to hell is broad, and its gate is wide for the many who choose that way. But the gateway to life is very narrow and the road is difficult, and only a few ever find it" (Matt 7:13-14); and in his response to the question, "Lord, will only a few be saved?" (Luke 13:23). This emphasis on the faithful few is also found in several of the New Testament letters and the book of Revelation. So in the Bible, generally, God's true people are often viewed as only a small minority who remain faithful. This emphasis challenges all claims that the Bible teaches a form of universal salvation, as well as the common assumption that the majority will be saved (see, however, Paul's qualification of this with regard to Jews in 11:25-26).

The idea that only a chosen few—a "faithful remnant"—are saved is one that many people today find disturbing and difficult to accept, but we must remember that behind this biblical emphasis lies a more radical view of God than most people in the modern world are prepared to accept—a view of God as the sovereign Holy One, the Judge of all the world, before whom sinful human beings must bow with deep reverence and fear. And this is the view of God that lies behind the words of Jesus and the biblical writers. The notion of the chosen few, then, is to be understood against the backdrop of the utter holiness and sovereignty of the Almighty. It is this that makes the message of God's grace such Good News in the writings of Paul. Those who are saved are saved undeservedly; they are saved only by the sovereign choice and mercy of God—"his undeserved kindness in choosing them" (11:5). From Paul's point of view, it is a mercy that anyone is saved.

As we observed earlier (see comments on 9:14-18), when Paul used predestination language or spoke of God's sovereign choice in the matter of salvation, his focus was generally on the predestination of the saved, not the predestination of the damned. He thought of predestination as a doctrine primarily for believers, not for unbelievers. It is a doctrine intended to evoke a sense of gratitude and praise in the hearts of the chosen, a doctrine of grace. But in this passage, he does not shy away from reflecting (even if briefly) on the darker side of predestination, the implications for those who have not been chosen. He hinted of this earlier, when he spoke of God's hand of judgment on Pharaoh and then concluded, "So you see, . . . he chooses to harden the hearts of others so they refuse to listen" (9:18; cf. his reference to "those . . . destined for destruction," 9:22). Here the reason the majority of Jews have failed to recognize Jesus as the Messiah is that their hearts have been "hardened"—God himself has made them unresponsive. But this is simply what Scripture itself says: "God has put them into a deep sleep. To this day he has shut their eyes so they do not see, and closed their ears so they do not hear" (11:8; cf. Deut 29:4; Isa 29:10). And David expresses the same sentiments when he prays, "Let their eyes go blind so they cannot see" (11:10; Ps 69:23). Here Paul draws on texts from all three parts of the Hebrew Bible (the law, the prophets, and the writings) to make his point: it is God himself who has darkened the understanding of the majority of Jews in a way that makes it impossible for them to respond.

But generally speaking, when Paul discusses the question of why Jews have not responded, his emphasis is on their own refusal to believe (11:20), not on God's darkening of their minds and hearts—and Paul does everything he can to woo them back. It is worth noting that it is their own disobedience that Paul highlights immediately prior to this passage (9:30-10:21), which leaves the strong impression that their being made unresponsive is a form of divine judgment on them for their obstinacy (cf. 1:21, 24, 28). As a general rule, then, though salvation is always viewed by Paul as the result of God's sheer mercy, divine judgment is spoken of more as the consequence of human disobedience than as the result of God's predestining choice.

When it comes to the question of why so many Jews are not saved, then, Paul leaves us with a paradox. Side by side lie statements that affirm both the sovereign choice of God and human responsibility (the consequences of human choice). Romans 9:6-29 and 11:1-10 focus on the role of God's sovereign choice, while 9:30-10:21 emphasizes the Jews' own disobedience. Nowhere does Paul tell us how to put the two together. It is a prime example of the way the Jewish mind could live with paradox. Both are portrayed as true perspectives—the focus is sometimes on one, sometimes on the other—but they cannot easily be put together logically. In the following section (11:11-24), the two perspectives are thoroughly mixed.

Modern minds find it difficult to live with this kind of paradox. We expect things to fit together logically, and our minds are constantly at work trying to understand how things relate rationally and coherently. As a result, modern Christians tend to come down on one side of the fence or the other, theologically—either on the side of God's sovereignty or on the side of human choice and responsibility. Thus, many Christians today speak of themselves as either Calvinists or Arminians, so named after classic defenders of the two positions, John Calvin and Jacobus Arminius. The Calvinists have built a coherent theological system (Calvinism) on the foundation of texts emphasizing the sovereignty of God and predestination. Classical Calvinism affirms that:

People are totally depraved.
God's election is unconditional.
Christ's atonement is only for the elect.
God's grace is irresistible.
Christians will persevere to the end.

The Arminians (and Wesleyans), on the other hand, have built a coherent theological system (Arminianism) on the foundation of texts emphasizing free choice and human responsibility. Classical Arminianism affirms that:

Salvation is for all who believe and persevere in obedience and faith.
Sanctification must accompany salvation.
Christ's atonement is for all.
God's grace is not irresistible.
Christians can fall from grace.

Neither Calvinism nor Arminianism, however, as a coherent theological system in itself, deals adequately with the element of paradox that we find in Paul. Though Scripture texts may be found in support of both theologies, both tend to ignore texts and emphases that do not fit well into their respective structures.

Therefore, if we wish to remain true to Paul and his teaching, we must learn to live with paradox. With regard to God's sovereignty and human responsibility, Paul implies that both are true, that we have to take both seriously. We cannot do away with either God's sovereignty or human responsibility and still have an adequate view of life. At the end of life, those of us who are saved can only bow down and acknowledge that it is solely by God's grace that we are among the saved, for everything is a gift of God—even the disposition of the heart to believe and saving faith itself. But in the meantime, we recognize that we are fully responsible for the choices we make and that there are serious consequences for our actions—these cannot be blamed on God. So we must learn to accept both the sovereign grace of God and the full weight of responsibility for the choices we make. In the end, this proves to be a more adequate view of life with all of its complexities than any strictly systematic theology ever could be. (For the paradoxical nature of Paul's thinking, see comments on 1:18-32; 6:1-14; 9:30–10:4; 11:11-24.)

Only God knows how all the pieces fit together. We have to embrace the element of paradox joyfully and learn to live in simple childlike trust, just as Jesus teaches—even when we don't understand ("Unless you . . . become like little children, you will never get into the Kingdom of Heaven," Matt 18:3). Our faith is based not on our ability to put the diverse pieces together logically but on the reliability of the word of God and the faithfulness of the one who alone knows the secrets of the mysterious universe he has made. Those who insist on fully understanding before believing run the risk of never coming to believe—they have made a god out of their demand for rational understanding. (Cf. the way Eve was led into sin by her perverse desire to understand everything just "like God," Gen 3:5ff.) One of Paul's most fundamental convictions is expressed in his statement, "We live by believing and not by seeing" (2 Cor 5:7). Pascal's famous saying, "The heart has its reasons, which reason does not know," reflects this awareness of the limitations of human understanding.

◆   F. Salvation Has Now Come to Gentiles (11:11-24)

[11]Did God's people stumble and fall beyond recovery? Of course not! They were disobedient, so God made salvation available to the Gentiles. But he wanted his own people to become jealous and claim it for themselves. [12]Now if the Gentiles were enriched because the people of Israel turned down God's offer of salvation, think how much greater a blessing the world will share when they finally accept it.

[13]I am saying all this especially for you Gentiles. God has appointed me as the apostle to the Gentiles. I stress this, [14]for I want somehow to make the people of Israel jealous of what you Gentiles have, so I might save some of them. [15]For since their rejection meant that God offered salvation to the rest of the world, their acceptance will be even more wonderful. It will be life for those who were dead! [16]And

since Abraham and the other patriarchs were holy, their descendants will also be holy—just as the entire batch of dough is holy because the portion given as an offering is holy. For if the roots of the tree are holy, the branches will be, too.

¹⁷But some of these branches from Abraham's tree—some of the people of Israel—have been broken off. And you Gentiles, who were branches from a wild olive tree, have been grafted in. So now you also receive the blessing God has promised Abraham and his children, sharing in the rich nourishment from the root of God's special olive tree. ¹⁸But you must not brag about being grafted in to replace the branches that were broken off. You are just a branch, not the root.

¹⁹"Well," you may say, "those branches were broken off to make room for me." ²⁰Yes, but remember—those branches were

broken off because they didn't believe in Christ, and you are there because you do believe. So don't think highly of yourself, but fear what could happen. ²¹For if God did not spare the original branches, he won't* spare you either.

²²Notice how God is both kind and severe. He is severe toward those who disobeyed, but kind to you if you continue to trust in his kindness. But if you stop trusting, you also will be cut off. ²³And if the people of Israel turn from their unbelief, they will be grafted in again, for God has the power to graft them back into the tree. ²⁴You, by nature, were a branch cut from a wild olive tree. So if God was willing to do something contrary to nature by grafting you into his cultivated tree, he will be far more eager to graft the original branches back into the tree where they belong.

11:21 Some manuscripts read *perhaps he won't.*

NOTES

11:11 *Did God's people stumble and fall beyond recovery?* Lit., "Did they stumble so that (*hina* [^{TG}2443, ^{ZG}2671]) they should fall?" The question implicitly expects the answer, "No." The purpose (or result) of their failure to respond to the Good News is not their irreversible ruin.

Of course not! This emphatic negation (*mē genoito* [^{TG}3361/1096, ^{ZG}3590/1181]) occurs ten times in Romans (3:4, 6, 31; 6:2, 15; 7:7, 13; 9:14; 11:1, 11) but nowhere else in Paul's writings.

But he wanted his own people to become jealous and claim it for themselves. Lit., "so that they would become jealous." The words "and claim it [salvation] for themselves" are not in the Gr. text but are implied. Here Paul appears to be drawing on a text from the Song of Moses (Deut 32:21), which he quotes in 10:19 also: "I will rouse your jealousy."

11:12 *think how much greater a blessing the world will share when they finally accept it.* Lit., "how much more, their fullness (*plērōma* [^{TG}4138, ^{ZG}4445])?" The word "fullness" may be interpreted in different ways: "complete conversion," "complete restoration," "perfection," and (most commonly) "full number" (as in 11:25, where it refers to the full number of converted Gentiles before all Israel is saved; so Moo 1996:688-690); cf. Cranfield 1981:557-558. The contrast with their failure suggests that "full restoration" may be the best interpretation.

11:13 *the apostle to the Gentiles.* Lit., "[an] apostle of Gentiles."

I stress this. Lit., "I exalt my ministry."

11:14 *to make the people of Israel jealous of what you Gentiles have.* Lit., "to make my flesh [my own people] jealous."

11:15 *For since their rejection meant that God offered salvation to the rest of the world.* Lit., "For if their casting-off [means] the reconciliation of the world."

It will be life for those who were dead! This disputed phrase (lit., "life from the dead," *zōē ek nekrōn* [TG2222/3498A, ZG2437/3738]) may be understood figuratively, as a great awakening, either of the Gentiles (Calvin 1960:248; Murray 1965:82-84; Stott 1994:298-299) or of the Jews themselves (Leenhardt 1961:285; Fitzmyer 1993:613; Mounce 1995:219), or, as most commentators interpret it, literally, as a reference to the final resurrection (Barrett 1957:215; Black 1973:144; Cranfield 1981:563; Käsemann 1980:307; Bruce 1985:205; Dunn 1988b:670). In Jewish tradition, the end is delayed until the full number of the elect are saved (cf. 11:25-27) and the Jews turn back to God (cf. Acts 3:19-21; Schreiner 1998:599).

11:16 *since Abraham and the other patriarchs were holy, their descendants will also be holy—just as the entire batch of dough is holy because the portion given as an offering is holy.* Lit., "if the [dough offered as the] first fruits (*aparchē* [TG536, ZG569]) is holy, so is the whole lump." This statement alludes to Num 15:17-21, where the Israelites were commanded to offer to God the first cake made from the flour of grain cut at the beginning of the harvest, an act that seems to have been interpreted as consecrating the whole harvest and ensuring God's blessing on it. (Cf. Lev 19:23-25 and the use of *aparchē* in 1 Cor 15:23, which speaks of Christ as "the first of the harvest," an allusion drawn from Lev 23:10). Though some take "first fruits" here to refer to the early Jewish Christians or to Christ himself, the following context suggests the phrase refers rather to Abraham and the patriarchs, to whom God made the original promises (cf. 11:28). The word "holy" (*hagia* [TG40, ZG41]) is used of things that belong to God.

11:17 *some of the people of Israel.* The NLT adds this for clarity.

wild olive tree. Such trees produced poor fruit with little or no oil.

grafted in. For the horticultural difficulties of grafting shoots from a wild olive tree into a cultivated tree and regrafting branches that have been cut off, see Bruce 1985:203-204; Cranfield 1981:565-566. Some see this as an example of Paul's unfamiliarity with common horticultural practices of the countryside—though there is evidence of such a strange procedure sometimes being done to reinvigorate unproductive trees. But Paul is less concerned with horticulture than with the issue of what God is doing among Jews and Gentiles, of which the broken-off branches and grafted shoots are but a metaphor (Moo 1996: 702-703).

So now you also receive the blessing God has promised Abraham and his children. The NLT adds this for clarity.

sharing in the rich nourishment from the root of God's special olive tree. Lit., "you have become a sharer (*sunkoinōnos* [TG4791, ZG5171]) in the rich root of the olive tree." This is the reading of ℵ* B C. Instead of "the rich root," some Gr. mss (ℵ² A D² 33 1739 𝔐) have "the root and the richness"; others (𝔓46 D* F G) read "the richness." For a biblical metaphor of Israel as an olive tree, see Jer 11:16.

11:18 *But you must not brag about being grafted in to replace the branches that were broken off.* Lit., "Do not boast [about your superiority to] the branches."

You are just a branch, not the root. Lit., "you do not support the root, but the root [supports] you."

11:20 *you are there because you do believe.* Lit., "by faith you stand." The words "by faith" (referring to faith in Christ) are emphasized.

but fear what could happen. Or, "but fear God." Lit., "but fear."

11:21 *he won't spare you either.* This is the reading of ℵ A B C P 81 1739 1881. Some Gr. mss (𝔓46 D F G 33 𝔐), followed by NA²⁷, read "perhaps he won't spare you either," a softer expression of the warning.

11:22 *if you continue to trust in his kindness.* Lit., "if you remain in [his] kindness"—that is, by continuing in faith in Christ.

But if you stop trusting, you also will be cut off. Lit., "otherwise you also will be cut off."

11:24 *You, by nature, were a branch cut from a wild olive tree.* The words "by nature" are often assumed to refer to the wild olive tree itself ("what is by nature a wild olive tree," NRSV; cf. NIV, NAB, NJB); more correctly, they refer to the original identity of the cut-off branch (Gentiles), which belongs "by nature" to a wild olive tree (Cranfield 1981:571-572).

COMMENTARY

When it comes to understanding the heartrending failure of Jews to respond to the Good News, we have to think more deeply about God's purposes in it all. And when we do, we realize that it is as a result of the Jews' rejection of the gospel that the precious gift of salvation has been extended to Gentiles. Historically, the same pattern may be observed in the Acts of the Apostles: when the Jews rebuffed the evangelistic preaching of the early missionaries, the missionaries typically turned to the Gentiles (cf. the words of Paul and Barnabas to the Jews in Antioch of Pisidia: "It was necessary that we first preach the word of God to you Jews. But since you have rejected it and judged yourselves unworthy of eternal life, we will offer it to the Gentiles," Acts 13:46; cf. Acts 28:25-28).

Using horticultural language, following his reference to roots and branches in 11:16, Paul speaks metaphorically of some of the Jewish branches of God's holy tree as having been broken off to accommodate the Gentile branches that God has now grafted in (11:17). So in this troubling "breaking off" of Jews, God has quietly been at work accomplishing his deeper purposes, including the "grafting in" of Gentiles. For the moment, at least, the divine focus seems to have shifted to Gentiles. However, we must not think of this turn of events as something entirely new in the mind of God. God's concern for the Gentile world and his desire to see them ultimately included in his people are hinted at throughout the Old Testament. When God made his original covenant with Abraham, for example, he promised to bless "all the families on earth" through Abraham (Gen 12:3). This more universal concern seems to have been forgotten in much of Israel's history as the people engaged in war with their neighbors and sought to protect their uniqueness by highlighting the exclusivity of Jewish religious claims. But Jews were reminded of their larger mission to the world when they suffered in exile. This is reflected especially in Isaiah 40–66, which says that God's Servant "will not falter or lose heart until justice prevails throughout the earth" (Isa 42:4). Addressing his Servant, God says, "You will be a light to guide the nations" (Isa 42:6); "You will do more than restore the people of Israel to me. I will make you a light to the Gentiles, and you will bring my salvation to the ends of the earth" (Isa 49:6). In these crucial chapters, God says, "I will also bless the foreigners who commit themselves to the LORD. . . . I will bring them to my holy mountain of Jerusalem and will fill them with joy. . . . My Temple will be called a house of prayer for all nations. . . . I will bring others, too, besides my people Israel" (Isa 56:6-8; cf. 56:3; the banquet prepared in Zion

"for all the people of the world," Isa 25:6; and the texts quoted by Paul in 15:9-12).
These words find their eventual fulfillment not in the missionary work of Judaism
per se but in the mission of the Messiah, who, though he devoted his initial work to
the evangelization of Jews exclusively (Matt 10:5-6; cf. Matt 15:24), later tells his
followers, "Go and make disciples of all the nations" (Matt 28:19; cf. Mark 16:15;
Luke 24:47). The intention of God from the beginning has been to include people
from all over the world in his family, and this is the mission he has now entrusted to
his church.

Even this seemingly unexpected shift of focus to Gentiles strangely serves the
purposes of God for his original people, the Jews. God's hope is that the enthusiastic response of Gentiles to his salvation will make Jews jealous; when they see others enjoying the goodness and grace of God that should be theirs, it will stimulate
them to seek it for themselves (11:11). And that was Paul's hope, too, even as he fulfilled his particular calling in ministering the message of God's grace to Gentiles
(11:13-14).

All of this is part of a larger story, the story of God's mysterious saving work that
finds its climax in the eventual return of the Jewish people themselves to God
(11:25-26). When God claimed Abraham and the early Hebrew patriarchs as his
own, he also claimed their descendants: "For if the roots of the tree are holy, the
branches will be, too" (11:16). When their final return to God comes, it will bring
unspeakable rejoicing to all who know God throughout the world, for it will bring
about the final day of resurrection (11:15). If God's rejection of the Jews results in
the outpouring of his eternal blessing on Gentiles, how much greater will the
worldwide blessing be when God accepts his own people back? It will mean nothing less than the full experience of eschatological glory!

Furthermore, this is only part of an even larger story—the story of God's Christ-
centered plan for the universe as a whole. Though we catch only glimpses of this
larger vision from Paul, it is clear that God's desire is to gather for himself a group of
people—a "family," including both Jews and Gentiles—who, by the Spirit of his
Son living within them, will grow to become like his Son and one day share his
Son's full glory (8:29-30; Col 1:27). In the end, God's desire is to unite the entire
universe under the authority of his Son, to the endless praise of his own glory and
grace (Eph 1:9-12; 3:5, 10). When we think of God's work of salvation, then, we
must think of it in the larger context of his ultimate plan for the entire universe.

Here Paul reminds us to see everything that happens as part of God's larger story
and to interpret it all eschatologically—that is, in light of the ultimate end. As
Christians, we seek to interpret historical events not simply through secular eyes
but through the eyes of Scripture and in light of God's ultimate purposes. And that,
for us, may result in quite a different perspective as we seek to discern what God is
doing in the world, behind the scenes. We must always remember that things may
look quite different from God's point of view, that there may be hidden purposes
of God at work in the seeming anomalies or tragedies of life. This difference of perspective is expressed well in the classic text from Isaiah: "'My thoughts are nothing

like your thoughts,' says the LORD. 'And my ways are far beyond anything you could imagine'" (Isa 55:8-9). So as we consider the events going on in the world around us and in our own lives, we must seek to understand them on a deeper level than that of mere human analysis; our task is to understand—as much as is humanly possible—what *God* is doing. That is why Paul says elsewhere, "From now on . . . we regard no one from a human point of view" (2 Cor 5:16, NRSV). As Christians, we seek to understand everything from a spiritual point of view, with spiritual sensitivity.

With this newfound blessing, Gentiles must be careful not to regard Jews with contempt or take their own status for granted—as if they themselves were somehow responsible for the grace they now enjoy. Yes, some of the original Jewish branches of God's holy tree were broken off. And yes, from one point of view they were broken off in order to make room for the Gentile branches God has now grafted in. But it is only by God's pure grace that Gentiles have now come to share in God's goodness. And in any case, they must remember that they are only branches that have been grafted in—they are not the root (11:17-18). They are a foreign addition to the holy tree, not the native essence of it. They are entirely dependent upon the grace that has made them a part of God's tree.

Further, Paul adds, they would do well to remind themselves of the reason the Jews were broken off—their refusal to believe in Christ—and then reflect on what could happen if they stray from their own trust in him. "For if God did not spare the original branches," warns Paul, "he won't spare you either" (11:21). Just as the Jews were broken off because of their unbelief, so Gentiles can be broken off, too. Salvation will be theirs only if they continue to trust firmly in Christ. It is always dependent on their continuing to stand firm in the faith and not letting themselves drift away from the Good News (11:22; Col 1:23). The situation calls not for smugness but for reverential fear before the one who in the end will be the Judge of all (Acts 10:42).

So we must always remember that God is both gracious and severe. We must always take into account both the love of God and the judgment of God. Those who refuse his ways will experience his judgment; those who open their heart to him and place their trust in his kindness will experience his compassion—but only if they continue to trust in his kindness. "If you stop trusting," Paul warns his Gentile readers, "you also will be cut off" (11:22; cf. Gal 5:2-4). And conversely, he adds, if Jews now in a state of unbelief come to trust in Christ, they will be reinstated and fully welcomed back. Indeed, if God was able to accomplish the difficult task of grafting in wild, non-native branches (Gentiles) to his domesticated tree, how much more will he be able to graft back in the branches that were originally a part of it (i.e., Jews, 11:23-24)? Because God has the power and authority both to graft in and to cut off, we must live in reverent fear of him at all times.

This passage is reminiscent of one of the major themes of the prophet Ezekiel. Ezekiel emphasizes that it is not the past that defines our relationship to God but the present. The question is not how we used to live and walk with God but how we live and walk with him now. No matter how disobedient or wicked people may have been in the past, if they turn around and begin to obey the ways of God, "They will surely live and not die. All their past sins will be forgotten, and they will live" (Ezek 18:21-22). At the same time, he warns, if righteous people revert to a life of sin, they will surely die. No matter how righteous they may have been in the past, "all their righteous acts will be forgotten, and they will die for their sins" (Ezek 18:24; cf. 33:12-16). Paul, like Ezekiel, emphasizes that we must never presume on God's grace because it is always our life and faith in the present that defines our relationship to God—not our experience of him in the past. This does not negate what he says elsewhere about the believer's security in Christ's grace (8:31-39; Phil 1:6) but simply highlights the need for believers to continue trusting in that grace. We are secure as long as we remain firmly trusting in Christ's unmerited kindness toward us.

Paul's twin emphases on God's sovereignty and human responsibility are thoroughly intertwined in this chapter. On the one hand, God, in his sovereign grace, is the one who has chosen the few Jews who are saved (11:2, 5-7)—they are the chosen few, the favored remnant. And he is the one who has made the others unresponsive by putting them into "a deep sleep," the one who has "shut their eyes so they do not see, and closed their ears so they do not hear" (11:8). He is the one responsible for their "rejection" (11:15). He is also the one who has opened the way for Gentiles to be saved (11:11) and who, in his sheer mercy, has grafted them into his holy tree (11:17, 24). So there is no room for pride; those who are saved are simply the blessed recipients of his undeserved kindness, his grace. On the other hand, Paul emphasized that it was the Jews' own refusal to believe that resulted in their being "broken off" (11:20); they turned down God's offer of salvation (11:12). So God's judgment on them is simply the result of their own disobedience (11:22). In the same way, whether Gentile believers continue in God's grace or fall under his judgment depends on whether or not they continue to trust in Christ (11:22). And when Paul talks about desiring to make Jews jealous in order to evoke in them an acceptance of the Good News, he is also clearly using the language of human choice.

Here we see, as clearly as anywhere, the paradoxical nature of Paul's thinking. His mind readily affirmed both the sovereign choice of God and the very real consequences of human decisions. His statements move freely from one to the other; the twin emphases lie side by side in his writing. As a good Jew, he can freely believe in two seemingly contradictory things at the same time and readily live with the paradoxical realities of both. Paul is not as bothered—or limited—by questions of logical consistency as modern Christians are. We, too, must learn to live with paradox. Indeed, any truly biblical theology must embrace paradox as a central element, for it is a part of the biblical writers' way of thinking. What the Bible gives us is not a simple theology centered on God's sovereignty or human choice alone, but a theology paradoxically embracing both. This is a reflection of the biblical writers' sense of having to deal with two different dimensions—the divine and the human, the coming age and the present age—at the same time. So the question of whether Paul believes (on the one hand) in God's sovereignty and predestination or (on the other) in free choice and human responsibility is the wrong question; he affirms the importance of both. (For more on the paradoxical nature of Paul's thinking, see comments on 1:18-32; 6:1-14; 9:30–10:4; 11:1-10.)

The crucial question, however, is this: when does he emphasize one as opposed to the other? As a rough generalization, I have already suggested that when Paul emphasizes God's sovereign choice, it is usually when he discusses the salvation of believers—it is a doctrine for the chosen, the saved. It is crucial that believers know that they are saved only by God's grace, not by what they do. When he emphasizes the seriousness of human choice, it is often when he discusses God's judgment—it is a doctrine for those in danger. It is crucial that those who profess faith in Christ feel the full weight of their responsibility to remain faithful to Christ and not turn away, lest they face the judgment of God. In other words, when Paul emphasizes God's sovereignty, it is the positive side that he highlights—God's saving grace for the elect. When he emphasizes human responsibility, it is the negative side that he highlights—the dire consequences of not believing or not living out one's professed faith. Generally speaking, salvation is the result of God's sovereign grace, but God's judgment is the consequence of unbelief and sin. Expressed differently, Paul believed both in salvation by grace and judgment by works. It is the paradox forced upon us by the necessity of living in two different dimensions—the divine and the human—at the same time.

◆   ## G. All Israel Will Be Saved One Day (11:25-32)

²⁵I want you to understand this mystery, dear brothers and sisters,* so that you will not feel proud about yourselves. Some of the people of Israel have hard hearts, but this will last only until the full number of Gentiles comes to Christ. ²⁶And so all Israel will be saved. As the Scriptures say,

"The one who rescues will come from Jerusalem,*
and he will turn Israel* away from ungodliness.
²⁷And this is my covenant with them,
that I will take away their sins."*

²⁸Many of the people of Israel are now enemies of the Good News, and this benefits you Gentiles. Yet they are still the people he loves because he chose their ancestors Abraham, Isaac, and Jacob. ²⁹For God's gifts and his call can never be withdrawn. ³⁰Once, you Gentiles were rebels against God, but when the people of Israel rebelled against him, God was merciful to you instead. ³¹Now they are the rebels, and God's mercy has come to you so that they, too, will share* in God's mercy. ³²For God has imprisoned everyone in disobedience so he could have mercy on everyone.

11:25 Greek *brothers*. 11:26a Greek *from Zion*. 11:26b Greek *Jacob*. 11:26-27 Isa 59:20-21; 27:9 (Greek version). 11:31 Other manuscripts read *will now share;* still others read *will someday share*.

NOTES

11:25 *I want you to understand*. Lit., "I do not want you to be ignorant." This is a common Pauline phrase that is rendered variously by the NLT; it occurs also in 1:13; 1 Cor 10:1; 12:1; 2 Cor 1:8; 1 Thess 4:13.

this mystery. For Paul, the word "mystery" (*mustērion* [TG3466, ZG3696]) refers to a long-hidden truth or "secret" that has now been revealed (see note on 16:25; cf. 1 Cor 15:51; Eph 3:3-11; Col 1:26-27; 4:3). Here the truth that is now revealed is that when the full number of Gentiles has been converted, "all Israel" (presently blinded and unresponsive) will finally come to "see" and be saved—that is, they will come at last to believe in Christ and the Good News.

dear brothers and sisters. Gr., *adelphoi* [TG80, ZG81] (brothers); cf. NLT mg.

so that you will not feel proud about yourselves. Lit., "so that you not be wise in your own estimation." The same phrase occurs in 12:16.

Some of the people of Israel have hard hearts. Lit., "a hardness (*pōrōsis* [TG4457, ZG4801]) has happened in part to Israel." The implication is that God has brought this about. For other references to hardening, see 9:17-18; 11:7-10; cf. John 12:40.

the full number of Gentiles. Lit., "the fullness (*plērōma* [TG4138, ZG4445]) of the Gentiles." See note on 11:12.

11:26 *all Israel will be saved.* The phrase "all Israel" means not every single Jew without exception but the Jews as a whole, in a general sense. In Paul's understanding, the salvation of "all Israel" does not occur throughout history but seems to be linked to the end of the age and the second coming of Christ (see the OT quotation that follows; cf. note on 11:15).

from Jerusalem. Lit., "from Zion," a traditional Jewish way of speaking of Jerusalem. This reference may suggest that Paul thinks of Jerusalem as the place of Christ's return.

he will turn Israel away from ungodliness. Lit., "he will turn away ungodliness (*asebeias* [TG763, ZG813]) from Jacob."

11:27 *this is my covenant with them.* This is God's promise to them. The "new covenant" in Jesus is really the fulfillment of an old one (cf. Jer 31:31-34; Ezek 11:19-20; 36:25-27). Up to this point, in vv. 26-27, Paul has been citing Isa 59:20-21, LXX.

I will take away their sins. Here Paul leaves the text of Isa 59:20-21, LXX, and merges it with wording from Isa 27:9, LXX ("purge away Israel's sin") and Jer 31:34[33] ("I will forgive their wickedness, and I will never again remember their sins"). See comments on 7:6; 8:4.

11:28 *Many of the people of Israel are now enemies of the Good News, and this benefits you Gentiles.* Lit., "As regards the gospel, [they are] enemies on your account"—that is, for your sake.

Yet they are still the people he loves because he chose their ancestors Abraham, Isaac, and Jacob. Lit., "but as regards election, [they are] beloved on account of the fathers." God will faithfully fulfill the promises he made to the patriarchs; cf. 11:29.

11:29 *For God's gifts and his call can never be withdrawn.* This means they are irrevocable. For the meaning of "call," see note on 1:1; cf. 1:6; 8:28, 30; 9:12, 24. God's "gifts" and "call" may be taken as a single idea (Calvin, Käsemann) or as two distinct items (Cranfield); or (perhaps preferably) the "call" may be understood as a special instance of God's "gifts" (Moo).

11:30 *you Gentiles were rebels against God.* Lit., "you were disobedient (*ēpeithēsate* [TG544, ZG578]) to God."

but when the people of Israel rebelled against him, God was merciful to you instead. Lit., "but now you have received mercy through the disobedience (*apeitheia* [TG543, ZG577]) of these."

11:31 *God's mercy has come to you so that they, too, will share in God's mercy.* This is the reading of 𝔓46^vid A D² F G 𝔐. Other Gr. mss (𝕏 B D*) read, "so that now they will share in God's mercy." This is a difficult reading because Paul has been arguing that Israel will be saved in the future. It is possible that, due to a scribal error, *nun* [TG3568, ZG3814] (now) was accidentally carried over from the previous two clauses. The final clause is expressed as the purpose of what precedes it, but the logic is not clear.

11:32 ***everyone.*** Gr., *tous pantas;* this is the reading of ℵ A B D[c] 𝔐. Some Gr. mss (𝔓46[vid] D*) read *ta panta* (all things).

so he could have mercy on everyone. "Everyone" refers to all peoples, both Jews and Gentiles—that is, everyone without distinction, not everyone without exception. Paul is not thinking of those who persistently refuse God's mercy.

COMMENTARY

At the end of this section, Paul expresses his confidence in the future return of the Jews to God. God will be faithful to keep the promises he made to his ancient people long ago. In spite of their present-day rejection of the Good News, they are still his special people because of the promises he made to Abraham and the patriarchs. And one day, when the number of Gentile Christians is complete, the Jews will surely come back to him—"all Israel will be saved." Just as Gentiles have now received God's mercy, so the Jews will one day receive his mercy because God desires to show mercy to all people.

Paul saw the tragic state of the Jews as only temporary—one day, after all the chosen Gentiles have been gathered in, the Jews will come back to God and receive his salvation, just as the prophets predict. "And so all Israel will be saved," he concludes (11:26; cf. 11:12, 15). But exactly how he understood this—who will be included in "all Israel," and how and when this will come to pass—is unclear. Unfortunately, he did not give us any details. (Note that he says nothing about a future Jewish government; see comments on 4:13.) Paul certainly did not conceive of this happening apart from the Jews coming to believe in Christ, for he consistently spoke of God's judgment on those who reject the Messiah; but it is unlikely that he had any more idea than we do of exactly how and when this will happen. He simply knew that God made a promise to Abraham and his descendants and that God can be trusted to keep his promises; "For God's gifts and his call can never be withdrawn" (11:29). On this basis, he was assured that God would one day save his people, just as he had promised. The new covenant will not be complete until it embraces the people of the old covenant.

On the face of it, this statement about ethnic Jews still being God's special people seems to conflict with his emphasis elsewhere that "true" Jews are not defined ethnically. ("You are not a true Jew just because you were born of Jewish parents or because you have gone through the ceremony of circumcision," 2:28; "Not all who are born into the nation of Israel are truly members of God's people! Being descendants of Abraham doesn't make them truly Abraham's children. . . . Abraham's physical descendants are not necessarily children of God," 9:6-8.) Here we seem to have two conflicting views of the Jewish people and their relationship to God—another example of Paul's paradoxical thinking. Behind this lie two conflicting considerations, both of which are true. On the one hand, because the Jews have refused to recognize God's Messiah, they stand outside of the promises God has made in the new covenant of Jesus Christ. On the other hand, because they are ethnically Jewish, they are still recipients of the promises God made to Abraham and his descendants under the old covenant. And because God honors his promises—and both promises are trustworthy—Jews end up in an ambivalent position in Paul's thinking (11:28), very much like the ambivalent position of believers as partakers of the present age and the age to come simultaneously. When two truths conflict (e.g., God's sovereignty and human responsibility), Paul seems to be able to hold the two in tension—that is, to affirm the truth of both simultaneously. The fact that this may be logically inconsistent is of no consequence, for, as we have observed, Paul's view of God is sufficiently large to embrace the element of paradox.

Paul's point is that God desires to show mercy to all. Just as disobedient Gentiles have now experienced God's mercy, so disobedient Jews will one day receive his mercy. God's desire is to pour out his mercy on both Jews and Gentiles—on all people, everywhere—for such is the nature of his kindness (11:30-32; cf. the story of Jonah, which emphasizes God's desire to show mercy even on his enemies). Earlier Paul concluded, "All people, whether Jews or Gentiles, are under the power of sin" (3:9; cf. 3:23), and they therefore stand guilty under the judgment of God (3:19). No one, neither Jew nor Gentile, can lay claim to his favor—no one deserves it. The only hope for salvation lies in his mercy. God has so ordered things that both Jews and Gentiles have become imprisoned in their own disobedience. He has brought both groups into a situation where their sin against him must be acknowledged and brought to light so that he might pour out his abundant, forgiving grace on both. "God has imprisoned everyone in disobedience so he could have mercy on everyone" (11:32). God's desire is always that people recognize that salvation is a gift of grace and mercy.

As mysterious as the ways of God are, and as difficult and painful as they sometimes seem to be, the end to which they lead is mercy, pure mercy—for such is the nature of God. This accords with what God proclaimed to Moses, following a time of Israelite disobedience at Mount Sinai: "Yahweh! The LORD! The God of compassion and mercy! I am slow to anger and filled with unfailing love and faithfulness. I lavish unfailing love to a thousand generations. I forgive iniquity, rebellion, and sin." (Exod 34:6-7). The sulking Jonah confessed the same truth: "I knew that you are a merciful and compassionate God, slow to get angry and filled with unfailing love" (Jonah 4:2). And in a time of much suffering and pain, the author of Lamentations affirmed, "The faithful love of the LORD never ends! His mercies never cease. Great is his faithfulness; his mercies begin afresh each morning" (Lam 3:22-23). The biblical God, the God of Jesus Christ, the God of the Good News, is above all a God of mercy and grace—a God who delights in forgiving people and showing them mercy! And those who have put their trust in Christ to save them are the blessed recipients of his mercy.

One final note is in order. Though the wording of this passage seems to reflect a strand of universalism in Paul's thinking ("so he could have mercy on everyone,"

11:32), the context makes it clear that it is a representative universalism that Paul is talking about—that is, a representative acceptance of the Good News by the different nations of the earth. Paul's writing expresses the consistent conviction that salvation is only for those who put their trust in Jesus Christ.

◆   H. The Mysterious Ways of God (11:33-36)

33Oh, how great are God's riches and wisdom and knowledge! How impossible it is for us to understand his decisions and his ways!

34For who can know the LORD's thoughts? Who knows enough to give him advice?*

35And who has given him so much that he needs to pay it back?*

36For everything comes from him and exists by his power and is intended for his glory. All glory to him forever! Amen.

11:34 Isa 40:13 (Greek version).   11:35 See Job 41:11.

NOTES
11:33 *Oh, how great are God's riches.* This is a reference to the abundance of his grace, not to wealth per se.

and wisdom and knowledge! This speaks of God's transcendent "wisdom" (*sophia* [TG4678, ZG5053]) and "knowledge" (*gnōsis* [TG1108, ZG1194]) expressed in his work of saving people. Some scholars would link the three terms in this verse differently as "the riches of his wisdom and knowledge" (cf. NIV).

his decisions. Lit., "his judgments" (*krimata* [TG2917, ZG3210]).

11:34 *For who can know the LORD's thoughts? Who knows enough to give him advice?* This is an allusion to Isa 40:13, LXX: "Who is able to advise the Spirit of the LORD? Who knows enough to give him advice or teach him?" Cf. also Isa 45:15; 55:8-9; Jer 23:18; Wis 9:13. God's ways transcend all human understanding.

11:35 *And who has given him so much that he needs to pay it back?* A close equivalent of the Heb. version of Job 41:11, which differs considerably from the Gr. version. God owes no one anything.

11:36 *For everything comes from him and exists by his power and is intended for his glory.* Lit., "Because from him and through him and for him [are] all things." Cf. Col 1:16, where the same is said of Christ. There is a close parallel in a statement of Marcus Aurelius (*Meditations* 4.23): "From thee are all things; in thee are all things; to thee are all things." All that happens has its origin in God and serves his purposes.

All glory to him forever! Amen. No matter what the perplexities of life (in this case, the difficulties of understanding the Jews' relation to God), God is to be praised in it all.

COMMENTARY
Paul concludes this parenthetical section (chs 9–11) with words of praise to God, whose mysterious ways are beyond the grasp of the human intellect, and upon whose mercy everything finally depends. "How impossible it is for us to understand his decisions and his ways! For who can know the LORD's thoughts?" (11:33-34). As humans, we are unable fully to comprehend either the mind of God or theenigmas of life—in this case, the failure of the Jews to receive Christ's salvation.

In the end, all we can do is bow in submission to him as Lord and give him our praise. "For everything comes from him and exists by his power and is intended for his glory. All glory to him forever! Amen" (11:36).

After concluding that God's desire is to have mercy on all people, Paul expresses his utter amazement at the sheer grace and greatness of God: "Oh, how great are God's riches and wisdom and knowledge!" (11:33). At the same time, he confesses his total confusion in trying to understand God's inscrutable ways: "How impossible it is for us to understand his decisions and his ways!" (11:33). He is at a loss to know how to put together the various factors to be considered in attempting to understand why Jews have turned their backs on Christ. Face to face with the paradox of God's sovereignty and human responsibility, Paul freely confesses the limitations of human understanding (11:34). But for Paul, this enigma is no occasion for frustration and skepticism; rather, it is cause for praise, for it reflects the profound and unfathomable nature of God himself in all his glory—the God whose ways and thoughts are as far beyond ours "as the heavens are higher than the earth" (Isa 55:8-9). The enigmas of life are rooted in the mysteries of God, which lie beyond human understanding. He is God and we are not—and because of that we bow before him in worship.

Appropriately, Paul concludes this section by reminding us of the incomprehensible greatness of God (11:36). Things are as they are because God has made them so for his own inscrutable purposes. He does not answer to us—we answer to him; God owes no one anything (11:35). In the end, everything is for him, not for us (cf. Isa 43:7, 21: "I have made them for my glory. . . . I have made Israel for myself"). And as people created and saved by God—and chosen for his purposes—we are infinitely indebted to him. Everything we have is a gift of God, and our life (physical and spiritual) is sustained only by his grace. So the real question for us is not how to *understand* the enigmas of life but how to *respond* to them. As people who owe him everything, we cannot challenge God and demand answers. On the contrary, with all of our unanswered questions, we can only bow in submission before him and give him our praise—for he alone is the Lord, the Sovereign One, and he has ultimate authority over all things. "All glory to him forever! Amen" (11:36).

The ending of this section is strangely reminiscent of the ending of the book of Job. To the perplexing question of why he has suffered so much, Job never receives an answer. But catching a vision of God in all his greatness, Job is humbled and silenced and bows his knee in submission to the sovereign will of God—and God blesses him for it. The unanswered questions no longer seem so important when one catches a glimpse of God in all his greatness.

In these three chapters, then, we see Paul wrestling with the agonizing question of how to understand the situation of the many Jews who are not saved. He gives us no simple answer but instead encourages us to look at the problem from multiple perspectives. We have to remember the following:

God has the right to choose whomever he wishes (9:15).
People have the freedom to accept or reject him (10:3, 12-13, 16).

It is only by God's grace that anyone is saved—thank God for the chosen few (11:5).

The Jews' non-response has resulted in salvation for the Gentiles (11:11-15).

One day, all Israel will be saved, for God will be faithful to his promises (11:26-27).

The most intriguing thing about Paul's discussion of this difficult issue is his conviction that one must take account of both God's sovereignty and human responsibility and his seeming acceptance of the unresolved tension between the two. Part of being human, Paul implies, is learning to live with paradox. We must acknowledge the limitations of human understanding and accept that we will never have all the answers—we must learn to live with the mysteries of God. In the end, "We live by believing and not by seeing" (2 Cor 5:7).

◆ III. Living the Good News (12:1–15:13)
A. A Fully Dedicated Life (12:1-21)

And so, dear brothers and sisters,* I plead with you to give your bodies to God because of all he has done for you. Let them be a living and holy sacrifice—the kind he will find acceptable. This is truly the way to worship him.* ²Don't copy the behavior and customs of this world, but let God transform you into a new person by changing the way you think. Then you will learn to know God's will for you, which is good and pleasing and perfect.

³Because of the privilege and authority* God has given me, I give each of you this warning: Don't think you are better than you really are. Be honest in your evaluation of yourselves, measuring yourselves by the faith God has given us.* ⁴Just as our bodies have many parts and each part has a special function, ⁵so it is with Christ's body. We are many parts of one body, and we all belong to each other.

⁶In his grace, God has given us different gifts for doing certain things well. So if God has given you the ability to prophesy, speak out with as much faith as God has given you. ⁷If your gift is serving others, serve them well. If you are a teacher, teach well. ⁸If your gift is to encourage others, be encouraging. If it is giving, give generously. If God has given you leadership ability, take the responsibility seri-

ously. And if you have a gift for showing kindness to others, do it gladly.

⁹Don't just pretend to love others. Really love them. Hate what is wrong. Hold tightly to what is good. ¹⁰Love each other with genuine affection,* and take delight in honoring each other. ¹¹Never be lazy, but work hard and serve the Lord enthusiastically.* ¹²Rejoice in our confident hope. Be patient in trouble, and keep on praying. ¹³When God's people are in need, be ready to help them. Always be eager to practice hospitality.

¹⁴Bless those who persecute you. Don't curse them; pray that God will bless them. ¹⁵Be happy with those who are happy, and weep with those who weep. ¹⁶Live in harmony with each other. Don't be too proud to enjoy the company of ordinary people. And don't think you know it all!

¹⁷Never pay back evil with more evil. Do things in such a way that everyone can see you are honorable. ¹⁸Do all that you can to live in peace with everyone.

¹⁹Dear friends, never take revenge. Leave that to the righteous anger of God. For the Scriptures say,

"I will take revenge;
   I will pay them back,"*
says the LORD.

²⁰Instead,

"If your enemies are hungry,
feed them.
If they are thirsty, give them
something to drink.

In doing this, you will heap
burning coals of shame on
their heads."*

²¹Don't let evil conquer you, but conquer
evil by doing good.

12:1a Greek *brothers.* **12:1b** Or *This is your spiritual worship;* or *This is your reasonable service.* **12:3a** Or
Because of the grace; compare 1:5. **12:3b** Or *by the faith God has given you;* or *by the standard of our God-
given faith.* **12:10** Greek *with brotherly love.* **12:11** Or *but serve the Lord with a zealous spirit;* or *but let
the Spirit excite you as you serve the Lord.* **12:19** Deut 32:35. **12:20** Prov 25:21-22.

NOTES

12:1 *so.* This represents the word *oun* [TG3767, ZG4036], sometimes translated "therefore";
it shows the crucial connection between Christian doctrine and Christian living in Paul's
thought (cf. Eph 4:1; Col 3:5) and thus marks the transition to the next major section
of Romans (chs 12:1–15:13). In view of the mercies of God described in chs 1–11, Paul
appeals for holy living in chs 12–15. Christian living is a grateful response to the grace of
God revealed in the Good News.

dear brothers and sisters. Gr., *adelphoi* [TG80, ZG81] (brothers); cf. NLT mg.

I plead with you. The verb *parakalō* [TG3870, ZG4151] has a wide range of meaning and may
be translated in different ways: "plead with" (NLT), "appeal to" (TEV, NRSV), "urge" (NIV,
NAB, NJB), "implore" (REB), "beg" (CEV), "encourage" (God's Word).

give your bodies to God. Or, "give yourselves to God" (cf. 6:13). Though Paul uses the
word "bodies" (*sōmata* [TG4983, ZG5393]), perhaps because of the imagery of sacrifice,
what he is calling for is nothing less than the dedication of a person's whole life to God
(cf. Calvin 1960:452: "By *bodies* he means not only our bones and skin, but the whole mass
of which we are composed").

because of all he has done for you. Lit., "through the mercies (*oiktirmōn* [TG3628, ZG3880]) of
God"—that is, because of the salvation he has so graciously given, spelled out in chs 1–11.

a living and holy sacrifice. For the idea of Christian "sacrifice," see Heb 13:15-16; 1 Pet
2:5. The whole of each believer's life, given back to God in response to his mercies to us,
is to be fully set apart and dedicated to him—"holy" in every way.

the kind he will find acceptable. Lit., "well pleasing (*euareston* [TG2101, ZG2298]) to God."
A life fully dedicated to God is the kind of sacrifice that pleases him.

This is truly the way to worship him. Lit., "[this is] your rational [or reasonable] service
[or worship]" (*tēn logikēn latreian* [TG3050/2999, ZG3358/3301]). This is a logical and appropriate response, in view of the greatness of the grace God has shown us in the Good News
(Evans 1979:18). Or, *logikēn latreian* may mean "spiritual worship," as distinguished from
traditional Jewish Temple worship. For various interpretations of the phrase, see Moo
1996:752-753, who concludes that the best translation may be "true worship" (TEV).

12:2 *Don't copy the behavior and customs of this world.* Lit., "don't be conformed to this
age" (*tō aiōni toutō* [TG165, ZG172])—that is, to the present world, in contrast to the world to
come (cf. Eph 1:21). The verb may be translated in different ways: "do not be conformed"
(NASB, NRSV; cf. KJV); "do not conform yourselves" (TEV); "do not conform" (NIV; cf.
REB, NJB).

but let God transform you into a new person. Lit., "be [continually] transformed"
(*metamorphousthe* [TG3339A, ZG3565])—ultimately into the likeness of Christ (8:29). Cf. 2 Cor
3:18: "All of us . . . are being transformed into the same image from one degree of glory to
another; for this comes from . . . the Spirit" (NRSV). As Paul thinks of it, this transformation

is not a single, once-for-all event but an ongoing process, the result of being continually filled with and directed by the Holy Spirit (Eph 5:18; Col 3:10).

by changing the way you think. Lit., "by the renewal (*tē anakainōsei* [TG342, ZG364]) of the mind." Our whole way of thinking needs to be transformed—reprogrammed—by the Spirit; cf. the promise of the new covenant in Jer 31:33: "I will put my instructions deep within them, and I will write them on their hearts" (cf. Ezek 11:19; 36:25-27).

Then you will learn to know God's will for you. The word "know" (*dokimazein* [TG1381, ZG1507]) implies "discern, accept, and obey," not simply "recognize." The work of God's Spirit in our hearts gives both a deeper understanding of God's will and a desire to obey it.

good and pleasing and perfect. Morally good (*agathon* [TG18, ZG19]), pleasing to God (*euareston* [TG2101, ZG2298]), and perfect, complete, or absolute (*teleion* [TG5046C, ZG5455]). Only by the transforming work of the Holy Spirit can one live a truly God-pleasing life.

12:3 *Because of the privilege and authority God has given me.* Lit., "through the grace given to me"—that is, the undeserved gift of being called to be an apostle (1:1, 5; 15:15-16).

Don't think you are better than you really are. Lit., "don't think [of yourself] more highly than you ought to think."

measuring yourselves by the faith God has given us. Lit., "each one, according to the measure of faith that God has given." Here "measure of faith" (*metron pisteōs* [TG3358/4102, ZG3586/4411]) is best taken as a reference not to the *quantity* of one's faith (either saving faith or special miracle-working faith), nor to the true faith itself as a standard (as in Cranfield 1981:613-616; Moo 1996:761), but to the spiritual gifts one has received. This interpretation is suggested by the immediately following context (12:4-8), which emphasizes the different functions and gifts that different individuals have in the church (so Dunn 1988b:721-722; Barrett 1957:235; Sanday and Headlam 1902:355; Hodge 1886:386). Here "faith" does not have its usual meaning but denotes "the spiritual power given to each Christian for the discharge of his or her special responsibility" (Bruce 1985:215). Cf. 12:6, where Paul speaks of ministering "in proportion to faith" (NRSV).

12:5 *We are many parts of one body.* Paul describes this analogy more fully in 1 Cor 12:4-31.

we all belong to each other. Lit., "individually we are members (*melē* [TG3196, ZG3517]) of one another."

12:6 *In his grace, God has given us different gifts for doing certain things well.* Lit., "And having different gifts according to the grace that has been given to us." The spiritual gifts we each have are an expression of God's grace to us individually, given for the work of Christian ministry (1 Cor 12:7). Of the gifts listed in 12:6-8, only two are found in Paul's other lists of gifts: prophecy (1 Cor 12:7-10, 28; Eph 4:11) and teaching (1 Cor 12:28; Eph 4:11); this may imply that, in addition to a few well-defined and widely used gifts, Paul thought of numerous other less-defined gifts (Moo 1996:764).

So if God has given you the ability to prophesy, speak out with as much faith as God has given you. Lit., "if prophecy, in proportion to faith" (*kata tēn analogian* [TG356, ZG381] *tēs pisteōs*)—a vague phrase that could be understood in different ways (see Cranfield 1981:620-621). In this context, "in proportion to faith" is best understood as "according to the spiritual gift you have received," much like "the measure of faith" in 12:3 (NRSV). The point of 12:6-8 is that Christians are to minister faithfully according to the gifts God has given them. In the NT, the gift of prophecy is not so much the ability to predict the future as the ability to deliver a specific word that God has for the church (note the way Paul speaks of it in 1 Cor 14; cf. Acts 13:1-3.)

12:7 *If your gift is serving others, serve them well.* Lit., "if serving, in the serving" (*en tē diakonia* [TG1248, ZG1355])—that is, give yourself to serving. The word *diakonia* is translated in different ways: "serving" (NLT, NIV), "ministry" (NRSV, NAB), "administration" (REB), "practical service" (NJB).

If you are a teacher, teach well. Lit., "if [you are] the one teaching, in the teaching" (*en tē didaskalia* [TG1319, ZG1436])—that is, give yourself to teaching.

12:8 *If your gift is to encourage others, be encouraging.* Lit., "if [you are] the one encouraging, in the encouraging" (*en tē paraklēsei* [TG3870, ZG4151])—that is, give yourself to encouraging. The word *paraklēsis* [TG3874, ZG4155] is translated in different ways: "encouragement" (NLT, TEV, NJB; cf. NIV), "exhortation" (NRSV, NAB), "counselling" (REB).

If it is giving, give generously. Lit., "the one giving, in generosity" (*en haplotēti* [TG572, ZG605]).

If God has given you leadership ability, take the responsibility seriously. Lit., "the one leading (*ho proistamenos* [TG4291A, ZG4613]), in diligence" (or "in earnestness"; *en spoudē* [TG4710, ZG5082])—that is, lead diligently. Though the reference is a general one, Paul is most probably speaking of elders and deacons (cf. 1 Thess 5:12; 1 Tim 3:1-13; Titus 1:5-9). Or, *proistamenos* may mean "one who serves [or helps] others," as a related term means in 16:2. For various interpretations, see Cranfield 1981:625-627.

And if you have a gift for showing kindness to others, do it gladly. Lit., "the one showing mercy (*ho eleōn* [TG1653, ZG1796]), in gladness" (*en hilarotēti* [TG2432, ZG2660]). This is probably a reference to one who cares practically for the poor, sick, aged, and disabled. Calvin (1960:270) comments, "As nothing affords more consolation to the sick or to anyone otherwise distressed than the sight of helpers eagerly and readily disposed to afford him help, so if he observes gloominess on the face of those who help him, he will take it as an affront." Cranfield (1981:627) adds, "A particularly cheerful and agreeable disposition may well be evidence of the special *charisma* [TG5486, ZG5922] that marks a person out for this particular service; but an inward *hilarotēs* [TG2432, ZG2660] in ministering will in any case come naturally to one who knows the secret that in those needy and suffering people whom he is called to tend the Lord Himself is present (cf. Matt 25.31ff), for he will recognize in them Christ's gracious gift to him and to the congregation, in whose name he ministers, of an opportunity to love and thank Him who can never be loved and thanked enough."

12:9 *Don't just pretend to love others. Really love them.* Lit., "Love (*agapē* [TG26, ZG27]) must be sincere" (*anupokritos* [TG505, ZG537], "without hypocrisy"). Up until now, the word *agapē* has been used of God's love for us (5:5, 8; 8:35, 39); here it is used of our love for others (as it is in 13:10; 14:15).

12:10 *with genuine affection.* Lit., "with brotherly love" (*philadelphia* [TG5360, ZG5789]).

take delight in honoring each other. Lit., "in [showing] honor, outdoing one another." Alternatively, "Regard others as more important than yourself" (NJB; so Bruce, Cranfield, Schreiner). Cf. Phil 2:3: "Be humble, thinking of others as better than yourselves."

12:11 *Never be lazy, but work hard.* Lit., "in eagerness, not being lazy."

serve the Lord. This is the reading of 𝔓46 ℵ A B D² 1739 𝔐. Some Gr. mss (D* F G) have "serve the time," with "time" (*kairō* [TG2540, ZG2789]) replacing "Lord" (*kuriō* [TG2962, ZG3261]).

enthusiastically. Lit., "boiling over [fervent] in spirit," a phrase that may refer either to the human spirit ("with a heart full of devotion," TEV; "fervent in spirit," NAB; "ardent in spirit," NRSV; cf. "keep your spiritual fervor," NIV; and the similar phrase in Acts 18:25 with regard to Apollos: "with an enthusiastic spirit") or the Holy Spirit ("aglow with the Spirit," REB; cf. RSV, Cranfield, Dunn, Moo). The work of the Holy Spirit and its effect on the human spirit merge in Paul's thinking (Schreiner 1998:665).

12:12 *Rejoice in our confident hope.* Or, "Let your hope keep you joyful" (TEV). For the eschatological nature of "hope" (*elpis* [TG1680, ZG1828]), see note on 5:2.

12:13 *Always be eager to practice hospitality.* This is a reference to the early Christians' practice of providing meals and lodging for fellow Christians traveling through their area. Church leaders especially were to demonstrate such hospitality (cf. 1 Tim 3:2; Titus 1:8; contrast 3 John 1:10).

12:14 *Bless those who persecute you. Don't curse them; pray that God will bless them.* To "bless" or "curse" others is to invoke God's blessing or judgment on them (cf. Luke 6:28). For Paul's practice of this, see 1 Cor 4:12-13. Some Gr. mss (𝔓46 B 1739) omit "you," which might imply Christians are to pray for God to bless persecutors generally.

12:15 *Be happy with those who are happy.* Lit., "Rejoice (*chairein* [TG5463, ZG5897]) with those who rejoice." Biblical rejoicing runs deeper than simply being happy. Whereas happiness is commonly defined by one's circumstances, biblical joy is rooted in one's relation to the Lord and can be experienced even in the midst of suffering (cf. the injunctions to rejoice in Phil 4:4-7 and 1 Thess 5:16-18, both of which are addressed to Christians being persecuted).

12:16 *Live in harmony with each other.* Or, "Be equally concerned for all" (cf. "Have the same concern for everyone," TEV). Cf. 15:5ff; 1 Cor 1:10; Phil 2:2.

Don't be too proud to enjoy the company of ordinary people. Or, "Do not be proud, but accept humble duties" (TEV). The word for "humble" (*tapeinois* [TG5011A/B, ZG5424]) could be either masculine or neuter in form. Cf. 11:18, 20; 12:3. If masculine, it probably refers to "ordinary people"; if neuter, it might refer to humble duties.

And don't think you know it all! Lit., "Do not be wise in your own estimation." The same phrase occurs in 11:25.

12:17 *Do things in such a way that everyone can see you are honorable.* Or, "Do things that everyone considers to be honorable."

12:19 *Dear friends.* Lit., "beloved ones" (*agapētoi* [TG27, ZG28]).

Leave that to the righteous anger of God. Lit., "but give place to wrath" (*orgē* [TG3709, ZG3973])—that is, God's wrath, either present or future.

I will take revenge; I will pay them back. This is a quotation from the Song of Moses (Deut 32:35), cited also in Heb 10:30. For other Pauline references to the Song of Moses, see 10:19; 11:11; 15:10; 1 Cor 10:20; Phil 2:15 (cf. Heb 1:6; 10:30; see note on 10:19).

12:20 *If your enemies are hungry, feed them. If they are thirsty, give them something to drink.* This is almost an exact quotation from Prov 25:21-22, with the final clause ("and the LORD will reward you") omitted by Paul, emphasizing a gracious, less self-seeking response to one's enemies.

In doing this, you will heap burning coals of shame on their heads. This idiom does not refer to the exacting of revenge by increasing their judgment on the day of wrath (as some early Christian writers wrongly thought) but to the evoking of a sense of shame. Some scholars trace the origin of the idiom to an early Egyptian practice of expressing penitence by carrying on one's head a pan of burning charcoal on a bed of ashes (Cranfield 1981:650; Moo 1996:789).

COMMENTARY

In the third major section of the letter (12:1–15:13), Paul shifts from instruction to exhortation—from the issue of salvation to practical matters of Christian living. In response to God's saving mercies (chs 1–11), he begins chapter 12 with a call to a fully dedicated and thoroughly transformed life, the kind of life that pleases God in every way. This is followed by an appeal for Christians to apply themselves seriously to the various ministries they've been given, to serve the Lord with enthusiasm, joy, patience, and perseverance, and to relate to others (whether Christians or non-Christians) in a gentle, kind, and loving way—a gracious, Christlike way.

The Complete Dedication of the Christian Life as an Expression of Gratitude to God. Several of Paul's letters follow a similar pattern: first he speaks of the Good News (or some issue related to it), then he gives instructions for Christian living. The order is significant because it shows how, in Paul's thinking, Christian living represents a logical response to the message of salvation. The essential relationship between the two is spelled out at the very beginning of this section, which follows logically from the end of chapter 8. The mercy of God, which lies at the very heart of the Good News expounded in chapters 1–8 (and which Paul emphasizes in chs 9–11 as well: 9:15-16, 18; 11:5-6, 30-32), now becomes the basis for Christian living: "I appeal to you therefore . . . by the mercies of God" (12:1, NRSV). Knowing that our salvation is entirely due to the mercy of God, we are to live in a way that shows our gratitude. This is why Pauline ethics have been called *ethik der dankbarkeit*, "ethics of gratitude." As Thomas Erskine put it, "In the New Testament religion is grace, and ethics is gratitude" (*Letters*:16, cited in Bruce 1985:213). Bruce adds, "It is not by accident that in Greek one and the same noun (*charis* [TH5485, ZH5921]) does duty for both 'grace' and 'gratitude.'" For Paul, the Christian life is not a dreary obligation or the customary following of a set of moral-ethical rules but a joyful response to God's kindness in saving us, a way of saying thank you for all that God has so mercifully given us in Christ. It is a way of life based not on law but on grace. How we live, then, is a measure both of how much God's grace means to us and of how grateful we are. The Christian life is an expression both of our dependence on God's grace and of our response to it.

And what does that grace ask of us? Nothing less than the sacrificial dedication of our whole life to God and to a way of living that pleases him in every way. We are to give ourselves to him as "a living and holy sacrifice" (12:1). Every part of our life is to be devoted to the Lord. Because forgiveness is such a costly thing ("God bought you with a high price," 1 Cor 6:20; cf. 1 Cor 7:23), we recognize that our whole life has been claimed by God for himself. Just as there is no cheap grace, there is no cheap sacrifice; just as Christ sacrificed his life for us, we are to sacrifice our lives for him. As Paul writes to the Corinthians, "He died for everyone so that those who receive his new life will no longer live for themselves. Instead, they will live for Christ" (2 Cor 5:15; cf. 1 Pet 1:18-19). The whole of life is to be understood as a sacrifice devoted to him, to be consumed for his purposes, not ours. (For submission to Christ as Lord, see comments on 1:1; 6:15-23; 14:7-9.)

In the Old Testament law, animals (sheep, goats, and cows especially; see Lev 1–7, 16; Num 28–29) constitute the sacrifices that are to be offered to God, and sacrifice is the work of the priests. In the New Testament, the concept of sacrifice is extended to include the activities of praising God, doing good, and giving to the poor (Heb

13:15-16), and sacrifice (in this sense) becomes the work of every believer. In the early Christian community, both sacrifice and priesthood were understood figuratively: "You are his holy priests. Through the mediation of Jesus Christ, you offer spiritual sacrifices that please God" (1 Pet 2:5). When Paul talks about sacrifice in this passage, however, he thinks of it even more broadly. Here it includes the giving of one's whole self back to God, the dedication of every part of one's life to the service of God, as an expression of thanks. (For the New Testament idea of "priest," see comments on 15:16.)

A Distinctly Different Way of Life. This dedication means living in a way that is distinctly different from the way the world lives (12:2). In Paul's letters, there is a sharp distinction between this age, which is passing away, and the age to come, which is eternal (cf. Eph 1:21). The unbelievers of this age are characterized by a vain, worldly perspective (1 Cor 1:18–2:16; 3:18) and dominated by sin and Satan, the "god" of this age who has blinded their minds (2 Cor 4:4; Eph 2:1-3). Christ came in order to rescue his people from this present evil age (Gal 1:4) and bring them into the experience of the coming age, dominated by the power of the Spirit. So even though believers continue to live in this age, it is now possible for them to live in a way that transcends the evil power of the present age—to live a transformed life by the power of the coming age. "This means," Paul writes, "that anyone who belongs to Christ has become a new person. The old life is gone; a new life has begun!" (2 Cor 5:17). To the extent that believers allow their lives to be transformed by the Spirit—the power of the coming age and their guarantee that one day they will know the full experience of it—to that extent they can experience here and now the life of the coming age, or "eschatological existence." This is how we find the power to resist the pressures and temptations of the present evil age.

The closest New Testament parallel to Paul's negative view of this age (*aiōn* [TG165, ZG172]) is the negative perspective on the "world" (*kosmos* [TG2889, ZG3180]) found in the writings of John. Just as Paul discourages believers from living their lives according to this age (12:2), so John admonishes believers not to love the things of the world (1 John 2:15). It is in John's Gospel that we find Jesus' words, "Those who love their life in this world will lose it. Those who care nothing for their life in this world will keep it for eternity" (John 12:25). And it is also in John's Gospel that Jesus, praying for his own people, reminds them that they do not "belong to the world," just as he does not (John 17:14; cf. John 15:19: "The world would love you as one of its own if you belonged to it, but you are no longer part of the world. I chose you to come out of the world"). Paul also speaks negatively of the "world" (*kosmos*): "My interest in this world has been crucified, and the world's interest in me has also died" (Gal 6:14). So there are strong similarities between Paul's view of "this age" and what both Paul and John say about the "world." As people claimed by Christ, we must no longer think of ourselves as people of the world (this age). As those who have been called out of the world, we must no longer live like the world or think like the world. Our lives are to be driven not by the values of the world but by the values of the coming age and the power of the Spirit. We have come to see life through different eyes. "From now on, therefore, we regard no one from a human [that is, worldly] point of view" (2 Cor 5:16, NRSV). Having become new people in Jesus Christ (2 Cor 5:17), we have stepped into a different dimension, so we must live in a new way. This requires nothing less than a reevaluation of every part of our lives and thinking, a reconsideration of all our traditional values and desires.

This emphasis on keeping our lives distinct from the ways of the world builds on a similar theme in the Old Testament that calls for God's people not to indulge in the pagan practices of the cultures around them. Leviticus 18:2-3 says, "I am the LORD your God. So do not act like the people in Egypt . . . or like the people of Canaan. . . . You must not imitate their way of life" (cf. the denunciation of mixed marriages in Ezra 9:1–10:44; Neh 10:30; 13:23-28). Instead, God's people were to separate themselves from the pagans and be obedient to the way of life decreed by the Lord. In the same way, Paul discourages Christians from relating too closely to pagans and specifically from marrying non-Christians (1 Cor 7:39). He even cites an Old Testament text that says, "Come out from among unbelievers, and separate yourselves from them" (2 Cor 6:17). But what Paul encourages is a kind of *moral* separation, not physical isolation (cf. 1 Cor 5:9-11, where he makes it clear that he is not suggesting that Christians avoid contact with the pagan world). Paul's concern is that Christians keep their lives pure and their lifestyle distinctive. So it is in the New Testament as a whole: the emphasis is on believers maintaining a distinctively Christian lifestyle, not on isolating themselves from the unbelieving world.

This kind of wholly dedicated life requires more than the correction of a few bad habits. It requires nothing less than a complete change of attitude and outlook—a transformation of our whole way of thinking, a change of heart on the deepest level. And that requires more than determined moral reformation; it requires the transforming work of the Spirit of God in our inner life (12:2). Only the Spirit of God can transcend the power of sin, and God has given us his Spirit precisely so that we can be changed—so that we can be increasingly shaped into the likeness of Christ himself. Our calling is to let his Spirit fill our lives and become the controlling influence in all things ("be filled with the Holy Spirit," Eph 5:18)—this is the real secret of Christian living. In ourselves, we have no power to reform our lives (7:14-25), but by the Holy Spirit, God gives us both the desire and the power to live as he wants us to. ("For God is working in you, giving you the desire and the power to do what pleases him," Phil 2:13.) Herein lies our hope of becoming fully sensitive to God's wishes, fully obedient to the kind of life he wants us to live—a life that pleases him in all things.

But this is not an instantaneous experience. It is the slow, continuous work of a lifetime as God's Spirit steadily shapes us into the likeness of Christ. "And the Lord—who is the Spirit—makes us more and more like him as we are changed into his glorious image," Paul writes to the Corinthians (2 Cor 3:18)—day by day, all life long. In Paul's understanding, being "filled with the Spirit" is not a once-for-all, instant transformation but a daily yielding to the full influence and control of the Spirit in all things. (For the role of the Spirit, see comments on 7:4-6, 14-25; 8:1-17; 26-30; 13:8-10; 15:13.)

Using Our Gifts for Ministry. Paul begins his discussion of practical Christian living by talking about the different roles we play individually in the body of Christ and the need to use our different gifts energetically to serve the body (12:3-8). Of all Paul's images of the church, the image of it as a body composed of different parts ministering together in a mutually dependent way, subject to Christ as the head, is perhaps the most unique and characteristic. Every Christian, Paul emphasizes, has been given special gifts for the good of the body as a whole (1 Cor 12:7) and is responsible for the full use of those gifts. The fact that our ministry abilities are a gift from God means there is no room for either pride or false denigration of our talents. Nor should we be jealous of one another's gifts. We all have different work to do, and we must appreciate our interdependence (12:3-5). Because spiritual gifts are given not just for our own edification but for the good of the body, our focus ought not to be on the gifts or talents themselves but on how we can use them most effectively to minister to the needs of the body. And because they are spiritual gifts, we must always rely on the guidance and power of the Spirit to make their use in the body effective. (For the church as a body, see 1 Cor 12:1-31 and Eph 4:4-16. For the relationship of the church to Christ as the head of the body, see Eph 1:22; 4:15; 5:23; Col 1:18; 2:19.)

In the writings of the earliest Christians, no formal distinction is made between "clergy" and "laity." The church is not a community passively dependent on the ministry of a few leaders who do most of the work. Instead, every Christian is actively involved in ministry. (For Paul's description of how this works when Christians get together, see 1 Cor 14:26-33.) What is important, then, is to assess the special gifts God has given us individually and to use those gifts diligently in ministering the grace of Christ to others, just as others minister the grace of Christ to us. This mutual dependence means there is no room for Christians who are loners, living on their own apart from the body; community life and active ministry are an essential part of what it means to be a Christian. We are together the living body of Christ, not just isolated Christians relating individually to our Savior. It also means that there is no room for passive Christians who expect all the ministry to be done by others.

The line between natural gifts or abilities and spiritual gifts in Paul's thinking is not entirely clear. For example, how do natural teaching abilities relate to the spiritual gift of teaching? And how do natural leadership/administrative abilities relate to the spiritual gift of leadership/administration? Nor is the line between spiritual gifts and character traits a clear one. For example, the criteria listed in the Pastoral Letters for choosing elders and deacons focus more on character traits than on spiritual gifts per se, though the gifts of teaching and leadership/administration seem to be assumed (1 Tim 3:1-13; Titus 1:6-9). Character traits seem closer to what Paul calls spiritual "fruit" (the fruit of the Spirit, intended for all Christians; Gal 5:22-23) than to what he speaks of as spiritual gifts. Though the lines are not clearly drawn and it is uncertain how broadly the apostle would define spiritual gifts, it is certainly true that he would think of everything that equips us for ministry as a gift from God—because "everything comes from him" (11:36). In general, Paul is less concerned with analyzing and defining spiritual gifts precisely than with encouraging the fullest possible use of them—whatever they are—in the service of Christ and his church.

There are several lists of special gifts or ministries in Paul's letters. The gifts listed in 12:6-8 are a very practical set: prophecy (see note on 12:6), service, teaching, encouragement/exhortation, generosity, leadership/administration, and compassion. Those listed in 1 Corinthians 12:8-10 have a more "charismatic" flavor: special wisdom and knowledge, special faith, healing, miracle working, prophecy, spiritual discernment, speaking in tongues, and interpretation of tongues speaking. The list of ministries that follows in 1 Corinthians 12:28-30 is somewhat similar: apostles, prophets, teachers, miracle workers, healers, helpers, leaders/administrators, tongues speakers and tongues interpreters. The list in Ephesians 4:11, which also speaks of ministries rather than gifts per se, is briefer: apostles, prophets, evangelists, pastors and teachers. We might compare these with the broader ministry categories of elders and deacons/deaconesses spoken of in 1 Timothy 3 and Titus 1. Clearly, there is some overlapping of gifts in these various lists, and some ministries would seem to make use of multiple gifts. It is important to remember that none of these lists of gifts or ministries is to be viewed as comprehensive, and there is no assumption that an individual is restricted to one and only one gift or ministry (Paul himself clearly had multiple gifts and ministries).

When Paul speaks of special gifts, he typically emphasizes the following points:

God has given all of us different gifts and ministries.
Each person's gifts and ministry are necessary and important.
Gifts are given for the edification of the body of Christ, not for ourselves.
The relative value of a gift lies in its potential to build up the body.
Whatever gifts we have, we are to use them energetically in the service of Christ.

In addition, as he emphasizes in 1 Corinthians 13, the ministry of God's gifts must always be expressed in love, or else it has little value. In the end, love is more important than any spiritual gift, and the usefulness of a gift is directly linked to the love it expresses (1 Cor 12:31–13:3, 8-10, 13).

Living a Good, Loving, Christlike Life. In the remainder of chapter 12, Paul speaks of the kinds of attitudes and behavior that should characterize Christian living more generally—his equivalent (some would say) of Jesus' Sermon on the Mount.[1] Here Paul gives instructions for relating both to believers and to unbelievers. The picture of the Christian life that emerges is a beautiful one. Characterized by goodness, passionate devotion, joy, patience, prayerfulness, generosity, empathy, humility, and—above all—real love and care for others, it is a life that reflects a Christlike spirit in all its relations with others. But that is exactly what we would expect because, in Paul's understanding, the Christian life is driven by the Spirit of Christ (7:6; 8:1-14), and these characteristics are simply the "fruit" of the Spirit, reflecting the nature of Christ himself. (Note how similar these characteristics are to those he speaks of as the Spirit's "fruit" in Galatians: "love, joy, peace, patience, kindness, goodness, faithfulness, gentleness, and self-control," Gal 5:22-23.) For Paul, these qualities define the shape of the Christian life.

The Christian life is to be, above all, a life of genuine love for others. The priority of this can be seen from the number of statements in this passage that deal, in one way or another, with the importance of expressing love. We must love others sincerely (12:9), express genuine affection for and appreciation of one another (12:10), be attentive and generous to those in need (12:13), be warmly hospitable (12:13), be deeply empathetic (12:15), be humble (12:16), and desire to live in peace with all (12:16, 18). Of all the Christian virtues, love is by far the most important. Paul places it at the very top of his list of the Spirit's fruit (Gal 5:22-23); he speaks of it as the essence and sum of all the moral commandments (13:8-10); and he places it side by side with faith when he summarizes the heart of the Christian faith ("faith expressing itself in love," Gal 5:6). What faith is to Christian theology, love is to Christian living—the key element, the heart of our response. So it is difficult to overstate the importance of love in Paul's thinking—or, for that matter, in the New Testament as a whole. Jesus himself identifies the two love commandments as the greatest of all God's commandments (Mark 12:30-31) and speaks of love as the identifying mark par excellence of his disciples (John 13:34-35). We can only conclude that Christian love—sacrificial, Christlike love—is very dear to the heart of God, a quality to be prized above all else in the Christian community. Paul concludes his famous chapter on love with the words, "Three things will last forever— faith, hope, and love—and the greatest of these is love" (1 Cor 13:13). (For more about love, see comments on 13:8-10; see also "Love" under the "Major Themes and Theological Concerns" heading in the Introduction.)

Responding Gently to Opposition. Addressing a community that may have been facing some opposition for its Christian beliefs, Paul emphasized the importance of responding to outsiders in a gentle, nonvindictive way: "Bless those who persecute you. Don't curse them; pray that God will bless them" (12:14); "Never pay back evil with more evil" (12:17); "Do all that you can to live in peace with everyone" (12:18); "Never take revenge" (12:19); "If your enemies are hungry, feed them. If they are thirsty, give them something to drink" (12:20); "Don't let evil conquer you, but conquer evil by doing good" (12:21). Christians are to be "patient in trouble" (12:12) and known for their gracious way of responding, modeled after the selfless response of Christ himself when he was persecuted. Such a response can itself be an expression of love (cf. Matt 5:44); it reflects a deep-seated trust in the personal care of God (see 1 Pet 4:19). Such a response is in line with the attitude toward opposition encouraged throughout the New Testament. Of all the New Testament writings, perhaps 1 Peter— addressed to Christians suffering persecution—has the most to say about the importance of responding to opponents graciously. Like Paul, Peter reminds us that suffering is part of our calling as Christians, just as Christ suffered (1 Pet 2:21; cf. Phil 1:29). Our response is to be nonretaliatory, gentle, and respectful (1 Pet 3:9, 16) so that people will have nothing to say against the Good News that we proclaim.

Such a gentle response seems strangely out of place in the modern world, where Christians are encouraged to stand up for their rights, to defend themselves and their convictions vigorously, and to use the courts aggressively, if need be, to achieve justice. Admittedly, we live in an entirely different society from that of the early Christians, and there may be times when an active and well-reasoned defense is both appropriate and necessary. But perhaps we have forgotten the value the early Christians placed on responding to opponents in a gentle, Christlike way. The hard-nosed, demanding attitude that has sometimes replaced it seems to reflect the self-centered ethos of modern culture more than the sacrificial, other-centered ethos of the New Testament.

There is something very attractive about the kind of Christian life that Paul describes here, something beautiful and appealing in its selfless simplicity, which transcends culture. It is a way of life that would be recognized as beautiful and noble in virtually any society. Self-sacrificing love—Christlike love—is a powerful witness in any culture because it is a universal virtue. And self-sacrificing love, more than any other quality, is what characterizes Paul's fine description of the Christian life in this chapter.

ENDNOTES
1. Though there are many parallels between the two (see Bruce 1977:336-337), how much of chapter 12 is derived from the oral tradition or written summaries of Jesus' teachings is unclear. In any case, it would be wrong to equate a set of instructions like this with what Paul calls "the law of Christ" in 1 Cor 9:21 and Gal 6:2, which refers rather to the law of love.

◆   B. Respect for Authority (13:1-7)

Everyone must submit to governing authorities. For all authority comes from God, and those in positions of authority have been placed there by God. ²So anyone who rebels against authority is rebelling against what God has instituted, and they will be punished. ³For the authorities do not strike fear in people who are doing right, but in those who are doing wrong. Would you like to live without fear of the authorities? Do what is right, and they will honor you. ⁴The authorities are God's servants, sent for your good. But if you are doing wrong, of course you should be afraid, for they have the power to punish you. They are God's servants, sent for the very purpose of punishing those who do what is wrong. ⁵So you must submit to them, not only to avoid punishment, but also to keep a clear conscience.

⁶Pay your taxes, too, for these same reasons. For government workers need to be paid. They are serving God in what they do. ⁷Give to everyone what you owe them: Pay your taxes and government fees to those who collect them, and give respect and honor to those who are in authority.

NOTES
13:1 *Everyone must submit to governing authorities.* Here the "authorities" (*exousiai* [ᵀᴳ1849, ᶻᴳ2026]) are not cosmic spiritual powers (as in 8:38; Eph 1:21; 3:10; 6:12; Col 1:16; 2:10, 15) but civil authorities or officials. Some see a double reference in this term, both to

civil authorities and to angelic powers that stand behind and act through the civil authorities. For a fuller discussion of the interpretation of "authorities," see Cranfield 1981:656-659; Moo 1996:795-796; for "submit" (*hupotassomai* [TG5293A, ZG5718]), see comments below. Cf. Moo 1996:797, who draws a distinction between "submit" and "obey."

For all authority comes from God. Lit., "for there is no authority (*exousia*) except by God." The following context suggests that the authorities are to be understood not as allowed by God but as ordained by God.

and those in positions of authority have been placed there by God. Lit., "and the ones that exist have been instituted (*tetagmenai* [TG5021, ZG5435], "appointed," "ordered," "designated") by God." The reference seems to be to government officials rather than to governments per se, though there is a very close link between the two.

13:2 *So anyone who rebels against authority is rebelling against what God has instituted.* Lit., "So the one who opposes the authority (*exousia*) resists the ordinance (*diatagē* [TG1296, ZG1408]) of God." However, in the NT, Christians are clearly instructed not to comply with human decrees that oppose the will of God (cf. Acts 4:18-20; Rev 14:9-12; see commentary below).

13:3 *the authorities.* Lit., "the rulers" (*hoi archontes* [TG758, ZG807]). No distinction is intended between "rulers" and "authorities" (*exousiai*) in the Gr. text.

do not strike fear in. Or, "hold no terror for" (NIV); or, "are no cause of fear for" (cf. NAB).

and they will honor you. Lit., "and you will have its [that is, the authority's] commendation" (*epainon* [TG1868, ZG2047]). Cf. 1 Peter 3:13: "Who will want to harm you if you are eager to do good?" This is a general truth, in need of the qualifying recognition that sometimes authorities can become perverse (cf. 1 Pet 3:14). Cranfield (1981:664-665) lists three possible explanations for this idealized view of government and concludes that whatever the government does (good or bad) will result in ultimate honor for God's faithful people.

13:4 *They are God's servants, sent for the very purpose of punishing those who do what is wrong.* Lit., "he is the servant (*diakonos* [TG1249, ZG1356]) of God as an executor of wrath (*ekdikos eis orgēn* [TG1558/3709, ZG1690/3973]) on the wrong-doer." Cf. 1 Pet 2:14. "The state is thus charged with a function which has been explicitly forbidden to the Christian (12:17a, 19)" (Bruce 1985:224). Here Paul seems to envisage two distinct spheres of service to God: the civil and the spiritual; one deals with the preservation of law and order in society, the other with the salvation and sanctification of individuals in the church.

13:5 *to keep a clear conscience.* By honoring what God has instituted, the Christian maintains a good conscience before God. For the meaning of "conscience," see note on 2:15 and comments on 14:23.

13:6 *Pay your taxes.* Or, "you pay taxes"; the phrase may be understood as either imperative (NLT, NJB, CEV) or indicative (NRSV, NIV, TEV, REB, NAB).

For government workers need to be paid. The NLT adds this for clarity.

They are serving God in what they do. Lit., "For they are servants (*leitourgoi* [TG3011, ZG3313]) of God, giving attention to this very thing." The word used here for "servants" is most commonly used of religious service.

13:7 *Pay your taxes and government fees.* The precise difference between the words for "taxes" and "government fees" (*phoros, telos* [TG5411/5056, ZG5843/5465]) is unclear, and translations of the second term vary: "toll[s]" (NAB, NJB), "revenue" (NRSV, NIV), "levy" (REB), "fees" (NLT, CEV). Other translations of the two terms: "personal and property taxes" (TEV); "property taxes and sales taxes" (Theodore of Mopsuestia, cited in Bray 1998:329).

give respect and honor to those who are in authority. The word "respect" is lit. "fear" (*phobon* [TG5401, ZG5832]). Cf. 1 Pet 2:17.

COMMENTARY

Beginning in chapter 13, Paul gives specific guidelines for dealing with a few practical issues. The first concerns the question of how Christians are to respond to non-Christians in positions of authority. In the first two decades of the Christian mission, when the church was still viewed, by and large, as a sect of Judaism, Christians were protected by the special privileges the Roman Empire granted to the Jewish community (see Schnelle 2005:161 n. 95). But the fact that Christianity was founded by a person executed by the Romans as an agitator and instigator of insurrection meant that his followers, as they proclaimed Christ more and more widely, were increasingly viewed with suspicion as potential fomenters of unrest like their master—a charge frequently made against them by their Jewish antagonists. The Roman historian Suetonius (*Claudius* 25.4) speaks of a riot in Rome in AD 49, stirred up "at the instigation of Chrestus" (probably a variant spelling of *Christus*)—perhaps as a result of the introduction of Christianity into the Jewish community in Rome—resulting in the temporary expulsion of all Jews from Rome not many years before Paul wrote this letter (cf. Acts 18:2). With both Jews and Romans increasingly wary of them, Christians were keenly aware of the need to live circumspect lives before the public and to show all due respect to the authorities.

In this letter to a church that may have been viewed with special suspicion because of the recent riot, Paul addressed the specific question of how Christians are to relate to secular authorities. Living blamelessly in the midst of a pagan society means living as compliant citizens in the eyes of the government, even if it is a pagan government. Therefore, Christians are to be obedient to the demands of the state—and they can generally do so in good conscience because government is an institution ordained by God to maintain order in the world. So Christians should be law-abiding citizens, respecting the civil authorities who (even though they may not be aware of it) are doing the work of God in carrying out their duties. For this reason Christians are to pay taxes and import duties like everyone else and to defer to the authorities set over them in society. To refuse to do so is to invoke upon oneself the wrath both of the civil authorities and of God, who has given the civil authorities their work to do.

Following his instructions on how to respond to suspicion and opposition (12:14, 17-21), Paul's advice on the specific question of how Christians are to relate to civil authorities (13:1-7) is simple and straightforward: as a general rule, Christians are to respect those who have authority over them and to live as compliant subjects. This is part of what it means to live blamelessly in society, part of one's witness to the world. This advice is very much in line with Jesus' response to those who questioned him about whether Jews should pay taxes to the Romans: "Give to Caesar what belongs to Caesar" (though he immediately qualifies this by pointing out the even greater obligation to God; Mark 12:17). Generally speaking, this emphasis on compliance with the laws of the state runs throughout the New Testament and the early church, even after Christians began to experience persecution (cf. Titus 3:1; 1 Pet 2:13-17).

In part, Paul's advice reflects the high value the early Christians placed on a gentle and submissive attitude generally. This emphasis may be seen throughout the New Testament: Christians are called to submit to God (Heb 12:9; Jas 4:7), to Christ (Eph 5:24), to church leaders (1 Cor 16:16), to government officials (13:1, 5; Titus 3:1; 1 Pet 2:13-14), and more generally to one another (Eph 5:21). More specifically, Christian wives are to submit to their husbands (Eph 5:22, 24; Col 3:18; Titus 2:5; 1 Pet 3:1, 5; cf. 1 Cor 14:34), Christian slaves to their masters (Titus 2:9; 1 Pet 2:18), and young men to their elders (1 Pet 5:5). A gentle and submissive spirit was understood by the early Christians to be a strong and attractive witness to the world, an appropriate response to the God-ordained structures of authority, and an expression of a Christlike life (Phil 2:5-8; cf. 1 Pet 2:21-23; 3:16-18).

Paul's advice also reflects his understanding of government as part of God's created order, an authority instituted by God himself in order to preserve the world from chaos (13:1-3). Those in government administration therefore indirectly serve God and the good of his people, whether they know it or not (13:4). And Christians, by their compliance with the laws of the state, are called to acknowledge that. Their duty is to help and not to hinder. Those who do wrong and break the law will suffer the consequences; they will be punished, both by the state and by God, who has instituted the state for his purposes. So Christians should comply with the demands of the state, both to avoid punishment and to honor the state as a God-ordained institution (13:5). This includes paying taxes and import duties (13:6-7), even (apparently) if they have some qualms about the things such revenue is used for. (Neither Paul nor Jesus, for example, was oblivious of the fact that such tax revenue supported state-endorsed paganism and the Roman army with its sometimes-oppressive practices.) As a general rule, then, Christians are to comply with the laws of the state, even as citizens of a pagan society.

But what if secular authorities go beyond their divinely ordained jurisdiction and make specific demands of Christians that clearly go against the will of God? What if the state requires Christians to do specific things that they cannot, in good conscience, do? Though Paul does not raise that question in this passage, other parts of the New Testament do—and they clearly imply that whenever there are conflicting demands or competing claims, Christians have no choice but to obey God rather than human authorities. Immediately after his affirmation that it is right to "give to Caesar what belongs to Caesar" (Mark 12:17), Jesus adds the strong qualification, "and give to God what belongs to God"—implying that the demands of God transcend all others. Thus, when Peter and John are ordered by the Sanhedrin (the Jewish supreme court) to cease their evangelism, they boldly reply, "Do you think God wants us to obey you rather than him? We cannot stop . . ." (Acts 4:19-20). Similarly, in the book of Revelation, Christians confronted by the government's demand to worship the image of Caesar are called to remain faithful even if it means they die (Rev 2:10), and anyone who bows to the pagan demands of the authorities is doomed forever (Rev 14:9-13). In the persecution setting of Revelation, quite a different view of government is expressed: there the government is portrayed as the "beast" (Rev 13:1-8), the "great prostitute," the "Mother of All Prostitutes and Obscenities in the World" (Rev 17:1, 5), and its authority is seen as deriving not from God but from Satan (Rev 13:2). So, the authority of the state is limited to the purposes for which it has been divinely instituted, and the demands of the state must be resisted when they conflict with the demands of God. The need for this kind of civil disobedience is taken for granted by the New Testament writers. The general rule of submission that Paul lays down in this passage, then, in no way negates the need for Christians to assess critically the demands that secular authorities make upon them. But it does encourage a posture of respect to authority generally, in acknowledgment of its God-ordained status. The cumulative effect of Christians saying no to the *unauthorized* demands of the state will be more effective if they have demonstrated their readiness to say yes to its *authorized* demands (Bruce 1985:221-222). There is no basis here for a militant antigovernment stance.

Some years later, in a letter written from Rome during a period of intense persecution, the advice of Paul is echoed in the advice of Peter:

> For the Lord's sake, respect all human authority—whether the king as head of state, or the officials he has appointed. For the king has sent them to punish those who do wrong and to honor those who do right. It is God's will that your honorable lives should silence those ignorant people who make foolish accusations against you. . . . So be happy when you are insulted for being a Christian. . . . It is no shame to suffer for being a Christian. Praise God for the privilege of being called by his name! (1 Pet 2:13-15; 4:14, 16)

Still later, 30 years after the death of both Paul and Peter in the grisly persecution of Nero, with the even more recent terror of the emperor Domitian perhaps still vivid in his memory, an elder in the church in Rome named Clement writes of the importance of obediently submitting to rulers who have received God-given "glory and honor" over earthly things and prays "that in peace and mildness they may put to godly use the authority thou hast given them" (*1 Clement* 60–61; cf. Radice 1968:55). So we see something of the seriousness with which the church in Rome took Paul's advice about respecting the civil authorities and the enduring effect it had. Generally speaking, this was the attitude encouraged throughout the early church.

So it is a fine line that Christians are called to walk. As people with one foot in this world, we are called to respect the God-ordained institutions of this world, even as we recognize their imperfections and failings in a world of sin. But as people for whom this world is no longer home, we freely acknowledge that the demands of heaven transcend the demands of the world. And whenever there is a serious conflict between the two, we know our primary calling is to be faithful to the Lord, whatever the price. We recognize that government, generally speaking, is an institution set up by God to serve him by maintaining order in a world of sin; but we also recognize that, at times, government may be so dominated by "the god of this world" (2 Cor 4:4) that it becomes a despotic tool in the hand of Satan—it becomes the enemy of God. One day the state will disappear; but the Kingdom of God will last forever, and it claims our ultimate loyalty. "The state can rightly command obedience only within the limits of the purposes for which it has been divinely instituted . . . The state not only may but must be resisted when it demands the allegiance due to God alone" (Bruce 1985:223).

> The obedience which the Christian man owes to the State is never absolute but, at the most, partial and contingent. It follows that the Christian lives always in a tension between two competing claims; that in certain circumstances disobedience to the command of the State may be not only a right but also a duty. This has been classical doctrine ever since the apostles declared that they ought to obey God rather than men. (T. M. Taylor, *The Heritage of the Reformation* 8–9, cited in Bruce 1985:224)

◆   C. The Importance of Love (13:8-10)

8Owe nothing to anyone—except for your obligation to love one another. If you love your neighbor, you will fulfill the requirements of God's law. 9For the commandments say, "You must not commit adultery. You must not murder. You must not steal. You must not covet."* These—and other such commandments—are summed up in this one commandment: "Love your neighbor as yourself."* 10Love does no wrong to others, so love fulfills the requirements of God's law.

13:9a Exod 20:13-15, 17.   13:9b Lev 19:18.

NOTES

13:8 *Owe nothing to anyone.* A repetition in negative terms of 13:7: "Give to everyone what you owe them." Christians are to leave no debts or obligations unpaid.

If you love your neighbor, you will fulfill the requirements of God's law. Lit., "The one who loves the other one (*ton heteron* [TG2087A, ZG2283]) has fulfilled the law"—that is, the law of Moses. Or, (less likely) "The one who loves has fulfilled the other law (*ton heteron nomon* [TG3551, ZG3795])"—that is, the second great commandment (Mark 12:31), the "law of Christ" (Gal 6:2), which is the law of love.

13:9 *You must not commit adultery. You must not murder. You must not steal. You must not covet.* In order, the seventh, sixth, eighth, and tenth of the Ten Commandments (Exod 21:13-15, 17; Deut 5:17-19, 21), here following the order of the Gr. version of Deut 5:17-21; all of these focus on relationships to others. It is not clear why Paul skipped the ninth commandment.

commit adultery. Gr., *moicheuō* [TG3431, ZG3658]—having illicit sexual relations with someone other than one's spouse. Though the original OT injunction against adultery was addressed primarily to married women, by NT times it had broadened to include any illicit sexual relations involving a married person (cf. Luke 16:18).

murder. Gr., *phoneuō* [TG5407, ZG5839]—taking another person's life illegally (as defined by the law of Moses); this is a more restricted term than "kill."

covet. Gr., *epithumeō* [TG1937, ZG2121]—desiring to have what belongs to someone else and/or engaging in an immoral activity ("lust," L&N 1.291). Some Gr. mss (א P 048), followed by the KJV and NKJV, have inserted the ninth command, "You shall not bear false witness," before the injunction against coveting, thereby following the Ten Commandments (Exod 20:15-19; Deut 5:19-21). Superior mss (𝔓46 A B D F G 1739) indicate that the words should not be added.

and other such commandments. Other moral commandments of the OT; Paul was not referring to the ritual commandments.

Love your neighbor as yourself. This is a quotation from Lev 19:18, spoken of by Jesus as the second most important of all the OT commandments (Mark 12:31). In James it is referred to as the "royal law" (Jas 2:8)—that is, the rule of the ultimate King (God or Christ) or the rule of the Kingdom of God.

13:10 *love fulfills the requirements of God's law.* "To love, then, is to obey the whole Law" (TEV).

COMMENTARY

In this section, Paul returns to the key theme of love as a way of relating to others, whether Christians or non-Christians. Paul's emphasis on love dominated his picture of the Christian life in 12:9-21, and he will return to it again in chapter 14. For Paul, love is the very essence of Christian living, the single most important trait to be expressed in a Christian's life. Love occurs first in the list of virtues he describes as the "fruit" of the Spirit (Gal 5:22-23). Love is more important than any charismatic gift—indeed, apart from love the gifts have little value in themselves (1 Cor 12:31–13:3). The whole Christian life may be summed up in terms of faith and love—"faith expressing itself in love" (Gal 5:6). Because the love commandment sums up the Old Testament moral law (Gal 5:14), a life of love essentially fulfills the moral demands of God, for the truly loving person will never intentionally wrong someone else. Thus, Paul speaks of love as "the law of Christ" (Gal 6:2); it is the quintessential moral expression of the eschatological life of the Kingdom. (This is why John Wesley spoke of pure love as the essence of Christian perfection.)

Like all other virtues, true Christian love—self-sacrificing, Christlike love (1 Cor 13:4-7)—comes only by the transforming work of the Holy Spirit, who pours God's own love into our hearts (5:5). This is why Paul speaks of love as "fruit" of the Spirit (Gal 5:22). Although believers are strongly encouraged to pursue a life of active love themselves (1 Cor 14:1; Eph 5:2, 25, 33; Col 3:14, 19; 1 Thess 5:8; 2 Tim 2:22), they are ultimately dependent on God for love. Like salvation, Christian love is a gift of God's grace, the result of being filled with his Spirit (Eph 5:18). A truly loving heart, then, is an expression of our new life in Christ brought about by the power of the Spirit. This is why Augustine said, "Love and do as you please" (*Homilies on 1 John* 7.8). A person motivated by pure love is driven by the Spirit of God and will do what pleases God in all things. (For the role of the Spirit, see comments on 7:4-6, 14-25; 8:1-17, 26-30; 12:2; 15:13.)

In Mark 12:30-31, Jesus speaks of two great commandments as summing up the law: "You must love the LORD your God with all your heart, all your soul, all your mind, and all your strength" (cf. Deut 6:5), and "love your neighbor as yourself" (cf. Lev 19:18). But Paul speaks only of the second of these (13:9; Gal 5:14). Though he occasionally refers to loving God (8:28; 1 Cor 2:9; 8:3; 16:22; cf. 2 Thess 3:5), his focus is rather on God's love for us—and the appropriate response to such love, in his thinking, is for us to trust Christ and love others (faith and love). In this passage, then, Paul is concerned primarily with the importance of loving others—

hence, his reference to the second table of the Ten Commandments (Exod 20:12-17; Deut 5:16-21), four of which are quoted here. These commandments (against adultery, murder, stealing, and coveting) forbid hurting others; and since one who loves never intentionally harms another person, the person who truly loves fulfills these commandments—and all the demands of the moral law.

Though sometimes (as here) Paul speaks of the importance of loving other people generally, his primary emphasis is on loving other Christians specifically—that is, the expression of love in the church. ("We should do good to everyone—especially to those in the family of faith," Gal 6:10.) Though Christians are to respond in a gentle and gracious way to all and to live in the world in a way that reflects well on the Good News in all they say and do, the deepest expression of their love is to be focused on the Christian community, the family of God. The emphasis is similar to that of the Johannine writings, where the consistent stress is on loving "one another" (John 13:34-35; 1 John 2:7-11; 3:11-23; 4:7-12, 20-21) and love for Jesus is expressed by showing love to his sheep (John 21:15-17). We are not to relate to other Christians, then, in the same way that people of the world relate to one another; we must love one another fervently. This, Jesus says, is what will prove to the world that we are his disciples (John 13:35). Mutual love is to be the distinguishing mark par excellence of true Christian believers. (For more about love, see comments on 12:9-21.)

◆   D. Being Ready for Christ's Return (13:11-14)

11This is all the more urgent, for you know how late it is; time is running out. Wake up, for our salvation is nearer now than when we first believed. 12The night is almost gone; the day of salvation will soon be here. So remove your dark deeds like dirty clothes, and put on the shining armor of right living. 13Because we belong to the day, we must live decent lives for all to see. Don't participate in the darkness of wild parties and drunkenness, or in sexual promiscuity and immoral living, or in quarreling and jealousy. 14Instead, clothe yourself with the presence of the Lord Jesus Christ. And don't let yourself think about ways to indulge your evil desires.

NOTES

13:11 *This is all the more urgent.* Lit., "And this" (*kai touto*)—a Gr. idiom introducing an additional factor reinforcing what has been said about the importance of exemplary living in 12:1–13:10.

you know how late it is; time is running out. Wake up. Lit., "knowing the time, that the hour has come for you to wake from sleep." "Sleep" implies unawareness of the demands of the time. Aware of rising persecution for Christians and growing political tensions in Jerusalem, perhaps Paul was thinking that the cataclysmic troubles of the end were nearing (cf. Mark 13:4-31) and that the divine restraining force against evil was about to be withdrawn (2 Thess 2:3-12).

13:12 *The night is almost gone; the day of salvation will soon be here.* The reference is to the second coming of Christ, the day of ultimate deliverance from the darkness of this age, when believers will come into the full experience of salvation (cf. 8:23; Heb 9:28; 1 Pet 1:5). Paul anticipated the return of Christ soon and would have been surprised at the long delay we now have experienced. "If knowledge of that day and hour was withheld even from the Son of man [cf. Mark 13:32], it was denied *a fortiori* to his servant" (Bruce 1985:227-228).

So remove your dark deeds like dirty clothes. Lit., "So let us put off (*apothōmetha* [TG659, ZG700]) the works of darkness." This is the reading of ℵ A B C D¹; other Gr. mss (𝔓46 D*·² F G) read, "Let us throw off (*apobalōmetha* [TG577, ZG610]) the works of darkness." "Darkness" connotes sin.

and put on. Lit., "let us put on" (*endusōmetha* [TG1746A, ZG1907]). Paul often encourages believers to "put on" certain virtues or a certain way of life (13:14; Eph 4:24; 6:11, 14; Col 3:10, 12; 1 Thess 5:8; cf. also 1 Cor 15:53-54; 2 Cor 5:3; Gal 3:27). This is often coupled with an emphasis on "putting off" (*apotithemai* [TG659, ZG700]) sinful practices or a life of sin, as it is here (Eph 4:22, 25; Col 3:8; cf. Col 3:5).

the shining armor of right living. Lit., "the armor of light," in contrast to the works of darkness just mentioned. "Light" connotes purity, goodness, and holiness. "Armor" suggests the imagery of war and the need for protection (from sin and Satan). (See Paul's more detailed description of the Christian's armor in Eph 6:13-18; 1 Thess 5:8).

13:13 Because we belong to the day, we must live decent lives for all to see. Lit., "Let us walk properly (*euschēmonōs* [TG2156, ZG2361], "honorably") as in the day." The lives of Christians are to reflect the light of Christ's glory, not the darkness of sin. Here the phrase "as in the day" may be understood either metaphorically (in contrast to "night" and "darkness," 13:12-13; cf. 1 Thess 5:7) or eschatologically (referring to the coming day of salvation; 13:12). In this passage, the two seem to merge.

13:14 Instead, clothe yourself with the presence of the Lord Jesus Christ. Lit., "But clothe yourselves (*endusasthe* [TG1746A, ZG1907]) with the Lord Jesus Christ"—not in a theological sense (with the imputed righteousness of Christ) but in a moral sense (with the character and purity of Christ). Christians are to manifest outwardly what they have experienced of Christ inwardly. Just as the preceding statement ("Don't participate in the darkness of wild parties and drunkenness, or in sexual promiscuity and immoral living, or in quarreling and jealousy") interprets "remove your dark deeds" (13:12a), so this statement interprets "put on the shining armor of right living" (13:12b). Note the contrast with the desires of the flesh in the immediately following context.

And don't let yourself think about ways to indulge your evil desires. Lit., "and give no forethought to the flesh, to [satisfy] its lusts (*eis epithumias* [TG1939, ZG2123])." Cf. 6:12ff. For "flesh" (*sarx* [TG4561, ZG4922]) as the locus of sinful desires, cf. 7:5, 18, 25; 8:3-9, 12-13.

COMMENTARY

The final rationale for living a life of love and holiness is an eschatological one: Christians are to live in constant readiness for the return of Christ, which is expected shortly. In both our personal lives and our relationships with others, we are to conduct ourselves becomingly, in an altogether good and moral way, as those ready for the "day of salvation." Refraining from sinful desires, we must continually live a Christlike life in light of the end.

Among the earliest Christians, there was the widespread expectation that Christ would return soon. Some of the words of Jesus himself seem to anticipate this (Matt 16:28; 24:33-34), though he emphasized that he had no precise knowledge of when this would be (Matt 24:36). In an earlier letter, Paul seemed to think that he himself would still be alive when it occurred (1 Thess 4:17; cf. 1 Cor 15:51-52). The expectation of Christ's imminent return is reflected even in the books considered by some to be among the later writings of the New Testament (Jas 5:8; 1 Pet 4:7; Rev 1:1, 3; 3:11; 22:6-7, 12, 20). The widespread persecution of Christians and growing political tensions in Jerusalem may have fueled this expectation, in light of Jesus' words about the signs of the end (Matt 24:3-35). As a result, the early Christians felt a sense of urgency.

The overall emphasis in the New Testament, however, is not so much on the timing of Jesus' coming as on the importance of being ready for it, whenever it happens—for it will come unexpectedly, and it will bring with it the final day of judgment (Matt 24:36-51; 25:1-13; Luke 17:26-35; 1 Thess 5:2-11; 2 Pet 3:10-14). So references to the return of Jesus are often accompanied by appeals for holy living. In the New Testament, references to the second coming of Christ serve two purposes: they provide hope and encouragement for Christians experiencing suffering and persecution (2 Thess 1:7, 10; 1 Pet 1:3-7, 13; 4:13), and they stimulate believers to holy living and responsible stewardship in light of the soon-coming day of judgment and reward (Matt 16:24-27; 24:45-51; 25:31-46; 2 Cor 5:9-10; 2 Tim 4:1-2; 2 Pet 3:11-14; 1 John 2:28).

Because the return of Christ will come unexpectedly, Christians should be alert and vigilant, ready for it at any moment. As people of light who "belong to the day" (13:13), we are to keep awake and not be found sleeping like those who live in darkness (13:11-12). This contrast between light and darkness is found throughout Paul's writings (2 Cor 4:6; 6:14; Eph 5:8-14; Col 1:12; 1 Thess 5:4-8), as it is in John's writings (John 1:5; 8:12; 12:35-36, 46; 1 John 1:5-7; 2:8-11) and the Dead Sea Scrolls. It most often expresses the contrast between holy living and sinful living.

Because of the danger of falling into sin, we are to clothe ourselves with the "shining armor of right living"—that is, a holy way of life (13:12). In a parallel passage in an earlier letter to the Thessalonians, Paul speaks of faith and love as our "armor" and the confidence of salvation as our "helmet" (1 Thess 5:8)—a passage which reflects the importance of faith, love, and hope as the three central elements in his view of the Christian life (cf. 1 Thess 1:3; 1 Cor 13:13). Being prepared for the coming of Christ is expressed both in the vitality of our faith and the holiness of our life. (For a more detailed description of God's armor, see Eph 6:10-18.)

Though Christians are exempt from condemnation because of their trust in Christ (8:1; cf. 5:1), Paul still encouraged his readers to live in a way that would leave them without embarrassment when Christ comes so that their hearts would be "strong, blameless, and holy as [they] stand before God our Father when our Lord Jesus comes again" (1 Thess 3:13; 5:23). This meant ridding themselves of all immoral and sinful ways and seeking to live a genuinely Christlike life: "Put on the Lord Jesus Christ, and make no provision for the flesh, to gratify its desires" (13:14, NRSV). More specifically, it is a life of ever-increasing love—the perfect fulfillment of God's law (13:8-10)—that Paul speaks of as the key to being found blameless and holy on that day (1 Thess 3:12-13; cf. Phil 1:9-10).

But what's the danger? Why should judgment be a concern if there is "no condemnation for those who belong to Christ Jesus" (8:1)? Are Christians not already declared innocent? It is important to recognize that when Paul speaks of judgment, he speaks of it in two different ways—he thinks of it on two different levels. First, there is the ultimate judgment, resulting in eternal condemnation for "those who don't know God . . . those who refuse to obey the Good News of our Lord Jesus" (2 Thess 1:8)—a judgment from which true Christian believers are exempt because of their trust in Christ to save them (3:21-26; cf. John 3:16-18, 36; 1 John 5:11-13). Second, there is a judgment of believers to assess the kind of lives they have lived. Here it is not their salvation that is at stake but certain unspecified rewards to be given to those who have lived a faithful life. This is what Paul is referring to, for example, when he says that Christian workers "will be rewarded for their own hard work" (1 Cor 3:8). The clearest instance of this judgment is found in 1 Cor 3:12-15, where he speaks of a fire that will test the work of Christians (in this case, Christian leaders specifically) for its durability—with the result that some will "suffer great loss," even though they are saved: "But on the judgment day, fire will reveal what kind of work each builder has done. The fire will show if a person's work has any value. If the work survives, that builder will receive a reward. But if the work is burned up, the builder will suffer great loss. The builder will be saved, but like someone barely escaping through a wall of flames" (1 Cor 3:13-15).

It may be this testing that Paul is referring to when he says to the Christians in Corinth, "We must all stand before Christ to be judged. We will each receive whatever we deserve for the good or evil we have done in this earthly body" (2 Cor 5:10); and to the Christians in Rome, "We will all stand before the judgment seat of God. . . . Yes, each of us will give a personal account to God" (14:10, 12). This may help to explain the seemingly paradoxical affirmation of the dual principles of salvation by faith and judgment by works that we find in at least some Pauline passages: the two may refer to different levels of judgment. So even though true Christians are assured of their salvation because of their trust in Christ, Paul still feels it entirely appropriate to stimulate them to pure and upright living so they will be found "blameless and holy" on the day when Christ returns to assess their lives.

It is also possible that Paul was addressing some in the church who were merely nominal believers. For them, the final judgment would reveal whether or not they were really among the regenerate family of God; in the end, the quality of their life would reveal whether or not they were among those who are considered righteous because of their faith. Paul's warning, then, may well serve a double purpose—to call authentic believers to show by their lives that they really are among the elect, and to challenge those with a merely nominal faith to take their commitment to Christ more seriously.

The thoroughly good and Christlike life that Paul calls for in this passage sums up his appeal for wholly dedicated living in chapters 12–13. In the end, it is nothing less than the life of the Lord Jesus Christ himself that we are to emulate; he himself is the model of perfect purity and love. Writing to the Ephesians, Paul encourages Christians to put on a "new nature, created to be like God—truly righteous and holy"

(Eph 4:24; cf. Eph 5:1; Col 3:10). Here he speaks more directly of putting on "the Lord Jesus Christ" (13:14; cf. 1 Cor 11:1; Eph 4:13, 15; 5:2). As Paul reminds us earlier, the final goal of Christian salvation is to be conformed to the likeness of Christ (8:29). To that end, our calling is to apply ourselves seriously to living an authentically Christlike life. But even as we do so, we are compelled to acknowledge on a deeper level that we are ultimately dependent on the Spirit of Christ to produce such a life in us (2 Cor 3:18; Gal 5:22-23). For only the Spirit of the living Christ within (Gal 2:20; Col 1:27) can produce in us the holy characteristics of Christ himself.

It was the latter part of this passage that first illuminated the heart of the early Christian theologian Augustine with the light of Christ. Deeply longing to be delivered from his sinful way of life, he heard the voice of a child singing, "Take up and read! Take up and read!" Augustine picked up a copy of Scripture and found himself looking at these words of Paul: "Don't participate in the darkness of wild parties and drunkenness, or in sexual promiscuity and immoral living, or in quarreling and jealousy. Instead, clothe yourself with . . . the Lord Jesus Christ. And don't let yourself think about ways to indulge your evil desires" (13:13-14). His response was immediate: "No further would I read, nor had I any need; instantly, at the end of this sentence, a clear light flooded my heart and all the darkness of doubt vanished away" (*Confessions* 8.29). His conversion in AD 386, brought about by this text, had a monumental influence on the whole of later Christian history.

◆   E. Respecting the Opinions of Others (14:1-23)

Accept other believers who are weak in faith, and don't argue with them about what they think is right or wrong. ²For instance, one person believes it's all right to eat anything. But another believer with a sensitive conscience will eat only vegetables. ³Those who feel free to eat anything must not look down on those who don't. And those who don't eat certain foods must not condemn those who do, for God has accepted them. ⁴Who are you to condemn someone else's servants? They are responsible to the Lord, so let him judge whether they are right or wrong. And with the Lord's help, they will do what is right and will receive his approval.

⁵In the same way, some think one day is more holy than another day, while others think every day is alike. You should each be fully convinced that whichever day you choose is acceptable. ⁶Those who worship the Lord on a special day do it to honor him. Those who eat any kind of food do so to honor the Lord, since they give thanks to God before eating. And those who refuse to eat certain foods also want to please the Lord and give thanks to God. ⁷For we don't live for ourselves or die for ourselves. ⁸If we live, it's to honor the Lord. And if we die, it's to honor the Lord. So whether we live or die, we belong to the Lord. ⁹Christ died and rose again for this very purpose—to be Lord both of the living and of the dead.

¹⁰So why do you condemn another believer*? Why do you look down on another believer? Remember, we will all stand before the judgment seat of God. ¹¹For the Scriptures say,

"'As surely as I live,' says the LORD,
'every knee will bend to me,
    and every tongue will confess and
        give praise to God.*'"

¹²Yes, each of us will give a personal account to God. ¹³So let's stop condemning

each other. Decide instead to live in such a way that you will not cause another believer to stumble and fall.

¹⁴I know and am convinced on the authority of the Lord Jesus that no food, in and of itself, is wrong to eat. But if someone believes it is wrong, then for that person it is wrong. ¹⁵And if another believer is distressed by what you eat, you are not acting in love if you eat it. Don't let your eating ruin someone for whom Christ died. ¹⁶Then you will not be criticized for doing something you believe is good. ¹⁷For the Kingdom of God is not a matter of what we eat or drink, but of living a life of goodness and peace and joy in the Holy Spirit. ¹⁸If you serve Christ with this attitude, you will please God, and others will approve of you, too. ¹⁹So then, let us aim for harmony in the church and try to build each other up.

²⁰Don't tear apart the work of God over what you eat. Remember, all foods are acceptable, but it is wrong to eat something if it makes another person stumble. ²¹It is better not to eat meat or drink wine or do anything else if it might cause another believer to stumble. ²²You may believe there's nothing wrong with what you are doing, but keep it between yourself and God. Blessed are those who don't feel guilty for doing something they have decided is right. ²³But if you have doubts about whether or not you should eat something, you are sinning if you go ahead and do it. For you are not following your convictions. If you do anything you believe is not right, you are sinning.

14:10 Greek *your brother;* also in 14:10b, 13, 15, 21.   14:11 Or *confess allegiance to God.* Isa 49:18; 45:23 (Greek version).

NOTES

14:1 *Accept other believers who are weak in faith.* This is a reference to those who have legalistic scruples about relatively unimportant things—in this case, those whose faith is not mature enough to realize that all foods are equally "lawful" and all days equally "holy." Most likely these were Jewish Christians with conservative convictions about the importance of traditional Jewish ritual practices rooted in the law of Moses. For alternative possibilities, see Cranfield 1981:690-698; Moo 1996:828-832.

14:2 *another believer with a sensitive conscience.* Lit., "the weak one" (*ho asthenōn* [TG770, ZG820]). The term itself makes it clear where Paul stands on this issue: he believes Christians may eat anything; see 14:14, 20.

will eat only vegetables. This means they refuse to eat meat. This issue seems to be a somewhat different one from that discussed in 1 Cor 8 and 10, the question of whether Christians ought to abstain from a particular kind of meat—meat that has been sacrificed to pagan idols. Though vegetarianism may be understood as an extreme position taken by Jews worried about buying any form of "idol meat" from butchers in the pagan world, Paul seems to treat them as two separate issues. (Note that in this passage there is no mention of meat offered to idols.) Vegetarianism may represent normal eating patterns taken over from some converts' backgrounds, or (more likely) a generalized hesitation on the part of some Jewish Christians to eat any meat that would be considered impure or improperly slaughtered by OT standards (Lev 11:3-47; 17:10-16; cf. the hesitations of Daniel and his friends in Dan 1:8-16); note the parallel concern to observe "holy days" in this passage. (For a detailed discussion of different ways to interpret the "strong" and the "weak," see Cranfield 1981:690-697; Moo 1996:828-833.)

14:3 *those who don't eat certain foods must not condemn those who do.* Cf. Col 2:16: "Don't let anyone condemn you for what you eat or drink."

14:4 *Who are you to condemn someone else's servants?* Cf. 14:10, 13. The emphasis on not condemning others runs throughout the NT (Matt 7:1-5; Luke 6:37-38, 41-42;

1 Cor 4:3-5; Jas 4:11-12). Because it is those who abstain from eating who are encouraged not to condemn others (14:3), this statement is most naturally taken as addressed to the "weak." The rest of v. 4 would then refer to the "strong."

They are responsible to the Lord, so let him judge whether they are right or wrong. Lit., "To his own Lord he stands or falls [i.e., will be approved or condemned]." "They" probably refers to the "strong." The term "judge" is used very broadly here; it should not be understood primarily as a reference to the final judgment.

And with the Lord's help, they will do what is right and will receive his approval. Lit., "and he will stand [be approved], for the Lord is able to make him stand." This is the reading of 𝔓46 ℵ A B C; other Gr. mss (D F G 048) have "for God is able to make him stand."

14:5 *some think one day is more holy than another day.* Probably a reference to Jewish holy days generally, not simply the Sabbath (cf. Col 2:16: "certain holy days or . . . Sabbaths").

every day is alike. For Paul, every day is to be viewed as holy—that is, regarded as sacred and lived for the Lord. Cf. Col 2:16: "So don't let anyone condemn you . . . for not celebrating certain holy days or new moon ceremonies or Sabbaths" (cf. Gal 4:10).

You should each be fully convinced that whichever day you choose is acceptable. Or, "You should each be fully convinced that what you are doing is right." Lit., "Each one must be fully convinced in his own mind." There is no virtue in weak indecision and vacillation, which only incapacitate people. Instead, believers are to aim for sure convictions, which "set [them] free for an obedience which . . . is firm, decisive, resolute, courageous, joyful" (Cranfield 1981:705-706).

14:6 ***Those who worship the Lord on a special day do it to honor him.*** Lit., "The one who observes the day observes [it] to the Lord."

Those who eat any kind of food do so to honor the Lord. Lit., "the one who eats, eats to the Lord." Those who feel free to eat anything do so out of the conviction that this is acceptable to the Lord (cf. 1 Cor 10:31).

they give thanks to God before eating. Or, "they give thanks to God for what they eat." Lit., "he gives thanks to God." The words "before eating" are not included in the Gr. text but may be implied. The invocation of God's blessing or prayer of thanksgiving was understood to sanctify the food, whatever kind of food it was (cf. 1 Tim 4:3-5).

And those who refuse to eat certain foods also want to please the Lord. Lit., "and the one not eating, to the Lord he does not eat." They also do what they do out of the conviction that this is what the Lord desires.

14:8 ***If we live, it's to honor the Lord. And if we die, it's to honor the Lord.*** Or, "For whatever we do—whether we live or die—we do it to honor the Lord."

So whether we live or die, we belong to the Lord. Or, "whether we live or die, we do so as those who are claimed by the Lord."

14:9 ***to be Lord both of the living and of the dead.*** Or, "to be Lord both of those who live and of those who die." "Christ died, and is Lord of the dead; Christ lives, and is Lord of the living" (Bruce 1985:231).

14:10 *another believer.* Lit., "your brother" (also in 14:13, 15, 21).

the judgment seat of God. This is the reading of ℵ* A B C* D F G 1739. Some Gr., mss (ℵᶜ C² 048 0209 33 𝔐) have "the judgment seat of Christ," as in 2 Cor 5:10. There is no significant difference between the two. It is the judgment of Christians especially that seems to be in focus here, not the universal judgment of all people. See comments on 13:11-14.

14:11 *"As surely as I live," says the* L\ORD\. This is a common OT phrase (Isa 49:18; cf. Num 14:28; Deut 32:40; Jer 22:24; Ezek 5:11). Paul has added it as an introduction to the quotation that follows.

every knee will bend to me, and every tongue will confess and give praise to God. This is a quotation from Isa 45:23, LXX, also alluded to in Phil 2:10-11, which speaks of the universal acknowledgment of Christ as Lord. Here the point is that every individual will be held personally accountable to God.

14:12 *each of us will give a personal account to God.* The words "to God" are omitted in some Gr. mss (B F G 1739 1881), resulting in the translation, "Each of us will be held personally accountable." The meaning remains essentially the same. See note on 14:10.

14:13-23 For the possible chiastic arrangement of these verses, see Dunn 1988b:816.

14:14 *I know and am convinced on the authority of the Lord Jesus.* Lit., "I know and am persuaded in the Lord Jesus" (NRSV). The phrase "in the Lord Jesus" may be translated in different ways: "All that I know of the Lord Jesus convinces me" (REB); "The Lord Jesus has made it clear to me" (CEV).

no food, in and of itself, is wrong to eat. Lit., "nothing, in itself, is unclean (*koinon* [TG2839, ZG3123])." Cf. 14:20: "all foods are acceptable"; cf. also 1 Cor 10:25-26; 1 Tim 4:4; Titus 1:15; and Mark's comment that Jesus "declared that every kind of food is acceptable in God's eyes" (Mark 7:19).

14:15 *distressed.* The word *lupeitai* [TG3076A, ZG3382] may also be translated "outraged" (REB) or "being hurt" (NAB; cf. TEV, NRSV).

14:16 *Then you will not be criticized for doing something you believe is good.* Lit., "Do not then let your good be blasphemed." This Gr. sentence may be interpreted in at least three ways, depending on how one understands (1) who is being addressed (the strong alone, or both the strong and the weak); (2) what "your good" means (the principle of freedom, the Good News, or good acts generally); and (3) who does the blaspheming (the weak, or outsiders). Some alternative interpretations: (1) "Don't let your actions bring criticism on the church"; (2) "Don't let your actions bring shame on the Good News"; (3) "Don't let your actions bring reproach on the principle of Christian freedom." Of these, the third fits the context best. (For a fuller discussion of the alternatives, see Cranfield 1981:715-717.)

14:17 *living a life of goodness.* Lit., "righteousness" (*dikaiosunē* [TG1343, ZG1466])—here, not in a theological sense but in an ethical sense.

peace and joy in the Holy Spirit. For the meaning of "peace" (*eirēnē* [TG1515, ZG1645]), see note on 1:7. The Gr. word for "joy" (*chara* [TG5479, ZG5915]) carries a deeper connotation than the more superficial English word "happiness" (see comments on 5:3-5; 15:13). Both peace and joy are classified by Paul as "fruit" produced by the Holy Spirit (Gal 5:22). The future blessings of the Kingdom of God can be experienced here and now by the power of the Holy Spirit.

14:18 *with this attitude.* Lit., "in this," i.e., in this way, with these as your priorities. For alternative interpretations, see Cranfield 1981:719.

14:19 *let us aim for.* Lit., "let us pursue" (*diōkōmen* [TG1377, ZG1503], a subjunctive verb). This is the reading of C D 1739 𝔐. Other Gr. mss (ℵ A B C F G L P 048 0209) read, "we pursue" (*diōkomen*, the same verb in the indicative mood).

harmony. Lit., "the things of peace" (*ta tēs eirēnēs* [TG1515, ZG1645])—that is, peaceful interpersonal relations.

14:20 *Don't tear apart.* Lit., "don't destroy" or "don't tear down."

the work of God. This is God's redeeming work in the life of other Christians.

all foods are acceptable. Lit., "all things are clean" (*kathara* [TG2513, ZG2754]). Any kind of food may be eaten. See note on 14:14.

but it is wrong to eat something if it makes another person stumble. Lit., "but it is bad [wrong] for the person who eats with offense." This ambiguous clause is usually understood as addressed to the person who causes someone else to sin by what he or she eats. Some, however, understand it as addressed to the person who causes himself to sin by what he eats—that is, by violating his own conscience (NJB). Cf. 1 Cor 8:13: "If what I eat causes another believer to sin, I will never eat meat again as long as I live."

14:21 *to stumble.* This is the reading of $\aleph^1$ A C 048 1739. It means to cause someone to sin. Some Gr. mss ($\aleph^*$ P) have "to be hurt"; others ($\mathfrak{P}46^{vid}$ $\aleph^2$ B D F G P 0209 $\mathfrak{M}$) add "or be led into sin [or be caused to lose his faith] or weakened" after the initial verb, which accurately conveys Paul's meaning.

14:22 *You may believe there's nothing wrong with what you are doing.* Lit., "the faith that you have"—that is, the deep-seated conviction that what you are doing is right.

Blessed are those who don't feel guilty for doing something they have decided is right. This is a difficult text, meaning "Blessed are those who, because they do what they believe to be right, do not condemn themselves"; or, "Blessed are those who, because they do what they believe to be right, stand uncondemned [or have a clear conscience]." They do not condemn themselves by doing something they believe to be wrong, or by doing something they're not sure is right. "He is a fortunate man who has no misgivings about what he allows himself to eat" (Moffatt 1935:202). The reference is to those who live with a good conscience. The condemnation may be understood either as self-imposed or as pronounced by God.

14:23 *you are sinning if you go ahead and do it.* Lit., "he is condemned if he eats."

For you are not following your convictions. Lit., "because it is not out of faith (*ek pisteōs* [TG4102, ZG4411])."

If you do anything you believe is not right, you are sinning. Lit., "and everything that is not out of faith (*ek pisteōs* [TG4102, ZG4411]) is sin." At the end of 14:23 some Gr. mss add 16:25-27, though it is unlikely the doxology was originally placed here, given the close relation between this chapter and the immediately following section (15:1-13). The ending of the letter varies in the different mss; see "Canonicity and Textual History" in the Introduction. For evidence that at least one Gr. ms ended here, see Metzger 1971:533-536; Bruce 1985:26-29; Moo 1996:6-9).

COMMENTARY

In this section, Paul gives some practical guidelines concerning two particular issues over which there was disagreement among Christians: (1) the eating of meat and (2) the religious observance of special holy days. Some Christians felt it was wrong to eat meat, while others (like Paul) felt free to eat anything. Some thought it was important to observe certain holy days—e.g., the Sabbath—while others (like Paul) were convinced such things were irrelevant. On minor issues such as these, of little theological or moral significance in themselves, Paul encouraged Christians to be tolerant of one another and to allow for differences of opinion. The important thing is to be charitable to those who believe differently and to refrain from either ridiculing or condemning them for their different beliefs or practices. In matters like these, each person is to be guided by his or her own conscience, but those with more liberated leanings must—as an act of love—restrain their liberties if in any way their actions would prove detrimental to those with more conservative (i.e., traditional Jewish) convictions.

Should Christians Eat Meat or Not? The issue of which foods may or may not be eaten was an especially sensitive one for Jewish Christians. For centuries, Jews had been instructed to observe the regulations pertaining to food in the law of Moses, which prohibit the eating of certain kinds of meat, the drinking of blood, and the eating of meat that is not slaughtered in a way that allows the blood to be drained off (Lev 11; 17:10-15). Though Jesus' teachings effectively abrogated the food laws ("It's not what goes into your body that defiles you"—to which Mark parenthetically adds, "By saying this, he declared that every kind of food is acceptable in God's eyes," Mark 7:15, 19), many Christians from a Jewish background did not feel free to abandon the traditional restrictions. Indeed, at an early meeting convened in Jerusalem to discuss these issues, Jewish Christian leaders decreed that at least some of the Mosaic regulations pertaining to food were to be observed by Gentile Christians as well (see Acts 15:20, 29), though Paul later seems to have rejected this decision in principle ("You may eat any meat that is sold in the marketplace without raising questions of conscience," 1 Cor 10:25). In Syrian Antioch, Paul disagreed publicly with Peter's decision not to eat with Gentiles because Paul felt such legalism amounted to a denial of the Good News (Gal 2:11-15). Disagreements over eating practices naturally arose, then, in churches comprising both Jews and Gentiles, and the issue often proved to be divisive: Jewish Christians refused to eat with their Gentile brothers and sisters because they could not be sure the food was kosher and did not want to offend God.

Though Paul was convinced that Christians are free from the ritual obligations imposed by the Mosaic legislation, he nonetheless encouraged his readers to be very sensitive to the concerns of those who still felt bound by such traditions and to do nothing that would lead their more conservative brothers and sisters to violate their conscience. Why? Because weaker or less mature Christians might be enticed into practices that for them would be sin, if they followed the practices of liberated Christians while still uncertain whether such practices are right. For any behavior that does not derive from a person's deepest convictions is sin (14:14, 23). In general, Christians are to refrain from doing anything that would prove detrimental to other believers out of a desire to live in love and harmony with their brothers and sisters (cf. 12:16, 18).

Guiding Principles. How are we to respond, then, when conflicts or sharp differences of opinion arise in the church today? What general principles might we derive from Paul's writings for dealing with such disagreements? (See the helpful discussion of this question in Moo 1996:881-884, for whom the overriding consideration is the unity of the church.) It depends, first, on how serious the conflict is. If there are major theological differences on issues so fundamental as our understanding of the Good News, these must be confronted straightforwardly as a matter of urgency—as, for example, Paul does in his letter to the Galatians, where he adamantly insists that we are saved by our faith alone and not by obedience to the law of Moses. On crucial theological issues such as this, concerned with ultimate matters of eternal salvation, there is no room for different opinions; here God himself has revealed to us what is true. Likewise, if there are major differences of perspective on basic moral issues such as sexual ethics, these also must be met head-on and dealt with in the most unequivocal way—as, for example, Paul does when he declares that those with immoral lifestyles will be excluded from the Kingdom of God (1 Cor 6:9-10; Gal 5:19-21; Eph 5:5-6; Col 3:5-6; cf. 1 Cor 5:1-7, 11-13). On fundamental issues of morality and ethics, there is no room for different opinions because God has revealed in the moral law of Scripture what is right and wrong. So in the most basic matters of theological and moral understanding, God has plainly revealed to us in the Good News and in Scripture what is true and right—what we are to believe and how we are to live—and these truths must be upheld firmly and unambiguously.

In areas of secondary importance, however, where major theological or moral issues are not involved (here, the questions of whether Christians ought to abstain from meat and whether they ought to observe special holy days), we must allow for differences of opinion and be gracious and charitable in all our responses to those with whom we differ. So, for example, Christians whose faith is immature or whose understanding is limited are to be warmly welcomed and not immediately confronted about areas of their life that remain unliberated (14:1). When it comes to questions of lesser importance like these, we are not to ridicule or condemn Christians who hold different opinions, for—like us—they are simply seeking to be faithful servants of the Lord in how they live (14:1-6).

The Principle of Doing Everything "to the Lord." In the middle of this discussion, Paul reminds us of a more fundamental truth: all Christians are claimed by the Lord for himself, so all of us are called to honor the Lord in how we live. "For we don't live for ourselves or die for ourselves. If we live, it's to honor the Lord. And if we die, it's to honor the Lord. So whether we live or die, we belong to the Lord. Christ died and rose again for this very purpose—to be Lord both of the living and of the dead" (14:7-9). Whatever we do, we are to be motivated by a desire to serve the Lord, recognizing that we no longer belong to ourselves but to him (1 Cor 6:19-20). We are to live, then, as people "under new management," and everything we do is to be done not for ourselves but for him who died for us. As Paul reminds us, he died "so that those who receive his new life will no longer live for themselves. . . . [but] for Christ" (2 Cor 5:15). That is what it means to confess Christ as Lord, and that is why Paul speaks of himself as a "slave" of Christ. Everything we do, then, is to be motivated not by self-interest but by our devotion to Christ as Lord, for we, too, live as his "slaves." This is the life to which all serious Christians are called.

So we must acknowledge that those with whom we disagree may also be driven by the desire to honor the Lord in what they do. That is why we must refrain from ridiculing or condemning them (14:3-4, 10, 13). As servants of Christ, they may simply be doing what they believe to be right in the eyes of the Lord. As conscientious Christians, they may be seeking to live by their principles and their devotion to the Lord just as we are—and we must honor that. Paul knew, for example, that certain religious observances (e.g., abstaining from meat and recognizing special holy days) may be a valid form of Christian worship for some, if they thereby seek to honor the Lord (14:6). So, those who observe such customs may be as serious about honoring Christ as those who do not observe them. Even though, to more mature Christians, their convictions may seem misguided and their understanding defi-cient, what they do may be motivated by the purest of intentions. God alone knows the hearts of his people, and since he judges people by the motivation of their hearts, he may be more troubled by our thoughtless condemnation of such people than by any deficient expression of faith on their part. (Bruce comments, "There is no sin to which Christians—especially 'keen' Christians—are more prone than the sin of censoriousness" [1985:232].) In secondary matters like these, then, we must focus on our own accountability to God, not theirs (14:10-12). And we must re-member that God will judge us the same way we judge others (Matt 7:1-2). The pri-mary responsibility for evaluating their convictions, then, lies with their Lord, not with us. And since he is far more concerned for them than we ever will be, we can rest assured that they are in good hands (14:4).

The Principle of Freedom. Still, Paul's own position on these particular questions is clear. "I know and am convinced on the authority of the Lord Jesus," he writes, "that no food, in and of itself, is wrong to eat" (14:14). He speaks of those who hold the more conservative point of view on such issues, those more rigidly bound by their traditions—Christians fearful of eating meat, for example—as "weak in faith" (14:1). Why? Because theirs is a more legalistic perspective on the Christian life. They still think in terms of rules and regulations, laws and observances; they fail to appreciate the real freedom inherent in the Good News. Though the moral de-mands of the Old Testament law retain their validity for Paul as an expression of the will of God (cf. 13:8-10), ritual observances such as circumcision, Sabbath-keeping, and food restrictions do not. Here Paul's perspective is similar to that of Jesus, who seems to place little importance on the ritual laws. (Jesus says little about circumci-sion, downplays the importance of the Sabbath, and emphasizes that food does not defile a person—see Mark 2:23-27; 7:1-8, 14-23.) People with oversensitive con-sciences, then, fail to appreciate the implicit distinction made between the moral law and the ritual law by Jesus, as well as by Paul. Even more serious, those with such legalistic tendencies may think that what they do or do not do in matters of ritual observance has some bearing on their achieving a right relationship with God. They run the subtle risk of failing to appreciate the full significance of grace in their understanding of the Good News.

The Principle of Love. Nonetheless, in minor areas of difference such as these, the important thing is not to insist on the principle of Christian freedom or to seek to convert others to our point of view but to be considerate of others' sensitivities (14:15-22). The love commandment—the "law of Christ" that takes precedence over all else—requires that we be charitable to everyone. So Christian liberty must always be tempered by Christian love; our sense of being liberated must always be subordinated to the more important concern of what is most helpful to others. And at all costs, we must avoid doing anything that would prove destructive to a Christian brother or sister (14:15, 20-21—an admonition clearly addressed to those who feel free to eat meat). For if we sin against the people of Christ, we sin against Christ himself (1 Cor 8:12). Our primary responsibility, then, is not to "shake up" those who are bound by their traditions and their conservatism but to show them love. As a result, Gentile Christians living alongside Jewish Christians should sympathetically refrain from eating meat when they sit down and eat together—if the latter find it offensive. In this way they will avoid leading their Jewish brothers and sisters into sin and encourage genuine fellowship between the two groups—and those are the important concerns. True Christian love is always sacrificial love, which implies a willingness to give up our own desires and rights for the good of others, just as Christ did for us (cf. 15:1-3). It is important to realize the truth of Christian freedom but even more important to be guided by the principle of love in all we do, as Christ was.

This principle of giving up one's personal rights for the sake of others is a precept that governs Paul's life and thinking in many areas. This is why, for example, he refrains from eating meat sacrificed to pagan idols in the presence of Christians who feel such meat is sinful (cf. 1 Cor 8, 10, esp. 8:13; 10:27-29), even though he is absolutely convinced on the authority of the Lord himself that Christians are free to eat anything (14:14, 20). This is also why he chose to remain single and to support himself in his missionary work, even though he had the right to marry and to be supported by others, like the other apostles (1 Cor 9:3-12). In general, his desire was to adapt his way of life as much as possible to the way of life of the people around him, in order to win as many as he could to Christ (1 Cor 9:19-23). His was not a self-centered perspective but an others-centered perspective. In Paul's thinking, the truth of Christian freedom must always be tempered by the awareness that we live not in isolation but in the presence of others, both Christians and non-Christians, whose decisions for or against Christ are constantly being influenced by our actions. For the sake of Christ's work, then—both the work of evangelism and the work of discipleship—we are called to give up our rights for the sake of others.

Today, influenced by the culture of a self-centered society, many modern Christians are much more concerned to assert their rights than to give them up. Self-abnegation is distinctly *passé* in a culture that venerates egoism—and yet, it is the life to which every true follower of Jesus is called. For Jesus himself says, "If any of you wants to be my follower, you must turn from your selfish ways, take up your cross, and follow me. If you try to hang on to your life, you will lose it. But if you give up your life for my sake and for the sake of the Good News, you will save it" (Mark 8:34-35). A life of self-denying, sacrificial love for Christ's sake is the way to true freedom.

The Principle of Conscience.   Behind Paul's emphasis on the importance of adapting to the sensitivities of others lies his firm conviction that if someone really believes a certain practice is wrong, then it is wrong for that person to engage in it (14:14; cf. 1 Cor 8:7, 10)—indeed, it is sin. Indulging in a practice that one really believes to be wrong, or that one is not sure is right, has the potential to destroy the life of the person who does it (14:15, 20; 1 Cor 8:11). A fundamental principle of Christian ethics, then, is that no matter what others may feel free to do, a believer should never violate his or her own conscience (14:23). For if Christians go against their conscience, they are going against what they really believe to be right. At that point, their actions are out of sync with their deepest convictions—and *that*, Paul warns, is always sin. People who go against their conscience stand self-condemned. So no matter what everyone else feels free to do, we do well to listen to our conscience and to respect it, remembering that the day is coming when God will judge even our secret life (2:16).

The Pastoral Letters especially emphasize the value of maintaining a good conscience before God. Paul advises Timothy, "Keep your conscience clear," and includes a clear conscience in his list of requirements for church elders (1 Tim 1:19; 3:9; cf. 2 Tim 1:3 and Paul's affirmation of his own clear conscience in Acts 23:1; 24:16; 2 Cor 1:12). Paul says that it is because of a good conscience that we are able to love others ("Love . . . comes from a pure heart, a clear conscience, and genuine faith," 1 Tim 1:5). Though the principle of following one's conscience is never a wholly reliable guide in itself (some people's consciences may be corrupted or "fried," if not dead; 1 Tim 4:2; Titus 1:15), it is an important, safe, conservative guide to Christian behavior and is in no way to be belittled. A clear conscience is a great aid to living life well, in fellowship with God. This, in turn, is why Christians must be so careful to respect the consciences of others when they differ with their own sense of what is right.

Summary. In this chapter, then, Paul gives us several basic principles to guide our responses when there are disagreements in the church over issues that are not of primary theological or moral importance:

1. We must be gracious and accepting of others' opinions (14:1, 3).
2. We must seek to honor the Lord in everything we do and allow others to do the same (14:6-8).
3. We must do nothing that would cause others to sin, even if it means restraining our liberties (14:15, 21).
4. Whatever others feel free to do, we must not go against our own conscience (14:23).

None of these principles, of course, is a sufficient guide in itself. Each has to be qualified by the others and interpreted as it is applied to specific issues. The principle of doing whatever we feel free to do for the Lord, for example, must be qualified by the need to be considerate of the consciences of others. But this concern, focused as it is on the qualms of individuals, must be qualified by the yet larger concern for what is best for the church as a whole. (The behavior of the church as a whole is not in every case to be dictated by the legalistic inhibitions of the weakest member in it if the freedom of the Good News is to be maintained.) And the principle of not violating our conscience must be qualified by the awareness that our conscience may comprise a strange mix of correct intuitions and incorrect feelings shaped by the distortions of our individual backgrounds—we always have to assess the validity of our feelings. So, none of these principles is to be followed simplistically and applied legalistically. Each must be interpreted in a thoughtful and spiritually sensitive way as we deal with sometimes-complex differences of opinion in the church today. Nevertheless, taken at face value, these simple principles provide a fine set of basic guidelines for Christians wondering how to respond to issues in the church on which there is no clear consensus or to situations in which there are sharp differences of opinion.

It is these underlying principles—this understanding of the proper *motivation* of Christian behavior—that underlies all that Paul writes about Christian living. These underlying principles are the most important points to note in passages dealing with the Christian life. For Paul, the Christian life is motivated primarily by love for others and by a strong sense of belonging to Christ. (This is seen even more strongly in 1 Corinthians, an earlier letter that gives us a window into Paul's view of the Christian life.) So life for the believer is never simply a matter of asserting one's own rights or fulfilling one's personal desires. Though the Christian life is a life of freedom, it is the freedom to serve not oneself but others (Gal 5:13)—and thereby to serve Christ himself. Martin Luther summed up Paul's understanding of this issue well when he juxtaposed the two sentences, "A Christian is a most free lord of all, subject to none. A Christian is a most dutiful servant of all, subject to all" (*On the Liberty of a Christian*, first sentences, cited in Bruce 1985:233). We are indeed free—free of all legalisms; but at every point we restrict our freedom to what would be most helpful to others, for that is what is most honoring to Christ. In the disputed secondary areas of Christian living, then, the important thing is not so much *what* we do or do not do but *why* we do it—the real question is one of motivation. In everything we do, we live as people who are claimed by Christ—slaves of Christ, who calls us to a life of love and service.

It is perhaps worth noting, however, that at least some of the early Christians—especially those with a more conservative, traditional conscience—would surely have disagreed with Paul on some of these issues. To them, issues relating to food and special holy days would have been important issues of principle defined by the law of Moses, not simply casual matters of opinion. (And they most certainly would not have appreciated the way Paul refers to them as those who are weak in faith!) In the same way today, those with a more conservative or traditional outlook may find themselves arguing for the absolute importance of issues that others may regard as mere matters of opinion or of secondary importance. This difference in emphasis is one of the factors that make the resolution of certain conflicts in the church so difficult. It raises the key question of how we are to distinguish between issues of primary importance and those of lesser significance—mere matters of opinion. And here, it's of crucial importance to realize that, generally speaking for Paul, the central issues are issues of theology and ethics, matters pertaining to the Good News and biblical morality. The less significant issues, on the other hand, typically concern externals—they tend to be issues of cultural form, not issues of theological or moral substance.

Paul's understanding of the priorities of the Christian life is reflected in his statement about the Kingdom of God being "not a matter of what we eat or drink, but of living a life of goodness and peace and joy in the Holy Spirit" (14:17). Christian living is not a matter of legalistically following certain customs at all costs but a matter of living a life of sacrificial love for others, in harmony with Christian brothers and sisters and in joyful fellowship with the Lord himself. In other words, the Christian life is a life dominated by the two great love commands: the command to love God with everything we have and are, and the command to love others in the same way we love ourselves (Mark 12:30-31). These represent the most basic of all New Testament ethical principles. In the church, then, the dominant concern of Christian living is to relate to others in a way that promotes both the glory of God and the ultimate good of all who belong to Christ (14:18-19; 1 Cor 10:31–11:1).

◆ F. Living Together in Love and Harmony (15:1-13)

We who are strong must be considerate of those who are sensitive about things like this. We must not just please ourselves. ²We should help others do what is right and build them up in the Lord. ³For even Christ didn't live to please himself. As the Scriptures say, "The insults of those who insult you, O God, have fallen on me."* ⁴Such things were written in the Scriptures long ago to teach us. And the Scriptures give us hope and encouragement as we wait patiently for God's promises to be fulfilled.

⁵May God, who gives this patience and encouragement, help you live in complete harmony with each other, as is fitting for followers of Christ Jesus. ⁶Then all of you can join together with one voice, giving praise and glory to God, the Father of our Lord Jesus Christ.

⁷Therefore, accept each other just as Christ has accepted you so that God will be given glory. ⁸Remember that Christ came as a servant to the Jews* to show that God is true to the promises he made to their ancestors. ⁹He also came so that

the Gentiles might give glory to God for his mercies to them. That is what the psalmist meant when he wrote:

"For this, I will praise you among
    the Gentiles;
I will sing praises to your name."*

¹⁰And in another place it is written,

"Rejoice with his people,
    you Gentiles."*

¹¹And yet again,

"Praise the LORD, all you Gentiles.
Praise him, all you people of
    the earth."*

¹²And in another place Isaiah said,

"The heir to David's throne* will come,
    and he will rule over the Gentiles.
They will place their hope on him."*

¹³I pray that God, the source of hope, will fill you completely with joy and peace because you trust in him. Then you will overflow with confident hope through the power of the Holy Spirit.

15:3 Greek *who insult you have fallen on me.* Ps 69:9.   15:8 Greek *servant of circumcision.*   15:9 Ps 18:49.
15:10 Deut 32:43.   15:11 Ps 117:1.   15:12a Greek *The root of Jesse.* David was the son of Jesse.   15:12b Isa 11:10 (Greek version).

NOTES

15:1 *We who are strong must be considerate of those who are sensitive about things like this.* Lit., "We, the strong, ought to bear (*bastazein* [TG941, ZG1002]) the weaknesses of the weak." The phrase "things like this" refers to the questions of whether Christians should abstain from eating certain kinds of food and whether they should observe certain holy days.

15:2 *We should help others do what is right.* Lit., "Each of us must please his neighbor for good."

and build them up in the Lord. Cf. 14:19; 1 Cor 8:1; 14:26; Eph 4:12; 1 Thess 5:11.

15:3 *The insults of those who insult you, O God, have fallen on me.* The words "O God" are not included in the Gr. text but are implied. A quotation from Ps 69:9 (see note on 11:9-10), in which the righteous person suffers abuse from those who disdain God; here it is understood as a reference to the abuse Christ suffered because of his commitment to pleasing God, not himself.

15:4 *Such things were written in the Scriptures long ago to teach us.* Cf. 1 Cor 10:6, 11.

And the Scriptures give us hope and encouragement as we wait patiently for God's promises to be fulfilled. Lit., "so that we might have hope through the patience and encouragement of the Scriptures"—that is, through the patience (endurance) and encouragement the Scriptures give us. The words "as we wait patiently" may be alternatively translated "and they teach us to wait patiently." The OT lessons of endurance encourage us to remain faithful.

15:5 *live in complete harmony with each other.* The phrase *to auto phronein* ("to have the same mind"), emphasizing the importance of harmony in the church, occurs also in 12:16; 2 Cor 13:11; Phil 2:2; 4:2.

as is fitting for followers of Christ Jesus. Lit., "according to Christ Jesus," which could be translated in different ways: "following the example of Christ Jesus" (NJB, TEV; cf. REB); "as you follow Christ" (NIV, CEV); "in obedience to the desire of Christ Jesus" (cf. NCV). Cf. Phil 2:5-8.

15:6 *Then all of you can join together with one voice, giving praise and glory to God.* Disharmony in the church inhibits the worship of God's people and the glory they give to him.

God, the Father of our Lord Jesus Christ. Lit., "the God and Father of our Lord Jesus Christ," which reflects a slightly different nuance than the NLT.

15:7 *just as Christ has accepted you.* Some Gr. mss have "us" instead of "you."

so that God will be given glory. Lit., "for the glory of God." This is an ambiguous phrase that may be understood as connecting either with the first part of the verse ("Therefore accept each other") or the second ("just as Christ has accepted you [or us]"); the first is more likely.

15:8 *Christ came as a servant to the Jews.* Cf. Matt 15:24: "I was sent only to help God's lost sheep—the people of Israel." For Jesus as a "servant" (*diakonos* [TG1249, ZG1356]), see Mark 10:45; Luke 22:27; cf. John 13:1-17.

15:9 *He also came so that the Gentiles might give glory to God.* Alternatively, "and the Gentiles are giving glory to God," or "(Christ came as a servant to the Jews) so that the Gentiles might give glory to God." The syntax is difficult: are v. 8 and v. 9a parallel assertions dependent on the very first words of v. 8 ("Remember that"; lit., "I say"; so Cranfield), or are v. 8b and v. 9a parallel purpose expressions dependent on v. 8a ("Remember that Christ came as a servant to the Jews"; so Dunn, Moo, Schreiner)?

Though the details are obscure, the overall point is clear: Christ came for the salvation of both Jews and Gentiles.

That is what the psalmist meant when he wrote. Lit., "As it is written," a phrase introducing four OT quotations that speak of the place of Gentiles in God's plan (in support of 15:9a). Some see the quotations emphasizing God's covenant blessing on both Jews and Gentiles (in support of 15:8-9a; so Cranfield, Dunn, Moo, Schreiner); but the only common element in the four quotations is the reference to Gentiles. Though the details of God's eternal plan of salvation were a "mystery" concealed from previous generations (Eph 3:2-6; Col 1:25-27), the inclusion of Gentiles in the plan is understood by Paul as something clearly predicted in the OT.

For this, I will praise you among the Gentiles; I will sing praises to your name. This is a quotation from Ps 18:49. The phrase *exomologēsomai soi* [TG1843A, ZG2018] can be translated in different ways: "I will praise you" (NLT, REB, NAB, NJB, TEV); "I will thank you"; "I will acknowledge you [publicly]"; "I will proclaim you." It is rendered most lit. as, "I will confess you" (NRSV).

15:10 *And in another place it is written.* Lit., "And again it says."

Rejoice with his people, you Gentiles. This is a quotation from the Song of Moses (Deut 32:43). For other Pauline references to the Song of Moses, see 10:19; 11:11; 12:19; 1 Cor 10:20; Phil 2:15; cf. Heb 1:6; 10:30; see note on 10:19.

15:11 *Praise the LORD, all you Gentiles.* This is a quotation from Ps 117:1.

15:12 *And in another place Isaiah said.* Lit., "And again Isaiah says."

The heir to David's throne. Lit., "the root of Jesse," that is, the descendant of Jesse. This is probably a messianic designation. (Jesse was the father of King David, and the Messiah was to be a descendant of David; see 1:3; cf. Rev 5:5.) The quotation is an allusion to Isa 11:10, LXX.

15:13 *God, the source of hope.* Or, "God, who is the ground of hope" (REB); or, "God, in whom we hope." Lit., "the God of hope." The title may be suggested by the reference to hope at the end of the preceding verse. For the meaning of "hope," see comments on 5:2-5; 8:18-25.

will fill you completely with joy and peace. Cf. 14:17: "The Kingdom of God is not a matter of what we eat or drink, but of living a life of goodness and peace and joy in the Holy Spirit." The word for "joy" (*chara* [TG5479, ZG5915]) carries a deeper connotation than the more superficial English word "happiness"; see comments below and on 5:2-5. For the meaning of "peace," see note on 1:7.

because you trust in him. Or, "as you trust in him [or in Christ]." Lit., "in believing" (*en tō pisteuein* [TG4100, ZG4409]).

Then you will overflow with confident hope. Lit., "so that you may abound in hope." A hope-filled life is the result of a heart filled with joy and peace arising from one's faith in Christ and the power of the Holy Spirit. For the eschatological meaning of "hope," see note on 5:2.

COMMENTARY

This section serves as a conclusion to chapter 14. It emphasizes the importance of relating in love to those with different backgrounds and convictions in the church and calls Jews and Gentiles to live together in harmony, reflecting the selfless love of Christ. Christians are called to look beyond their own interests to the needs of those around them, to be considerate of the doubts and fears of less mature Christians, and to do everything they can to strengthen others in the Lord. As followers of Christ, Jews and Gentiles must accept one another and learn to live together in love, for Christ came to save them both. They are to live together in peace and joy, by the power of the Holy Spirit, as they look forward to their glorious future.

Living Together in Love and Harmony. In this passage, Paul calls on the more mature Christians to be patient and gracious in their dealings with more conservative brothers and sisters—those still bound by the traditions of their past—and to be considerate of their misgivings and fears. In everything, Christians are to live not simply for themselves but for others—to help one another sacrificially and to build one another up in the Lord. They are to model their lives after that of Christ himself, who sacrificed his own life for the sake of others. In this way, they will all come to live together in a harmonious, Christlike spirit, praising God "with one voice" (15:6).

With strong ethnic differences in the church, Paul places great emphasis on the importance of harmony in the body of Christ (12:16; 14:19; 15:5-6). The church is to be known as a warmly welcoming place, a tangible expression of the harmonious fellowship that is to characterize the family of Christ. This is one of the reasons Paul placed so much importance on the expression of love among believers. It is also the reason for his strong warnings against anything or anyone that would be divisive (see comments on 16:17). Today, his words apply equally well to churches experiencing the tension of doctrinal differences (or any other kind of differences) that are not of major theological or moral significance. Where Christians have different convictions about secondary issues like these, they must learn to live together in love. In matters like these, love is not divisive but warmly accepting.

Though Paul does not often refer to Christ as an example, when he does, his focus is usually on the sacrificial love of Christ—not the compassion shown in his earthly ministry, but the self-sacrificing love expressed in his suffering and death (2 Cor 8:9; Phil 2:5-8; Col 3:13). For therein lies the deepest significance of Christ's life. And just as sacrificial love is the quintessential characteristic of Christ, so it is to be the quintessential mark of the followers of Christ. This concurs with what Jesus said: "I am giving you a new commandment: Love each other. Just as I have loved you, you should love each other. Your love for one another will prove to the world that you are my disciples" (John 13:34-35; indeed, Jesus implied that the love of believers for one another is a significant factor in unbelievers coming to know Christ; John 17:21, 23). For Paul, then, "sacrificial love" (*agapē* [TG26, ZG27]) is the single most important character trait for Christians to develop—the virtue to be sought above all others.

Accepting One Another with Our Differences. The priority of the love command means that Christians from different ethnic backgrounds (here, Jews and Gentiles) must accept one another, just as Christ has accepted us, and must learn to live together in love (15:7). Christ came to save both Jews and Gentiles (15:8)—and Paul quotes texts from all three major parts of the Old Testament (the law, the prophets, and the writings) to validate the inclusion of Gentiles in his plan (15:9-12; cf. Gal 3:8). So, as Paul writes to the Galatians, in God's eyes "there is no longer Jew or Gentile, slave or free, male and female. For you are all one in Christ Jesus" (Gal 3:28). As Christians, then, we must learn to see each other through new eyes—as part of the "family." Our fundamental identity is defined no longer by our ethnicity, gender, or social status but by our adoption into the family of Christ—we are *Christians*. And in this new Christian family, it is not our ethnic diversity that we celebrate but our oneness in Christ.

Paul nowhere encourages believers to focus on their ethnic or racial diversity; his consistent emphasis is rather on the unity of the body of Christ:

> For Christ himself has brought peace to us. He united Jews and Gentiles into one people when, in his own body on the cross, he broke down the wall of hostility that separated us. . . . He made peace between Jews and Gentiles by creating in himself one new people from the two groups. . . . So now you Gentiles are no longer strangers and foreigners. You are citizens along with all of God's holy people. You are members of God's family. . . . We are his house. . . . We are carefully joined together in him, becoming a holy temple for the Lord. (Eph 2:14-15, 19-21)

Paul's emphasis on the unity of Christians from different backgrounds challenges a great deal of contemporary thinking about the importance of affirming our diversity. It represents a fundamentally different way of dealing with the issue of ethnic and racial diversity in the Christian community, and behind it lie a different set of values and a different goal. Paul highlights not the differences between Christians but the bond that ties them together in Christ. He encouraged them to see each other not as distinct from one another but as brothers and sisters who share the same bloodline. His goal was not to distinguish them from one another but to bind them together as members of the same family—interconnected parts of the same body. Christian love does not divide but unites.

Living a Life of Joy, Peace, and Hope. Paul concludes this section on living out the Christian faith (12:1–15:13) by praying that God would fill the Christians in Rome with joy and peace so that they may overflow with hope by the power of the Holy Spirit (15:13). It is the transforming power of the Spirit that produces all distinctively Christian qualities and attitudes. So, to the list of the Spirit's fruit recorded in his letter to the Galatians ("love, joy, peace, patience, kindness, goodness, faithfulness, gentleness, and self-control," Gal 5:22-23), Paul here adds "hope," the joyful, faith-filled anticipation of the glorious future God has promised to his people. (For the eschatological meaning of "hope," see comments on 5:2-5; 8:18-25.) The Spirit of God provides a different worldview for the Christian, a different way of thinking—a completely different outlook, reflecting the change of heart that takes place when one receives the life of Christ. The result is the gradual transformation of one's character.

In the New Testament, "joy" implies something deeper than mere happiness. As the term is commonly used in English, "happiness" is a more superficial phenomenon, something more dependent on one's circumstances; it is something we feel when everything is going well. New Testament "joy," on the other hand, is frequently spoken of in the context of suffering and persecution; it is less dependent on circumstances. It is something that may be experienced even in the midst of pain because a believer's joy is in the Lord. This is why Paul encourages Christians—even Christians experiencing persecution—to seek the experience of continual joy: "Always be joyful" (1 Thess 5:16); "Always be full of joy in the Lord. I say it again—rejoice!" (Phil 4:4). In light of all the goodness and grace God has shown us and his promise never to forsake us (8:31-39), our hearts are to be filled with joy. (About joy, see comments on 5:1-5.)

◆ IV. Conclusion (15:14–16:27)
A. Paul's Missionary Calling (15:14–22)

[14]I am fully convinced, my dear brothers and sisters,* that you are full of goodness. You know these things so well you can teach each other all about them. [15]Even so, I have been bold enough to write about some of these points, knowing that all you need is this reminder. For by God's grace, [16]I am a special messenger from Christ Jesus to you Gentiles. I bring you the Good News so that I might present you as an acceptable offering to God, made holy by the Holy Spirit. [17]So I have reason to be enthusiastic about all Christ Jesus has done through me in my service to God. [18]Yet I dare not boast about anything except what Christ has done through me, bringing the Gentiles to God by my message and by the way I worked among them. [19]They were convinced by the power of miraculous signs and wonders and by the power of God's Spirit.* In this way, I have fully presented the Good News of Christ from Jerusalem all the way to Illyricum.*

[20]My ambition has always been to preach the Good News where the name of Christ has never been heard, rather than where a church has already been started by someone else. [21]I have been following the plan spoken of in the Scriptures, where it says,

"Those who have never been told
　　about him will see,
and those who have never heard
　　of him will understand."*

[22]In fact, my visit to you has been delayed so long because I have been preaching in these places.

15:14 Greek *brothers;* also in 15:30.　15:19a Other manuscripts read *the Spirit;* still others read *the Holy Spirit.*
15:19b *Illyricum* was a region northeast of Italy.　15:21 Isa 52:15 (Greek version).

NOTES
15:14 *You know these things so well.* Lit., "you are . . . filled with all knowledge." Paul reassures them of his confidence in them, even though he has felt it necessary to speak straightforwardly to them about certain issues.

you can teach each other. The term *nouthetein* [TG3560, ZG3805] is translated in different ways: "instruct" (NIV); "give advice to" (NEB); "correcting" (NJB); "admonish" (NAB).

15:15 *knowing that all you need is this reminder.* Or, "as a reminder," "by way of reminder."

15:16 *a special messenger.* Or, "minister." Lit., "servant" (*leitourgon* [TG3011, ZG3313]). In the NT, the term often denotes religious service and sometimes priestly service. See note on 15:27 (cf. 1:5; 12:3). Cranfield 1981:755-756, following Barth, argues that Paul speaks of himself as a Levitical servant of Christ the Priest rather than as a priest himself; but the sacrificial language of 15:16b suggests the work of a priest.

I bring you the Good News so that I might present you as an acceptable offering to God. Lit., "doing the priestly work (*hierourgounta* [TG2418, ZG2646]) of the gospel of God in order that the offering of the Gentiles might be acceptable."

made holy by the Holy Spirit. Lit., "sanctified (*hēgiasmenē* [TG37, ZG39]) by the Holy Spirit." This is why the offering is acceptable. In contrast to those who thought of Gentiles as "unclean" because they were uncircumcised, Paul (like Peter in Acts 15:8-9) clearly sees them as "clean" because of the sanctifying work of the Spirit.

15:17 *I have reason to be enthusiastic about all Christ Jesus has done through me in my service to God.* Lit., "I have [reason for] boasting in Christ Jesus [about] the things [I have done] for God." The following verses make it clear that Paul understands Christ to be working through him to accomplish these things.

15:18 *bringing the Gentiles to God.* Lit., "for the obedience of the Gentiles"; cf. 1:5; 16:26.

by my message and by the way I worked among them. Lit., "by word and deed" (*logō kai ergō* [TG3056/2041, ZG3364/2240]).

15:19 *by the power of God's Spirit.* Instead of "God's Spirit," some mss have "the Spirit" or "the Holy Spirit."

I have fully presented the Good News of Christ. Lit., "I have completed [the task of preaching] the Good News of Christ"—not to every individual but in every province from Judea to Illyricum, thus fulfilling his preaching commission in the northeastern Mediterranean area.

from Jerusalem. Jerusalem represents the origin of the Christian movement (cf. Luke 24:47; Acts 1:4, 8). Early Christians may have understood this as the fulfillment of the prophecies of Isa 2:3; Mic 4:2.

all the way to Illyricum. A Roman (Latin-speaking) province northwest of Macedonia, lying along the Adriatic coast east of Italy—the region of modern Albania. There is no mention of Illyricum in Acts or Paul's other letters. It is not clear from the text whether Paul means that he preached "in" Illyricum or "all the way to the border of" Illyricum. He probably reached Illyricum by traveling west on the Egnatian highway from Thessalonica and then turning north.

15:20 *rather than where a church has already been started by someone else.* Lit., "so I don't build on someone else's foundation." Cf. 2 Cor 10:16.

15:21 *Those who have never been told about him will see, and those who have never heard of him will understand.* This is a quotation from Isa 52:15, LXX.

15:22 A number of translations (NRSV, TEV, REB, NAB, NJB, CEV), as well as NA[27], begin a new section (or paragraph) with this verse. The NLT begins the new section—Paul's Travel Plans—with 15:23. As a transition between the two sections, the verse could be joined to either, depending on how it is translated.

delayed so long. Or, "delayed so many times (*ta polla*)." Cf. 1:13.

COMMENTARY
As Paul prepares to end his letter, he reassures his readers of his confidence in them and emphasizes that the authority with which he writes stems from the missionary calling God has given him to proclaim the Good News to the Gentile world. His

calling had been attested by the miraculous things that God had done through him all across the northeastern end of the Mediterranean. His missionary work had extended all the way from Jerusalem right around to Illyricum and for many years had been guided by his desire to preach Christ in the unreached areas, especially to people who had never heard of Christ.

Though Paul wanted the believers in Rome to know that he was confident of their Christian maturity, he still felt it necessary to speak quite straightforwardly to them about certain issues. This, he reminds them here (as he did at the very beginning of the letter; 1:1, 5), is because of the authority God has given him as a missionary commissioned to serve the cause of Christ and the Good News among the Gentiles (15:15-16).

In accordance with his Jewish background, Paul likened his calling to that of a priest. His task was to present the Gentiles as a pure and holy offering to God, set apart for God by the transforming work of the Holy Spirit in their lives. This word may have been directed to strict Christian Jews who viewed Gentiles as inherently unclean because they were uncircumcised. Paul's point was that Gentile converts have been made clean by the sanctifying work of the Spirit. As he wrote earlier, "True circumcision is not merely obeying the letter of the law; rather, it is a change of heart produced by God's Spirit" (2:29; cf. Acts 15:8-9; Phil 3:3; Titus 3:5). When Paul spoke of his desire to present the Gentiles as a pure and holy "offering," he was thinking of more than mere conversion and the presence of the Spirit in their lives; he wanted to see their lives changed and fully transformed by the power of the Spirit. That's why he earlier wrote so extensively about the work of the Spirit and God's ultimate desire that they be conformed to the likeness of his Son (7:4-6; 8:1-17, 26-30; 12:2).

As a "priest," Paul took his calling seriously—a priest's work is holy work, done in the sacred service of God. Although there is no formally designated role for priests in the New Testament church, those who serve God are likened to priests several times. In the book of Hebrews, Christ himself is pictured as the perfect priest, the ultimate fulfillment of the Old Testament priesthood—just as the sacrifice he offered is viewed as the ultimate and perfect sacrifice, good for all sins forever (see Heb 7:15–10:18). His work now is the priestly work of intercession for his people in the presence of God himself. His faithful people are also spoken of as priests because they, like Christ, are the ones specially called and set apart to do the work of God in the world. Thus, Peter speaks of Christians as God's "holy priests" who offer spiritual sacrifices; they are "royal priests, a holy nation" in the world (1 Pet 2:5, 9; cf. Rev 1:6; 5:10; 20:6). Whereas in the Old Testament, priests are a special caste (the descendants of Aaron), in the New Testament, all of Christ's people serve as priests. Anointed by his Spirit, all Christians are set apart for God's holy work in the world, offering up their daily sacrifices to him. Like Paul, they must take their calling absolutely seriously because a priest's work is holy; indeed, every part of a priest's life is considered holy, set apart for God.

Paul attributed the widespread results of his ministry not to himself but to the living Christ who worked in and through him, sometimes in miraculous ways (15:17-19). Paul knew that effective Christian ministry is always the work of God (or Jesus Christ, or the Holy Spirit—when Paul refers to the divine power at work within, he speaks of the three interchangeably). The apostle spoke of himself as a simple channel through which the Lord worked: "It is no longer I who live, but Christ lives in me" (Gal 2:20; cf. Col 1:27). Paul encouraged Christians to take their call to ministry seriously but never to forget that they too are simply instruments through which the Lord ministers his grace (1 Cor 3:5-7; 2 Cor 4:7; 12:8-10; cf. 1 Cor 2:1-5). "I have worked harder than any of the other apostles," he claimed— but then immediately added, "yet it was not I but God who was working through me by his grace" (1 Cor 15:10). Here Paul teaches us both humility and trust; for apart from the Lord and his power, we and our ministry are nothing. We are always dependent on him to use us, to work in and through us, if our ministry is to be effective.

By the power of God's Spirit, Paul's work resulted in a strong and effective witness for Christ, expressed both in the message he preached and in the life he lived—and also in the miraculous things God did through him (15:18-19). His witness had spread all the way from Jerusalem (where it all started) to Illyricum (modern Albania, above the northwestern coast of Greece). And because the evangelistic needs of the northeastern end of the Mediterranean had been so great, he had little time for anything else. That's why his long-anticipated visit to Rome had been delayed so long (15:22; cf. 1:13).

As a pioneer missionary, Paul's desire had always been to preach Christ to those who had never heard of him before. So he aimed for the difficult, unreached areas, not the places where others had already preached the Good News (15:20-21; 2 Cor 10:16). The priority Paul gave to taking the Good News to the unreached has served as a model for pioneer missions in the last two centuries—and rightly so. If we take seriously Jesus' charge, "Go into all the world and preach the Good News to everyone" (Mark 16:15-16; cf. Matt 28:18-20; Luke 24:47), and if we really believe the world is "subject to God's anger," "without God and without hope," apart from the saving message of the Good News (Eph 2:3, 12), then we *must* give priority to taking the message of Christ to unreached areas all over the world. Although not all of us are called to be pioneer missionaries like Paul, all of us are called to share in the pioneering work of the Good News worldwide and to do everything we can to forward it—to pray for it, give to it, support it in every way. For it is the most urgent work in the world and dear to the heart of God—"For God loved the world so much that he gave his one and only Son, so that everyone who believes in him will not perish but have eternal life" (John 3:16). If these words are true, it is crucial that we do everything we can to see that the saving message of Christ is heard by everyone, everywhere. It is the responsibility of each new generation of Christians to seek to reach the people of their generation, all over the world—especially those who have never heard the Good News.

◆ **B. Paul's Travel Plans (15:23-33)**

23But now I have finished my work in these regions, and after all these long years of waiting, I am eager to visit you. 24I am planning to go to Spain, and when I do, I will stop off in Rome. And after I have enjoyed your fellowship for a little while, you can provide for my journey.

25But before I come, I must go to Jerusalem to take a gift to the believers* there. 26For you see, the believers in Macedonia and Achaia* have eagerly taken up an offering for the poor among the believers in Jerusalem. 27They were glad to do this because they feel they owe a real debt to them. Since the Gentiles received the spiritual blessings of the Good News from the believers in Jerusalem, they feel the least they can do in return is to help them financially. 28As soon as I have de-livered this money and completed this good deed of theirs, I will come to see you on my way to Spain. 29And I am sure that when I come, Christ will richly bless our time together.

30Dear brothers and sisters, I urge you in the name of our Lord Jesus Christ to join in my struggle by praying to God for me. Do this because of your love for me, given to you by the Holy Spirit. 31Pray that I will be rescued from those in Judea who re-fuse to obey God. Pray also that the believers there will be willing to accept the donation* I am taking to Jerusalem. 32Then, by the will of God, I will be able to come to you with a joyful heart, and we will be an encouragement to each other.

33And now may God, who gives us his peace, be with you all. Amen.*

15:25 Greek *God's holy people;* also in 15:26, 31. 15:26 *Macedonia* and *Achaia* were the northern and southern regions of Greece. 15:31 Greek *the ministry;* other manuscripts read *the gift.* 15:33 Some manuscripts omit *Amen.* One very early manuscript places 16:25-27 here.

NOTES

15:23 *I have finished my work in these regions.* Lit., "no longer having a place in these regions." Paul viewed his pioneering evangelism in the northeastern end of the Mediterra-nean as basically completed. See note on 15:19.

15:24 *Spain.* Clement, an elder in the church in Rome, writing about AD 96 (only three decades after the death of Paul), observed that Paul eventually traveled "to the furthest lim-its of the west"—which to a Roman would surely mean Spain (*1 Clement* 5). The Muratorian Canon (lines 34-39) asserts explicitly that Paul went to Spain from Rome. The implication is that, after spending two years in prison in Judea and two years under house arrest in Rome (Acts 21-28), Paul was eventually released and then continued his missionary work in the western end of the Mediterranean, as he had originally planned. Later, Paul was rearrested and executed by the Romans around AD 65. Eusebius (*History* 22) mentions that Paul was released from Rome and rearrested there but does not specify where he was between his release and rearrest. Aus thinks that Paul's desire to go to Spain is linked to the prediction in Isa 66:19-20 of representatives from Tarshish being taken to Jerusalem as an offering to the Lord in the last days, ushering in the Parousia (for a critique, see Schreiner 1998:775).

you can provide for my journey. Lit., "I hope . . . to be sent on my way by you." Paul hoped the Roman Christians would be a means of support as he began his mission work in the Latin-speaking West.

15:25 *to take a gift to the believers there.* Lit., "serving the saints" (*tois hagiois* [TG40A, ZG41])—that is, the Christians (cf. 1:7).

15:26 *the believers in Macedonia and Achaia have eagerly taken up an offering.* For details of this offering, see 1 Cor 16:1-4; 2 Cor 8:1-9:15. Macedonia and Achaia are, respec-tively, the northern and southern Roman provinces of Greece. Paul had organized a similar collection from the Christians in Galatia (central Turkey, 1 Cor 16:1), and the presence of

Trophimus with him later in Jerusalem may imply that the Christians of Ephesus and the surrounding area (western Turkey) had contributed money as well (Acts 20:4; 21:29).

for the poor among the believers in Jerusalem. See note on 15:25. Jewish Christians, in time, came to be called "the poor," and there later arose an ascetic Jewish-Christian sect called the Ebionites (from Heb. *'ebyonim* [TH34, ZH36], "the poor").

15:27 *they feel . . . they feel.* Both phrases, not in the Gr., are added by the NLT for clarity.

they owe a real debt to them. Whether Jerusalem Christians thought of this as something more than voluntary, as a duty owed by the daughter churches to their mother, is not clear. Paul's point is simply that Gentile Christians are inherently indebted to the Jewish community who brought the Good News to them.

to help them financially. Lit., "to serve (*leitourgēsai* [TG3008, ZG3310]) them in the physical things." See note on the related term *leitourgon* (servant) in 15:16. Cf. the use of *leitourgia* [TG3009, ZG3311] (service) in 2 Cor 9:12.

15:28 *As soon as I have delivered this money and completed this good deed of theirs.* Lit., "Then, having completed this [task] and having sealed to them this fruit"—a difficult phrase that might refer to the "fruit" of the Gentile mission, of which many Jerusalem Christians were skeptical.

15:29 *Christ will richly bless our time together.* Lit., "I will come in the fullness of the blessing of Christ"—that is, with the full blessing of Christ. This reading is supported by 𝔓46 ℵ* A B C 81 1739. Some Gr. mss (ℵ² 𝔐), followed by the KJV and NKJV, read, "in the fullness of the blessing of the Good News of Christ."

15:30 *Dear brothers and sisters.* Gr., *adelphoi* [TG80, ZG81] (brothers). Omitted in some Gr. mss.

join in my struggle by praying to God for me. Or, "struggle together with me in [your] prayers to God for me." For other references to prayer as a "struggle," see Luke 22:44; Col 4:12-13.

because of your love for me, given to you by the Holy Spirit. Lit., "because of the love of the Spirit"—that is, the love that the Spirit gives (cf. 5:5; Gal 5:22).

15:31 *those . . . who refuse to obey God.* Those who reject God's revelation in Christ—that is, the unbelievers. Lit., "the disobedient."

the donation I am taking. This is the reading of B D* F G. Most Gr. mss (𝔓46 ℵ A C D¹ 𝔐) read, "my ministry." The reading underlying the NLT probably represents a later gloss explaining more precisely the nature of Paul's ministry to the believers in Jerusalem.

15:32 *by the will of God.* Or, "if it is God's will" (cf. NJB). Lit., "through the will of God" (*dia thelēmatos theou* [TG2307, ZG2525]).

with a joyful heart. Lit., "in joy." For the meaning of "joy," see comments on 5:2-5; 15:13; cf. 14:17.

we will be an encouragement to each other. Lit., "I will be refreshed together with you" (*sunanapausōmai humin* [TG4875, ZG5265]). The Gr. verb implies both rest and refreshing of one's spirit (Newman and Nida 1973:289).

15:33 *God, who gives us his peace.* Or, "God, our source of peace" (TEV). Lit., "the God of peace." This title is used also in 16:20; 2 Cor 13:11; Phil 4:9; 1 Thess 5:23; Heb 13:20; cf. 2 Thess 3:16.

Amen. This word is found in ℵ B C D 𝔐 but not in 𝔓46 A F G 1739 1881. The second-century ms 𝔓46 has 16:25-27 here. See "Canonicity and Textual History" in the Introduction. Cranfield, noting that all the concluding greetings in Paul's letters include the word "grace," argues on this basis that 15:33 cannot be considered the final prayer of the letter (1981:780).

COMMENTARY

Now that his mission work in the northeastern Mediterranean area appeared finished (after more than 20 years of active service), Paul was at last free to think of visiting the Christians in Rome, something he had long wanted to do. His plan was to pay them a brief visit on his way west to Spain, which was beginning to produce some of the great men of the Roman Empire at this time (Seneca, Trajan, and Hadrian all had Spanish ancestry). His hope was to recruit the help and support of the Roman church for his work of preaching the Good News in the western (Latin-speaking) end of the Mediterranean world (15:23-24). (Paul's view of the mission work the Lord had given him to do seems to have encompassed the whole of the Roman world.) In the meantime, however, he had a task to complete in Jerusalem— the delivery of the money that had been collected for the poor Christians in Jerusalem by the believers in Greece. Because his anticipated trip to Jerusalem was a risky one due to the strong anti-Christian sentiment there, he asked for the special prayers of the Roman Christians for his protection. His hope was that all would go well so he could come see them in Rome with a joyful heart, in full anticipation of Christ's blessing on his ministry to them.

Paul's request for prayer was a poignant one because, as we know from Luke's account in Acts 21-28, things did not work out in Jerusalem as Paul had hoped. The violence of the mob in the city led to his arrest and incarceration in Judea for two years. When he finally reached Rome, it was not as a free man en route to Spain but as a prisoner of the state awaiting his trial before Roman officials. But even in these difficult circumstances, Paul attempted to be a faithful witness to the Good News, both in prison in Judea (Acts 24:10-25; 26:1-29) and under house arrest in Rome (Acts 28:17-31). As Luke records it, "For the next two years [after arriving in Rome], Paul. . . . welcomed all who visited him, boldly proclaiming the Kingdom of God and teaching about the Lord Jesus Christ" (Acts 28:30-31).

Several years later (assuming that Paul was released and later rearrested; see note on 15:24; cf. 15:28), Paul was once again in Rome as a prisoner of the state, this time awaiting execution. According to early Christian tradition, he was beheaded in Rome during the anti-Christian pogrom of Nero at about the time Peter was killed in AD 64-65. Happily for the Christians in Rome, his unexpected stays in the capital of the empire may have meant that the believers there had more opportunities to be blessed by Paul's ministry than they ever anticipated. (See "Date and Occasion of Writing" in the Introduction.)

Paul's immediate plans were to go to Jerusalem with the money that had been collected from the churches in Greece for poor Christians in Jerusalem (15:25-26)—something the leaders of the Jerusalem church had encouraged him to do when they first put their stamp of approval on his wider ministry to the Gentiles (Gal 2:10). Paul had delivered a gift to the poor believers in Jerusalem once before, in a time of famine, from the newly founded church in Damascus (Acts 11:29-30). Since the Jewish church was their "mother" in the Lord (because the Good News was first sent out from Jerusalem), it was only appropriate, he reasoned, for the

Gentile church to assist poverty-stricken Jerusalem Christians with their financial needs (15:27). Paul may also have hoped that such a gift would be a means of allaying the suspicion with which so many Jerusalem Christians viewed him and his mission to the Gentile world (see Acts 21:20-24). It may also represent, in his thinking, a tangible expression of God's blessing on the entire Gentile mission, which skeptical Jerusalem believers, in need of material help, could not deny. In addition, this might be one way of evoking the Jewish "jealousy" that Paul speaks of in 11:11, 14—the desire to have the blessing the Gentiles have experienced.

The Need to Care for the Poor. The need to provide for the poor is emphasized in both the Old and New Testaments. Concern for the needy, especially widows and orphans, is evidenced throughout the Old Testament, and the law of Moses makes specific provision for the poor (e.g., Lev 19:9-10; Deut 14:28-29). In the New Testament, it is Luke's Gospel and James especially that highlight the importance of caring for those in need. Luke emphasizes Jesus' special concern for the poor (Luke 4:18; 6:20-21) and includes several of Jesus' teachings on the importance of caring for the needs of the poor (Luke 11:41; 12:33; 14:12-13; 18:22; 19:8). In Luke's Gospel, giving to the poor is the best thing people can do with their money—the best investment a person can make (Luke 12:33-34). James emphasized that true faith must be expressed in one's care for the poor, including widows and orphans who are suffering (Jas 1:27; 2:15-16)—and needy employees as well, for whom God himself is concerned (Jas 5:1-6). Indeed, to accumulate money for oneself without regard to the needs of those less well-off renders a person liable on the day of judgment (Jas 5:3).

The needs of the poor is not one of the more dominant themes in Paul's letters, but his writings do evidence his commitment to raising money for the poverty-stricken Jerusalem church in particular and his encouragement of Christians to give generously to that (15:25-27, 31; 1 Cor 16:1-4; 2 Cor 8–9; Gal 2:10). According to the Pastoral Letters, he also organized care for needy widows in the church (1 Tim 5:3-16) and encouraged Christians to devote themselves to "meeting the urgent needs of others" (Titus 3:14). In addition, Acts records Paul's desire to be a hard-working example of the way Christians can help the poor, remembering the words of Jesus: "It is more blessed to give than to receive" (Acts 20:35). So although Paul's writings do not focus on the needs of the poor per se, he made it clear that God's people are to show their concern by giving to those in need, especially needy Christians. ("We should do good to everyone—especially to those in the family of faith," Gal 6:10.) As in the Johannine writings, the focus of Paul's letters is on the needs of Christ's people especially.

Although Paul was diligent to take care of poor Christians and to support individuals in need, he did not emphasize the larger needs of society as a whole. For him, the broader social needs of the culture are entirely secondary; eternal salvation and the spiritual-moral-relational life of those who belong to Christ are the most important issues. The awareness that the Lord will return soon and that the things of the world are transitory only reinforced his focus on the things that have eternal value. This world, dominated by "the god of this world" (2 Cor 4:4), stands under the judgment of God and will not endure. Thus, Paul says to the Corinthians, "We look not at what can be seen but at what cannot be seen; for what can be seen is temporary, but what cannot be seen is eternal" (2 Cor 4:18, NRSV). Nowhere does he focus on the large-scale social needs of the culture or encourage Christians to become actively involved in transforming the structures of secular society. On the contrary, he seemed to discourage Timothy from becoming too involved in secular issues, reminding him that soldiers of Christ "don't get tied up in the affairs of civilian life" (2 Tim 2:4). However he might assess the problems of modern culture, Paul (were he here) would almost certainly still remind us of the ultimate priority of eternal issues and the urgency of addressing the deepest needs (the spiritual needs) of human beings above all else. For Paul—and for the New Testament writers as a whole—personal salvation and the spiritual-moral-relational life of Christ's people are the issues of supreme importance.

Was It God's Will for Paul to Go to Jerusalem? In any event, Paul asked the Romans to pray for him because going to Jerusalem was risky business. The anti-Christian sentiment was strong, and many people had it in for Paul. Aware of the potential dangers, Paul asked that they pray for his safety so that he might arrive safely in Rome with a joyful heart, ready for the ministry God had for him there. But given the fateful outcome, one might wonder whether it was really God's will for Paul to travel to Jerusalem at all.

Interestingly, although Acts leaves the impression that Paul was convinced that God wanted him to go to Jerusalem (Acts 20:22; cf. Acts 21:13), it also leaves the impression that a number of other Christians were convinced he should not go. Indeed, Luke says it was *through the Holy Spirit* that the believers in Tyre warned Paul not to go to Jerusalem (Acts 21:4; cf. Acts 21:11)—a statement that is especially significant in light of Luke's emphasis on the Spirit as the God-ordained guiding force of the early missionary evangelists. This statement of Luke, together with the fact that Paul was soon arrested in Jerusalem and spent the next four years confined in jail or under house arrest, leaves us wondering whether the apostle misread the will of God. With his independent spirit and strength of will, did he fail to hear what the Spirit was saying to him through his fellow believers? If this is Luke's intended point, his account in Acts also reminds us of the gracious way that God is able to take even the mistakes and misjudgments of his servants and turn them into good for his purposes (Acts 23:11; Rom 8:28)—for in one way or another, Paul gets to Rome. (Note, however, that most commentators assume it is the believers in Tyre who misinterpreted God's will rather than Paul. For discussion of this, see Fernando 1998:551; Larkin 2006:580-583; Wall 2002:289). In any case, here we are reminded that, in the mysterious providence of God, not all prayers get answered in the way we think they should (15:30-32).

Prior to his final greetings, Paul closes this section with a common blessing—the invocation of God's presence and peace upon the Christians to whom he writes (15:33). If our lives are to reflect the glory of the Lord as they ought, we need a strong sense of his presence and peace in all we do.

◆   ## C. Personal Greetings and Final Instructions (16:1-24)

I commend to you our sister Phoebe, who is a deacon in the church in Cenchrea. ²Welcome her in the Lord as one who is worthy of honor among God's people. Help her in whatever she needs, for she has been helpful to many, and especially to me.

³Give my greetings to Priscilla and Aquila, my co-workers in the ministry of Christ Jesus. ⁴In fact, they once risked their lives for me. I am thankful to them, and so are all the Gentile churches. ⁵Also give my greetings to the church that meets in their home.

Greet my dear friend Epenetus. He was the first person from the province of Asia to become a follower of Christ. ⁶Give my greetings to Mary, who has worked so hard for your benefit. ⁷Greet Andronicus and Junia,* my fellow Jews,* who were in prison with me. They are highly respected among the apostles and became followers of Christ before I did. ⁸Greet Ampliatus, my dear friend in the Lord. ⁹Greet Urbanus, our co-worker in Christ, and my dear friend Stachys.

¹⁰Greet Apelles, a good man whom Christ approves. And give my greetings to the believers from the household of Aristobulus. ¹¹Greet Herodion, my fellow Jew.* Greet the Lord's people from the household of Narcissus. ¹²Give my greetings to Tryphena and Tryphosa, the Lord's workers, and to dear Persis, who has worked so hard for the Lord. ¹³Greet Rufus, whom the Lord picked out to be his very own; and also his dear mother, who has been a mother to me.

¹⁴Give my greetings to Asyncritus, Phlegon, Hermes, Patrobas, Hermas, and the brothers and sisters* who meet with them. ¹⁵Give my greetings to Philologus, Julia, Nereus and his sister, and to Olympas and all the believers* who meet with them. ¹⁶Greet each other in Christian love.* All the churches of Christ send you their greetings.

¹⁷And now I make one more appeal, my dear brothers and sisters. Watch out for people who cause divisions and upset people's faith by teaching things contrary to what you have been taught. Stay away from them. ¹⁸Such people are not serving Christ our Lord; they are serving their own personal interests. By smooth talk and glowing words they deceive innocent people. ¹⁹But everyone knows that you are obedient to the Lord. This makes me very happy. I want you to be wise in doing right and to stay innocent of any wrong. ²⁰The God of peace will soon crush Satan under your feet. May the grace of our Lord Jesus* be with you.

²¹Timothy, my fellow worker, sends you his greetings, as do Lucius, Jason, and Sosipater, my fellow Jews.

²²I, Tertius, the one writing this letter for Paul, send my greetings, too, as one of the Lord's followers.

²³Gaius says hello to you. He is my host and also serves as host to the whole church. Erastus, the city treasurer, sends you his greetings, and so does our brother Quartus.*

16:7a *Junia* is a feminine name. Some late manuscripts accent the word so it reads *Junias*, a masculine name; still others read *Julia* (feminine).   **16:7b** Or *compatriots;* also in 16:21.   **16:11** Or *compatriot.*   **16:14** Greek *brothers;* also in 16:17.   **16:15** Greek *all of God's holy people.*   **16:16** Greek *with a sacred kiss.*   **16:20** Some manuscripts read *Lord Jesus Christ.*   **16:23** Some manuscripts add verse 24, *May the grace of our Lord Jesus Christ be with you all. Amen.* Still others add this sentence after verse 27.

NOTES

16:1 *I commend to you our sister Phoebe.* It is possible that Phoebe carried this letter with her when she traveled to Rome.

a deacon in the church. Or, "who serves the church" (TEV). It is not clear whether *diakonon* [ᵀᴳ1249, ᶻᴳ1356] is used here as a general term (i.e., "servant") or as a specific technical term for an office in the church ("deacon," as in Phil 1:1; 1 Tim 3:8, 12; so Cranfield 1981:781; Bruce 1985:252; Dunn 1988b:886-887). First Timothy 3:11 may suggest that women, as well as men, functioned in this office if "the women" are to be understood as deacons.

Cenchrea. One of the two seaports of Corinth, just a few miles away on the eastern (Aegean) side of the isthmus (cf. Acts 18:18). The church there was probably a daughter church of the church in Corinth.

16:2 *Welcome her in the Lord.* The common phrase "in the Lord" (*en kuriō* [TG2962, ZG3261]) is an ambiguous phrase that, in this case, could mean "as a Christian sister" (because of Phoebe's relationship to the Lord), or "as Christian brothers and sisters" (because of the Roman Christians' relationship to the Lord), or "in a Christian way."

as one who is worthy of honor among God's people. Lit., "in a way that is worthy of saints" (*axiōs tōn hagiōn* [TG516/40A, ZG547/41]). The phrase modifies the verb but could be understood as a reference to the saintliness either of Phoebe (cf. NLT) or of the believers in Rome (cf. TEV: "as God's people should"); Moo (1996:915) suggests that Paul may have been thinking of both. It was considered important for believers to extend hospitality to fellow believers visiting or traveling through their area.

Help her in whatever she needs. This presumably includes financial assistance.

she has been helpful to many, and especially to me. Lit., "a helper (*prostatis* [TG4368, ZG4706]) of many, and of me myself." See note on the related term *proistamenos* [TG4291A, ZG4613] in 12:8. Exactly how she helped Paul is not clear, but the term may well suggest hospitality and financial assistance.

16:3 *Priscilla and Aquila.* A Jewish Christian couple, originally expelled from Rome by the edict of Claudius against Jews (in AD 49), whom Paul first met and with whom he stayed in Corinth (as a fellow leatherworker or tentmaker) during his original evangelistic work there. They then relocated in Ephesus, where a church met in their home; later, they returned to Rome. They are mentioned together in Acts 18:2, 18, 26; 1 Cor 16:19; 2 Tim 4:19. The unusual fact that Priscilla's name precedes Aquila's in four of the six instances may imply that she was a Christian before him (and perhaps instrumental in his conversion), or that she was the more active of the two in Christian work, or simply that hers was the dominant personality (cf. Cranfield 1981:784). Paul used the name *Prisca*, while Luke used the more familiar form, *Priscilla*, in Acts.

my co-workers in the ministry of Christ Jesus. Lit., "my fellow-workers in Christ Jesus." The ambiguous phrase "in Christ Jesus" may refer either to Priscilla and Aquila or to their ministry (as in the NLT).

16:4 *they once risked their lives for me.* Though we have no account of the details, this may have happened at a crisis during Paul's difficult, two- or three-year stay in Ephesus (described in Acts 19:1-41); cf. 2 Cor 1:8-9.

16:5 *the church that meets in their home.* The Christians to whom this letter is addressed may, in fact, comprise a number of small house churches (see "Audience" in the Introduction).

the province of Asia. Western Turkey.

16:6 *Mary.* One of seven women named Mary in the NT; there appears to be no other reference to her in the NT.

16:7 *Andronicus and Junia.* In Greek, *Iounian* is frequently taken to be the accusative of Junias (which may be the short form of *Junianus* [TG2458A, ZG2687], a man's name) but is perhaps better taken as the accusative of *Junia* [TG2458, ZG2686] (a woman's name). The name *Junia* occurs often in Gr. writings, but the name *Junias* occurs nowhere else. A few mss (𝔓46 cop^bo, some Old Latin mss) read *Ioulian* [TG2456, ZG2684], the accusative of *Julia.* Junia is probably to be understood as the wife of Andronicus. The names suggest that the two were Hellenistic Jews—that is, native Greek-speaking Jews (see Cranfield 1981:788-789; Dunn 1988b:894-895).

my fellow Jews. A phrase (*sungeneis mou* [TG4773, ZG5150]) also found in 9:3; 16:21; cf. 16:11.

who were in prison with me. Perhaps during Paul's tumultuous two- or three-year ministry in Ephesus. (Cf. 2 Cor 11:23, written shortly after Paul left Ephesus. See note on 16:4.)

highly respected among the apostles. This means either "well known (*episēmoi* [TG1978, ZG2168]) among the apostles" (i.e., highly respected by the apostles; cf. TEV) or (less likely) "outstanding [or prominent] among the apostles," with the implication that Andronicus and his wife Junia (or Junias, if a man) were considered apostles themselves (so NRSV, REB, NAB, NJB, NIV). The term "apostles" (*apostoloi* [TG652, ZG693]) may be understood either in the more limited, early sense (as in "the Twelve") or—more likely—in the wider, later sense of commissioned missionary evangelists (see note on 1:1).

16:8 Ampliatus. Possibly a slave or freedman; a common slave name.

16:9 Urbanus. Possibly a slave or freedman; a common slave name. The fact that he is spoken of as "our co-worker" (instead of "my co-worker") may imply that Paul knew him only by reputation.

Stachys. Nothing is known about this person.

16:10 Apelles, a good man whom Christ approves. Or, "one whose loyalty [faithfulness, commitment] to Christ has been proved" (cf. TEV). Lit., "the approved one in Christ."

the believers from the household of Aristobulus. Lit., "the ones from [the people of] Aristobulus." The fact that Aristobulus himself is not greeted may imply that he was not a Christian or that he was dead; it's possible that he is to be identified as Aristobulus the grandson of Herod the Great and brother of Agrippa I, a friend of the Emperor Claudius; see the following reference to Herodion (Cranfield 1981:791-792).

16:11 Herodion, my fellow Jew. Possibly a slave or freedman who may have served Herod.

the Lord's people from the household of Narcissus. Lit., "the ones from [the people of] Narcissus." The fact that Narcissus himself is not greeted may imply that he was not a Christian or that he was dead; it's possible that he is to be identified with Narcissus, the influential freedman of the Emperor Claudius, who had been forced to commit suicide shortly before Paul wrote this letter (Cranfield 1981:792-793).

16:12 Tryphena and Tryphosa. The names of two women, possibly sisters or twins who were slaves or freedwomen. (Twins were often given names deriving from the same root; Bruce 1985:260.)

the Lord's workers. Those "who work in the Lord's service" (TEV).

dear Persis, who has worked so hard for the Lord. Possibly a slave or freedwoman; a common slave name meaning "Persian woman."

16:13 Rufus. Possibly the same Rufus referred to by Mark as the son of Simon of Cyrene, who carried the cross of Jesus, and the brother of Alexander (Mark 15:21). The fact that Mark alone of the Gospel writers makes mention of Rufus may imply that Rufus was known to the Christians in Italy to whom Mark (according to the earliest tradition, the anti-Marcionite prologue to the Gospel) was writing (see Cranfield 1981:793-794).

whom the Lord picked out to be his very own. Lit., "chosen in [or by] the Lord." Some suggest this implies he was a "choice" or "outstanding" follower of the Lord (REB).

his dear mother, who has been a mother to me. When and where her motherly care for Paul would have been expressed is not clear. If Simon of Cyrene (Rufus's father, according to Mark 15:21) is the same as Simeon "the black man" (Acts 13:1), his wife may have included Paul in their family during Paul's early days in Syrian Antioch (Bruce 1985:261).

16:14 *Asyncritus, Phlegon, Hermes, Patrobas, Hermas.* Nothing is known about these men; *Hermas* was a common slave name.

the brothers and sisters. Gr., *adelphoi* [TG80, ZG81] (brothers). These were fellow members of the same house church.

16:15 *Philologus, Julia, Nereus and his sister.* Julia is probably the wife of Philologus, or his sister. In the Gr. text, the phrase "Philologus and Julia" and the following phrase "Nereus and his sister" are parallel. The latter may have been children of Philologus and Julia.

Olympas. Nothing is known about this person, the only one named of those who met in the same house church with Philologus and Julia, and Nereus and his sister.

16:16 *in Christian love.* Lit., "with a holy kiss" (also in 1 Cor 16:20; 2 Cor 13:12; 1 Thess 5:26); cf. "with a kiss of love" (1 Pet 5:14, NASB). The "kiss of peace," which to this day is a part of the liturgy of the Eastern Orthodox Church, is first mentioned as a regular practice in Christian gatherings in Justin Martyr's *First Apology* 65: "When we have ceased from our prayers, we greet one another with a kiss."

All the churches of Christ send you their greetings. Paul may be thinking especially of the churches represented by those who were about to accompany him to Jerusalem (some of whom are listed in Acts 20:4) with their gift for the poor.

16:17 *I make one more appeal.* Cf. the use of the same word (*parakalō* [TG3870, ZG4151], "I plead," "I urge," "I implore," "I beg") in 12:1; 15:30.

my dear brothers and sisters. Gr., *adelphoi* [TG80, ZG81] (brothers).

people who cause divisions. "Divisions" (*dichostasiai* [TG1370, ZG1496]) are listed among the works of evil that exclude people from the Kingdom of God in Gal 5:19-21. Elsewhere Paul has strong warnings against those who are divisive (14:20-21; 1 Cor 1:10-11; 3:3-4; Titus 3:9-11; cf. 1 Cor 11:17-22; Gal 5:19-21; 1 Tim 6:3-5).

upset people's faith. Or, "lead others astray" (REB). Lit., "do things that cause stumbling (*ta skandala* [TG4625, ZG4998])"—i.e., things that lead others into sin or away from true faith in Christ (cf. 14:13, 20).

by teaching things contrary to what you have been taught. Paul does not specify the teaching or behavior that concerns him, but its substance may be similar to what he criticizes elsewhere (cf. 1 Cor 5:11; 6:9; 10:21; Gal 1:6-9; 5:19-21; Eph 5:3-7; Phil 3:2, 18-19; Col 2:4, 8, 16-23; 1 Thess 4:3-8; 1 Tim 1:19-20; 4:1-3; 6:3-5, 20; 2 Tim 2:14-26; 3:1-9; Titus 1:10-16; 3:9-10).

Stay away from them. Several times Paul instructs Christians not to associate with those in the church who are causing moral or theological problems (1 Cor 5:1-13; 2 Thess 3:6, 14; 2 Tim 3:1-5; Titus 3:9-11). The point is to make both them and the church aware of their sin. In extreme cases, the offending person is to be excluded from the fellowship (1 Cor 5:3, 5; cf. Matt 18:17).

16:18 *they are serving their own personal interests.* Lit., "they are serving their own belly" ("serving . . . their own appetites," TEV; cf. Phil 3:19). Though some understand this as a reference to eating meat when it might offend others (see 14:1-6, 14-23; cf. 1 Cor 8:4-13; 10:14-33), it is probably best taken in a nonliteral sense: to serve one's "belly" is to serve oneself or one's own desires. On a deeper level, such people serve the cause of Satan (2 Cor 11:13-15).

glowing words. Or, "flattery" (NRSV).

16:19 *I want you to be wise in doing right and to stay innocent of any wrong.* This verse is parallel to 1 Cor 14:20: "Be innocent as babies when it comes to evil, but be mature in understanding matters of this kind."

16:20 *The God of peace.* Or, "God, our source of peace" (TEV; see note on 15:33)—in contrast to Satan, the instigator of dissension in the church (cf. 16:17).

will soon crush Satan under your feet. Satan is understood as the instigator of those who teach wrong things (16:17; cf. 2 Cor 11:13-15). The imagery derives from Gen 3:15, where the snake is told, "He will strike your head."

our Lord Jesus. This is the reading of 𝔓46 ℵ B. Some Gr. mss (A C 33 𝔐), followed by the KJV and NKJV, read, "our Lord Jesus Christ"; a few mss (D*vid F G) omit the entire sentence (see "Canonicity and Textual History" in the Introduction).

16:21 *Timothy, my fellow worker.* Timothy was a native of Lystra and a convert of Paul who became Paul's close assistant (Acts 16:1-3). Of him Paul said to the Philippians, "I have no one else like Timothy, who genuinely cares about your welfare. . . . Like a son with his father, he has served with me in preaching the Good News" (Phil 2:20, 22). Compare what is said of him in 1 and 2 Timothy.

Lucius. Probably not to be confused with the one Paul calls "Luke, the . . . doctor," in Col 4:14.

Jason. Perhaps the Jason with whom Paul stayed in Thessalonica (Acts 17:6-9).

Sosipater. Perhaps the Sopater of Berea mentioned in Acts 20:4.

my fellow Jews. This phrase (*sungeneis mou* [TG4773, ZG5150]) is found also in 9:3; 16:7; cf. 16:11.

16:22 *I, Tertius, the one writing this letter for Paul.* Here is evidence that Paul used secretaries to write his letters (see "Author" in the Introduction). In some letters, Paul wrote the final words himself to authenticate the letter (1 Cor 16:21; Col 4:18; 2 Thess 3:17; cf. Gal 6:11; Phlm 1:19).

send my greetings, too, as one of the Lord's followers. Or, "I send my Christian greetings, too." Lit., "I greet you in the Lord." The ambiguous phrase "in the Lord" may be connected either with "the one writing this letter" or with "send my greetings."

16:23 *Gaius.* One of Paul's first converts in Corinth (1 Cor 1:14). If he is to be identified with the Titius Justus who took Paul in when he was first rejected by the synagogue in Corinth (Acts 18:7), his full name would then be Gaius Titius Justus (Bruce 1985:265).

He is my host and also serves as host to the whole church. Paul was staying in his home, and the church met in his home.

Erastus, the city treasurer. This is very possibly the Erastus mentioned in a late first-century stone inscription found at Corinth, which speaks of him as the commissioner of public works. Whether he is to be identified with the Erastus of Acts 19:22 or 2 Tim 4:20 is unclear; the name was a common one (Bruce 1985:266).

16:24 This verse is not included in the NLT (cf. NIV) because it is not found in the earliest Gr. mss (𝔓46 𝔓61 ℵ A B C). In "Western" mss (D F G) the verse is added as, "May the grace of our Lord Jesus Christ be with you all. Amen." The Western text, which omits 16:25-27 (the final doxology), ends here.

COMMENTARY

In this closing section, after asking the Romans to warmly receive Phoebe, a deacon coming to visit them from the church in Cenchrea, Paul sent his greetings to a number of individuals he knew personally in the church in Rome. These personal regards are followed by (1) greetings from several Christians who are working together with Paul or who are key people in the church in Corinth, (2) a final warning to beware of people who cause problems and divisions, and (3) a final word of praise to God, the source of all the blessings proclaimed in the Good News.

The inclusion of such a long list of personal names in a letter addressed to a church Paul had never visited has led some scholars to question whether chapter 16 was really a part of the original letter sent to Rome. Some have suggested that the chapter might be better understood as an attachment to a later copy of the letter addressed to the Christians in Ephesus, where Paul spent more than two years (see "Canonicity and Textual History" in the Introduction).[1] But with the widespread travel that was common in the Roman Empire, it is very possible that a good number of Christians whom Paul had known elsewhere had traveled to the capital city, for a variety of reasons. After Claudius's death in AD 54, his earlier decree expelling the Jews from Rome in AD 49 (cf. Acts 18:2) was relaxed and former residents with Jewish backgrounds who were on the list (like Priscilla and Aquila) could have returned to their homes then. If the greetings were indeed addressed to people in Rome, the omission of Peter's name would seem to imply that Peter was not in Rome at that time.

Paul's Endorsement of Phoebe and Greetings to Christians in Rome. Paul's encouragement of the church to give a warm reception to the visiting Phoebe (who may have carried this letter with her when she traveled to Rome) shows something of the warm bond of Christian love that is to distinguish the Christian fellowship from all others. She is to be welcomed not simply as an ordinary guest, as people of the world would welcome one another, but "in the Lord"—that is, in a way that shows the deep appreciation and respect that Christian people are to feel for one another and the loving, Christlike care that is to characterize all relationships among the people of God. The church is to be the place where God's love is showcased and felt in tangible ways.

From the detailed personal greetings that Paul gives to a number of individuals in the church (16:3-16), we can learn several things. First, life was not easy for the early Christians; there was occasional persecution and imprisonment of those who openly bore witness to Christ (16:4, 7). The shared experience of suffering for Christ would have bound them together as a fellowship of the persecuted.

Second, many Christians—not just the apostles—were considered active workers in the service of the Lord, including a number of women (16:1-3, 6-7, 12-13, 15). Note the way Paul speaks of people as "co-workers" or "the Lord's workers" (16:3, 9, 12) and his special appreciation of those who have "worked so hard" for the Lord and his people (16:6, 12). Exactly what kind of work they did for the Lord (evangelism, ministry, or practical service of others) is often not clear, but it is evident that they took their work for the Lord seriously. The fact that nine of the twenty-six names in this section are names of women shows the important role women played in the ministry of the early church, and Paul's appreciation of their hard work and commitment to the gospel.

Third, many early Christians undertook extensive travel. Though Paul had never been to Rome, he seems to have had a personal acquaintance with many of the people he greeted. How much of the travel was due to business or family interests and how much to persecution or more specifically Christian interests (evangelism and ministry) is not clear.

Fourth, the Christians were probably divided up into a number of smaller groups meeting in people's homes (16:5, 14, 15, 23), perhaps along ethnic lines. These groups would not have centered around a single pastor or priest, as many churches do today, but would have engaged in the mutual sharing of their various gifts, probably according to the pattern of 1 Cor 14:26-33.

Fifth, the early Christians viewed one another as family, and the expression of warmth and closeness was considered important. Paul spoke of Phoebe as "our sister" (16:1), and he called Rufus's mother his own "mother" (16:13). He spoke of several as "dear" to him (16:5, 8-9, 12). Christians are to show their affection for one another with Christian love (16:16). The entire family is to live together as a fellowship of love. It is clear that the warm regard Paul felt for specific believers is determined not by their social status or secular credentials but by the intensity of their love for Christ and by their service to him. Whatever their different backgrounds and ethnicity, it was their devotion to the Savior that united them in the family of Christ. For Paul, there was nothing else ultimately important in life. Jesus Christ makes all other interests and concerns relative—he is the sole reason for living (Phil 1:21). Devotion to Christ is the measure of all else.

One Final Warning. Before ending his letter, Paul felt he had to warn his readers of one specific danger: the threat posed by people who upset others' faith and cause divisions by the wrong things they teach. Though the people Paul had in mind are not precisely identified, it is clear that their smooth and ingratiating words had the potential to mislead the gullible. These deceivers, Paul cautioned, were driven by their own personal interests and agendas, not by a genuine concern for Jesus Christ and the welfare of his church (16:17-18). (The true shepherds of God's people are driven by a selfless concern for the work of the Savior and for his sheep.) It is this problem that Paul seems to have anticipated when he cautioned the elders of the Ephesian church, "So guard yourselves and God's people. Feed and shepherd God's flock. . . . I know that false teachers, like vicious wolves, will come in among you after I leave, not sparing the flock" (Acts 20:28-29).

For Paul, true faith and genuine love are the key elements of the Christian life (1:8) and thus the hallmarks of a healthy Christian community. Those who seek to undermine these cornerstones are to be strictly avoided: "Watch out for people who cause divisions and upset people's faith. . . . Stay away from them" (16:17; cf. his other strong warnings against those who are divisive in 14:20; 1 Cor 1:10; 3:3; Titus 3:9). Christians who seriously seek to be obedient to Christ must learn to be discerning (16:19) and protect themselves from the subtle and persuasive influence of such people; for behind such influence lies the evil one himself, who seeks to destroy the faith and unity of Christ's church. Our protection lies in the power of

God, who will soon destroy Satan, and in the grace and blessing that the Lord Jesus Christ pours out on his people (16:20).

The twin concerns to maintain true faith and Christian unity require a fine balance, for they often appear to pull in opposite directions. Those most concerned to maintain the purity and truth of the Good News are often prone to be divisive. Those who most value the unity of the church, on the other hand, are often prone to compromise the truth of the message in order to avoid discord. Christians must always remember that both truth and unity are important to God. God's people must work hard to preserve the unity of the church, even as they strive to uphold the truth of the Good News. Both faith and love are dear to God, and both are to be held dear by the people of God, too. In the Christian community, faith and love are always married—and "let no one split apart what God has joined together."

Final Greetings. The final greetings were sent by those with Paul at the time of writing. These greetings reflect his practice of working with a team rather than on his own (cf. Acts 20:4). The mention of Tertius as the one who actually penned the letter (16:22) reveals Paul's use of secretaries. (For the implications of such a practice, see "Author" in the Introduction.) The greetings sent from Erastus, the city treasurer of Corinth, suggest that at least some prominent and well-to-do people were among the believing community in Corinth (cf. 1 Cor 1:26).

In many of the Greek manuscripts, the letter is closed—as it began—with the invocation of Christ's grace upon his people (16:20, 24; cf. 1:7; for the manuscript differences, see "Canonicity and Textual History" in the Introduction). Christians live and die by the grace of the Lord Jesus Christ—and that is what this letter is all about.

E N D N O T E S
1. Bruce (1985:253-257) provides further discussion of the names in chapter 16 as they relate to arguments for Ephesus or Rome as destinations for this epistle.

◆   **D. Paul's Closing Words (16:25-27)**

[25]Now all glory to God, who is able to make you strong, just as my Good News says. This message about Jesus Christ has revealed his plan for you Gentiles, a plan kept secret from the beginning of time. [26]But now as the prophets* foretold and as the eternal God has commanded, this message is made known to all Gentiles everywhere, so that they too might believe and obey him. [27]All glory to the only wise God, through Jesus Christ, forever. Amen.

16:26 Greek *the prophetic writings.*

N O T E S
16:25 The closing benediction (16:25-27, a single sentence in Gr.) occurs at different places in the early Gr. mss: after 14:23, after 15:33, after 16:23 (24), or after 14:23 and 16:23 (24). Some mss do not include any benediction. See "Canonicity and Textual History" in the Introduction.

all glory to God. Lit., "to God be the glory" (16:27 in the Gr. text).

This message about Jesus Christ. Lit., "the preaching of Jesus Christ," that is, the message (Good News) about Jesus Christ.

a plan kept secret. Lit., "mystery." The word *mustērion* [TG3466, ZG3696] refers to a long-hidden secret that has now been revealed (see note on 11:25). The substance of the "mystery" varies with the context. Here it is the Good News itself (as in Col 4:3). In 11:25-26, it refers to the final salvation of all Israel—but only when the full number of Gentiles is complete. In Col 1:26-27, it is the presence of the resurrected Christ himself in the believer's life. In Eph 3:3-11, it refers to the inclusion of Gentiles in God's eternal plan of salvation. In each case, however, the term refers to some aspect of God's saving work in Christ.

from the beginning of time. Lit., "for eternal ages" (cf. Eph 3:9; Col 1:26).

16:26 *as the prophets foretold.* Though the prophets predicted the coming of the Good News, many of the details remained hidden as a "mystery." Calvin (1960:328) comments, "Although the prophets had formerly taught all that Christ and the apostles have explained, yet they taught with so much obscurity, when compared with the shining clarity of the light of the Gospel, that we need not be surprised if those things which are now revealed are said to have been hidden."

so that they too might believe and obey him. Lit., "for the obedience of faith" (*eis hupakoēn pisteōs* [TG4102, ZG4411]). This phrase could be understood as a reference either to the obedience that results from faith, or (more likely, in the context of Romans) epexegetically, to the obedience that consists of faith. See note on 1:5.

16:27 *forever.* This reading is supported by 𝔓46 B C 33. Other Gr. mss (𝔓61 ℵ A D) read "forever and ever" (*aiōnas tōn aiōnōn* [TG165, ZG172]).

COMMENTARY

The letter closes with a doxology in which Paul appropriately praises God for the Good News of salvation that has now been revealed to the Gentile world so that people everywhere might believe and obey it. He concludes with the words, "All glory to the only wise God, through Jesus Christ, forever. Amen." For the amazing wonder of the salvation he has given us in Jesus Christ, God deserves the praise of his people forever.

BIBLIOGRAPHY

Achtemeier, Paul
1985 *Romans.* Atlanta: John Knox.

Aus, R. D.
1979 Paul's Travel Plans to Spain and the Full Number of the Gentiles of Rom. XI:25. *Novum Testamentum* 21:232–262.

Barclay, William
1978 *The Letter to the Romans.* Rev. ed. Philadelphia: Westminster.

Barrett, C. K.
1957 *A Commentary on the Epistle to the Romans.* New York: Harper & Row.

Barth, Karl
1933 *The Epistle to the Romans.* Oxford: Oxford University Press.

Baur, F. C.
1873, 1875 *Paul.* 2 vols. London: Williams & Norgate.

Beker, J. C.
1986 The Faithfulness of God and the Priority of Israel in Paul's Letter to the Romans. *Harvard Theological Review* 79.

Best, Ernest
1967 *The Letter of Paul to the Romans.* Cambridge: Cambridge University Press.

Black, Matthew
1973 *Romans.* Greenwood, SC: The Attic Press.

Bray, Gerald, editor
1998 *Ancient Christian Commentary on Scripture: New Testament VI, Romans.* Downers Grove: InterVarsity.

Bruce, F. F.
1977 *Paul: Apostle of the Heart Set Free.* Grand Rapids: Eerdmans.
1985 *The Letter of Paul to the Romans.* 2nd ed. Grand Rapids: Eerdmans.

Brunner, Emil
1959 *The Letter to the Romans.* Philadelphia: Westminster.

Bultmann, Rudolf
1951, 1955 *Theology of the New Testament.* 2 vols. Translator, Kendrick Grobel. New York: Scribners.

Bunyan, John
1962 *Grace Abounding to the Chief of Sinners.* Oxford: Clarendon.

Calvin, John
1960 *The Epistles of Paul the Apostle to the Romans and to the Thessalonians.* Grand Rapids: Eerdmans.

Carson, D. A.
1994 *God's Sovereignty and Human Responsibility: Biblical Perspectives in Tension.* Grand Rapids: Baker.

Comfort, Philip W.
2007 *New Testament Text and Translation Commentary.* Carol Stream, IL: Tyndale House.

Cranfield, C. E. B.
1980 *The Epistle to the Romans, Vol. I: Romans I–VIII.* Corrected ed. Edinburgh: T & T Clark. (Orig. pub. 1975)
1981 *The Epistle to the Romans, Vol. II: Romans IX–XVI.* Corrected ed. Edinburgh: T & T Clark. (Orig. pub. 1979)

Denney, James
1900 St. Paul's Epistle to the Romans. Pp. 555–725 in *The Expositor's Greek Testament,* vol. 2. London: Hodder & Stoughton.

Dodd, C. H.
1932 *The Epistle to the Romans.* London: Collins.

Donfried, Karl P.
1991 *The Romans Debate.* Rev. ed. Peabody, MA: Hendrickson.

Dunn, James D. G.
1988a *Romans 1–8.* Dallas: Word.

1988b *Romans 9–16.* Dallas: Word.

1993 Letter to the Romans. Pp. 838-850 in *Dictionary of Paul and His Letters.* Editors, G. Hawthorne, R. Martin, and D. Reid. Downers Grove: InterVarsity.

1998 *The Theology of Paul the Apostle.* Grand Rapids: Eerdmans.

Edwards, James R.
1992 *Romans.* Peabody, MA: Hendrickson.

Elwell, Walter A.
1993 Election and Predestination. Pp. 225-229 in *Dictionary of Paul and His Letters.* Editors, G. Hawthorne, R. Martin, and D. Reid. Downers Grove: InterVarsity.

Eusebius
1965 *The History of the Church.* Translator, G. A. Williamson. Harmondsworth: Penguin.

Evans, Christopher
1979 *Romans 12:1-2: The True Worship.* Rome: Abbaye de S. Paul h.l.m.

Fee, Gordon D.
1994 *God's Empowering Presence: The Holy Spirit in the Letters of Paul.* Peabody, MA: Hendrickson.

Fernando, Ajith
1998 *Acts.* Grand Rapids: Zondervan.

Fitzmyer, Joseph A.
1993 *Romans.* New York: Doubleday.

Fung, R. Y. K.
1978 The Impotence of the Laws: Toward a Fresh Understanding of Romans 7:14-25. Pp. 34-48 in *Scripture, Tradition, and Interpretation.* Editors, Gasque and La Sor. Grand Rapids: Eerdmans.

Günther, W.
1976 Sebomai. Pp. 91-95 in *The New International Dictionary of New Testament Theology,* vol. 2. Grand Rapids: Zondervan.

Guthrie, Donald
1970 *New Testament Introduction.* Downers Grove: InterVarsity.

Harris, Murray
1992 *Jesus As God.* Grand Rapids: Baker.

Harrison, Everett F.
1976 Romans. Pp. 1-171 in *The Expositor's Bible Commentary,* vol. 10. Grand Rapids: Zondervan.

Hennecke, Edgar
1965 *New Testament Apocrypha.* 2 vols. Philadelphia: Westminster.

Hodge, Charles
1886 *Commentary on the Epistle to the Romans.* Repr. Grand Rapids: Eerdmans.

Howard, George
1992 Faith of Christ. Pp. 758-760 in *The Anchor Bible Dictionary,* vol. 2. New York: Doubleday.

Hunsinger, George
1998 Hellfire and Damnation: Four Ancient and Modern Views. *Scottish Journal of Theology* 51, no. 4:406-434.

Hunter, Archibald M.
1966 *The Gospel According to St Paul.* Rev. ed. Philadelphia: Westminster.

Käsemann, Ernst
1980 *Commentary on Romans.* Grand Rapids: Eerdmans.

Kaylor, R. David
1988 *Paul's Covenant Community: Jew and Gentile in Romans.* Atlanta: John Knox.

Kelly, J. N. D.
1963 *A Commentary on the Pastoral Epistles.* London: Adam & Charles Black.

à Kempis, Thomas
1903 *Of the Imitation of Christ.* Oxford: Oxford University Press.

Knox, John and Gerald R. Cragg
1954 The Epistle to the Romans. Pp. 353-668 in *The Interpreter's Bible*, vol. 9. New York: Abingdon.

Kümmel, Werner Georg
1975 *Introduction to the New Testament*. Nashville: Abingdon.

de Lacey, D. R.
1993 Gentiles. Pp. 335-339 in *Dictionary of Paul and His Letters*. Editors, G. Hawthorne, R. Martin, and D. Reid. Downers Grove: InterVarsity.

Ladd, George Eldon
1974 *A Theology of the New Testament*. Grand Rapids: Eerdmans.

Larkin, William
2006 Acts. Pp. 311-596 in *Cornerstone Biblical Commentary*, vol. 12. Carol Stream: Tyndale House.

Leenhardt, F. J.
1961 *The Epistle to the Romans*. London: Lutterworth.

Louw, Johannes P. and Eugene A. Nida
1989 *Greek-English Lexicon of the New Testament Based on Semantic Domains*. 2 vols. 2nd ed. New York: United Bible Societies.

Luther, Martin
1954 *Commentary on the Epistle to the Romans*. Grand Rapids: Zondervan.

1960 *Luther's Works*, vol. 34. Philadelphia: Muhlenberg.

Metzger, Bruce M.
1971 *A Textual Commentary on the Greek New Testament*. London: United Bible Societies.

Minear, Paul S.
1971 *The Obedience of Faith*. London: SCM.

Mitton, C. L.
1953–1954 Romans 7 Reconsidered. *Expository Times* 65:78-81, 99-103, 132-135.

Moffatt, James
1935 *The Bible. A New Translation*. New York: Harper & Row.

Mohrlang, Roger
1984 *Matthew and Paul: A Comparison of Ethical Perspectives*. Society for New Testament Studies Monograph Series 48. Cambridge: Cambridge University Press.

1993 Love. Pp. 575-578 in *Dictionary of Paul and His Letters*. Editors, G. Hawthorne, R. Martin, and D. Reid. Downers Grove: InterVarsity.

2003 Paul. Pp. 679-688 in *Jesus in History, Thought, and Culture: An Encyclopedia*. 2 vols. Editors, J. L. Houlden and Leslie Houlden. Paperback ed. Oxford: ABC-CLIO.

2005 *Jesus: The Complete Guide*. New York: Continuum.

Moo, Douglas J.
1996 *The Epistle to the Romans*. Grand Rapids: Eerdmans.

Morris, Leon
1988 *The Epistle to the Romans*. Grand Rapids: Eerdmans.

1993a Salvation. Pp. 858-862 in *Dictionary of Paul and His Letters*. Editors, G. Hawthorne, R. Martin, and D. Reid. Downers Grove: InterVarsity.

1993b Sin, Guilt. Pp. 877-881 in *Dictionary of Paul and His Letters*. Editors, G. Hawthorne, R. Martin, and D. Reid. Downers Grove: InterVarsity.

Mott, S. C.
1993 Ethics. Pp. 269-275 in *Dictionary of Paul and His Letters*. Editors, G. Hawthorne, R. Martin, and D. Reid. Downers Grove: InterVarsity.

Mounce, Robert H.
1981 *Themes from Romans*. Ventura: Regal Books.

1995 *Romans*. Nashville: Broadman & Holman.

Munck, J.
1967 *Christ and Israel: An Interpretation of Romans 9–11*. Philadelphia: Fortress.

Murray, John
1965 *The Epistle to the Romans*. 2 vols. Grand Rapids: Eerdmans.

Newman, Barclay M. and Eugene A. Nida
1973 *A Translator's Handbook on Paul's Letter to the Romans.* New York: United Bible Societies.

Nygren, Anders
1949 *Commentary on Romans.* Philadelphia: Fortress.

O'Neill, J. C.
1975 *Paul's Letter to the Romans.* Harmondsworth: Penguin.

Paige, T.
1993 Holy Spirit. Pp. 404-413 in *Dictionary of Paul and His Letters.* Editors, G. Hawthorne, R. Martin, and D. Reid. Downers Grove: InterVarsity.

Radice, Betty, editor
1968 *Early Christian Writings: The Apostolic Fathers.* Harmondsworth: Penguin.

Räisänen, H.
1983 *Paul and the Law.* Tübingen: J. C. B. Mohr.

Rhys, H.
1961 *The Epistle to the Romans.* New York: Macmillan.

Robinson, John A. T.
1979 *Wrestling with Romans.* Philadelphia: Westminster.

Rupprecht, A. A.
1993 Slave, Slavery. Pp. 881-883 in *Dictionary of Paul and His Letters.* Editors, G. Hawthorne, R. Martin, and D. Reid. Downers Grove: InterVarsity.

Sanday, William and Arthur C. Headlam
1902 *A Critical and Exegetical Commentary on the Epistle to the Romans.* 7th ed. New York: Charles Scribner's Sons.

Sanders, E. P.
1977 *Paul and Palestinian Judaism.* London: SCM.
1983 *Paul, the Law, and the Jewish People.* Philadelphia: Fortress.

Schlatter, Adolf
1995 *Romans: The Righteousness of God.* Peabody, MA: Hendrickson.

Schnelle, Udo
2005 *Apostle Paul: His Life and Theology.* Grand Rapids: Baker Academic.

Schreiner, Thomas
1986 Proselyte. Pp. 1005-1011 in *International Standard Bible Encyclopedia,* vol. 3. Grand Rapids: Eerdmans.
1998 *Romans.* Grand Rapids: Baker.
2001 *Paul: Apostle of God's Glory in Christ.* Downers Grove: InterVarsity.

Scott, E. F.
1947 *Paul's Epistle to the Romans.* London: SCM.

Sherwin-White, A. N.
1963 *Roman Society and Roman Law in the New Testament.* Oxford: Oxford University Press.

Shulam, Joseph and Hillary Le Cornu
1997 *A Commentary on the Jewish Roots of Romans.* Baltimore: Lederer.

Stewart, James S.
1954 *A Man in Christ.* New York: Harper & Brothers.

Stott, John R. W.
1994 *Romans: God's Good News for the World.* Downers Grove: InterVarsity.

Stuhlmacher, Peter
1994 *Paul's Letter to the Romans: A Commentary.* Louisville: Westminster.

Thielman, F.
1993 Law. Pp. 529-542 in *Dictionary of Paul and His Letters.* Editors, G. Hawthorne, R. Martin, and D. Reid. Downers Grove: InterVarsity.

Thomas à Kempis
See à Kempis, Thomas.

Thomas, W. H. Griffith
1946 *Commentary on Romans.* Grand Rapids: Eerdmans.

Travis, S. H.
1993 Judgment. Pp. 516-517 in *Dictionary of Paul and His Letters.* Editors, G. Hawthorne, R. Martin, and D. Reid. Downers Grove: InterVarsity.

Vermes, G.
1975 *The Dead Sea Scrolls in English.* 2nd ed. Harmondsworth: Penguin.

Wall, Robert
2002 The Acts of the Apostles. Pp. 1-391 in *The New Interpreter's Bible,* vol. 10. Nashville: Abingdon.

Watson, D. F.
1993 Diatribe. Pp. 213-214 in *Dictionary of Paul and His Letters.* Editors, G. Hawthorne, R. Martin, and D. Reid. Downers Grove: InterVarsity.

Wedderburn, A. J. M.
1988 *The Reasons for Romans.* Edinburgh: T & T Clark.

Wenham, David.
1995 *Paul: Follower of Jesus or Founder of Christianity?* Grand Rapids: Eerdmans.

Wesley, John
1879 *The Journal of the Rev. John Wesley, A.M.,* 4 vols. London: Wesleyan Conference Office.

Williams, Charles B.
1952 *The New Testament. A Translation in the Language of the People.* Chicago: Moody.

Wright, D. F.
1993 Homosexuality. Pp. 413-415 in *Dictionary of Paul and His Letters.* Editors, G. Hawthorne, R. Martin, and D. Reid. Downers Grove: InterVarsity.

Wright, N. T.
2002 The Letter to the Romans. Pp. 393-770 in *The New Interpreter's Bible.* Nashville: Abingdon.

Yinger, Kent L.
1999 *Paul, Judaism, and Judgment according to Deeds.* Society for New Testament Studies Monograph Series 105. Cambridge: Cambridge University Press.

Ziesler, John
1989 *Paul's Letter to the Romans.* London: SCM.

Galatians

GERALD L. BORCHERT

INTRODUCTION TO
Galatians

SEVERAL DECADES AGO, I taught New Testament at a college in Jerusalem. During those years, I often visited the Temple Mount and the Western Wall, walking the busy streets and browsing in bookstores. During that time, I had an experience that carried my thoughts back almost two millennia to the time when the Apostle Paul wrote his letter to the Galatians. In a certain bookstore, I picked up a book of ancient Jewish prayers, and as I was thumbing through it, a particular prayer caught my attention:

> *Blessed art thou, Lord our God, King of the Universe,*
> *Who hast not made me a Gentile.*
> *Who hast not made me a slave.*
> *Who hast not made me a woman.*

A footnote then added what women should pray for the last line:

> *Who hast made me according to thy will.* (Birnbaum n.d.:15-18)

I had two immediate reactions. One was to feel sorry for women who had to thank God for status as second-class citizens. The other was to realize that the prayer was in the same order as Paul's reversal of discrimination, stated in Galatians 3:28: "There is no longer Jew or Gentile, slave or free, male and female. For you are all one in Christ Jesus."

Leaving that bookstore, I walked to the Western Wall and put on my yarmulke. I went into the place under the arch where the men were praying and the women were not permitted, and I began to ponder these two realizations. Thereafter, I returned to my office and read Galatians again. It seemed like a very different book than the one I had read before. As I read, many memories flooded my mind— memories of classes in which I had studied Galatians but not fully understood why Paul was so vehement in his reaction to the Judaizers, memories of attending a synagogue where the women were only allowed to sit in the balcony while the men welcomed me to sit with them and even asked for my opinion on prospective rabbis that they were interviewing.

Something revolutionary happened to me at that time. Living in Israel, among all the restrictions of the Jews, I discovered liberty in Christ. I experienced an undeniable affinity with Paul, who became one of my foremost teachers.

Since then, Galatians has been one of my favorite books of the Bible, and I can easily understand why Luther named it his "Katerina" after his beloved wife,

Katerina von Bora (Luther 1955–1975:40.2). It is a believer's *Magna Carta* of Christian liberty (Borchert 1994:145). Accordingly, I welcome you to the adventurous study of Paul's first epistle, which argues the centrality of the gospel and its message of faith and freedom in Christ with powerful clarity.

AUTHOR

Although scholars differ on many points in interpreting Galatians, there has been an almost complete consensus that if the Apostle Paul wrote any epistle, he must have written Galatians. Even F. C. Baur (the nineteenth-century founder of the Tübingen Hypothesis, which posited that many of the Pauline epistles were pseudonymous) constructed his thesis about the early church on the basis that Paul must have written Galatians, Romans, and the two Corinthian letters (Baur 1875:1.246).

Paul's authorship does not necessarily mean that Paul actually penned the document, because his pattern was apparently to dictate his ideas to an amanuensis or secretary (cf. Rom 16:22, where Tertius identifies himself as Paul's scribe). This practice was common, as indicated by its occurrence in thousands of documentary Greek papyri (see Longenecker 1974; 1990:lix). An amanuensis could be strictly a penman (like Tertius) or could be given some latitude in suggesting the form or content of the letter.[1]

At the end of a letter, the person who was dictating material would usually add a few words in his own handwriting so that the recipient would recognize that the letter was truly from the person who claimed to be writing. Paul also followed this way of authenticating his letters (2 Thess 3:17; cf. also 1 Cor 16:21; Col 4:18; Phlm 1:19). This practice is clearly seen in Galatians: in concluding his letter, Paul stopped dictating, took up the quill himself, and added in his own "large letters" (see commentary at 6:11), a firm authentication of his harsh censure upon the Judaizing false teachers who were leading his Galatian children into error (6:12-13). As a result of this personal addition, none of the Galatian deviants could claim that the stinging words in this epistle had not originated with Paul.

The name of Paul's amanuensis for Galatians is not given. While some of these secretaries were given a degree of freedom to fill out the particulars in customary acknowledgements, orders, letters of condolence, and so on, it is unlikely to have been the case in emotionally packed and tersely formulated documents such as Galatians. The book vibrates with energy and displays amazing rhetorical skill. It must have come from the mind of an incredibly gifted person who was completely conversant in both Jewish and Hellenistic styles of argument. These qualities suggest that Paul had a very direct role in forming the structure and content of the entire letter.

DATE, OCCASION OF WRITING, AND AUDIENCE

While the authorship of Galatians raises few questions, other matters of introduction are not so easily treated, and some of these issues remain extremely controversial. One of the foremost of the debated points involves the timing of Paul's visits to

Jerusalem (cf. 1:17-18; 2:1-2) as they correspond to the journeys of Paul recorded in Acts. Most particularly, scholars debate whether Galatians was written before or after the Jerusalem Council (c. AD 50; Acts 15:1-35). Scholars have also wondered whether the recipients of this epistle were living in northern Galatia or in southern Galatia. The two positions are known, sensibly enough, as the "Northern Galatia Theory" and the "Southern Galatia Theory."

Until the twentieth century, it was commonly believed that Paul must have made a trip into the mountainous regions of north central Asia Minor where the ethnic Galatians lived (the Northern Galatia Theory). Although such a trip is not recorded in Acts, it was forcefully argued that Paul, under inspiration, would not have misidentified his intended recipients, wrongly referring to Iconians and Phrygians as Galatians. In the decade prior to the twentieth century, however, William Ramsay began his journeys and research into the areas of Paul's travels, which at that time were little known, at least to Westerners. Although Ramsay began as a disciple of Baur (who questioned the historical accuracy of Acts), Ramsay ultimately concluded that Baur had erred and that Acts was a trustworthy guide to the geography of the area. He found that the term "Galatia" was sometimes used for the residents of the Roman province of Galatia, which included Iconium, Lystra, and Derbe—regions that Paul passed through on his first missionary journey (Acts 14). Accordingly, there was little need to posit an unknown visit to the ethnic Galatians of the north in order to make the name "Galatians" satisfactory for this epistle. Many modern scholars now affirm the Southern Galatia Theory—they consider that Paul wrote to the churches in southern Galatia some time after his first missionary journey, which probably occurred no later than AD 45–47.

The remaining question is when exactly Paul wrote this letter, especially in correlation to the events of Acts 15 (which are dated AD 50). If the Jerusalem Council took place prior to Paul's letter to the Galatians, Paul certainly would have cited the council's declarations of liberty for the Gentile believers. Because Paul makes no mention of the council, some scholars believe that Galatians was written prior to AD 50.

Granted this assumption, the next task is to line up Paul's mention of a visit to Jerusalem (2:1-10) with one of the five Jerusalem visits reported by Luke in the book of Acts. The five Luke records are: (1) after his conversion (Acts 9:26; cf. Acts 21:17-18), (2) to bring relief to the church in Jerusalem from the church in Antioch (Acts 11:27-30), (3) for the Jerusalem Council (Acts 15:1-29), (4) when Paul "went up" (the usual designation for going to Jerusalem; Acts 18:22), and (5) at his final visit and arrest (Acts 21:15-30). By contrast, Paul records only three visits—the two mentioned in Galatians (1:18-21; 2:1-5) and the so-called contribution visit (Rom 15:25-28; 1 Cor 16:1-4; cf. 2 Cor 1:16), which could be identical with his final visit.[2] The crucial issue for our purposes is to determine how the early visits recorded in Galatians and the ones in Acts are related.

From my understanding of these texts, the most helpful way to resolve the discrepancies is to order the sequence of events as follows:

1. Jesus was crucified sometime between AD 26–30, inasmuch as his ministry
   began at about age 30 (Luke 3:23), and Herod the Great, who was alive at the
   time of Jesus' birth (Matt 2:1), died in 4 BC. Dionysius Exiguus, who established the Christian calendar (c. AD 525), miscalculated the years related to
   the Roman calendar.
2. Paul was probably converted on the Damascus Road within two or three years
   after Jesus' death (Acts 9:1-19a).
3. Paul testified about Jesus in Damascus (Acts 9:19b-22) and thereafter went into
   Arabia for a three-year period before returning to Damascus (Gal 1:16-17).
4. After those three years, Paul went to Jerusalem for a 15-day period (1:18), probably sometime between AD 30 and 33, depending on the death of Jesus. The followers of Jesus there were fearful of him (Acts 9:26), but Barnabas convinced
   them that Paul's bold witness was authentic. At this time, Paul would have met
   with Cephas (Peter) and James before being hurried off to Caesarea and Tarsus
   to avoid confrontation with the Jewish authorities (1:18-20; Acts 9:26-29).
5. Then, Paul spent 11 or 14 years in ministry (depending on whether the three
   years in Arabia of Gal 1:18 are part of the 14 years counted from his conversion
   in Gal 2:1 or are prior to the 14 years). This period of ministry possibly lasted
   until about AD 44. "Syria" and "Cilicia" (1:21) were regional names; the first was
   the area around Antioch, and the second could have included any place in Western Asia Minor or Tarsus and probably included the locations of the first missionary journey.
6. Thereafter, Paul apparently went to Jerusalem again privately with Barnabas and
   Titus. Paul claimed that God had revealed that he should make this trip and that
   it was not forced upon him (2:1-2, 6) by some need for counsel. At that time,
   circumcision does not seem to have been a burning issue because there was apparently no compelling argument that Titus needed to be circumcised (2:3).
   That issue, however, did become important later (2:11-16). Luke apparently did
   not discuss this segment of Paul's life in Acts because he was only highlighting
   what he saw as the strategic points in Paul's ministry.

With what visit in Acts, then, does the visit mentioned in Galatians 2:1-3 best correlate? Calvin and many other scholars have thought it coincided with the visit of Acts
15 (the Jerusalem Council), but there are problems with this view. First, the visit in
Galatians 2:1 was only Paul's second visit (probably c. AD 47), whereas the Jerusalem Council (Acts 15:1-29) was his third visit (AD 49–50). Second, Barnabas was
clearly regarded as a member of the missionary team in Galatians 2:1, just as he was
in the second visit of Acts 11:27-30. He is even mentioned first in this second Acts
reference. Paul and Barnabas did not separate until the second journey, when they
were to carry the council's decision to Syria and Asia Minor. It was precisely at this
time that Silas, who was to report the decision, actually became Paul's partner rather
than Barnabas (Acts 15:22, 37-40). It seems clear, then, that Galatians 2:1-3 corre-
lates with Acts 11:27-30 and not with Acts 15 and the Jerusalem Council.

Thus, it seems that the Epistle to the Galatians was written after Paul's second visit and probably soon after Paul's confrontation with Peter at Antioch (2:11-16) but before the Jerusalem Council (Acts 15:1-29), when a kind of peaceful coexistence was finally agreed upon between Paul and his Gentile converts on the one hand and the Jerusalem leaders and their Jewish converts on the other.

Assuming that the foregoing analysis is correct, Galatians is logically the earliest of Paul's letters, preceding the Thessalonian epistles by three or four years.[3] Galatians was probably written in the late 40s AD, prior to the exclusion of the Jews from Rome in AD 49 by Emperor Claudius. That event is noted both in Acts 18:2 and in Suetonius's *Claudius* 25.4 (see Bettenson 1963:3).[4]

CANONICITY AND TEXTUAL HISTORY

The Epistle to the Galatians has long been considered one of Paul's major epistles and, as such, has been included as part of the New Testament canon since about the end of the first century or beginning of the second century AD. For example, 𝔓46, dated to the second century, is a codex that includes Romans, 1 Corinthians, 2 Corinthians, and Galatians. Galatians is the third epistle in this collection.

The few minor issues of concern in the Greek text of Galatians will be discussed at the appropriate points in the commentary. Bruce Metzger offers only a few pages of comment on the text of Galatians in his detailed textual analysis of the New Testament (1971:589-599). The Greek critical texts, the Nestle-Aland 27th edition of *Novum Testamentum* and the United Bible Societies' fourth edition of the *Greek New Testament*, are quite reliable. The idea that Galatians is a compilation of other documents (which was once proposed) has virtually been abandoned, as Kümmel cogently states (1984:304).

LITERARY STYLE

As a former lawyer, I often compare Galatians to a legal brief in which Paul clearly expressed his frustration with the "foolish Galatians" (3:1). They had fallen for the skewed logic of legalistic teachers who were probably threatened by Jewish zealots or nationalists and had therefore resorted to a "circumcision drive" to prove their faithfulness to Jewish teaching. In so doing, they perverted the Christian gospel and emptied the grace of Christ of its meaning (1:6-7). In this epistle, Paul used the patterns of Greek rhetoric to develop a series of arguments focusing on the great principle of freedom in Christ (5:1) and on God's acceptance of all people through their faith in Christ—whether Jew or Gentile, slave or free, male or female (3:28). Paul believed that Christ's coming marked a new era; he firmly advocated to his straying followers that the era of the law had passed (3:24-25) and that, in the gift of the Spirit, all persons could call God their Father and inherit God's promise to Abraham (3:29; 4:6-7). These Judaizing teachers were totally wrong in trying to make Gentiles into Jews.

The process of composing this theological brief undoubtedly prepared Paul for the later Council of Jerusalem, where the gauntlet was thrown down by Judaizers there who argued that apart from circumcision, no one could be saved (Acts 15:1, 5).

Paul's opponents probably did not realize that the former rabbinic scholar turned Christian (1:13-15) was ready for their arguments. Peter's responses in that council—to the effect that the Holy Spirit made no distinction between Jew and Gentile and that even Jews were unable to keep the yoke of the law and had to be saved by grace (Acts 15:8-11)—were clearly echoes of Paul's basic arguments in Galatians (cf. 2:14-15; 3:28). The Jerusalem Council and its resulting accord, though not accepted by all, is both a model for conflict resolution among Christians (Acts 15:16-19) and an indelible memorial to the wisdom and insight of the man who wrote the incredible argument called Galatians.

H. D. Betz (1979:44-46, 113-114, 128-130, 253-254) makes an intriguing analysis of how Galatians (especially in the first two chapters, beginning with 1:6) can be understood in terms of the elements of classical rhetoric. Galatians 1:6-11 appears to be a classical *exordium*, or a statement of cause. A *narratio*, or statement of facts, follows in 1:12–2:14, and 2:15-21 is the *propositio*, the summary proposition or thesis being argued. Perhaps less convincingly, Betz likens 3:1–4:31 to the *probatio*—the proofs, or arguments, supporting the thesis, and he takes 5:1–6:10 to be the *exhortatio*—the rhetorical exhortations or emotive implications that might accompany the argument. While Betz, in a manner reminiscent of Bultmann's early thesis on the Cynic and Stoic diatribe (1910), no doubt presses the rhetorical model too far, these studies do establish that Paul was a learned writer who used both Hellenistic and rabbinic patterns of argument. Paul was skilled in using the methods of the Jewish and Gentile intelligentsia, but he was not bound by them. The content and form of his message were determined by his purpose.

MAJOR THEOLOGICAL THEMES

Galatians revolves around the issue of gaining acceptance or status with God. More precisely, the question is about how one gains such acceptability. Does a person work for it, or is acceptance a gift? If it is a gift, what is its relationship to responsible, moral living? Should such living flow naturally as an outcome of the gift? The difference between what is acquired by human effort and what is a gift from God is basic to Paul's understanding of the nature of authentic Christian freedom, authentic Christianity, and even the gospel message itself.

God's existence was not the question for Paul or the Galatians that it might be for contemporary skeptics. Humans were assumed to be accountable to God for how they lived, and such accountability is assumed in this letter. The way in which one is answerable, however, was the issue at hand.

Paul's concerns for the Galatians can be summarized in three broad thematic topics or theological themes: the law and circumcision, Christ and the gospel of salvation, and new life in the Holy Spirit. These themes or topics are not isolated concerns; they are intimately related, and when combined, they form an amazingly holistic message. Moreover, there is a natural progression to these themes that moves our thinking through the transformation process from self-centeredness to wholeness of life in Christ.

The Law and Circumcision. As a former Jewish leader, Paul understood very well the importance of obedience to the law. The Hebrew term *halakha* (see the commentary at 5:14 and 5:16), which defines the legal prescriptions to be obeyed by observant Jews, is derived from the idea of a person's "walk" (cf. Heb. *halak* [TH1979/1980, ZH2142/2143]). In becoming a Christian, Paul was forcefully confronted by Christ with the radical difference between having a relationship with God as a person and trying to do God's will as defined by rules, rites, and traditions, such as circumcision. Walking with God was far different for Paul than just obeying rules.

Paul sternly rejected the idea of following the "works of the law" as a self-oriented and slavish attempt to gain credit with God (4:8-11, 21-31). Acceptance by God does not come from obedience to the law or by performing an external rite such as circumcision. The Galatians wrongly thought that they could add these factors to faith in Christ as marks of superior Christian status. In his response to this idea, Paul used four specific arguments, or proofs, in Galatians 3:1-18 to clarify why reliance on the law was doomed to failure. His arguments were based on experience, the biblical example of Abraham, the scriptural category of curse, and an analogy developed out of the biblical understanding of covenant promise.

By arguing in this manner, Paul was not denying the historical value of the law in the development of Israel's faith. He circumscribed or limited its role, however, to a preparatory function that directed persons to their need for Christ (3:23-24). In other words, law is useful in pointing out human inadequacy, but it is not God's ultimate answer to such inadequacy. Therefore, according to Paul, for a person to choose the way of law and circumcision as a mark of status with God was to misunderstand God's intention in salvation, to pervert the gospel, and to reject the grace of God's free gift in Christ (1:6-7).

In Paul's mind, anyone who advocated such a perversion of the gospel should be cursed and condemned. He spared no one in this analysis—not an angel from heaven (1:8-9), nor other Christian leaders such as Cephas (Peter) and Barnabas (2:11-13), and not even himself (1:8), should he turn from the gospel that he first presented to them. Accordingly, he spoke strongly when he scolded the foolish Galatians (even figuratively suggesting they were under a spell; 3:1-3) for having abandoned the truth of the gospel. Moreover, he did not hesitate to recommend that the false teachers who proclaimed the virtues of circumcision should carry their "cutting" to the point of castrating themselves (5:12).

Law and circumcision were not, however, to be identified with sin, as Paul firmly stated later in Romans 7:7—the law faithfully served its God-ordained purpose. For the Galatians, however, Paul had to establish that one cannot rely on works of the law or on the marks of circumcision to gain status with God. Acceptance with God is not a matter of human achievement but comes in an entirely different way. That way is the focus of the next theological theme.

Christ and the Gospel of Salvation. If, as Paul argued, the means of acceptance with God was not reliance on the works required by the law or on circumcision, then it was Paul's duty to spell out the basis for genuine acceptance with God. The basis he presents is God's own provision for acceptance through Christ. Christ's sacrificial death (1:4; 3:13) and his powerful resurrection (1:1) are at the core of Paul's theology. So central is Christ's role in Paul's thinking that one could easily sum up his theology in terms of being "in Christ" (e.g., 2:16, 17; 3:14, 22, 26). He viewed himself as having been "crucified with Christ" and recognized that Christ was living in him (2:19-20).

Paul firmly believed that Christ Jesus was the unique, divine Son of God, specifically sent from God in God's time, yet born fully human and in full conformity to the biblical expectations for the coming Messiah (4:4). As Paul stated, God's purpose for sending the Son was to liberate and redeem the people of the world. They were slaves to the various powers of the world—powers to which people give their allegiance, even though these powers are not divine (4:3, 8-9). The death and resurrection of Christ allows all humans—regardless of their race, status, or sex (3:28)—to be adopted into the family of God (4:5) and to call God their Father (4:6).

Paul identified this adoption process by the technical term "justification," which means being "made right with God," or being "reckoned as acceptable to God" (2:16-17). This idea of justification has been the subject of considerable debate in the history of scholarship from Luther to the present time in terms of what God really did in Christ's "atoning" for our sins. Did Christ actually make us righteous before God or merely declare us righteous? What actually changed for us as the result of Christ's death and resurrection? However we choose to define the status of our new life in Christ, the answer must recognize the effective change that has resulted from Christ's work for us as well as the continuing nature of our human frailty. Paul addressed this twofold reality, providing both teaching on Christ's atoning work and instructions for authentic Christian living in the concluding segments of this epistle (5:1–6:10).

Adoption or acceptance by God is not achieved through human goodness but by having faith in Jesus Christ and in what he did for us (2:16). What Jesus did for us was motivated by God's mercy, grace, and love (1:6; 2:21; 5:4). Christ's gracious work is thus to be understood as a righteous replacement for our sinfulness (1:4; 2:16-17). "Faith" describes our personal response when we hear and receive the proclamation of this unique work of Christ for us (3:2, 11, 22). Our response of faith to the work of Christ is the basis for the forgiveness of our sins, our abandonment of the ways of the world, and our victory over the powers of evil (1:4; 3:10-14, 22; 4:3, 8-11). It is the beginning of a new way of life—life in the Holy Spirit.

New Life in the Holy Spirit. For Paul, salvation was not just a technical "beginning" with Christ, like an isolated initiation into the divine. He knew that much more was expected—and that salvation entailed an ongoing transformation of life with Christ and within a Christian community. His longing was that those who had found freedom in Christ would abandon the pseudo life patterns associated with external status-seeking and, among the Galatians, represented by the works of the law. Instead, they should adopt a new pattern of walking with the Spirit (5:16). A return to the old bondage of legalistic prescriptions, such as those that separated Jews from Gentiles, was totally unacceptable. Paul forcefully condemned such behavior because those old ways had been torn down by the crucifixion of Christ (2:18). Christians were now to live the "crucified" way (2:20) so that they would not negate the death of Christ (2:19-21; 5:2-4).

To live the crucified way means for Christians to live in the world but not participate in the ungodly ways of the world. Christians are freed to live for Christ (5:1) and to conduct their lives (or "walk") according to the directions of the Spirit (5:16). In chapters 5–6, Paul makes it clear that freedom in the Spirit is not license to follow the ways of the world (5:13). Accordingly, Christians are in fact part of two worlds, or two realities. They do not live in a completely protected environment and therefore Paul summons them to reject the transient, confused, and hostile ways of the world and to commit themselves to hope in the coming era of righteousness (5:5).

Paul was convinced that this hope in the coming era would provide the framework for following the transformed life of the Spirit and not for returning to the old way like the Galatians were doing (5:7-10). The presence of the Spirit in the Christian, Paul elsewhere asserted, is God's "guarantee" of hope, or the "first installment" of what is yet to come (2 Cor 1:22; 5:5; cf. Eph 1:14).

Accordingly, he spelled out the contrast of these two orientations, or ways of living, by a vivid differentiation not totally unfamiliar to either the Hellenistic world or to the twenty-first century. Paul illustrated the "works of the flesh" by referring to 15 tragic vices in humans (5:19-21); at the same time, he illustrated the "fruit of the Spirit" (or the results of being led by the Spirit) with nine godlike virtues which were in harmony with God's will (5:22-23). Paul's obvious purpose in making this radical distinction was to make it clear to his deviating converts that being identified with Christ's crucifixion meant putting the old way of life to death.

Having set out the parameters of these two diverse ways of living, Paul provided the Galatians with brief exemplary statements of what it should mean for a person to walk by the Spirit. They should show love for others in society, especially to those of the Christian community (5:25–6:10).

THEOLOGICAL CONCERNS

The letter to the Galatians has historically been a foundational building block in the Christian theology of salvation. Accordingly, it provides a refreshing interpretive journey for the people of God, with some intriguing exercises along the way. In dealing with the fine points of the book, readers may scratch their heads as they try to understand Paul's logic in his allegory about Hagar and Sarah as depicting two different Jerusalems (4:21-31). They may be shocked at Paul's blunt declaration that his opponents should castrate themselves (5:12) or at his demand that they quit troubling him because he carried in his body the scars of having suffered for Jesus (6:17).

These and other vivid expressions enhance the forcefulness of the letter and help readers to realize that Paul was locked in what he regarded as a life-and-death struggle for the fundamentals of the Christian gospel. It should be patently obvious to every reader of Galatians that Paul was totally unwilling to capitulate to those who wanted to maintain adherence to the formal laws of Moses as the basis for Christianity. He courageously took this stand despite the fact that it would at times bring him into conflict with the earliest disciples of Jesus (such as Peter; 2:11; cf. also James and John; 2:9), his own colleagues (such as Barnabas; 2:13), and even, possibly, an angel from heaven (1:8)! To say that Paul was convinced that he had the correct understanding of the gospel would be a magnificent understatement—he was willing to be anathematized (totally cursed) if he were found to have altered the message of the gospel (1:8).

This epistle, then, is not just about theological ideas. It is about each Christian's life of commitment to their ongoing salvation. It is about how Christ, through the Spirit of God, can transform human life into a great journey of responsible freedom. It is about a life of self-giving service (6:1-10) that far supersedes rigid obedience to law or tradition (5:13-14). Internalizing the significance of Paul's thunderous message to the Galatians should be a life-changing event—may it be so! (This last expression captures the meaning of "Amen"—the last word of the epistle.)

OUTLINE

ENDNOTES

1. Though it has been subject to debate among scholars, I suggest that Ephesians is a letter of this type, in which the amanuensis had some influence on content. In particular, it seems to evidence some Lucan patterns of writing. To mention only a couple examples, it has the idea of a dividing wall between Jews and Gentiles drawn from the Temple imagery that is so important to Luke (cf. Eph 2:14), and it contains the only mention in the New Testament of being "filled with the Holy Spirit" outside of Luke and Acts (Eph 5:18).

2. This apparent discrepancy between Paul and Luke has prompted some scholars to think that Acts is chronologically unreliable (Haenchen 1971:400-439; Funk 1956:130-136; Beare 1943:295-306). While space and the focus of this commentary do not permit discussion of these views, it is clear that Baur's ghost has not yet vanished (cf. Baur 1875). The works of Hemer (1977:81-88; 1989:159-220, 277-307) and Polhill (1992:50-52, 320-332) give helpful treatments on the reliability of Acts in this section.

3. A brief reading of Paul's writings might suggest that the Thessalonian correspondence was the earliest of the epistles since it deals with an issue that the early church faced almost immediately—namely, the problem of Christians dying unexpectedly prior to the anticipated early return of Christ. The church, however, was faced with the issues in Galatians before there was general anxiety about eschatological matters. Many scholars date 1 and 2 Thessalonians at the beginning of the 50s AD (see Borchert 1986a:14-15).

4. This dating raises the issue of theological kinship between Galatians and Romans. The letter to the Romans was written in the mid- to late 50s AD, but theological kinship does not necessitate chronological kinship—the two books could have been written ten years apart. Galatians does appear to be an earlier form of some arguments that are later revisited and expanded in Romans. Some of the typically rabbinic arguments of Galatians are not revisited in Romans, probably because circumcision was not the main issue there. Instead, there are additional emphases on both Jewish and Hellenistic patterns of logic and psychology in Romans (see Borchert 1986b:81-92).

COMMENTARY ON
Galatians

◆ I. Introduction (1:1–5)

This letter is from Paul, an apostle. I was not appointed by any group of people or any human authority, but by Jesus Christ himself and by God the Father, who raised Jesus from the dead.

²All the brothers and sisters* here join me in sending this letter to the churches of Galatia.

³May God our Father and the Lord Jesus Christ* give you grace and peace. ⁴Jesus gave his life for our sins, just as God our Father planned, in order to rescue us from this evil world in which we live. ⁵All glory to God forever and ever! Amen.

1:2 Greek *brothers*; also in 1:11.   1:3 Some manuscripts read *God the Father and our Lord Jesus Christ.*

NOTES

1:1 Paul. The epistle opens with a reference to Paul, its primary sender. Jewish parents in Paul's time frequently gave their sons two names so that they could function easily in both the Jewish and the Hellenistic worlds. Thus, Saul was his Jewish name and Paul his Hellenistic one. (The same practice applied, for example, to John Mark; cf. Acts 12:12.)

an apostle. This word is derived from the Gr. verb, *apostellein* [TG649, ZG690] (to send), which is parallel to the Latin *missus,* from which we get the English word "missionary." In the NT, *apostolos* [TG652, ZG693] may carry this broad meaning (see Rom 16:7), but in the Pauline letters, it generally refers to a select group of "sent ones" who were commissioned personally by Jesus to act as his ambassadors in proclaiming the gospel. Paul was included in this group (see comments below).

I was not appointed by any group of people or any human authority. Lit., "neither by men nor through man." Two different Gr. prepositions are used: *apo* [TG575, ZG608] ("from," used as a preposition of source) and *dia* [TG1223, ZG1328] ("through," used here as a preposition of derivative agency). The Gr. behind the NLT's "any group" and "human authority" is a generic rendering of *anthrōpos* [TG444, ZG476] (humanity). Paul's commissioning had been directly from the risen Lord, apart from any human sources or agents (cf. Acts 26:14-18).

1:2 All the brothers and sisters. It is not entirely clear who this includes, whether the missionary team with Paul or a particular church. In this case, it could well have included all the Christians, or alternatively, the leaders of the church at Antioch in Syria, if that is where the letter originated (see Dunn 1993:29-30). In other letters, Paul added the names of one or two colleagues who joined him in writing a letter (Phil 1:1; 1 Thess 1:1); the expansive reference here is unusual.

the churches of Galatia. This expression is very brief in comparison with other Pauline letters; it does not identify the churches of Galatia as churches "of God" or "of God and Christ" or call the Christians "saints" or "faithful ones." This lack of positive attributions fits well with the glaring lack of commendation from Paul for the recipients of this letter. This becomes more apparent in 1:6, where Paul typically provides a thanksgiving statement after the greeting (cf. Col 1:3-10; 1 Thess 1:2-10)—here it is completely omitted.

1:3 *God our Father and the Lord Jesus Christ.* This reading has the support of certain mss (ℵ A P 33), but it is just as likely that Paul wrote "from God the Father and our Lord Jesus Christ" (as found in 𝔓46 𝔓51 B D F G H 1739 𝔐). While the difference in the two readings is minimal, the emphasis in the latter seems to accentuate the Christian's personal relationship with the Godhead through Christ. The linking of "God" with "Jesus" (as in 1:1) is a Christian affirmation of their oneness of purpose, which is further explained in 1:4. The term *Lord* (*kurios* [TG2962, ZG3261]), used with the names of *Jesus* and *Christ*, emphasizes the post-Resurrection confession of Jesus as victorious Lord. The synoptic Gospels suggest that this designation could have been used by Jesus himself (see Matt 22:44; Mark 12:36; Luke 20:42). In any event, the term became a building block in the Christian proclamation of the reigning Christ (see Acts 2:34-35; 1 Cor 15:25).

grace and peace. These words introduce the greeting part of the letter. The typical Gr. greeting, *chairein,* has been altered slightly to "grace" (*charis* [TG5485, ZG5921]), a weighty Christian word. It connotes God's marvelous self-giving love and forgiveness to us through Jesus and has its theological roots in the OT concept of the "lovingkindness" of God (*khesed* [TH2617, ZH2876]). The second element of the greeting, "peace" (*eirēnē* [TG1515, ZG1645]), is the typical Semitic greeting of welcome, which pronounces rest and peace (*shalom* [TH7965, ZH8934]). The combination of these two greetings was undoubtedly an early Christian innovation used by Paul and others, as is evident in Peter's letters (1 Pet 1:2; 2 Pet 1:2) and in the Apocalypse of John (Rev 1:4). Sometimes "mercy" is inserted between the two words (cf. 1 Tim 1:2; 2 Tim 1:2; 2 John 1:3), and sometimes mercy is substituted for grace (cf. Jude 1:2), but the meaning is basically the same. Early Christians quite consistently maintained this order of the words, suggesting their theological awareness that God's grace precedes peace.

1:4 *Jesus gave his life for our sins.* The preposition "for" is in question. Some mss (𝔓51 ℵ¹ B H 0278) read *huper* [TG5228, ZG5642] (on behalf of), while others (𝔓46 ℵ* A D F G 1739 𝔐) read *peri* [TG4012, ZG4309] (concerning). Manuscript evidence is in favor of the second reading, as is the observation that scribes would have been more likely to change *peri* to *huper* because *huper* is the more frequently used preposition in expressions pertaining to Jesus' death "on behalf of" our sins. While *huper* may enhance a substitutionary view of the Atonement (the sacrifice of Christ), *peri* is an elastic term that can also include such a view.

1:5 *forever and ever.* The Greeks had no word for eternity because their idea of time was not linear but cyclical. Gradually, the Hebrews enhanced their linear concept of time and added prefixes to *'olam* to express their expanded ideas which emerged from the earlier idea of Sheol. (For an extended discussion on eternity, see excursus 33 in Borchert 2002:360-367.) Christians such as Paul, therefore, had to speak of eternity or "foreverness" using such descriptions as "unto the eons of eons" or "ages of ages." (For a further discussion of *aiōn* see TDNT 1.197-209.)

COMMENTARY

Paul used a typical Hellenistic format in his letter writing. The introduction to this epistle thus includes (1) the writer (Paul), (2) the recipients (the churches of Galatia), (3) a greeting (from all the brothers and sisters), and (4) a blessing (grace and peace). The body of such a letter usually began with some gracious remarks to or about the recipients, such as thankfulness for the relationship which the writer had or hoped to have with them (see, e.g., Col 1:3-10; 1 Thess 1:2-10).

While Paul used the general Hellenistic form, the content of his introductions conformed to his Christian perspectives, with a somewhat different focus for each epistle. The beginning of the Epistle to the Romans, for example, is quite extended and shows a very gracious spirit on Paul's part. The beginning of Galatians is just the opposite—it is brief and omits the usual Pauline statement of thanksgiving, signaling Paul's very different purpose and spirit in this letter.

In the opening line, Paul identifies himself as an apostle because he was commissioned by the risen Christ to proclaim the gospel (1 Cor 15:8-11), not by any human agent. In saying this, Paul was laying the groundwork for a defense of his apostleship, the authoritative role that allowed him to affirm the truths of the gospel in contradiction to the falsehoods the Galatians had heard from various Judaizing opponents. As discussed in the introduction, Paul had raised up the churches of Galatia on his first missionary journey (see Acts 13:1-14:28). Evidently, some time soon after Paul's visit, the Galatians had been diverted from the simple tenets of the gospel: faith in Jesus Christ—his death for their sins and his resurrection. These two important events are mentioned by Paul in his introduction (1:1, 4).

The expression "Jesus gave his life for our sins" is a clear reference to the crucifixion. The Greek emphasizes the fact that Jesus gave himself willingly in his death rather than indicating that humanity had power to overcome him (cf. John 10:18). Paul added "for our sins" because he viewed Jesus' death as having a purpose—namely, accomplishing God's plan of salvation. This Jesus who was crucified was ultimately victorious because he was raised from the dead.

The death and resurrection of Jesus are intended to save believers from this evil age (1:4). Paul firmly believed in the Jewish idea of two ages: the present age, in which the powers of evil are rampant, and the age to come, in which they will be destroyed (cf. Jewish apocalypses such as *2 Baruch* and *4 Ezra* for their ideas on the present evil age). For Paul, the crucifixion and resurrection of Jesus marked a decisive moment in history when God made it clear to the evil powers that they would not ultimately triumph. Their end is destruction (see, e.g., 1 Cor 2:6-9; 15:20-28; Eph 1:18-2:7; 2 Thess 2:1-8; Rev 19:11-20:15).

The concluding doxology (1:5) reminds readers that God is the ultimate center in Paul's theology. All things will ultimately be subject to God (cf. 1 Cor 15:28). The idea of "glory" recalls Old Testament descriptions of God's presence on Mount Sinai, in the Tabernacle, or Tent of Meeting, and in the Temple (Exod 24:16; 40:34; 1 Kgs 8:11). Glory (*doxa* [TG1391, ZG1518]) usually, though not always, carries the ideas of radiance and splendor generally associated with majesty. Ascribing glory to God is a rightful recognition of God's rule over all things. Such praise belongs to God forever.

In this introduction, Paul addressed his straying children in Galatia, setting out with crystal clarity exactly who he was: a divinely appointed agent of Jesus, the resurrected Messiah. The Galatians had accepted some deceptive teachers who had annulled the power of the gospel by their teaching and openly criticized Paul. He thus began his letter by announcing to them—in no uncertain terms—that he had received his apostolic commission directly from Christ and from the God who raised

Jesus from the dead, not from mere mortals. In the process, he also summarized the crucial theological assertions about Jesus that he would later bring to bear on their error. He referred to the recipients as "churches" but reminded them that the present age was filled with evil. The answer to evil is not human effort but the self-giving death of Jesus, who died and was raised in accordance with God's divine purpose.

When the reader realizes that the Galatians had turned away from the gospel, it is clear why Paul's introductory words are so terse and straightforward. Paul was angry with the Galatians, and he was about to rebuke them severely.

◆ II. An Exposing Rebuke (1:6-10)

6I am shocked that you are turning away so soon from God, who called you to himself through the loving mercy of Christ.* You are following a different way that pretends to be the Good News 7but is not the Good News at all. You are being fooled by those who deliberately twist the truth concerning Christ.

8Let God's curse fall on anyone, including us or even an angel from heaven, who preaches a different kind of Good News than the one we preached to you. 9I say again what we have said before: If anyone preaches any other Good News than the one you welcomed, let that person be cursed.

10Obviously, I'm not trying to win the approval of people, but of God. If pleasing people were my goal, I would not be Christ's servant.

1:6 Some manuscripts read *through loving mercy.*

NOTES

1:6 The introduction of this section is reminiscent of other Gr. letters of rebuke (cf. Longenecker 1990:11, 14), though its focus is particularly theocentric.

I am shocked. Gr., *thaumazō* [TG2296, ZG2513]; perhaps more forcefully translated, "I am stunned."

turning away so soon. It is debated whether these "turncoats" were apostate. The use of the present tense may suggest that the process was still going on (so George 1994:91), but it could also be the historical present tense. The note of "so soon" (*tacheōs* [TG5030, ZG5441]) is also intriguing. It may be that Paul was recalling how soon, after the Passover and the crossing of the sea, the Israelites had deserted God for the golden calf in the wilderness (Exod 32:7-8)—the situation appears to be quite parallel.

the loving mercy of Christ. There are several variants in the mss related to the phrase "of Christ"; some add "Jesus" (D syr^h**—so TR and KJV) and others substitute "of God" (327). The most significant variant is the omission of "of Christ" ($\mathfrak{P}$46vid F* G Hvid), but an impressive combination of witnesses ($\mathfrak{P}$51 ℵ A B 33 1739) do include "of Christ." I am inclined to agree with most English translations that it belongs in the text.

1:8 *curse.* This idea has its roots in the OT concept of *kherem* [TH2764, ZH3051], which connotes condemnation and utter destruction.

an angel. Some Jews and Christians of the first century were not hesitant to speak about angelic visitations. During the intertestamental period, discussions concerning angels had multiplied. Drawing upon Dan 12:1, Jews named archangels such as Michael, Uriel, Gabriel, Raphael, and Raquel (each name ended with the suffix "el," indicating that they were agents of God; cf. *1 Enoch* 1:20; *4 Ezra* 2–4).

1:9 *I say again.* This announcement is an emphatic repetition of the curse.

you welcomed. Lit., "you received" (*parelabete* [TG3880, ZG4161]). Paul used this technical rabbinic term in his epistles to denote the passing on of tradition in a completely faithful or unaltered state. He used two terms for this process: *paralambanō* ("receive," as in this verse) and *paradidōmi* [TG3860, ZG4140] ("pass on" or "deliver"; cf. 1 Cor 11:23 and 15:3).

1:10 *Obviously.* The argument in 1:10 completes the rebuke by implicitly excluding Paul from the curse and making a transition to the next section, in which Paul provides insights into his own pilgrimage with God. It is like a saddle between two mountains that enables climbers to move from one peak to another. I have pointed regularly to the phenomenon of saddle texts in my commentary on John (Borchert 1996:167, 217). In this transition, Paul uses a couple of Gr. questions that are reminiscent of Cynic and Stoic diatribes. In that method of argument, a person asked leading questions in such a way that the answers would be apparent, and any opponent to the questioner would quickly realize that he would likely appear foolish or misinformed if he were to persist in his opposition (cf. Rom 2:21-23; 3:1-3; 4:1-2, 9-10; 6:1, 15; 7:7, 13; 8:31-34).

servant. Paul most often characterized himself as a servant or slave. Here he identifies himself as a slave (*doulos* [TG1401, ZG1528]; cf. Rom 1:1). Paul's goal was to imitate the self-giving servant model of Christ (Phil 2:5-8), which in turn would provide a model for others (Phil 3:17). This perspective is the exact opposite of seeking prestige through people-pleasing (cf. Matt 20:25-28).

COMMENTARY

Paul's first statement is shocking. Instead of thanking God for the recipients, as one might expect from his other letters (cf. Col 1:3-10; 1 Thess 1:2-10), he rebuked the Galatians, charging them with incomprehensible desertion. The metaphorical use of *metatithesthe* [TG3346A, ZG3572] normally means changing one's place; here it implies exchanging one's relationship with God for something else. The Galatians had abandoned their commitment to God's loving and gracious message of salvation in Jesus Christ to adopt, instead, counterfeit substitutes preached by those who claimed to have a better message of salvation.

The Galatians were not just deserting Paul—they were departing from God. From Paul's point of view, the Galatians had abandoned the real meaning of Christ's gracious love that was embodied in the gospel. The Galatians' claim to a "different kind of Good News" was not acceptable to Paul. Two Greek words used in 1:6-7 make an important distinction: the Galatians were advocating a "different" (*heteron* [TG2087, ZG2283]) gospel message, but Paul refused to accept this "other" (*allo* [TG243, ZG257]) gospel message as being the true gospel. The Galatians might have argued that these were different forms of the true gospel and that theirs was actually preferable to Paul's because it included Old Testament patterns. Paul rejected their view and denied it any legitimacy. In fact, he objected to the idea that their new message was Good News at all. Instead, Paul said that those who proclaimed this other message were perverters of the authentic gospel.

The plural use of "those" (*tines* [TG5100, ZG5516], "certain ones") at 1:7 indicates that there were a number of false teachers who continued to disturb the Galatian churches by deliberately "twisting" (*metastrepsai* [TG3344, ZG3570]) Paul's earlier presentation of the gospel. Because of their adulteration of the gospel, Paul wished that they would be utterly cursed and destroyed. Such an *anathema* (curse) brought with it the terrible expectation that the wrath of God would fall on anyone who was so cursed (TDNT 1.354).

Paul's commitment to the authentic gospel was absolute. He permitted no alteration of the gospel proclamation: salvation is based on the death of Jesus and freely available to all people—a gift of God's grace received by faith. Paul emphatically cursed anyone who would bring a different gospel, even if the messenger were an angel. At that time, the Jews viewed God as being so high and lifted up that communication from God was expected to come through the mediation of angels (see IDB 1.132-133). When Jesus became the mediator between God and humanity, however, the role of angels was greatly reduced. The book of Hebrews clearly places angels in a role subordinate to the Son (1:5-9) and even to those who are being saved (1:14). Paul, however, had little interest in explaining his theology of angels at this point but rather stated that even the claim of an angelic visitation was not grounds to alter the message of the gospel—such an angel deserved God's curse. Not only did Paul proclaim a curse on any human being or superterrestrial angelic messenger who might alter the gospel, but he also specifically included himself as a potential object of this curse if he should present a different gospel. However, Paul also stated unambiguously that the Galatians had received the correct traditions concerning the gospel. Unfortunately, the Galatians had not been faithful to this gospel but had adopted counterfeit ideas.

Paul concluded this section by forcing the Galatians to face the issue of his own integrity. Did he merely manipulate words to gain human status or praise? Paul asked in two ways whether the reader supposed that he was actually trying to score popularity points with people or with God. If the reader had any doubt that the answer should be "no," it would be removed by the end of the epistle as it became clear that it was Paul's opponents who were seeking adulation, not Paul. Instead, Paul's life had been full of suffering for Jesus (6:17).

In short, Paul was a God-pleaser, not a people-pleaser. The expression "win the approval of people" translates the Greek word *peithō* [TG3982, ZG4275] (persuade), which was associated with a rhetorical strategy that was viewed negatively by many ancients as a contorted and deceptive manner of speaking (Betz 1979: 54-55). Calling Paul a people-pleaser would be to say that Paul was an insincere flatterer, but Paul completely denied using such manipulative tactics. As a servant of Christ, he was determined to follow Christ's example of humility (cf. 2:20; 5:24; 6:2).

The force of this section was to charge the Galatians and their teachers with a major deviation from the gospel that merited divine condemnation. This section also made it absolutely clear that the Galatian problem did not reside with Paul, who had faithfully delivered the authentic Good News to them even as he had received it. Therefore, neither the original message nor the messenger could be held responsible for the Galatians' having become turncoats. They were therefore liable to come under the curse Paul pronounced.

◆ III. Paul's Defense of the Gospel: A Historical Rehearsal (1:11–2:13)
A. Paul's Divine Call to Mission (1:11-17)

¹¹Dear brothers and sisters, I want you to understand that the gospel message I preach is not based on mere human reasoning. ¹²I received my message from no human source, and no one taught me. Instead, I received it by direct revelation from Jesus Christ.*

¹³You know what I was like when I followed the Jewish religion—how I violently persecuted God's church. I did my best to destroy it. ¹⁴I was far ahead of my fellow Jews in my zeal for the traditions of my ancestors.

¹⁵But even before I was born, God chose me and called me by his marvelous grace. Then it pleased him ¹⁶to reveal his Son to me* so that I would proclaim the Good News about Jesus to the Gentiles.

When this happened, I did not rush out to consult with any human being.* ¹⁷Nor did I go up to Jerusalem to consult with those who were apostles before I was. Instead, I went away into Arabia, and later I returned to the city of Damascus.

1:12 Or *by the revelation of Jesus Christ.* 1:16a Or *in me.* 1:16b Greek *with flesh and blood.*

NOTES

1:11 *Dear brothers and sisters.* The NLT leaves the conjunction here untranslated, and the ancient mss are quite evenly divided as to whether the conjunction should be *de* [TG1161, ZG1254] (but, now) or *gar* [TG1063, ZG1142] (for). The first has the support of 𝔓46 ℵ*·² A D¹ Ψ 𝔐, and the second appears in ℵ¹ B D*·ᶜ F G. In the context I find a stronger case for *de*, a mild adversative; it unites this statement with 1:10 and expands the positive aspects of Paul's ministry over against the negative perspective communicated in the earlier questions.

I want you to understand. This section opens with a familiar rabbinic, classical, and legal expression that signifies a formal transfer of information: "I want to make known to you" (*gnōrizō* [TG1107, ZG1192]). It is solemnly addressed to those whom Paul is convinced do not know the facts (cf. 1 Cor 12:3; 15:1; see also 2 Cor 8:1; Eph 6:19). This word is also used of God's making his divine purpose known to humans (see Rom 9:22-23; 16:26; Eph 1:9; 3:3, 5, 10; Col 1:27).

the gospel message I preach. In Gr., the expression lumbers along (lit., "the evangel which was evangelized by me"); it is similar to many Heb. statements in which there is a repetition of etymologically related words in order to emphasize the idea (such as, "coming, he came"). The effect is to strongly affirm that Paul and the gospel are intimately related.

1:11-12 *not based on mere human reasoning. I received my message from no human source, and no one taught me.* This reading is a free-flowing, contemporary rendering of a complex, three-part denial of human involvement in Paul's reception of the gospel— literally, "not according to man, nor did I receive it from man, nor was I taught it." The force of "not according to man . . . nor did I receive it from man" in 1:11-12 is similar to the double denial of 1:1 (see note).

1:12 *received.* This word (*parelabon*) calls to mind the first part of the rabbinic pattern for passing down a tradition. See note on 1:9.

direct revelation. The Gr. term for "revelation" (*apokalupsis* [TG602, ZG637]) means to draw aside a curtain in order to unveil something hidden. This term is used only once in the LXX translation of the canonical OT (1 Sam 20:30) but occurs a few other times in the later, apocryphal books of the LXX (e.g., Sir 11:27; 22:22). During the intertestamental period it became an important term for describing books that had an eschatological message. In the NT, the term is concentrated in Paul's epistles (cf. Moulton and Geden

1926:92, who indicate that 13 out of 18 NT uses are in Paul) and usually refers to the unveiling of a mystery with eschatological significance.

from Jesus Christ. It is debated whether the genitive form of "Jesus Christ" in this passage is objective or subjective. If it is objective, then Jesus Christ is the content of the revelation or, as Dunn (1993:54) argues, "the gospel is not simply 'from Christ' but *is* Christ"; how that revelation was spelled out "caused the difference between Paul and the others." If the genitive is subjective, however, then Jesus Christ is the source of the revelation and as Longenecker (1990:24) argues, "the question Paul faced at Galatia was where his message of a law-free gospel came from." The NLT renders the subjective genitive in the text (using the preposition "from") while showing the objective sense in the NLT mg ("of Jesus Christ").

1:13 the Jewish religion. The Gr. word translated "Judaism" is used only here and at 1:14 in the NT. It represents a post-Maccabean understanding of Israel and stands against the Hellenization that had been imposed on the people by their Seleucid conquerors (cf. 2 Macc 2:21; 4:13).

1:14 I was far ahead of my fellow Jews. Paul describes a second aspect of his former life—his superior personal development within Judaism. The continuing force of the imperfect *proekopton* [TG4298, ZG4621] (was advancing [continually]) is significant (cf. TDNT 6.704-711). By comparison with colleagues of his own age, Paul excelled, having advanced by virtue of his zeal.

1:15 But. Lit., "but when" (*hote de* [TG3753/1161, ZG4021/1254]). These words clearly signal Paul's personal transition in the past from unbelief to belief.

1:16 to reveal. It is probably not profitable to try to distinguish between an internal subjective experience and an external objective experience (cf. Burton 1921:50; Wikenhauser 1960:134-137). Paul's experience may have involved both, which may explain the slightly different ways in which it is described in Acts (9:4-5; 22:7-9; 26:13-18).

his Son. This Christological designation (TDNT 8.383) clearly refers to the person who was the focus of Paul's revelatory experience—the crucified, risen, and living Messiah. Some have argued that the term "Son of God" has its roots in apocalyptic Judaism (see the critique of Stanton 1989:227-233) or Hellenistic and non-Jewish Christian thinking, but the scholars promoting this view seem predisposed to find the sources of Christological affirmations in the "heavenly man" (*theos anēr*) construct of later Hellenistic writing, influenced by Diaspora Jews, or in the concepts of "sons of the gods," such as those attributed to the divine Augustus (for a critique, see Schillebeeckx 1986:424-429), rather than in early Christian affirmations about Jesus (cf. discussions in Kim 1981:100-230; Marshall 1977:111-123).

1:17 go up to Jerusalem. For the Jews, "going up" always implied the Holy City because Jerusalem is in the mountains. In the minds of Jews, it was geographically and theologically "up" (cf. Acts 15:2; the simple expression "went up" is used without direct mention of Jerusalem in the Gr. of Acts 18:22).

Arabia. This country was part of the Nabatean kingdom, ruled by Aretas IV from 4 BC to AD 40 (cf. Betz 1979:73-74). The Romans generally called this area "Arabia" (BAGD 104). The exact size of the territory varied depending on battles among the roving tribes. Arabia sometimes included Damascus and the cities of the Decapolis.

COMMENTARY

Because his authority as an apostle (cf. 1:1) and the correctness of his message (1:6-7) had been seriously challenged, Paul found it necessary to state that his gospel did not come through the mediation of others (1:11, 16-17). He wanted to counter any misguided notions of the Galatians (1:6) that he was merely a second-generation disciple or a subapostle. Paul asserted his divine call and claimed no dependency on the Jerusalem church or the earlier apostles. His calling had not been "according to man" and had not come "from man." Therefore, Paul insisted that he had not learned his gospel from any human source.

Instead, Paul's calling had come by divine revelation in his encounter with the risen Lord, which then became the basis for his dynamic preaching (cf. 1:15-16; Acts 9:1-19). As noted, the revelation of Jesus Christ could be about Jesus Christ (i.e., Jesus Christ was himself the revelation) or it could mean that the revelation came from Jesus Christ. Both options are valid because Jesus Christ is both the source and the content of the revelation Paul received.

Having established that his message came by revelation, Paul reminded the Galatians of his past. He states in 1:13 that the Galatians had already heard about his former "way of life" (*anastrophē* [TG391, ZG419]). He had been a zealot for Judaism, a Hasidic-type Jew whose zealous commitment was to assure faithfulness to the law by the people of the covenant, much like the hymn writer from Qumran who claimed inspiration for his zeal through the Holy Spirit (Acts 9:1-2; cf. 1QH 14:13 [see Vermes 1995:229]), even if it meant dealing violently with those he viewed as deviants. Even later in life, as a Christian, Paul considered his life as a Jew to have been excellent (cf. Phil 3:4-6), though he deeply regretted his persecution of Christians (cf. 1 Cor 15:9; Eph 3:8; 1 Tim 1:13-15). He had done so because he considered Christians to be deviant Jews and therefore sinful lawbreakers. The goal of his persecution was their utter destruction (cf. the sentiment of Ps 101:8).

Paul described the group he once persecuted as "God's church" (1:13). This expression is rather unusual for Paul, who usually uses the term "church" to refer to local congregations. The generic use of the term implies a universal perspective; from his self-righteous stance, Paul would have attacked both Jewish Christians and Gentile converts such as the Galatians, who were part of the church and would thus have come under the protective Roman rights of the Jews as members of a licensed religion (see Josephus *Antiquities* 14.10ff; 16.6; for comments on the Jews as a *religio licita*, see Blomberg 1997:19, 23-24). Exposing such illegitimate Jews to the Romans became one of the goals of zealous, Pharisaic Jews.

As a young Jewish rabbi, Paul had clearly committed himself to the "traditions of the fathers," a Greek description of the rabbinic pattern in which rabbinic students learned the teachings of their elders by rote memory. These legal teachings were in oral form until they were codified in the Mishnah after the fall of Jerusalem and destruction of the Temple. Paul probably made such a strong point of his model status in Judaism because he thought that the Galatians were trying to appropriate some aspects of Paul's past. Not only did they not do it as well as Paul did, they did so without realizing that such a turn was, in fact, a denial of the believer's freedom in Christ (cf. 2:17-19; 3:1-2; 5:1).

At this point, Paul reminded them that something revolutionary had taken place in his life (1:15). The God whom he sought to serve from birth was not only in the scrolls of the Bible that he had studied; this God had come to Paul directly through his Son

(1:16). Moreover, God not only revealed his Son *to* Paul but also *in* Paul. Christ had come to dwell in Paul and live *through* him as Paul preached him to the world.

This revelation occurred during Paul's trip to Damascus, when the risen Christ told him, "I am Jesus, the one you are persecuting!" (Acts 9:5). Paul saw Jesus at this time (1 Cor 9:1; 15:8) and received from this life-altering event a sense of freedom from human striving and a divine commission (Acts 26:16). The Greek verb in 1:16 (*euangelizōmai* [TG2097A, ZG2294]) means to "proclaim" or "preach about something good." In its transliterated form, it becomes the English word "evangelize." The content of the proclamation, Paul indicated, was "him" (*auton*)—that is, the Lord Jesus.

The audience for Paul's proclamation was "the Gentiles" (*tois ethnesin* [TG1484, ZG1620]])—literally, "the nations," (i.e., any non-Jews). Later, Paul explained that his mission was to the uncircumcised, whereas Peter's mission was to the circumcised (2:7). While Acts indicates that Paul typically began his preaching among the Jews, he seems to have gained a greater hearing among the Gentiles (cf. Acts 14:1-4; 17:1-5; 28:17-28), a fact which often angered the Jews. While the focus of Paul's mission remained primarily on the Gentiles, Paul, particularly in his letter to the Romans, indicated that his goal was the evangelization of both Jews and Gentiles, a goal evident both in his use of logic (Rom 1:16-17; 2:9–3:26) and in his stated desire (Rom 9:3). Paul's goal for the gospel was thus universal in scope, though his particular role was to evangelize Gentiles.

In looking back over his life, Paul was convinced that God had been fully active from his birth in setting him apart for his calling (1:15). Texts such as this one, which involve questions of determinism, frequently create problems for Western readers. Here, the conflict is between Paul's apparently free, sinful actions and God's foreordained purpose for his life. The fundamental hermeneutical issue is whether one reads such texts with a Hellenistic, Western mindset or from a Semitic point of view. Western readers are inclined to assume that Paul thinks like people of our time—in a deductive, syllogistic manner. Paul may write in Greek, but behind his words one must always be conscious of his Semitic way of thinking in pictures and stories. For Paul, everything goes back to God's person and creativity, but he also knows that humans have a will and are disobedient—he holds ideas in tension. Both of these ideas are embedded in the way that Paul, as a Hebrew, thinks about himself and God.

The memory of Paul's earlier persecution of Christians never left him. Nonetheless, he could rejoice that God had been gracious and given him a new life story that reflected God's liberating kindness and grace (*charis* [TG5485, ZG5921]) rather than human effort and self-promotion. Understanding Paul's story is vital to gaining the right perspective on Galatians because Paul realized that the Galatians were asserting ideas akin to those he had abandoned when he left Judaism to become a Christian. Their proposal for self-advancement was, for Paul, a rejection of grace and a loss of freedom. It was not the gospel!

Unfortunately, the Galatians had been deceived by some Judaizers who were undoubtedly seeking to deprecate Paul by saying that he was a subordinate of the apostles and by suggesting that his message was inadequate. This prompted Paul to affirm that his preaching of Jesus did not originate with other humans and that he did not need other humans to help him understand the gospel. He denied two possible claims of his opponents. First, he denied a Jerusalem source for his gospel. Christ was at the center of Paul's thinking as a Christian, not Jerusalem. Therefore, in Paul's mind, the Jerusalem church neither provided nor authenticated his message. Second, Paul understood himself to be an apostle through his direct experience with Christ and refused to consider himself a subordinate or derivative apostolic preacher. While his opponents may have claimed some form of apostolic succession or confirmation for their views, Paul vehemently denied any indebtedness to Peter, James, John, or any other early disciples or relatives of Jesus for his knowledge of the gospel (cf. 2:6, 9, 11-12). Paul rejected the idea that priority in time meant superiority in message; he also denied any preliminary association with the early church's headquarters or its earliest leaders.

After describing what he did not do, Paul turned to what he did do: he went into Arabia (1:17). "Arabia" probably refers to a large area, much of it desert but some of it quite prosperous, stretching from parts of Mesopotamia to the Sinai and lying east of the Jordan River. Paul's exact location, his activities, and how much of the three years (1:18) he actually spent there before returning to Damascus are matters of speculation. He may not have gone far from Damascus (cf. Burton 1921:58), and it is improbable that he would have gone as far south as the Sinai and then have returned all the way north to Damascus before going to Jerusalem. Whether he did mission work at this time or was in a period of spiritual retreat is not known. What seems likely is that he achieved further clarity about the gospel there before he went to Jerusalem. Otherwise, he could hardly have claimed thereafter that his gospel was not influenced by Jerusalem or by the apostles.

It is evident throughout the stories of the Bible that the blessings of God are always accompanied by a call to obedient service. For any reader to miss the twofold pattern—that grace and commission belong together—is to miss the main theological thrust of this section. None of us is an apostle Paul, but each of us has been called by God and commissioned to have Jesus Christ revealed in us and through us to the world.

◆ B. Paul's First Visit as a Christian to Jerusalem and Beyond (1:18-24)

¹⁸Then three years later I went to Jerusalem to get to know Peter,* and I stayed with him for fifteen days. ¹⁹The only other apostle I met at that time was James, the Lord's brother. ²⁰I declare before God that what I am writing to you is not a lie.

²¹After that visit I went north into the provinces of Syria and Cilicia. ²²And still the Christians in the churches in Judea didn't know me personally. ²³All they knew was that people were saying, "The one who used to persecute us is now preaching the very faith he tried to destroy!" ²⁴And they praised God because of me.

1:18 Greek *Cephas.*

NOTES

1:18 *Then three years later.* "Then" (*epeita* [TG1899, ZG2083]) is Paul's signal to his readers that these events followed in successive order, with no breaks in the historical account. For a discussion of the sequence of events recorded both in Acts and Galatians in Paul's life, see "Date, Occasion of Writing, and Audience " in the Introduction.

to get to know. This word, rendered "to get to know" (*historēsai* [TG2477, ZG2707]), can be translated in various ways, but there is good support for translating it as "to meet," "for an initial visit," or "to become acquainted" (Cole 1989:55; BAGD 383). The visit after three years is best identified as the visit mentioned in Acts 9:26.

Peter. Lit., "Cephas," Peter's surname. In the context, it is interesting to note the use of Peter's Semitic name, *Cephas,* at 1:18; 2:9, 11, rather than his Gr. name, *Peter,* as at 2:7. Could Paul have been suggesting that he had differences with Peter in the three uses of *Cephas,* whereas in the one clear statement where he mentioned a cooperative mission pattern with the other apostle, he referred to him by his Hellenistic name, *Peter* (cf. "Cephas" in 1 Cor 1:12; 3:22; 9:5; 15:5)? While this idea may seem conjectural, there is a similar pattern on Luke's part in Acts when dealing with John Mark. He is introduced in Acts 12:25 and 15:37 with both his Semitic and Hellenistic names. When he deserts the mission to the Gentiles, however, he is called by his Hebrew name, *John* (Acts 13:13; see also 13:5, which is probably a foreshadowing of his abandoning the mission), but when he rejoins Barnabas in a mission to the Gentiles in Cyprus, he is called "Mark" (Acts 15:39, NASB).

1:19 *James, the Lord's brother.* This James should not be confused with the other two men named James who are listed among the Lord's apostles in the synoptic Gospels (cf. Mark 3:17, 18). This James was Jesus' brother. The argument that this James could not be a brother of Jesus through Mary cannot be substantiated by Scripture and likely arose to defend the Roman Catholic doctrine of the perpetual virginity of Mary.

1:20 *I declare before God that what I am writing to you is not a lie.* In this oath, Paul calls upon God to witness to the truthfulness of his statement. The use of oaths, as Sampley (1977:477-482) has incisively argued, was a common practice in Roman law and implied that the oath-maker was willing to argue the case to the full extent of the law. Paul's oath is reinforced by his forceful claim that he was not lying, a claim that was tantamount to opening himself up to the severe judgment of God if the claim proved to be false (cf. TDNT 9.599-601). Concerning Jesus' warning against oaths in Matt 5:34, we must remember that the Jews had developed a complex hierarchy of oaths, some of which were stated in such a way that they could be later withdrawn without consequence. The intent of Jesus was to insist on truthfulness and to eschew word games. For a discussion of Jesus and oaths, see Guelich 1982:211-219.

1:22 *didn't know me personally.* This Gr. imperfect periphrastic construction (lit., "I was continuing to be unknown by face") indicates that the Judean Christians knew about Paul (as indicated in 1:23) but did not know him personally.

1:23 *the very faith.* Use of the term "faith" to designate a belief pattern is a little unusual in Paul's main epistles (cf. Rom 1:5; Titus 1:13; see BAGD 664). Its use here may support the view that Paul was providing an authentic reminiscence of what others had said.

COMMENTARY

Paul asserted that the first time he visited Jerusalem as a follower of Jesus was three years after his Damascus road experience. The purpose of that trip was primarily to get acquainted with Peter and James, among the apostles. In their discussions, Paul probably asked Peter about the historical life of Jesus (Kilpatrick 1959:144-149).

This initial visit reflects the visit reported in Acts 9:26-28. The fifteen days mentioned in 1:18 are certainly not a problem in correlating the two accounts. The report in Acts 9:27-28 indicates that Paul met a number of Christians in Jerusalem and that Barnabas introduced him to "the apostles." Paul said that he met only two apostles, Peter and James. For some readers, it may seem unusual that this James would be designated as an apostle, since he, Jesus' brother, was not listed among the twelve apostles Jesus chose during his earthly ministry. Furthermore, Luke suggests that the substitute chosen to replace the apostate Judas would not only need to have been called by Jesus from the beginning but also have been a witness to the Resurrection (see Acts 1:21-22). In Paul's mind, James (having seen the risen Christ; 1 Cor 15:7) met the requirements for being an apostolic leader.

Paul left Jerusalem and went north into the provinces of Syria and Cilicia. This journey corresponds with Acts 9:30, which states that Paul went north to Caesarea and then to his home of Tarsus in the Roman province of Cilicia (the eastern part of modern Turkey). Thereafter, Luke reports that Barnabas went to Tarsus and brought Paul to Antioch in the province of Syria, located on the southern side of the mountain pass known in the ancient world as the Syrian Gates, since it connected Cilicia with Syria (Acts 11:25-26).

Paul further emphasized his limited contact with the Jerusalem church by pointing out that even after his visit with Peter, when some Christians in Jerusalem got to know him personally (see Acts 9:28-30), the churches throughout Judea only knew of him by report—they had only heard that he was a chief persecutor of Christians who had made an about-face (1:22-24). These churches were now precious to Paul; they were no longer the object of his persecutions. He called them "the churches in Christ," one of his favorite phrases. For him, being in Christ was the epitome of authentic Christianity, as an eschatological goal and as a present reality. This phrase clearly defined the context of his life commitment and expressed his experience. It summarizes the nature of Pauline mysticism, which is not only personal, but, as Sydney Cave (1929:50) has argued, is also corporate. Thus, to speak of churches as being "in Christ" is a genuine Pauline perspective and one of the foundations for all Christian life and thought.

Paul concludes this section by noting the amazement of the churches at his conversion. He even includes a direct quote from the Judean churches (as marked by the use of *hoti* [TG3754, ZG4022]): "The one who used to persecute us is now preaching the very faith he tried to destroy!" This verse may be one of the earliest surviving recorded statements directly from the Judean churches (cf. Bammel 1968:108-112). What a transformation! The persecutor of Christians had become a preacher of Christ.

What more could Paul do than give glory to God? The only true response to the work of God in the world was praise to the Lord. Paul set the response of the Judean Christians in direct contrast to those of the Galatians, who now sought to undermine his teaching on Christian liberty instead of praising God for his transformation. This statement sets in bold relief two reactions that are often present when God is at work—praise and criticism (or opposition).

◆   ## C. Paul's Second Visit: A Strategic Conference (2:1-10)

Then fourteen years later I went back to Jerusalem again, this time with Barnabas; and Titus came along, too. ²I went there because God revealed to me that I should go. While I was there I met privately with those considered to be leaders of the church and shared with them the message I had been preaching to the Gentiles. I wanted to make sure that we were in agreement, for fear that all my efforts had been wasted and I was running the race for nothing. ³And they supported me and did not even demand that my companion Titus be circumcised, though he was a Gentile.*

⁴Even that question came up only because of some so-called Christians there—false ones, really*—who were secretly brought in. They sneaked in to spy on us and take away the freedom we have in Christ Jesus. They wanted to enslave us and force us to follow their Jewish regulations. ⁵But we refused to give in to them for a single moment. We wanted to preserve the truth of the gospel message for you.

⁶And the leaders of the church had nothing to add to what I was preaching. (By the way, their reputation as great leaders made no difference to me, for God has no favorites.) ⁷Instead, they saw that God had given me the responsibility of preaching the gospel to the Gentiles, just as he had given Peter the responsibility of preaching to the Jews. ⁸For the same God who worked through Peter as the apostle to the Jews also worked through me as the apostle to the Gentiles.

⁹In fact, James, Peter,* and John, who were known as pillars of the church, recognized the gift God had given me, and they accepted Barnabas and me as their co-workers. They encouraged us to keep preaching to the Gentiles, while they continued their work with the Jews. ¹⁰Their only suggestion was that we keep on helping the poor, which I have always been eager to do.

2:3 Greek *a Greek.*   2:4 Greek *some false brothers.*   2:9 Greek *Cephas;* also in 2:11, 14.

NOTES

2:1 *Then fourteen years later I went back to Jerusalem again.* The first word in this section, the Gr. *epeita* [TG1899, ZG2083] (then), introduces the third consecutive statement (cf. 1:18, 21). It implies that, for Paul, the "fourteen years later" followed directly after the previous statement. The question that perplexes scholars is whether or not these fourteen years include the earlier three years (cf. 1:18) and thus should be dated from the Damascus road experience (so Jewett 1979a:52-54 and Longenecker 1990:45; contra Ogg 1968:56-57 and Dunn 1993:87). For my reconstruction of the events in Paul's life, see "Date" in the Introduction.

2:2 *I went there because God revealed to me that I should go.* This sentence is a somewhat expanded form of the Gr., which can be rendered, "I went up according to revelation," or perhaps, "I went up as a result of (*kata* [TG2596, ZG2848]) revelation."

privately. The Gr. idiom *kat idian* [TG2596/2398, ZG2848/2625] emphasizes that even Paul's second meeting was private.

those considered to be leaders of the church. Lit., "those who seemed to be somebodies" (*tois dokousin* [TG1380, ZG1506]). A similar expression is used in 2:6, where it clearly refers to the Jerusalem leaders. The Gr. text actually introduces this group earlier in the verse, simply as "them" (*autois*). Though this could syntactically be taken to denote a separate group of people, it is generally agreed that it is another reference to the "seeming somebodies." Betz (1979:86-87) differs, however, thinking that the two statements in 2:2 refer to two different groups of people, but he is unable to say exactly who is referred to by "them" (*autois*).

shared with them the message I had been preaching. Lit., "I laid out before them the gospel which I proclaim." This statement should not be interpreted as Paul's submission to Jerusalem authority (contra Schlier 1949:67-68), because it does not imply subordination. In some circumstances, *anatithēmi* [TG394, ZG423] can imply just the opposite (BAGD 62), but here it is doubtful that Paul was attempting to elevate himself above other preachers.

I was running the race for nothing. Paul was fond of using race/running imagery (1 Cor 9:24-27; Phil 3:12-14). The expression "for nothing" or "empty" (*kenon* [TG2756, ZG3031]) is familiar in Paul's writings. In one context, he reminds us that if Christ had not been raised from the dead, both preaching and faith would be empty (1 Cor 15:14, 58).

2:5 But we refused to give in to them for a single moment. "Give in" (*hupotagē* [TG5292, ZG5717]) lit. means "submit." The Gr. underlying "single moment" (*pros horan* [TG4314/5610, ZG4639/6052]), lit. means "for an hour," and reflects a Semitic way of thinking; in actuality, it should be rendered as implying a very brief period, since time was generally reckoned in hours. The precise Gr. word signifying the smallest amount of time—like our concept of a split second—is *atomos* [TG823, ZG875]. It is used only once in the NT, in 1 Cor 15:52, where Paul is making an argument for instantaneousness.

The expression *hois oude* (not to them) was omitted in D* and several Latin sources, including it[b], Irenaeus (in Latin), Tertullian, and one ms known to Jerome. It yields the rendering, "we submitted for an hour." This aberrant text suggests that Paul seemingly relented for a short period and circumcised Titus, but that idea runs counter to Paul's entire stance in this argument. If it were true, it would render the next statement in this verse both confusing and contradictory—how would Paul's giving in have "preserved the truth" for the Galatians?

We wanted to preserve the truth. The Gr. introduces this statement by *hina* [TG2443, ZG2671], which can imply either purpose or result. Here, purpose is primary: Paul was very clear that his stance was absolutely necessary in order to assure the integrity of the gospel.

2:7 they saw that God had given me the responsibility of preaching . . . to the Gentiles, just as he had given Peter the responsibility . . . to the Jews. The word translated "Gentiles" is, lit., "uncircumcised," and the word rendered "Jews" is "circumcised." This is the way that Jews divided humanity in their thinking. The word translated "given" is *pepisteumai* [TG4100, ZG4409] (entrusted), which is relatively unusual for Paul, occurring only two other times in his writings (1Cor 9:17; 2 Tim 1:12); it may indicate a recollection of the words used at this early consultation (Betz 1979:96-97).

2:8 For the same God who worked through Peter as the apostle to the Jews also worked through me as the apostle to the Gentiles. This verse reiterates the previous one with a few intriguing features. The expression "as the apostle to" stands for the Gr. *apostolēn* [TG651, ZG692], which could be used technically as "apostleship" or probably more generally as an expression of "mission" (so the RSV). It is not repeated in Gr. with reference to Paul, which may or may not have had significance in the consultation and which may have been implied by Paul, as suggested by the NLT rendering. In addition, whereas "the circumcision" is once again used for the Jews, the term used for their opposite here is "Gentiles" rather than "uncircumcision" as before. Since "the circumcision" was how Jews usually referred to themselves, this might be an instance of Paul using insider language from his days as a Pharisee.

2:9 James, Peter, and John. The "apparent somebodies," the reputed ones mentioned in 2:2 and 2:6, are here identified as James (undoubtedly the Lord's brother, as in 1:19), John (probably the son of Zebedee; cf. Mark 1:19-20), and Peter (actually "Cephas"; see note at 1:18). Longenecker (1990:56) suggests that Peter was probably the recognized leader in these discussions on apostolic mission (as in 2:7; also 1:18; 2:11; cf. the lists of the Twelve; e.g., Mark 3:14-19), but James seems to have been in charge of administrative matters (cf. Acts 15:13), which probably explains the reason for his being listed first here. These "apparent somebodies" are not only identified but are also designated as "pillars," which suggests that they were accorded a place of honor in the Jerusalem church as representing a secure tradition. But linking "pillars" with the rather ironic expression "those who are reputed" (*hoi dokountes* [TG1380, ZG1506]; here rendered as "who were known as") leaves the impression that Paul is speaking tongue-in-cheek. In light of Peter's actions in 2:11-14, it is likely that Paul is speaking ironically to make the point that all believers, regardless of earthly status, only stand firm insomuch as they reflect the authentic gospel.

they accepted Barnabas and me as their co-workers. Lit., "they extended to us the right hand of fellowship." The right hand was regarded by the ancients as the hand of acceptance (cf. Rev 1:17; Josephus *Antiquities* 8.387; 18.328-329). In the ancient world, the right hand was contrasted with the deceptive left hand, the Latin word for which was *sinister.*

They encouraged us to keep preaching to the Gentiles, while they continued their work with the Jews. Lit., "so that (*hina* [TG2443, ZG2671]) we [would go] to the Gentiles and they to the circumcision." Does the text imply a mission strategy involving either a geographical distinction (Burton 1921:97-99) or an ethnic difference (Longenecker 1990:58-59), or does it simply refer to two representative authority roles (Dunn 1993:111-112)? Paul's shorthand, which omits the verbs, unfortunately leaves the case unsettled. The NLT rendering emphasizes ethnic differences.

2:10 *keep on helping the poor.* The visit recorded in Acts 11:28-30 is also a relief effort; this statement strengthens my argument in the Introduction that it is the same visit as the one Paul mentions here (cf. Bruce 1982:126-127).

COMMENTARY

Paul's meeting in Jerusalem probably best coincides with his carrying financial assistance to Jerusalem during the famine (Acts 11:28-30; see "Date, Occasion of Writing, and Audience" in the Introduction for discussion). While some think that this visit is similar to that described in Acts 15:1-35, I find it difficult to conceive that Paul would have overlooked a second visit (described in Acts 11:29) or that Luke would have purposely constructed a sequence involving Paul that had no basis in fact. Moreover, I am convinced that the official decision of Acts 15 had not yet occurred when Paul wrote to the Galatians and that Gentiles such as the Galatians had not yet received a communiqué concerning the resolution of differences between Paul and certain Jerusalem leaders.

In this famine visit, Barnabas accompanied Paul; in fact, Barnabas is mentioned first in Acts 11:30, suggesting that at that time he was the leader of the two. Following the departure of John Mark, however, Luke's order changed in favor of Paul (Acts 13:43). In Acts, Barnabas is pictured as a significant donor to the church, a Cypriot Levite whose birth name was Joseph. His new name, given by the apostles, meant "son of encouragement" (Acts 4:36-37). He rescued Paul (9:27), and he also rescued Mark after his conflict with Paul (15:39).

Titus, Paul's coworker, is not mentioned in Acts in connection with either the second or third visits to Jerusalem, although in the third visit Luke mentions that Paul and Barnabas were accompanied by some other persons (Acts 15:2). In the very brief account of the second visit, no additional persons are mentioned as traveling with them, though this certainly does not rule out the possibility that others went to help protect the famine gift for Jerusalem (Acts 11:29-30). While Titus's presence on this trip was not of great importance for the Acts narrative, Paul makes a point of it in Galatians (2:3) because Titus serves as the test case for his gospel of freedom.

In going up to Jerusalem, Paul believed that he was acting in response to the revealed direction of God (2:2). Once he arrived in Jerusalem, he had a private meeting with the church leaders, which confirms that this visit was the event identified in Acts 11:29 rather than the more public debate suggested for the Jerusalem Council in Acts 15:2-7.

Paul called these leaders "the seeming somebodies" or "the apparently reputable ones." In doing so, he was employing a familiar rhetorical device: he reused the Judaizers' cherished designations for the leaders of the Jerusalem church in an ironic manner to disparage their argument that they could appeal to a greater authority than Paul. He called his opponents' reliance on the "pillars" into question and ultimately showed it to be invalid support for their argument. In 2:6, Paul refers to the "reputation" of the Jerusalem church leaders and then contrasts that idea with God's point of view in that "God has no favorites." This deconstruction laid the foundation for dealing honestly with the nature of the church "pillars" and the Judaizers' appeal to their authority (2:9). Thereafter (in 2:11-12), Paul demolished their argument by showing that those authorities had behaved in a way that was quite unlike Christ in regard to the issue at hand.

The sequence of events that Paul recounts in Galatians 2 shows why the expression was at least ironic, if not disparaging. In his report on the meeting with "the pillars," Paul told the Galatians that they affirmed his joint mission with Barnabas to the Gentiles. Furthermore, the Jerusalem leaders' acceptance of the Gentile Titus was a significant gesture toward not requiring circumcision for Gentile Christians (2:1-3). The issue would probably not have been raised except that some troublesome, sinister Judaizers upset the harmony of the meetings (2:4). So, Paul presents Titus as a test case against his Judaizing opponents. Titus, a Greek Gentile, had not been circumcised, and no one at Jerusalem required it of him. Some Judaizing opponents at Jerusalem had attempted to make circumcision a basis for Christianity (cf. 2:4), but this view did not prevail concerning Titus. (The strict Jewish opinion was that unless a man was circumcised, he did not belong to the covenant community; cf. McKnight 1991:80-82). Apparently, the views of the troublemakers were summarily dispatched, and agreement prevailed in this private meeting (2:2). But later, the "pillars" were apparently swayed by the erring and irritating Judaizers so that when Peter came to Antioch, he was waffling on the issue of Gentile fellowship and afraid to eat with them while "some friends of James" were there (2:11-12).

Sometimes readers are troubled by the comparison between the noncircumcision of Titus (2:3) and Paul's later insistence that Timothy be circumcised (Acts 16:3). Paul's rationale was probably that Timothy had a Jewish mother (Acts 16:1) and should therefore have been regarded as a Jewish Christian, not a Gentile Christian. Although Paul clearly advocated that there should be no distinctions in the gospel understanding (3:28), he also did not want to place hindrances in the presentation of the gospel. Thus, he was willing to eliminate possible hang-ups the Jews might have in order to win them for Christ (cf. 1 Cor 9:19-23). While the story in Acts evidently occurred after Galatians was written, it is important to recognize that Paul was neither anti-Jewish nor anti-Gentile (cf. 3:28), but pro-Christ! Whether someone was Jew or Gentile was not the point for him—they both needed Christ!

It seems clear from 2:4 that the pressure for circumcision did not come from the Jerusalem leaders but from "so-called Christians" (*pseudadelphous* [TG5569, ZG6012], "false brothers"), whom Paul vividly portrayed as sneaking spies (*pareisaktous . . . kataskopēsai* [TG3920/2684, ZG4207/2945]). Their goal was to discredit and destroy Paul's gospel. Their evil intent was focused on the missionaries' teaching about liberty "in Christ."

Paul pinpointed the spies' sinister goal as enforcing slavish adherence to Jewish laws and regulations for all Christians. But Paul completely refused to submit to them at all (2:5). He firmly denied any authority or credence to these imposters in their goal of subverting the gospel so that the Galatian Christians—and, by implication, all Gentile believers—would receive an uncontaminated gospel message. Paul's goal was the continuing preservation of the gospel's authenticity or integrity (Lightfoot 1865:107).

Once again, he reminded the Galatians that he owed his message to no human being (cf. 1:1, 11-12); in fact, not even the "reputable ones" supplemented his message (2:6). Nonetheless, he sought the apostles' blessing on his mission to the Gentiles. His desire for consultation proves that he was not a lone ranger. For Jerusalem and Paul to have been presenting different messages would have had disastrous consequences for evangelism (cf. Bruce 1982:111).

While Paul acknowledged the importance of the Jerusalem leaders, he nevertheless made it absolutely clear that human honor and prestige meant nothing. In dealing with his opponents, he realized that they might claim chronological precedence as being on their side if they could base their arguments on the authority of the Jerusalem leaders. Paul completely dismissed this line of thought. He followed this dismissal with a strong counterargument about God's impartiality (2:6), a familiar Pauline theme (e. g., Rom 2:11; 3:22; 10:12; Eph 6:9). This idea is foundational to Paul's thesis that there should be no distinctions among humans (3:28).

Paul's report about his relationship with the Jerusalem leaders is stunning (2:7-8). Not only did the leaders not add to Paul's gospel requirements, but they recognized that God had divided the responsibility for proclaiming the gospel (not two gospels) between Peter and Paul. Paul named Peter along with himself, indicating that he viewed Peter and himself as the leaders of two distinct areas of mission (for the use of *Cephas* and *Peter,* see note on 1:18).

It is probably very difficult for many Western Gentile Christians to grasp the importance of such an irenic spirit of cooperation. The meeting was composed of Jewish Christians who had grown up with a commitment to the Jewish practice of circumcision as the basis for receiving the promises to Abraham. Thus, it was revolutionary for them not to insist that Titus be circumcised. These verses stand alongside the remarkable verses of Acts 11:17-18 in demonstrating the changed mindset of Jewish Christians about Gentiles receiving the gospel.

In the last part of 2:9, Paul concluded his argument against his opponents by indicating that "the pillars" knew that he had been specially gifted by God and that they therefore extended to him and Barnabas "the right hand of fellowship." This affirmation of their apostolic commission ensured mutuality between Paul and the Jerusalem leaders rather than any kind of subordination.

This consultation visit was concluded with a directive to remember (a present subjunctive denoting continuing activity) the poor (2:10). It represents a familiar biblical injunction for believers to take care of the economically disadvantaged (cf. Luke 6:20). This practice became identified with holiness and humility (cf. Matt 5:3).

In summary, we need to understand that Paul presented his argument by clearly detailing the sequence of events that had taken place. It is not dissimilar to the report in Acts 11, where Peter had to report on the events concerning Cornelius to the Jerusalem leaders so that they could understand that God was doing something new within the church (Acts 11:17-18). Detailing information does not always lead to the resolution of different points of view, but it is an important element in enabling the church to reach greater consensus. Private events and meetings do not always yield merely private outcomes. The implications of such events often have ramifications far beyond the immediate circumstances, and, if the Spirit of God is evident in those events, they can provide insight for the church as a whole and affect the broader history of Christianity.

◆   ## D. The Confrontation at Antioch (2:11-13)

11But when Peter came to Antioch, I had to oppose him to his face, for what he did was very wrong. 12When he first arrived, he ate with the Gentile Christians, who were not circumcised. But afterward, when some friends of James came, Peter wouldn't eat with the Gentiles anymore. He was afraid of criticism from these people who insisted on the necessity of circumcision. 13As a result, other Jewish Christians followed Peter's hypocrisy, and even Barnabas was led astray by their hypocrisy.

N O T E S

2:11 *I had to oppose him to his face.* Paul said that he stood against Peter "to the face" (*kata prosōpon* [TG2596/4383, ZG2848/4725]). Peter and Paul thus had a face-off. Paul's judgment was that Peter "was condemned" (*kategnōsmenos* [TG2607, ZG2861]) for fracturing the fellowship between Jewish and Gentile Christians.

2:12 *who were not circumcised.* This colloquial expression is implied from the context.

people who insisted on the necessity of circumcision. It is quite possible that this text refers to radical Jews, who evoked fear, and to fearful Jewish Christians. If Acts is any indication of fear in the early church, then it should not be forgotten that before AD 70, the hostility against Christians arose from Jewish traditionalists who viewed Christians as heretical Jews. They not only killed Jesus and Stephen (Acts 7:54-60), but they also rejoiced when Herod Agrippa I (Acts 12:2) put James, the brother of John, to death. He also arrested Peter (Acts 12:3). People under pressure can act strangely, and it is clear that the infant church was struggling for existence within the powerful Jewish context in which they were living. Still, we must be careful not to read the power of the church in the post-Constantinian era back into early Christian times (F. C. Baur and his Tübingen ideas about powerful political struggles in the early church are dead! It is time to bury them).

2:13 *other Jewish Christians.* The "other" or remaining (*hoi loipoi* [TG3062, ZG3370]) Jews (*Ioudaioi* [TG2453A, ZG2681]) were probably Jewish Christians, seemingly distinct from "the circumcision," or non-Christian Jews. Accordingly, when James's associates came, the Christian Jews in Antioch joined in playing the hypocrite (*sunupekrithēsan* [TG4942, ZG5347]). "Hypocrisy" is a word taken from the Gr. theater; it implies "pretense" or "outward show" (BAGD 845).

even Barnabas was led astray by their hypocrisy. Peter's action influenced even Paul's associate, Barnabas. Paul never forgot how his close coworker was led astray (*sunapēchthē* [TG4879, ZG5270]; cf. BAGD 784).

COMMENTARY

The focus in this section shifts from Jerusalem to Antioch, where Peter visited the church that was on the forefront of the gospel mission to the Gentiles. In the first century, Antioch was the capital of the large imperial province of Syria. Situated on the Orontes along with its seaport, Seleucia (both cities were named after significant Seleucid figures), Antioch was one of the leading cities of the Roman Empire. It had piped water, a nighttime lighting system, and a Las Vegas-style entertainment center known as Daphne. It was *the* cosmopolitan city of Syria.

The coming of Peter and some Jewish believers to Antioch was nothing unusual—there was a significant Jewish population in Antioch, and Jews traveled regularly between Jerusalem and Antioch. It was most common there, as in Alexandria and elsewhere, for Jews to live in Jewish enclaves. The church in Antioch, however, also had many Gentile believers, thereby creating a new community outside of Judaism. In this new community, Jews and Gentiles ate together.

In the ancient world, eating together was a sign of acceptance, but Israel's restrictive food practices had prevented Jews from eating in Gentile homes for fear of eating forbidden food (see Lev 11:1-47) or of being too closely involved with idolatrous worship. These restrictions had expanded to the point that just eating with Gentiles was a violation of purity rules (*m. Tohorot* 7:6; 8:6; cf. *m. Berakot* 7:1; 8:6). Such practices reinforced the Gentile image of the Jews as a suspect and exclusivist subculture. Paul's insistence on the acceptance of Gentiles into community fellowship was directed against any similar Jewish Christian exclusivity. (Peter's experiences in Acts 10-11 argue toward this same end.) At the Antioch church, Jewish and Gentile Christians ate together—at least until some friends of James arrived.

The arrival of James's friends caused Peter to withdraw and separate from the Gentiles. How could Peter have been intimidated by James's friends when Peter had earlier been instructed by God in a vision that Gentiles should be treated as clean (or kosher; Acts 10:15)? Why did Peter separate from the Gentiles? The text does not say that Peter was afraid of James. Nor does the Greek say that he was afraid of the Jewish Christians, although the present rendering in the NLT suggests this idea by identifying them as "these" legalists. The word use in 2:15, as Longenecker (1990:73-75) has pointedly argued, shows that "the circumcision" (*peritomēs* [TG4061, ZG4364]) were Jews, although one might possibly argue that they were traditionalist Jewish Christians.

The Jewish Christians were probably not the ultimate source of the problem. Perhaps James's associates brought bad news of developing hostility by Pharisaic Jews against Jewish Christians who were seeking to remain in the fold of Judaism while also associating with Gentiles (see note on 2:12). (It is important at this point to remember that a later synagogue curse against the Nazarenes and *minim* or "heretics" was added to the Eighteen Benedictions [see Barrett 1961:166-167].) If persecution by radical Jews was an imminent possibility, then Cephas's fear would be understandable. It is certainly worth noting that Paul was seized in the Temple, according to Acts, on the charge that he had associated with Gentiles (Acts 21:21, 28-29; cf. Acts 22:21-22). While we cannot be sure of Paul's shorthand here, this certainly is a more meaningful alternative than arguing that Peter was afraid of James and his associates. From Paul's perspective, Peter would nevertheless stand condemned. The Greek text says nothing about what "the circumcision" were saying. Were these Jews in contrast to Jewish Christians? Could such a scenario still fit Paul's face-to-face confrontation with Cephas? I believe that the answer is "yes" because the possibility of being persecuted was not an adequate reason for turning away from the truth of the gospel. In Paul's mind, real truth included the freedom to have fellowship with Gentiles. Paul reminded the Galatians in this letter that he had experienced persecution (5:11) and bore in his body the scars of belonging to Jesus (6:17). To turn from the truth because he feared persecution would have meant rejecting the way of Christ.

Similar to his earlier denial of Jesus in the midst of a hostile setting (e.g., Mark 14:66-71), Peter again responded poorly to the pressure of hostile circumstances. In this crucial situation, Paul was God's man of the hour. He confronted Peter directly with his hypocritical actions, which had led other Christian Jews, including Barnabas, into an insincere relationship with the Gentile Christians. Therefore, the text provides a forceful illustration of the power of fear in immobilizing Christians— even Christian leaders—and offers an example of Christian integrity in the face of weakness and the possible collapse of community fellowship.

This meeting between Paul and Peter was a very critical moment in Christian history because it was a crucial point in defining Christianity. This section also explains why Paul had earlier categorized the Jerusalem leaders as having an apparent reputation (2:2, 6, 9). The so-called pillars did not always faithfully represent Christ— the same can be equally true of leaders today.

◆ IV. The Significance of Antioch: A Statement of the Issue (2:14-21)

[14]When I saw that they were not following the truth of the gospel message, I said to Peter in front of all the others, "Since you, a Jew by birth, have discarded the Jewish laws and are living like a Gentile, why are you now trying to make these Gentiles follow the Jewish traditions?

[15]"You and I are Jews by birth, not 'sin-ners' like the Gentiles. [16]Yet we know that a person is made right with God by faith in Jesus Christ, not by obeying the law. And we have believed in Christ Jesus, so that we might be made right with God because of our faith in Christ, not because we have obeyed the law. For no one will ever be made right with God by obeying the law."*

¹⁷But suppose we seek to be made right with God through faith in Christ and then we are found guilty because we have abandoned the law. Would that mean Christ has led us into sin? Absolutely not! ¹⁸Rather, I am a sinner if I rebuild the old system of law I already tore down. ¹⁹For when I tried to keep the law, it condemned me. So I died to the law—I stopped trying to meet all its requirements—so that I might live for God. ²⁰My old self has been crucified with Christ.* It is no longer I who live, but Christ lives in me. So I live in this earthly body by trusting in the Son of God, who loved me and gave himself for me. ²¹I do not treat the grace of God as meaningless. For if keeping the law could make us right with God, then there was no need for Christ to die.

2:16 Some translators hold that the quotation extends through verse 14; others through verse 16; and still others through verse 21.   2:20 Some English translations put this sentence in verse 19.

NOTES

2:14 While Betz (1979:113) and others (Bruce 1982:135; Longenecker 1990:80) argue that the narrative segment of Paul's rhetorical presentation concludes at 2:14, I see the propositional section of Paul's *apologia* as beginning at this point. I recognize, however, that this verse is transitional to the proposition. Scholars debate whether Paul's quotation should end at this verse or continue to 2:16 or even to the end of the chapter. Here, Paul seems to have merged a dialogical discourse with a more assertive monological argument, so it is difficult to be sure of the precise format. Paul has also made skillful use of questions (2:14, 17) in the familiar style of the Gr. diatribe (cf. Bultmann 1910). In these verses, Paul has very clearly defined the issues in terms of justification by faith (being regarded as right with God).

When. Lit., "But when." This section is introduced by a strong contrast to the general agreement described before. The words contextualize the forthcoming discourse as Paul's response to Peter's hypocrisy.

why are you now trying to make these Gentiles follow the Jewish traditions? Lit., "why force Gentiles to 'Judaize' [or 'become like Jews'] (*Ioudaizein*[TG2450, ZG2678])?" Did this argument have any effect on Peter? It is interesting to reflect on the similarity between this argument and the one that came from Peter's mouth before the Jerusalem Council as recorded in Acts 15:10 (which I hold to be a later event).

2:15 ***You and I are Jews by birth, not 'sinners' like the Gentiles.*** To understand Paul's argument here—about not being "sinners" and yet still being "sinners" (cf. 2:17)—it is necessary to turn to Paul's own testimony in Phil 3:6, where he claims to be "free of blame" or not "accused of any fault." If the Jews regarded the law as ultimate and perceived themselves as obedient, then the natural conclusion was that they were not sinners. The Gentiles did not even try to keep the law, so the conclusion was that they were sinners. When Paul met Jesus, however, he realized that this evaluative argument was flawed because the law was not the ultimate judge. God was! The law was only a means to God. Once Paul became a Christian, he could say that all of his Jewish efforts to keep the law were failures, a "manure pile," or "garbage" (Phil 3:8). That is why he knew that he and Peter were also sinners.

2:16 ***For no one will ever be made right with God by obeying the law.*** Paul universalized his thesis by collecting everyone into the scope of his argument with the words *pasa sarx* [TG3956/4561, ZG4246/4922] (all flesh) and then by negating the possibility of being justified or being judged right with God through human effort, epitomized in obedience to the law. He supported this idea with reference to Ps 143:2 (cf. Rom 3:20).

2:17 Those familiar with Rom 2–3 and with the ancient diatribe or debating techniques in both Jewish and Hellenistic traditions will recognize a similar pattern of argument in

Gal 2:17ff. The reader is guided through a possible critique of Paul's thesis by means of leading questions for which the final answer should be obvious, even to the novice. The way in which the argument is phrased in Gr. is intriguing, however, because the first question in English may be interpreted either as two parts of a single protasis or as both parts of a first class condition. In the first instance, one would understand the logical connections as "*If* we seek to be made right in Christ, and *if* we are found to be sinners, *then* would that mean Christ led us into sin?" The second option would be understood as "*If* we seek to be made right in Christ, *then* we are found to be sinners. Has Christ, then, led us into sin?"

Absolutely not! The final question that asks whether Christ is a servant or agent (*diakonos* [TG1249, ZG1356]) of sin can hardly be answered in the affirmative. Paul responds with his familiar, abrupt negation, *mē genoito* [TG3361/1096, ZG3590/1181] (variously translated as "absolutely not!" "ridiculous!" or the authoritative "God forbid!"). The implication is that there can be no acceptable contrary argument (cf. Rom 3:6, 31) for such a hypothesis. Whatever one might argue, there is no possibility that Christ is the agent of sin! Christ cannot be blamed for human failure.

2:18 Rather, I am a sinner. This expression (*parabatēn* [TG3848, ZG4127]) signifies a "transgressor" (BAGD 612), or one who stands under judgment (cf. Rom 2:25, 27).

if I rebuild the old system of law I already tore down. Using a building motif in argument to represent destruction and reconstruction was familiar to Jews; they viewed the Temple as a major focus of Israel's history and the wall that separated Jews from Gentiles on the Temple grounds as the symbol of their faithfulness to the God of Israel (cf. Acts 21:27-30; ISBE 4.759-776, especially at 772).

2:19 This verse points beyond itself to what I have elsewhere called the key passage of Galatians—namely, 3:23–4:7 (Borchert 1994:145-151)—and to Paul's later reasoning as to why the law could not accomplish what he had earlier thought it could (3:19-22).

I died to the law—I stopped trying to meet all its requirements. This expansion helps to interpret Paul's abbreviated Gr., "for through law I died to law."

2:20 My old self has been crucified with Christ. The use of the perfect tense here signifies that the crucifixion of Paul's old self with Christ has continued effects in his life. The Gr. prefix (*sun* [TG4862, ZG5250]) of *sunestaurōmai* [TG4957, ZG5365] means "together"; Paul was picturing himself as following his master in a life of self-sacrifice. He viewed himself as copying or imitating Christ (cf. Phil 3:8,10,17; 1 Pet 4:13). Paul did not thereby exalt himself but accepted Christ's death as his model for life.

It is no longer I who live, but Christ lives in me. The contrasting pattern of life and death is a thematic Pauline image that is also found in a number of texts in Romans (on baptism, Rom 6:1-11; the Christian struggle, Rom 7:7-25; living in the Spirit, Rom 8:1-17). This contrast between life and death is clearly drawn from the choice God set between the two ways (cf. Deut 30:15; Jer 21:8; cf. also Matt 10:39; 25:46; John 3:16-18), with the way of life being the only acceptable alternative.

So I live in this earthly body by trusting in the Son of God. In some important Gr. mss (𝔓46 B D* G), there is a variant that reads, "the Son of God and Christ," but the use of such an expression for the object of faith is unusual and makes such a reading unlikely (cf. Longenecker 1990:94).

2:21 the grace of God. This statement parallels OT expressions of the loving and tender mercy (*khesed* [TH2617, ZH2876]) of God. It contributes to Paul's thesis that the Judaizers had misunderstood both God's grace and the role of the law since they envisioned earning status with God through their view of obedience to the law.

COMMENTARY

Because of the Galatians' attempt to win God's favor through human effort, Paul's task was to reduce any kind of legalism to absurdity. In this section, he reminded the Galatians that both he and Peter were members of God's covenant with Israel. Yet he stressed that neither he nor Peter were able to depend on obedience to the law as the basis for being justified or declared right with God. Such a declaration comes only through faith in the faithfulness of Jesus Christ, God's Son, and not by trying to obey the law or keep a set of rules.

Paul confronted Peter about his two-faced behavior publicly, before "all" the Christians in Antioch. Paul did so for the sake of the gospel and because earlier he had been the model of strict adherence to Jewish traditions (cf. 1:14). Accordingly, he knew how to evaluate Peter. He judged Peter as not following the strict Torah requirements of a Christian Jew (*Ioudaikōs* [TG2452, ZG2680]), which probably meant that he was not eating according to strict kosher food laws. Paul could easily regard him as living like a Gentile on the one hand but refusing table fellowship with Gentile Christians on the other.

Evidencing his ability in rhetorical argument, Paul joined himself with Peter and differentiated Jewish Christians from Gentiles according to historical Jewish understanding. Gentiles were, in that understanding, rejected by Jews as "sinners" (cf. Matt 5:43-48/Luke 6:27-36; Matt 6:7, 32; Rom 1:18; cf. also 1 Macc 2:44; *Jubilees* 23:23-24; 1QH 10[2]:8-12), as "dogs" (cf. Matt 7:6; Mark 7:28), and as those outside the covenant with Abraham. By contrast, Jews believed that they were a privileged people because they were, by birth, members of the covenant community (cf. Rom 9:4-5).

To understand Paul's argument about not being sinners (2:15) and yet still being sinners (2:17), it is necessary to turn to Paul's own testimony in Philippians 3:6, where he claims to be free of blame and not accused of any fault. If the Jews regarded the law as the ultimate standard and perceived themselves as obedient to it, then the natural conclusion was that they were not sinners. But the Gentiles did not even try to keep the law. Therefore, the conclusion of such an argument would be that they were sinners. When Paul met Jesus, however, he learned that this evaluative argument was flawed because the law was not the ultimate judge. God was! The law was only a means to God. Indeed, as a Christian, he could then say of all of his Jewish efforts with the law that they were a failure, a manure pile, or "garbage" (Phil 3:8). That is why he knew that he and Peter were also sinners.

Following this argument, Paul set out his basic thesis: a person, such as Peter or Paul, cannot depend on "works of the law" or on Jewish religious activity to become rightly related to God. Peter and Paul agreed on this issue: their birth and religious activity did not make them Christians; what enabled them to become Christians was their relationship to Jesus. Unlike the Qumran covenanters who organized their community to promote and test the fulfillment of legal obligations (cf. 1QS 5:20-23) and the rabbis who formulated the Oral Law (later codified as the Mishnah) to assure responsive faithfulness to the covenant,[1] Paul purposely emphasized that a relationship with God begins with faith in Jesus Christ and continues by that same faith. This idea is expressed in Romans 1:16-17 as "out of faith, to faith" (*ek pisteōs eis pistin* [TG4102, ZG4411]), an idiom for something that begins and continues to the end (cf. also the classic statement in Gal 3:11).

Paul clearly articulated that he was a Jew by birth. He knew that God had given to Israel the gift of a relationship with God by means of his covenant with them. Building upon that understanding, he recognized that becoming rightly related to God did not come through traditional Jewish obedience to the law. Rather, it came "through faith in Jesus Christ" and/or "by Jesus Christ's faithfulness." This expression (Gr., *dia pisteōs Iesou Christou*) is capable of several meanings, depending on whether it is viewed as an objective genitive (our faith in Jesus Christ) or a subjective genitive (Jesus Christ's faith or faithfulness). In his discussions about faith, Paul was emphasizing either one or the other and perhaps even intended to encompass both ideas, depending on whether his concern was for his readers to understand their faith in Christ or Christ's faithfulness. For contemporary readers, it is probably best to realize that our faith is dependent upon the faithfulness of Jesus and to take these statements as purposefully ambiguous.

Paul strengthened his argument by emphasizing that both he and Peter believed in Christ Jesus so that they, like all other Christians, might be justified (or be declared righteous) by Christ's faithfulness (or their faith in Christ) and not because of any human effort related to their Jewish heritage. The capstone of Paul's argument is, "For no one will ever be made right with God by obeying the law" (2:16). Paul confessed that he had died to the hopeless goal of keeping the law so that he might be crucified with Christ and live for God.

The meaning of "becoming right with God" or "being justified" has been debated frequently throughout the history of the church. Summarizing the fundamental issue, the point here is whether believers have been made righteous by some infusion (or infusions) of God's grace (so Ritschl and the Roman Catholic view) or have been declared/regarded as righteous by God through the death and resurrection of the righteous Jesus Christ (so the Protestants, with Luther and Calvin, who called this "imputed righteousness"). More recently, some discussions have focused on whether or not Paul was using transfer terminology (so Sanders 1977:470-472)—that is, that Christ's righteousness has been transferred to us. There has also been recent attention on whether the idea in Paul's writings is "relational" or "ethical" (cf. Bruce 1982:138 and Longenecker 1990:84-85). In the final analysis, the meaning of the verb *dikaioō* [TG1344, ZG1467] (justify) probably has both relational and ethical implications for Paul (so Ziesler 1972; cf. Seifrid 1992 for a historical study).

Paul then addresses a common question: how can we seek to be right in Christ and then discover that we are still sinners (2:17)? The precise meaning of this question is uncertain: Does the discovery of being a sinner come from being right with God? Or is the discovery an ethical discovery so that although we seek to be justified, we find ourselves still sinning? Or does it mean that when Paul and Peter ate with the Gentiles, they were judged by strict Jews to be disobedient or "sinners"?

These and other possibilities have been suggested by various scholars, and there may be some truth or basis for argument in all of them, depending on one's presuppositions. In any case, Paul is masterful in frustrating Jewish logic but clearly expresses that Christians, though justified by Christ, still sin. Sinful Christians, however, do not make Christ the source of sin. Rather, he is the justifier.

Ironically, Paul stated that he would be a sinner if he rebuilt the old systems he had torn down. Normally, Jews thought of themselves as sinners when they failed to obey the law. Once Paul was converted, he took the opposite stand—it would be a sin for him to try to keep the law. That would be like rebuilding a structure he had already torn down. It is possible (esp. with the Gentile fellowship issue at hand) that Paul was here alluding to the wall of the Temple that separated Jews from Gentiles—a wall that Christ broke down by his death on the cross (Eph 2:14). In any event, Paul was not about to return to his former Judaism. Why? Paul gives his answer in 2:19. He insisted on the helpless state of the law and his determination to abandon the law (dying to the law) as the means of realizing his goal of living for God. His hope of acceptance by God could not be achieved merely by obeying rules. Moreover, Paul epitomized his critique of the law with a dynamic image of reversal. He had died to the law by being crucified with Christ. Paul then viewed his living for God as a death to the old way of the law, which he had abandoned since it was ineffective for salvation. To accept it again would be to deny Christ. To assume that obedience to the law could effect salvation would be to make Christ and his death totally irrelevant!

Instead of giving one iota of credence to the views of the Galatian legalists, Paul declared that since he had been crucified with Christ, he no longer lived except by the Christ who lived in him, the one who loved him and died for him (2:20). The force of the statement is shocking and must not be toned down or spiritualized. Paul genuinely believed himself to be a transformed person (cf. 2 Cor 5:17), a member of a new created order in which life and death are seen from an entirely different perspective (cf. Phil 1:21) and the old fear of condemnation is removed by living in Christ. Such freedom could never come from relying on human endeavor to obey the law (cf. Rom 8:1-4).

Paul declared that his new life was based on the reality that Christ lived in him. This relationship has often been called "Pauline mysticism."[2] However one understands this mysticism, it carries no hint of self-absorption or seclusion. Paul's view of a relationship with Christ always involves a dynamic relationship with the community of faith. Moreover, Paul made it clear that while he was talking about life and death, he was not proclaiming a theology of escape from the body. Rather, Paul viewed the body positively as a vehicle for expressing the presence of Christ.

It is important to recognize that Paul could use the term "flesh" both positively and negatively. When Paul used the term negatively, he meant that the human physical nature had become an end in itself or served a selfish, evil purpose (cf. Rom 7:14-8:17). But the body or flesh could also be a positive vehicle for expressing faith in the Son of God and for honoring him in one's life. Paul was motivated to live positively because the Son of God loved him and delivered himself up for Paul. Paul viewed the love-motivated death of Jesus for him (*huper* [TG5228, ZG5642] *emou*, "on my behalf") as a very personal event that changed him from being a legalist. But it was hardly an exclusive event for Paul, since he also included the Galatians as recipients of the crucifixion (3:1) and the power of Christian freedom (5:1).

Finally, Paul confronted the Galatian legalists directly in 2:21 by completely denying that he had negated the significance of God's grace. In doing so, he set the stage for asserting that it was not he, but the "foolish" Galatians, who had treated the grace of God as null and void. Paul summarized the ridiculous legalist argument: If the legalists assumed that righteousness (or acceptance by God) could be attained through obedience to the law, there could be no other conclusion than that the death of Christ was extraneous to salvation. If this argument were true, the entire rationale for Christian faith and salvation would be destroyed, and the Galatian legalists would have won the case—but then they could hardly be called Christians! All Christians, therefore, who read this section of Galatians should pause and reflect on whether they are trying to live by laws and rules as a substitute for living by grace.

ENDNOTES
1. For an extended discussion of covenantal law-keeping, see Sanders 1977:511-515, expanded in Sanders 1983, especially at 17-29.
2. I know of three classifications: Deissmann's "reacting mysticism" (1926:149-157; cf. 135-139); Schweitzer's "sacramental mysticism" (1931:118-124); and Cave's "community mysticism" (1929:50).

◆ V. Paul's Rationale for Salvation by Faith in Christ Jesus (3:1–4:31)
    A. Four Proofs against Legalism (3:1-18)
        1. A shocking rebuke (3:1-5)

Oh, foolish Galatians! Who has cast an evil spell on you? For the meaning of Jesus Christ's death was made as clear to you as if you had seen a picture of his death on the cross. ²Let me ask you this one question: Did you receive the Holy Spirit by obeying the law of Moses? Of course not! You received the Spirit because you believed the message you heard about Christ. ³How foolish can you be? After starting your Christian lives in the Spirit, why are you now trying to become perfect by your own human effort? ⁴Have you experienced* so much for nothing? Surely it was not in vain, was it?

⁵I ask you again, does God give you the Holy Spirit and work miracles among you because you obey the law? Of course not! It is because you believe the message you heard about Christ.

3:4 Or *Have you suffered.*

NOTES
3:1 *Oh, foolish Galatians! Who has cast an evil spell on you?* Some mss (C D² Ψ 0278 33ᶜ 1881 𝔐) add "not to obey the truth." This scribal addition was an attempt to harmonize this verse with 5:7. The Gr. verb translated "has cast an evil spell" (*ebaskanen* [TG940, ZG1001]) does not appear elsewhere in the NT, but in other Gr. writers it means to come

under the power of the "evil eye" or to be "bewitched" (cf. Betz 1979:131). The treatment for this spell was supposedly "spitting 3 times" (BAGD 137).

the meaning of Jesus Christ's death was made as clear to you as if you had seen a picture of his death on the cross. This sentence expands Paul's Gr. shorthand concerning the Galatians' previous knowledge of Christ's death.

3:2 Let me ask you this one question. In typical diatribe fashion, this statement opens the way to a question with an answer that Paul knows will be obvious to his readers.

Of course not! The NLT supplies, for modern English readers, the implied response.

You received the Spirit because you believed the message you heard about Christ. This statement expands the very truncated expression, "out of hearing by faith."

3:4 Have you experienced so much for nothing? Commentators are divided as to whether *epathete* (from *paschō*) is to be interpreted in a positive sense (as "experience") or a negative sense (as "suffering"); see NLT mg. While there are some uses of the verb among Gr. writers that seem to indicate a positive or at least a neutral sense, the most frequent uses in the LXX and particularly in the NT refer to difficult experiences of suffering (cf. Luke 22:15; Acts 1:3; 1 Cor 12:26; Heb 2:18; 1 Pet 2:20; BAGD 633-634). A question is raised by Paul's use of *paschō* [TG3958, ZG4248] because there is no record of the Galatians suffering except in this text and possibly in 6:12.

3:5 work miracles among you. It is not clear to what specific miracles Paul was referring; he may have been reminding them of such acts as the healing of the cripple in Lystra (Acts 14:8-10), which would presuppose a southern Galatian context for the letter (see "Date, Occasion of Writing, and Audience" in the Introduction).

COMMENTARY

In this section (3:1-4:31), Paul moves to the heart of his argument with the Galatians. He readily accepts the challenge of supporting his arguments about abandoning the law and adopting faith in Christ as the basis for being declared righteous and acceptable to God. While commentators differ variously as to how the remainder of Galatians is organized, it is quite apparent that Paul, like an able attorney, used supporting proofs to build his case. While some of the arguments, such as 3:1-5 and 4:8-11, resemble Hellenistic rhetoric, other parts, such as 3:15-18 and 4:21-31 are very Jewish in their format. Taken as a whole, this section is a magnificent synthesis of two styles of thinking that can be found elsewhere in Paul (see Rom 1:18-3:19).

Paul begins his defense of the gospel by rebuking the Galatians for their irrational defection from their transforming experience of receiving the Holy Spirit through faith in Christ. Rebuke was familiar in Hellenistic rhetoric. What follows, however, indicates that Paul was not just using a rhetorical ploy. He was absolutely serious when he said that their actions were stupid and their logic was irrational. But did Paul go too far in calling them "fools"? Didn't Paul open himself to the condemnation of Jesus for calling someone a "fool" (Matt 5:22)? If Paul had rejected them because he assumed superiority, he might have been in danger of Gehenna, as Jesus said. But his goal was exactly the opposite; his intentions were to rescue the Galatians from apostasy. Paul used five incisive rhetorical questions to demonstrate to the Galatians that they stood self-condemned for abandoning the way of faith and for foolishly following the way of legalism.

Question 1: Who has cast an evil spell on you? This question at 3:1 is the first of five strategic questions in the style of the Greek diatribe, a rhetorical device that showed opposing views to be illogical. When Paul asked if they had come under a magician's spell, he was probably using the term figuratively, since it would be pressing the rhetoric too far to suggest that Paul's opponents had actually used magic upon the Galatians. Nevertheless, Paul's discussion of the role of the Spirit in what follows reminds us that he was more sensitive to spiritual realities than most people in today's Western world (cf. Neyrey 1988:72-100). He did not treat the power of evil lightly.

The pithy, picturesque language of Paul's depiction of the crucified Jesus suggests that he must have been a fascinating preacher. It was hard for Paul to understand how the Galatians could stray from his vivid presentation of the gospel. They were indeed foolish for substituting obedience to the law for Christ's sacrificial death, which accomplished complete reconciliation for all who believe and thereby receive the Spirit.

Question 2: Did you receive the Holy Spirit by obeying the law of Moses? Paul's mention of the Holy Spirit in the context of believing indicates that Paul considered "faith in Christ" to be a completely different orientation than "obedience to the law." According to their experience, the Galatians should have known that the Spirit was directly linked to faith-acceptance and not to legalistic works. That was where they went astray. Indeed, the experience of the Spirit was, for the early Christians, proof positive that they were regenerated people of God (see 4:6; Acts 10:45; Rom 5:5).

Some scholars have argued that this mention of the Spirit is almost an aside (cf. Lightfoot 1890:133-136), but Longenecker (1990:101-102) correctly, I believe, sees the role of the Spirit as the underlying presupposition to Paul's argument for a law-free gospel. Without the presence of the Spirit, their understanding of Christ and faith would be carnal or worldly (3:3; 4:3, 9).

Question 3: How foolish can you be? After starting your Christian lives in the Spirit, why are you now trying to become perfect by your own human effort? This third question (3:3) has two parts. Paul first returned to the subject of their foolishness (*anoētoi* [TG453, ZG485]), or irrational behavior, by asking if they had lost their minds. The second part presents another set of incompatible opposites. Normally, the beginning and end of the Christian life should go down the same path, but the Galatians had bifurcated their lives into two orientations. They had begun their Christian experience, through Paul's preaching, oriented to the Spirit (*pneumati* [TG4151, ZG4460]), but then they had switched loyalties in midcourse to other teachers and were trying to reach perfection (*epiteleisthe* [TG2005, ZG2200]) by an orientation that Paul called the "flesh" (*sarki* [TG4561, ZG4922]; see 3:3). Paul details the contrast between these two orientations most clearly in Romans 8:2-9. For Paul, the orientation to the flesh involved making the created order and its ways the focus of life (cf. Moo 1991:510-523; Dunn 1988:419-429).

Question 4: Have you experienced so much for nothing? Surely it was not in vain, was It? The fourth rhetorical question at 3:4 asks what the Galatians' abandonment of their previous experience of faith and orientation to the way of the Spirit would mean. Paul said that they had made their earlier experiences or sufferings (see note on 3:4) empty by their subsequent adoption of legalism.

Question 5: I ask you again, does God give you the Holy Spirit and work miracles among you because you obey the law? This fifth and final rhetorical question completes Paul's logical argument. It points the Galatians to God and then asks them, "How did God commence your new Christian life—by obedience to the law or by the hearing of faith?" This question does not merely summarize the previous question, as some commentators have suggested; rather, it emphasizes the centrality of God's activity by using two powerful verbs that represent God's provision (*epichorēgōn* [TG2023, ZG2220]) and God's effective working (*energōn* [TG1754, ZG1919]). The giving of the Spirit and the working of miracles among the Galatians provided an indisputable testimony. How could they deny their experience of God's presence through his saving and sustaining power? All human effort pales in significance before the power of God.

These questions continually serve to warn contemporary Christians against adopting a life of rule-keeping and legalism as a substitute for God's gracious provision in Christ for all who live in the Spirit.

◆   ## 2. A biblical example: Abraham (3:6-9)

6In the same way, "Abraham believed God, and God counted him as righteous because of his faith."* 7The real children of Abraham, then, are those who put their faith in God.

8What's more, the Scriptures looked forward to this time when God would declare the Gentiles to be righteous because of their faith. God proclaimed this good news to Abraham long ago when he said, "All nations will be blessed through you."* 9So all who put their faith in Christ share the same blessing Abraham received because of his faith.

3:6 Gen 15:6.   3:8 Gen 12:3; 18:18; 22:18.

NOTES

3:6 For the contemporary reader to perceive the logic of Paul's discussions here and later in such passages as the Hagar argument (4:21-31), it is essential to have some understanding of Jewish thought and rabbinic exegetical logic. I will supply some brief background comments at relevant points, but those interested in pursuing rabbinic logic further are encouraged to consult other discussions (e.g. Barrett 1976:1-16; Longenecker 1975:19-50, 104-132; Sanders 1983:18-29). The arguments that follow are based on Paul's exegesis of Scripture and challenge the arguments of the Galatians and their erroneous teachers (Barrett 1985:22-24; Bruce 1982:155, Longenecker 1990:109-110).

3:7 In Gr., this verse begins with the phrase "you know, then." It might be taken as a signal that an announcement is being made, such as, "know then!" (which I tend to prefer), or it could be a simple statement of fact: "you know, then." The NLT seems to take this second view, omitting the phrase for smoother English.

3:8 *What's more, the Scriptures looked forward to this time when God would declare the Gentiles to be righteous because of their faith. God proclaimed this good news to Abraham long ago when he said, "All nations will be blessed through you."* This statement is not meant as an explanation of the argument of 3:7 but as an addition to it, joined to it by the conjunction *de* [TG1161, ZG1254] ("what's more"). This addition asserts that the real children of Abraham are not restricted to Jews but include Gentiles who, like Abraham, accept God's promise in faith. The Scripture is personified as having the ability to "look forward." Scripture is not detached from God, however; it is identified with God's will and God's ability to foresee the future (cf. TDNT 1.754). As such, Paul expressed a very high view of Scripture.

COMMENTARY

In this section, Paul uses the example of Abraham, a man of faith, to show that this Jewish forefather's example would not support an argument that human activity could make a person accepted or justified by God. As the starting point for his argument, Paul cites Genesis 15:6 to emphasize Abraham's faith (cf. Rom 4:3) in an exemplary proof-text that confirms the difference between works of the law and the hearing of faith discussed in the previous section. In contrast to Paul's understanding of Abraham's faith, the rabbis would have argued that Abraham was judged righteous because he had been faithful in the time of testing and was consequently rewarded (cf. Targum Pseudo-Jonathan on Gen 15:6; *Exodus Rabbah* 3:12; see also Longenecker 1990:113-114). The rabbis understood the reward as the establishment of the everlasting covenant of Genesis 17:1-8 with its unbreakable sign of circumcision (Gen 17:9-14; cf. Sir 44:19-21; 1 Macc 2:52; *Jubilees* 17:15-18). James, who also comments on Abraham's faith (Jas 2:22-24), has a different starting point. He assumes Christian faith and then questions the actuality of that faith if it does not evidence the reality of a transformed life. To understand James correctly, one needs to consider Christians who assume that nothing more is needed than faith— Christians who misunderstand Paul.

Paul had been brought up with a rabbinic perspective, but when he became a Christian, he realized that Abraham did not merit the covenant. Instead, the covenant was a promise from God that Abraham accepted by faith. This distinction was foundational for Paul; it went to the heart of his conflict with the Galatians and their misguided teachers because they had undoubtedly relied on Abraham as their role model for the place of both circumcision and human effort in being justified (see Lightfoot's classic comparison of Paul and Philo at this point; 1865:159-163). Not only did Paul assert that circumcision and human effort were of no avail, but he also presented faith not as an alternative type of good work but simply as the acceptance of God's generosity. Abraham did nothing to warrant the promise; rather, he became a model for all time as one who heard the promise and believed God. Abraham's faithfulness flowed from and did not precede the promise uttered by God.

In complete harmony with the scriptural prediction, all authentic children of Abraham, whether Gentiles or Jews, are accepted by God, not on the basis of their human status or activity, but on the basis of their faith. Paul clearly identified the issue at 3:7 as going beyond Abraham to those who would be his authentic descendants.

One important issue in this entire argument is how often Paul uses the concept of faith or believing; the people of faith, not the legalists, were the genuine children of Abraham. Moreover, Paul's use of the generic *huioi* [TG5207, ZG5626] (sons, children) is obviously used in contrast to "seed" (*spermati* [TG4690, ZG5065]), both because of his concern for the Gentiles who did not need to be circumcised (3:8), and his basic thesis that there was only one legitimate "seed" of Abraham (namely, Christ; see comments on 3:16).

The Galatians and their misguided teachers (3:8) undoubtedly viewed themselves as being true heirs of the promise to Abraham (Gen 12:3; 18:18; 22:18; 26:4). But their view of being children of Abraham was dependent on their reformulation of the promise in Genesis 12:3 and on their understanding that both circumcision and the law were required. Paul emphatically declared that these requirements were outside the scope of acceptance by faith. He staunchly rejected the idea that the blessing to "all the nations" (*panta ta ethnē* [TG1484, ZG1620]) meant that all Gentiles had to become Jews in order to be accepted by God. Instead, the promise was extended to all persons who were united with Christ by faith.

In 3:9, Paul concludes his argument with a general declaration that places all believers, both Jews and Gentiles, into the same universal community. This community has its origin and existence in faith (*ek pisteōs* [TG1537/4102, ZG1666/4411]; cf. Rom 1:17), together with the forefather of faith, Abraham (cf. Rom 4:1-3, 16-17). Not only did Paul reject the idea that Gentiles had to become Jews, but he also rejected the idea that Jews had to deny their Jewish heritage to become Christians (Rom 11:1-2). Instead, he firmly maintained that all were called to faith as Abraham was, and all those of faith should be included in the blessing that came to Abraham.

Paul was neither anti-Jewish nor anti-Gentile; he was an advocate of faith in Christ, and he found in Scripture an ideal model of what faith and believing really mean. Abraham's faith was a positive response to God's promise. He heard and believed. Everyone must understand that faith is the fundamental basis for Christianity; a person does not need to have faith plus something else. Faith alone—*sola fide*—makes a person right with God.

◆   ## 3. The curse of the law (3:10-14)

10But those who depend on the law to make them right with God are under his curse, for the Scriptures say, "Cursed is everyone who does not observe and obey all the commands that are written in God's Book of the Law."* 11So it is clear that no one can be made right with God by trying to keep the law. For the Scriptures say, "It is through faith that a righ-teous person has life."* 12This way of faith is very different from the way of law, which says, "It is through obeying the law that a person has life."*

13But Christ has rescued us from the curse pronounced by the law. When he was hung on the cross, he took upon himself the curse for our wrongdoing. For it is written in the Scriptures, "Cursed is everyone who is hung on a tree."* [14]Through Abraham, so that we who are believers Christ Jesus, God has blessed the Gentiles might receive the promised* Holy Spirit with the same blessing he promised to through faith.

3:10 Deut 27:26.   **3:11** Hab 2:4.   **3:12** Lev 18:5.   **3:13** Deut 21:23 (Greek version).   **3:14** Some manuscripts read *the blessing of the.*

N O T E S

3:11 *So it is clear that no one can be made right with God by trying to keep the law.* Sanders (1983:18-29) has proposed that Paul would hardly have suggested that it was impossible to keep the law, even though that is what Paul said. Instead, Sanders argues that this statement was merely a polemic against the misguided teachers of the Galatians, who were concerned primarily with circumcision as a means of gaining acceptance with God and reception into the covenant people. While Sanders has corrected some categorical misconceptions about the law and Second Temple Judaism, his interpretation misses the point of Paul's logic here (cf. Schreiner 1985:245-278).

For the Scriptures say, "It is through faith that a righteous person has life." Paul did not repeat the formula *gegraptai* [TG1125, ZG1211] (it has been written), but there is no question that it is implied here following 3:10. Habakkuk 2:4 (the quoted text) is also cited at Rom 1:17 and in Heb 10:38 (though "my" is added there as in the LXX).

3:12 *It is through obeying the law that a person has life.* This rendering expands on the terse quote from Lev 18:5, "the one doing them will live by them."

3:13 *For it is written in the Scriptures, "Cursed is everyone who is hung on a tree."* This statement is not an exact quotation of Deut 21:23, which stipulates burial of an executed person on the same day to prevent defilement of the land (cf. the exposure of Saul's body at Beth Shan in 1 Sam 31:10-13). By the first century AD, however, this text was applied not only to exposed corpses but also to living persons who were put to death on wooden poles, as in crucifixion (Fitzmyer 1978:493-513).

3:14 *the same blessing he promised to Abraham.* Although there is no mention of the Holy Spirit as a promise to Abraham, Christians are given the Holy Spirit as a sign that they have become heirs of Abraham.

C O M M E N T A R Y

At this point in his argument, Paul turns from the model of Abraham to focus on the negative aspect of the law—he speaks of the law's curse. He highlights this idea with three strategic statements, each with its scriptural proof-text (Garland 1994:175), and thus attacked the Galatians' positive view of the law and legalism. At the same time, he made an important statement about the meaning of Christ's death.

In the first of his three scripturally-based assertions (3:10), Paul focused on those who, like the Galatians, had placed their confidence in works of the law (*ergōn nomou* [TG2041/3551, ZG2240G/3795]). They may well have quoted to Paul the curse of Deuteronomy 27:26 (and its positive parallel in Lev 18:5) to support the necessity of keeping the law. But instead of applying the curse to the non-law-keeping Gentiles, as the legalists might have argued, Paul responded by applying the curse to all who attempted to keep the law—for Paul knew that no one could really do so successfully.

The Galatians may have been surprised that, instead of avoiding the anticipated problem text of Deuteronomy 27:26, Paul actually quoted it. But then he emphasized "all things" (*pasin* [TG3956, ZG4246]) and the keeping or "doing" (*poiesai* [TG4160, ZG4472]) of every single thing in the book of the law, not just being generally law-abiding. The Galatians, like the rabbis, hardly expected to have to keep the law so completely to obtain its blessings and avoid its curses (Dunn 1993:171-173). A determined young Pharisee such as Saul might have tried to do better than most (cf. 1:14), but he probably also had to rely on the means of forgiveness when he realized that he had fallen short. The misguided Galatians, however, must have thought that they could pick and choose among the laws, whereas Paul was ready to hold them to every word of the law. He knew that they had put their necks in a legalistic noose, and he was ready to make them hang by their own weak logic.

Because Paul, the former Jewish fanatic, knew the impossibility of absolute obedience to law (3:11), he was a powerful spokesman for the very different way of righteousness, a way that relied on God's grace rather than on human effort. Gaining acceptance with God does not come by legalistic obedience. Instead, justification comes by faith in the "cursed" and crucified Christ who set people free from the curse of the law (3:13).

The time-honored expressions, "to be justified," or "to be declared righteous" (*dikaioutai* [TG1344, ZG1467]), mean being made right with God. In Greek, "with God" can also be rendered "before God," which suggests a court scene with a person standing before the judge (God) who hears the verdict. But the hoped-for verdict of acquittal and acceptance before God could never come on the basis of keeping the law. There had to be another way.

Significantly, this way had already been written in the Old Testament, in Habakkuk 2:4, but the Jews had not understood this text to mean that justification comes by faith. For example, the Qumran scribes, following the typical Jewish tradition in which faith was interpreted as faithfulness, applied the same text to themselves as obedient Jews (1QpHab 7:17–8:3). Paul's interpretation of Habakkuk 2:4 (here and at Rom 1:17) is that faith is reliance on God. This verse was crucial to Paul's logic of justification and is widely regarded as a key text in the Protestant Reformation (cf. Luther 1955–1975: 26.268-270; 27.257-258 [published in 1519 and 1535 on Galatians 3:11]; 1955–1975:25.9, 151-153 [on Romans 1:17]). C. H. Dodd has also argued that the early Christians selected this Old Testament text for inclusion in their early *testimonia* (lists of verses used by Christians in preaching and apologetics) to prove that Jesus was the fulfillment of the promises in Scripture (Dodd 1952:50-51).

Paul's continuing insistence that faith rather than law is the basis for justification makes it clear that his reliance on faith could not be compromised. Those who lived by the law had to fulfill all of it (Lev 18:4) or suffer God's curse (Deut 27:26). The Galatians had to realize their plight. They also had to understand that Christ had taken away the curse of the law by becoming a curse for us as part of our redemption (cf. 4:5).

This representation of the crucifixion as a redeeming event for us has prompted theological images of redemption in terms of a slave-market price being paid. These word pictures, however, must not be pressed too far. For example, neither Paul nor this analogy really speak to the question of who received the price that was paid in order to effect redemption (cf. 1 Cor 6:20; 7:23). The point is that an exchange occurred in which Christ, in redeeming us, became a curse for us, who were under a curse (Deut 27:26) because of our disobedience.

The idea of the death of Jesus the Messiah by crucifixion (and the curse that implied) must have been horrendous to the former rabbinic Jew, Saul of Tarsus. Yet once he became a Christian, the cross became the focal point of his preaching (cf. 1 Cor 1:18). Paul saw Jesus' becoming the curse for us as having two important implications (3:14), both of which are introduced by the Greek word *hina* [TG2443, ZG2671] (an identifier for purpose or result clauses). The first implication is that, in Christ, outsiders (the Gentiles) can become insiders to the blessings of Abraham. The great division between Jew and Gentile was rendered inoperative by Christ, who took upon himself the curse that belongs to everyone. The second important implication is that by faith, a person can become a child of Abraham and receive the promised Holy Spirit. The Spirit's presence is not earned by legalistic obedience or by pious activity. The Holy Spirit is a pure and simple gift received through faith. Accordingly, even if we are Gentiles, we receive the blessings foretold to Abraham and the Holy Spirit in our lives when we become Christians.

◆　　## 4. Analogy from the promises of the covenant (3:15-18)

¹⁵Dear brothers and sisters,* here's an example from everyday life. Just as no one can set aside or amend an irrevocable agreement, so it is in this case. ¹⁶God gave the promises to Abraham and his child.* And notice that the Scripture doesn't say "to his children,*" as if it meant many descendants. Rather, it says "to his child"— and that, of course, means Christ. ¹⁷This is what I am trying to say: The agreement God made with Abraham could not be canceled 430 years later when God gave the law to Moses. God would be breaking his promise. ¹⁸For if the inheritance could be received by keeping the law, then it would not be the result of accepting God's promise. But God graciously gave it to Abraham as a promise.

3:15 Greek *Brothers.*　3:16a Greek *seed;* also in 3:16c, 19. See notes on Gen 12:7 and 13:15.　3:16b Greek *seeds.*

N O T E S

3:15 *Dear brothers and sisters.* The use of *adelphoi* [TG80, ZG81] (brothers, friends) at the beginning of a paragraph frequently signals that Paul is switching his style or tone (cf. 1:11; 4:12; 5:13).

here's an example from everyday life. Lit., "I am speaking as a human," or "humanly speaking." In other words, Paul is going to use human logic and analogies (Cosgrove 1988:543-545).

3:17 *This is what I am trying to say.* The expression is intended for emphasis as well as to signal a clarification.

430 years later. These 430 years have generated some discussion because Gen 15:13 (cf. Acts 7:6) identifies the duration as 400 years, while Exod 12:40 speaks of 430 years in the land of Egypt. As Longenecker (1990:133) indicates, the early rabbis also wrestled with the differences in the records and thought that they solved it by concluding that the lesser length might refer to the time that the Israelites were in Egypt, while the greater number also included the period up to the giving of the law (cf. the contrast between Deuteronomic and Priestly perspectives in Clements 1967:57-58). Even if Paul adopted a rabbinic solution to this difference, his point is the same, namely, that the law came much later and could not effectively replace the force of the earlier covenant and promise.

3:18 *For if the inheritance could be received by keeping the law, then it would not be the result of accepting God's promise. But God graciously gave it to Abraham as a promise.* Building on the idea of a will or testament from 3:15, Paul introduces the idea of inheritance (*klēronomia* [TG2817, ZG3100]) that will become important to his discussion in 3:29-4:7. Such inheritance, however, should not be interpreted according to OT ideas of land but in terms of NT ideas of acceptance with God and the future hope of Christians. In any case, Paul's overarching point is that legalistic obedience can in no way substitute for God's gracious way of dealing with humanity. Our inheritance of God's promise is rooted in something other than law.

COMMENTARY

In this section, Paul concludes his fourfold proof against legalism by turning to the human analogy of covenant or testamentary promise. Having supported his thesis against legalism with arguments based on experience, the biblical example of Abraham, and exegesis of the biblical idea of curse, Paul now uses his rabbinic expertise to drive home the idea that legalism and God's gracious promise are rooted in two very different perspectives.

The argument at 3:15 is based on an analogy taken from the law courts. It involves a document, covenant, or will (*diathēkē* [TG1242, ZG1347]) that has been ratified (*kekurōmenēn* [TG2964, ZG3263])—or, to use a popular saying, is "signed, sealed, and delivered." Using an example from probate, Paul makes the point that no one should be able to vitiate or set aside (*athetei* [TG114, ZG119]) a legitimate will or even add a codicil (*epidiatassetai* [TG1928, ZG2112]) to a will after a testator (a will-maker) has died. Paul's purpose in using such technical legal terminology was for comparison. If the Galatians could understand basic legal procedures, then they might grasp the logic involved in God's covenant with Abraham, particularly as discussed in 3:17.

Before discussing 3:17 further, we need to examine two important words in 3:16: "promise" and "seed" (or "child," NLT), the former being further explained in 3:18. Paul repeatedly emphasized the Greek singular form of *sperma* [TG4690, ZG5065] (seed). This method of argument—appealing to exegetical constructions, such as the fine distinctions made here—was quite common among rabbis of Paul's time. Most Jewish rabbis understood that "seed," as it concerned the covenant, should be understood as a singular collective, referring not to one person but to Israel, specifically to Abraham's descendants through Isaac (cf. Daube 1956:439-444; Wilcox 1979:2-20). Paul recognized this interpretation when he wrote that all who were in Christ should be regarded as Abraham's seed (3:29), but he also declared that

Christ alone was the true seed of Abraham. In true rabbinic fashion, therefore, Paul could use a text in more than one way, depending on the point to be made.

Contemporary readers who think that words have only one meaning may wince at such rabbinic exegesis, but Paul began this section by indicating that he was going to use human logic in these verses. Such a methodology, therefore, was not viewed by Paul, the former rabbi, as an inappropriate exegesis of the sacred Bible. He would have regarded it as fully in keeping with the spirit of Holy Scripture, which points to the coming of God's anointed one—namely, Christ, the epitome of Abraham's seed.

In bringing together the important terms "covenant" (*diathēkēn* [TG1242, ZG1347]; 3:15) and "promise" (*epangelian* [TG1860, ZG2039]; 3:16), Paul affirms in 3:17-18 that they are superior to the law because they preceded the law. Moreover, since the will or covenant had been fully ratified, the coming of the law could not be considered a legitimate codicil (addition) to the covenant and promise to Abraham (cf. 3:15) and therefore could neither negate nor alter it. Paul differentiated between law and promise by asserting that the former involves human effort, whereas the latter is simply obtained as a gracious gift from God. We receive the promise as one receives an inheritance—with gratitude to the Giver for his gift.

◆   B. The Purpose of the Law (3:19-22)

19Why, then, was the law given? It was given alongside the promise to show people their sins. But the law was designed to last only until the coming of the child who was promised. God gave his law through angels to Moses, who was the mediator between God and the people. 20Now a mediator is helpful if more than one party must reach an agreement. But God, who is one, did not use a mediator when he gave his promise to Abraham.

21Is there a conflict, then, between God's law and God's promises?* Absolutely not! If the law could give us new life, we could be made right with God by obeying it. 22But the Scriptures declare that we are all prisoners of sin, so we receive God's promise of freedom only by believing in Jesus Christ.

3:21 Some manuscripts read *and the promises?*

NOTES

3:19-22 A number of interpreters have argued along lines similar to Betz (1979:163) that what follows, even through 4:7, is tangential to Paul's thought. In agreement with Longenecker (1990:135-163), however, I have argued that these verses are not a digression but are crucial to Paul's argument, and that the next section is, in fact, key to Paul's complete argument (Borchert 1994:145-151).

3:19 *God gave his law through angels to Moses.* The Gr. text does not name "Moses" here but simply "a mediator" as in 3:20. For many contemporary readers, the reference to angels in the giving of the law may seem strange since the Heb. text (and thus most English translations) of Exod 19:16-25 gives no hint of an angelic presence at this event. But in Deut 33:2-4, the presence of the heavenly host with flaming fire at the right hand of the Lord is related to Sinai and the giving of the law through Moses. The LXX (Old Greek translation) of Deut 33:2-4 calls this heavenly army or host "angels" (*angeloi* [TG32, ZG34];

cf. Ps 68:18 [67:18 in the LXX]; for a further discussion see Longenecker 1990:139-141).
Paul and many early Christians were quite familiar with this translation.

3:20 Now a mediator is helpful if more than one party must reach an agreement. But God, who is one, did not use a mediator when he gave his promise to Abraham. Lit., "Now a mediator is not for one, but God is one." Since 3:20 is so brief in the Gr., there have been countless (cf. Lightfoot 1865:146-147) ideas as to what Paul was saying. Suggestions have involved angels, individuals, or parties and various ways that Moses or some other mediator may have been related to them. The view adopted by the translators of the NLT reflects a rather long scholarly tradition that includes both Lightfoot (1865:147) and Burton (1921:191-192). It views Moses as the mediator between God and the people in the giving of the law (cf. 3:19).

The second half of 3:20 can be simply (and perhaps best) translated, "God is one." This brief affirmation of monotheism was included in the ancient confession of Israel, the Shema (Deut 6:4). Paul seems to be linking Abraham's direct communication with God to the most revered confessional statement of the Jews. In Paul's statement, then, the giving of the law, with Moses as mediator, takes a back seat in light of God's direct promise to Abraham.

3:22 But the Scriptures declare that we are all prisoners of sin. This text is reminiscent of Rom 3:23 (cf. Rom 11:32) in stating the fact that all have sinned. But why did Paul move from the subject of law to Scripture? Did he have a particular text in mind? One is tempted to suggest a specific text (e.g., Deut 27:26) to fit the context. But perhaps the solution lies in understanding the law as Torah. For a rabbi such as Paul, the Torah was the Scripture.

COMMENTARY

Having stated his proofs against legalism (3:1-18), Paul now identifies the genuine function of the law as over against the errant claims of the Galatians. On the basis of its function, he is then able to clarify its role in relation to Christ. In the whole New Testament, there is no clearer statement of the law's purpose than this one.

Galatians 3:19 opens with a leading question in which Paul directs the Galatians to reflect on the real purpose of the law: "Why, then, was the law given?" He answers the question by proposing a positive function for the law. God gave the law not to nullify or alter the covenant promise but to show people their sinfulness. It was a temporary institution, existing until the coming of the promised "child" (or "seed," *sperma* [TG4690, ZG5065]), who was Christ. Of course, most Jews would not accept the idea of a temporary role for the law, because they regarded it as the eternal and unchanging will of God (see, e.g., Bar 4:1; *Jubilees* 1:27; 6:17; *1 Enoch* 99:2).

The Jews had a high regard for the law; they even boasted that God had given it to Moses by the hands of angels (see note on 3:19). It is possible that the erring Galatians had heard of such a Jewish tradition (*Jubilees* 1:29–2:1; cf. Josephus *Antiquities* 1.136; Philo *De Somniis* 1.142-143), and they may have viewed such angelic presence as further confirming the law's significance (Callan 1980:549-567). Paul mentioned angels, however, not to elevate the law but to contrast this delivery system with God's direct communication. (One should also note the lower status of angels in relation to Christ: Heb 1:5-8; cf. Burton 1921:189.) The mention of a "mediator" in 3:19 ("Moses," NLT) indicates that the law was not delivered directly from God to the people, but required a mediator, who, in Jewish thought, was Moses (Philo *Life of Moses* 2.166; *Assumption of*

Moses 1.14). The giving of the law is contrasted with the singleness or oneness of God in communicating his promise to Abraham.

Paul then asks the critical question, "Is there a conflict, then, between God's law and God's promises?" His response, "Absolutely not!" (3:21), shows that he did not equate the law with evil phenomena in the world, such as those proposed by the heretic Marcion. In spite of the subordinate role of the law, Paul still recognized that it came from God.

The human situation is pictured here by Paul as being like that of an incarcerated person confined to a limited pattern of life without genuine freedom to respond adequately to God. While the law was viewed as a gift of God and is to be regarded as good (cf. Rom 7:12), it did not give humans the power to escape imprisonment. It gave only the knowledge of sin (cf. Rom 7:13-20) and a glimpse of the alternative—the way of God.

True life is not initiated by the law, nor does it result from obeying the law. True spiritual life comes from God. The infinitive *zōopoiēsai* [TG2227, ZG2443] (to make alive) refers to God's life-giving power (3:21). The law never had such power! As the NLT suggests, to be made alive is virtually synonymous with being accepted or made right with God (Bruce 1982:180). Whereas Paul once thought that obedience to Torah would provide life, he had learned as a Christian that he was in bondage, or imprisoned (*sunekleisen* [TG4788, ZG5168]), under sin (3:22). Since the law did not have power to give life (3:21), the purpose of the law was to make clear the reality of the curse (3:10) and the imprisoning nature of sin (3:22). It pointed beyond itself to the need for a solution to the human predicament.

According to 3:22, the solution to human sinfulness is not the law, but the promise that is realized by faith in Jesus Christ. While law and promise may at first glance appear to be at odds, they are actually partners in providing a solution to the human problem.

In summary, the law was a temporary parenthesis to the basic promise that was given to Abraham; the law functioned to identify human sin and to prepare people for God's solution of faith in Christ Jesus. The law could never replace the expected promise; it did not enable direct communication with God, and it never had the power to give life. Rather, the law judged humanity by showing the divine standard. It pointed beyond itself to the coming promise of life through faith in Christ. This way of faith in the living Christ is the only way that leads to life.

◆   C. The Nature of God's Authentic Children (3:23–4:7)
        1. Guardianship prior to Christ (3:23–25)

²³Before the way of faith in Christ was available to us, we were placed under guard by the law. We were kept in protective custody, so to speak, until the way of faith was revealed.

²⁴Let me put it another way. The law was our guardian until Christ came; it protected us until we could be made right with God through faith. ²⁵And now that the way of faith has come, we no longer need the law as our guardian.

NOTES

3:22-23 Both 3:22 and 3:23 use the verb *sunkleiō* [TG4788, ZG5168] (imprisoned) to signify the bondage of the old era and the contrasting noun *pistis* [TG4103, ZG4412] (faith) to designate the liberating perspective of the new era.

3:23 *Before the way of faith in Christ was available.* While there is no direct reference to Christ in the Gr., the NLT correctly infers "in Christ" from the context of 3:22 and 3:24.

COMMENTARY

In this section, Paul describes the temporary nature of the law by comparing it to a household guardian who has responsibility for children during a limited period of their lives. Paul thereby divides religious history into two epochs or eras with "the coming of faith" (*elthein tēn pistin*) as the dividing line; the change in eras came at "the right time" (4:4; lit., "the fullness of time"). The law as a protective guardian is probably related to the rabbinic concept of the oral law as a protective fence (*m. Avot* 1:1), the rules of which were codified in the Talmud (for more on this concept, see Borchert 1994:146-147). For Paul, a liberated rabbi, his past life under the law served as its own evidence that it was the way of the old era. Christ's coming had effectively ended the disciplinary role of the law as guardian.

In Hellenistic times, the *paidagōgos* [TG3807, ZG4080] (guardian) was not really a teacher (as in the KJV). He or she was usually a slave who served a household by being a companion to the children—accompanying them to school and making sure that they did their studies and stayed out of trouble (Longenecker 1990:146-148). The guardian had significant authority over the children and was responsible to mete out discipline as necessary. But when the child reached maturity, the entire situation changed and the slave-guardian served his or her former charge. (On this relationship, see Plato *Lysis* 208c; *Laws* 7.808-810; for a similar pattern among the Jews, see *Genesis Rabbah* 29.6 and 31.7; also Strack and Billerbeck 1922:3.339-340, 557.) The implication is that for those who have experienced the new era in Christ, the guardianship of the law has ceased. The temporary services of the law are therefore no longer needed because God has provided something better.

As indicated in 3:19-22, the function of the law was not to provide a way for people to become acceptable to God but to provide God's standard so that humans might understand their sinfulness and seek God's solution. Here Paul indicates that the purpose for which Christ came was to provide the way for people to be made right with God by faith. This theological idea is usually termed "justification by faith." Since the old era (the law) had come to an end, Paul concluded this segment of his argument by dismissing the guardian that was no longer needed (3:25). For anyone to turn to the law after receiving Christ is to return as an adult to a disciplinary system intended for young children; it is tantamount to turning away from Christ's grace.

◆   2. The new community in Christ (3:26-29)

26For you are all children* of God through faith in Christ Jesus. 27And all who have been united with Christ in baptism have put on Christ, like putting on new clothes.*

²⁸There is no longer Jew or Gentile,* slave or free, male and female. For you are all one in Christ Jesus. ²⁹And now that you belong to Christ, you are the true children* of Abraham. You are his heirs, and God's promise to Abraham belongs to you.

3:26 Greek *sons.*   3:27 Greek *have put on Christ.*   3:28 Greek *Jew or Greek.*   3:29 Greek *seed.*

NOTES

3:26 *For you are all children of God through faith.* Paul signals the importance of unity in Christ in this verse by moving "all" (*pantes*) to the beginning of the sentence. He also delivers this statement to the Galatians with commanding force, shifting his words from the first person plural used in the previous verses to second person plural, implicitly pointing his finger and saying, "You, pay attention!"

in Christ Jesus. Paul uses his familiar expression "in Christ," which is often discussed under the rubric of mysticism. As Sydney Cave has correctly observed (1929:51), however, Paul's mysticism is corporate rather than individual and solitary (cf. Borchert 1994:147-148).

3:28 *male and female.* This phrase reflects the unity of humanity found in the creation story of Gen 1:27, which places primary emphasis on the fact that God made humans in his image and then states that he made them male and female.

3:29 *And now . . . you are . . . children of Abraham.* The conclusion is introduced by *ara* [TG686, ZG726], which means "then," "therefore," or "as a result." It is rendered in the NLT as "now."

that you belong to Christ. In Gr., this statement is a conditional clause, assumed to be unquestionable: "if you belong to Christ [as you indeed do]." What follows as a conclusion is thus presumed to also be a certainty.

the true children. This phrase renders the Gr. *sperma* [TG4690, ZG5065] (seed), used here as a singular collective. This is a different use than in 3:16, where Paul uses the term in a linguistic argument that Christ alone is Abraham's seed.

COMMENTARY

This section contains one of Paul's major thesis statements; it is key to understanding Galatians. Besides containing one of the best known verses in Paul's writings (3:28), the entire section is beautifully constructed and has three significant verses about our relationship in Christ.

The first verse is potent: "For you are all children of God through faith in Christ Jesus." The age-old quest to become a child of God is thus realized through faith in Christ and certainly not through human effort. Faith is foundational to a relationship with God.

The next statement, in 3:27, uses a clothing metaphor (*enedusasthe* [TG1746A, ZG1907], "you put on") to remind the Galatians that baptism had vividly portrayed their changed lives. The Greek behind "united with Christ in baptism" is literally "baptized into Christ," which seems to point to a metaphorical idea: "immersed in Christ." Acceptance as God's children and as heirs of Abraham is not gained through human effort but through faith in Christ, of which baptism is a picturesque representation.[1] Baptism into Christ unifies all believers in their belonging to Christ by dissolving the usual human discriminatory relationships—those between Jew and

Gentile, slave and free, male and female. These three distinctions are part of ancient Jewish tradition and are still maintained by many Jews today, as evidenced by recently published works such as the Jewish *Daily Prayer Book, Ha-Siddur Ha-Shalem.* This prayer book includes the traditional benediction, "Blessed be thou, Lord our God, King of the Universe who hast not made me a heathen [Gentile]. . . who hast not made me a slave . . . who has not made me a woman." As the footnote there indicates, women are required to pray "who hast made me according to thy will" in place of the last line (Birnbaum, n.d.: 15-18). Paul's rejection of these distinctions was revolutionary.

While his primary argument with the Galatians was focused on the first distinction, it is clear that Paul wanted them to realize that life in Christ means rejection of all such human patterns of discrimination. In Christ, such distinctions are now "irrelevant" (Bruce 1982:187)! Unfortunately, such human distinctions and protectionist perspectives have been responsible for national and ethnic wars, for the disregard of the poor and economically disadvantaged, for the manipulative restriction of women into minority roles within society, and for patterns of slavery. The community of faith needs to learn how to deal with manipulative human distinctions as the body of Christ, constantly seeking to heal divisive relationships while at the same time maintaining high standards of morality (cf. Eph 2:14-20; 1 Cor 6:9-11).

These verses articulate a fundamental Christian truth in declaring the full acceptance and equality of all Christians in the community of Christ. But in the history of the church, Christians have repeatedly failed to accept the radical implications of this new community by failure to acknowledge communal equality of those with a different skin color or ethnic background, those of different economic and social status, or those of different gender. Repeatedly and tragically, the church has separated believers on the basis of superficial characteristics, confining certain kinds of people to one side of the church, to the balconies, or to separate assemblies. The result is that human distinctions rather than unity in Christ have often become the identifying marks of Christian communities. Such distinctions will not exist in the new heaven and the new earth, and Paul's vision was that they should be removed from our community on this earth.

In concluding this section, Paul asserts that Christians, as a collective unit, are Abraham's seed. He could make this assertion because Christians are united to Christ and are thus derivatively the seed of Abraham and heirs of God's promises to Abraham. What was promised to Abraham is now received by all who believe in Christ.

ENDNOTES

1. In the early church, white robes were frequently worn by those who were baptized, which is probably why clothing imagery is used here (cf. Longenecker 1990:155-156; TDNT 2.319; Moule 1961:51-53). Betz considers that this verse, as well as the next, may be rooted in an early baptismal liturgy (1979:181-184).

◆ ## 3. The great transition: from slavery to adoption as children of God (4:1-7)

Think of it this way. If a father dies and leaves an inheritance for his young children, those children are not much better off than slaves until they grow up, even though they actually own everything their father had. ²They have to obey their guardians until they reach whatever age their father set. ³And that's the way it was with us before Christ came. We were like children; we were slaves to the basic spiritual principles* of this world.

⁴But when the right time came, God sent his Son, born of a woman, subject to the law. ⁵God sent him to buy freedom for us who were slaves to the law, so that he could adopt us as his very own children.* ⁶And because we* are his children, God has sent the Spirit of his Son into our hearts, prompting us to call out, "Abba, Father."* ⁷Now you are no longer a slave but God's own child.* And since you are his child, God has made you his heir.

4:3 Or *powers;* also in 4:9. **4:5** Greek *sons;* also in 4:6. **4:6a** Greek *you.* **4:6b** *Abba* is an Aramaic term for "father." **4:7** Greek *son;* also in 4:7b.

NOTES

4:2 *guardians.* The use of this term reminds us that in early Roman law under *patria potestas,* fathers had control over their domains and families in matters of property, slaves, and inheritance. In the later *Code of Justinian* (1.22-23), the general time for reaching maturity was set at age 20, but fathers were still permitted to designate the time of inheritance according to their own preference (*Code of Justinian* 1.14).

4:3 *that's the way it was with us before Christ came.* "Us" may possibly refer to Jewish Christians, such as Paul, but it more likely includes both Jewish and Gentile Christians. The expression "before Christ came" in the NLT is more literally rendered, "when we were children." Both translations indicate a time prior to Christian salvation, but each has a different focus.

the basic spiritual principles of this world. The expression *stoicheia tou kosmou* [TG4747/2889, ZG5122/3180] permits a number of meanings, including the "basic elements of the world," such as air, earth, water, and fire; spiritual beings (including spirits, angels, and demons); basic philosophical principles; even pre-Christian, proto-Gnostic spiritual structures of the universe; and planetary and stellar bodies in space (cf. citations of *stoicheia* in Betz 1979:204-205; BAGD 768-769; TDNT 8.670-687; and Bandstra's detailed study in 1964; for a survey of various views, see Mussner 1977:293-297). Paul would undoubtedly have included in this list the misused idea of the principles of law (see 4:5; cf. Reicke 1951:259-261).

4:4 *when the right time came, God sent his Son.* This idea appears nowhere else in Paul's writings. Much speculation, therefore, has developed as to whether the statement in 4:4, 5 introduces an early Christian confession and what the theological roots of such a confession might be. Could it have been based on an early wisdom tradition? Does it imply a preexistence theology? However one answers these questions, these verses are an extremely significant statement about Christ and his authentic community of followers.

While Paul asserts the preexistence of Christ elsewhere (e.g., 1 Cor 8:6; Col 1:15-16), Dunn argues that these statements are in themselves hardly an affirmation of preexistence or, for that matter, virgin-birth traditions. I would note, however, that they are consistent with those traditions and are clearly related both to earlier Jewish messenger/mission (Gen 24:40; Jer 7:25) and full humanity (Job 14:1; 1QH 18:12-16) traditions (cf. Dunn 1990:39-43, 107-123 and 1993:215). Paul probably also had in mind the Adam–Christ contrast that is more clearly presented elsewhere (Rom 5:12-21; 1 Cor 15:45-49).

4:5 *to buy freedom for us who were slaves to the law, so that he could adopt us as his very own children.* This verse contains two *hina* [TG2443, ZG2671] (in order that, so that) clauses that define the purpose or result of the Son's mission. Because the first clause does not actually define the recipients as "us" (a lit. translation would be "those"), some have proposed that the first clause applies to the Jews and the second to all persons in successive stages (cf. Bruce 1982:197; Dunn 1993:216). Others opt for the idea that the defined recipients in the second clause also relate to the first clause (cf. Longenecker 1990:172), since the roots of the statement may reflect a very early Christian confession. The latter view is represented by the NLT rendering.

4:7 *you are no longer a slave but God's own child.* Paul is drawing this major section to a conclusion, as indicated by the Gr. word *hōste* [TG5620, ZG6063] (as a result, therefore). He uses the second person singular as though he were addressing each reader individually and then adds a conditional sentence which spells out the Christian's inheritance as "everything." Beginning with *ei* [TG1487, ZG1623] (if), the condition (sonship) is presumed to be true; there should be no question concerning the result that follows.

COMMENTARY

In this section, Paul focuses on the great transition in history that enabled human beings to be liberated from slavery to the law and to become authentic children of God. Paul's argument reminds one of a Chinese puzzle, whereby one idea emerges out of an earlier one. It is all held together by Paul's overarching concern that the Christian community in Galatia should realize that they had left the old slavery of law and were now, in fact, children of God.

This section of Galatians makes a powerful theological statement about Christ and the Christian life. The mention of "heirs" in 3:29 provides a word link with 4:1, in which Paul contrasts a child-heir (who is legally not much different than a household slave) and a fully mature heir, who can take possession of estate property. (It is not very productive to argue about whether Paul had Jewish or Hellenistic probate laws in mind, since the metaphor is applicable to many ancient legal traditions.) Of course, a slave and a young heir are in reality quite different, but relative to possessing the estate, Paul's point is that neither is in a position to exercise its possession or its disposition.

Paul further develops the idea of slavery that he mentioned in 4:1 and in 4:3 when he says that we used to be enslaved "to the basic spiritual principles of this world." The word "principles" (*stoicheia* [TG4747, ZG5122]) is used again at 4:9 to suggest spiritual forces opposed to God. Thus, the NLT renders the term as "spiritual principles" (or, "spiritual powers"—see NLT mg) both at 4:3 and 4:9. Paul fully believed that spiritual forces, such as principalities and powers, are at work in this world (cf. 1 Cor 2:4-13; 5:4-5; 10:20-21; Eph 2:1-2; Col 2:8); thus, he also took the work of the Holy Spirit very seriously (cf. Rom 15:13; 1 Cor 2:10-13; 6:19; 12:4-13). It is incumbent on modern readers to understand Paul's clear commitment to the power of the Holy Spirit and to discover the reality of that power in their lives.

History changed dramatically at "the fullness of time" (4:4, ESV), for that is when God sent his Son to be "born of a woman." The three clauses Paul uses in 4:4 ("God sent his Son, born of a woman, subject to the law") identify three important aspects of Christology. First, Jesus was God's special envoy or agent (see Borchert 1996:236), sent by God to represent God on earth. This sending is strategic to both John's and Paul's pictures of Jesus (TDNT 8.354-357, 384-385). Second, the Son was "born of a woman," which means that he was truly human. The third clause, literally "born under the law," affirms that the Son not only died under the curse of the law but truly fulfilled the intention of the law. This perspective clashed with the perspectives of the Jewish legalists with whom Paul was arguing.

Several things must be recognized about 4:5-6 to prevent incorrect interpretations. The text of Galatians 4:5 is theologically significant because these two clauses assert two very crucial aspects of salvation: redemption and adoption. Both are strategic analogies, but we must not push them beyond their intended emphasis. The first comes from the context of the slave market, where a slave could be set free by the payment of the redemption price. Christ set people free from bondage to sin and the law (i.e., legalism) by his redemptive death on the cross. Paul's picture does not attempt to account for who received the purchase price—the focus is on freedom from slavery. The second image reflects the common ancient practice of important patrons adopting people—even adult colleagues—and giving them full inheritance, as when Emperor Vespasian adopted Titus. Paul's point is that Christ gives all people who trust in him the full status of God's beloved children without regard to their previous spiritual or ethnic heritage. Paul is not concerned with other aspects related to the issue of adoption and does not draw out the analogy any further—to do so would only prove again the axiom that there is no such thing as a perfect analogy. Unfortunately, theological debates and speculations continue to take place concerning these unanswerable issues.

In view of the causal conjunction *hoti* [TG3754, ZG4022] at the beginning of 4:6, great care must be taken not to think that Paul was arguing that the presence of the Spirit in one's life or heart was consequent upon or subsequent to the experience of salvation. Such an idea separates the gift of salvation from the gift of the Spirit, but Paul would not have conceived of the two as separate. Elsewhere in Paul's letters (cf. 3:2; Rom 8:14-16), the presence of the Spirit is linked directly to the act of regeneration. Paul undoubtedly regarded the Spirit as present at all stages of the salvation process. We are children of God, born of God because God sent the Spirit into our hearts. As Longenecker writes (1993:173), "For Paul, it seems, sonship and receiving the Spirit are so intimately related that he can speak of them in either order." Paul uses an unusual formula for the Spirit here: "the Spirit of his Son." This expression unites the Son with the Spirit, even as they are united in their mission to save mankind. God sent the Son for redemption, and then he sent the Spirit of his Son for regeneration and adoption. The Spirit, as united to Christ, is elsewhere referred to in Paul's writings as "the Spirit of Jesus Christ" (Phil 1:19), "the Spirit of Christ" (Rom 8:9), and "the Spirit of the Lord" (2 Cor 3:17).

Jesus' Spirit enables humans to call upon God as Father. Paul uses *abba* [TG5, ZG5] (a Greek transliteration from Aramaic; cf. Jesus' use of the term in Mark 14:36) along with the Greek *patēr* [TG3962, ZG4252] here and in Romans 8:14; both of these words mean "father." That an Aramaic term is used in this letter to Greek-speaking, Gentile congregations is a powerful testimony that the idea of God's fatherhood goes back to Jesus' teachings, since Jesus spoke in Aramaic. When Jesus came to Israel, the Jews viewed God as remote; they had ceased to use the name "Yahweh" for fear of taking the Lord's name in vain. But the consistent testimony of John and the Synoptics is that Jesus called God his Father. That familiarity with God was viewed by the Jewish establishment as desecrating God's holiness. What is even more surprising is that Jesus also taught his disciples to call God "Father" (see Matt 6:9; Luke 11:2; cf. Borchert 1983:15-16). This sense of God's personal, parental concern for Christians is foundational to an adequate understanding of the Christian life.

Paul's final point is that each believer, through Christ, has entered a new dimension of relationship with God. Whether legalistic Jew or seeking Gentile, each believer in Christ has become a daughter or son of God. No one should ever again be enslaved to the task of trying to become right with God through human effort. For Paul, it meant that if a person was an authentic child of God, then his or her status as an heir, through God's grace, should be presupposed (cf. Rom 8:16-17). But it is important to understand that Paul did not advocate possessing things after the manner of contemporary "prosperity thinking." His concern was focused on acceptance by God with its attendant blessings.

In an era in which the Jewish view of God overemphasized transcendence, and the pagan views of the gods rendered them impotent (cf. Murray 1951), the Christian view of God as a personal, caring Father supplied a new dynamic to the religious scene. The strategically timed coming of Christ rendered invalid the age-old view that people gained status with the divine (or with the fates) by exerting human effort. Yet the Galatians still sought self-realization and worth through good works and philosophies. In addressing his readers directly as "you" (both plural and singular), Paul called on them to recognize that they had been fully accepted by God. The Spirit would enable them to recognize the significance of their adoption as God's children and the blessings of a God-given inheritance. This message was timely for Paul's day, and it continues to have great meaning for our times, characterized as they are by solutions based on seeking to "find" oneself and quests for self-realization.

◆   ## D. Paul's Pastoral Concern for the Galatians (4:8-20)

8Before you Gentiles knew God, you were slaves to so-called gods that do not even exist. 9So now that you know God (or should I say, now that God knows you), why do you want to go back again and become slaves once more to the weak and useless spiritual principles of this world? 10You are trying to earn favor with God by observing certain days or months or seasons or years. 11I fear for you. Perhaps all my hard work with you was for nothing. 12Dear brothers and sisters,* I plead with you to live as I do in freedom from these things, for I have become like you Gentiles—free from those laws.

You did not mistreat me when I first preached to you. 13Surely you remember that I was sick when I first brought you the Good News. [14]But even though my condition tempted you to reject me, you did not despise me or turn me away. No, you took me in and cared for me as though I were an angel from God or even Christ Jesus himself. [15]Where is that joyful and grateful spirit you felt then? I am sure you would have taken out your own eyes and given them to me if it had been possible. [16]Have I now become your enemy because I am telling you the truth?

[17]Those false teachers are so eager to win your favor, but their intentions are not good. They are trying to shut you off from me so that you will pay attention only to them. [18]If someone is eager to do good things for you, that's all right; but let them do it all the time, not just when I'm with you.

[19]Oh, my dear children! I feel as if I'm going through labor pains for you again, and they will continue until Christ is fully developed in your lives. [20]I wish I were with you right now so I could change my tone. But at this distance I don't know how else to help you.

4:12 Greek *brothers;* also in 4:28, 31.

NOTES

4:8 *so-called gods that do not even exist.* The expression *phusei mē ousin* [TG5449/3361, ZG5882G/3590] (are not by nature) may be related to Gr. philosophical concepts of reality. Paul denied that the gods fit the category of reality.

4:9 *now that you know God (or should I say, now that God knows you).* The Gnostics made knowledge (*gnōsis*) the basis for their theories of salvation (see Borchert 1974:79-93; 1996:76-80).

4:10 *trying to earn favor with God.* This statement is not based in the Gr. text, but the NLT supplies the full import of Paul's sparse statement here. The issue was not simply that certain days were observed but that the Galatians continued to seek God's favor by these works.

4:12 *Dear brothers and sisters, I plead with you to live as I do . . . for I have become like you.* The NLT rendering fills in the very brief Pauline shorthand that involves a plea for the Gentiles to remain in their law-free state. "Dear brothers and sisters" is a generic rendering of the Greek *adelphoi* [TG80, ZG81] (brothers) because the emphasis is on Paul's pastoral concern for the entire community.

Longenecker thinks that this verse begins a major section that goes through 6:10. He titles it very generally as a "Request Section," or a section of exhortations (Longenecker 1990:184-186).

4:13 *sick.* Lit., "through the infirmity of the flesh" or "in the weakness of the flesh." The context, involving Paul's recollection of his earlier time with the Galatians, seems to favor the NLT rendering here.

4:16 *Have I now become your enemy because I am telling you the truth?* Most scholars, concurring with the KJV, RSV, and NIV, have viewed this sentence as a rhetorical question. I was formerly of that opinion, but having participated in the work of the NLT, I am now convinced that *hoste* [TG5620, ZG6063] (so, so that) does not introduce a question here (cf. Burton 1921:244-245; Longenecker 1990:193). Rather, it is a firm castigation of the Galatians: "So! I have become your enemy because I tell the truth!"

4:18 *If someone is eager to do good things for you, that's all right.* The Gr. is in the form of a maxim (Burton 1921:247) and should read something like, "to be zealous in good is always good."

4:19 *Oh, my dear children! I feel as if I'm going through labor pains for you again . . . until Christ is fully developed in your lives.* Some mss (א[2] A C D[1] 0278 33 𝔐) read *teknia*

[TG5040, ZG5448] (little children) here rather than *tekna* [TG5043, ZG5451] (children), as in NA²⁷ and UBS⁴ (following ℵ* B D* F G 1739). The change to *teknia* probably shows the influence of John's phraseology (cf. 13:33; 1 John 2:1, 12, 28, but nowhere else in Paul). The sense, however, is not much different, and so the NLT reads, "my dear children."

COMMENTARY

Throughout this section, Paul's pastoral heart is evident, whether in commending the Galatians for the initial kindness they showed him when they received him during a time of illness, or in scolding them for turning away and following after the deceptive teachers who wooed them. That they accepted such teachings and turned again to slavish ways was very troubling to Paul, and he was genuinely pained by the actions of those who once honored him and his ministry. In the midst of his stern critique of the Galatians' departure from the truth, Paul continued to show his pastoral heart (see esp. 4:11-12). At the same time, whenever Paul spoke of something being "in vain" (using the term *eikē* [TG1500, ZG1632] in 3:4, 4:11, or *kenos* [TG2756, ZG3031] in 2:2), readers should understand that he was absolutely serious, because he was dealing with crucial matters of Christian life and thought (cf. Rom 13:4; 1 Cor 15:2, 10, 14, 58; 2 Cor 6:11; Phil 2:16; 1 Thess 3:5).

Paul began his critique of the Galatians' problem by reminding them that they had been enslaved to paganism—worshiping nonexistent gods or idols like those described in Romans 1:19-23. Although Paul did not recognize idols as real deities, he realized that their worshipers became enslaved in the process of worshiping them. Paul asked the Galatians how they could now turn away from the living God—and not for the hope of freedom, but to be enslaved again! The Greek present tense of *epistrephete* [TG1994, ZG2188] (turn to, turn back) in such a religious context implies that they were presently "apostatizing" from God (4:9). They were turning away from God by going back to the *stoicheia* [TG4747, ZG5122] (powers, principles) mentioned in 4:3. For Paul, these elements included all facets of the pre-Christian way of life—from reliance on the law (cf. Col 2:20-23) to pagan trust in idols. Paul regarded these elements as completely powerless and deficient. Jews would hardly have placed the law in the same category as idols, but Paul made it quite clear in Romans 1-3 that the way of the Jews was just as ineffectual in gaining acceptance with God as pagan efforts.

Paul confronted them directly with their practice of observing the calendar (4:10), which undoubtedly was modeled in some way on scrupulous Jewish observances (cf. Betz 1979:217; cf. also George 1994:317-318 for similar church patterns). Paul no longer followed the Jewish rules for which he was once a fervent advocate (cf. 1:14). Instead, he found a new liberty that enabled him to identify with the Gentiles he had formerly despised. Paul was distressed that his labor for the Galatians might have been in vain, so he begged them to become as he was— free from the law and free in Christ. He felt no threat from their legalistic position, but he was concerned for their condition. They were on the verge of reversing all that he had done when he was first among them.

Reminiscing about the time that he labored among them, he recalled how well they had received him, even in his weak physical condition, which was probably due to illness. Bruce (1982:208-209) posits three possibilities concerning this illness: (1) malaria, contracted in the marshy areas of Pamphylia; (2) epilepsy, against which spitting (*exeptusate* [TG1609, ZG1746]; 4:14) was used to prevent spreading the effects of the evil eye; or (3) some vision-related problem. The reference to the Galatians' former willingness to pluck out their eyes (4:15) has prompted certain scholars to think that Paul's problem was near blindness. This theory is usually supported with reference to his writing with large letters (cf. 6:11), but the idea remains speculation. Paul's statement in 4:15 is actually a testimony of the Galatians' former kindness to Paul. Willingness to give one's eyes for another was regarded as the height of a self-giving spirit (apart from sacrificial death) since sight was so highly prized and blindness was regarded as a living death. A classic example of this is found in Samson's story. The worst possible fate the Philistines could envision for Samson was to make him a blind slave (Judg 16:21).

Whatever Paul's illness was, he had pondered the possibility of being rejected (*exouthenēsate* [TG1848, ZG2024]) and spat upon (*exeptusate;* see 4:14). Sick people were often rejected in the ancient world (see, for example, some of the stories of Jesus in Luke 16:19-23; John 5:2-7; 9:1-2). It would have been tempting for the Galatians to simply reject Paul because of his appearance or physical condition, but they had given Paul hospitality, the memory of which he described in glowing terms. He likened it to the reception worthy of an angel or even of Christ. But the blessed joy of that earlier period had passed (4:16). Paul could not help but wonder why they had exchanged their former enthusiastic acceptance of him and of freedom in the gospel for the slavery of legalism. Consequently, he exhibited some "tough love" in an effort to unshackle them again.

Paul's criticism of the Galatians provides a twofold model for how constructive criticism can operate within the Christian community. On the one hand, Paul was extremely honest with the Galatian converts. He reminded them of their former way of life—that they once were pagans who did not know the living God but had since been touched with divine, transforming power. Paul insisted that their return to worship practices focused on human effort was useless and, in fact, a rejection of his ministry of grace to them. Accordingly, he charged them with changing their loyalties and abandoning their former high regard for him and for the gospel.

On the other hand, we see that—in spite of his obvious frustration with the straying Galatians—Paul's harshest criticisms were reserved for the undermining work of his insidious opponents. Galatians 4:16-17 forms a transition from Paul's pastoral concern for the Galatians to his castigation of the methods and purposes of the false teachers who distorted the truth and led the Galatians into error. Paul denied credence to the false teachers by refusing to mention them by name, but his readers certainly knew to whom he was referring. Paul condemned the false teachers' zeal in currying the Galatians' favor; they were deceptive and did not act in the interests of the Galatian church. The scheming false teachers established tight fellowship boundaries around the Galatians so that they could shut out the people that they wanted to exclude. Whether it was Paul or other Gentiles is not actually stated in the Greek, but the NLT rendering implies that the boundaries were set against Paul.

Having made his critique, Paul once again revealed the gentle side of his pastoral heart. He reminded the Galatians that they were his babies and that he longed for them to mature. While some may find it strange that Paul used feminine imagery to portray his concern for the Galatians, this pattern was not a problem for Paul. He elsewhere referred to himself as a gentle, nursing mother (1 Thess 2:7) and, in the same context, as a caring father (1 Thess 2:11). Paul's pastoral heart ached for the Galatians to become Christ-formed people—that is, people transformed into the image of Christ (cf. Rom 8:29).

Paul's attitude towards the Galatians pulsates with patient kindness, the goal of which was restoration rather than long-term condemnation. He concludes his pastoral words at 4:20 with an emotionally charged desire to be present so that they could really sense the change in his tone and recognize that his concern for them was genuine. That Paul was frustrated by the situation is very evident; accordingly, he continues his attempts at bringing understanding to his deviating children in the next section. His pattern of dealing with problems in the community by means of both a stern critique and gentle grace should be emulated in the church today.

◆   ## E. An Illustrative Appeal from the Old Testament: Abraham's Two Children (4:21-31)

21Tell me, you who want to live under the law, do you know what the law actually says? 22The Scriptures say that Abraham had two sons, one from his slave wife and one from his freeborn wife.* 23The son of the slave wife was born in a human attempt to bring about the fulfillment of God's promise. But the son of the freeborn wife was born as God's own fulfillment of his promise.

24These two women serve as an illustration of God's two covenants. The first woman, Hagar, represents Mount Sinai where people received the law that enslaved them. 25And now Jerusalem is just like Mount Sinai in Arabia,* because she and her children live in slavery to the law. 26But the other woman, Sarah, represents the heavenly Jerusalem. She is the free woman, and she is our mother. 27As Isaiah said,

"Rejoice, O childless woman,
    you who have never given birth!
Break into a joyful shout,
    you who have never been
        in labor!
For the desolate woman now has
        more children
    than the woman who lives with
        her husband!"*

28And you, dear brothers and sisters, are children of the promise, just like Isaac. 29But you are now being persecuted by those who want you to keep the law, just as Ishmael, the child born by human effort, persecuted Isaac, the child born by the power of the Spirit.

30But what do the Scriptures say about that? "Get rid of the slave and her son, for the son of the slave woman will not share the inheritance with the free woman's son."* 31So, dear brothers and sisters, we are not children of the slave woman; we are children of the free woman.

4:22 See Gen 16:15; 21:2-3.   4:25 Greek And Hagar, which is Mount Sinai in Arabia, is now like Jerusalem; other manuscripts read And Mount Sinai in Arabia is now like Jerusalem.   4:27 Isa 54:1.   4:30 Gen 21:10.

N O T E S

4:21-31 The variation in pronouns used throughout this entire section is most interesting. This section begins in 4:21 with a harsh tone of address in the second person plural. The allegory proceeds thereafter without further personal reference until the introduction of the heavenly Jerusalem; the city is said to be "our mother" or "mother of all of us" in 4:26 (depending on the variations among the mss). It then identifies the children of promise in 4:28, not only with Isaac, but also with the Galatians in the second person plural (though a number of the ancient mss read first person plural, probably from the influence of 4:31; see note below). There is no question that Paul identifies with the Galatians in 4:31 through the clear use of the first person plural.

4:21 *do you know what the law actually says?* The Gr. is, "Do you not hear the law?" A few mss (D F G cop^sa) have "read" (*anaginōskete* [TG314, ZG336]) instead of "hear" (*akouete* [TG191, ZG201]), but this reading is inferior. Judaism was primarily an oral culture, and the law was read aloud so one could hear it, even when one read to oneself (for a discussion of orality, see Borchert 1996:31-33; Daube 1956:55-62).

4:22 *The Scriptures say.* The verse opens with the formula, "It is written" (*gegraptai* [TG1125, ZG1211]), normally used for authoritative direct quotations. Here Paul did not use a direct quotation from Scripture in his storyline; nevertheless, he wanted to convey that the same authority was present.

Abraham had two sons. While the text indicates that Abraham had two sons, Ishmael and Isaac (Gen 16:15; 21:2-3), it is clear from Scripture that Abraham also had other sons (Gen 25:1-6). Yet for the purpose of defining his principal heir, Paul maintained that the issue involved a choice between his first two sons (cf. Barrett 1976:1-16). Paul's point seems to be to confront the Galatians directly with the necessary choice between the radically different freedom-tradition of the children of promise and the slave-tradition of the children of law.

4:23 *The son of the slave wife was born in a human attempt to bring about the fulfillment of God's promise. But the son of the freeborn wife was born as God's own fulfillment of his promise.* The rendering of the NLT fills out Paul's shorthand. The rendering "human attempt" conveys Paul's use of *sarx* [TG4561, ZG4922] (flesh). The contrast between flesh and promise in 4:23 should not be understood to mean that Isaac was not conceived through sexual relations. Rather, the point is that Ishmael was the result of human determination alone. Perhaps Paul saw Abraham's fleshly efforts as similar to those of the false teachers who, in emphasizing circumcision, were also relying on the flesh (cf. Dunn 1993:246).

4:24 *These two women serve as an illustration of God's two covenants. The first woman, Hagar, represents Mount Sinai where people received the law that enslaved them.* The NLT rendering again expands Paul's words to supply important background for modern readers: Sinai was the place where the law was given (Exod 19-20; Lev 26:46; cf. TDNT 7.282-284).

Some modern readers may wonder why Paul uses such a strange argument. While one may differ with Longenecker's organization of this part of the letter, he quite plausibly suggests that Paul may have used this illustration because the false teachers had charged Paul with being in the wrong tradition (Longenecker 1990:199-200). Paul, the former rabbi, was quite up to the task of arguing that it was the false teachers who were in the wrong tradition, not Paul. The use of Hagar and Sarah as a contrasting pair is found in other rabbinic arguments (cf. Longenecker's helpful extended excursus [1990:200-206]).

4:25 *And now Jerusalem is just like Mount Sinai in Arabia, because she and her children live in slavery.* The ancient Gr. mss are split as to whether or not Hagar's name is included here: 𝔓46 ℵ C F G 1739 omit it; A B D 062^vid 33 1881 𝔐 include it. If the name

Hagar was not originally in the text, it was likely carried over from the previous verse (Comfort 2007:[Gal 4:25]).

Jerusalem. Contrast the spelling *Ierousalēm* [TG2419, ZG2647] 4:25, 26 with *Hierosoluma* [TG2414, ZG2642] in 1:17-18; 2:1. The latter spelling is the familiar geographical spelling of the city, which Paul uses in his earlier references to his visits, whereas the former spelling here is usually the designation used in the LXX for the "Holy," or divinely selected, City. Perhaps Paul was seeking to focus on the intention of God in selecting the city as his place of visitation and thus move his readers to consider God's ultimate holy city (cf. Longenecker 1990:33-34, 213).

4:27 This verse is a direct quotation from the LXX of Isa 54:1.

4:28 And you, dear brothers and sisters, are children of the promise, just like Isaac. This reading is supported by 𝔓46 B D* F G 33 1739. Other mss (ℵ A C D² 062 𝔐) read, "And we, dear brothers and sisters, are children of the promise, just like Isaac." The variant is probably the result of scribes attempting to retain unity with the first person plural in 4:26, 31 (Comfort 2007:[Gal 4:28]).

4:31 we are not children of the slave woman; we are children of the free woman. Did Paul intend this rabbinic argument to convince his misguided followers of the correctness of his view so that they would no longer see themselves as children of slavery but of freedom? Or was it just another rhetorical device used to convince them that they did not need to pursue the route of legalism? The answer is not really clear, but the argument in ch 5 seems to suggest that, while Paul was absolutely convinced of his own logic and viewed the Galatians as children of promise, he lacked confidence that the Galatians would receive his message quickly.

COMMENTARY

In this section, Paul uses a rabbinic style of argumentation to convince the law-oriented Galatians that they have become part of a slave-tradition that began with Hagar. Instead, they must choose the promise-tradition that began with Abraham's wife, Sarah (the tradition that Paul's gospel advocates). Paul uses an extended allegory to spell out his perspective, a method that is foreign to most contemporary readers.

The Greek participle *allēgoroumena* [TG238, ZG251] ("interpreted allegorically"; the NLT reads "illustration") is used in the New Testament only here at 4:24. As one might expect, the use of this term has led to much scholarly discussion. Allegories usually use surface terms as symbols for deeper meanings in a text. This interpretive method has been primarily associated with the city of Alexandria, as represented by the Jew Philo, a near contemporary of Paul, and in later centuries with Christian interpreters such as Origen, who expanded its possibilities greatly. In the Middle Ages, interpreters developed a pattern in which scriptural texts were said to have four meanings, of which the literal was often regarded as the least significant. The school of Antioch attacked Alexandrian proponents such as Origen, and much later, Luther inveighed against the medieval allegorical exegetes. The word allegory has thus come to have some negative connotations, raising in many minds the specter of weird meanings that are historically irrelevant. Recently, scholars have realized that allegory was not confined to Alexandria and that rabbis often used allegorical methods (cf. Ellis 1957:51-54; Hanson 1959:80-83; Longenecker 1975:43-50, 120-132).

A number of scholars have been anxious to distinguish Paul from the allegorists and the Alexandrian school by defining his method primarily as typological and showing that he did not abandon historical contexts (see Mussner 1977:319-320; Longenecker 1990:209-210). Although by comparison to the Alexandrians, Paul is quite reserved in his treatment and highly aware of the historical relatedness of his symbolic interpretations, his method is a far cry from a contemporary literal-historical method and much more akin to the allegorical interpretations of the Jewish rabbis. Today, we might not find Paul's argument in the following verses the best way of interpreting Scripture, but it was fully acceptable among the rabbis when they were seeking support for their views. Paul's discussion must be viewed in light of such rabbinic appropriateness. An allegorical interpretation, accordingly, helped him to fix the noose on the false teachers' deceptive practices.

Paul's mention of two covenants in 4:24 was probably meant to refer to the Old and New Covenants according to the Christian way of thinking. There is, however, no covenant with Ishmael or with Hagar mentioned in the Old Testament (contra Dunn 1993:249-250), and reaching such a conclusion is a bit involved. The contrast, as it is spelled out here, is really between freedom and its alternative, slavery, which Paul obviously linked to the activities of the false teachers. As the argument is explicated, Paul identifies freedom with promise (4:23, 28) and with spiritual regeneration (4:29). The slave option is not spelled out so precisely, but it is certainly related to the law (4:21), as shown by the Sinai reference.

The logic of 4:25 is straightforward, if one accepts Paul's unusual symbolic equations of Hagar, Jerusalem, and Sinai. McNamara (1978:24-41), followed by others, has argued with some force that a place near Petra bears the name of El Hagra, or Hagar, and that there are some hints in the Jewish Targum that suggest that Sinai may have been in the same area. Such geographical associations would have supplied more than enough material for a capable rabbi like Paul to build an argument based on a Hagar link to the law, especially since he had spent some time in Arabia (cf. 1:17). Ridderbos (1953:176-177), however, denies these geographical identifications and opts for an allegorical link alone. Whatever method one chooses, the Jewish establishment would hardly have accepted Paul's linking of the law with Ishmael, but Paul's style of argument would have been quite familiar to the rabbis. Undoubtedly, it greatly disturbed the Judaizing false teachers in Galatia who were actively advocating obedience to the law.

The secondary link, which places Jerusalem and her children in the same order with Sinai, is not as difficult to understand since Paul regarded Jerusalem as the headquarters of the law and the place where Jesus was crucified. While Sarah is not noted by name in the Greek at 4:26, the connection is obvious. Paul clearly intended the contrast of this verse with the preceding one to highlight the great difference between his gospel and the message espoused by his Judaizing opponents. The symbolism of the heavenly Jerusalem or mother city of God is contrasted to the earthly city. This contrast is also pictured in Hebrews (Heb 11:10, 16; 12:22, 13:11-14) and Revelation (Rev 3:12; 11:8; 21:2, 10–22:5). The idea of the heavenly Jerusalem may originally have grown out of a theory about a divine archetype in heaven being associated with the Tabernacle and Temple (Exod 25:40; 1 Chr 28:19; cf. Bruce 1982:221). Such ideas were given greater shape during the pessimistic times of the apocalyptic writers, when hope did not seem to lie within the world order (e.g., *1 Enoch* 90:28-29; *2 Enoch* 55:2; *2 Baruch* 4:2-6; *4 Ezra* 7:26; 10:7, 25-28; cf. also 1 QM 12:1-2). These thoughts of a divinely ordained mother city were probably suggested to writers by verses such as Psalm 87:3, 5 and Isaiah 54:1 (cited by Paul in the next verse).

It may seem to contemporary readers that 4:27 is an unrelated proof-text, but to a rabbi like Paul, it was perfectly legitimate because the barrenness of Sarah in the biblical story could be related to any other reference in Scripture. The conclusion of the citation, then, was important to Paul because of the prediction that the barren one, here interpreted as Sarah, would bring forth more children than the other woman, here identified with the slave woman Hagar, whose children Paul linked to the law.

Following the reference to children in the textual citation at 4:27, Paul used the word-link principle in 4:28 to return to the idea that the barren one's children are in reality, like Isaac, children of promise. Moreover, with the positive perspective of the proof-text as a basis, he addressed the Galatians directly as members of the promise. From Paul's perspective, the Galatians had to make the crucial choice between the line of Hagar (associated with Mount Sinai/slavery/present Jerusalem/law) and the line of Sarah (associated with Mount Zion/freedom/heavenly Jerusalem/Spirit/promise).

Having aligned the Galatians with himself, Paul turns to the two types of children as the next stage in his argument. At this point, he distinguishes between those born of the "flesh" (*kata sarka* [TG2596/4561, ZG2848/4922]), whom he linked with law, and those born of the "Spirit" (*kata pneuma* [TG2596/4151, ZG2848/4460]), whom he identified with promise. His final stage in the argument was to return to the Abraham story for the theme of persecution. In that story, Ishmael is a troublesome young man who "sported with," "made fun of," or "willfully teased" (*metsakheq* [TH6711, ZH7464]) the child Isaac (Gen 21:9). Sarah was angry with Ishmael's behavior, and the later rabbis made much of his hostility (cf. the Targums *Onqelos* and *Pseudo-Jonathan* on Gen 21:9). Paul was thus completely within the rabbinic point of view as he identified Ishmael with the way of the flesh. Because they were Christians, Paul showed the Galatians that they were already in the promise-tradition and were therefore subject to persecution or intimidation by those from the slave-tradition like Ishmael—a group that implicitly included the Judaizing teachers.

Paul could hardly have found better support for his cause than the next verse of Genesis (21:10). Sarah herself supplied the anathema: "Get rid of the slave and her son, for the son of the slave woman will not share the inheritance with the free woman's son" (cf. Gen 21:10). Paul was quick to use this statement as a Scriptural warrant for the exclusion of the false teachers (4:30). Bruce (1982:225) suggests that Paul's opponents, in their defense, may actually have pushed Paul into the use of this text. Whatever the reason, Paul had his proof-text, but his purpose involved more than the exclusion of the false teachers. It seems that he was equally concerned to give a rationale for the right of inheritance, a point which is not usually highlighted in commentaries on this verse. God's riches are not inherited by keeping the law but by believing in Christ.

Every generation must learn the lesson that exerting human effort to gain acceptance with God and having faith in Christ are mutually exclusive ways of life. One of them must give way to the other. A Christian, by definition, is committed to freedom in Christ. To choose the other way is to deny and pervert the gospel (cf. 1:6-7). For Paul, the gracious God revealed in Jesus Christ was the way to responsible freedom. To choose the way of law, then, was to reject Christ and take the law as a substitute for God in Christ. Paul would never again capitulate to such a slavish way of life, and so it should be with all Christians.

◆ VI. The Way of Liberty (5:1–6:10)
A. The Threat to Liberty Epitomized in Circumcision (5:1-12)

So Christ has truly set us free. Now make sure that you stay free, and don't get tied up again in slavery to the law.

²Listen! I, Paul, tell you this: If you are counting on circumcision to make you right with God, then Christ will be of no benefit to you. ³I'll say it again. If you are trying to find favor with God by being circumcised, you must obey every regulation in the whole law of Moses. ⁴For if you are trying to make yourselves right with God by keeping the law, you have been cut off from Christ! You have fallen away from God's grace.

⁵But we who live by the Spirit eagerly wait to receive by faith the righteousness God has promised to us. ⁶For when we place our faith in Christ Jesus, there is no benefit in being circumcised or being uncircumcised. What is important is faith expressing itself in love.

⁷You were running the race so well. Who has held you back from following the truth? ⁸It certainly isn't God, for he is the one who called you to freedom. ⁹This false teaching is like a little yeast that spreads through the whole batch of dough! ¹⁰I am trusting the Lord to keep you from believing false teachings. God will judge that person, whoever he is, who has been confusing you.

¹¹Dear brothers and sisters,* if I were still preaching that you must be circumcised—as some say I do—why am I still being persecuted? If I were no longer preaching salvation through the cross of Christ, no one would be offended. ¹²I just wish that those troublemakers who want to mutilate you by circumcision would mutilate themselves.*

5:11 Greek *Brothers;* similarly in 5:13.   5:12 Or *castrate themselves,* or *cut themselves off from you;* Greek reads *cut themselves off.*

NOTES

5:1 Some scholars have attached this verse to the end of ch 4 (cf. Bruce 1982:226-227), while others have begun a new section with it and attached it to the verses that follow, thereby softening the abruptness of 5:2 (among the many using the term "abrupt," see Betz 1979:255; Longenecker 1990:223; Dunn 1993:261). But it is the very nature of this "saddle text" that it participates both in what has gone before and in what follows. Notice that "therefore" or "now" (*oun* [ᵀᴳ3767, ᶻᴳ4036]) is in the middle of the Gr. sentence and links both sections. George (1994:352, following Longenecker 1990:223) is correct in emphasizing that the first part is in the indicative, whereas the second part is imperative.

So Christ has truly set us free. Following the lead of Deissmann (1909:326-328) and others, I think the dative (*eleutheria* [TG1657, ZG1800]) should be rendered as "for freedom," followed by the statement "Christ has set us free." The NLT emphasizes the fact of the Christian's liberation by using the word "truly."

Now make sure that you stay free, and don't get tied up again in slavery to the law. The summons in the verse includes both a positive and a negative imperative, "stand up" (*stēkete* [TG4739, ZG5112]), which the NLT epitomizes in "make sure" (the positive), and the negative, "don't get entangled" or "tied up" (*enechesthe* [TG1758A, ZG1923]). The warning is to avoid being "again" (*palin* [TG3825, ZG4099]) ensnared or tied up in "slavery," which Paul literally calls "a yoke of slavery." "Yoke" (*zugō* [TG2218, ZG2433]) was a term then commonly used by observant Jews to refer to the law or Torah.

5:2 *Listen! I, Paul, tell you this.* Paul initiates the discussion in 5:2 with a forthright call for the Galatians' attention (*ide*; "behold," "notice") along with a direct reference to himself ("I, Paul" is emphatic). The impact is like that of an orchestral drum roll introducing something exceedingly important. The conditional sentence (a third class condition, grammatically speaking) that follows makes Paul's concern in this letter absolutely straightforward.

If you are counting on circumcision to make you right with God, then Christ will be of no benefit to you. The future *ouden ōphelēsei* [TG5623, ZG6067] (benefit) with the negative, "to be worthless," is not merely futuristic, but completes the condition and refers to the time when they might make such a decision.

5:5 *But we who live by the Spirit eagerly wait to receive.* The shift from the second person plural "you" to the first person plural "we" indicates Paul's shift in attitude in this verse and the next.

5:8 *It certainly isn't God, for he is the one who called you to freedom.* The idea that God calls us is a consistent biblical theme. It goes all the way back to God's calling the disobedient Adam in the garden (cf. Gen 3:9) and continues with God's call of Abraham, Moses, Samuel, and the prophets.

5:9 *This false teaching is like a little yeast that spreads through the whole batch of dough!* The NLT rendering is an explanatory interpretation of Paul's shorthand, which is an exceedingly brief maxim: "A little leaven [yeast] leavens the whole lump."

5:10 *that person.* The Gr. grammar is singular here, perhaps implying that Paul had one specific false teacher in mind. In light of the plural references in 1:7 and 5:12, the singular could be taken as a collective reference or as a reference to a known leader of the opponents. See discussion in the commentary below.

5:11 *If I were no longer preaching salvation through the cross of Christ, no one would be offended.* The NLT unfortunately loses the Gr. idea of scandal in this verse, which surely was important to Paul (Longenecker even suggests that Paul may have coined the idea [1990:233]; cf. 1 Cor 1:23; cf. also Rom 9:33; 1 Pet 2:8). Moreover, when Peter rejects Jesus, he is called a *skandalon* [TG4625, ZG4998] in Matt 16:23; contrast the true disciple in 1 John 2:10 who is not an offense (for a fuller discussion, see TDNT 7.339-343).

5:12 *I just wish that those troublemakers who want to mutilate you by circumcision would mutilate themselves.* This verse begins with a formalized wish on Paul's part. "Wish" (*ophelon* [TG3785, ZG4054]) is derived from the idea of owing something to someone, and it became a Gr. expression for a heart-longing or deeply felt wish.

COMMENTARY

Standing like a bridge between two land masses or like a saddle between two mountain peaks, 5:1 is both a summary of Paul's extended theological analysis of the Galatian problem and his summons to follow a life of liberty. Paul's thesis encompasses his theological analysis and his resulting imperative for the Galatians in one determinative idea: freedom! In their quest to obtain assurance and status with God, the Galatians had sacrificed liberty. They had chosen a law-oriented substitute for Christ. Knowing that this quest would lead them into slavery, Paul summoned them to return to the Christ-given way of freedom. This verse should be highlighted in every Christian's life; every believer should know that the law or legalism cannot set them free. Only Christ can bring liberty to humanity.

In this major section, Paul first confronts the threat of the law in terms of the symbolic role of circumcision. In the minds of the Galatians, circumcision was a symbolic sign of having attained status with God under the law, so Paul begins this section by confronting the issue directly. Paul tells his misguided children that such a route is ineffective in gaining God's approval, and even worse, it is a rejection of God's grace. For the Christian who is led by the Spirit and walks in love, circumcision is an irrelevant factor, but the Galatians had yielded to the insidious pressure of these troublesome teachers of the law and had allowed their infectious teaching to spread to the point that they began to believe that Paul also promoted circumcision. Paul sternly challenged this by referring to his own experience of persecution. He reaffirmed his commitment to the scandal of the cross and asserted that the perverters of his Good News stood condemned. Indeed, he longed for an end to their intimidating influence concerning circumcision, preferring that they should be destroyed. With cutting sarcasm, Paul declared his hope that they would castrate themselves (5:12).

Paul warned that circumcision would vitiate Christ's effectiveness in their lives (5:2, 4). This attack was not directed against circumcised Jewish Christians but was meant to establish the sufficiency of Christ for Gentile Galatians. The failure of either Jews or Gentiles to recognize Christ's sufficiency was, in Paul's mind, tantamount to discrediting Christ. Paul continues his argument in the style that the law courts used to build a case. Apparently, the Judaizing teachers had not been forthright with the Galatians. Therefore, Paul was prepared to give his audience a lesson in Jewish jurisprudence. Beginning 5:3 with the formal declaration, "I bear witness," he made the point that in the law circumcision does not stand alone; it carries the obligation of complete obedience to the whole law, to all the laws.[1]

Galatians 5:4 is perhaps Paul's strongest warning yet; his word to the Galatians was that by seeking status with God through the law, they would in fact have breached their relationship with Christ and fallen from grace! To follow such a course, as Luther correctly judged, would be insanity (Luther 1955–1975:27.18). The severity of Paul's judgment here mirrors the intensity of his opening salvo at 1:6-9. His goal in both cases was to rescue his Galatian children from the pit of separation from Christ.

Paul quickly changes his tone in 5:5, however, as he reminds the believers that they will attain their hope by faith and through the Spirit. This movement from harsh criticism to caring concern is a frequent phenomenon in Galatians (cf. 4:8-20 and the allegory in 4:21-31). Paul apparently thought that the most effective way to deal with his erring children was to be both a pastoral friend and a forthright disciplinarian. In this case, Paul highlights the consequences of the two different ways of life. Through the law, the Galatians would fall away from grace (5:4), but the hope of righteousness by faith (5:5) remained for those living by the Spirit, which is the focus of 5:16-25. Returning to the issue at hand, Paul again mentioned circumcision in 5:6, dismissing it in favor of something better. In place of the law and circumcision, Paul's principle for life was "faith expressing itself in love," which some have rephrased by the maxim, "faith as root and love as fruit" (cf. Bruce 1982:232; cf. also Lightfoot 1865:204-205). This love is the focus of Paul's thesis for action in 5:13-15 and the foundation for properly assisting those who are ensnared by sin and worldly concerns (6:1-10).

In 5:7, Paul shifts back to a disciplinary critique of the Galatians. In 5:7-8, he uses athletic imagery to represent the Christian life, as is often found in the New Testament (cf. 1 Cor 9:24-27; Phil 3:13-14; 1 Tim 6:12; 2 Tim 4:7; Heb 12:1-2, 12; cf. also TDNT 8.226-235). Here and in 2:2, Paul uses the picture of a marathon to represent the Galatians' and his own life with Christ. It was evident that roadblocks had been erected on the Galatians' racecourse, but who was responsible? Paul's question, "Who has held you back?" (5:7) is intriguing because he uses the word *enekopsen* [TG1465, ZG1601] ("Who cut in?"). Certainly this term could be used of someone cutting in on a race (cf. De Vries 1975), but when one realizes that Paul wanted the Judaizing circumcisers to "cut" or "mutilate" (*apokopsontai* [TG609, ZG644]) themselves (5:12), then the image must be understood to have other vivid implications. The "cutting in" of the false teachers deterred or detoured the Galatians from their pursuit of "the truth," which refers to the gospel as proclaimed and defended by Paul. Instead of following the truth, the Galatians had been sidetracked by human persuasion that was out of keeping with God's calling.

Paul then uses the image of leaven in his critique of the Galatians. This maxim ("A little leaven leavens the whole lump") was a familiar Jewish expression for contamination. Prior to the first Passover, the Israelites were instructed to get rid of leaven, or yeast, in their homes (cf. Exod 12:14-20; Deut 16:4, 8) as a sign of their hasty departure from Egypt. Paul found the maxim significant in illustrating the infectious power of evil. He told the Corinthians that the sexually deviant sinner in their midst was a leaven to them—badly infecting the entire church (1 Cor 5:6). Here it is used to warn against the infectious idea that status with God could be gained through circumcision.

Galatians 5:10 returns to the positive tone of 5:5, and Paul here tells the Galatians of his conviction in the Lord that they would not disagree with his perspective. He was equally convinced that "that person" who had troubled them would have to "endure" (*bastasei* [TG941, ZG1002]; third person singular) judgment. Did Paul think that the Galatian problem was initiated by a particular person—perhaps some outspoken leader of the opponents? Or could this word be a singular collective? The idea of a single leader is rather intriguing since Paul referred earlier to a number of agitators (cf. 1:7), and in just a few verses he says that he wishes that *they* would castrate themselves (5:12).

Paul then confronted what was evidently a false charge leveled against him—namely, that he had been advocating or preaching circumcision. It is not improbable that the Judiazers viewed the charge as a real possibility since Paul seems never to have renounced his Jewish heritage and had once been a fiery advocate for Jewish traditions (1:14; for other possible reasons, see Dunn 1993:278-279). Paul countered this idea with the facts of his own subsequent persecution (probably at the hands of circumcision defenders) and his insistence that "preaching circumcision" rather than preaching Christ would in effect nullify the "offense" (*skandalon* [TG4625, ZG4998]) of the cross. Paul then lashed out at those who preached circumcision with one of the most crass statements made in the New Testament: "I only wish that those troublemakers who want to mutilate you by circumcision would castrate themselves" (*apokopsontai*; 5:12, NLT mg). This wish is indicative of Paul's grave feelings toward those who were altering the gospel and leading Christians astray. *The Living Bible* avoided the real meaning of this text by the wording, "cut themselves off from you" (cf. NKJV). This fuzziness has been corrected in the NLT by the use of the word "mutilate" (so also NASB, RSV), but even this term is euphemistic when compared to the harshness of Paul's expression.

Of course, being castrated would have subjected the Judaizers to the harsh judgment of the Torah, which excluded all eunuchs from the worshiping congregation of Israel (cf. Deut 23:1), and Paul probably thought that these false prophets deserved such treatment. Yet it is important to add that such a perspective concerning eunuchs should hardly be the view of Christians because it was not the view of Jesus (cf. Matt 19:12). Jesus was, however, very harsh towards those who led helpless ones into sin. He even said that being dumped into the sea with a millstone tied around one's neck would be preferable to enduring his wrath on this point (Mark 9:42).

All readers of Galatians need to recognize that the foundation for Paul's theology and decision-making is Christ, not the law. This text provides a strategic principle for interpreting other things that Paul wrote that are less clear, such as the dialogical sections of 1 Corinthians (Paul sometimes speaks with tongue in cheek or quotes arguments by the Corinthians in order to reject them, as he does in 1 Cor 14:33b-36). The book of Galatians makes it clear that neither law nor circumcision was fundamental to Paul's thinking. As a transformed Jew, he was rooted in Christ's death and resurrection.

With respect to the present text, we conclude by noting that this section is so vibrant that contemporary readers can sometimes miss the point of its dynamic interplay with the argument against bondage. The point is that enslaving substitutes for the scandal of the cross are ever present. The purveyors of an easy bondage are never far from Christians or the church. This letter and this particular text therefore continue to reprove legalistic advocates and those who espouse self-centered religious worship. God in Christ offers his love to the world. Therefore, humans are charged to take God's answer to human sin seriously. Christians who have found new life in Christ are, according to Paul, expected to live in freedom with a faith that expresses itself in love (5:6). This concern for faith that is manifested in love is basic to the rest of the Galatian letter.

ENDNOTES

1. Some recent scholars have been attracted by arguments such as covenantal nomism, which emphasize relationship rather than legalism. They tend to be unhappy with Paul's understanding of the law and Judaism, but Paul's analysis of his contemporary Judaism is probably better than recent reconstructions suggest. The rabbis of the Tannaim often debated at length the effects of minor breaches of the law. Texts such as Deut 27:26 would have formed for them, as for Paul, the basis for favoring strict adherence (cf. the helpful analysis of Daube 1956:250-252; cf. also 4 Macc 5:20-21). In his statement here and at 3:10, Paul argues like a skilled rabbi of his time.

◆   B. The True Model of Freedom to Love (5:13-15)

¹³For you have been called to live in freedom, my brothers and sisters. But don't use your freedom to satisfy your sinful nature. Instead, use your freedom to serve one another in love. ¹⁴For the whole law can be summed up in this one command: "Love your neighbor as yourself."* ¹⁵But if you are always biting and devouring one another, watch out! Beware of destroying one another.

5:14 Lev 19:18.

NOTES

5:13 *serve one another in love.* The variant reading, "love of the Spirit" (found primarily in Western mss: D F G it), is undoubtedly a later addition, probably through the influence of 5:16-22. The shorter reading has the support of the best witnesses: 𝔓46 ℵ A B C.

5:14 *the whole law.* One is tempted to ask whether Paul was reestablishing the role of the law. Was he inconsistent in his presentation, as Räisänen (1983:199) has argued? Or is Sanders (1983:4-6, 94-114) correct in his idea that Paul was establishing a new "covenantal nomism" by a distinction in Galatians between how one gets into the covenant (chs 1–4) and how one stays in the covenant (5:13–6:10)? The answer to all of these questions must be a resounding "No!" because Paul can in no way be building a new system of legalism. What he and other NT writers have done is to employ the idea of halakha ("walk," or "way of life") from the rabbis to give "law" a new focus. Love is not merely a rule to be obeyed; it is a new way of life (cf. commentary on 5:16-26).

When Paul spoke of the "whole law," he was not advocating keeping every command. What then is the *pas nomos* [TG3551, ZG3795] (whole law) here? Is it similar to *holon ton nomon* (the whole law) in 5:3, as suggested by the RSV and Dunn (1993:289-290), implying some continuing relationship between the two statements, or is it to be conceived differently, as suggested in Hübner (1984:36-40) and the NLT? The "whole law" is a new way of living, namely, "walking" in love with God and one's neighbor. It is not a set of rules.

command. In Gr., this word is *logos* [TG3056, ZG3364] (word). This term has been rendered by the expression "command" or "commandment" in a number of versions, including the NIV and the NLT. Paul's use of it here is reminiscent of the Heb. "Ten Words," a reference to the Ten Commandments.

COMMENTARY

My beloved teacher, Otto Piper of Princeton, would often say that it is not sufficient to attack another person's position without providing another rationale or model in its place. By the end of chapter 4, Paul had destroyed his opponent's argument that keeping the law would make a person right with God. In 5:1-12, he demolished the notion that circumcision made anyone acceptable to God. It was now mandatory for Paul to explain how one lives meaningfully in light of God's righteousness coming through Christ and apart from the prescriptions of the law. Without such an alternative, the Christian life might be considered aimless. Jesus told a brief parable concerning the cleansing of a house with an unclean spirit. If the house was merely left empty, it could be threatened with reoccupation by an additional seven spirits who were worse than the first (Matt 12:44-45). What would fill the house for the Galatians now that the law had run its course? Paul's replacement for the law was love, which is not a set of rules—a truth discovered by the rich man who came to Jesus, asking what new rule he needed to perform in order to be acceptable to God (Mark 10:17-24). Jesus, like Paul, insisted that self-giving love for God and one's neighbor encompasses the whole law (cf. Matt 12:34-40).

Paul also knew that freedom without responsibility is a prescription for chaos; thus, he set parameters, or limitations, on the use of that freedom. God's calling always carries an element of mission or responsibility. Even the early blessing of Abraham was accompanied by the understanding that all humanity would benefit from it (Gen 12:3; cf. Paul's reflection on this verse in 3:8). Accordingly, Paul firmly rejected self-centered (*sarki* [TG4561, ZG4922], "sinful nature, flesh") activity in the name of freedom. Instead, he commanded Christians to follow the way of love (*agapē* [TG26, ZG27]). Paul identified this love as the basis for serving others. The contrast between self-centeredness and service for others is almost too obvious to require comment. Such service is not to be oriented toward oneself but toward Christ. Thus, Paul referred to himself as a servant (*doulos* [TG1401, ZG1528]) of Christ (1:10; Rom 1:1). This idea of servitude for Christ stands in stark contrast to the slavery of the law: service to Christ is motivated by love, but the law entails obligation for acceptance.

Paul makes a surprising, positive assertion about the law. He says that the whole law is summed up in the saying "Love your neighbor as yourself" (Lev 19:18). Rabbis were known for their attempts to summarize the law. Hillel discoursed on the converse or negative golden rule: "Don't do to others what you wouldn't want them to do to you" (*b. Shabbat* 31a). Akiba, after Jesus, also commented on Leviticus 19:18 (cf. *Genesis Rabbah* 24:7; see also Daube 1956:65-72 and Theilman 1989:55-59). Paul was convinced that the command "Love your neighbor as yourself" encapsulated God's will for human beings. In adopting this position, Paul was following Jesus' use of Leviticus 19:18 to sum up the essence of the law. Prior to Jesus' notable use of Leviticus 19:18 (cf. Matt 22:39-40; Mark 12:31), little attention was given to that text. Paul's interpretation, therefore, represents the general Christian tradition's interpretation of the so-called "law command" (cf. Rom 13:9-10; James 2:8, where it is called the "royal law"; cf. also *Didache* 1:2). The way of love is the way of Christ.

Love, therefore, is to be the basic principle of the Christian walk. To state the idea in Jewish rabbinic terms, it is a fundamental element of Christian halakha (cf. *halikah* [TH1979, ZH2142]; and *halak* [TH1980, ZH2143], "walk")—the Halakha being those teachings of the rabbis that were legally to be obeyed as coming from God; this categorization is in contrast to the Haggadah (related to *nagad* [TH5046, ZH5583], "tell"), which refers to those statements, instructions, interpretations, and patterns of worship that were regarded as helpful in relating appropriately to God but not legally binding. What Paul and James (as Jews) meant in using the term "law" in relation to love was that love is not merely a "helpful" element in a Christian's life— it is absolutely crucial to the Christian way of life. The authentic Christian does not merely talk about love but is a model of love (John explains the same idea in 1 John 4:7-21). Therefore, the freedom to love that comes from a new relationship with Christ does not build a new set of laws or rules. Love is a transformed way of living.

In 5:15, Paul provides a vivid illustration of what the love command does not mean. The form of the first class condition ("if you bite and devour one another" = "since you are biting and devouring one another") suggests that Paul actually believed that the Galatians were engaged in internecine battles that were bitterly tearing apart the fellowship. He pictured the Galatians as wild animals ripping each other to pieces and warned them of the destructive consequences of their actions. To what extent this was rhetorical exaggeration for effect and what the exact issues were that they were fighting about are unclear. Probably, issues related to various views of the law and the significance of circumcision were fragmenting the church.

When freedom is mentioned in the contemporary world, it is often divorced from the concept of responsibility. Paul knew that a person should not talk of one without the other because self-oriented freedom is a recipe for disorder and confusion. Paul strongly exhorted the Galatians to abandon self-centeredness and follow the way of loving service to others. Truly loving one's neighbor represented for Paul and the other New Testament writers the fulfillment of God's will. This perspective came from Jesus (Mark 12:31) and is poorly represented by contentious attitudes, which usually devastate a Christian community. The correct perspective is not merely saying, "I love you," or even, "In Jesus, I love you," but engaging in genuine self-giving for other persons. Words can be very cheap, and Christians often contradict their words by their actions. Genuine love, as Paul said elsewhere (1 Cor 13:1-13), is not self-seeking. The model of freedom expressed in love is therefore basic to the Christian life. When one truly seeks the way of Christ, freedom to follow the way of love will be evident.

◆   ## C. The Resource of the Spirit for the Life of Liberty (5:16-26)

16So I say, let the Holy Spirit guide your lives. Then you won't be doing what your sinful nature craves. 17The sinful nature wants to do evil, which is just the opposite of what the Spirit wants. And the Spirit gives us desires that are the opposite of what the sinful nature desires. These two forces are constantly fighting each other, so you are not free to carry out your good intentions. 18But when you are directed by the Spirit, you are not under obligation to the law of Moses.

¹⁹When you follow the desires of your sinful nature, the results are very clear: sexual immorality, impurity, lustful pleasures, ²⁰idolatry, sorcery, hostility, quarreling, jealousy, outbursts of anger, selfish ambition, dissension, division, ²¹envy, drunkenness, wild parties, and other sins like these. Let me tell you again, as I have before, that anyone living that sort of life will not inherit the Kingdom of God.

²²But the Holy Spirit produces this kind of fruit in our lives: love, joy, peace, patience, kindness, goodness, faithfulness, ²³gentleness, and self-control. There is no law against these things!

²⁴Those who belong to Christ Jesus have nailed the passions and desires of their sinful nature to his cross and crucified them there. ²⁵Since we are living by the Spirit, let us follow the Spirit's leading in every part of our lives. ²⁶Let us not become conceited, or provoke one another, or be jealous of one another.

NOTES

5:16 *Spirit . . . sinful nature.* For a discussion of Paul's ethical dualism, see Davies 1980:17-34. This dualism is briefly and artfully articulated in this verse, which is a preview to the brilliant, extended contrast Paul develops in Rom 7:16–8:16 (see Borchert 1986b:85-87).

Then you won't be doing what your sinful nature craves. The NLT is correct here; the second clause is focused on an expected result and should not be made into another imperative, as in the RSV.

5:17 *These two forces are constantly fighting each other, so you are not free to carry out your good intentions.* Paul's point is that within each person, a battle is raging between two opposing orientations.

5:20-21 A number of scholars have seen in this statement something like a liturgical formula (consisting of a recital of patterns to be avoided) to be used when candidates were being prepared for baptism in the early church (cf. Betz 1979:284-285; Longenecker 1990:258; Dunn 1993:306). If Colossians was also related to such Christian instruction, then the presence of another form of the two ways of life in Col 3:5-17 would further support such an idea.

5:25-26 A number of scholars have not been quite certain where to place these verses (cf. Longenecker 1990:264-265, who details the scholarly dilemma). Fung clearly illustrates this dilemma when he groups these verses along with 5:24 in a separate section that he simply calls "Application and Appeal" (1988:274-278). Other scholars have been induced to join these verses to 6:1-10, supposing that they begin the next section (e.g., Betz 1979:291-293; Dunn 1993:316-317), even though they do not really bear the literary marks of a new section. I reject this latter view. For similar reasons, I reject the idea that these verses might be a saddle text like 5:1. Instead, 5:25 seems to be a positive exhortation attached to the list of virtuous spiritual characteristics and parallel to the forceful warning that follows the rejection list of vices or sinful activities (5:21b). To his positive exhortation, Paul added a further concluding exhortation (5:26), directed against those who might regard themselves as having achieved a high spiritual status and thereby be tempted to be proud.

COMMENTARY

In this section, Paul focuses on the wonderful divine resource available to Christians for the life of freedom. That resource is the Spirit of Christ, upon whom they need to depend for their everyday lives. Paul literally told the Galatians to "walk by the Spirit." The verb for "walk" (*peripateite* [TG4043, ZG4344]) is translated "live" at 5:16; it is used frequently by both Paul and John to refer to the way a person conducts his or her life, and it is drawn from the Old Testament word *halak* [TH1980, ZH2143], which can be used similarly. For example, Genesis 5:24 says that "Enoch walked with God" (KJV). There, the verb *halak*, as in many other places, means to do something habitually (cf. Gen 6:9 concerning Noah or Gen 17:1 in God's command to Abraham). This idea of the habitual walk was linked by the biblical writers, and even more by the rabbis, with the habitual following of the law by God's people (cf. E. Merrill in VanGemeren 1997:1.1033). The rabbis would have argued that even God walked habitually in this manner, according to their understanding of Leviticus 26:12 and Deuteronomy 23:14.

The term *Halakha* then came to be used by rabbis to refer to binding precepts for the faithful Jewish life (see Danby 1933:xvii-xxiii for more on Halakha). This concept was distinguished from Haggadah—nonbinding comments, such as worship information, liturgies, and the like. Paul's exhortation to his Galatian children to "walk by the Spirit" had the form of a rabbinic prescription, but the Spirit is not an external set of rules to be followed. It is an internal way of being that is directed by God, and as such, it concerns the personal adaptation of the way of love to one's neighbors.

The opposition of the flesh (*sarx* [TG4561, ZG4922]; sinful nature) to the Spirit (*pneuma* [TG4151, ZG4460G]) is a common theme in Paul's writings. The conflict is epitomized in the Greek verb *epithumei* [TG1937, ZG2121], which means "rises in desire against." The most significant part of the verse is the statement about the dilemma each Christian faces: "so you are not free to carry out your good intentions." Those familiar with Romans 7:15-18 will recognize the close parallelism of Galatians 5:17 to Paul's articulation of his own inner struggles there. The solution, of course, is not to be found in one's self any more than salvation is to be discovered in one's own resources.

The powerful answer to the human dilemma is to be found only in God and in the leading of the Spirit (cf. 5:18; Rom 7:25–8:9; cf. Borchert 1986b:87-88). The verb *agesthe* [TG71, ZG72] (5:18; "directed" in the NLT) stands in striking contrast to the verb "walk" (*peripateite* [TG4043, ZG4344]; 5:16). The important point is divine direction in dealing with the frustrations of life. This sentence, however, is not a mere assertion; it is a first-class condition that assumes the correctness of the conclusion if the condition is met. Thus, the person directed by the Spirit can assume release from the need to be governed by law. In drawing this conclusion, Paul was not merely developing a theological argument unrelated to the issues of life. He was very much aware of human temptations to sin. But Paul asserted that the Spirit enables Christians to confront and overcome the evil and sin in their lives.

While the Old Testament writers inveighed against human sins, they were not inclined to provide lists of sins (cf. Betz 1979:282). Listing vices and virtues was of particular interest to the Greco-Roman writers from Plato and Aristotle, to Stoics such as Zeno, and to others of Paul's contemporaries such as Seneca and Epictetus.

There are similar lists among the writings of Philo (*Sacrifices* 30–33) and in texts such as 4 Macc 1:26-27; Wis 14:23-27; *Testament of Reuben* 3:3-8; and *Testament of Issachar* 7:2-5 (cf. Longenecker 1990:249-251). As the idea became resident in Jewish thought, the concept of the "two ways" developed and is found at Qumran (cf. 1 QS 3:25–4:11) as well as in early Christian writings such as the *Didache* (4–5, esp. 5:1-2) and *The Epistle of Barnabas* (18–20). Such lists are well known throughout Paul's writings (Rom 1:29-31; 1 Cor 5:9-11; 6:9-10; Eph 4:31-32; 5:3-5; Col 3:5; 2 Tim 3:2-5) and are also found in other parts of the New Testament, such as Mark 7:21-22; James 3:15-17; Revelation 21:8; 22:15. Proper behavior was the goal of these lists, and reprehensible behavior was clearly to be avoided. Paul and other early Christians found such lists helpful in the instruction of catechumens, or new Christians, but they were also used to remind believers of the acceptable way of Christian living—undoubtedly the purpose of the negative list here (5:19-21) and the positive list later (5:22-23).

Paul opened his list of sins in 5:19 by referring to the vices as "works of the flesh" (*ta erga tēs sarkos* [TG204/4561, ZG2240/4922]), a shorthand expression for evil activity. Paul argued in Romans 1:32 that such activities warrant the death penalty! The list includes 15 specific vices and the catchall comment, "other sins like these" (5:21). The list resists ordering, though it is possible to recognize in the list the following: concerns about loose living (items 1–3); opposition to Christian faith (items 4–5); patterns of conflict (items 6–13); and lack of sobriety (items 14–15). The vices are as follows:

1. Sexual immorality (*porneia* [TG4202, ZG4518]) includes adultery and prostitution (cf. 1 Cor 5:1-5; 6:18).
2. Impure thoughts (*akatharsia* [TG167, ZG174]) could refer to that which was ritually unclean, such as unclean food, but came to be a general term for sexual misconduct. Undoubtedly, Paul would have included impure thoughts and contemporary sexually explicit humor in this category (cf. Rom 1:24 for sexually dirty living).
3. Lustful pleasures (*aselgeia* [TG766, ZG816]) included sexual excess, wantonness, perverted and reckless living, and the idea of complete disregard for all ethical standards (cf. Mark 7:22; 2 Pet 2:18).
4. Idolatry (*eidōlolatria* [TG1495, ZG1630]) refers to the worship of an image or any God-substitute (cf. 1 Cor 8:4-7; cf. also Acts 4:7; Rev 9:20).
5. Sorcery (*pharmakeia* [TG5331, ZG5758]). Originally related to the dispensing of drugs (hence, English "pharmacy"), this term became directly associated with potions and poisons and was thus related to those who practiced witchcraft or used evil and demonic spirits to affect others (cf. Rev 18:23).
6. Hostility (*echthrai* [TG2189, ZG2397]) includes hatred and was associated with troublemakers (cf. Eph 2:14-16, where Christ came to bring an end to such hostile ways).
7. Quarreling (*eris* [TG2054, ZG2251]) includes rivalry and divisiveness (cf. 1 Cor 1:11; 3:3).

8. Jealousy (*zēlos* [TG2205, ZG2419]) can mean zealousness in a positive sense, but in the negative, it is closely related to envy and involves an unhealthy longing for that which belongs to others (cf. 1 Cor 3:3; Jas 3:14-16).

9. Outbursts of anger (*thumoi* [TG2372, ZG2596]; cf. Luke 4:28; Acts 19:28; Eph 4:31).

10. Selfish ambition (*eritheiai* [TG2052, ZG2249]), a word that originally meant earning money but came to have a negative meaning associated with self-seeking (cf. Phil 2:3-4).

11. Dissension (*dichostasiai* [TG1370, ZG1496]) or divisions (cf. Rom 16:17).

12. Division (*haireseis* [TG139, ZG146]) originally carried the meaning of a choice and later developed the sense of belonging to a party or group in either a positive or negative sense. Here the term has the definite negative connotation of party divisiveness (cf. 1 Cor 11:19). The term was used later during early Christian debates and has come down to us in the word "heresy."

13. Envy (*phthonoi* [TG5355, ZG5784]) implies a malicious spirit that vies for another's status or possessions (cf. Matt 27:18; 1 Tim 6:4).

14. Drunkenness (*methai* [TG3178, ZG3494]) denotes intoxication (cf. Luke 21:34; Rom 13:13; Eph 5:18).

15. Wild parties (*kōmoi* [TG2970, ZG3269]) means participation in orgies, usually associated with drunkenness (cf. Rom 13:13; 1 Pet 4:3).

The list is not exhaustive, so Paul adds his catchall statement covering other similar activities (5:21). Apparently, Paul had given the Galatians similar advice at a previous time because after listing these vices, he reminded them that he had told them before that practicing such evils would prevent them from inheriting the Kingdom of God.

Paul initiated his contrasting list of virtues at 5:22 in a very significant manner. Whereas he had designated the negative activities as "works" (*erga* [TG2041, ZG2240]) of the flesh (NLT uses "desires" here), the positive characteristics of the Christian life he calls the "fruit" (*karpos* [TG2590, ZG2843]; not "fruits") of the Spirit. The list of vices implicitly results from human effort, while the virtues are the product of God's graciousness and the spontaneity of the new life (cf. Burton 1921:313; cf. also Barrett 1985:75-76). Dunn (1993:308) pushes the images even further to suggest that the plural "works" reflects human divisiveness and the singular "fruit" the unity of the Spirit.

The New Testament contains a number of lists of virtuous characteristics; the most commonly cited are among Paul's writings (cf. 2 Cor 6:6; Eph 4:2; Phil 4:8; Col 3:12-15; 1 Tim 4:12; 6:11; 2 Tim 2:22; 3:10). This list of nine virtues resists ordering even more stubbornly than the list of vices, though it seems significant that most of Paul's lists begin with or emphasize the virtue of love, undoubtedly the characteristic Paul prized above all others (cf. 5:14; 1 Cor 13:13). The virtuous characteristics are as follows:

1. Love (*agapē* [TG26, ZG27]). This word is used rarely in extant pagan sources. It has multiple meanings and should not be limited to the motif contrast proposed by Nygren in his work on *Agape and Eros*. The term *eros* (passionate love) does not even appear in the New Testament. While the word *agapē* can refer to various human relationships, such as love between parent and child or husband and wife, the term in the New Testament highlights the relationship between God the Father and the Son (e.g., John 15:10) and God's love for human beings (John 5:20; Rom 5:8; see Borchert 1996:238). This love of God for humans is intended by God to be reciprocated by humans (e.g., 2 Thess 3:5) and derivatively to be directed to other human beings (e.g., 1 John 4:7). Christian love is to be modeled on the love of God and is to be a distinguishing mark of the Christian (cf. John 13:34-35; 15:12, 17-26). Paul expects such love of the Galatians (5:14), and he identifies it as the first characteristic of the life of the Spirit.

2. Joy (*chara* [TG5479, ZG5915]). Happiness was regarded by the Greco-Roman writers as a virtuous characteristic and as the goal of life. In John's Gospel, joy is understood as a principal result of obedience (John 15:10-11). In Paul's writings, joy is in the triad of "righteousness, peace, and joy," which all reflect the presence of the Holy Spirit (Rom 14:17; cf. also Rom 15:13, where joy and peace are found in the context of Christian hope).

3. Peace (*eirēnē* [TG1515, ZG1645]). In the Hellenistic world, this implied a sense of well-being. In Paul's writings, peace is related to the Hebrew *shalom* [TH7965, ZH8934], which for a group of nomads originally meant "acceptance into the camp" and was the basis for covenants and agreements between people (see Pedersen 1926:2.263-322). Theologically speaking, peace is the result of salvation as a person is accepted by God through Christ (cf. Rom 5:1). It goes far beyond our current secular meaning of the cessation of hostilities. Jesus identified peacemakers as children of God (Matt 5:9).

4. Patience (*makrothumia* [TG3115, ZG3429]). Patience is little discussed by Greek writers, but it was regarded as a quality of the "slow-to-anger," "long-suffering" God of the Old Testament (cf. Exod 34:6; Ps 103:8 [102:8 LXX]; cf. also NT texts such as Rom 9:22; 1 Pet 3:20; and 1 Tim 1:16; 2 Pet 3:15, concerning Christ). This characteristic is also expected of Christians (cf. Col 1:11; 3:12; 1 Thess 5:14).

5. Kindness (*chrēstotēs* [TG5544, ZG5983]). Among the Greek writers, this had a variety of meanings, including goodness and generosity. In the first century, some Romans mistook Christians as followers of someone called "Chrestus," undoubtedly a confusion for Christos (i.e., "Christ"). They probably assumed that his name meant something like "a good guy" (cf. Suetonius *Claudius* 25:4; Bettenson 1963:3). In the Old Testament, God is identified as kind or good and this designation is picked up by New Testament writers in their references to God (e.g., 1 Pet 2:3; cf. Ps 34:8 [see 33:8 LXX] or Ps 136:1 [135:1 LXX]; cf. also Rom 2:4; 11:22). As a quality expected of Christians, see 2 Cor 6:6.

6. Goodness (*agathōsunē* [TG19, ZG20]). This concept, not widely used outside of Jewish and Christian sources, was developed from the frequently used, general word *agathos* [TG18, ZG19] (good, right, useful), which has a wide range of meaning. The term is used only four times in the New Testament (also at Rom 15:14; Eph 5:9; 2 Thess 1:11) and here is probably equivalent to generosity.

7. Faithfulness, or faith (*pistis* [TG4102, ZG4411]). It is not completely clear which meaning is most appropriate here. The focus of *pistis* throughout this letter has been on the idea of faith. While Paul used this word in Rom 3:3; 1 Cor 1:9; 10:13; 2 Cor 1:18; 1 Thess 5:24 to speak of God's faithfulness, he used the term more frequently to speak of people's faith in God. Sometimes the two notions overlap.

8. Gentleness (*prautēs* [TG4240, ZG4559]). Seen in contrast to arrogance, this virtue was highly regarded among the Greeks. In the Old Testament, its use marks humility or meekness (Num 12:3 LXX). Jesus had a gentle spirit (Matt 11:29; cf. 2 Cor 10:1), and in the Beatitudes, he extolled people who were meek (Matt 5:5). Paul regarded this characteristic as particularly significant in assisting others (cf. 6:1; 2 Tim 2:25; cf. also Eph 4:2; Col 3:12; Titus 3:2). This trait is sometimes described as "strength under control."

9. Self-control (*enkrateia* [TG1466, ZG1602]). This characteristic was highly regarded during the classical period as ethical moderation or as avoiding an indulgent way of life. Paul used the verb form for avoiding sexual activity when unmarried (1 Cor 7:9) and for the Christian lifestyle in general, which he likened to that of an athlete in training (1 Cor 9:25). Betz (1979:288) considers that the idea of self-control epitomizes the Christian fulfillment of the Old Testament law but finds that it was also a concern central to the Greek ethic. The Greek noun (used only here and in Acts 24:25; 2 Pet 1:6) was more frequently used by the Apostolic Fathers (cf. TDNT 2.339-342). In the second century it became associated with asceticism and celibacy and with the avoidance of meat and strong drink by the desert sectarians known as the Encratites.

In summing up this list of virtuous characteristics at 5:23, Paul returned to his concern for the way of liberty. His shorthand use of *kata* [TG2596, ZG2848] (against), however, needs some explanation. Most likely the Greek clause (lit., "against such things is no law") means that these characteristics were, in fact, outside the purview of law, but they nonetheless fulfilled the intention of the law (5:14; see the comments there). In other words, Paul told the Galatians that God's will could be done by Christians through the Spirit's impartation of these divine characteristics without any reference to legal prescriptions.

Paul concluded his discussion of spiritual resources for the life of liberty by directly attacking what he did not mean by "liberty." The freedom Paul advocated was not freedom for the flesh (the "sinful nature") to fulfill its "passions and desires" (5:24). Paul declared that these inappropriate desires were killed with Christ in the crucifixion. He assumed that his Christian readers no longer lived in the realm of the flesh and were rather manifesting positive spiritual characteristics by living in the Spirit. He did not simply repeat his exhortation to "walk" in the Spirit (5:25; cf. 5:16). Rather, this exhortation (to them and to himself: "let us") was to "follow directly in the steps" (*stoichōmen* [TG4748, ZG5123]) set by the Spirit. This instruction answers both the legalist and the libertine. The way of Christ's followers is not the way of undirected liberty (libertinism) nor the way of direction by a code or list of prescriptions (legalism); it is a direct, personal, step-by-step leading of the Spirit in the Christian's life.

In an era when "bad" is sometimes slang for "good" and sadly misguided sexual choices can come under the banner "gay," it is important to rediscover this text, which defines virtue and vice in clear terms and does not manipulate meanings or pander to deviant patterns of behavior. Paul was particularly lucid in his call for accepting the direction of the Spirit and avoiding the sinful patterns of humanity.

Paul explicitly defined these evil patterns in terms of 15 degenerate activities. Although the list is not complete, it is so encompassing and so precise that it touches upon nearly every sin. Paul similarly listed nine characteristics of those being led by the Spirit. While the list may again not be complete, it is sufficiently indicative of what proper alignment with God means for a person's lifestyle. Paul closes each list with a strong exhortation. He directly warns that following the way of sin will deprive a person of an inheritance with God. He commissions Christians to accept the step-by-step leading of the Spirit and to avoid self-centeredness, superiority, and various improper attitudes toward others.

For Paul, the horrible crucifixion of Christ was not merely an event in history involving Jesus of Nazareth. As indicated in 5:24, it was equally an event that personally involved all "those who belong to Christ Jesus" (*hoi tou Christou Iēsou*). As Paul told the Galatians earlier, he had "been crucified with Christ" (2:20). The Christian accepts the terrible event of the crucifixion as bringing all of life's motives and actions into conformity with the crucified Savior (cf. Phil 2:5-8). Thus, all desires and passions are nailed to the cross and a new way of life emerges—life in the Spirit of God. Paul intended nothing less than a transformation of life.

To say that the verses of this section are relevant for our era is an understatement. The text challenges the church to recover its role of establishing standards of behavior for its members in a world that has lost its guidelines and boundaries. At the same time, the Christian church must not attempt to do so from a pedestal of superiority, fearful reaction, or self-preservation. As Paul instructed, it must flow from a genuine sense of following Christ and of loving service to others. Clearly, Christians have been called to live by and for the God and Father of our Lord Jesus Christ, who leads each person by the Spirit. Only in this way can Christians experience the characteristics of the Spirit and exhibit them in daily life.

◆   D. The Freedom to Serve (6:1-10)

Dear brothers and sisters, if another believer* is overcome by some sin, you who are godly* should gently and humbly help that person back onto the right path. And be careful not to fall into the same temptation yourself. ²Share each other's burdens, and in this way obey the law of Christ. ³If you think you are too important to help someone, you are only fooling yourself. You are not that important.

⁴Pay careful attention to your own work, for then you will get the satisfaction of a job well done, and you won't need to compare yourself to anyone else. ⁵For we are each responsible for our own conduct.

⁶Those who are taught the word of God should provide for their teachers, sharing all good things with them.

⁷Don't be misled—you cannot mock the justice of God. You will always harvest what you plant. ⁸Those who live only to satisfy their own sinful nature will harvest decay and death from that sinful nature. But those who live to please the Spirit will harvest everlasting life from the Spirit. ⁹So let's not get tired of doing what is good. At just the right time we will reap a harvest of blessing if we don't give up. ¹⁰Therefore, whenever we have the opportunity, we should do good to everyone—especially to those in the family of faith.

6:1a Greek *Brothers, if a man.*   6:1b Greek *spiritual.*

NOTES

6:1-10 These verses resist any substantial organizing principle except that the four uses of *gar* [TG1063, ZG1142] (for) in 6:3, 5, 7, and 9 seem to introduce the use of popular wisdom sayings or maxims to support some of the ethical exhortations contained therein. Another view is that all of these ethical statements are rooted in Paul's polemic with the Galatians (cf. Betz 1979:298). Yet another opinion is that the verses are general hortative statements (advice and commands), strung together without any basic relationship to the Galatians (cf. Longenecker 1990:269-271). These verses obviously had some relationship to the Galatians or they would not have been included, but not everything has to be polemical.

6:3 *If you think you are too important to help someone, you are only fooling yourself. You are not that important.* The NLT rendering expands the maxim's pithiness: "If anyone thinks he is something, being nothing, he deceives himself." Paul's purpose in using this maxim seems to be to condemn empty self-importance. One reason for regarding the saying as a common Gr. maxim is that it uses the word *phrenapata* [TG5422, ZG5854] (deceive), which appears nowhere else in the NT or in Jewish-Greek literature.

6:4 *Pay careful attention to your own work.* The translation in the NLT could be made a little stronger by focusing more on evaluation (*dokimazetō* [TG1381, ZG1507]) and less on doing. It should probably read, "Be sure to evaluate what you are doing."

6:7 *Don't be misled.* NA²⁷ indicates that Marcion read this statement as "You are misled," an obvious alteration on his part.

6:9 *let's not get tired.* The Gr. word *enkakōmen* [TG1573A, ZG1591] was altered in later Byzantine mss to read *ekkakōmen* [TG1573, ZG1707] (lose heart), apparently because the first word was unfamiliar to later copyists (cf. the similar phenomenon at Luke 18:1; 2 Cor 4:1, 16; cf. also Longenecker 1990:281). The basic meaning, however, varies little.

6:10 *Therefore.* The presence of *ara* [TG686, ZG726] (so then, consequently) and *oun* [TG3767, ZG4036] (therefore) signals that Paul has come to his concluding statement in this section.

opportunity. This word (*kairon* [TG2540, ZG2789], "opportunity," "specific occasion/time") serves as a word link to the previous verse; it occurs in the phrase "right time" (6:9). Here, it emphasizes that Christians had strategic opportunities at their disposal to help others.

we should do good to everyone. The exhortation is again given as a cohortative subjunctive involving Paul as well as the Galatians (cf. 6:9), though a few mss (A B² 1881) have the indicative, "we do good to everyone."

COMMENTARY

In this section, Paul provides a model for effective exhortation. He encourages believers to exhibit a spirit of Christian humility in their relationships with others. He opens with an endearing address by calling them *adelphoi* [TG80, ZG81] (brothers and sisters). Then he speaks to them about helping to restore those who are overtaken by sin. The verb *prolēmphthē* [TG4301, ZG4624] (overcome) allows for various meanings; in this context, it probably suggests bondage or lack of freedom. The NLT rendering "overcome" is certainly close to the idea of sin capturing or enslaving a person. It should be obvious that the role of spiritual persons (*pneumatikoi* [TG4152A, ZG4461]) in such a context should not be one of detachment but of caring involvement. Such is the way of love and concern.

Paul exhorts the Galatians to be agents of restoration, but not in a way that exhibits superiority. The characteristic to be exemplified is gentleness, the eighth in the category of virtues listed in 5:22-23. Then, in order to make his point eminently clear, Paul adds a warning note to the rescuers to be careful lest they succumb to temptation themselves. Paul's picture of blind guides or teachers who need teaching (cf. Rom 2:19-21) reminds us that careless helpers may themselves need to be rescued. Critical self-reflection is an important practice for anyone assuming this role, no matter how spiritual.

Paul then tells his readers to "share each other's burdens." This statement speaks of the interrelatedness between those who are burdened and those who are seeking to help them (i.e., sharing in troubles). In the ancient world, as throughout the world today, people had many troubles (not simply financial as suggested by Strelan 1975:266-276). The concern does not need to relate only to the sin of 6:1 but could include many other matters, such as illness, loss of loved ones, problems of oppression, persecution, hunger, family and work issues, and many others. The spiritual person is exhorted by Paul to be a burden-bearer, to be one who exhibits the overarching characteristic of love, as well as the other virtues (cf. Rom 12:5; Eph 4:12-14).

Paul concludes his exhortation by saying that the person bearing others' burdens is fulfilling the law of Christ. Whatever "the law of Christ" means, it is not a reference to law as the Judaizers viewed it. For Paul, that was bondage. It meant either the Torah, the will of God as affirmed by Jesus, or perspectives and principles that Paul perceived as inherent in the gospel message. Hays's idea of a paradigm built on the loving, self-giving actions of Christ also seems to capture the meaning here (1987:268-290).

As indicated in the notes, 6:3 contains one of the four uses of *gar* [TG1063, ZG1142] (for) that introduces a wisdom saying or maxim. The maxim, "If you think you are too important to help someone, you are only fooling yourself. You are not that important," seems to have been a popular adage about those who think they are superior if they bear the burdens of others. Paul's use of "burden" shows his desire to lighten the loads of Christian pilgrims who find their journey difficult. Paul wanted to see Christians find personal satisfaction from genuine evaluation of their own work, not from comparison with others. It follows that one might have a reason for personal satisfaction or boasting, not in a negative sense, but in the sense of genuine self-worth.

Christians often express a horror at having a good feeling of self-worth, a view that has resulted from what could be called "worm theology"—thinking of oneself as a worm in the light of God's saving grace. Granted, our actions are worthless in obtaining salvation (cf. Paul's statement in Phil 3:9), but even Paul, as a Christian, hardly regarded himself as a worm (cf. 1 Cor 15:10), though his former attempts to gain God's approval were not very highly regarded (Phil 3:8). The point for Paul was to have a sane estimate or authentic evaluation of one's own actions and capabilities that gives a foundation for satisfaction, but that is no reason to become involved in the game of comparison. When Paul wrote these words, he undoubtedly knew that authentic self-analysis was highly regarded by the Greeks; knowing oneself was a principle goal of philosophy.

Galatians 6:5 is the second verse in this section that uses the Greek word *gar* [TG1063, ZG1142] to introduce a popular moral adage. This adage, "For we are each responsible for our own conduct," supports Paul's view in the previous verse. Like the prior maxim, this one also contains an unusual word (*phortion* [TG5413, ZG5845], "burden, oppressive weight") not found elsewhere in Paul's writings (though it is found in Matt 11:30; 23:4; Luke 11:46; Acts 27:10; and in other contexts). The significance is undoubtedly to be found in the link with *hekastos* [TG1538A, ZG1667] (each) in both verses. Each person should do an authentic self-evaluation of his or her work, and each person is counseled to bear the weight of that evaluation (i.e., its success or failure).

The contrast between the two images for a burden in this section is extremely important. On the one hand, Paul exhorted the Galatians to assist those who were weighed down by the burdens and cares of life (6:1-2); on the other hand, he exhorted them to evaluate their own work honestly and to accept the burden or responsibility for their own actions.

It may seem that 6:6 digresses from Paul's argument, since it is not directly connected to the logic of what precedes or follows it. It seems that in talking about assuming one's own burden, Paul had the striking thought that he could also comment on the legitimacy of paying teachers (church workers) their salaries. The participial expressions *ho katēchoumenos* [TG2727, ZG2994] (the one being taught, from which comes the English word "catechumen") and *to katēchonti* (the teacher, catechist) are significant because they refer to two classes of people belonging to the church. The catechists were teachers in the church in Galatia, and they apparently deserved to be paid more money than they were receiving. The catechumens were persons in need of instruction, though they were not necessarily prebaptismal candidates, as might be the case today.

Betz (1979:304-306) thinks that Paul's language is rooted in the basic perspectives of the philosophical schools and that they were developed on the principle of common life and sharing among the participants. He accepts the possibility that there might have been "some kind of educational institution" functioning at Gala-tia. While an actual school may be stretching the words here, it is quite likely that Paul had in mind the continuing need for the support of those who were preaching and teaching (cf. 1 Cor 9:3-12a), though he himself did not require such help (cf. 1 Cor 9:12, 15-18; 2 Cor 11:7-11; 1 Thess 2:9; 2 Thess 3:8-9). His reference, of course, was not meant to apply to the false teachers, but to those who were faithfully teaching the authentic gospel (cf. 1 Cor 1:18; 14:36; cf. also Acts 17:11). Perhaps if the Galatians had paid their teachers more, they might not have been so susceptible to the Judaizing false teachers.

Paul next develops his ideas by using a number of interrelated pithy statements in 6:7-9, with 6:8 as the focus or core around which the short statements are posi-tioned. The argument begins with a forceful negative warning in the second person plural: "Don't be misled!" This warning is followed by another short warning: "You cannot mock the justice of God." These statements are followed by the third maxim (again introduced by *gar* [TG1063, ZG1142], "for"), "[For] at just the right time we will reap a harvest of blessing" (6:9; cf. Prov 22:8; Hos 8:7; John 4:8; and the reverse per-spective in Jer 12:13; Luke 19:21-22).

The point of the warnings in 6:7 becomes clear in 6:8 as Paul relates these verses with word links involving sowing and reaping. Paul's metaphor envisions two life-styles of sowing, one "to the flesh" or sinful nature, and the other "to the Spirit" (flesh and Spirit are contrasted elsewhere in this letter at 3:3; 4:29; and 5:16-25). The expected results, according to Paul, would be apparent at the time of reaping; those oriented to the flesh should expect to harvest the tragedy of destruction (iden-tified in the NLT as "decay and death"), whereas those oriented to the Spirit should expect a harvest of eternal life.

Because Christians tend to dissect any New Testament texts referring to the eschaton (end times), it is important to note that Paul makes no specific reference to a time frame here, nor does he speak about the nature of the end, the state of the wicked (beyond a general concept of destruction or ruin), or the nature of eternal life. Speculators must turn elsewhere for answers to these questions. What can be said is that the pictures of harvest indicate two very different results arising from the two different styles of life (for an extended discussion on eternal life, see Borchert 2002:360-367).

Having thus mentioned the two ways of life and their expected results, Paul encourages the Galatians not to succumb to fatigue in the service of doing good. The last clause of 6:9 contains the fourth and final *gar,*which introduces a final statement from popular wisdom to bolster Paul's exhortation. The statement emphasizes that the harvest comes to us at the "appropriate time" (*kairō idiō* [TG2540/ 2398, ZG2789/2625]), but its coming is conditioned upon a person's not "giving up." Persevering in hardship is Paul's formula for success, and endurance is the recipe for reigning with Christ (2 Tim 2:12; cf. Jas 1:12; Matt 10:22; 24:13).

Paul especially encouraged believers to do good to those who were members of the household of faith. This designation of the Christian community as a household reminds us that in the Roman Empire, people thought in terms of households, and the emperor was regarded as the head of the whole Roman household. Each household had household rules or codes (see Eph 4:17–6:9; Col 3:18–4:1; 1 Pet 2:11-20; 3:1-7), and each person was expected to assist others in the household.[1] Paul here calls on the members of the Christian community to support one another as a household would (cf. Eph 2:19-22).

Christianity is not just a religion of creeds and ideas; it also involves genuine concern for people. Accordingly, Paul linked a number of statements that called the Galatians to rescue those that had fallen victim to sin and to assist those who were burdened by the concerns of their lives. In exhorting them to do good, he repeatedly warned them about their own weaknesses, temptations, and inability to evaluate themselves adequately. He charged them to remember God's continual watchfulness—they would reap according to the way that they had sown. He challenged them to live in the Spirit rather than pursue a fruitless, sinful life. He encouraged them not to give up when doing good and helping others, especially members of the community of faith. As a matter of community integrity, he added that they should not forget to support authentic teachers of the word.

While these exhortations are brief by comparison with those in some of the other epistles, and while they address only a few specific issues, they are nonetheless extremely powerful in their directives and clearly pertinent in supplying an exemplary pattern for Christian action in any generation. To understand the interrelationship of a caring, ethical life with ultimate Christian reality is absolutely crucial. Words without life are hollow. Christian witness without Christian concern is a pseudo-gospel. We see here that Paul was not only concerned about the initial faith of Christians but about their entire way of life.

ENDNOTES
1. For a helpful interpretation of 1 Peter in terms of household language, see Elliot 1981:21-58.

◆ VI. Paul's Conclusion (6:11-18)

[11]NOTICE WHAT LARGE LETTERS I USE AS I WRITE THESE CLOSING WORDS IN MY OWN HANDWRITING.

[12]Those who are trying to force you to be circumcised want to look good to others. They don't want to be persecuted for teaching that the cross of Christ alone can save. [13]And even those who advocate circumcision don't keep the whole law themselves. They only want you to be circumcised so they can boast about it and claim you as their disciples.

[14]As for me, may I never boast about anything except the cross of our Lord Jesus Christ. Because of that cross,* my interest in this world has been crucified, and the world's interest in me has also died. [15]It doesn't matter whether we have been circumcised or not. What counts is whether we have been transformed into a new creation. [16]May God's peace and mercy be upon all who live by this principle; they are the new people of God.*

[17]From now on, don't let anyone trouble

me with these things. For I bear on my
body the scars that show I belong to
Jesus.

¹⁸Dear brothers and sisters,* may the
grace of our Lord Jesus Christ be with
your spirit. Amen.

6:14 Or *Because of him.*   6:16 Greek *this principle, and upon the Israel of God.*   6:18 Greek *Brothers.*

NOTES

6:12 *the cross of Christ.* This reading is supported by most mss. 𝔓46 and B, however, read, "the cross of Christ Jesus."

6:13 *those who advocate circumcision.* Lit., "the one being circumcised." The rendering in the NLT picks up the advocacy role from 6:12.

6:15 The interpretive *gar* [TG1063, ZG1142] has played a significant role in the strategy of this letter. It is used to introduce important principles or maxims at 3:26, 27, 28; 5:5, 6; 6:3, 5, 7, and 9 (though its presence is not always evident in the NLT). In ch 3, *gar* was used to enunciate the universal nature of the Christian message that unites all people in Christ and eliminates human distinctions, a section which I designate as a key to all of Paul's thought (Borchert 1994:145-151). In that context, Paul articulates his view that time is divided into two eras by the coming of Christ (3:24 and 4:4). Through the uses of *gar* at 5:5 and 5:6, Paul makes it clear that the new era of the Spirit has made the distinctions between circumcision and uncircumcision passé for the Christian. In the maxims introduced by *gar* in ch 6, Paul confirms the reality of new ways of acting through the direction of the Spirit. Finally, in 6:15, Paul uses the *gar* to encapsulate all of these ideas in a new creation perspective with a direct focus on the major concern of this letter, namely, the Judaizers' attempt to retain the old, especially by means of mandatory circumcision.

6:16 *the new people of God.* As discussed below, this phrase is lit., "the Israel of God." Scholars have often puzzled over its referent. The NLT rendering (esp. the word "new") could give one the impression that, in a context like Rom 9–11, Paul himself might wince at this statement, but cf. Eph 2:14-15.

COMMENTARY

It is my usual practice to tell my students to read the beginning and ending of a book in order to discover how they should interpret what is in the middle. Such a pattern may not serve the readers of suspense novels well, but it can be a fruitful method for analytical reading. It can be a helpful strategy for the study of the New Testament. For example, this approach is quite a useful introduction to the basic differences of focus in each of the four Gospels. Similarly, it is an insightful method for handling this epistle, addressed by Paul to deviant Galatians.

The conclusion of this epistle conforms, with slight variations, to the general structure of the conclusions or subscriptions of Paul's letters in four of the six basic elements: the autographical certification, the concluding exhortations, the peace blessing, and the grace benediction (cf. Longenecker 1990:287-289). The two elements not included are the personal greetings and the aspects of rejoicing and praise associated with the exhortations. These last two elements are omitted because this letter was primarily an unhappy critique of Paul's straying children in Galatia. This fact mirrors the obvious omission of any "thanksgiving" section in his stern introduction.

These verses bring Paul's letter to a dramatic conclusion: Taking the quill into his own hand to personally write his summation, Paul did not mince words in directing several stern warnings to anyone who opposed him. He stated his absolute attachment to Jesus Christ his Lord and to the way of the cross as the supreme pattern for the Christian life.

In the ancient world, people who used a secretary for writing their letters often added a concluding remark in their own handwriting to indicate the authenticity of the letter. In the concluding statement of 2 Thessalonians, Paul gives us an insight into his practice, especially since in that letter there seemed to be a question of fraudulent letters arriving from a pseudo-Paul (2 Thess 2:2). In that letter he wrote, "HERE IS MY GREETING IN MY OWN HANDWRITING. . . . I DO THIS IN ALL MY LETTERS TO PROVE THEY ARE FROM ME" (2 Thess 3:17). Although there is no personal greeting at Galatians 6:11, there is a personal word from Paul: "I wrote" (*egrapsa* [TG1125, ZG1211]; an epistolary aorist). But why did he write this in such large letters? And why did he draw attention to this with the directive to "Notice" (*idete* [TG3708B, ZG1625])? Was this due to poor eyesight (based on an interpretation of 4:15)? Or was it that Paul's hands had been injured or were so rough from working as a tentmaker that he was unable to handle the task of delicate writing? These and other speculative ideas have been proposed, but their validity seems questionable, especially since Paul, in this harsh letter, was not seeking empathy from the recipients. The most likely scenario is that Paul was specifically reaffirming his argument against circumcision (6:12-13) in his own handwriting and in large words (cf. Lightfoot 1865:221; Betz 1979:314; Bruce 1982:268). It would be akin to underlining our writing or italicizing and boldfacing our printing.

In this section, Paul attacks even the motives of his Judaizing opponents. His charge against the false teachers (again referring to them indirectly rather than directly to avoid giving them status) was that their only motivation in attempting to force the Galatians into being circumcised was personal self-interest. Given the growing Jewish nationalism in Judea and its neighboring provinces such as Galilee—a nationalism that was spurred on by militant Zealots during that period—the Jewish Christians must have come under intense pressure not to have any friendly relations with the *goyim* [TH1471, ZH1580], or hated Gentiles. To bring Gentiles within the fold of Judaism (namely, to have them circumcised) was one tangible way that Jewish Christians could prove to the Zealots and others that they were still faithful Jews and should not be persecuted. Although they were Christians, such a theory argues that these false leaders were attempting to prove their loyalty to Judaism (cf. Jewett 1971:198-212). Paul, however, considered such self-interested motivation to be reprehensible and a serious blow to the meaning of the gospel ("the cross of Christ").

According to Paul, the legalists were to be viewed not merely as his enemies but also as opponents of the cross of Christ. They were apparently seeking to escape the harsh implications of a crucifixion-oriented faith. They were abandoning identification with the crucified Savior in favor of acceptance from the Jewish establishment.

They sought status with others by reconverting Gentile Christians to their legalistic perspectives. In so doing, they were proving themselves to be like all self-centered persons in that they were oriented to the ways of the world and grasping after praise.

Instead of succumbing to their rationale, Paul dealt a knockout punch to their selfish motivation. Paul asserted at 6:13 that they who "advocate circumcision" did not themselves keep the law (cf. the implications of 5:3). This charge amounts to designating the Judaizers as "sham Jews," a charge that Paul had earlier leveled at Peter (2:14). To make matters worse, they were trying to make sham Jews out of Gentiles (2:14) with the motive of glorying in how many followers they had won over.

Paul initiates his rebuttal in 6:14 with what was probably his favorite negative expression, *mē genoito* [TG3361/1096, ZG3590/1181], translated variously as, "May it not be!" "God forbid," "It can never be," or "Absolutely not!" (cf. 2:17; 3:21; Rom 3:4, 5, 31; 6:2, 15). Here, he personalizes this rejection with reference to his own views. Then he relates 6:14 to the previous verse by means of a word-link: the Judaizers *boasted* in the personal conquests of their followers' flesh, but Paul excluded *boasting* on his part, except in "the cross of our Lord Jesus Christ." This statement about boasting is in harmony with his statements elsewhere, though expressed differently, as for example in his boasting not of his achievements but of his own weakness (2 Cor 11:30) or in the exclusion of boasting because of faith (Rom 3:27). The mention of the cross is also a word-link with 6:12, where Paul has already condemned the false teachers for seeking to avoid the persecution attached to the cross.

As noted by Bruce (1982:271), it is a major problem for us after centuries of seeing the cross as a positive symbol in Christianity "to realize the unspeakable horror and loathing" which the mere thought of the cross would have provoked in Paul's day. It was probably difficult for early Christians to admit that their loving Savior had died on a despicable cross, yet that is exactly one of the central affirmations of early Christian preaching (Acts 10:39; 1 Cor 1:17-18; Phil 2:8; Heb 12:2). The despised and rejected things of the world, however, became Paul's focus for boasting (Rom 5:2-3; 1 Cor 1:27-31), and the crucifixion became for him a symbol of the world's rejection of Christianity and the Christians' rejection of the world.

When Paul reaches the conclusion of his letter, the significance of his words is not diminished but heightened. At first glance, 6:15 may seem simply to repeat the strategic statement at 5:6, but attached to the revolutionary statement about the insignificance of circumcision and uncircumcision is the more explosive phrase, "but a new creation" (*alla kainē ktisis* [TG2937, ZG3232]). The Judaizers were living in the old way, while the new way had been inaugurated by Christ; they were attempting to reestablish the role of circumcision in the new era. Such an attempt was hardly new-era thinking; it was old-era politics in which they were trying to save their own necks by sacrificing both the message and the recipients of the gospel.

In 6:16, Paul introduces what is sometimes called the "peace blessing" (also represented in Rom 15:33; 2 Cor 13:11; Eph 6:23; Phil 4:9). But there are a few matters that are a little unusual here. The first is that the statement includes a mercy blessing as well. This word is certainly understandable as a theme inherited from the Old Testament, which often refers to the mercy or loving kindness (*khesed* [TH2617, ZH2876]) of God (cf. TDNT 2.479-481). What is truly unusual here, in contrast to the normal greetings, is that peace precedes mercy instead of following grace and mercy. In the usual order, it is generally assumed that peace is the result of grace and mercy. What is even more significant here is the appearance of the expression, "Israel of God" (NLT, "the new people of God"; see note on 6:16). In most contexts, this phrase would be regarded as a reference to the Jewish people, but here it appears to refer to the Galatians, most of whom are Gentile Christians. Would Paul refer to Gentiles in this way only here, and not in his other writings? In his extended discussion of Israel in Romans 9–11, the term "Israel" seems to be reserved for Jews, particularly in the strategic texts of Romans 9:6-9 and 11:11-32.

Two basic ways of resolving these issues have emerged among scholars. The first way is to divide the verse into two parts and argue that those who follow the rule of the cross receive the blessing of peace, while those that are the Israel of God receive the blessing of mercy (cf. Dunn 1993:344-345). The problem with such a view is that it seems completely out of joint with the whole argument of Galatians—Christians are unified in their justification, so why give a divided blessing? The second solution suggests that those who follow the rule of the cross are here called the Israel of God (cf. Longenecker 1990:297-298; cf. also the NLT rendering). But then how does one solve the problem of applying the name "Israel" to Gentiles?

The answer for those taking this second view probably lies in the context of the Galatian situation. Much of the argument in Galatians is focused on the fact that Christians are children of promise and thus children of Abraham (3:9, 14; 4:31). If the argument of the Judaizing false teachers was an incentive to become children of Abraham and join in the rite of circumcision, then Paul's counterargument would make sense—namely, that to accept Abraham's seed (Jesus) and follow in the way of faith makes one a true child of Abraham and therefore a member of "the Israel of God." In a parallel picture, Paul illustrated the Gentile relationship to Israel by viewing the Gentiles as wild olive branches that had been grafted into the main trunk of Israel's historical tree in order to replace some broken branches (Rom 11:17-26). While this second view may not solve all the exegetical problems, it seems to conform to the general pattern of Paul's argument in this letter and is therefore preferable to the first view.

Paul directed a final imperative in 6:17 against the Judaizers, who were continuing to trouble him by disturbing his children in the faith. The close connection pictured here between Paul and the Galatians is reminiscent of the close connection between Jesus and the Christians that Paul had been persecuting. Jesus confronted Paul on the Damascus Road by asking Paul why he was persecuting him (Acts 9:1-5). This final exhortation is addressed to anyone engaged in such Judaizing activity, and it is supported by a somewhat strange warning that the one who is writing to them is marked as a "Jesus-man," so they should take notice. What is meant by the reference to the marks (*stigmata* [TG4742, ZG5116]) has led to the speculation that Paul had been tattooed or branded as a slave (cf. TDNT 7.657-664). Most likely, the statement refers to injuries sustained during some of the early mistreatments listed in 2 Corinthians 11:21-33. Paul probably had lasting physical indicators of being roughly treated for the sake of the gospel; he specifies that the marks were on his body (*sōmati* [TG4983, ZG5393]). Paul regarded these marks as a strong confirmation of his apostolic calling.

Taking up the cross of Christ in one's life is costly. It was costly for Jesus, and it was costly for Paul, as he bore the marks of commitment to Christ in his own body. The way of the cross will also be costly for contemporary Christians, who may be tempted to seek the praise and admiration of the world or to add rules and requirements to the way of God. To these Paul would again thunder, "Quit troubling Christians with such human perspectives. Discover anew the freedom that comes in a living attachment to the crucified Jesus!"

The benediction of grace closes the epistle (6:18); it reminded the Galatians that, in spite of the severe tone in much of the letter, Paul cared intensely for the "spirit" (*pneumatos* [TG4151, ZG4460]) of his Christian children. His mention of their spirit probably reminded them that they belonged to the Spirit and not to the flesh. If this was Paul's earliest letter, then it provided a model for all his other epistles. Two elements, however, are not repeated in his later letters. The first is the direct address by the generic *adelphoi* [TG80, ZG81] (brothers), rendered here as "Dear brothers and sisters," and the second is the final word "Amen," a standard Jewish affirmation meaning, "Let it be so!"

For my own readers I would add: May the lovingkindness of the gracious Lord be with you all everywhere. May you hear the great apostle's words and choose liberty in Christ rather than law and legal prescriptions. And may every believer respond with a convincing "Amen!"—let it be so!

BIBLIOGRAPHY

Bammel, E.
1968 Galater i.23. *Zeitschrift für die neutestamentliche Wissenschaft* 59:108-112.

Bandstra, A. J.
1964 *The Law and the Elements of the World: An Exegetical Study in Aspects of Paul's Teaching.* Grand Rapids: Eerdmans.

Barrett, C. K.
1961 *The New Testament Documents.* New York: Harper & Brothers.

1976 The Allegory of Abraham, Sarah and Hagar in the Argument of Galatians. Pp. 1-16 in *Rechtfertigung.* Editors, J. Friedrich et al. Tübingen: J. C. B. Mohr.

1985 *Freedom and Obligation: A Study of the Epistle to the Galatians.* London: SPCK.

Baur, F. C.
1875 *Paul: His Life and Works.* London: Williams & Norgate.

Beare, F. W.
1943 The Sequence of Events in Acts 9–15 and the Career of Peter. *Journal of Biblical Literature* 62:295-306.

Bettenson, Henry
1963 *Documents of the Christian Church.* 2nd ed. London: Oxford University Press.

Betz, Hans D.
1979 *Galatians.* Hermeneia. Philadelphia: Fortress.

Birnbaum, P., editor and translator
n.d. *Daily Prayer Book, Ha-Siddur Ha-Shalem.* New York: Hebrew Publishing Company.

Blomberg, Craig L.
1997 *Jesus and the Gospels.* Nashville: Broadman & Holman.

Borchert, Gerald L.
1974 Insights into the Gnostic Threat to Christianity as Gained through the Gospel of Philip. Pp. 79-93 in *New Dimensions in New Testament Study.* Editors, R. N. Longenecker and M. C. Tenney. Grand Rapids: Zondervan.

1983 The Lord of Form and Freedom: A New Testament Perspective on Worship. *Review and Expositor* 80:5-18.

1986a *Discovering Thessalonians.* Carmel, NY: Guideposts.

1986b Romans, Pastoral Counseling, and the Introspective Conscience of the West. *Review and Expositor* 83:81-92.

1994 A Key to Pauline Thinking: Galatians 3:23-29. *Review and Expositor* 91:145-151.

1996 *John 1–11.* New American Commentary. Nashville: Broadman & Holman.

2002 *John 12–21.* New American Commentary. Nashville: Broadman & Holman.

Bruce, F. F.
1982 *The Epistle to the Galatians: A Commentary on the Greek Text.* Exeter: Paternoster.

Bultmann, Rudolf
1910 *Der Stil der paulinischen Predigt und die kynisch-stoische Diatribe.* Göttingen: Vandenhoeck und Ruprecht.

Burton, E. DeWitt
1921 *The Epistle of Paul to the Galatians.* International Critical Commentary. Edinburgh: T & T Clark.

Callan, Terrance
1980 Pauline Midrash: The Exegetical Background of Gal 3:19b. *Journal of Biblical Literature* 99:549-567.

Cave, Sydney
1929 *The Gospel of St. Paul.* New York: Doubleday.

Clements, Ronald E.
1967 *Abraham and David.* Studies in Biblical Theology 5. London: SCM.

Clements, Roy
1997 *No Longer Slaves: Set Free by Christ.* Leicester: Inter-Varsity.

Cole, R. Alan
1989 *Galatians.* 2nd ed. Tyndale New Testament Commentaries. Leicester: Inter-Varsity.

Comfort, Philip W.
2007 *New Testament Text and Translation Commentary.* Carol Stream, IL: Tyndale House.

Cosgrove, Charles H.
1988 Arguing Like a Mere Human Being: Galatians 3.15-18 in Rhetorical Perspective. *New Testament Studies* 34:536-549.

Cullman, Oscar
1962 *Christ and Time.* Translator, F. Filson. Philadelphia: Westminster.

Daube, David
1956 *The New Testament and Rabbinic Judaism.* London: Athlone.

Danby, Herbert, editor
1933 *The Mishnah.* London: Oxford University Press.

Davies, W. D.
1980 *Paul and Rabbinic Judaism: Some Rabbinic Elements in Pauline Theology.* Philadelphia: Fortress.

Deissmann, Adolph
1909 *Light from the Ancient East: The New Testament Illustrated by Recently Discovered Texts of the Greco-Roman World.* Translator, L. Strachan. London: Hodder & Stoughton.

1926 *Paul: A Study in Social and Religious History.* Translator, W. E. Wilson. London: Hodder & Stoughton.

De Vries, C. E.
1975 Paul's Cutting Remarks about a Race: Galatians 5:1-12. Pp. 115-120 in *Current Issues in Biblical and Patristic Interpretation.* Editor, G. Hawthorne. Grand Rapids: Eerdmans.

Dodd, C. H.
1952 *According to the Scripture: The Substructure of New Testament Theology.* London: Nisbet & Co.

Dunn, James D. G.
1988 *Romans 1–8.* Word Biblical Commentary, vol. 38a. Dallas: Word.

1990 *Jesus, Paul and the Law. Studies in Mark and Galatians.* Louisville: Westminster.

1993 *The Epistle to the Galatians.* Black's New Testament Commentary. Peabody, MA: Hendrickson.

Elliot, John
1981 *A Home for the Homeless.* Philadelphia: Fortress.

Ellis, E. Earl
1957 *Paul's Use of the Old Testament.* Grand Rapids: Eerdmans.

Fitzmyer, Joseph A.
1978 Crucifixion in Ancient Palestine, Qumran Literature, and the New Testament. *Catholic Biblical Quarterly* 40:493-513.

Fung, Ronald Y. K.
1988 *The Epistle to the Galatians.* New International Commentary on the New Testament. Grand Rapids: Eerdmans.

Funk, Robert W.
1956 The Enigma of the Famine Visit. *Journal of Biblical Literature* 75:130-136.

Garland, David E.
1994 Paul's Defense of the Truth of the Gospel Regarding Gentiles (Galatians 2:15–3:22). *Review and Expositor* 91:165-181.

George, Timothy
1994 *Galatians.* New American Commentary. Nashville: Broadman & Holman.

Grant, Robert M. and David Tracy
1984 *A Short History of the Interpretation of the Bible.* London: SCM.

Guelich, Robert A.
1982 *The Sermon on the Mount: A Foundation for Understanding.* Waco: Word Books.

Haenchen, Ernst
1971 *The Acts of the Apostles.* Translator, R. Wilson. Philadelphia: Westminster.

Hanson, R. P. C.
1959 *Allegory and Event: A Study of the Sources and Significance of Origen's Interpretation of Scripture.*
Richmond: John Knox.

Hays, Richard B.
1987 Christology and Ethics in Galatians. *Catholic Biblical Quarterly* 49:268-290.

Hemer, Colin J.
1977 Acts and Galatians Reconsidered. *Themelios* 2:81-88.

1989 *The Book of Acts in the Setting of Hellenistic History.* Editor, C. H. Gempf. Tübingen: J. C. B. Mohr.

Hübner, H.
1984 *Law in Paul's Thought.* Edinburgh: T & T Clark.

Jewett, Robert
1971 The Agitators and the Galatian Congregation. *New Testament Studies* 17:198-212.

1979a *A Chronology of Paul's Life.* Philadelphia: Fortress.

1979b *Dating Paul's Life.* London: SCM.

Kilpatrick, G. D.
1959 Galatians 1:18, 27. Pp. 144-149 in *New Testament Essays.* Editor, A. J. B. Higgins. Manchester:
University of Manchester Press.

Kim, Seyoon
1981 *The Origin of Paul's Gospel.* Tübingen: J. C. B. Mohr.

Kümmel, Werner
1984 *Introduction to the New Testament.* Translator, H. C. Kee. Nashville: Abingdon.

Lightfoot, J. B.
1865 *Saint Paul's Epistle to the Galatians.* London: MacMillan.

Longenecker, Richard N.
1974 Ancient Amanuenses and the Pauline Epistles. Pp. 281-297 in *New Dimensions in New Testament
Study.* Editors, R. N. Longenecker and M. C. Tenney. Grand Rapids: Zondervan.

1975 *Biblical Exegesis in the Apostolic Period.* Grand Rapids: Eerdmans.

1990 *Galatians.* Word Biblical Commentary, vol. 41. Dallas: Word.

Luther, Martin
1955-1975 *Luther's Works.* 56 vols. Editor, J. Pelikan. St. Louis: Concordia.

MacDonald, D. R.
1987 *There Is No Male and Female.* Philadelphia: Fortress.

McKnight, Scott
1991 *A Light among the Gentiles: Jewish Missionary Activity in the Second Temple Period.* Minneapolis:
Fortress.

McNamara, Martin
1978 to de (Hagar) Sina oros estin en te Arabia (Gal. 4.25a): Paul and Petra. *Milltown Studies* 2:24-41.

Marshall, I. Howard
1997 *The Origins of New Testament Christology.* Leicester: Inter-Varsity.

Martyn, J. Louis
1997 *Galatians.* Anchor Bible, vol. 33A. New York: Doubleday.

Metzger, Bruce M.
1971 *A Textual Commentary on the Greek New Testament.* London and New York: United Bible Societies.

Moo, Douglas
1991 *The Wycliffe Exegetical Commentary: Romans 1-8.* Chicago: Moody.

Moule, C. F. D.
1961 *Worship in the New Testament.* Ecumenical Studies in Worship 9. Richmond: John Knox.

Moulton, W. F. and A. S. Geden
1926 *A Concordance of the Greek Testament.* Edinburgh: T & T Clark.

Murray, Gilbert
1951 *Five Stages of Greek Religion.* 3rd ed. Boston: Beacon.

Mussner, Franz
1977 *Der Galaterbrief.* Herders theologischer Kommentar zum Neuen Testament 9. Freiburg: Herder und Herder.

Neyrey, Jerome H.
1988 Bewitched in Galatia: Paul and Cultural Anthropology. *Catholic Biblical Quarterly* 50:72-100.

Nygren, Anders
1953 *Agape and Eros.* Philadelphia: Westminster.

Ogg, George
1968 *The Chronology of the Life of Paul.* London: Epworth.

Pedersen, Johannes
1926 *Israel: Its Life and Culture.* Copenhagen: Branner og Korch.

Polhill, John
1992 *Acts.* New American Commentary. Nashville: Broadman & Holman.

Räisänen, H.
1983 *Paul and the Law.* Wissenschaftliche Untersuchungen zum Neuen Testament 29. Tübingen: J. C. B. Mohr.

Ramsay, Sir William M.
1895 *St. Paul the Traveler and the Roman Citizen.* London: Hodder & Stoughton.

Reicke, Bo
1951 The Law and This World According to Paul: Some Thoughts Concerning Gal 4:1-11. *Journal of Biblical Literature* 70:259-276.

Ridderbos, Herman N.
1953 *The Epistle of Paul to the Churches of Galatia.* New International Commentary on the New Testament. Grand Rapids: Eerdmans.

Robinson, J. A. T.
1976 *Redating the New Testament.* Philadelphia: Westminster.

Russell, Walter B., III
1997 *The Flesh/Spirit Conflict in Galatians.* Lanham, MD: University Press of America.

Sampley, J. P.
1977 Before God, I Do Not Lie (Gal I.20): Paul's Self-defense in the Light of Roman Legal Praxis. *New Testament Studies* 23:477-482.

Sanders, E. P.
1977 *Paul and Palestinian Judaism: A Comparison of Patterns of Religion.* Philadelphia: Fortress Press.

1983 *Paul, the Law, and the Jewish People.* Philadelphia: Fortress.

Schillebeeckx, Edward
1986 *Jesus: An Experiment in Christology.* New York: Crossroad.

Schlier, Heinrich
1949 *Der Brief an die Galater.* (Meyers) Kritisch-exegetischer Kommentar über das Neue Testament. Göttingen: Vandenhoeck und Ruprecht.

Schreiner, T. R.
1985 Paul and Perfect Obedience to the Law: An Evaluation of E. P. Sanders. *Westminster Theological Journal* 47:245-278.

Schweitzer, Albert
1910 *The Quest of the Historical Jesus.* Translator, W. Montgomery. London: Adam & Charles Black.

1931 *The Mysticism of Paul.* Translator, W. Montgomery. London: Adam & Charles Black.

Seifrid, Mark
1992 *Justification by Faith: The Origin and Development of a Central Pauline Theme.* Leiden: Brill.

Stanton, Graham
1989 *The Gospels and Jesus.* Oxford: Oxford University Press.

Stendahl, Krister
1963 The Apostle Paul and the Introspective Conscience of the West. *Harvard Theological Review* 56:199-215.

Strack, H. L. and P. Billerbeck
1922–1928 *Kommentar zum Neuen Testament aus Talmud und Midrash.* Munich: Beck.

Strelan, J. C.
1975 Burden-bearing and the Law of Christ: A Re-examination of Galatians 6:2. *Journal of Biblical Literature* 94:266-276.

Theilman, Frank
1989 *From Plight to Solution: A Jewish Framework for Understanding Paul's View of the Law in Galatians and Romans.* Leiden: Brill.

VanGemeren, William A.
1997 *New International Dictionary of Old Testament Theology and Exegesis,* vol. 1. Grand Rapids: Zondervan.

Vermes, Geza
1995 *The Dead Sea Scrolls in English.* London: Penguin Books.

Wikenhauser, Alfred
1960 *Pauline Mysticism: Christ in the Mystical Teaching of St. Paul.* New York: Herder.

Wilcox, M.
1979 The Promise of the "Seed" in the New Testament and the Targumim. *Journal for the Study of the New Testament* 5:2-20.

Witherington, Ben, III.
1994 *Paul's Narrative Thought World: The Tapestry of Tragedy and Triumph.* Louisville: Westminster / John Knox.

Ziesler, J. A.
1972 *The Meaning of Righteousness in Paul.* Cambridge: Cambridge University Press.